## Special Allyn & Bacon Online Suppleme...

In addition to the supplements available with *The Language A...* ...
online supplements to help students explore language arts furth... ...

### Research Navigator™ Guide for Education with Access Code

Designed to help students select and evaluate research from the Web to find the best and most credible information available. The booklet contains:

- A practical and to-the-point discussion of search engines
- Detailed information on evaluating online sources
- Citation guidelines for Web resources
- Web activities for education
- Web links for education
- A complete guide to Research Navigator™ (access code required)

Allyn and Bacon's new Research Navigator™ is the easiest way for students to start a research assignment or research paper. Complete with extensive help on the research process and three exclusive databases of credible and reliable source material: EBSCO's ContentSelect Academic Journal and Abstract Database, *New York Times* Search by Subject Archive, and "Best of the Web" Link Library. Research Navigator™ helps students make the most of their research time quickly and efficiently. Each Research Navigator™ Guide contains an access code allowing individual users entry into this wonderful resource for research assistance.

### Allyn & Bacon Language Arts Literacy Zone SuperSite (access code required) (http://www.ablongman.com/literacy)

A website with a wealth of information for pre-service and in-service teachers—whether you want to gain new insights, pick up practical information, or simply connect with one another! It includes state standard correlations; teaching resources; ready-to-use lesson plans and activities for all grade levels; subject-specific Web links for further research and discovery; information on Allyn and Bacon professional titles to help you in your teaching career; up-to-date "In the News" features; a discussion forum; and much more.

### Themes of the Times

By visiting the Companion Website (www.ablongman.com/cramer1e) for *The Language Arts,* students can link directly to specially selected *New York Times* articles presenting differing perspectives on contemporary literacy topics.

# The Language Arts

## A Balanced Approach to Teaching Reading, Writing, Listening, Talking, and Thinking

**Ronald L. Cramer**

Oakland University

With Foreword by W. Dorsey Hammond

PEARSON

Boston • New York • San Francisco
Mexico City • Montreal • Toronto • London • Madrid • Munich • Paris
Hong Kong • Singapore • Tokyo • Cape Town • Sydney

*Dedicated, with love, to my children Amy, Jen, Ben and my grandson Max.*
*Their journeys to literacy have informed my thinking and delighted my soul.*

Series Editor: Aurora Martínez Ramos
Editorial Assistant: Erin Beatty
Senior Development Editor: Mary Kriener
Senior Marketing Manager: Elizabeth Fogarty
Production Administrator: Anna Socrates
Photo Researcher: Katherine S. Cook
Composition and Prepress Buyer: Linda Cox
Manufacturing Buyer: Andrew Turso
Cover Coordinator: Linda Knowles
Text Design and Composition: Glenna Collett
Editorial-Production Service: Susan McNally

For related titles and support materials, visit our online catalog at www.ablongman.com.

Between the time Website information is gathered and then published, it is not unusual for some sites to have closed. Also, the transcription of URLs can result in typographical errors. The publisher would appreciate notification where these errors occur so that they may be corrected in subsequent editions.

CIP data not available at time of publication.

ISBN: 0-321-08724-0

Printed in the United States of America
10  9  8  7  6  5  4  3  2     RRD-IN  07  06  05

**Photo Credits**
All photos by Amy Ronelle Cramer and Juan Libon except for pages 3, 94, 133, 255, T. Linfors; page 309, Laima Druskis; and page 417, Will Hart.

# Contents

# 3   Assessing Writing and Reading   88

## 4 Listening and Talking   132

## 5 Emerging Literacy   170

## 6 Literature and Literacy   204

## 7   Content Literacy: Reading and Writing in the Content Areas   254

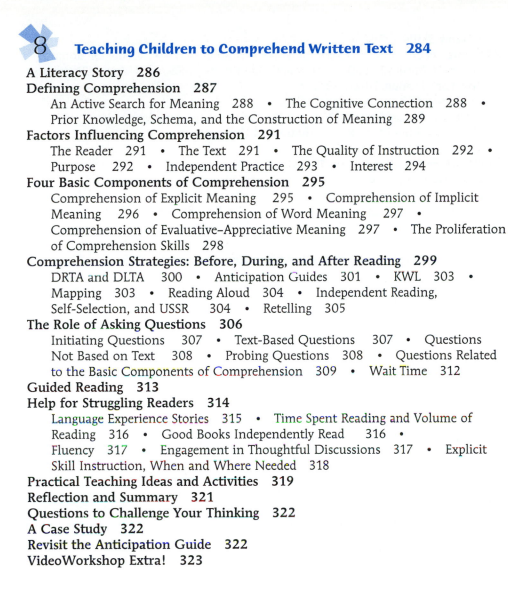

## 12   The Mechanics of Writing: Grammar, Punctuation, Capitalization, and Handwriting   454

## 13 The Spelling Connection: Integrating Reading, Writing, and Spelling  492

# Preface

It's a rare person who can't recall a favorite teacher who made a difference in his or her life. Decades ago, Ms. Anderson wrote five words I have never forgotten: "Ron, you have wonderful ideas." It was my first encouragement to write, and it sunk in deeply. I think of her often. I wonder if she remembers the fateful words she bestowed as a gift I would forever treasure? Probably not. Thousands of students have passed through her classroom over the decades: teachers, doctors, writers, pastors, lawyers. The fate of teachers is not to march victoriously at the head of the column; our role is to prepare others for the journey into the land of promise and possibility—the land of literacy and literature. Teach children to love literature and literacy; be the hero or heroine of their literary lives; help children know that all things spiritual and material are enriched through a life in literature and literacy. Literature bestows a storehouse of knowledge, a world of experience, an arsenal of language.

Just as ancient mariners needed stars to steer by, so teachers need a philosophy—a set of principles—to guide their instructional decisions. *The Language Arts: A Balanced Approach to Teaching Reading, Writing, Listening, Talking, and Thinking* reflects my philosophy concerning children, teachers, and the language arts.

- *I believe* that creativity is as natural to children as breathing. The challenge for teachers is to learn how to identify and release children's native creativity.
- *I believe* that teachers work hard to release the creative potential children possess and are often successful.
- *I believe* that language arts instruction works best when children are led to construct their own knowledge in settings where prior knowledge is the bridge to acquiring new knowledge.

This text presents an array of strategies, models, research, and well-established best practices for teaching reading, writing, talking, listening, and thinking. Its research, ideas, and information will inform and, I hope, inspire preservice teachers as they grapple with the complexities and challenges of learning to teach the language arts. Experienced teachers know a great deal about teaching the language arts, yet day-to-day realities often interfere with their best intentions and efforts. This text speaks to teachers' needs as they confront the challenges of teaching under all circumstances. No textbook can address every teaching challenge; yet it is my fervent hope that the philosophy, ideas, and information that infuse this text will inspire and inform all teachers, both new and experienced educators, as they teach the language arts to children.

So, if it is your fate to be a teacher, love your fate—*amori fati*. You have chosen the noblest profession. You will face many challenges, but tomorrow a new day will dawn. You will stand before your class and steadfastly continue the work you were fated to perform. *Teachers are my heroes, my heroines.*

# How This Book Is Organized

This first edition of *The Language Arts: A Balanced Approach to Teaching Reading, Writing, Listening, Talking, and Thinking* was written in the belief that literature and literacy provide the essential foundation of children's world knowledge and that the teacher's role is crucial in conveying this legacy to children. Each chapter focuses on a central language arts concept, and the Blue Pages at the back of the text complement this content with related activities, bibliographies, and other resources.

The unifying themes of this text include the following: the need for balance in instructional approaches and practices, the foundational role of literature in the language arts, respect for the diversity and capabilities of children, the importance of integrating the language arts throughout the curriculum, the central role of critical and creative thinking in language arts instruction, and the crucial role teachers play in implementing effective instruction. This combination of topics and themes provides the rationale for a language arts text that extends a friendly and respectful voice to preservice and experienced teachers alike.

- Chapter 1, "Foundations and Approaches to Teaching the Language Arts," concentrates on foundations of language arts and three approaches to language arts instruction that have influenced current philosophy and practices. Discussion revolves around integrating the language arts, literature, the influential teacher, and instructional technology.

- Chapter 2, "Organizing Learning Environments," focuses on ways to create inviting environments for learning, classroom management, thinking, and construction of meaning.

- Chapter 3, "Assessing Writing and Reading," explores the basic principles and types of assessment and the procedures and instruments needed to assess reading, writing, and language arts.

- Chapter 4, "Listening and Talking," explains why listening and talking are crucial skills for promoting growth in reading and writing and provides practical ideas for integrating listening and talking skills into lessons.

- Chapter 5, "Emerging Literacy," explores the reading–writing relationship, home literacy, emergent writing and reading concepts, and assessment of emergent reading and writing.

- Chapter 6, "Literature and Literacy," explores issues involved in selecting and using literature, literary elements, genres and responses to literature, establishing classroom libraries, and how and why reading aloud influences literacy.

- Chapter 7, "Content Literacy," examines the principles, strategies, and concepts essential to successful content literacy.

- Chapter 8, "Teaching Children to Comprehend Written Text," defines and describes the factors that influence comprehension as well as the components and strategies for teaching comprehension; it discusses how to help struggling readers.

- Chapter 9, "Word Study," concentrates on word study issues, such as word recognition, dictionary skills, and the development of meaning vocabulary, as well as exploring phonics instruction.

- Chapter 10, "The Writing Process in a Workshop Environment," provides an overview of a writing workshop environment, including incorporation of Donald Graves's writing principles and stages of the writing process.

- Chapter 11, "Poetry for Children," focuses on preparing children for poetry, responding to poetry, sources of inspiration for writing poetry, and the language and technical devices of poetry; it also describes 17 poetic forms.

- Chapter 12, "The Mechanics of Writing," stresses the value of contextualizing the teaching of grammar and mechanics in learning to speak, read, and write.

- Chapter 13, "The Spelling Connection," stresses the integration of reading, writing, and spelling by exploring spelling stages, various instructional strategies, word selection, invented spelling, and assessment of spelling.

 ## Special Features

Each chapter includes a rich set of features that enhance the general text. Some have been written by teachers, students, and professionals to provide varying perspectives on the classroom. Together with the text, they create a comprehensive blueprint for teaching the language arts, following a solid instructional strategy of *preparation, instruction, reinforcement,* and *application.*

- **Chapter openers** include "Big Ideas" that outline the objectives for the chapter, a chapter content–specific philosophy, and an anticipation guide provide students with a preview of major topics and an opportunity to assess their own readiness prior to reading the chapter.

**Prepare**

- **Literacy Stories** begin each chapter and tell the story of transforming literacy experiences to inspire and motivate students' pursuit of literacy goals.

- **A Matter of Standards** features examine pertinent International Reading Association/National Council of Teachers of English standards for reading and language arts as they relate to chapter content.

**A MATTER OF STANDARDS**

**Emergent Literacy**

**Standard:** The IRA/NCTE standards document does not list a specific standard for emerging literacy. However, the preamble to the standards document states that "literacy growth begins before children enter school as they experience and experiment with literacy activities—reading and writing, and associating spoken words with their graphic representation."

Emergent literacy is not one of the 12 official standards listed in the IRA/NCTE Standards for the English Language Arts. However, the introduction speaks to the issue of emergent literacy as quoted above. This statement implies that schools have a role to play in

 **STANDARD**

sponsoring and fostering emergent literacy. Literacy emerges in tiny bursts of enlightenment as parents read to young children, engage them in meaningful conversations, sing the alphabet with them, recite nursery rhymes, and encourage drawing and writing. While a culture of home and family literacy aids and abets emerging literacy, not all children receive a sufficient measure of home literacy experiences. Such children need emergent literacy experiences developed and sponsored by educational institutions such as Head Start as well as kindergarten and primary-grade instruction. When given rich emergent literacy experiences, children make the transition to conventional literacy much more successfully. This literacy wave in chapter describes ways in

## Instruct

- A **Themes of the Times** icon at the start of each chapter directs readers to the Companion Website (www.ablongman.com/cramer1e) with a direct link to specially selected *New York Times* articles, which present differing perspectives on contemporary education topics.

**The New York Times**
expect the world®
nytimes.com

**Themes of the Times**
Expand your knowledge of the concepts discussed in this chapter by reading current and historical articles from *The New York Times* by visiting the "Themes of the Times" section of the Companion Website.

- **Margin notes** and **section summaries** serve to check learning and supplement key points as students work their way through each chapter.

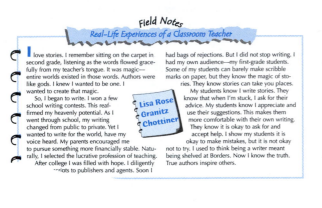

**Field Notes**
*Real-Life Experiences of a Classroom Teacher*

I love stories. I remember sitting on the carpet in second grade, listening as the words flowed gracefully from my teacher's tongue. It was magic—entire worlds existed in those words. Authors were like gods. I knew I wanted to be one. I wanted to create that magic.

So, I began to write. I won a few school writing contests. This reaffirmed my heavenly potential. As I went through school, my writing changed from public to private. Yet I wanted to write for the world, have my voice heard. My parents encouraged me to pursue something more financially stable. Naturally, I selected the lucrative profession of teaching.

After college I was filled with hope. I diligently ⸱⸱⸱ripts to publishers and agents. Soon I

*Lisa Rose Granitz Chottiner*

had bags of rejections. But I did not stop writing. I had my own audience—my first-grade students. Some of my students can barely make scribble marks on paper, but they know the magic of stories. They know stories can take you places.

My students know I write stories. They know that when I'm stuck, I ask for their advice. My students know I appreciate and use their suggestions. This makes them more comfortable with their own writing. They know it is okay to ask for and accept help. I show my students it is okay to make mistakes, but it is not okay not to try. I used to think being a writer meant being shelved at Borders. Now I know the truth. True authors inspire others.

- **Field Notes** boxes present real-life experiences of classroom teachers and parents, who provide practical tips for succeeding in the language arts classroom.

- **Connecting Technology to Teaching** boxes, written by teacher Lisa Kunkleman, appear in every chapter and present perspectives and ideas for applying technology to teaching the language arts.

**Point ▆ Counterpoint**
**A Debatable Issue**
**Imitation**

**Background**
Imitation has a bad reputation but an honorable history. Artists and writers frequently speak of the value and necessity of the imitative stage in their own careers. Nevertheless, some educators fear that imitation in storytelling and writing will adversely influence children's creativity and originality.

**The Debatable Issue**
Encouraging imitation in storytelling and writing prevents children from developing their own creative and original ideas.

**Take a Stand**
Argue the case for or against the debatable issue. Is there a legitimate distinction between certain forms of imitation and plagiarism? Do our ideas about the role of imitation in learning need to be reconsidered? What arguments might you propose for or against the debatable issue? Marshal your arguments based on your philosophy, experience, relevant research, and expert opinion. After you have discussed these questions among colleagues, debate the issue in your class.

- **Point–Counterpoint** boxes present readers with topics at issue in literacy and literature and ask students to consider both sides, take a reasoned stand, and then defend it.

**Standing on the Shoulders of Giants**
**Historical Contributions to Literacy**
**Donald Graves and Donald Murray**

A quiet revolution occurred in American schools in the 1980s and 1990s. Not in whole language, as you may think, but in *writing*. Revolutions are often difficult to trace, but in the case of the writing revo⸱⸱⸱ ⸱ing its origins is not difficult. Two Don⸱⸱⸱

fessor at the University of New Hampshire. And he did write books—17 at last count. He has written poetry, novels, articles, and columns, but perhaps his finest contribution has been that of teacher and mentor. The measure ⸱⸱ great teachers ⸱⸱⸱

- **Standing on the Shoulders of Giants** boxes relate stories of accomplished individuals whose contributions to the field of literacy serve both to inspire and to educate.

- Each chapter ends with a **Reflection and Summary,** an interactive **Case Study, Questions to Challenge Your Thinking,** and a **Revisit** to the opening anticipation guide.

**Reinforce**

- **Teaching Tips** throughout the book and a featured set of **Practical Teaching Ideas and Activities** at the end of each chapter provide students with suggestions that can be used immediately in the classroom.

**Apply**

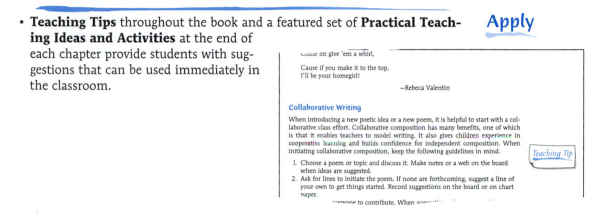

Come on give 'em a whirl,

Cause if you make it to the top,
I'll be your homegirl!

—Rebeca Valentin

**Collaborative Writing**

When introducing a new poetic idea or a new poem, it is helpful to start with a collaborative class effort. Collaborative composition has many benefits, one of which is that it enables teachers to model writing. It also gives children experience in cooperative learning and builds confidence for independent composition. When initiating collaborative composition, keep the following guidelines in mind.

1. Choose a poem or topic and discuss it. Make notes or a web on the board when ideas are suggested.
2. Ask for lines to initiate the poem. If none are forthcoming, suggest a line of your own to get things started. Record suggestions on the board or on chart paper.

*Teaching Tip*

- **VideoWorkshop Extra!** activities (for students whose books are packaged with the special VideoWorkshop for Literacy CD-ROM) direct readers to the Companion Website, where critical thinking questions correlate the text with video clips on the CD-ROM, which encourage the application of general concepts to the classroom. (VideoWorkshop is available as a value-pack option with this book.)

- **The Blue Pages** are a special section at the back of the book, offering students a compendium of resources for each chapter: (1) teaching activities keyed to chapter topics and issues, (2) annotated lists of children's books selected to build on chapter topics and issues, and (3) annotated professional references related to chapter topics and issues, as well as additional materials for some chapters. (Even more resources can be found on the Companion Website at the online version of the Blue Pages.)

**The Blue Pages**

**Teaching Activities, Children's Literature, and Professional Resources**

**1**

**Foundations and Approaches to Teaching the Language Arts**

**Teaching Activities**

**1.** *Focus on language arts in staff development and staff meetings.* As a staff, choose one or two specific areas of language arts on which to focus the entire year of teacher in-servicing and focus studies. Ask your principal or building administrator to regularly set aside 10 to 15 minutes of each staff meeting for substantive conversation about language arts instruction. Teachers could share specific classroom experiences, model lessons, or discuss a prechosen topic.

**2.** *Establish a professional library.* Ask the teachers in your building to share their professional literature. Create a teachers' resource library, with a checkout system, in an easily accessible area such as the teach-

bimonthly. Use this opportunity to exchange ideas, share experiences and teaching practices, inquire, gain multiple insights, and plan in a collaborative manner. Inspiration, empowerment, and effective growth and change often result from opportunities in which teachers collaborate and learn from one another.

**5.** *Review research with a critical lens.* Use these questions as you evaluate a piece of research:
- What exactly was accomplished by the study?
- What population was used?
- At what time of the school year was it done?
- How long was the study?
- Can the results be

# Supplements and Learning Aids

To get the most use of *The Language Arts: A Balanced Approach to Teaching Reading, Writing, Listening, Talking, and Thinking,* students and instructors can choose from a  number of useful supplements:

For the Instructor:

- **Instructor's Manual with Test Items,** written by George Coon and Geraldine Palmer Coon of Oakland University, provides a variety of instructional tools, including chapter summaries, student objectives, activities and discussion questions, vocabulary, test questions, and reflections inspired by the text.
- **VideoWorkshop/My Lab School** is a new way to bring video into your course for maximized learning! This total teaching and learning system includes quality video footage on an easy-to-use CD-ROM plus a Student Learning Guide and an Instructor's Teaching Guide. The result? A program that brings textbook concepts to life with ease and helps students understand, analyze, and apply the objectives of the course. VideoWorkshop is available for students as a value-pack option with this textbook. (The special package ISBN is required from your representative.) VideoWorkshop will eventually become part of an exciting new online package called "My Lab School," which is currently under construction. Watch for details.

For Students:

- **The Companion Website** (www.ablongman.com/cramer1e) provides a wealth of resources including additional study items, a link to special articles from the  *New York Times,* annotated weblinks, a complete guide to conducting research on the Internet, and an online extension of the Blue Pages, with additional resources for the preservice teacher.

# Additional Supplements

In addition to the supplements available with *The Language Arts: A Balanced Approach to Teaching Reading, Writing, Listening, Talking, and Thinking,* Allyn and Bacon offers an array of student and instructor supplements on the overall topic of literacy. Speak with your representative about obtaining these supplements for your class!

- **Allyn & Bacon Digital Media Archive for Literacy.** This CD-ROM offers still images, video clips, audio clips, weblinks, and assorted lecture resources that can be incorporated into multimedia presentations in the classroom.
- **Professionals in Action: Literacy Video.** This 90-minute video consists of 10- to 20-minute segments on phonemic awareness, teaching phonics, helping students become strategic readers, organizing for teaching with literature, and discussions of literacy and brain research with experts. The first four segments provide narrative along with actual classroom teaching footage. The

final segments present, in a question-and-answer format, discussions by leading experts in the field of literacy.

- **Allyn & Bacon Literacy Video Library.** Featuring renowned reading scholars Richard Allington, Dorothy Strickland, and Evelyn English, this three-video library addresses core topics covered in the literacy classroom: reading strategies, developing literacy in multiple intelligences classrooms, developing phonemic awareness, and much more.

# Acknowledgments

Most people skip prefaces; acknowledgments, on the other hand, are usually read, at least by those who expect to see their names there. I hope I haven't left anyone out who deserves acknowledgment. If so, I apologize. Writing is a lonely task, but I did not long for company as I wrote. I sought advice and help and received it.

I wish to acknowledge those teachers who contributed pieces to the Field Notes and technology notes, provided samples of children's work, suggested book lists, and offered many practical teaching ideas found in the Blue Pages. I sought out teachers who knew the landscape of the classroom and asked them to help me make this book relevant for classroom teachers. While you will be the judge of the success of this effort, I know these teachers have added to the validity of the ideas, suggestions, and strategies described in this book. I deeply appreciate their time, effort, and kindness in helping me make this book more teacher friendly than it otherwise would be: Kathy Brimmer, Melissa Schade Brendt, Erin Caldwell, Lisa Rose Granitz Chottiner, Margaret Dudley, Peggy Elson, Kelly Emmer, Dawn Hayes, Kourtney Hamilton, Gayle Hileman, Jennifer Hill, Megan Hussein, Shevy Jacobson, Sue Jacobson, Cathy Kochanski, Michelle Krzeminski, Lisa Kunkleman, Ann Marie Laskowski, Ann Llewellyn, Gail Marinelli, Liz Molnar, Vanessa Morrison, Gail Pottinger, Rebecca Roberts, Ellie Russell, Adnan Salhi, Sarah Ziegler Stevenson, Mary Ann Sturken, Jamie Sweeney, JoAnne Vazanno, Danhua Wang, Margaret Weber, Kristin Wilson.

The faculty of the Reading and Language Arts Department at Oakland University are my friends and colleagues. They were supportive and generous in offering their help and advice. I cannot imagine working in a better collegial environment: Richard Barron, Jennifer Berne, Jane Bingham, Gloria Blatt, Sigrid Brandt, Hal Cafone, Jim Cipielewski, Bob Christina, Kathleen Clark, George Coon, Harry Hahn, Dorsey Hammond, Joan Henderson, Ledong Li, Mary Lose, John McEneaney, Gwen McMillon, Annette Osborne, Geraldine Palmer, Linda Pavonetti, Anne Porter, Robert Schwartz, Toni Walters, and Joyce Wiencek.

I've had excellent editors on many occasions. Good editors spin gold out of straw; bad ones reverse the process. Good editors find errors and soothe egos. I've had excellent editors on this project—acquisitions editor Aurora Martinez, senior development editor Mary Kriener, and production editor Anna Socrates. I appreciate their patience, and their faith that I would, eventually, finish this book.

Reviewers' comments made me smile and frown. Either way, they helped make this a better book. A special thank you to Charlotte E. Black, California State, San

Bernadino; Maria A. Ceprano, Buffalo State College; Margaret Bell Davis, Eastern Kentucky University; Barbara Morgan-Fleming, Texas Tech University; Mary Louise Gomez, University of Wisconsin, Madison; F. Todd Goodson, Kansas State University; Rosalind Horowitz, University of Texas, San Antonio; Ellen Jampole, SUNY–Cortland; Rebecca Kaminski, Clemson University; Patricia Leek, University of Texas–Dallas; Janelle Mathis, University of North Texas; Karl Matz, Minnesota State University; Michael Moore, Georgia Southern University; Barbara Rahal, Edinboro University of Pennsylvania; Michelle Southerd, Illinois State University; and Elizabeth Witherspoon, Stephen F. Austin State University.

I'm grateful to the children whose photographs and works appear throughout this book. I'm sentimental about children but a realist as well. Their ways and their language are beautiful, often extraordinary. Teaching children is hard work, but for all of its difficulties, headaches, and heartaches there is a compensating reward.

My daughter, Amy, did most of the photography that appears throughout this book, and I am grateful for her help. I thank my dear friends, George Coon and Geraldine Palmer Coon. They read every word of my manuscript. They found the usual sprinkling of miscues and provided substantive suggestions as well. I can't help but think that they have taken their philosophy from Gene Autry's famous song, *Home, Home on the Range.* I seldom heard a discouraging word from them.

I also thank Barbara Wilson who read the entire manuscript and made many important contributions and suggestions. I also appreciate the steadfast help given me by Annette Osborne, Danielle Reid, Dorothy Goetz, and Kris Allen, who made important contributions to the side notes and the Blue Pages of this book.

My children, Amy, Jen, and Ben have been a source of inspiration through many seasons and for numerous reasons. I first learned to love the language of childhood from my children, and to appreciate the challenge literacy imposes upon children. Now my grandson, Max, has succeeded my children as childhood language model. Each child is unique; each child hurdles over different obstacles as they learn the language, literature, and literacy of their generation. I love them all most dearly.

# Foreword

This fine book on the language arts is particularly timely. In an era of mandates, multiple professional standards, and in some cases even scripted programs, Ron Cramer has given us a book that speaks directly to the best in classroom teachers or to any educator who cares deeply about the literacy issues that impact young students.

This work is scholarly, research-based, practical, and thoughtful. The author writes with particular clarity and insight. The book has a nice sense of voice. Cramer communicates with us teacher to teacher, researcher to researcher, and scholar to scholar. He asks something of us as we read this book: to be reflective and introspective. He leads us into each chapter with an effective anticipation guide, engages us during the reading, and asks us to reflect after it. You will like, among the many features, the section in each chapter called Practical Teaching Ideas and Activities as well as Questions to Challenge Your Thinking. One cannot read this book without getting a strong sense of the fascinating history of language arts, putting in meaningful context the literacy issues and challenges of our times.

Central to this book is the theme of thinking—that language and thinking are inextricably tied together. Thinking goes to the very heart of engaging students in the language arts.

Though highly readable, this is not a recipe book with a dozen strategies to pull off the shelf for easy use. It is a book deeply grounded in scholarship, carefully reasoned positions, and best teaching practices.

Master teachers will profit from this book because it will affirm what they are doing and stretch their thinking. New and less experienced teachers will profit from its candor and its clear discussion of important issues and practices.

The book addresses all the components of the language arts, with special emphasis on writing and revision, word study and vocabulary, spelling, and reading comprehension. Notably it presents an excellent treatment of the too-often-neglected topic of teaching grammar and language usage.

I would caution undergraduate and graduate students that this is not a book to sell back to the bookstore at the end of the semester. This is one of those special works that you will return to frequently for both guidance and inspiration.

In an era of reading wars and battles of "who is right," this book is a scholarly work about "what is right," or at least what we in education should be thinking about to make the teaching of language arts "more right."

Knowing Ron Cramer's work and career, I would expect his work to be scholarly, thoughtful, practical, and civil. He has succeeded on all counts.

As you begin reading, be prepared to think, to be informed, to be entertained, to be enlightened, and most important, to be educated by a scholar and masterful teacher.

W. Dorsey Hammond
Salisbury University

### A Philosophy and Approach for Teaching the Language Arts

**P**hilosophy guides practice. But sometimes it seems our philosophy is deaf and dumb. This is because we seldom articulate it. Yet, like the air we breathe, it is there—an invisible presence that we cannot escape. Our philosophy is embedded in our approach to teaching—what we say, what we do, and how we do it. A philosophy is a set of underlying principles that guide conduct. An approach lays out the practices, procedures, activities, and manner of implementing a philosophy. Teachers need a philosophy, stars to steer by as they navigate the currents and tides of teaching.

Have you ever written a statement of your beliefs about children and teaching? Do any of the following statements resonate with your beliefs? Care deeply about children; respect their language, culture, and diversity; apprise them often of their dignity, talents, and worth; effective teaching is more than passing on knowledge and skill; good teaching creates independent learners who will learn more than you can possibly teach them.

# 1 Foundations and Approaches to Teaching the Language Arts

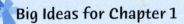

## Big Ideas for Chapter 1

1. Teachers need a foundation of beliefs about teaching and children.

2. Language arts instruction works best as an integrated whole.

3. Literature is the catalyst for integrating the language arts.

4. Influential teachers are recognized by their caring attitude and their professional competence.

5. Language experience, whole language, and balanced literacy instruction are three important approaches to teaching the language arts.

6. Technology supplements, but does not replace, teachers. When used wisely, it can promote learning to read and write.

7. Language experience emphasizes children's language and experience as foundational in teaching and learning the language arts.

8. Whole language emphasizes wholeness over isolation, meaningful practice, and the value of cultural and social communication.

9. Balanced literacy emphasizes the harmonious and proportional arrangement of all relevant components of the language arts curriculum.

## Anticipation Guide

*Consider each of the following statements, and determine whether you agree or disagree with each. Save your answers, and revisit this guide at the end of this chapter.*

1. A philosophy of teaching must be put into writing before it can be useful.  agree  disagree
2. Integrating the language arts is difficult and complex.  agree  disagree
3. Influential teachers are quite rare in this day and age.  agree  disagree
4. The six language arts should be equally emphasized.  agree  disagree
5. Technology has revolutionized the teaching of the language arts.  agree  disagree
6. Literature is the core around which the language arts revolve.  agree  disagree
7. Listening and responding to children will influence their language learning.  agree  disagree
8. All children have experiences useful for language learning.  agree  disagree
9. Breaking language into small pieces makes learning language easier.  agree  disagree
10. Balanced literacy brings together different philosophies of instruction.  agree  disagree

I read everything I could get my hands on, murder mysteries, *The Good Earth*, everything. By the time I was thirteen I had read myself out of Harlem. I had read every book in two libraries and had a card for the Forty-second Street branch.

—*James Baldwin*

## A Literacy Story

Harper Lee created a masterpiece of American literature in her novel *To Kill a Mockingbird*. The story, set in a small Southern town, is a testament to the courage and decency of a small-town lawyer, Atticus Finch. Atticus defends a black man accused of raping a white woman. This dramatic tale of prejudice and hatred is also a love story and even, in part, a literacy story involving a charming and precocious little girl named Scout.

Atticus has two children, Jem and Scout. Scout has learned to read by sitting on her father's lap as he read aloud from his newspaper, *The Mobile Register*. Scout is reluctant to go to school, suspecting it will ruin her carefree life. But, guided by her brother, Jem, she submits and takes her seat in Miss Caroline's first-grade classroom. Miss Caroline writes the alphabet on the board and asks Scout if she knows what it says. Scout reels off the alphabet, then reads aloud from *My First Reader* and *The Mobile Register*. But Miss Caroline is upset. Someone has interfered with her responsibilities, and this is dangerous. She tells Scout, "Now you tell your father not to teach you any more. It's best to begin reading with a fresh mind. You tell him I'll take over from here and try to undo the damage." Later, having caught Scout writing a letter, Miss Caroline proclaims, "We don't write in first grade, we print. You won't learn to write until you're in the third grade."

Scout meditates on these admonitions and wonders how she learned to read. Turns out she can't remember ever *not* knowing how to read. She thinks that reading just came to her like ". . . learning to fasten the seat of my union suit without looking around." For Scout, learning to read was associated with family and love. Atticus was Scout's model. She absorbed reading through the pores of her skin as she sat on her father's lap. Scout's trouble on her first day of school reminds us that learning to read can be made easy or hard. We can adopt Miss Caroline's theory of literacy, or we can adopt Atticus' theory. The choice is ours.

The defense had gone well; the committee seemed pleased. The topic had been well received; the design and statistical procedures had raised no objections; the results and conclusions set off no alarm bells. I had answered all questions put to me about my dissertation. "Yes! Home free," I thought. Then came the final request: "Ron, tells us about your philosophy of reading." My premature celebration came to a halt. "My philosophy of reading? Well, um, let's see. I think everyone should be a good teacher, and well, you know. . . ." I stumbled on for a while as rudderless as a dinghy in a heavy sea. I had never been asked to state my beliefs; I had never asked myself what I believed about reading. I know now what I didn't know then; I had a philosophy, but it was unarticulated. The philosopher Ludwig Wittgenstein said, "Philosophy is not a theory but an activity." His statement suggests that our beliefs and principles are defined by what we do, not just by what we say. Nothing defines your philosophy more explicitly than your actual deeds.

To read more about educational philosophies, visit
http://carbon.cudenver.edu/~mryder/itc_data/etexts.html

## A Philosophy for Teaching the Language Arts

Everyone subscribes to some beliefs, even if one's beliefs are a kind of agnostic neutrality. While the word *agnostic* is often used in a religious context, it simply means "without knowledge." Another way of putting it is "I'm neutral on that issue; I don't know enough to have an opinion." But neutrality is not a tenable position for the teaching profession. Teachers cannot be neutral; they must have a foundation of beliefs. *And they do.* Our beliefs are revealed in our actions, even if we do not state or claim them (Au, 1997).

I wish to state my foundational beliefs about language arts. They are articulated in this chapter (see Table 1.1) and throughout this book. Like all beliefs, they are

### Table 1.1

**A Statement of Belief: Teaching the Language Arts**

1. Language, whether oral or written, is best learned in active and meaningful social contexts.
2. Language is acquired and retained through meaningful use and practice.
3. Learning the language arts is dependent on effective use of the existing language, knowledge, and culture of the learner.
4. Language arts instruction focuses on the language and experiences of the learner.
5. Language is easiest to learn when it is presented whole rather than in isolated pieces.
6. Language learning is facilitated by active mental, emotional, and physical involvement.
7. The language arts must be integrated with one another and with content subjects.
8. Literature, diverse and varied, provides the models, means, and motives for language arts learning.
9. Teachers' expectations influence student outcomes; students' expectations also influence outcomes.
10. Meaningful practice is essential to succeed in any undertaking that requires skill; this applies as certainly to language arts as to any other skill.
11. All children have creative potential. Teachers must apprise children of their creative potential in an atmosphere of respect and approval.
12. It is crucial for teachers to understand and appreciate the value that cultural and racial diversity contribute to schooling and society.

debatable; but I do not debate them—I state them. They are fundamental to my life and practice as a teacher of children and adults. My beliefs are not arranged in any hierarchy of importance, since I consider them as a whole rather than as isolated pieces of a philosophy.

## Integrating the Language Arts

Four questions set the scene for integrating the language arts. The first question is *What are the components of the language arts?* For decades, the discussion revolved around *four* language arts: reading, writing, talking, and listening. Often thinking was considered the fifth language art. But thinking is not a language art per se; rather, it is the glue that binds the language arts.

In 1996, the National Council of Teachers of English and the International Reading Association recognized two additional language arts: viewing and visually representing. While they are newly recognized by professional societies, they are not actually new. Both have existed, without official sanction, for as long or longer than the original four.

The second question is *Is integration a new idea?* No. But credit must be given to teachers for calling it forth. Integration cannot happen in the ivory towers of academe. It has to happen in classrooms where teachers reign supreme. Teachers,

See "Integrating the language arts" by Carl B. Smith, 1997. Bloomington, IN: ERIC Clearinghouse of Reading English and Communication. (ERIC Document Reproduction Service No. ED402629.

exercising their instincts for good literacy instruction, are responsible for what success there has been in integrating the language arts. I have known teachers who have successfully done so. I witnessed integration of the language arts in the open classroom movement popular in England in the 1970s. I'd seen it in schools in the early 1960s. There is no doubt that the current movement to integrate the language arts has historical roots. So, it is not new; but it is powerful, important, and highly desirable.

The third question is *Does integrating the language arts mean that all six arts should be emphasized equally?* No again. Reading and writing are the most essential language arts. Teachers understand this; observe how much time and attention they devote to reading and writing. Anecdotal evidence supports this assertion as well. For instance, count the number of books and articles devoted to reading and writing. They number in the tens of thousands. Compare this count with studies of the other four language arts: the four together do not come close to the attention devoted to reading and writing. There is reason for this emphasis. Reading and writing form the foundation of literacy. I am not, however, suggesting that listening, talking, viewing, and visually representing are unimportant. Rather, I am stating the obvious: reading and writing are the king and queen of the language arts; the other four are members of the royal family. All must be viewed with respect, but two outrank the other four.

The fourth question is *Is integrating the language arts complex?* No. Well, yes and no. Integration requires careful organization, motivation, and engagement in order to be effective (Guthrie & McCann, 1997; Pappas, Kiefer, & Levstik, 1999). Further, integration requires a commitment to its value. Assuming you believe integration has merit, you have to organize instruction so that listening, talking, viewing, and visually representing work together with reading and writing. It is also crucial to integrate content instruction into the mix (Gavelek, Raphael, Biondo, & Wang, 2000). Throughout this book, integration is a continuing theme because integrating the language arts adds extraordinary value to literacy instruction.

The essential elements of the six language arts, plus the unofficial one, thinking, are described and defined below.

## Reading

Reading has two main branches, comprehension and word recognition. Comprehension is the gold standard of reading, word recognition the facilitator. When words are readily recognized, comprehension is facilitated; when words are not readily recognized, comprehension is impeded. Reading instruction must pay significant attention to word recognition since it is prerequisite to comprehension. But this does not mean that comprehension should be put on the shelf while decoding skills are acquired. On the contrary, comprehension must be taught side by side with word recognition. The notion that first you learn to read, then you read to learn, is incorrect, since it advances the idea that word recognition is *the* primary objective of early reading instruction. It is not; it is one of two objectives—comprehension and word recognition.

> Teaching mental imaging with comprehension puts words with images to enhance comprehension. For more information, visit http://www. understandmore.com/

Essential concepts of reading include the following:

1. Comprehension, in all of its facets and features, is king, queen, and royal court of reading instruction—everything else is elevator music.
2. Reading centers on the construction of meaning through the use of prior knowledge, reasoning, and text.
3. Word recognition instruction is crucial since it provides the code necessary to access meaning.
4. Reading skill is acquired and retained through meaningful use and practice.
5. The purpose of reading is to acquire knowledge, enjoy literature, and participate in society's intellectual, spiritual, and economic benefits.

## Writing

Writing is a process that involves a method of doing writing, a number of operations involved in writing, and continuing development that requires change (Kane, 1988). Writing usually ends in an outcome, such as publishing or sharing. Writing is organized around recursive stages, typically identified as prewriting, drafting, revising, and publishing or sharing. These stages are sometimes thought of as linear: start with prewriting, move to drafting, on to revising, and finally to publishing or sharing, in a straight line from start to finish. But few writers follow this sequence (see Figure 1.1). Actually, stages in writing recur again and again in a nonlinear sequence; writing changes and shifts with the dynamics of each writer's purposes, practices, and preferences.

> For more information on the writing process, see Chapter 10.

*Snoopy is famous for his many variations on the theme "It was a dark and stormy night." He uses all the steps in the writing process, too (see Snoopy's Guide to the Writing Life, edited by B. Conrad and M. Schulz, 2000, Cincinnati, OH: Writer's Digest Books).*

Writing instruction is often conducted in a workshop environment in which all participants are learning to write and are pursuing specific objectives. Writing workshops are led by a teacher in a collegial atmosphere. Children may be working individually or in partnerships. The teacher's role includes organizing minilessons, coaching, listening, modeling, and choreographing the entire writing experience (Cramer, 2000).

Essential concepts of writing include the following:

1. Writing is modeled by using literature and teacher demonstration.
2. Children usually choose their own topics, though topics and genre may also be assigned.
3. Conferences, student- or teacher-led, are organized to guide and motivate writing.
4. Revision is a central goal of writing instruction.
5. Writing has outcomes, such as publication and sharing.
6. Writing occurs four or five times a week for periods of 40 to 60 minutes.
7. The mechanics of writing are best taught and learned within the context of meaningful writing practice.

*Teaching Tip*

## Listening

Children are skilled listeners; they are also skilled at ignoring what they hear. Very young children have significant listening capability. They can, for instance, respond to many oral requests and commands, though they may choose to ignore what does not suit their interests. A child who is unable to utter a single word may, nevertheless, understand hundreds of words. From the onset, listening vocabulary outpaces speaking vocabulary, and this remains true into adulthood. Listening comprehension seems to involve the same or similar mechanisms as reading comprehension. For this reason, listening capacity is often used as a measure of reading potential. Consequently, children whose word recognition skills lag behind their cognitive capacity can receive instruction when written material is read aloud to them.

"The most basic of all human needs is the need to understand and be understood. The best way to understand people is to listen to them."
—Ralph Nichols, President, Dale Carnegie Training®, Michigan

Essential concepts of listening include the following:

1. Listening has direct practical applications to reading, writing, and talking.
2. Listening is most effective when listeners establish their own purposes, as in prediction.
3. Organized dialogue around books, stories, and informational material develops skill and knowledge across all of the language arts.
4. Reading aloud strengthens listening capacity, content knowledge, and language arts skills.
5. Different areas of content require different listening purposes, strategies, and skills.

## Talking

I prefer the term *talking* over the term *speaking* when describing oral language facility, since it conveys more accurately the informal manner in which oral language is most often encountered.

A famous comedienne often introduced her monologues with the plaintive line "Can we talk?" Her question suggests that talk is necessary if we are going to connect with one another. Talk is the sine qua non, the essential condition, for building and sustaining healthy relationships. Little can be accomplished among teachers and children without talk—not one-way talk, as in lectures, but genuine conversations. Through conversations that children first learn to construct meaning from the welter of stimuli and experiences that surround them. And nothing contributes more to children's immediate and long-term understanding of how to construct meaning from their world than good conversation early in life (Tough, 1973).

> "Listen, learn, change."
> —David Gergen, editor-at-large for *US News & World Report*

Essential concepts of talking include the following:

1. Talk is the catalyst that builds and sustains dynamic learning communities.
2. Language and social skills are developed and strengthened through talk.
3. Talk is a crucial medium through which children extend their thinking and learning skills.
4. Literature provokes talk that leads to more effective language arts instruction.
5. Talk strengthens and reinforces learning of the content subjects.

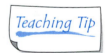

For more information on integrating talk and curriculum, read *Book Club Plus: A Conceptual Framework to Organize Literacy Instruction*, by Taffy E. Raphael, Susan Floria-Ruane, and MariAnne George.

## Viewing

Viewing is a crucial component of learning; indeed, viewing precedes reading and writing in human development (think babies and toddlers) as well as in human history (think cave paintings). Viewing is more pronounced among today's generation of children than previous generations. Increasingly, children gain extensive viewing experiences through television, movies, computer games, the Internet, CD-ROMs, advertising, photography, and art. More important, viewing opportunities are integrated with text in more contexts than they were in the past. There are, for example, thousands of picture books for young children, and texts for older children contain more art, graphs, photographs, and other visual media than in the past.

Essential concepts of viewing include the following:

1. Viewing skills must be integrated with the skills of comprehending text.
2. The Internet provides a powerful forum for integrating viewing with text.
3. Critical analysis of viewing experiences is needed since both sound and unsound information is present in many viewing situations.
4. Strategies for interpreting and analyzing visual text are available and should be taught.

## Visually Representing

The word *represent* means to "depict or portray an image or likeness" of something or someone. Humans of the ancient world portrayed the animate and inanimate world on cave walls. Their visual representations expressed the universal human desire to communicate, not just to those immediately present but to those who might "read" their visual representations at some future time. Cave dwellers portrayed a text through art. Children, too, can portray their verbal and written texts through art, craft, drama, and dance. Visually representing experiences adds power to the other language arts. True, some folks think of the activities associated with visual representation as a frivolous waste of limited academic time, but this is not so.

See "Storytelling, Drama, Creative Dramatics, Puppetry, Choral Speaking, and Reader's Theater for Children and Young Adults," located at http://falcon.jmu.edu/~ramseyil/drama.htm

The activities associated with visual representation arouse, stimulate, and enlarge interest and knowledge. For these good reasons, they must not be neglected.

Essential concepts of visual representation include the following:

1. These activities advance knowledge of words and ideas through the arts, crafts, and other media.
2. Visual representation makes for a more fully rounded education.
3. It enlists mind and body in the portrayal of imaginative ideas.
4. It increases children's confidence in their abilities.
5. It augments the growth of language.
6. It advances the development of multiple intelligences.

Figure 1.2 shows an example of two young students using visual representation. They tell the story of a confused Octopus named Hector who has the misfortunate of miscounting his tentacles. The story goes on to explain how Hector solves his dilemma.

## Thinking

Thinking is not a language art in itself, though it is an indispensable ingredient of all language arts. Thinking has a creative component; it also has a critical component. Creative thinking leads to new ideas, new ways of looking at old ideas, and different ways of understanding the world or some aspect of it. Critical thinking is often intuitive and subjective. For example, the impressionist painters saw the world subjectively and created a new way of representing animate and inanimate objects that was startlingly different from the techniques of the realistic artists who preceded them. The impressionists were creative; so were the realistic artists. Writing stories and poems is generally considered creative work, but a dry tome on building suspension bridges may also be creative (Bruner, 1962; Cramer, 1979).

Critical thinking is different from creative thinking, but it does not exclude creativity. The critical thinker seeks evidence for ideas and checks the evidence to determine whether an idea is true or false, right or wrong, good or bad. Where possible, empirical evidence is sought to confirm or disprove an idea. Thus, critical thinking tends to be more objective than subjective. Whether critical or creative thinking is involved, words are usually the medium through which the thinker operates, though there may be exceptions (Tierney, 1990). Einstein said that his ideas about the universe were not always represented in his mind through words.

Essential concepts of thinking include the following:

**Figure 1.2**

**Hector the Octopus**

*Kim and John, two fifth-graders, worked as coauthors to create the book* Hector the Octopus. *The fine story is enhanced by outstanding visual representation of the text.*

1. Creative thinking focuses on discovering new or unusual ways of solving problems or representing the world of experience.
2. Critical thinking focuses on logical inquiry wherein evidence is sought and analyzed to determine truth or falsity.
3. While distinctions exist between creative and critical thinking, they are not mutually exclusive operations of the mind.
4. Growth in the language arts is enhanced when teachers provide abundant opportunities for children to engage in both critical and creative thinking (Foster, Sawicki, Schaeffer, & Zelinski, 2002).

For more information see "How Can We Teach Critical Thinking?" by Kathryn S. Carr, in *Childhood Education* (Winter 1988): pages 69–73.

For further information and examples of how to foster critical and creative thinking within various school subjects, visit http://www.sasked. gov.sk.ca/policy/cels/e14.html

## Section Summary: Integrating the Language Arts

1. There are six official language arts: reading, writing, listening, talking, viewing, and visually representing. Thinking, while not considered a language art, is the glue that binds together the language arts.
2. Reading has two main branches: (a) word recognition—that is, the decoding of language, and (b) comprehension—that is, constructing meaning through reasoning, prior knowledge, and text.
3. Writing is a process that involves a method of doing writing, a number of operations involved in writing, and continuing development that requires change.
4. Listening is a comprehension capability whereby meaning is derived by constructing meaning from oral messages.
5. Talking builds and sustains learning communities. It is a medium through which children extend their thinking and learning skills.
6. Viewing is a skill requiring the integration and comprehension of information derived from visual images such as art, photography, graphs, and images on the Internet.
7. Visually representing is the ability to create images as in art or photography. This ancient skill preceded reading and writing in history and human development.

## Literature-Based Language Arts

### A Brief History

Literature defines us. It defines our culture, nation, history, and aspirations as a people. When we think of literature, we tend to think of books, and rightly so, since most stories, novels, poems, essays, and informational materials are enclosed within two covers. But the book format is not the only venue for literature. Magazines and newspapers publish literary works. Already we see electronic venues for literature, such as the Internet, e-books, and books on cassettes. Additional electronic formats, not yet imagined, will surely appear.

For nearly two centuries, literacy instruction in America used basal texts. Basal materials of the 20th century included student texts, workbooks, teacher's manuals, and related ancillary materials. The McGuffey *Readers* were the first widely used basal texts. Dr. McGuffey was a moral philosopher. His texts did contain some worthy literature, but the overriding theme was moralistic and religious. During the latter half of the 20th century, basal readers came under harsh criticism for neglecting authentic literature, particularly at early levels. In a misguided attempt to make early texts "easy," publishers tried two well-known approaches, word control and linguistic pattern control. Word control gave us the Dick and Jane text: "Look, look, look, Dick . . ." Linguistic pattern control gave us "The cat sat on a hat." Though many children learned to read from these texts, many did not. The most serious criticism of such texts, however, is not pragmatic (did they work?) but aesthetic (did they offer a rich diet of literature?—they did not).

As a result, a movement, sometimes referred to as *literature-based curriculum,* took hold in many schools. A literature-based curriculum strives to integrate the language arts, and often content subjects as well, based on literary themes. This movement forced publishers to include more literature in their basals. But the cat had gotten out of the bag. Curricular movements devoted to introducing good literature into the curriculum have proliferated, and in some venues they have completely replaced basal readers as the primary vehicle for delivering reading instruction.

> To learn more about literature-based instruction, visit http://www.eduplace.com/rdg/res/literacy/lit_oms0.html

Now for a little history. Early literature-based instruction had two names: individualized reading and personalized reading. Lyman Hunt (1966), Walter Barbe (1961), Jannette Veatch (1959), and Russell Stauffer (1969), among others, stressed the idea that a basal reader could never substitute for a good library. They developed and implemented principles and practices for literature-based reading. Of course, that term did not exist then. Nevertheless, the concept of literature-based language arts did exist, and in certain venues it flourished. It is important to acknowledge the historical roots of any educational movement lest we conclude that no history, no pioneers, no intellectual giants preceded us. More often than not we replicate and innovate based on the ideas of others. It is right and crucial for today's educators to recognize that we stand upon the broad shoulders of those who preceded us.

The one big idea that the current literature-based movement has in common with its historical predecessors is this: *good literature is an essential component of an effective language arts program.* Today, literature circles and book clubs have become vehicles for spreading the word that literature matters, that good books should be the coin of the language arts realm (Evans, 2001; Morrow, 1997; Raphael & McMahon, 1994). The modern literature-based curriculum uses literature, usually books, as the primary materials for teaching the language arts. Implementation varies widely but always includes settings in which students meet to discuss books and devise ways of integrating what they have read or are reading with the other language arts and their content subjects.

> For more information on Book Club and Book Club Plus, visit http://www.ciera.org; search with the key words *book club.*

Teaching literature-based language arts requires a library, and sometimes it also requires a diplomatic teacher. Censorship issues can disrupt a teacher's instructional plans. But when such an issue arises, respectful discussion with parents and community trumps confrontation. In the Field Notes feature, Mrs. Schade Brandt describes how she dealt with a censorship issue that arose in her classroom.

## Why Literature Matters

The British politician William Gladstone said, "Books are a delightful society. If you go into a room filled with books, even without taking them down from their shelves, they seem to speak to you, to welcome you." *Books matter.* The writer Katherine Anne Porter said, "Just the knowledge that a good book is waiting one at the end of a long day makes that day happier." *Literature matters.* The short story writer Katherine Mansfield said, "The pleasure of all reading is doubled when one lives with another who shares the same books." *Sharing literature matters.* Book col-

## Field Notes
### Real-Life Experiences of a Classroom Teacher

**M**rs. Wilkinson* called me the second week of school and angrily complained about the book her daughter, Mary, had checked out from the library. Since our picture book collection was hardly controversial, I was surprised at her vehemence. It turned out that Mary had chosen a Native American creation story containing magic. Mrs. Wilkinson felt that it conflicted with her family's religious beliefs.

I explained that although our library would continue to offer stories from various cultures, I would work with Mrs. Wilkinson to reach a solution that would best meet her family's needs. I had to concentrate to keep my voice neutral as I outlined the options, some of which disagreed with my own beliefs about students' book selections. Finally, Mrs. Wilkinson herself chose my favorite option: Mary

**Melissa Schade Brandt**

would be allowed to choose any books, and her mother would review them before reading them with Mary.

I anticipated another conflict in October, when I began planning our traditional Halloween activities. Rather than wait for the expected complaint, I wrote Mrs. Wilkinson a note describing our plans and inviting her to come in and review the activities before the holiday began. I was apprehensive about the meeting, but she arrived with a smile. She told me that everyone in her church had been pressuring her to homeschool her children and that her pastor had said that public schools would not accommodate her beliefs. Mrs. Wilkinson had taken great pleasure in showing them my note. She said her pastor had been impressed with my willingness to be flexible. She thanked me for showing her that a public school could meet her needs and did not exclude Mary from any activities.

* Names are fictitious except that of the author of this piece.

lectors will understand political theorist Harold Laski's blatant thirst for literature: "Books are the one element in which I am personally and nakedly acquisitive. If it weren't for the law I would steal them. If it weren't for my purse I would buy them." *Collecting books matters.* But literature alone cannot redeem the unredeemable. George Christoph Lichtenberg, the 18th-century writer and scientist, expressed this truth naughtily but delightfully: "A book is a mirror; if an ass peers into it, you can't expect an apostle to peer out." *Wisdom matters.*

Every culture has its literature. These stories define a culture in more ways than we might expect. Literature reveals our values and traditions, our prejudices and ideals. It may be written or oral, factual or fictional, prose or verse. Literature probably started with oral stories told around the hearth or the campfire or within a cave or wigwam, tent or house. Stories are as old as human history, and storytellers have always held an honored place in human affairs. Stories constitute an important part of the collective memory of a culture (Hirsch, Kett, & Trefil, 1988; Temple, Martinez, Yokota, & Naylor, 2001).

It is not by coincidence that the great writers often refer to themselves as storytellers. It is not by coincidence that many children and adults close the covers of a book prematurely if they sense that a good *story* is not being told. Stories have a transforming, almost magical, effect on children. Story time is often children's favorite time in school. And stories have a practical academic purpose in that they are a powerful way of conveying information to children. Flood (1986) has shown that the best way to convey historical information to children is through a combination of story and expository text. The next most effective way is through story text alone. The least effective way is through expository text alone.

Literature is the fountainhead. Every writer owes a debt to those who wrote the literature on which today's readers and writers are nourished. The novelist William Faulkner pointed out that quality literature is not the only source of useful information; one can learn from any genre or classification of literature. Nonfiction, for example, is a rich vein to be mined by serious readers and writers. Children need a storehouse of knowledge, a world of experience, an arsenal of language, and an archive of resources. Literature is the goddess who bestows these treasures.

## Section Summary: Literature-Based Language Arts

1. A literature-based curriculum integrates the language arts and content subjects based on themes drawn from literature.
2. Literature-based language arts have their historical roots in movements referred to as individualized reading and personalized reading. Currently, literature-based instruction goes by names such as literature circles, book clubs, and literary themes.
3. Literature matters because it helps define cultural values, traditions, prejudices, and ideals.

## The Influential Teacher

Years ago, a colleague placed this sign upon his door: PHILOSOPHER, LOGICIAN, COUNSELOR TO THE MULTITUDES. He was a 26-year-old, newly minted PhD, and just starting his first year of teaching. He could scarcely have counseled a handful yet, let alone a multitude. I've laughed at this harmless braggadocio over the years. Yet I see now that his statement might well describe the roles good teachers fulfill. There kneels Ms. Vazzano, first-grade teacher, quietly comforting Brian, whose dog died yesterday. Yonder sits Mr. Schwartz, eighth-grade English teacher, admiring a poem Katie wrote. Down the corridor I see Mrs. Kaufman, 11th-grade science teacher, explaining the logic of biological diversity to Kris, her prize pupil. So there is a sense in which teachers are philosophers, logicians, and counselors to the multitudes of children who pass in and out of their doors. And multitudes they are. If you teach elementary school for 30 years, you'll directly influence a thousand or more children, four times that many if you teach middle school or high school. Come to think of it, experienced teachers might, with all humility, hang my colleague's statement on their doors: PHILOSOPHER, LOGICIAN, COUNSELOR TO THE MULTITUDES.

### The Caring Teacher

Mark Medoff, at age 35 a successful playwright and winner of a Tony Award for *Children of a Lesser God,* returns to his high school and asks to visit his 12th-grade English teacher, Miss Roberts. He remembers her as the quintessential selfless teacher, recalls her respect for language, ideas, writing. She steps into the hall, looks into the forgotten face of Mark Medoff. He says to her, "I want you to know you were important to me." She embraces him, weeps, and soon disappears back into

"Never believe that a few caring people can't change the
world. For, indeed, that's all
who ever have."
—Margaret Mead,
anthropologist

the classroom to do what she has done thousands of days through all the years of her adult life. There are thousands of caring teachers like Miss Roberts. Some have passed on, some are still teaching, some aspire to teach. There is no formula for being a caring teacher, but perhaps the secret lies in cultivating a compassionate heart. Most of us have had car-ing teachers. An influential teacher sees potential where others do not, discerns gifts where others see only annoying behavior. Teachers who so choose can be influential; they can implant memories that influence students long after the caring teacher who implanted them has passed from the scene.

## The Professional Teacher

Teachers are professionals in the same class as doctors, lawyers, and engineers. They are members of a group with specialized training and knowledge. Teaching is a noble profession. Teachers care deeply about their work. They strive to master what-

"The price of success is hard work, dedication to the job at hand, and the determination that whether we win or lose, we have applied the best of ourselves to the task at hand."
—Vince Lombardi,
longtime coach of the
Green Bay Packers

ever subject they are asked to teach. They attend university classes at night and during their summers; they attend workshops, read books, buy unreimbursed teaching materials, collaborate with one another, worry about their students, read papers at night, prepare for the next day's class. Because teachers are professionals, they do their work under good and bad conditions; often they work with meager resources and insuffi-cient administrative support. While teachers are indeed professionals, they may be excused if they sometimes say, like the comedian Rodney Dangerfield, "I get no respect." What teachers often get instead are great expectations and modest salaries. Still, they chose to be teachers, and most do not regret their decision. Regardless of their status in society, most teach-ers strive to uphold the highest standards of their profession.

**Seekers**. The Latin root of *inquire, quaerere,* means "to seek." A teacher is a seeker. An inquiring mind is the finest asset a teacher can possess. Inquiring teachers seek to improve their teaching, continue their education, develop their professional con-nections. They attend workshops and conferences when circumstances permit, sub-scribe to journals that provide teaching advice, search the Internet for ideas and information. Seekers are not satisfied with what they learned yesterday; they seek to learn what recent research has revealed. Seekers are not content with yesterday's good ideas; they want to learn what good ideas may have been hatched today. Unafraid of risky ideas, seekers know that failure nearly always precedes success. Will Marion Cook, a composer of jazz and classic music, once told Duke Ellington, the "King of Jazz," "Try to go against what is easy for you. Test yourself." Good advice for teachers, too.

**Researchers**. Teachers are researchers, whether they think of themselves in that vein or not. The Old French word *oerchier* means "to search," and it is much like the Latin word *quaerere*—to seek. To do research means to study something thoroughly, in a detailed, accurate manner. Teachers can conduct their own research to improve their own teaching, better understand their students, and add to the body of knowledge that others may find useful.

With all that teachers have to do, one might reasonably ask, "Why add to the burden teachers already bear?" A fair question. But I do not propose research as a required formal pursuit for teachers. Formal qualitative or quantitative research, while rewarding, requires an enormous commitment of time and energy; therefore, I do not recommend it unless appropriate support, through the school district or a nearby university, is available (and I work with teachers who undertake this). Rather, I propose research of a more informal nature—studying something or someone within the classroom that might be useful for enhancing daily classroom experiences. Here are two examples.

**1.** Have your students keep a record of every book they have read. Did they like it or not? Why? Would they recommend the book to others? What books have they read outside of school? inside school? Are there books unavailable at school they would recommend adding to the class library? Periodically review the information obtained. Use the information to change, redirect, or supplement the literature instruction you provide. Share your findings with colleagues.

**2.** Collect a sample of writings over the course of one or two semesters. Keep the sample small. For example, choose three of your best writers, three of your average writers, and three of your weakest writers. Ask questions you want answered, such as these: What topics were chosen? What examples of good ideas and interesting language are present in each group's writing? What writing conventions gave the least trouble? the most trouble? What strengths and weaknesses are most common in each group's writing?

## Section Summary: The Influential Teacher

1. Caring teachers often leave their students with enduring legacies of influence that can last a lifetime.
2. Teachers' professional responsibilities include developing inquiring minds and conducting informal research to aid their own professional growth.

## The Promise of Technology

The word *technology* has become a synonym for computers and their applications. But technology was not invented during the digital era. Some ancient farmer sharpened a stick to plow ground and harvested a better crop. Some brave hunter drove the first spear into a mastodon, killing the fearsome creature at a safer distance. No, technology is not new, but that does not make it any less scary. My first computer, a gift, sat in its box for six months before I reluctantly unpacked it. A colleague told me I'd like it better than my typewriter. I doubted it. Like the 19th-century Luddites, I mistrusted modern technology, and gave up my Luddite-ish tendencies only

# A MATTER OF STANDARDS

## An Introduction

Over the past decade, an educational *standards movement* has sprung up, representing a diverse group of individuals and institutions—some favoring, others critical of, the standards movement. Standardized tests are typically used to determine whether schools have met achievement targets. Standards are general statements or goals for teaching and learning. The word *standard* in the context of education suggests a level of attainment used as a measure of adequacy. A standardized test's specified tasks, procedures, and norms can be compared across groups and geographical regions.

Standardized tests have uses, but their focus is often too narrow to fully and fairly assess achievement across a robust curriculum. The intention behind the standards movement is to raise student achievement—a laudable goal. However, opponents point out that teaching in an environment preoccupied with scoring well on a standardized test can make it difficult for schools to implement a well-balanced and comprehensive curriculum. High-stakes tests encourage "teaching to the test" and overreliance on multiple-choice questions and are often misaligned with local school curricular objectives. Furthermore, such testing cannot assess certain crucial skill and knowledge domains, such as critical thinking, creative thinking, writing, and higher-order comprehension. Opponents also feel such tests cannot measure performance in the arts—music, drama, art, and dance. Consequently, overreliance on standardized tests to determine how well a school is performing can be highly misleading. These and other issues have led to controversy regarding the standards movement.

While serious problems have accompanied the standards movement, educators cannot ignore it. All educators, especially classroom teachers, should participate in answering two important issues raised by the standards movement: (1) Are there ways in which schools can measure and report educational progress without relying too much on standardized tests? (2) Are schools willing to be held accountable for student achievement?

The federal government, most states, and many professional organizations have promulgated written standards for all academic disciplines. The standards that appear at the beginning of every chapter of this book are those set forth by the International Reading Association (IRA) and the National Council of Teachers of English (NCTE). Each A Matter of Standards feature contains a brief discussion of one or more of the IRA/NCTE *Standards for the English Language Arts* and is intended to help you correlate the content of this book with the IRA/NCTE standards. The full text of the standards is reproduced on the inside front cover of this book. The first feature examines the role technology plays in today's classrooms.

**IRA/NCTE Standard 8:** Students use a variety of technological and informational resources (e.g., libraries, databases, computer networks, video) to gather and synthesize information and to create and communicate knowledge.

Standard 8 emphasizes the importance of technology and libraries as resources for information and ideas. The Internet, e-mail, interactive video, and other technological innovations are changing the way we teach and learn. For example, certain aspects of writing, particularly spelling, graphics, revising, and publishing, have been significantly influenced by technology. More changes are on the way.

Students are often more comfortable with technology than teachers are. This suggests the need for greater emphasis on professional development for teachers. In the meantime, students are sometimes the teachers of teachers. We should welcome this switch in roles, for it gives students a feeling of pride and pleasure. Nor need we feel ashamed that our students sometimes know more than we do, although this circumstance does tell us that more professional development to enhance teachers' technological savvy is needed.

reluctantly. Now I refuse even to address an envelope on a typewriter. (Come to think of it, I no longer own a typewriter.) Write a book without a computer? Impossible.

The word *technology* is derived from the Latin root *texere,* which means "to weave or fabricate." And weaving is an apt metaphor for technology since the thoughtful teacher must now ask, "How can I weave technology into the language arts curriculum?" It is not just a question of the availability of technology, though such problems still persist. There are challenges far more daunting than obtaining resources. Two questions are particularly challenging: (1) How readily will teachers adapt to the use of technology? (2) What are the best uses of technology, especially in teaching the language arts?

> See "America Calls: Technology-Based Interdisciplinary Planning and Instruction," by J. K. Bryan, C. Merchant, and K. Cramer, 1999, in *Classroom Leadership Online,* 2(5).

Technology has its wise early users, its reluctant late users, and its stubborn refuseniks. Never forget that many educational innovations have been widely hyped, quickly adopted, and happily abandoned. Remember teaching machines? But technology is not destined to fade away. Like paper and pencil, technology is here for the long haul. Nevertheless, we must not let the technology zealots lead us down the primrose path. There is no wisdom in chiding reluctant late users, nor even refuseniks, for their skepticism. What is needed is a slow hand, gradually adapting to technology's innovations, patiently demonstrating technology's benefits, respectfully drawing the skeptics into the sticky web of technological advancement.

> "If we don't change, we don't grow. If we don't grow, we aren't really living."
> —Gail Sheehy, author

## Technology for Teaching Reading and Writing

Technology supplements teachers: it cannot replace them. Teachers are *the* most important variable in children's learning. They are irreplaceable; they do not need expensive upgrading in memory capacity or speed of response. Technology cannot determine the teachable moment with the precision of a sensitive teacher; technology cannot serve as social, emotional, and intellectual role models or deliver that enduring first encouragement that sets off a storm of creative engagement in a child. But technology can provide educational opportunities that no teacher, no matter how fine, can provide. Technology can send children to the Internet to experience the presentation of text, audio, and graphics that no teacher and no book can duplicate. Technology can put children in touch with their peers in the Australian outback to exchange letters, share ideas, explore concepts. Technology can allow children to navigate their own learning trails, access information unavailable in classrooms, "hire" their own teachers. Technology can be an extraordinary teacher and often is. Still, whoever would choose a good computer over a good teacher is just the person most in need of a good teacher.

Each chapter in the book includes a special Connecting Technology to Teaching feature written by classroom teacher Lisa Kunkleman, who shares thoughts and suggestions for incorporating technology into your language arts classroom. Ms. Kunkleman became a classroom technology specialist by dint of her own superior intellect and her determination to move from knowing nothing about technology to assuming leadership among her colleagues in connecting technology to teaching.

## Technology in the Classroom

Advocates of technology believe that the technology revolution will ultimately transform the educational environment. Many believe that the "redemption" of public education lies in the acquisition and use of the latest technologies. Certainly numerous applications for technology exist within the school setting. In fact, The International Society for Technology in Education (ISTE) has created, through NETS (National Educational Technology Standards), standards that recognize effective technology goals. (See the Blue Pages for NETS Standards for English Language Arts.)

Many school districts have invested large sums of money in the purchase of technology while failing to develop adequate technology plans. Consequently, it is often left up to the classroom teacher to integrate new technologies into the existing curriculum. Most teachers, however, lack software-specific skills and knowledge of program capabilities, making it hard to effectively infuse them into their teaching. Additionally, most schools fail to provide adequate user training and support.

The prime directive in using technology must be to improve student learning. Without this guiding principle, we merely change how we do things and fail to truly impact students' education. Most teachers currently use "computer time" for activities that are already done effectively in other ways. For example, they have students write a story and type it into a word-processing program. The students then illustrate their writing with Clip Art. Couldn't the same thing be accomplished using paper, pencil, and a 69¢ box of crayons? In fact, this type of computer activity has probably taken away some learning opportunity by keeping students from the creative and tactile experiences that occur when one puts crayon to paper.

Throughout this book, this feature will provide ways to offer students new learning opportunities and experiences by integrating technology into your teaching. The information and ideas are only suggestions and should be used as a springboard to your own vision of technology. As a teacher of the 21st century, you will be a pioneer on this new frontier. It will be up to you to create and develop this new environment.

Contibuted by Lisa Kunkleman

**Reading.** Research shows that technology is an effective means of engaging children in learning (Kirkpatrick & Cuban, 1998). Many children have computers in classrooms and at home. Children are learning to view print in a nonlinear fashion. The world of icons, animation, and audio supports comprehension of text in ways not known only a decade ago. Electronic books are available on CD-ROM, the current best technology. They can also be downloaded from the Internet, though these versions are not as interactive as CD-ROMs. Electronic books are available to children even in primary grades, though they have not yet lived up to the hype that accompanied their introduction. Many types of Learning Adventure software are useful for developing comprehension and vocabulary. For example, the Trail series engages children in simulation activities requiring strategic planning and decision making as they progress along the trail (Oregon Trail, Yukon Trail, etc.). Phonics, spelling, and vocabulary software abounds. Some of it is acceptable, some awful. Teachers can consider what is available and decide which programs might be useful when children require supplemental tutorial help.

**Writing.** Software programs designed to teach writing are available. Some are faithful to the writing process. They are interactive and lead students step by step through prewriting, drafting, revising, and publication. Computer-assisted composition programs are more valuable after children have experienced the writing process in the traditional fashion. There is no substitute for an excellent writing teacher. Writers need human interaction, especially in the formative stages of learning to write. However, once children have gained a foothold on the writing process, the computer can supplement writing instruction and provide useful practice. Three software programs for teaching writing are worthy of consideration.

**1.** *Microsoft Office.* Published by Microsoft Corporation and available in Apple and IBM formats, this software package includes Microsoft Word for word processing, Microsoft Excel for spreadsheet and graphing, and PowerPoint® for presentation capabilities. Students use Word for all of their writing, revising, and editing. They can scan pictures into their writing, create their own artwork, and set up tables and graphs for reports and insert them into the written text. PowerPoint® allows the student to create a formal presentation. Excel allows students to develop charts and spreadsheets, which, for example, may be used for making calculations for a unit on the stock market.

*Teaching Tip*

**2.** *Hyper Studio.* Published by Roger Wagner, this hypermedia program comes in Apple and IBM formats. Students can use it for writing, animation, graphics enhancement, drawing, and presentations. The teacher can use it to develop portfolios; narratives, poems, and student books may be published or saved in a portfolio record. This program takes time and patience to learn.

**3.** *Children's Writing and Publishing Center.* Published by the Learning Company for Apple and IBM formats, this writing program is less challenging and is especially useful for younger students. It has simple graphics and easy-to-follow directions. Students in middle school may find this software too simplistic; the same company has programs available for older students.

Head (2000), a middle-school English teacher, has conducted research comparing computer revision with paper and pencil revision. She describes some of the problems and opportunities associated with teaching middle schoolers to compose and revise on a computer.

See Chapter 10 for more information on writing and technology.

## Section Summary: The Promise of Technology

1. Technology, though it cannot replace good teachers, can play a supplemental role in teaching and learning the language arts.
2. Technology can be especially useful in teaching reading and writing, though at present its uses remain limited.

## Three Approaches to Language Arts Instruction

There are three approaches to language arts instruction that stand on the foundations of research, knowledgeable authority, and teacher practice: language experience, whole language, and balanced literacy. One might ask, "Why these three?" The answer is that the principles and practices of these three approaches have influenced language arts instruction in recent decades more than others. Many of the principles and practices of these three approaches have been adopted or adapted, in various guises, by other approaches to literacy. They can serve as a foundation for any approach to literacy. Balanced literacy, now in the ascendancy, adopted or adapted many of its principles and practices from those of language experience and whole language.

The 1950s and 1960s saw the emergence of language experience. Though it never achieved a large following among teachers, it has significantly influenced the development of other approaches to literacy, including whole language. The 1980s saw the emergence and gradual decline of whole language. Many of its best practices and principles have been adapted in an approach called balanced literacy. The principles and practices of balanced literacy are still in flux; its configuration is firming but is not yet fully formed. Likely to remain on the stage for the next several decades, balanced literacy is having a profound influence on literacy instruction. This approach remains open to ideas and influences from either side of the literacy wars, which have damaged relationships among literacy educators and the general public.

## The Language Experience Approach to Literacy Instruction

The decades of the 1950s, 1960s, and 1970s brought language experience into the mainstream of language arts instruction. Sylvia Ashton-Warner (1963), Russell Stauffer (1970), Mary Ann Hall (1970), Jeannette Veatch and colleagues (1973), and Roach Van Allen (1976) represent just a few of the men and women who wrote the books, conducted the research, and developed the foundational philosophy of the language experience approach. It embraces two fundamental principles: (1) the child's oral language constitutes the key linguistic knowledge for learning to read and write, and (2) the child's experiences are the content around which literacy is organized. The name itself derives from these two principles. The learner's oral language determines the linguistic structure of the initial reading material, and the learner's experience establishes the content.

**Principles of Language Experience**. Philosophy implies and guides practice; practice implies and reveals philosophy. All approaches to instruction have a philosophy, whether stated or implied. They also have practices by which their philosophical principles are implemented. The following principles outline the major premises of language experience as a philosophy and approach to literacy instruction.

1. **Oral language and personal experience bridge the gap between spoken and written language**. When children's language and experience are accepted as a starting point for literacy, learning to read and write is easy. When this is not the case, learning to read and write can be difficult. Language experience exploits the two major resources children possess—their language and their experience. It is one of the most efficient ways to initiate reading and writing. Learning to read and write had been difficult for Jamal, a third-grader who came to the Oakland University's Reading Clinic able to read only three words on a pre-primer list. He stumbled through a primer passage and said, "I can't read this, either." So I asked Jamal to tell me about something he had done recently. He described his attendance at a Pis-

tons' basketball game. I recorded his account and read it back to him. Then we read it together. Finally, I said, "Jamal, read your story to me." He read it fluently, though I helped him on two or three words. Why was this so easy? Why could Jamal read words such as *basketball, Pistons, scored, Jerry Stackhouse* in the context of his own account and not read a seemingly simple list and passage? *There is a reason.* Words describing personal experiences provide a context of maximum support; words written by someone else may not. The reception of Jamal's language and experience was instrumental in turning him into a reader and writer.

> "A major purpose of this approach is to impart the understanding that anything that can be said can be written, and anything that can be written can be read or said." See http://www.sasked.gov.sk.ca/docs/ela/e_literacy/language.htm

2. **Early literacy instruction is organized around the personal experiences of the learner.** The child who sees the Great Mojave Desert from the backseat of an air-conditioned Lexus may have a more luxurious ride than the child who sees that same desert from the bed of a pickup truck, but both children have their own personal experience of the desert. Why do we persist in thinking that the experience of the child in the Lexus is somehow richer than that of the child in the pickup? Actually, the child riding the pickup might, under the right circumstances, give a more vivid account of the Mojave Desert than would the other child. Personal experience, when connected to personal language, is much more easily remembered and understood than someone else's language and experience. The language experience approach thus makes learning to read and write accessible for nearly any child—or adult, for that matter.

3. **The language arts must be integrated.** Integrated language arts create a corridor for mutual listening and talking. Talking and listening are present in nearly every aspect of the language experience approach. Book talks, sharing writing, responding to literature, comprehension discussions, dictating accounts, and peer discussions lead to an abundance of opportunities to talk and listen in situations directly connected with reading and writing. Research supports writers' intuitive understanding that reading influences writing (Tierney & Shanahan, 1991). Katie, a first-grader, gave me a lesson in integrated language arts. I've always been fascinated by hummingbirds. I've watched them hover over a flower, wings beating so rapidly they appear to have no wings at all. Katie had read a book about hummingbirds, and it was her turn to share her book with the class. She came prepared with props. She held up a penny and said, "A hummingbird can weigh about as much as this penny." She continued, now holding up a thimble: Several baby hummingbirds can fit into this tiny thimble." Then she read a page from her book, showed us a picture she had drawn, and read a report she had written. I didn't realize it at the time, but I had witnessed a first-class demonstration of the integrated curriculum—art, literature, writing, reading, and oral language shared with fascinated first-grade listeners. A tiny bundle of six-year-old elegance shared a few vividly illustrated facts about hummingbirds, and I've never forgotten them.

4. **Language is for making meaning and is best acquired through meaningful use and practice.** Acquiring language, in all of its subtleties, is the special province of childhood. As children acquire language, they acquire more than a set of words and sentences. They also acquire thought structures and learning strategies that aid in

learning to read and write. As children develop, language becomes instrumental in directing thinking and learning. The richer language becomes, the more bountiful thinking and learning can be. The language experience approach involves children in their own language learning, acknowledges the worth of their language, and organizes the curriculum around their experiences. Children probe language to acquire its meaning. No one does this better than a young child. A colleague of mine, Jim Cipielewski, had gone to a local school to read aloud to children. Ann, searching through Jim's book bag, expressed definite opinions about certain books as she read off the titles, rejecting first this one, then that one. Surprised, Jim asked this strong-willed kindergartner to read aloud and discovered she could read books suitable for third- and fourth-graders. Then this exchange occurred:

**Jim:** Ann, your mother must be a good teacher.

**Ann:** My mother is a teacher?

What's remarkable about this snippet of conversation? Just this. Ann has closely monitored this conversation, and she is surprised at Jim's implication that her mother is a teacher. In effect, Ann has said, "I didn't know my mother was a teacher." Until now she has operated on a narrow meaning of the word *teacher*—a person who presides over classrooms in her school. Now she begins the process of acquiring an extended meaning for the word *teacher*—someone who helps you learn, not necessarily one of those folks who preside over school classrooms.

**5. Writing knowledge is acquired most easily in company with the acquisition of reading.** Writing is a fundamental component of language experience, and dictation is a forerunner of independent writing. Dictation is oral composition, and oral compositions are the language experience child's first reader. The step beyond oral composition is independent writing, which has requirements that young children are only partly prepared to emulate. For instance, they have only rudimentary knowledge of spelling. Invented spelling, therefore, must be encouraged because it enables children to write early.

Recording dictated accounts gives children a model of how written language is produced as they observe how the teacher records their accounts. As teachers record speech, they can talk about writing and model it as they talk. I'm always amazed at how much children retain from these modeling experiences. They soon begin incorporating dialogue and punctuation into their writing. Sometimes their first efforts are accurate; sometimes, partly accurate. Alisha's first independently written story provides an example of each:

*Accurate:* the racoon sayd "non av the anam can halp you"
*Partly accurate:* the snail "sayd you are so sad b cas no bdey lics you y not" sayd the
             bear

In the first example, Alisha put quotation marks around the raccoon's exact words and did so correctly. In the second example, where snail and bear are speaking, Alisha incorrectly places the word *said* (*sayd*) within quotation marks and doesn't separate the words of the two speakers. But her work is partly accurate; she knows that quotation marks are used in the context of conversation. She has the concept but not the refinement. The refinement of writing knowledge results from much authentic writing and reading practice.

6. **Literature models and motivates language arts instruction**. Where literature is a priority, books must be available. Books shape our minds and stretch our thinking. They are, as the writer Caroline Gordon said, ". . . a magic carpet on which we are wafted to a world we cannot enter in any other way." Through books, children may meet any person, visit any place, live in any era. Reading books enhances children's ability to function in a literate society. Literature helps children think about what writers do and how they do it. As literacy grows, children read and write their own books, talk about what they have learned, create art related to the literature they have ingested. Classrooms without books are like bicycles without wheels. They won't take you anywhere. To lack a library is to lack something crucial.

> "Magic carpets are provided in my room."
> —Karen Capanyola, teacher, on how she uses magic carpets to demonstrate to students that books can take you anywhere

7. **A sight vocabulary is derived from dictated accounts to support growth in word recognition**. Word recognition is a means to an end—comprehension. Until a child can read written words fluently, meaning cannot be reliably derived from text. An initial sight vocabulary is necessary so that word recognition can be taught from known words. Language experience is an efficient way to establish a sight vocabulary. After reading their dictated accounts, students make word cards, choosing only those words they recognize in and out of context. Word study activities begin once a child has acquired a few sight words.

**Practices of Language Experience**. Language experience is not limited to dictation activities. Other instructional components are part and parcel of the language experience approach. They include dictation, comprehension, writing, literature-based individualized reading, word recognition, talking and listening, art and drama, sharing and publishing, and the mechanics of literacy—spelling, handwriting, and punctuation.

1. **Dictation**. There are three phases to dictation: recording the account, rereading the account, and drawing words from accounts for word study. The language experience approach introduces children to reading through dictated accounts, the initial source of reading material. Dictation may be taken from groups or individuals. Groups typically have seven to nine children. Group dictation accustoms children to talking about their experiences, and it helps them understand the procedures for rereading dictated accounts. Individually dictated accounts can be started once children are comfortable talking about their experiences and are familiar with rereading procedures. Dictation can be gradually phased out as children become fluent readers. Those who are progressing more slowly continue until they, too, can read fluently. Some children are less eager to dictate than others; some need the stimulus of a recent class experience: a book read aloud, a nature walk, a discussion of pets. After a time, children come to class able to discuss their personal experiences and have less need for a specific classroom stimulus.

*Teaching Tip*

Lauren and Mykala, first-graders, wrote a dictated experience story together about going to see *The Nutcracker* ballet. They made a booklet, with included a picture of themselves along with their story, as shown in Figure 1.3.

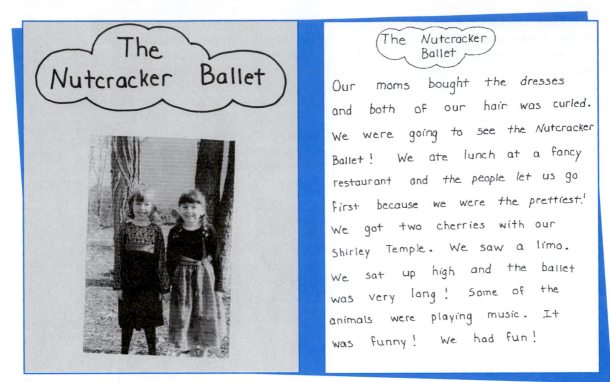

**Figure 1.3**

**A Dictated Language Experience Story**

*Lauren and Mykala reread their jointly dictated experience story perfectly and with enthusiasm. Experience stories connect language with personal experience so directly that children seldom have difficulty rereading them.*

2. **Comprehension**. Any approach to language arts that does not include a strong comprehension component has an intolerable weakness. Comprehension instruction must be deliberate, intensive, and direct. It can't be left to chance or limited to shallow questioning before, during, or after reading. Comprehension instruction must be planned and organized. Comprehension strategies, of the sort described elsewhere in this book, can be used with fiction and nonfiction materials. Instruction can occur in small groups and whole-class settings. Reading materials should include short stories, essays, reports, books, magazines, newspapers—any materials that children find interesting. Since multiple copies of reading materials may be needed, literature-based basal readers provide a convenient source of useful reading material. However, using the full basal program is counterproductive to a comprehensive language experience approach. Time will not permit simultaneous use of a complete basal approach and a complete language experience approach. Furthermore, the two approaches are philosophically incompatible.

3. **Writing**. Writing intensifies life and slows it down, which allows for reflection. Reflection analyzes the unexamined or underexamined issues of life, thus opening

doors to alternative ways of imagining life. For these reasons and others, writing is a crucial component of language experience. Schedule writing for no fewer than 40 minutes every day. Those who cannot write can draw and have their drawings labeled by the teacher. The writing process and the writing workshop, described in Chapter 10, are essential parts of a strong writing component. Children need support in their writing; consequently, it is necessary to use invented spelling, which enables children to use the full range of their oral vocabulary. Writing is valuable in itself, but it also contributes to comprehension, word recognition, and spelling. Writing also gives multiple opportunities for reading, talking, listening, viewing, and visually representing.

4. **Individualized reading, the literature base**. Individualized reading relies on children to self-select books as their primary reading material. Children read at their own pace and keep a record of the books they have read. Individual and group conferences are held to discuss books and monitor comprehension. When not otherwise engaged, children read books, write about books, or work on projects related to the books they have read. Literature circles and book clubs provide opportunities to share experiences and work on book-related projects. Activities such as drama, choral reading, and read-alouds are organized at the teacher's discretion. A good way to introduce books to children is to read all or part of the books aloud.

5. **Word recognition**. In the language experience aproach, 20 to 30 minutes a day are spent on word recognition activities; these continue until word recognition fluency is achieved. Sight words, learned through language experience accounts, are a starting point. Auditory and visual discrimination can be taught by using the text of dictated accounts and words drawn from these accounts. Word study activities such as showing children how to categorize words by meaning, sound, structural pattern, and other word features, are especially valuable. After a sufficient number of words have accumulated in word banks, children can work in groups or individually to construct and exchange short messages using words from their word banks.

*Michael, a first-grader, is reviewing words from his language experience word bank with his teacher, Ringo Mukhtar.*

6. **Talking, listening, viewing, and visually representing**. Oral and written language are parallel systems for communicating meaning. Talking and listening sometimes get short shrift in the language arts curriculum since reading and writing tend to dominate class activities. It is far better when oral and written language work together to create literacy events. Art and drama projects are excellent vehicles for connecting reading and writing with talking, listening, and viewing. The language experience and whole language approaches have an advantage in that their ways of teaching reading and writing afford multiple opportunities to integrate listening and talking with reading and writing, and with viewing and visually representing.

7. **Art, drama, and music**. Before children are capable of recording their ideas through the more abstract medium of print, they are able to represent their impressions of the world in the concrete forms of visual art, drama, and music. Artistic expression allows children to use their senses, and this, in turn, adds substance to experience. Writing, reading, talking, listening, viewing, visually representing, and thinking are enhanced when children express themselves with paint, fabric, clay, drama, and dance.

8. **Sharing and publishing**. Publication and oral sharing of writing is an essential component of the language experience approach. Book talks, book making, and the author's chair are forums for sharing language arts experiences, though these activities can easily degenerate into routines devoid of vitality if not monitored closely. Book talks and author's chair stimulate critical listening when the format is varied and fresh. If they become too routine, children lose interest.

For more information on sharing and publishing see Chapter 10.

9. **Mechanics: spelling, handwriting, and punctuation**. Children need to experience the writing process so they can draft, revise, and edit their writing, and in the final stages, proofread for miscues. They also need systematic spelling instruction, beginning in the first or second grade and continuing until a high level of spelling proficiency is acquired.

Legibility is the key issue in handwriting. It takes time for children to acquire the eye–hand coordination needed to write legibly. Whether teachers choose to use handwriting materials or teach handwriting on their own, it does no harm and much good to show children how to form letters and space them so that their audience can read them.

Punctuation becomes increasingly important as children move from early to later stages of writing. Dictation provides opportunities to informally talk about the symbols we call punctuation. Casual comments about punctuation can be made now and then as an account is recorded. Punctuation minilessons aimed at needs observed from analyzing children's writing are also helpful.

**A Critique of Language Experience**. Language experience has been criticized as difficult to manage because it is less structured, for instance, than a basal reader approach. Actually, management is no more or less a problem than it is in any other approach—all require organizational skills. I have worked with teachers who tried and failed to install language experience in their classrooms, and I have worked with teachers who have succeeded. The most common reason teachers fail with language experience is lack of support, not difficulties with management. Support has two dimensions, both of which are crucial to success: (1) teachers must be grounded in the principles and practices of language experience, and (2) teachers need the support of administrators and colleagues. To lack either is to miss something crucial.

The first requirement for success with language experience is solid grounding in its principles and practices. Without this, you may become discouraged before you have given the approach a chance to work. The solution is to acquire a proper grounding by reading the works of those who advocate the approach, seeking the counsel of teachers who have used it successfully, or taking a university course from someone well acquainted with language experience. Then you have to give it a go and stick with it long enough to discover whether it will work for you.

A second requirement for success is the support of administrators and colleagues. If you work in a school where all teachers are required to use the same materials and approach, opportunities for experimentation are nonexistent. Lack of administrative support has kept many fine teachers from exploring alternative instructional approaches. Language experience is not for the faint-hearted or for those content to drift through the teaching day in a routine way. Language experience requires a strong commitment from teachers and administrators. When there are commitment, support, and solid grounding in the premises and practices of language experience, it works.

## Standing on the Shoulders of Giants
## Historical Contributions to Literacy
### Ken and Yetta Goodman

Sigmund Freud remains controversial decades after his death. Freud can be judged by his work or by his influence, or both. His work is judged wanting by many, but even his critics recognize that few scholars have had a more profound impact on 20th-century thought: psychiatry, psychology, the arts, and literature are forever indebted to Freud's fecund mind. Whether his theories were right or wrong doesn't matter nearly so much as the influence he had on thought, research, and institutions of learning.

So it is with Ken and Yetta Goodman. They influenced thought, research, teaching, and learning within the literacy profession. Ken and Yetta are a team, personally and professionally. Ken says so in his book *On Reading:* "There is no idea in this book that has not been shared with, interrogated by, contributed to by Yetta." There have been other teams in the history of education; Paul and Jean Hanna come to mind. But none has made a more important and lasting contribution to literacy. The books, articles, chapters, presentations, and leadership provided by this scholarly team are more than just impressive. They are massive.

Ken and Yetta were and are the backbone of the whole language movement. Their ideas, writing, and leadership guided its destiny throughout its rise to national and international prominence. Ken's book *What's Whole in Whole Language?* sold well over a quarter million copies and in many respects became the bible of the movement. The two originated and led miscue analysis, which provides a window into the way in which readers process print and construct meaning.

Since I have known Ken and Yetta Goodman for more than three decades, I want to say a personal word as well. I have sometimes disagreed with specific aspects of their work; nevertheless, I have profound respect for them personally and professionally. Their contributions, passion, and genuine love of the profession they have served so well have been extraordinary. Like Freud, their work has had a great influence on thought and practice within and beyond the literacy profession.

For additional information, visit Ken and Yetta Goodman's homepage: http://www.u.arizona.edu/~kgoodman

## The Whole Language Approach to Literacy Instruction

The terms *whole* and *language* are crucial to understanding the whole language approach. When language is whole, it is easy to learn; when language, either oral or written, is broken into bits and pieces, it is difficult to learn. Language is crucial to learning and communicating; it reflects experience and culture. Experience and culture, when harnessed to instruction, make learning meaningful; when ignored, learning becomes difficult. Goodman (1986, p. 27) describes wholeness of language in these words: "Language is language only when it's whole. Whole text, connected discourse in the context of some speech or literacy event, is really the minimal functional unit, the barest whole that makes sense."

So, what is whole language? Altwerger, Edelsky, and Flores (1989, p. 10) define it as follows: "First and foremost: Whole Language is not practice. It is a set of beliefs, a perspective. It must become practice but it is not the practice itself. Journals, book publishing, literature study, thematic science units and so forth do not make a classroom 'Whole Language.' Rather, these practices become Whole Language–like because the teacher has particular beliefs and intentions."

Whole language stands for principles and practices that have enriched literacy instruction. It appeared on the literacy scene in the 1980s; the 1990s saw its decline. At the height of its prominence, many teachers regarded themselves as whole language teachers, and many still do. But, as in any prominent educational movement, many latched onto the label without subscribing to the principles. Publishers, for example, produced materials that claimed whole language parentage. These claims, often misleading, were seldom based on authentic whole language principles. Controversy muddled the message and interfered with its implementation. Eventually, charges and countercharges about its efficacy were issued back and forth. Whole language was blamed for school failure with little regard for accuracy or fairness. Questions engendered fierce arguments among its adherents and its detractors: Should phonics be taught? What is the role of skill instruction in whole language? How should literacy be assessed?

The blame game has a long history in American educational circles. Such debates usually generate more heat than light, but the current debate may be an exception. The debate has caused whole language advocates to sharpen their focus; it has caused teachers and researchers to reassess literacy instruction; it has led to a movement loosely identified as balanced literacy, which is discussed in detail later in this chapter.

**Principles of Whole Language.** The following principles outline the major premises of whole language as a philosophy and approach to literacy instruction.

1. **Language is easiest to learn when it is whole rather than fragmented or isolated.** Whole language is based on the observation that oral language is learned whole and in natural circumstances. Virtually all children learn to speak their native language competently and do so without formal instruction. Children learn oral language in their homes and their neighborhoods. Most oral language learning occurs prior to schooling. Once children start to school, written language

instruction is often accomplished by breaking language instruction into smaller pieces. For instance, phonics is often taught from part to whole—*ruh–uh–tuh = rat*. Whole language proponents argue that this approach makes learning difficult, unnatural, and nonmeaningful. The role of phonics in early reading instruction is, undoubtedly, the most contentious issue. But phonics is not the only teaching technique that violates whole language principles. For example, according to whole language philosophy, most skill instruction violates the wholeness principle (Goodman, 1986).

**2. Language is acquired and refined through meaningful use and practice.** Even an infant uses language in whole, meaningful ways. Picture 1-year-old Sarma, sitting in his high chair, face covered with cereal, repeating a single word—*muk*. *Muk* may be unintelligible to a casual visitor, but *muk* conveys a complete message to Sarma's mother. Mother knows that Sarma is saying, "I want milk." Whole language advocates argue that even a single word, like *muk*, is not only meaningful but whole in the context of its utterance (Goodman, 1986). Over the next few years, Sarma will expand and refine his language, but even at the age of one, he uses language to convey and receive meaningful messages.

Whole language extends this example to all aspects of acquiring language, whether oral or written. Since language is refined and extended through meaningful use and practice, instruction must follow this principle. Such instruction is called authentic; instruction that departs from this principle is inauthentic. Children should read books, genuine literature; this is authentic. They should not receive instruction from controlled basal readers; this is inauthentic. Children should write for their own purposes; this is authentic. Copying the news of the day from the chalkboard is inauthentic. A workbook page on short vowels violates the authenticity rule because it breaks reading instruction into pieces of language. Literacy instruction, according to whole language philosophy, must strictly adhere to the principle of meaningful use and practice.

**3. Language learning must focus on meaning.** All language functions revolve around the intent to convey or receive meaning. Failure to focus on meaning results in miscommunication (Halliday, 1975). When this happens, teachers and children talk past one another instead of with one another. Miscommunication can damage prospects for literacy. Tough (1973) recorded conversations between preschool children and their mothers. She found that miscommunication adversely affects oral language development and diminishes prospects for literacy. Conversely, focusing on meaning strengthens children's oral language and improves their prospects for learning to read and write. Teachers and parents sometimes send messages that implicitly say to children: don't inquire, don't be curious, don't make connections, don't explore, don't focus on meaning. This is seldom done on purpose, but children infer meaning as much, or more, from our behavior as from our words. Teachers and parents can also send messages that say: seek information, be curious, make connections, explore past experience, always seek meaning. Deeds trump words in conveying messages to children.

4. **There are three language cuing systems: graphophonic, syntactic, and semantic**. Three cuing systems operate during reading: graphophonic, syntactic, and semantic. The graphophonic system refers to the sounds and symbols of written language, including spelling patterns, the phonology, or sound system, of oral language, and the relationship between the two. The syntactic system, often called grammar, refers to the interrelationship of words, sentences, and paragraphs within a text and a context. Word order, tense, and number are aspects of the syntactic system. The semantic system refers to the meanings of language. Meaning is the key component of the cuing system and is strongly influenced by culture, beliefs, and prior knowledge. These three linguistic cuing systems are interrelated within the social–cultural context, which is called the pragmatics of language. Pragmatics is the study of language as it is used in a social context and the influence this has on behavior. How language is used within a social context reveals what it actually means. People adapt their language to fit the social context. Teenagers, for example, are apt to use language differently when communicating with other teenagers than when communicating with adults. When the language cuing systems and the pragmatics of the social situation work together, comprehension and communication can occur more effectively.

5. **Instruction should focus on the language and experience of the learner**. All children bring two assets to the classroom: their language and their experience. Language and experience are the raw material out of which the teacher and the child, working in harmony, fashion literacy. Teachers must plan an approach to literacy instruction suitable to the language and experiences of their children. The plan must include the activities, events, procedures, and practices consistent with the philosophy they wish to implement.

6. **Assessment focuses on observation of children rather than on testing**. Useful information about children is best obtained from informal tests, keen observation, and valid inference. According to whole language philosophy, close observation best reveals how well children are progressing. The purpose of observation is to modify instruction, meet short- and long-range student needs, plan ongoing instruction, and apply authentic assessment practices (assessment focused on real-world classroom instructional activities in naturalistic settings, e.g., portfolios of classroom work). Such observation is sometimes called *kid watching*.

Observation takes many forms: mental notes, written notes, checklists, conversations, conferences, interactions between and among children, meetings with parents and colleagues, portfolios. Good teachers, like good detectives, must be skilled observers. But observation requires more than just noting what's going on or marking a checklist. Effective teachers penetrate below the surface of what they observe. This requires sensitivity to the nuances of behavior and awareness of detail as well as the big picture. Teachers need ways to assess students' progress and needs without resorting to standardized tests, since most standardized tests provide little beyond a few numbers, useful mainly for comparing one student or one group of students with another. This seldom provides useful instructional information. You need more than a few numbers to understand children's instructional needs.

**7. Risk taking is essential to language learning.** When Robert Morris was warned that he might lose his property if he signed the Declaration of Independence, he replied, "Damn the consequences. Hand me the pen." All the men who signed the Declaration of Independence that fateful day had something to lose, and something even greater to gain—a free nation. There are various kinds of risks one might take, some foolish, some wise. Jumping out of airplanes seems foolish, but if you have a parachute and have been instructed by experts, the risk is reduced to an acceptable level—at least for some daring souls.

Learning a new academic skill is risky business. Fortunately, children are risk takers by nature, unless this ability has been drummed out of them. Even children whose behavior in the physical world is bold may shy away from academic risks. Fear of failure, self-protection, lack of confidence may motivate such behavior. But these emotions can be overcome when teachers make classrooms safe for risk taking. Curiously, risk taking and safety go hand in hand. Stunt coordinators spend enormous amounts of time and money making risky stunts as safe as can be. They work on safety precisely because they know the extent of the risk involved. Stunt coordinators want a safety net, an edge in case things go wrong. A safety net is what teachers can provide so children can say, along with Robert Morris, "Damn the consequences. Hand me the pen."

**8. Prior knowledge determines the meanings learners construct.** What you already know determines how well and how readily you will learn something new. Our knowledge of the world and its conventions is vast, and it varies with age, experience, and culture. Knowledge is organized into schemata—the organized networks of knowledge about objects, events, situations, and actions. Each schema (the singular of *schemata*) is related the others in complex interrelationships. Prior knowledge, our network of schemata, is brought into play whenever we read, write, talk, or listen. For example, if we ask children to read about dinosaurs, those with the most prior knowledge about dinosaurs are in the best position to comprehend the dinosaur text; they are most likely to incorporate new information into their existing dinosaur schema. Students with no previous knowledge of dinosaurs may acquire new knowledge to initiate a dinosaur schema, but since they are starting from scratch, they may have difficulty understanding and using whatever ideas and information the dinosaur text contains. Therefore, before, during, and after reading or writing, it is important to draw out children's prior knowledge through prediction, questioning, and discussion. This puts prior knowledge to work and provides a foundation on which to construct new knowledge. It also lets a teacher know whether prior knowledge is adequate or inadequate. The better and broader the information already possessed, the greater the likelihood that new information will stick and be integrated with information already possessed; the opposite is also true.

**9. Mistakes are instrumental in the construction of knowledge.** Beginnings are hard and mistakes inevitable. But mistakes are normal, and they are often instrumental in constructing knowledge. Teachers must expect and accept mistakes, and how they do this will influence how learning proceeds. Monitor your own attitude toward mistakes. If you react positively, new horizons may be opened; if negatively, new learning may be hindered.

Children can learn by monitoring their own mistakes. Dwayne knew the basketball court was a place where he could, through coaching, correct his mistakes. The classroom, however, was alien territory for Dwayne. He couldn't read, so he decided the best policy was to say little. He came to the Reading Clinic supposing he could maintain the same policy. We had a heart-to-heart: "Dwayne, you get the same thing here that you get on the basketball court—good coaching—but you have to play by the rules. You have to practice reading just as you have to practice basketball. *That's what I expect of you, but it's okay to make mistakes. I'll show you how to correct your own mistakes.*" Soon he was taking home books, reading them, listening to his mates, asking questions, and making some mistakes. I saw Dwayne a year after he left the clinic: "How's it going, Dwayne?" I asked. He replied, "Good, Dr. Cramer. I'm beginning to like reading."

**10**. **Language arts must be integrated**. Whole language advocates, like language experience advocates, believe in the necessity of integrated language arts. I have described this principle sufficiently under language experience, so I will not repeat it here.

*Teaching Tip*

**Practices of Whole Language**. All approaches to instruction have a philosophy, whether articulated or not. A philosophy allows for certain practices and rules out others. Whole language philosophy, some purists would say, rules out workbooks, spelling books, basal readers, word study, assigned writing, skills instruction—any practice deemed not whole or not authentic. Whole language philosophy allows for, but does not mandate, activities such as writing conferences, reading aloud, silent reading, self-selected literature, thematic units, art and music, journal writing, book making, invented spelling, the writing process. This is whole language in its philosophical perspective, but not necessarily whole language as teachers may actually practice it.

Some whole language advocates would not consider the components described below as constituting whole language practices unless these practices are wedded to a whole language philosophy (Altwerger et al., 1989). In other words, you have to subscribe to the whole language philosophy before the components described below could be considered components of a whole language approach.

*Teaching Tip*

**1**. **Writing process**. Whole language emphasizes the importance of the writing process, focuses on the operations by which writing is accomplished rather than the product. The writing process is organized in stages through which writing usually, though not always, progresses: prewriting, drafting, revising, and publishing or sharing. Kane (1988, p. 15) describes the writing process in these words: "As you work on a composition you will be, at any given point, concentrating on one phase of writing. But always you are engaged with the process in its entirety."

Though the writing process emphasizes the operations by which writing is accomplished, it would be wrong to assume that the final product is of no concern.

Product, not process, is the goal of writing. Process is the business of writers; product, the business of readers. Process should lead to a better product, and if it does not, then it has failed. Overemphasis on product can sabotage good writing; so can overemphasis on process. Process sometimes undervalues correctness to the detriment of the product. Neither condition is healthy, though it is clear that good ideas are more important than correctly expressed mundane ones. Figure 1.4 illustrates the concept of multiple revisions during the writing process.

2. **Writing conferences**. Conferences are a crucial component of writing instruction because they provide an outside audience for writing. Children know things about their writing that their teachers do not. Conferences help children understand what they know about their writing, and they give direction to future writing. Conducting effective conferences requires understanding children's perspectives. Consequently, comments, questions, and conversation must reflect children's perspectives: What are you writing about? What have you written so far? That's an interesting idea. What will you write next? Some conferences have a predetermined purpose. Others are spontaneous, intended to provide on-the-spot guidance. Some conferences are peer directed. All conferences encourage children to show what they know and reflect on what they will write next.

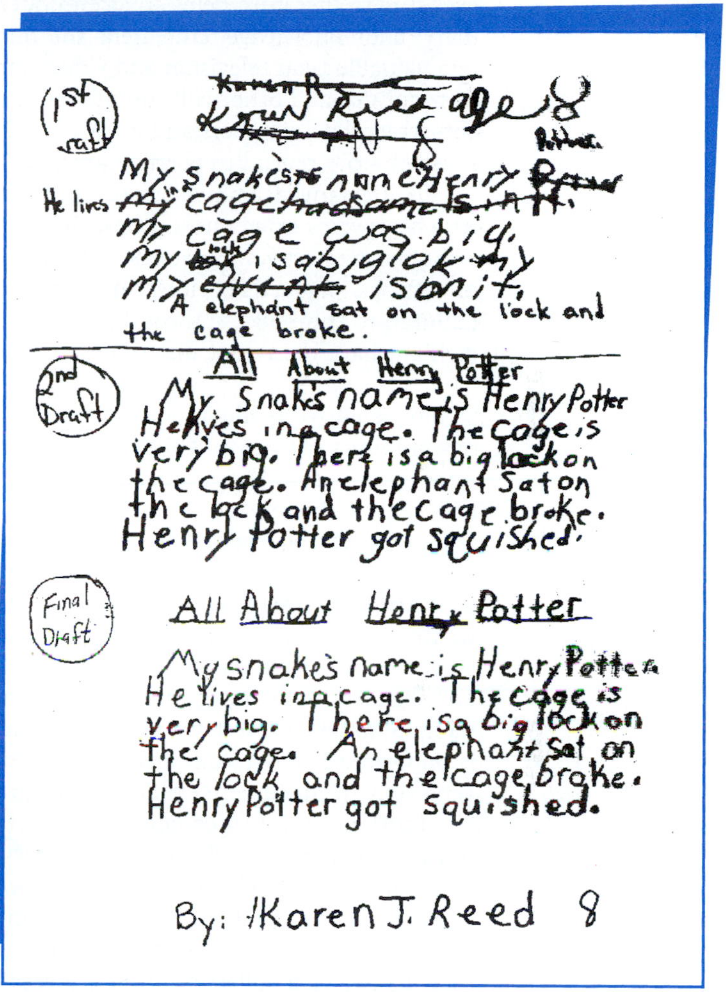

3. **Journal writing**. Journals are a valuable writing format, useful for exploring ideas that may later become more formal pieces. Children can use their journals to jot notes about interesting and unexpected events, explore topics, write drafts, and so on. It is a good idea to make journal entries almost daily. An important benefit of journal writing is that you are your

**Figure 1.4**

**Multiple Revisions in the Writing Process**

*Karen, age 8, wrote three drafts of her story. Draft 1 actually represents two drafts: it includes changes and an additional sentence. Draft 2 adds a concluding sentence and punctuation, and the handwriting is neater. Draft 3 contains no major changes but is written in Karen's best handwriting.*

own audience. Journals are a nonthreatening, productive way to build fluency and confidence in writing—a place to "learn to write like a writer."

4. **Literature study**. Many values are attributable to the study of literature. Wide exposure to literature helps children understand the writer's craft, expands vocabulary, adds knowledge, enlightens the mind, and entertains in ways more varied and valuable than television and video games. Literature imparts knowledge of our own culture and other cultures as well. Shared cultural knowledge provides referents essential to understanding oral and written language. Literature imparts a sense of story crucial to poetic, narrative, and even some expository writing.

Whole language philosophy emphasizes the importance of authentic literature, which provides experiences, knowledge, and language that help children read and write more effectively. Literature stimulates reading and writing, providing models of settings, characters, plots, and language structures. Discussion of books leads children to think like authors, to see what the author has done and how and why it might have been done differently.

5. **Individualized reading**. Few activities are more important than providing generous amounts of time for children to read silently. Individualized reading meets this important need. Whole language advocates, like language experience advocates, believe in its importance. Individualized reading was described earlier in this chapter, so I need not repeat that description here.

6. **Portfolio assessment**. A portfolio is a selection of works drawn from reading, writing, and other classroom activities. Pieces are usually chosen to represent the student's best work. Portfolios provide the perfect forum for helping children assess and monitor their own progress as well as material for teachers to use in assessment. Standardized tests may have their value, but they do not reflect much of what is important in day-to-day learning. Portfolios enable teachers to document literacy achievement much better than standardized tests do.

Portfolios can be a collaborative effort between teachers and children. Children must have a stake in selecting and reflecting on the contents. Ownership creates a willingness to participate, independent work habits, and healthy attitudes toward learning. The more children participate in creating their portfolios, the more likely they are to use them as meaningful tools for self-assessment. One of the best portfolio models is a collection of best pieces chosen by the student. A more complex model includes not only finished pieces of writing but the related work that preceded the final product: drafts, notes, and outlines. This type of portfolio enables teachers and children to assess both the process and the final product.

7. **Reading aloud to children**. It is well established that reading to children supports learning to read. It is less well recognized that reading aloud also supports writing, since it supplies models for writing and enriches the store of language available for writing. Chomsky (1972) found that children who were read many linguistically complex books developed greater linguistic capabilities than children who were not read to. Trelease (1995) cites dozens of highly successful read-aloud school and

*Teacher Gail Pottinger is taking a group experience story from a group of her students. First, she'll read the story, then they'll read the story together. She'll then ask for a volunteer to read the story. Finally she'll do five or ten minutes worth of follow-up discussion and word recognition.*

community programs that have been organized throughout the United States. After an extensive review of the literature, Anderson, Hiebert, Scott, and Wilkinson (1985) concluded that reading aloud to children constituted the single most important experience for reading success. Elley (1992) collected data from 32 countries, looking for factors that influence learning to read, and found that classroom and school libraries, regular book borrowing, silent reading, and reading aloud differentiated high- from low-scoring countries. Light (1991) found that parents who regularly read aloud had a significant positive effect on their children's attitude toward reading. The common denominator in all these read-aloud programs and experiments is the beneficial influence they exert on literacy and learning.

8. **Cooperative learning**. Whole language advocates see literacy as a social undertaking. Group instruction and experiences conducted in a social situation are crucial to learning the language arts. Activities that emphasize cooperative learning are, therefore, preferred. Many effective strategies fall into this category: writing workshops, group writing conferences, book clubs, peer editing, choral reading, and interactive literacy games.

9. **Bookmaking**. There are many ways to help children publish books. Parents and volunteers help in making books for special purposes. But for everyday book publishing, it is best to teach children how to make their own. A simple book cover can be made from pieces of cardboard cut to the same size as the pages on which a story, poem, or report has been written. Writing paper can be cut into shapes that symbolize a book's content or theme. For example, suppose you've written a book about

cats. Cut pages in the shape of a cat so the shape stands for the theme or content of the book. There are many kinds of books, but the most important thing is what goes into them. Children are always proud when they have expressed their ideas in books.

**A Critique of Whole Language.** Whole language has come under attack in recent times. Much of the criticism is unjustified and uninformed; some is related to strongly expressed views held by its advocates. Much has focused on questions regarding skill instruction, particularly phonics. Two other issues are often raised: (1) sampling text versus assaying text completely, and (2) the role of context in determining meaning. These latter issues are hotly debated by researchers though are arguably of lesser interest to classroom teachers. Krashen (1999) deals with these issues in *Three Arguments Against Whole Language and Why They Are Wrong.* In this section, only the broadly controversial issue, skills instruction is addressed.

A debate has continued for decades as to whether skills instruction, particularly phonics skills, is superior to more holistic approaches to learning to read. Krashen, defining his terms carefully, argues that "when Whole Language is defined as providing comprehensible text, it is a consistent winner" over the skill-building approaches to learning to read (Krashen, 1999, p. 27). Krashen came to this conclusion after reviewing studies of older and younger children who had received long-term instruction in holistic classrooms.

Whole language advocates object to skills instruction on the premise that it breaks language into bits and pieces to teach a skill or concept such as letter–sound relationships. And phonics, whether analytic or synthetic, requires breaking words into their constituent parts, although there are significant differences between these two approaches (see p. 331).

Does skills instruction make learning more difficult? A skills advocate might answer, "Yes, but a higher purpose is served since learning to decode words will benefit the learner down the road a piece." A whole language teacher might answer, "I can achieve the same outcome in a more holistic way through the use of literature, predictable books, and language experience stories." Does skills instruction violate the rule that language learning should focus on meaning? A skills teacher might say, "Yes, I suppose it does, but this is a temporary problem. As my children become readers, they soon forget the struggle they had in putting the pieces together to come up with the whole." A whole language teacher might reply, "Practice nonmeaningful language activities long enough, and you will inevitably teach children that language is not fun, not whole, not meaningful. You become what you practice."

How do teachers and researchers come to such conflicting views? Perhaps the answer lies in this Talmudic advice: "We do not see things as they are; we see things as we are." The Talmud, a book of rabbinic authority, suggests that "seeing things as we are" is part of the human condition. This may explain why literacy professionals are unable to resolve the ancient debate regarding literacy learning. Both sides act as though truth and wisdom reside in absolute dictums. Some whole language advocates ignore everyday instances of effective learning based on isolated practice of subskills. For instance, professional golfers routinely practice golfing

## Point ⟶ Counterpoint

### A Debatable Issue
### Skill Instruction

**Background**

Skills instruction is a hotly debated issue. Often the debate revolves around questions such as these: Should skills be taught directly? Should skills be taught in isolation or within an instructional context of meaningful use and practice?

**Debatable Issue**

Skills, such as phonics and the conventions of writing, should be taught within the context of meaningful use and practice rather than in isolation.

**Take a Stand**

Argue for or against the debatable issue. Marshal your arguments based on your philosophy, experience, relevant research, and expert opinion. After you have discussed the debatable issue informally among colleagues, consider debating the issue in your class.

---

subskills precisely because it leads to improvement in their whole game. Isn't it possible, even likely, that certain reading and writing subskills may be beneficially practiced outside of a wholeness context? The experience of many teachers answers yes to this question. On the other hand, some skills advocates operate on the premise that the more you isolate and fragment the subskills of reading and writing, the more effective instruction will be. This seems unlikely.

The answer may lie somewhere in the middle. A balanced approach consists of principles and practices drawn from a variety of instructional approaches, including whole language. Most teachers, myself included, want to make learning as whole and meaningful as they can make it. On the other hand, teachers should not be made to feel guilty if they introduce skill work that seems justified in light of their experience. The balanced middle seems best, and that is where a balanced literacy philosophy comes into the picture.

## The Balanced Literacy Approach to Literacy Instruction

Visit your local courthouse and you may see a statue of a blindfolded lady holding a set of balance scales—Ms. Justice. The blindfold and scales convey the message that equal, unbiased consideration of all issues is essential to the dispensing of justice. Everyone understands the need for a balanced, equitable system of justice, but vigorous debate ensues concerning how to structure the system to ensure fair outcomes. This view of justice is analogous to views about literacy instruction —agreement about ends, disagreement about means.

The term *balanced literacy* describes a literacy movement that brings together diverse philosophies of literacy instruction. It is an old idea with a recent facelift. Balanced literacy advocates dislike the term *eclectic*, though this term simply means to draw from several sources. Balanced literacy is not a collection of instructional concepts thrown together without a guiding philosophy. It avoids the extremes of whole language, which advocates little or no direct instruction in phonics. It also avoids the extremes of those who advocate explicit, intensive phonics instruction with insufficient emphasis on meaning and context. Balanced literacy recognizes that word study and phonics are necessary but insists on a broad instructional context, emphasizing writing process, meaningful use and practice, strategy instruction, response to literature, and recognition of the diverse needs of children.

Much good is expected to come of the balanced literacy movement. The need to reconcile the warring factions of literacy education is obvious, even to the casual observer. Debates, divisions, and distrust among groups with a legitimate stake in literacy policy have risen to an unhealthy level. Politicians castigate teachers; researchers war with one another; parents wonder what's gone wrong with their schools. Debate is good, but comity among stakeholders is needed. It is natural for stakeholders to wish to influence literacy policy. Like the old-time butcher, they can't resist putting a thumb on the balance scale to tip it in their direction. That's natural enough and probably healthy since, in a democratic society, everyone is entitled to put a thumb on the scale of educational policy. Democracy is messy but vibrant. If all goes well, the shakeout from the literacy debates will result in a healthier, more balanced philosophy of literacy instruction.

**Principles of Balanced Literacy**. Balanced literacy draws from existing philosophies of literacy, based on the premise of balance. Its principles and practices are derived from language experience, whole language, and traditional basal approaches. Balanced literacy is eclectic. It selects components of instruction from a variety of sources, systems, and styles and operates on the premise that students should be taught what they need to be taught, based on individual needs and stage of development. Its principles are described below.

**1. Balanced literacy strives for authenticity but acknowledges a legitimate debate about what is authentic**. An act or object is said to have authenticity if it is real, not counterfeit; genuine, not fake; true, not false; original, not copied. *Authentic* is a good word, but it has fallen prey to cliché. The term became a sort of battle cry with the advent of the whole language movement. It has been used pejoratively to ridicule certain practices; it has been used propagandistically to burnish a favored concept; it has been used properly to distinguish among appropriate and questionable instructional practices. When used properly, the word is powerful; when used to ridicule, the word is debased; when used to propagandize, the word is cheapened.

The term *authentic* is useful as long as we recognize that authenticity is a personal judgment arrived at through one's own experience and study of valid and reliable research. But experience and research must be interpreted—filtered through the philosophy one espouses and the biases one possesses. With these cautions in mind, three guidelines for determining authenticity are proposed. First, teachers should adopt instructional principles and practices that foster intellectual growth among students; those that discourage intellectual growth result in inauthentic instruction. Second, valid assessment is aligned with the instruction teachers provide; assessment that is independent of what has been taught is inauthentic. Third, the skills taught and the work assigned must be applicable to the real world students inhabit; if not, the skills taught and the work assigned are inauthentic.

2. **Children must own their own work**. Capitalism, America's economic system, is based on private ownership. The mantra of capitalism is that ownership breeds responsibility and stimulates growth. Can ownership accomplish similar results in schools? Perhaps, yet schools have tended to restrict ownership where students are concerned. Politicians and the state have gotten into the act as well, finding children too immature to own their educational goals and products.

*Co-ownership* is a better term—it suggests a *partnership* between teachers and children. A balanced view of ownership means that teachers have general responsibility for establishing the curriculum, setting goals, and assigning work; yet children must also have ownership responsibilities and rights based on the choices offered to them. For instance, individualized reading requires that children select the books they will read. This is essential, but it need not mean that teachers give up responsibility for making assignments, specifying genre, or selecting certain books for class discussion. Similarly, children should choose their own writing topics, but teachers can also suggest writing assignments and genre. Co-ownership implies that teachers and children have responsibilities and rights and an ownership stake in the work that falls to each.

3. **Teaching and learning work best when skill instruction is contextualized**. Does context facilitate learning to read? In other words, do picture and language clues help readers, particularly young readers, figure out the pronunciation and meaning of unknown words? This question is the focus of a long-running debate with no end in sight. Though it carries over into other areas of the curriculum, it focuses primarily on phonics and word study. Explicit phonics advocates argue that context does not facilitate word recognition. Whole language, language experience, and balanced literacy advocates argue that context does facilitate word recognition. Each side cites research purporting to support its position. Each side questions the validity of the other research. Each side makes straw-man arguments about the other's position. Explicit phonics advocates are said not to care about meaning. Context effects advocates are said to deny the value of phonics. Surely these accusations stretch the truth, yet they supply the ammunition that divides reading professionals into warring camps. Wars, as we all know, are declared by leaders but fought by the troops, and the troops, not the leaders, suffer the casualties. Teachers and children are the troops, and it is they who pay the debts of war.

Surely it can be said, after centuries of experience and reams of research, that phonics and word study should be an essential component of any comprehensive reading program. Likewise, learning the skill of analyzing context for clues to pronunciation and meaning can only add to a reader's repertoire of knowledge that facilitates reading. These are complementary ideas, and classroom teachers nearly always hold both views. Perhaps that's because they know what works with the children they teach.

4. **Instruction must adhere to the meaningful use and practice rule**. Since meaning is the ultimate goal of literacy, it makes sense to start children off expecting to make meaning of the texts they encounter or produce on their own. Balanced literacy advocates believe that insufficient attention is paid to meaning among those who advocate early intensive phonics. Balanced literacy advocates believe that word

recognition can be taught side by side with comprehension, so there is no reason to hold off on comprehension until children have learned to decode text. Similarly, balanced literacy advocates argue against extreme natural learning advocates, since the logic of natural learning implies a personalized curriculum for every child, a task many teachers find unmanageable.

5. **Since children's needs are diverse, and sometimes unique, the literacy curriculum must be flexible enough to meet the needs of all.** It is unrealistic to believe that any single utopian philosophy of literacy will fit all circumstances that may arise in classrooms across this diverse nation. A little humility is called for. There may well be a situation in which a given principle or practice, no matter how sound, will prove unsuitable for some teachers and children. A teacher may, for instance, find synthetic phonics works best for a given child or class. Who am I to say to that teacher, "You have committed a grievous instructional error"? I have never said such a thing. I don't expect ever to do so. If I truly believe in the principle of teacher ownership and professionalism, I must give teachers the same rights and responsibilities that I wish teachers to give to children. Instead, I would give this advice: *make informed choices; then carry out your responsibilities to the best of your ability.*

6. **Students need instructional support across a range of text types or genres.** While most children are familiar with story formats, they may not have significant exposure to expository or poetic texts. Furthermore, there are genres within genres. For instance, Padgett (2000) describes and illustrates 67 poetic forms ranging from the acrostic to the villanelle. While no one would argue that children need exposure to 67 different poetic text types, it is surely valuable to move beyond quatrain, haiku, and cinquain. Exposition also has genres within genres; the most common types are persuasive, explanatory, descriptive, and narrative. Further, any one of these traditional expository types may appear in fiction or nonfiction. A judicious balance of fiction, nonfiction, essays, and poetry is essential. Teachers must make choices while ensuring a balance of opportunity for children to make choices also. Wide reading is essential, and children may not always choose "high-quality" literature. Furthermore, much of the practice materials for early reading may not meet a strict test of "authentic" literature. Pearson and Raphael (1999, p. 14) point out that "Neither high quality trade books nor practice books can serve as the sole diet of books if young readers are to become proficient in literacy activities."

**Practices of Balanced Literacy.** Balanced literacy practices differ more in degree than in kind from practices adhered to by language experience and whole language advocates. For instance, writing process, literature study, individualized reading, portfolio assessment, reading aloud, journal writing, and cooperative learning are philosophically compatible with balanced literacy. On the other hand, word study (vocabulary and word recognition) and the conventions of writing (handwriting, grammar, usage, spelling, punctuation) are part of the direct but contextualized study in the literacy curriculum in language experience and balanced literacy, but not necessarily in whole language. Perhaps it would be more accurate to say they are not understood or taught in the same way.

**Table 1.2**

The Practices of Language Experience, Balanced Literacy, and Whole Language: Where They Converge and Diverge

| Practice | Language Experience | Balanced Literacy | Whole Language |
|---|:---:|:---:|:---:|
| Comprehension | ✔ | ✔ | ✔ |
| Writing process | ✔ | ✔ | ✔ |
| Literature study | ✔ | ✔ | ✔ |
| Literature-based approach | ✔ | ✔ | ✔ |
| Individualized reading | ✔ | ✔ | ✔ |
| Reading aloud | ✔ | ✔ | ✔ |
| Journal writing | ✔ | ✔ | ✔ |
| Writing conferences | ✔ | ✔ | ✔ |
| Portfolio assessment | ✔ | ✔ | ✔ |
| Cooperative learning | ✔ | ✔ | ✔ |
| Invented spelling | ✔ | ✔ | ✔ |
| Writing conventions (spelling, handwriting, mechanics, grammar) | * | * | ** |
| Word study (vocabulary, word recognition) | * | * | ** |
| Literary elements | * | | ** |
| Dictated experience stories | * | * | ** |

*Contextualization of instruction is important to both language experience and balanced literacy, but there is no taboo on direct instruction of these practices when deemed necessary or appropriate.

** These items are not checked under whole language, but this does not mean that they are considered unimportant. Rather, it means they are not taught directly. It is presumed they will be learned "naturally" through contextualized writing and reading practice.

Balanced literacy, like language experience and whole language, is not practiced in exactly the same way by all those who consider themselves within the camp. Table 1.2 identifies the principles and practices that unite and divide the three approaches to literacy instruction.

**Critique of Balanced Literacy.** The balanced literacy movement is a reaction to the perceived extremes of the traditional and whole language approaches to literacy instruction. The traditional approach depended largely on basal readers, was thought to pay insufficient attention to literature-based instruction, and tended to rely too much on workbooks to teach skills. Workbooks are an example, it is thought, of the failure to adhere to principles of meaningful use and practice. Whole language, on the other hand, was perceived to pay too little attention to skills instruction, particularly word recognition. On the surface, it seemed disorganized, perhaps due to overreliance on natural learning. It is debatable whether these criticisms were justified. Nevertheless, to the extent that perception is reality, the criticisms caused reactions within communities of influence (politicians, educators, parents) and stimulated the move to the middle path that balanced literacy represents.

Some have argued that balanced literacy is old wine in new bottles. But old wine may be good or bad, and so may new bottles. Balanced literacy must be judged on the merit of its principles and practices and the results that its practitioners experience when working with children. Balanced literacy does indeed derive many of its principles and practices from other approaches, such as whole language, traditional, and language experience. It could hardly be otherwise—this does not constitute a justified criticism. Balanced literacy must be judged, in the final analysis, on results. Is it good for children and teachers? Do children and teachers prosper under its practices and principles?

Balanced literacy is a solid citizen; it will work well if teachers understand its philosophy and implement its principles and practices, and many have. As a class, teachers are wise and thoughtful. They know when a principle and a practice are congenial, they know when children prosper or fail, and they have the wisdom and foresight to adjust instruction to what they believe is best for children and what they know works for children.

## Practical Teaching Ideas and Activities

*Teaching Tip*

**1.** *Articulate what you do and why you do it.* Examine and actually write out your own set of beliefs about literacy teaching and learning. Is your personal theory based on solid research? Reflect on what these beliefs will mean for your classroom practices. Involve the children in understanding your beliefs, which constitute the purpose behind their everyday activities. Analyze any discontinuity between your articulated theory and actual classroom practice; refine where appropriate. Revisit your articulated philosophy often as you use it to navigate your planning and decision making.

**2.** *Choose a yearly focus.* Rather than become overwhelmed with what you don't know, identify one focus area in language arts and develop a deeper understanding of it. Within this area, seek professional literature and in-servicing for further information, collaborate with others, and experiment in your classroom practices.

**3.** *Subscribe to a professional journal and join a professional organization.* Learning is a dynamic, lifelong journey. Stay informed of relevant research, connect it with your beliefs, and then apply it purposefully to your classroom practices. As professionals, we must be able to articulate the solid research that supports our classroom practices.

**4.** *Be collegial.* Establish partnerships with colleagues to model, observe, question, and discuss various teaching practices. Some teachers are superb at writing workshops, others at oral language activities, still others at guided reading instruction. Capitalize on the diversity of experiences and expertise within your own building or district. Enlist your principal to give release time or coverage to facilitate this teacher-to-teacher collaboration.

**5.** *Use "jigsaw."* Choose a professional book or article, and ask teachers on your staff to read different chapters or sections. Then present the findings in jigsaw fashion: each teacher briefly describes to the entire instructional staff the high points of the text he or she has read.

**6.** *Keep a reflective journal.* Regularly record classroom literacy experiences and the resultant student responses and learning outcomes. Reflect on these journal entries, considering what is working well and what could be done more effectively. Approach these experiences as a researcher: inquire, analyze, solve problems, rethink principles and practices, adopt new ideas, and refine them.

**7.** *Create an uninterrupted literacy block.* Schedule a daily block of uninterrupted time for integrated instruction in all areas of the language arts. Two and a half to three hours will allow for independent, shared, and small-group work in reading, writing, oral language, and visual literacy. Ensure that the children are spending most of this time engaged in authentic reading and writing practices, rather than insignificant activities, isolated and meaningless skill work, or "busy work."

**8.** *Allow ownership.* Allow children some control of and responsibility for their own literacy development and experiences. This includes opportunities such as self-selecting books, initiating personal decoding and comprehension strategies while reading, having choice in giving response to reading, self-selecting writing topics, approximating unknown spellings (invented spelling), inquiring into topics or areas of interest, and setting their own purposes for reading and writing experiences.

See the Blue Pages at the back of the book and on the Companion Website for additional activities.

## Reflection and Summary

### Reflection

Shangri-La, the Land of Oz, Dracula's castle: literature evokes these imaginary places. We know they are not real, but in our minds they are as compelling, perhaps more so, than the real world. Can we cultivate the imagination of children? Absolutely. That is what literature and art do best and why they are crucial companions in teaching the language arts. They spark the imagination.

Why is it important to do this? Because what we want most from our children is resourcefulness—not simply the accumulation of knowledge, but the ability to imagine what questions need to be asked. The art of the imaginative life consists not merely in solving problems, though this is important. Imaginative thinkers ask questions that have not been thought of before; they perceive things not readily visible to the material senses. Cultivating the imaginative mind is no easy task, and no teacher can do it alone. Teachers must invoke the powers of art and literature to refine sense and sensibility. Perhaps that is why the mother of one of the world's most imaginative scientists never asked him, "What did you learn today, Izzy?" Instead, she asked, "Izzy, did you ask any good questions today?"

## Summary

This chapter has presented the following main ideas:

- Teachers benefit from having an articulated set of principles and practices to guide the language arts instruction they provide.
- There are six recognized language arts: reading, writing, talking, listening, viewing, and visually representing. While thinking is not a language art per se, it is the glue that binds together the language arts.
- Integration strengthens language arts teaching and learning, but this does not mean that each requires equal instructional emphasis. Reading and writing require more emphasis than do the other four.
- Literature-based instruction is the catalyst for learning the language arts. Literature-based instruction can be organized and implemented through literature circles, book clubs, and individualized reading.
- The influential teacher exhibits the characteristics of caring and professional competence.
- While technology cannot replace teachers, it can provide supplementary training in selected aspects of language arts learning.
- Three approaches to teaching the language arts were described: language experience, whole language, and balanced literacy.

## ◄ Questions to Challenge Your Thinking

1. Do you agree or disagree that teachers have a philosophy of teaching even if they have never stated one? Explain.
2. Which of the language arts do you consider most important? Explain.
3. How does literature enhance the teaching of the language arts?
4. What, in your opinion, makes a teacher influential?
5. What role should technology play in teaching the language arts?

6. What advantages or disadvantages do you see in using the balanced literacy approach?
7. Do you agree or disagree with the whole language approach? Explain.
8. Which of the three approaches to literacy do you find most appealing? Explain.
9. What five or six principles would you subscribe to as elements of your personal philosophy of teaching the language arts?
10. What have you learned that you didn't know before you read this chapter?

## ◄ A Case Study

Read the following true case study, and then discuss the questions below with your classmates or colleagues.

Craig, a seventh-grader, is one of your more interesting students. He is pleasant with you and his classmates, yet at times he seems withdrawn. Today you noticed that he had been staring out the window while the rest of the class was occupied with an assignment. You saw him scribbling on a piece of paper from time to time, and you thought, "I should go back and urge him to get on with his work." But other things intervened and you did not get around to it. The bell rang, and your students filed out. As Craig passed near your desk, he threw a wadded piece of paper into the wastebasket. You're not a snoopy teacher, but you couldn't resist. You fished the paper out of the wastebasket. This is what you found.

### Future

As I look out the window
And stare into the dreary space
I wonder.
The future,
The future.
I see millions of dead people

Scattered along the plain.
The day before
Was a beautiful spring day,
But one bomb
One bomb
Destruction
If this is the present
What of the future?
Think.
If your mind is big enough to engross it
Think.

1. What is your first reaction to this case study?
2. As you read the poem, did you think, "No seventh-grader wrote this poem." If so, what made you doubt its authenticity?
3. What does Craig's poem imply about his thinking and language capability?
4. What would you say to Craig, if anything, the next time you see him?

## ◄— Revisit the Anticipation Guide ———————

Turn back to the Anticipation Guide in the chapter opener, and review your original responses to the questions. Having finished Chapter 1, complete the guide again, and then consider these questions.

1. Did you change your mind about any items? Which ones? Why?
2. Which ideas did you find most useful? Least useful? Why?
3. Which idea did you encounter with which you most strongly agree? Explain.

4. Which idea did you encounter with which you most strongly disagree? Explain.
5. What ideas would you propose as alternatives or additions to the ideas presented in this chapter?
6. What did you learn that most surprised or interested you?
7. If you had written this chapter, what would you have done differently? Explain.

## VideoWorkshop Extra!

If your instructor ordered a package including VideoWorkshop, go to Chapter 1 of the Companion Website (www.ablongman.com/cramer1e) and click on the VideoWorkshop button. Follow the instructions for viewing the appropriate video clip and completing the accompanying exercise. Watch the Companion Website for access to a new interactive teaching portal, My Lab School, currently under construction.

## A Philosophy for Organizing Classroom Environments

*Paul Brooks, environmentalist, said, "We shall never understand the natural environment until we see it as a living organism." Scientific evidence proves the soundness of his argument. Though no scientific evidence supports the following statement, it is just as sound:* We shall never understand teaching and learning until we come to see that a classroom is a living organism. *You can feel the good vibrations in a well-managed classroom; you sense that it is a living, thriving organism. The opposite is true of a badly managed classroom; you sense that it is a dead, dying, or malnourished organism.*

*While it takes the cooperation of everyone in a classroom to make it vibrant, the teacher is the prime mover, the first cause, the ecologist who shapes a learning community in which children flourish. A learning community is many things: a forum where creativity is welcome, a soapbox where ideas are freely exchanged, a theater where laughter is heard, a workshop where business is conducted, an arena where risks are taken, a society where interests are shared, a club whose membership includes everyone.*

# 2 Organizing Learning Environments: Language, Learning, and Diversity

## Big Ideas for Chapter 2

1. Teachers and children are mutually responsible for creating effective teaching and learning environments.

2. Teachers and children work together to create disciplined classrooms with effective work procedures and organizational arrangements.

3. Inviting physical arrangements of classrooms foster learning.

4. Psychologists Piaget, Vygotsky, and Bruner proposed complementary theories of how language and thought interact in learning.

5. Creative thinking focuses on new ideas and rethinking old ideas; critical thinking solves problems through careful evaluation of facts, data, and information.

6. Intelligence is multidimensional and includes verbal, mathematical, spatial, kinesthetic, and other types of intelligent behaviors.

7. Children of diverse racial, ethnic, language, and cultural backgrounds enrich classrooms when differences are understood and respected.

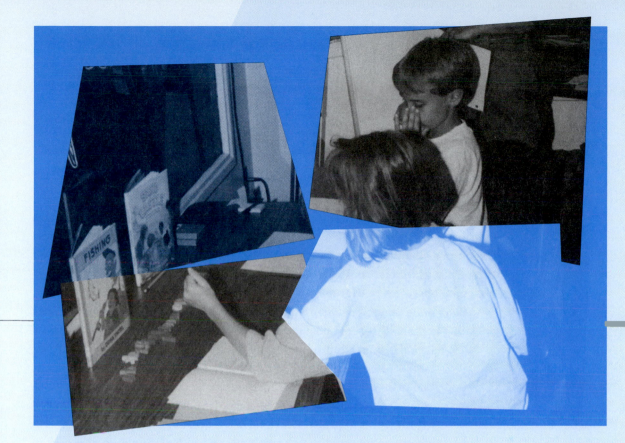

### ✦ Anticipation Guide

*Consider each of the following statements, and determine whether you agree or disagree with each. Save your answers, and revisit this guide at the end of this chapter.*

1. Classroom environments can be deliberately cultivated.                          agree     disagree
2. Children work best in quiet classrooms.                                          agree     disagree
3. Only teachers should create rules for classroom discipline.                      agree     disagree
4. A physically attractive classroom improves language arts achievement.            agree     disagree
5. Research shows that parents in classrooms create problems for teachers.          agree     disagree
6. All children are capable of creative thinking.                                   agree     disagree
7. High IQ children are more creative than average children.                        agree     disagree
8. Everyone speaks a dialect.                                                        agree     disagre
9. Diversity is mainly concerned with minority children.                            agree     disagree
10. Second-language learners should be taught only in English.                      agree     disagree

A language is not a finite resource or precious artifact in need of vigilant protection lest it wear away, fall apart, or get used up. It is constantly being renewed, and therefore changed, by living speakers, with all their cleverness, pride, and insatiable need to communicate.

—Steven Pinker

## A Literacy Story

Journeys. They can be long and dangerous, as when pioneers traversed this continent in covered wagons. An intrepid man once rowed across the Atlantic Ocean in a small boat. These were physical journeys, but a journey of the mind can be just as heroic. The journey to literacy has many pathways; for some, there are many obstacles to overcome.

A boy grew up in Sacramento, California, in a home where only Spanish was spoken. He started school speaking fewer than 50 English words. At age 9 he embarked on a journey to literacy: "Give me the names of important books, " he would say to his teachers. By important books, he meant books for adults, not children: *Great Expectations, Gone with the Wind, Moby-Dick*. As he read, he reported his progress to his teachers, thirsting for words of praise, which he often got. Like hungry readers everywhere, he haunted the library, and read in bed, in public parks, or in the shade of a tree. Like some other hungry readers, he found that his habit mystified his family. *You'll ruin your eyesight. What do you see in those books, anyway? Is my son a genius?*

So began the long journey for a boy of 9. It eventually led to graduation from Stanford University and Columbia University. Perhaps you know the rest of the story. The boy who started school with a vocabulary of 50 English words now makes his living with words. Richard Rodriguez now lives the life of a writer (*Hunger of Memory*). He often reads his essays on National Public Radio. He journeys around the world on lecture tours. Richard Rodriguez's journey to literacy started with the daring request to his teachers: "Give me the names of important books." Now he writes his own important books.

# A MATTER OF STANDARDS

## The English Language Arts

**Standard 9:** Students develop an understanding of and respect for diversity in language use, patterns, and dialects across cultures, ethnic groups, geographic regions, and social roles.

**Standard 10:** Students whose first language is not English make use of their first language to develop competency in the English language arts and to develop understanding of content across the curriculum.

Today's students are growing up in a more diverse society than any previous generation. As diversity has increased, so has our recognition of its importance in schooling. Every child must learn to appreciate and respect the value of diverse linguistic, cultural, racial, and ethnic differences. Students have an advantage when their teachers model essential behaviors and concepts related to diversity. Most

STANDARD

teachers are willing to meet this challenge, but it requires heartfelt commitment and explicit preparation. Teachers must avail themselves of resources related to diversity. They must understand that children are not fundamentally different merely because they bring different physical, linguistic, and cultural characteristics to the classroom. Diversity enriches learning when teachers are flexible and caring in their approach to teaching children of diverse backgrounds. We know, for example, that second-language learners learn to speak, read, and write English best in a supportive emotional and intellectual environment. This holds true for learning content as well. Teachers have the primary responsibility for providing a learning environment that makes success possible. This chapter suggests ideas and resources that can help teachers and students as they consider ways to improve teaching and learning in a context of diversity.

---

*Ecology* comes from the Greek word *oikos*—meaning "a house or dwelling." Ecologists study the relationships between organisms and their environments. For example, scientists study the relationship between rain forests and climate; sociologists study the relationships between human groups and their environments. Teachers are ecologists, too. Teachers create, manage, and organize the physical and social environments in which children dwell. Children spend more time dwelling in classrooms than any other environment except for their homes. The ecology of the classroom influences those special organisms we call children.

## Intellectual, Therapeutic, and Cultivated Environments

I've taught in universities for decades. I love the university; I wouldn't have spent my life in any other place. Still, I offer this heresy: *Excellent teachers do not come out of universities, though there they may learn the basics of excellent teaching. Excellent teaching comes out of the minds and hearts of those artist–teachers who have taught themselves how to be excellent teachers.*

I have taught long enough to know that I cannot teach another person how to teach. I can share my knowledge and experience with another

> "Good teaching is one-fourth preparation and three-fourths pure theater."
>
> —Gail Godwin, writer

person; I can influence another person. But in the end, *every tub rests on its own bottom*. Everyone who enters the teaching profession must take responsibility for him- and herself.

Excellent teaching is as mysterious as the smile on the *Mona Lisa*. Perhaps the Skin Horse had the answer to this mystery. When the Velveteen Rabbit asked the veteran of the nursery, the Skin Horse, "What is real?" he answered, "Real isn't how you are made, it's a thing that happens to you. When a child loves you for a long, long time, not just to play with, but REALLY loves you, then you become Real. It doesn't happen all at once. You become." Perhaps that's what happens to excellent teachers. *They become*. They grow into their specialized knowledge and skills. They become what it is they want to become through hard work, assuming full responsibility for their own growth. They have learned how to create and control the environments needed for REAL teaching and learning. They become, I want to say, REAL teachers.

## The Intellectual Environment

Gandhi, a man who changed the world forever, said, "You must be the change you wish to see in the world." If you wish to shape your classroom's intellectual environment, you must be the change you wish to see in your classroom. You can create an intellectual environment where ideas are valued—no one else can do it for you. An intellectual environment means openness to ideas and opinions that may conflict with your own ideas and opinions. Respect children's ways without abandoning your own perspective and without relinquishing discipline. Acquire a working knowledge of your children's abilities and aspirations while remaining alert to their limitations and uncertainties. Respect individual initiative, recognize individual achievement, encourage self-expression, establish fair standards of conduct, and develop a spirit of community within your classroom. Model the traits you want children to exhibit, as Gandhi did.

> "It is today that we create the world of the future."
> —Eleanor Roosevelt

An intellectual environment values diversity of thought and behavior (Carreiro, 1998). Perhaps you have walked into classrooms where quietness and orderliness prevailed: children in their seats, desks arranged in orderly rows. Questions are asked, hands raised, answers politely given. Such arrangements will not stimulate intellectual give and take (Temple, Nathan, Temple, & Burris, 1993). A challenging intellectual environment generates noise, bustle, argument and counterargument. Children thrive in busy but purposeful classrooms. Classrooms in which interaction among students is forbidden are unnatural, uncomfortable, and unhealthy. They do not promote learning or concentration. On the contrary, they produce a dislike for learning and a spirit of indifference. Still, at times students and teachers need a respite from the bustle of the working classroom. Therefore, spaces for quiet retreat are needed, but they cannot be the dominant mode in an intellectually healthy classroom.

## The Therapeutic Environment

Children crave security and stability. They need the assurance of acceptance and sympathetic understanding and to know that their ideas and feelings count. While teachers cannot hand out emotional security as if they were handing out pencils,

**Table 2.1**

**Ideas for Creating a Therapeutic Environment**

- Tell the truth. If a child asks, "Do we have to study grammar?" your truthful answer might be, "Yes, but not the kind you're used to. We don't study nouns and verbs here, but we learn to use them properly in our writing and conversation."
- Encourage laughter. I don't mean that you should tell jokes. If you can't, don't. But be as fun loving as your nature allows. The class clown can be an asset if you learn to use the laughs to your advantage.
- Don't be afraid of tears. A good story or poem generates emotions. An honest tear is as welcome as an honest laugh.

- Children are inherently risk takers, but risk taking requires a stable environment that builds self-confidence. A safety net is essential if we wish to get children to take academic and social risks.
- Keep hope alive. Hope is faith, confidence, belief; its opposite is dread, despair, doubt. Hope anticipates good outcomes. But once hope has departed, restoration is difficult. Keep hope alive; restore hope if it has faded.

*Teaching Tip*

they can eliminate unfavorable influences. A teacher's emotional demeanor will be reflected in the emotional tenor of the children. Kindness, courtesy, and respect for others can be modeled but not coerced. A classroom cannot always be tranquil, nor should it be. But it can be a place where children know the security of acceptance and the tranquility of humane consideration.

> Linus: "I guess it's wrong to be worried about tomorrow; maybe we should only worry about today?"
> Charlie Brown: "No, that's giving up. I'm hoping that yesterday will get better!"

The underlying premise of the film *Field of Dreams* is "You have to believe." This is also an underlying premise of teaching. You can build a field of dreams in your classroom; you can bring forth all the good things that faith in children generates. Table 2.1 suggests some ideas for creating a therapeutic environment in your classroom.

## The Cultivated Environment

Teaching and learning environments include all the conditions, circumstances, and influences surrounding and affecting the development of children in schools and classrooms. Institutions, whether schools or prisons, have environments that are either *cultivated or perpetrated* by those in charge of it; an institution's environment is established either in cooperation with or in opposition to its inhabitants. A cultivated environment promotes the development of individuals. A perpetrated environment, on the other hand, is imposed by the authorities in charge, sometimes involving neglect, thoughtless regimentation, or even brutality. Such an institution is, at best, offensive and at worst, evil. In prisons, the environment is perpetrated upon the inmates as a form of punishment. Bad schools, like prisons, have environments that have been imposed upon the "inmates." Good schools have cultivated environments, thoughtfully developed, carefully nurtured, and dedicated to the growth of children.

> "In an effective classroom students should not only know what they are doing, they should also know why and how."
> —Harry Wong, *Harry Wong's First Days of School*

Schools are institutions and classrooms are subunits within the larger institutional framework. Teachers, to the degree that they have the freedom to do so, can cultivate good environments within bad institutions. But it is far easier to cultivate good environments within a good institution. Unfortunately, teachers do not always have a choice or a voice in the larger institutional framework. Fortunately, they nearly always have some choice and a voice within their own classrooms.

## Section Summary: Intellectual, Therapeutic, and Cultivated Environments

1. An intellectual environment cultivates openness to ideas and respect for the opinions and ideas of others.
2. Children need a secure, stable therapeutic environment where they receive sympathetic understanding and acceptance.
3. Environments are cultivated through active, continuous effort to shape the conditions and atmosphere in which children learn.

## Classroom Management

### Managing Conduct and Work Procedures

Business and industry executives have learned a valuable lesson over the past decade. The foreman, the owner, the boss, so to speak, can achieve greater productivity, engender a sense of responsibility, and boost morale not by bossing people around but by creating teams of workers who have a significant say in how work is done. Teamwork works. Old-fashioned bossing doesn't work nearly as well. Teamwork works in schools just as it does in industry (Dyson & Freedman, 1991). Not only does teamwork make for a more pleasant and productive classroom, but it also prepares children for the workplace they will occupy when school days are over. Therefore, teachers have a double reason for creating mutual-responsibility classrooms wherein teamwork takes front and center. It makes today's work more pleasant and productive, and it prepares children for the world they will inhabit later.

Teachers are facilitators of learning; they make learning possible in carefully crafted ways. Ultimately, they are responsible for both means and ends. While teachers manage the overall learning environment, it is not their responsibility alone. There must be mutual responsibility, a community of learners building a responsible classroom environment together. For example, who cleans up the messes that inevitably occur in a working environment? It can't be the teacher alone; it shouldn't be the children alone. It should be a mutual responsibility. Who sets the rules of the working community? It can't be the teacher alone; it shouldn't be the children alone. It is a mutual responsibility. Who brings ideas to classroom discussions? It can't be the teacher alone; it shouldn't be the children alone either. It is a mutual responsibility. In a mutual-responsibility classroom, children can be trusted; so can the teacher. Everyone has a role to play and a say in how the work is to be accomplished. In a mutual-responsibility classroom, children are responsible for themselves and for one another. And children are responsible to the teacher, who is the person in charge—the boss, if you like. But there are many kinds of bosses.

## Field Notes
### Real-Life Experiences of a Classroom Teacher

I work to create a classroom that has a sense of purposeful activity and focused enthusiasm. We establish rules: I will be kind; I will be safe; I will work hard. Beyond these expectations, other components also facilitate the learning environment in my classroom.

1. I establish procedures for routine tasks, such as lining up or using the restroom. I do this in the first week of school. The students practice the procedures, and groups of students model the appropriate behavior.

2. Students get a copy of the three class rules the first week of school, sign them, and take them home for their parents to review. When students break a rule, I ask them which rule they think they have broken and what they might have done instead.

3. My instructional plans are scheduled to minimize transition and unstructured time. I know what I want students to do next. Well-thought-out lesson plans are my best weapon against misbehavior.

**Melissa Schade Brandt**

4. I follow the discipline of logical consequences. If students use materials inappropriately, they cannot use the materials for the rest of the day. If students disrupt people around them, they are moved. Students respect consequences.

5. When students seriously misbehave, I speak directly to them, stating the inappropriate behavior and asking the student for better alternatives. I make sure they understand what they did wrong, what a better choice would have been, and what the consequences will be.

6. Students who have chronic behavior problems need additional support. I meet with the parents, establishing one or two goals. I make a daily behavior chart indicating whether or not the goals were met. When goals are met, rewards are given.

7. Learning new behavior is motivating. Most students want to succeed, and I reinforce this attitude by giving praise for effort, behavior, and work well done. Students share work of which they are proud. I have not found other motivators, such as tokens or tickets, necessary.

Managing conduct and work procedures requires diplomacy and organization. Many teachers do this well. I asked someone whom I know to be an excellent teacher how she manages conduct and work procedures. Mrs. Schade Brandt describes ideas that work for her.

## Parents in the Classroom

Parents can be partners in your classroom. They can monitor homework, support instruction, work in centers, reinforce discipline, and support school and district goals and activities. Getting parents on your team can lighten the workload and provide support when difficult personal or professional issues arise. Some parents are reluctant to get involved in schools because they feel unwelcome. Seek ways to make parents feel welcome; involve them in as many school experiences as possible. Start by writing a letter to parents at the beginning of the school year. Explain how your instructional program will help children, what they should expect, and how you want to

For more information and guidance on parent–teacher collaboration, visit http://www.teachervision.com/lesson-plans/lesson-3730.html

Teaching Tip

## Field Notes
### Real-Life Experiences of a Parent Volunteer

During my years as a teacher and the following years as a parent, my passion has been sharing children's literature with young people and helping them become writers. As my children reached school age, I was drawn to volunteering my time and expertise to our school's publishing center—the Woodland Publishing Center.

The Woodland Publishing Center provides projects linked with classroom curriculum and assists students and staff in publishing young authors' works resulting from the writing process. Over the past eight years, the center has offered a variety of publishing opportunities, including these:

**Shevy Jacobson**

1. Woodland Wild Writers: a collection of short stories and poetry
2. Individual Stories: stories published in a variety of customized formats
3. Audio Authors: written group stories retold on audiotape
4. Seasonal Projects: writing focused on seasons and holidays

Our monthly flyer advertises projects that tie into the schoolwide curriculum theme. Volunteers are assigned to classrooms to assist teachers and young authors. Our Woodland Publishing Center has been successful because of the support it has received. Our parent–teacher organization provides a generous yearly budget to cover the cost of materials and technology. Twenty to thirty volunteers assist young authors with dictation, word processing, binding, and formatting. The Woodland faculty and staff support us by encouraging students to participate in the writing process.

The publishing center has had an impact on the Woodland community. We have played a role in the growth of our children's writing. We have created projects that encourage writing and publication. Parent volunteers have participated in their children's education.

Personally, my involvement as chairperson of the publishing center includes developing projects, communicating with faculty and staff, and assisting individual authors. I have developed a strong relationship with teachers, students, and principal. In addition, I have the personal satisfaction of sharing my passion for publishing with others.

> "After the verb 'to Love,' 'to Help' is the most beautiful verb in the world."
> —Bertha von Suttner, Australian novelist and first woman awarded the Nobel Peace Prize

involve them in their child's education. Include a parent volunteer form along with your letter.

Shevy Jacobson is a former teacher with a master's degree in reading and language arts. She is now a full-time homemaker, raising four boys. Still, she finds time to volunteer. I know she's busy, and I wondered how she found time to volunteer. She explains some of her volunteer work in the Field Notes piece. Figure 2.1 suggests ideas for using parent volunteers. Modify them to fit your instructional activities and philosophy.

## Section Summary: Classroom Management

1. Effective classroom management facilitates learning, fosters self-responsibility and cooperative working arrangements.
2. Inviting parents to act as classroom aides can enrich instruction when the arrangements are carefully prepared and organized.

Figure 2.1

**Parent Volunteer Form**

Parent's Name _____    Child's Name _____

Phone/e-mail _____

Please place a check mark beside the activities in which you can participate.

1. Working with children
   Reading to children
   Listening to children read
   Storytelling
   Tutoring individual children
   Working with small groups
   Preparing instructional materials
   Working in a teaching learning center
      Library center
      Publishing center
      Science center
      Math center
      Computer center
      Arts and crafts center

2. Assisting in class or school projects
   Going on field trips
   Fund raising
   Office assistance
   Helping at special school events

_____  Sorry, I am unable to participate.

_____  I will be glad to help. I'm available on the following days and times.

      M    T    W    T    F      Morning _____    Afternoon _____

Signature _____

## Creating Physically Inviting Environments

What sort of environment do you most enjoy? I have favorite places at home and at work. At home, my favorite place is a tiny room (5 by 6 feet) where I read. It has a leather chair, two bookcases, my favorite Civil War pictures on the wall, and a tiny side table—crowded but pleasant. I love that room, and I always anticipate pleasant experiences when I enter it. A spacious library would not seem half so grand. Schools and classrooms can be made inviting, too, when teachers and children cooperate to make them positive places for teaching and learning.

Pleasing physical arrangements create an ambience that fosters learning. Of course, teachers must accommodate the physical environment to the resources available to them. Limited space, unmovable furniture, and inadequate budgets

## Field Notes
### Real-Life Experiences of a Classroom Teacher

**O**ver the years, I have come to realize how much the physical layout of my classroom influences the learning activities, noise level, and independence of my students. I follow guidelines when setting up or changing the physical environment of my classroom. For example, I begin each school year by creating a detailed list of materials and furniture to be set up. Next, I create a list of centers for the room. I then draw a map, placing centers, using furniture, tables, carpets, and bookcases as natural dividers. Once my map is complete, I move the furnishings to their designated spots.

**Ann Marie Laskowski**

One thing to keep in mind when setting up your classroom is to remain flexible. Don't be afraid to readjust the physical environment if you find that it is not working. Remember to eliminate blind spots, since you want your students in view at all times.

I label every bin my students use daily. I clip pictures from teacher catalogs, which I mount and laminate on index cards. It is time consuming to create picture cards for bins, but it helps eliminate improper placement of items during cleanup. I try to create a pleasant physical environment with an established routine that my students find consistent and comforting.

limit what a teacher can do. The following suggestions are somewhat ideal, though many teachers work under severely limited conditions. Do as much as you can with what you have.

Arrangement of your classroom reflects your philosophy of teaching and learning. The traditional classroom, with fixed seating in rows, may suit some teachers perfectly well, but such arrangements do not allow the flexibility needed for the most effective organization of a literature-based, integrated language arts curriculum. In the Field Notes feature, a kindergarten teacher explains how she organizes her classroom.

Teachers take pride in the physical environment of their classrooms. They want their children to invest in it as well. Teachers provide a model that children can at first imitate; with this base of experience, they can then suggest their own innovations. Stimulating surroundings make for productive work. Attractive, interesting classrooms feature places for independent work and for cooperative learning. Carefully arranged furniture, well-designed centers, and displays of children's work stimulate ideas and promote interest in learning. Centers where children can go to read or write are especially important. Other desirable accommodations include display centers, science and math centers, and collections of children's work. The more inviting and stimulating a center is, the more likely it will be used to good purpose.

The physical configuration of a classroom can take many shapes. When resources are limited, the teacher must make do. But when

"Elementary school teachers spend more than $500 of their own money each year on school supplies," according to the National Education Association. New elementary school teachers spend about $700 a year to help stock their classrooms. http://www.mea.org: Pressroomonline

**Table 2.2**

**Organizing Space and Resources for Instruction**

1. Furniture arrangements: pleasing and varied placement of furniture
   - Arrange desks or tables in groups to accommodate cooperative work.
   - Determine seating arrangements to accommodate curricular goals.
   - Change arrangements from time to time.
2. Library: the heartbeat of the literature-based classroom
   - Books are crucial to effective language arts instruction.
   - Work toward acquiring six or seven times as many books as students.
   - Work toward acquiring books across four levels of readability.
   - Work toward acquiring a collection of multicultural books.
   - Acquire a diverse collection: fiction, nonfiction, poetry, picture, and so on.
   - Accommodations can include rugs, cushions, chairs, and so on.
   - Work toward acquiring books written by students.
   - Decorate with posters: authors, illustrators, medal winners.
3. Centers: activity areas suited to the curriculum and children's interests
   - Provide science kits, texts, and general science equipment for experiments.
   - Stock manipulatives, posters, and stories about math and mathematicians.
   - Set up tables and chairs and resources such as paper, pencils, and crayons.
   - Secure art supplies for drawing, painting, and pasting.
   - Provide supplies for making books, including a printer, if possible.
   - Add centers that fit your instructional goals.
4. Displays: arrangements of interesting artifacts
   - Make seasonal arrangements for fall, winter, spring, and summer displays.
   - Seek special collections and displays organized by students or parents.
   - Initially, you might model ways to make pleasing arrangements.
   - Later, students or parents can take charge of preparing displays.
5. Discussion center: author's chair, literature circles, group discussions
   - Floor seating is preferable, to avoid moving furniture.
   - Provide a chair or podium to accommodate author's chair sharing.
6. Computer center: computers, desks, and chairs
   - Strive for a computer–child ratio of 1:4, with appropriately sized furniture.
   - Post rules for Netiquette and appropriate computer use.
   - Create a trouble-shooting poster.
   - Provide list of expert students who can lend assistance.
   - Create bookmarked sites.
   - Provide laminated activity cards for various software.
   - Design an accountability form for summarizing work.

*Teaching Tip*

resources are ample, the possibilities for physical arrangement are limited only by imagination and the ambience you wish to create. It amazes me how often teachers spend their own money to create an environment that accommodates their own need for organization, beauty, and comfort, always thinking about how their plans will make learning more pleasant for children. Table 2.2 suggests ideas for physical arrangement of furniture, centers, library, displays, and group discussion areas. Figures 2.2 and 2.3 (pp. 60 and 61) illustrate possible arrangements of a first-grade classroom and a fifth-grade classroom.

**Figure 2.2**

**Map of First-Grade Classroom**

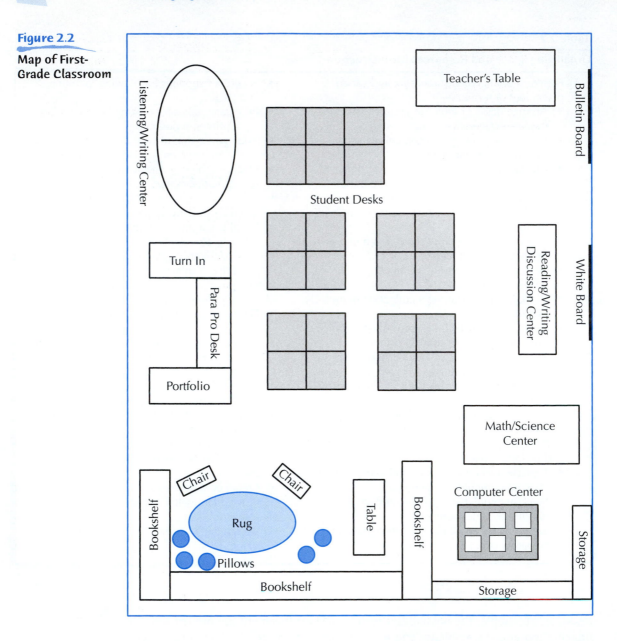

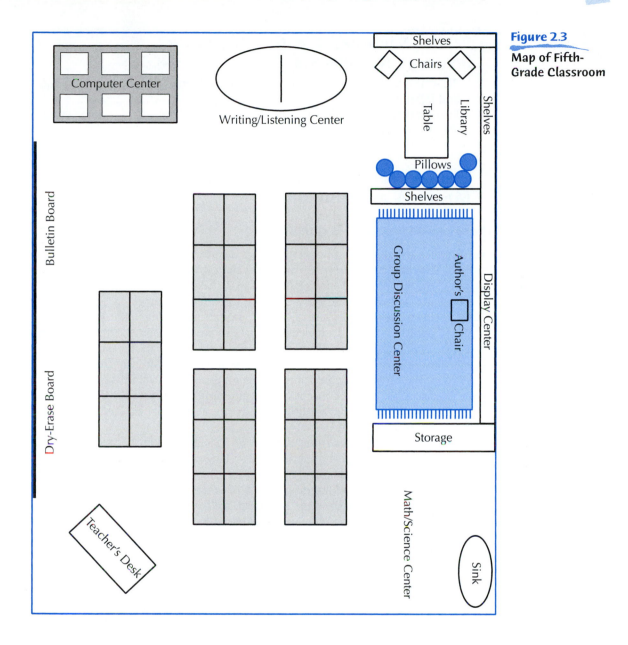

**Figure 2.3**
Map of Fifth-Grade Classroom

## Section Summary: Creating Physically Inviting Environments

1. Pleasing physical arrangements create an ambience that fosters teaching and learning.
2. Encourage children to contribute their ideas for designing and furnishing the classroom.

# Environments for Developing Language, Meaning, and Thinking

## Theories of Language Acquisition

Linguists seek to understand how language is acquired and how it works once it is acquired. The three best-known theories are referred to as behaviorist, nativist, and cognitivist. The behaviorists hold that children learn language by imitating adult models, gradually shaping their language to adult norms. Behaviorists cite generalization, imitation, reinforcement, successive approximation, and mediation to explain language learning (Skinner, 1957). Critics disagreed with behavioral explanations, and Chomsky (1959) delivered the coup de grâce: he argued that everything of interest in language acquisition centers on generalization, yet behavioral theorists define this concept vaguely and have not empirically demonstrated how it works. Few linguists today accept behaviorist explanations of language acquisition.

A second theory of acquisition is called nativist, or biological. It posits a biological inheritance for language capability unique to the human species (Lennenberg, 1967). Humans are innately predisposed to acquire language; learning to talk is as natural and inevitable as learning to walk. Nativist theorists argue that language is unique to the human species, has universally similar principles, and is acquired in similar ways throughout the world. They emphasize what occurs inside the child, whereas the behaviorists emphasize the role of the environment.

Cognitive theorists postulate innate biological structures that make language learning possible, but with a difference; they emphasize an inheritance of thought structures rather than linguistic universals (Pinker, 2002; Slobin, 1968). But whereas Lennenberg emphasized linguistic universals as the crucial inheritance, cognitivists posit inborn cognitive mechanisms, which enable children to process linguistic information gleaned from the environment. Cognitive theorists, such as Piaget, Vygotsky, and Bruner, were primarily concerned with explaining cognitive development, not with describing how language is acquired. They interpret linguistic data consistent with the view that general cognitive development determines language acquisition. The cognitivist's view is compatible with the interests of teachers and parents since it leaves room for environmental influences on language acquisition—the environments of home, school, and community.

To learn more about language acquisition theories, visit Steven Pinker's website at Massachusetts Institute of Technology: http://cogsci.soton.ac.uk?~harnad/Papers/Py104/pinker.langacq.html

For more information regarding behaviorist theory, visit http://www.sil.org/lingualinks/literacy/implementaliteracyprogram/Behaviorist

For additional information on various views of language acquisition, visit http://www.hausarbeiten.de/archiv/anglistik/angl-acq/angl-acq.shtml (Scroll down for the complete article. It is a wonderful resource!)

## Four Features of Language

There are four features of the language system: phonological (sound), syntactic (grammar), semantic (meaning), and pragmatic (social and cultural). Many linguists believe that an infant starts with a biological inheritance that makes language learning possible. The environment makes a contribution to language learning as well. As children develop and interact with their environment, they learn language naturally through the two interacting influences of biology and environment. Young children do not have to be *formally* taught to speak their language; it comes naturally, unlike learning to read and write, which requires a more formal learning environment.

**Phonology**. Phonology refers to the sound system of a language—the distribution, patterning, and tacit rules governing pronunciation. Linguists have identified 44 English speech sounds, though English has only 26 letters. This makes for some irregularity of letter–sound relationships, though English is not as irregular as is commonly believed (Venezky, 1999). Having more sounds than letters means that certain letters represent more than one sound in the written language system. Vowels are more irregular than consonants and often represent several sounds.

For more information on Venezky, visit http://www.literacyonline.org/sltp/presntr/venezky.htm

Knowledge of the phonology of English serves as a platform for learning to read and write. The written language system takes longer to master, but given opportunity, children can begin writing by kindergarten. Many write before kindergarten, using invented spelling (Cramer, 2000). Children's early writing paints a picture of the relative regularity of consonants, in contrast to vowels. The three kindergarten stories that follow illustrate how much easier it is for young children to spell consonant sounds than vowel sounds. Notice that vowels are omitted except for the word *a* and the long *e* in *me*.

For an interesting article on invented spelling, see "Invented Spelling," by Margaret Y. Phinney. This article was first published in the Spring 1987 issue of *Mothering*. It is reprinted here with permission of the author and the editors. See <http://naturalchild.com/guest/margaret_phinney2.html>

| | |
|---|---|
| Surhin: | a lt brd (original story) |
| | a little bird (translation) |
| Collin: | snt brt me a swtr (original story) |
| | santa brought me a sweater (translation) |
| Wendy: | mm rd jc ad me a str t wz t bdtm (original story) |
| | mom read Jessie and me a story it was at bedtime (translation) |

**Syntax**. The Greek word *suntassein* means to put in order. Syntax refers to the rules whereby words are arranged in an orderly structure to form grammatical English sentences. All languages have implicit rules by which native speakers easily generate grammatical sentences. Yet even fluent speakers may find formal grammar intimidating, especially when linguists attempt to explain the grammar of English in their esoteric texts, which are often only slightly more readable than the Rosetta Stone, the key to the deciphering of Egyptian hieroglyphics.

While all normally developing first-graders have an implicit knowledge of English grammar, they do not know the *rules* of traditional school grammar as described, for example, in Patricia O'Conner's (1996) marvelous little grammar primer: *Woe Is I: The Grammarphobe's Guide to Better English in Plain English*. Grammars of this sort are normative or prescriptive. They describe the rules of usage prescribed for polite speech. Traditional grammar is arbitrary and changes with the shifting sands of time. A classic example of arbitrary grammar is the rule *two negatives make a positive*. Really? Sam tells his mom, "No, I'm not going to no school today." No mother interprets this sentence to mean "I'm going to school today."

We owe that "rule" to a theologian cum mathematician turned to grammar maven—Bishop Lowe. That two negatives make a positive is a mathematical truism. But dragging math into grammar is arbitrary and illustrates the point that traditional grammar consists of agreed-upon conventions, even foolish ones, concerning written and spoken English. *Traditional grammatical rules are useful, and an educated person needs to know and use them.* Still, one needs to distinguish between natural oral English and traditional grammatical conventions.

**Semantics**.  Semantics deals with meaning. The semantic system of English enables us to construct meaning from written or spoken language. Nothing in language learning is more important than the semantic, or meaning, system. The meaning of an English sentence is derived partly from our vocabularies, but words alone will not take us across the bridge from words into meaning. Syntax, phonology, and pragmatics are also involved. Meaning is constructed from prior world knowledge—the sum total of what we know, believe, and understand. How we construct meaning also depends on the social context in which language is used.

> "Learning a definition is not equal to knowing the word. Definitions are insufficient."
> —From W. E. Nagy, "Research on Learning from Context: Major Findings and Implications," a talk presented at Prairie School, Urbana, IL, October 23, 1989.

The Book of Genesis says, "In the beginning was the word." Words are the lingua franca of communication. They can cut like a sharp knife or soothe like a baby's blanket. They can be as muddy as a swamp or as clear as mountain lake. They can entertain: "I am a Bear of Very Little Brain, and long words Bother me," says Pooh Bear. They can puzzle: "Anything reticulated or decussated at equal distances, with interstices between the intersections," which is the British writer Samuel Johnson's definition of words. They can inspire: "Words without thoughts never to heaven go," says Shakespeare.

Everyone has words at their command, and the sum total constitutes one's vocabulary. Words have multiple denotative and connotative meanings; words are used figuratively, metaphorically, and ironically; words are spoken with degrees of emphasis and inflection; words have emotional and social loading. How we use them influences meaning, and there are many to be used. There are nearly a million English words, but only a fraction of that number are required to speak, read, write, and listen effectively. First-graders have vocabularies ranging from 3,000 to 12,000 words; they may add as many as 3,000 new words each year, mostly derived from reading (Anderson & Nagy, 1992). These are estimates, since there is no way to count vocabulary precisely, and for good reason. First, researchers cannot agree on what constitutes a word. If Kathleen knows the word *walk,* chances are she knows *walks, walking,* and *walked.* Does this count in Kathleen's vocabulary as one word or four? Second, accurately estimating vocabulary size is difficult. You can't follow Kathleen around with a tape recorder day and night. You have to estimate the size of her vocabulary by taking a sample. But what sample will yield valid estimates? If you sample Kathleen's writing vocabulary, you get a better estimate than if you sample her spoken language. So we settle for best guesses. But it is sufficient to know that children like Kathleen have ample oral language. And Kathleen's words and general oral language knowledge constitute the key to effective literacy instruction.

**Pragmatics**. Pragmatics deals with the language choices people make in social and cultural contexts and interactions. Lamont greets his friend Ramon on the street with the question "Hey man, how yuh doing?" Ramon replies, "None yo' bidness, Piggy." Lamont didn't expect a recitation of how life was proceeding; Ramon didn't intend an insult. The exchange is just casual street conversation between two cool dudes. We shape language so that we can communicate meaning that fits the social and cultural situation in which conversation occurs. Thus the conversations we have with our dentist differ from the ones we have with a friend on the street.

There are varieties of English. Language differs among regional, cultural, social, and ethnic groups. Dialects represent one such difference, but there are others.

## Using Technology for Promoting Learning

Whether your school provides you with a single computer for your classroom, a traditional computer lab, a set of laptops, or PDAs for each student, your job is to use technology to support learning. You must always be able to answer "the why," "the how," and "the what now" of technology integration.

Technology should support curriculum and objectives. The first step in a technology integration is to determine your lesson objectives. Once they are set, evaluate the technology tools available to determine whether they can help your students attain the desired outcomes. In other words, ask, Can technology contribute something to my lesson that is otherwise unavailable? If you can answer yes, you're on the way to using technology to its full potential.

Once you know *why* you want to use technology for a lesson, the next step is figuring out how to integrate technology into it. First, become familiar with the types of technologies available to you and their potential uses in your classroom. Second, develop a technology management plan for your classroom. Whether you have one computer or thirty, successful management begins with you. Management strategies will vary depending on

resources, but here's one strategy that is always pertinent: *always have a back-up lesson in case the technology fails.* If things can go wrong, they will. The day you do not have a back-up plan will be the day the website you *must have* is unavailable. Keep in mind this adage: if you fail to plan, you plan to fail.

After you have planned and executed a successful technology integration activity, you still have one critical task to complete: You must R2 your lesson. R2 does not mean to breathe a sigh of *relief* now that it is over and then kick back and *relax*. R2 stands for *review* and *revise*. Did the lesson go the way you expected? What were its strengths and weaknesses? Was the reason for using technology apparent to the students? Did the lesson achieve the desired outcomes? How can you do it better next time? Never R2ing your lesson means never improving it.

Technology integration requires planning. You cannot simply log on to the Internet, download a technology lesson, and provide an enriched learning experience. Successful use of technology involves (1) planning—the why; (2) execution—the how; and (3) R2, reviewing and revising—the what now.

Contributed by Lisa Kunkleman

Language can be formal or informal, polite or impolite, suited to school or the street. English is sometimes divided into two categories—standard and nonstandard. This arbitrary distinction classifies language use as good or bad, right or wrong. A better way to understand language usage is to think of different *registers*, which vary according to the social situation at hand. Thus, when Coach yells during practice, she might say, "Bumblehead, you stink. Run that play again." But when Coach introduces so-called Bumblehead at the awards banquet she says, "Linda Ciponi is the best point guard in the conference."

For an interesting article dealing with dialect education, read "Dialect Education: Not Only for Oakland," by Carolyn Adger, Center for Applied Linguistics. Find it at http://facultyweb.cortland.edu/ANDERSMD/VYG.html

Linguists have pointed out that dividing language into standard and nonstandard usage is neither an accurate nor useful distinction. Dialects, for instance, are not substandard; they represent different registers perfectly suited to communicate meaning within the social and cultural contexts in which they exist. Thus, school and work registers differ from street and casual registers. It is useful, at times crucial, to have the linguistic flexibility to change registers to fit different social and cultural contexts. Language is intended to communicate meaning; when it does so, it performs its function. When it does not, it misses the mark.

## Seven Functions of Language

Language serves different purposes. For instance, Anne Marie may want her dad to read a book to her, so she uses language to convey her desire: "Dad, I want to hear the Animal Book again." This is called the *instrumental* function of language. Anne Marie uses it as a tool to get what she wants. I remember three clever little children who often used nonverbal language to get a book read to them. They arrived at my chair with a kiss and a book in hand—and got the same result as Anne Marie's verbal request. Children use language for many purposes, and it doesn't take them long to acquire the seven language functions that Halliday (1975) describes. You can find this out for yourself by observing kindergarten children. Chances are, you'll see all seven language functions put to use within an hour or two. Here are examples of each:

1. *Instrumental.* Todd says, "Dad, I want a drink of water." He's using language as a tool to get what he wants.
2. *Regulatory.* Mom says, "Ernie, turn off the television, and do your homework." Mom uses language to control Ernie's behavior.
3. *Interactional.* Ellie says to Toni, "Let's write this report together." Ellie uses language to propose a cooperative relationship with Toni.
4. *Personal.* Frank says to the world, "I did it my way." Frank is expressing his personal identity in this expressive manner.
5. *Heuristic.* Kathleen asks, "Dad, why do dogs bark?" Kathleen is trying to understand how and why the world works as it does.
6. *Imaginative.* Ashleigh says to her little sister, "You play Mom, and I'll play Dad." Ashleigh imagines a pretend world of her own making.
7. *Informative.* Billy tells his teacher, "Mr. Barron, an eagle can see a fish a mile away." Billy communicates recently acquired information to his teacher.

## Language and Thought

Jean Piaget, Lev Vygotsky, and Jerome Bruner, who rank among the 20th century's most influential psychologists, proposed related but somewhat different theories of language and thought. Language profoundly influences children's intellectual development. As children acquire language, they gain more than a set of words. They also acquire thought structures that can be applied in learning to read and write. As children develop, language becomes instrumental in directing thinking and learning. The richer the language, the more bountiful thinking and learning can be.

**Vygotsky**. Vygotsky (1962) assigned language a major role in the development of thinking and learning. He believed that children gain understanding and meaning through their exposure to language models supplied by adults and more advanced peers within social contexts. Concrete experiences with the world, accompanied by simultaneous experiences with language, provide the milieu within which children's thinking develops.

Vygotsky emphasized a concept known as the *zone of proximal development* (ZPD). He believed children learn best when they are "in the zone." The ZPD is conceptually similar to what Emmet Betts (1947) called the *instructional level* in reading. The ZPD is that space between independence and the need for instructional support. As one area of challenge is conquered, another lies ahead, where instructional support will again be needed. The ZPD is a moving, not a stationary, target. For example, a child who has learned the alphabet may next need assistance in connecting letters to sounds; once that challenge is mastered, continuing support will be required as the child advances, stage by stage, through increasingly mature literacy challenges. Growth in language and thought is analogous to clearing a forest from the middle outward. While the clearing grows ever larger, the forest remaining to be cleared is vast.

For more information and application of Vygotsky's theory, visit http://snycorva.cortland.edu/~ANDERSMD/VYG.HTML

**Piaget**. Piaget (1955) maintained that thinking stimulates language learning. Language acquisition is dependent, in Piaget's theory, on the presence of sensorimotor schemata. He believed that children's thinking stems from their actions upon the concrete world. For example, children understand the uses of a rattle before they give it a name; they know a needle is sharp before they have language to describe the property of sharpness. Language, for Piaget, is a way of labeling stored cognitive schemata. Seeing, hearing, touching, smelling, and tasting objects in the concrete world enable children to understand the functions and properties of objects before they have language to describe them. Piaget argued, therefore, that language does not organize thinking; it transmits it. He recognized, however, that language refines and elaborates thinking. Language and thought are interactive; they influence each other.

For more biographical information on Jean Piaget, visit http://www.ship.edu/~cgboeree/piaget.html

**Bruner**. Bruner's (1966) conclusions about language and thought closely parallel Vygotsky's. Bruner believed that it is only through the use of language that children learn to think abstractly. Thinking capability grows through the use of language.

Like Vygotsky, Bruner recognized the importance of adult language models. Through talk with adults, children learn to examine, structure, and reflect on their experiences. As children engage in learning activities under adult supervision, support is gradually withdrawn and children assume more responsibility for their learning. This concept is called scaffolding by Bruner (1963), the zone of proximal development by Vygotsky (1962), and the instructional level by Betts (1947). Bruner stressed that, while language stimulates thought, the strategies learned during language learning are useful for

For additional information on Jerome Bruner, visit http://tip/ psychology.org/bruner.html

### Table 2.3

**Applying the Theories of Vygotsky, Piaget, and Bruner to Classroom Instruction**

*Teaching Tip*

**Vygotsky**

1. Model language by interacting with children as listener, speaker, questioner, and friend.
2. Extend and expand children's thinking beyond the limits they may have constructed for themselves.
3. Stress social interaction with adults and peers, since it focuses children's attention on elements of their experience that might otherwise elude them.
4. Recognize that social interaction and the need to communicate are essential components in the development of language.
5. Create learning communities where the teacher and children work cooperatively and collaboratively through sharing, think-aloud modeling, and teacher-student conferences.
6. Emphasize imaginative play, role playing, experimentation, and manipulation.

**Piaget**

1. Provide activities and experiences which emphasize experimentation within the physical and social environment.
2. Use art, dance, music, drama, and play in group and individual settings to motivate language and provide experiences that give language concrete and direct referents in the physical and social environment.
3. Encourage children to actively participate in real-world events so that language and experience fit together naturally.
4. Activate prior knowledge, since only concepts for which the child is ready will be understood.

**Bruner**

1. Stress active experimentation and interaction with the physical and intellectual world on children's own terms.
2. Apply children's oral language knowledge to literacy instruction.
3. Exploit the natural relationship that exists between oral and written language in teaching of reading and writing.
4. All present learning is intended to serve the learner in the future; therefore, create activities that serve both pleasurable and practical purposes.
5. Make extensive use of independent reading, process writing, display centers, learning stations, cooperative study, computers, and educational games.

other types of thought maturation. Like Piaget's, his theories suggest the importance of discovery learning and problem solving. Table 2.3 suggests classroom applications of Vygotsky's, Piaget's, and Bruner's educational theories.

## Creative and Critical Thinking

I'm a fan of Calvin and Hobbes, cartoon characters created by Bill Watterson. Calvin is a kid, Hobbes an imaginary tiger. Only Calvin knows that Hobbes is real. In one strip, Calvin says to his teacher, "Miss Wormwood, could we arrange our seats in a circle and have a little discussion? Specifically, I'd like to debate whether cannibalism ought to be grounds for leniency in murders, since it's less wasteful." Miss Wormwood vetoes Calvin's proposal, and Calvin is shown sitting in a corner, saying, "For some reason, they'd rather teach us stuff that any fool can look up in a book." Learning excites Calvin, but not school learning. He is an example of childhood creativity, a kind of child outlaw living outside the normal boundaries of acceptable behavior. Creative thinking often exists on the edge of normal social behavior.

> "Creative minds have always been known to survive any kind of bad training."
> —Anna Freud, psychologist

Thinking can be *critical* as well as *creative*. Though not mutually exclusive, these two modes of thought work in different ways and are applied differently to problem solving. Creative thinking focuses on getting new ideas and considering old ideas in new ways. Creative thinkers must operate in the absence of sufficient information about what is right or wrong, wise or foolish, possible or impossible. Consequently, creative thinking tends to be more speculative than critical thinking.

> "Schools should be a mirror of a future society."
> —Anonymous

Critical thinking is characterized by careful evaluation and judgment. The critical thinker seeks to determine what is right or wrong, wise or foolish, possible or impossible on the basis of data, facts, and other information. While critical thinking can be wrong, foolish, or impossible, its intention is not speculative. Faced with a problem, the critical thinker is likely to take a different approach to solving it than would the creative thinker.

*Calvin is a rebel, the kind of child who can give a teacher a headache. Yet outside of school, he's articulate and imaginative. Though a challenge, students like Calvin can also be rewarding—don't give up on them.*

"Critical thinking is the intellectually disciplined process of actively and skillfully conceptualizing, applying, analyzing, synthesizing, and/or evaluating information gathered from, or generated by, observation, experience, reflection, reasoning, or communication, as a guide to belief and action."
From *Defining Critical Thinking: A Draft Statement for the National Council for Excellence in Critical Thinking,* by M. Scriven and R. Paul, 1996. Find it at http://www.ncte.org

Perhaps the nature of work inclines people to one type of thinking over another. For example, engineers typically solve problems that have right or wrong answers. They must ask questions such as these: How much weight will this bridge hold? What stresses will wind and water place upon this bridge? Teachers, on the other hand, face quite different problems. They must ask, Will this story interest seventh-graders? How can I present this story to stir their interest? No mathematical formulas are available to answer these questions. Experience with literature and seventh-graders helps, but will this year's seventh-graders react like last year's? The answer remains unknown until the story is tried. Teachers have to be creative, and they face a greater probability of being wrong than do engineers figuring stresses. This does not mean that engineers do not think creatively or that teachers do not think critically. But it marks a distinction in their everyday routines.

Teachers face the task of creating environments in which creative and critical thinking flourish. Fortunately, supporting critical and creative thinking requires neither exotic nor esoteric teaching skills. Creative thinking comes naturally in poetry and art. Critical thinking emerges naturally when one works with facts and information. Creative thinking is nourished through prediction at the beginning of a story; critical thinking comes into play as a story nears its end and facts and information have been revealed. Thinking of any sort is challenging, but creative work is especially fragile since it involves greater risks than critical thinking. There is no avoiding the possibility of failure. But failure often precedes success and makes success all the sweeter.

## Multiple Intelligences

How should we understand human intelligence? One school of thought treats intelligence and giftedness as synonymous. For instance, if you score at or above a certain number on the IQ test, perhaps 130, you are considered "gifted" in this school of thought. Some schools use the Stanford-Binet and the Wechsler Intelligence Scale for Children (WISC) to identify "gifted" children. High scorers get in, average scorers seldom qualify, and low scorers are shut out.

*Multiple Intelligences: Gardner's Theory.* ERIC Digest. Document Type: Information Analyses—ERIC Information Analysis Products (IAPs)(071); Information Analyses—ERIC Digests (Selected) in Full Text (073); Available from: ERIC Clearinghouse on Assessment and Evaluation, 210 O'Boyle Hall, The Catholic University of America, Washington, DC 20064. Phone: (800) 464-3742.

IQ tests are largely measures of verbal and mathematical reasoning. *They do not measure creativity or creative potential.* Some argue that IQ tests are objective, but this sort of objectivity is merely subjectivity dressed up in objective clothing. Every item on an IQ test represents a subjective judgment of some sort made by someone. Traditional understanding of intelligence is largely based on verbal and mathematical reasoning, and it assumes a one-dimensional view of intelligence. There is a broader view of human capability.

Gardner (1991a, 1993) proposes a multifaceted view of human potential, which he calls multiple intelligences. This concept formalizes what parents and teachers have known for decades: *many children have intellectual potential that traditional intelligence tests do not measure.* Gardner describes his theory of multiple intelligences in the following statement:

Multiple intelligences theory, on the other hand, pluralizes the traditional concept. An intelligence entails the ability to solve problems or fashion products that are of consequence in a particular cultural setting or community. The problem-solving skill allows one to approach a situation in which a goal is to be obtained and to locate the appropriate route to that goal. The creation of a *cultural* product is critical to such functions as capturing and transmitting knowledge or expressing one's views or feelings. The problems to be solved range from creating an end for a story to anticipating a mating move in chess to repairing a quilt. Products range from scientific theories to musical compositions to successful political campaigns. (Gardner, 1993, p. 15)

Gardner and his colleagues have identified seven intelligences: musical, bodily–kinesthetic, logical–mathematical, linguistic, spatial, interpersonal, and intrapersonal. Though Gardner identifies seven intelligences, he believes other intelligences are likely to be identified as research continues. Chapman's (1993) treatment of multiple intelligences suggests creative activities for implementing the seven intelligences in her book *If the Shoe Fits: How to Develop Multiple Intelligences in the Classroom.*

IQ is a cultural concept. Valued behavior must be relevant to a culture's needs. For example, expert Native American trackers of the 18th century could track a person or animal across plains, forests, or bare rock and do it unerringly. An expert tracker could read subtle signs and disturbances in the terrain that would be indiscernible to a highly "intelligent" physicist in today's society. But in a culture in which tracking is crucial, tracking might represent the peak of intelligence. A limited definition of intelligence inevitably leaves out certain valuable and underappreciated creative potentials, and this can be harmful.

Teachers routinely observe children demonstrating creative potentials that are not measured by IQ tests. Bob, a fifth-grader, is an example. Bob was a mechanical virtuoso. His father ran a junkyard where Bob learned to salvage parts and make minor repairs on cars, trucks, and tractors. Bob's teacher discovered his talent and used it as an instructional lever. Privileges granted required reciprocal responsibilities. In exchange for granting Bob the status of chief mechanic of room 12, his teacher expected and got a better academic effort, though not spectacular results. Bob's teacher sometimes imagines that Bob, who quit high school, is out there somewhere making mechanical things run smoothly—a man with the creative intelligence needed to make things work. Bob's special talent, his special *intelligence,* is not unique. He is representative of millions of children whose potential would not show up on a traditional IQ test. And good teachers seek to identify many such students. Teachers are like gardeners. They plant and cultivate, ever watchful for the blossoming of their flowers. They look beyond the obvious for gifts their children have to offer—gifts that may be obscured by shyness, awkwardness, or uncertainty. They seek to identify not only the gift of intelligence but the softer gifts, the gifts that get insufficient attention: thoughtfulness, kindness, empathy, humor, tolerance. These underappreciated gifts of the human spirit deserve more attention and appreciation than they usually get.

All this leads to the following hypothesis: *There is a much greater range of intellectual inventiveness, imagination, and intelligence among children than has been generally recognized; traditional IQ tests do not fully and completely measure human potential.* If teachers operate on this hypothesis they will see more potential, more imagination, more artistic and intellectual inventiveness among their children than they had previously believed possible.

## Section Summary: Environments for Developing Language, Meaning, and Thinking

1. Three significant theories of language acquisition are behaviorist (stresses environmental influences), nativist or biological (stresses biological predisposition), and cognitivist (assigns a role to both environmental and biological influences).
2. There are four major features of language: phonological (the sound system), syntax (the grammatical system), semantic (the meaning system), and pragmatics (the influence of social and cultural interaction on language).
3. Language has seven functions: instrumental, regulatory, interactional, personal, heuristic, imaginative, and informative.
4. Piaget, Vygotsky, and Bruner proposed theories of how language and thought develop in children and how language and thought influence children's intellectual development.
5. Creative thinking focuses on new and unusual ways of problem solving; critical thinking emphasizes evaluation of data, facts, and information in problem solving.
6. There are multiple intelligences. This idea broadens our concept of intelligence beyond the traditional view of IQ, which focuses on verbal and mathematical reasoning.

## Environments in Which Diversity Flourishes

*Unique* is a word that grammarians love to argue over. They say it is the perfect example of a word that does not allow for comparison or modification by an adverb of degree. So if the grammarians are right, it would be incorrect to say that someone is *very* unique or *more* unique than someone else. The *Mona Lisa* is unique, in a class by itself. You cannot compare it with any other painting. Every child is unique, in a class by himself or herself. I can say that Timmy is in a class by himself, so is Bonnie, and so is their teacher, Mrs. Tavi. You cannot compare them with any other human beings. Microbiologists, who study human DNA, agree. Every human being is unparalleled in the universe of human beings.

"The secret to education is respecting the pupil."
—Ralph Waldo Emerson

This peroration has a point. *Differences are good; differences are right; differences enrich the culture of a classroom.* Children have different colored faces, different textured hair, different cultural backgrounds, different native languages, different dialects, different genders, different learning dispositions. Differences can complicate teaching and learning; at the same time differences enrich the ambience of the

## Standing on the Shoulders of Giants
## Historical Contributions to Literacy
### Albert Harris

Over a quarter century ago, a young assistant professor had the good luck to have dinner with Albert Harris shortly before the publication of the *fifth* edition of Harris's classic reading textbook *How to Increase Reading Ability*. Awed by his vast knowledge of everything related to reading, I asked Professor Harris, "How's the fifth edition coming along?" His delightful answer still resonates in my memory. He chuckled as he said, "Ron, the book now knows more than I know." It took me a while to appreciate the profound truth of his remark, but I now know exactly what he meant: *memory fades; the written word endures.*

Albert Harris's book was my first reading textbook (fourth edition). It has endured as the reading textbook of record for half a century. His book, now co-authored with Edward Sipay, has gone through twelve editions, undoubtedly a record in its field. No textbook on reading has ever matched his absolute fidelity to scholarship. The reference section in recent editions typically contains nearly 3,000 references and consumes 130 pages. The books, articles, and chapters written by Harris are legion. I doubt anybody in the profession knows more about what was once called *remedial reading.*

His knowledge of reading stems from his research and his longtime directorship of a reading clinic in New York City. Listening to a lecture or having a conversation with him was always an education. His name is synonymous with excellence in research. Every year, the International Reading Association selects the best research article of the year. How fitting that this award is named in honor of one of the great teachers, researchers, and humanitarians in the field of reading.

Albert Harris is scholarship personified. His knowledge of research was legendary. I once heard a student teacher pose this question: "Professor Harris, what drugs are helpful for children with behavior problems?" I expected a brief remark or two. Instead, the young man got a full-blown ten-minute recital of the names, complications, and potential dangers of drugs then in use. The young man, along with the rest of us, was stunned by the ease with which he cited chapter and verse from the research then available. If research had been done, he knew it—in detail.

classroom. Celebrating differences does not mean forgetting that children have much in common: talents, interests, hopes, minds. We can appreciate differences while recognizing the human qualities that bind us together. An 8-year-old child put the idea of differences and likenesses into perspective in a way that few adults, myself included, could manage so beautifully:

### The Colors of the Rainbow

The people of the world are like
The colors of the rainbow.
The colors work together
to make a beautiful sight!
With one color, would the world be as lovely?
With one color, would the world be right?

—Michael

Table 2.4 on page 74 suggests ideas for putting differences in perspective.

**Table 2.4**

**Putting Differences in Perspective**

1. Cultures and languages are indeed different, but none is inferior by virtue of being different. This is the first premise for understanding diversity.
2. Every ambassador to a foreign country must learn as much as possible about the language and culture of the host. Teachers are ambassadors. They must know the parents, community, and institutions from which their students come.
3. Children need to know that their culture and language are honored and respected. Collect books, artifacts, and posters that reflect the stories, poetry, myths, mysteries, and achievements of all ethnic, linguistic, and cultural groups in your classroom.
4. Children learn new languages and cultural customs best when they are part of a learning community that honors differences.
5. Children develop confidence when they see that their educational achievements are real. Feeling good about learning without genuine achievement is delusional.

## Diversity and Equity

Diversity and equity must be acknowledged and acted upon. There are no easy answers, and the ground rules are debatable, as one would expect, since the topic is complex and controversial. I see the following ground rules as useful. First, acknowledge differences of race, gender, ethnicity, language, and culture. It is pointless and dishonest not to do so. Second, note that differences influence how children learn, how they respond to instruction, and how they understand what teachers think they have taught. Third, see that instruction and interaction with children fit the differences observed. Fourth, view differences as strengths rather than weaknesses. Fifth, be aware that expectations influence how we teach and how children learn. We get the best from children and teachers when expectations are positive.

For information on second-language learners and their implications for the classroom teacher, read "Re-Thinking the Education of Teachers of Language Minority Children: Developing Reflective Teachers for Changing Schools," by R. Milk, C. Mercado, and A. Sapiens, 1992. Find it at http://www.ncela.gwu.edu/ncbepubs/ focus/focus6.htm

A hundred years ago, most U.S. immigrants came from Europe. Today most come from Mexico, Central and South America, Asia, and the Middle East. Some states have more immigrants than others, but every state has children who are second-language learners, some of whom have limited English or no English. These children represent different races, ethnicities, languages, and cultures.

Diversity is both an opportunity and a challenge. Effective instruction in a diverse society requires changes in values and attitudes, adjustments in the methods and materials of teaching, and an approach that recognizes the challenge of diversity. The following ideas suggest responses to these challenges.

1. While diversity may challenge your values and require an attitude adjustment, diversity can enrich your classroom and stretch your teaching repertoire in interesting new directions.
2. Children with special learning needs often require a more flexible approach to teaching and learning than your training has provided. Filling these gaps may require additional training.

3. Children are not fundamentally different because they have diverse physical, linguistic, and cultural characteristics. Children everywhere understand and respond to respect, trust, caring, and teaching competence.
4. Substantive resources are available on diversity. This literature can help those interested in understanding and responding to the challenges of diversity (see professional references at the end of this section).
5. The books children read, the pieces they write, and the artifacts they create can make a powerful contribution to understanding diversity.

## Dialect

Everyone has a dialect; it is a matter of degree. Every dialect region in America has its own peculiar brand of English, distinguished from others by certain features of pronunciation, vocabulary, and syntax. You may park your car on the streets of Boston and Austin, but residents don't pronounce *park* and *car* the same way in these two cities. A hungry kid in Philadelphia may eat a grinder, but his counterpart in New York is more likely to eat a hero—same sandwich, different names. New Yorkers wait *on* line but Detroiters wait *in* line. These differences illustrate the three features of dialect: pronunciation, vocabulary, and syntax.

All Americans have a regional dialect, but we have no difficulty understanding one another. But do dialect differences interfere with learning to read and write? Reading failure, to the extent it exists among nonstandard speakers, may be partially attributed to a mismatch between the dialect of the learner and the dialect of instruction. Goodman (1965) said, "The more divergence there is between the dialect of the learner and the dialect of learning, the more difficult will be the task of learning to read."

Since dialect may sometimes adversely influence the acquisition of initial reading ability, how should reading instruction be structured for children whose dialect may pose this challenge? Several approaches have been suggested: (1) write instructional materials in the dialect of the individual reader, (2) teach children to speak standard English before commencing reading instruction, and (3) allow children to read standard English instructional materials in their own dialect (Cramer, 1971; Goodman, 1965).

Goodman (1965) endorsed the third approach since it avoids most of the objections to the other two alternatives. But all have serious practical limitations. Goodman's alternative is useful but depends on teachers' acceptance of the dialect speaker's language. For example, a black dialect speaker might read, "The dog, he look funny," when the text reads, "The dog looks funny." The first sentence is a meaningful realization of the second sentence for some dialect speakers. Though the insertion of *he* and omission of *s* from *looks* are typically considered word recognition errors, Goodman's work on miscue analysis has shown that such miscues are not reading errors in the traditional sense. Rather, they are deep-structure translations that go directly to meaning—which is encoded in the dialect itself. But teachers cannot succeed with this approach if they regard such language divergence as evidence of sloppy, incorrect, and ineffective communication. Yet linguistic science has established that divergent language is none of these things. In fact, the opposite is true.

But a fourth, and possibly better, alternative is available. In the language experience approach, the mismatch between spoken language and written language is eliminated when a speaker's language is recorded accurately through dictation. The language experience approach is ideal for overcoming the mismatch that occurs when the dialect speaker reads standard English. This alternative avoids the problem of procuring materials written in dialect, and it incorporates Goodman's idea that it is desirable to avoid mismatches between spoken language and written language (see Chapter 1).

## Second-Language Learners

America's history and destiny are tied to immigration. From its inception, America has been blessed with cultural and linguistic diversity. America is a cultural and linguistic paradise. Walk the streets of New York, Chicago, or Detroit, and you will hear that beautiful Tower of Babel—languages from around the world melding into the English language. What language, other than English, has been so enriched by tens of thousands of foreign words? What culture, other than American, has been so lavishly endowed with the traditions, cuisine, and entrepreneurship of its immigrants? No other nation on earth has been so blessed.

We live in a multicultural world. Unfortunately, too often we have regarded cultural and linguistic diversity as a handicap; too often learners have struggled because their educational needs went unmet; too often children have felt unwanted in America's classrooms. Second-language learners have special needs that must be recognized. At the same time, these children have special traits and capabilities that enrich our classrooms. Working with second-language learners does require a significant expenditure of energy and present a challenge to the intellect, but when teachers succeed, they present a gift not only to the children in class but to American culture.

To see how and why multicultural day is celebrated at one high school, visit http://www.ar.com.au/~unistar/celebration/multiday/default.htm

I usually have three Jamaican and four Chinese students in my graduate classes because of an exchange program we have with universities in China and Jamaica. Jamaicans read, write, and speak English, but their spoken dialect is distinct. While my Chinese students can read, write, and speak English, their command of phonology, semantics, and syntax usually needs refinement. Even though these students are well educated, and often brilliant, they usually go through a period of language adjustment that may take several years.

In addition to second-language issues, my students must adapt to cultural norms that run counter to those of their native culture. Yet these second-language learners are typically among the best students in my classes. I have come to appreciate how much their native culture contributes to their success in the American academic setting. They have a steep mountain to climb, steeper than I had previously understood. I have learned as much or more from them as they have learned from me. And this is the crucial point: *Teaching second-language learners is a two-way street. Open yourself to the language and culture of those students, and you will discover that you can learn as much or more from them as you are capable of teaching them.*

Learning a second language has parallels with learning a first language. Language learning has universal similarities. For example, a native-born child can converse rather easily at around age 2, but there are still language concepts to be learned: extending vocabulary, syntax, and pronunciation. By ages 5 to 7, all children are fluent in their native language. Syntax, phonology, and vocabulary are in place. Only vocabulary continues to grow throughout life. Children go through stages of language growth, but with exposure to appropriate language models, they learn the language. Second-language learners go through similar stages of growth in their second language. After two years, they can speak the language easily; after four or five years they are usually fluent, though progress depends on having relevant opportunities.

Learning a language requires interaction with people who speak the target language. But second-language learners may have few appropriate models. School may be the primary or only source of interaction with other speakers of the target language. Any reduction in opportunities to practice meaningful language use makes learning more difficult. Fortunately, there are solutions to this problem.

Languages have universal similarities, but important differences exist in features and details. For example, differences in the pronunciation of vowels between the first and second languages may make it more difficult for a second-language learner to readily distinguish English vowel sounds. Consequently, phonics programs that depend heavily on auditory discrimination put the second-language learner at a disadvantage. Syntactic differences also create problems. For example, how adjectives relate to nouns or how verbs are inflected may work differently in English than in a child's native language. Such differences make learning a new language challenging. Fortunately, young second-language learners navigate language issues far more competently than adults do. Difficulties notwithstanding, teachers play a key role in easing the burden second-language learners face. Ideas for helping them are suggested in Table 2.5.

**Table 2.5**

**Teaching Second-Language Learners**

*Teaching Tip*

1. Learn about the culture and language of your children. You can't learn everything, but learn the basics that will help you identify with your students.
2. Honor the culture and language of your children. Show appreciation for their language and culture. Respect given earns respect in return.
3. Be a language model. The manner in which you use English will help your children develop their own language skills.
4. Never forbid children to speak in their native tongue. Anything that disparages a child's native language and culture is an implicit rejection of the child.
5. Invite children to share their customs, traditions, holidays, and special occasions. Use this information as part of the curriculum in your classroom.
6. Appreciate and respect your own culture and language; this is the first step in appreciating the culture and language of others.
7. Make friends with folk of other cultures. Come to know them, and you will find that you share many of the same dreams, hopes, and aspirations.
8. Seek the counsel of experienced second-language teachers. They can share ideas that will make your work more successful.

## Point ═══ Counterpoint

### A Debatable Issue
### English Immersion

**Background**

Some second-language learners may come to school with little or no English proficiency. Some say these children should first learn to read and write in their native language. Others say this doesn't work. They advocate immediate immersion in English with little or no reference to a child's native language.

**The Debatable Issue**

Should second-language learners receive immediate immersion in English with little or no reference to

their native language, or should they first achieve literacy in their native language?

**Take a Stand**

Argue the case for or against the debatable issue. What arguments can you make for either side of the second-language learning debate? Marshal your arguments based on your philosophy, experience, relevant research, and expert opinion. After you have discussed the issue among colleagues, debate it in your class.

## Children with Special Needs

It would be a mistake with sad consequences if we failed to recognize the talents of children who have been labeled as learning disabled, dyslexic, having attention disorders, and so on. While I am skeptical about the validity of these labels, I do not

*Struggling readers come in all ages and sizes. Joe has struggled with reading, but is now making good progress thanks to the special tutoring he received from his teacher, Michelle Finamore.*

question the good intentions of those who diagnose and label these children. Often they are required to do so by law. But the "science" behind the diagnostic instruments used to identify special needs is questionable, the prescriptions dubious, and the categories fuzzy.

More than most, these children need our full attention and require consistently good instruction over an extended period of time. They do not need exotic instructional strategies, and this is fortunate, since none exists. Children with special needs can learn to read and write. I've worked with such children for decades. I've never known one who did not make progress in reading and writing when given good instruction over an extended period of time. Progress is sometimes slow, but now and then progress is rapid and dramatic. Children with special needs require skilled and sympathetic instruction by caring teachers. But often the instructional circumstances teachers face are difficult. Many teachers struggle valiantly to help these children, but they need more resources than are typically provided.

Like other children, those with special needs possess creative potential. They may have an intelligence that goes unnoticed, especially if this talent is neither verbal nor mathematical. Gardner (1991b) has described the intelligences that often go unnoticed, especially among children with special needs. They may, for example, possess artistic, leadership, or athletic skills. While we must provide basic literacy skills for these children, we also owe them the opportunity to develop the other intelligences they often possess. Table 2.6 suggests ideas for helping them.

> "There is a brilliant child locked inside every student."
> —Marva Collins, from *Great Quotes from Great Teachers*, 1996

## Table 2.6

### Helping Children with Special Needs

1. Do not count of the accuracy of labels and diagnoses given to children with special needs. The examiners, instruments, and procedures used to identify disabilities are not based on irrefutable science.

2. Trust your professional judgment when you have reason to doubt the accuracy of a diagnosis. An outside examiner may observe a child for a few hours, whereas a classroom teacher may observe that same child for hundreds of hours.

3. Strive for small successes in the early stages of instruction to build the confidence needed for larger successes later.

4. Pay special attention to children's ideas. As children gain confidence in the worthiness of their ideas, their skills in reading, writing, and content subjects are likely to grow more rapidly.

5. Don't assume that low or moderate achievement precludes other talents. Children possess many gifts; identify each child's strength and use it to leverage other skills.

6. Some children with special needs require a slower instructional pace and more individual attention than normally progressing children, especially if they have fallen far behind, as is often the case.

7. Unique strategies do not exist for children with special needs. They do not require exotic instruction; they require patient instruction by a good teacher over an extended period of time.

8. Teach to the heart and you will reach the head. Children who learn more slowly than others need their confidence restored; they need to know you care for them.

*Teaching Tip*

## Delpit's Ten Principles

Native English speakers have five or more years of oral language and cultural background before they enroll in school. Second-language learners also have an oral language and cultural background before they enroll in school. *We must not assume that different means deficient.* On the contrary, different backgrounds enrich the classroom when they are perceived as enriching. Second-language learners are not blank slates; they have a language and culture; it is merely different, not absent. The challenge is to appreciate, use, and build on the heritage children bring with them. They possess strengths and weaknesses just as native English speakers do. Strengths may be less obvious and should be sought out; weaknesses are all too obvious—they must not, for that very reason, be judged as the whole of what a child brings to the classroom. Teachers do not always possess the tools necessary to appreciate and use strengths; when this is the case, the only remedy is to acquire knowledge and sensitivity.

Second-language learners need to develop oral language and conceptual skills that will enable them to become fluent readers and writers of English. They need to build their English vocabulary to strengthen their ability to express what they already know. They need to build knowledge of syntactical structures of English for the same reason. Children also need to extend their conceptual knowledge of their new culture. As these pieces of the puzzle are acquired, second-language learners can begin to verbalize their existing knowledge more clearly and completely while gaining more knowledge.

Delpit (1995) has suggested ten principles of instruction for urban children. An examination of her principles suggests their applicability to second-language learners who face the same uphill struggle as urban children.

*Teaching Tip*

**1.** *Demand critical thinking.* Expectations have a role in determining how children learn. Expect much, and you're likely to get it; expect little, and you're likely to get that as well. It takes keen observation to identify talents that are not obviously displayed. But they are there for those who expect to find them.

**2.** *Recognize children's strengths.* Delpit urges teachers not to teach less content, but if anything, to teach more. Second-language learners do not know less, though they may express less because of limited English language facility. As second-language facility grows, they gain a firmer grasp on the conceptual knowledge needed to understand and extend content knowledge.

**3.** *Teach the basics.* Foundational skills are crucial, and nothing is more crucial than reading and writing. Reading and writing are the gateway skills that open or close the door to future possibilities. Phonics and comprehension are the gateway skills to reading; words, ideas, and conventions are the gateway skills to writing.

**4.** *Identify and build on strengths.* Strengths are not always apparent unless one deliberately looks for them. The child who draws but does not read has a talent that can be turned to academic excellence. The child who leads, even if using leadership in ways that may appear misdirected, has a strength.

**5.** *Use familiar experiences and metaphors.* Every child has background experiences derived from home and community. For example, holidays and customs are celebrated in children's homes and communities. These experiences are touchstones for extending home and community language and experiences into new language and experiences.

**6.** *Teach children to challenge racist views of their competence and worthiness.* Children lose confidence in their abilities when they perceive themselves as inferior. It is a teacher's duty to convey to children a strong sense of identity with their race and culture and to reject racist views that denigrate or demean their worthiness and right to be treated with respect, dignity, and equality.

**7.** *Create a sense of family and caring.* We often think of family as those living in the same household, but the concept has broader implications. Family includes the sense that you belong, that you have a caring relationship with those around you. Classrooms can be a place where you belong, where you have privileges as well as responsibilities. Richard Rodriguez, writer and lecturer, had a caring family at school and home. He started school, knowing only a few English words, yet he hungered to read challenging books. His teachers aided and abetted his ambitions and heaped praise upon his efforts. He tells of "basking" in the praise his school family provided.

**8.** *Assess children's needs, and meet them with diverse learning strategies.* Knowing what children know is more important than knowing what they do not know. The secret to assessment is identifying strengths that can be built upon. It doesn't work as well the other way around. For instance, phonics skills are best built from the known to the unknown. Start with known letters, sounds, and words and build outward to the unknown. Some might say, "This child doesn't know *any* letters, sounds, or words." This is almost never true, since few children lack oral language. If the student's oral language base is not in English, try working with dictated language-experience stories—they work just as well in a second language (see Chapter 1).

**9.** *Help children connect to their community and beyond.* Everyone owes a debt to their home community. Role models exist in every community and may have connections to extended communities. Role models need not be celebrities. Often they are local heroes, more accessible than celebrities. Bring them into your classrooms so that children can glimpse the possibilities for their futures.

**10.** *Respect children's home cultures.* Most of what children know derives from their home and community background. Support children's understanding of their culture, honor it, and use it to support their movement into new cultures. For example, knowing the major holidays children celebrate provides opportunities for connecting these identity points with new traditions.

## A Bibliography on Diversity

Dr. Toni Walters, professor of reading and language arts at Oakland University, has worked with diverse populations throughout her teaching career. Her commitment to eradicating racism and educating teachers on its insidious effects has been the hallmark of her career. She provided the professional references on diversity listed in Figure 2.4 as well as the Bibliography of Multicultural Literature for Younger and Older Children (2nd edition), listed in the Blue Pages at the back of this book.

### Section Summary: Environments in Which Diversity Flourishes

1. Racial, ethnic, cultural, and linguistic differences are good and right, and they enrich the culture of a classroom.
2. Diversity and equity must be acknowledged and acted upon.
3. One of the best ways to initiate reading for dialect speakers is to use their own language experience accounts as beginning reading material.
4. Respecting and valuing the language and culture of second-language learners is a crucial step in advancing the growth of English language skills.
5. Children with special needs make progress when given good instruction over an extended period of time.
6. Delpit has suggested ten principles for working with urban children that are applicable to second-language learners as well.

## Practical Teaching Ideas and Activities

*Teaching Tip*

**1.** *Negotiate community expectations.* Read aloud *What a Wonderful World* by George David Weiss and Bob Theile, a beautifully illustrated book based on Louis Armstrong's famous song lyrics. Brainstorm things that would and would not make your classroom a wonderful place to learn and grow. Use this dialogue as a springboard for negotiating your learning community's expectations in a shared writing activity. Have each of the children sign this chart and keep it posted in the classroom for the entire year as a reminder of everyone's responsibility in fostering an inviting, respectful, collaborative, and engaging classroom community.

**2.** *Establish clear routines and expectations—an essential precursor to effective teaching and high academic achievement.* Spend the first four to six weeks of the school year establishing routines and behavioral expectations and helping children understand the *how* and *why* behind them. Model, model, model! Demonstrate exactly how procedures and activities should look and sound and how to access and put away materials. Practice, practice, practice! Children should have extensive opportunities to practice these modeled routines and procedures, with the teacher directly supervising to provide specific feedback. Continue to reflect and revisit them until the students demonstrate the ability to self-monitor and take responsibility for their engagement in meaningful learning activities.

Anderson, R. C. (1994). The role of the reader's schema in comprehension, learning and memory. In R. B. Ruddell, M. R. Ruddell, & H. Singer (Eds.), *Theoretical process and processes of reading* (pp. 469–482). Newark, DE: International Reading Association.

Banks, J. A., & Banks, C. A. (Eds.). (2001). *Handbook of research on multicultural education.* New York: Jossey Bass.

Daniels, M. (2001). *Dancing with words: Signing for Hearing Children's Literacy.* Westport, CT: Bergin & Garvey.

Delpit, L. (1995). *Other people's children.* Paper presented at the National Reading Conference, New Orleans, LA.

Delpit, L., & Dowdy, J. K. (Eds.). (2002). *The skin that we speak: Thoughts on language and culture in the classroom.* New York: New Press.

Freire, P., & Macedo, D. (1987). *Literacy: Reading the word and the world.* Westport, CT: Bergin & Garvey.

Fuerstein, R. (1995). The bell curve: Getting the facts straight. *Educational Leadership, 52* (7), 69–74.

Gay, G. (2001). *Culturally responsive teaching.* New York: Teachers College Press.

Howard, G. R. (1999). *We can't teach what we don't know: White teachers, multiracial schools.* New York: Teachers College Press.

Irvine, J. J. (2002). *In search of wholeness.* New York: Palgrave Macmillan.

King, J. (1991). Dysconscious racism: Ideology, identity, and the miseducation of teachers. *Journal of Negro Education, 60* (2), 133–146.

Ladson-Billings, G. (2001). *Crossing over Canaan: The journey of new teachers in diverse classrooms.* New York: Wiley.

Macedo, D. (1994). *Literacies of power.* Boulder, CO: Westview Press.

Meier, D. (2002). *In schools we trust.* Boston: Beacon Press.

Nieto, S. (2002/2003). Profoundly multicultural questions. *Educational Leadership, 6* (4), 6–10.

Nieto, S. (1999). *The light in their eyes: Creating multicultural learning communities.* New York: Teachers College Press.

Rummel, M. K,. & Quintero, E. P. (1997). *Teachers' reading /teachers' lives.* New York: State University of New York Press.

Sacks, P. (1999). *Standardized minds.* Cambridge, MA: Perseus.

Walters, T. S. (1998). The language of a literate classroom: Rethinking comprehensive dimensions. (ERIC document Reproductions Series No ED 418 430.)

Walters, T. S. (1994). Multicultural literacy: Mental scripts for elementary, secondary, and college teachers. *Equity and Excellence in Education, 27* (2), 45–51.

**Figure 2.4**

**A Bibliography on Diversity**

**3.** *Set up centers.* Careful thought, planning, and organization are essential to the success of meaningful center-based activities during the literacy block. Room size will play a role in determining whether centers will be designated areas of the classroom or consist of tubs of materials students take to open spots in the room. Most classrooms can accommodate at least a few centers. When planning a center, consider how many students will use it simultaneously and allot space accordingly. For example, in a preprimary or primary classroom, blocks and art centers require more space. Display a visual reminder of the number of children who may work in that area at one time. Color-coded shelves or areas with coordinating tubs, trays, and baskets help maintain organization and independent access to materials and encourage activities. For very popular centers, or centers you expect every student to use in a given week, you may set up a clipboard with a sign-in sheet.

**4.** *Post a daily schedule.* A familiar, predictable routine will promote independence. Post a daily schedule using actual photographs of children in the classroom engaged in each of the scheduled activities, along with the expected time frame for each.

**5.** *Foster parental involvement.* Put forth the effort to make parents feel welcome in the classroom and suggest a variety of ways they can get involved. Invite parents to share diverse cultural backgrounds or special skills. Invite family members to come in as guest readers. Plan brown-bag lunches, inviting parents to join you for lunch to discuss classroom issues and supporting children's literacy development at home. Encourage classroom volunteers to participate in party planning, shopping for supplies, publishing children's writing, or lending support in the computer lab, literacy, or math activities, or an inquiry group. Suggest prep-work tasks for parents who feel more comfortable working behind the scenes or whose employment makes classroom work inconvenient. At home they might make blank books, or complete laminating, copying, cutting, or stapling tasks. As opportunities arise, solicit help through a "classified ad" section in your newsletter. List specific needs, explain what the role entails, and provide a way to reply.

See the Blue Pages at the back of the book and on the Companion Website for additional activities.

## Reflection and Summary

### Reflection

"What took you so short?" 4-year-old Ben asked his dad, who had returned much sooner than expected. "Bring on the empty horses," Michael Curtiz, the Hungarian-born film director, shouted to his film crew. These two sentences have something in common. *They are perfectly logical linguistic expressions.* The trouble is, they also constitute unexpected uses of English. Ben and Mr. Curtiz face a similar challenge. They are learning the strange twists and turns of the English language. Ben is learning his native language; Mr. Curtiz is learning English as a second language. Ben reversed the expression "What took you so *long?*" Mr. Curtiz wanted his crew to "Bring on the *riderless* horses." Mr. Curtiz was filming *The Charge of the Light Brigade*—thus the need for empty horses.

We can't help loving the English language, and we can't help loving those who risk its subtle snares. They remind us that learning our native language as a second language is a challenge, that English is a tangled miracle, that the brain is a malleable instrument of thought. As Mrs. Malaprop said, in Richard Brinsley Sheridan's play *The Rivals,* "If I reprehend anything in this world, it is the use of my oracular tongue, and a nice derangement of epitaphs!"

## Summary

This chapter has presented the following main ideas:

- Teachers are responsible for fostering intellectual, therapeutic, and cultivated environments within their classrooms. This must be done in cooperative work with the children and resources available in a classroom.
- Effective classroom management facilitates learning and fosters cooperative working arrangements among teachers and children. Parents can contribute to effective classroom management.
- Inviting physical arrangements and work procedures create an environment that fosters effective teaching and learning. Physical elements of an inviting classroom include attractive and functional arrangement of furniture, learning centers, and artistic displays.
- Language, thinking, meaning, and multiple intelligences are key concepts in teaching and learning the language arts.
- There are seven language functions: instrumental, regulatory, interactional, personal, heuristic, imaginative, and informative.
- Vygotsky, Piaget, and Bruner proposed theories of language and thought that have influenced instruction.
- Creative thinking focuses on unusual ways of solving problems. Critical thinking emphasizes evaluation of relevant information.
- There are multiple dimensions to intelligence. The idea of multiple intelligences moves beyond the narrow view of IQ as primarily verbal and mathematical.
- Racial, ethnic, cultural, and linguistic differences can aid teaching and learning when differences are valued.
- Second-language learners benefit from exposure to good English language models. Valuing the language and culture of second-language learners advances growth in English language skills.
- One of the best ways to initiate reading for dialect speakers is to use their own language experience accounts as beginning reading material.
- Children with special needs make progress when given good instruction over an extended period of time.
- Children of various cultural and linguistic backgrounds flourish in classrooms in which their differences are seen as enriching the teaching and learning environment.

# Questions to Challenge Your Thinking

1. As a teacher, what would you do to advance the intellectual environment in your classroom?
2. If you had the resources, how would you physically arrange your classroom?
3. In drawing up rules of conduct for your classroom, would you ask your children to participate in suggesting rules? Why or why not?
4. How would you use parent volunteers in your classroom to help in your language arts program?
5. Lev Vygotsky emphasized a concept called the zone of proximal development. What does this mean, and how is it similar to Betts's concept of instructional level?
6. You have a problem to solve. You want to raise money to buy books for the class library. Write two ideas that focus on creative thinking and two that focus on critical thinking to help raise money.
7. Why should a teacher focus closely on children's meanings during conversations with them?
8. You teach second grade. A Chinese boy shows up in September. He cannot speak English. What would you do to advance his English language skills?
9. Maggie is assigned to your fifth-grade class. She has been diagnosed as learning disabled. She reads at the second-grade level and dislikes writing intensely. What will you do to accommodate her needs and advance her reading and writing skills?
10. Do you think dialect has an adverse influence on learning to read? Explain.

# A Case Study

Read the following case study, and then discuss the questions below with your classmates or colleagues.

Jose's parents immigrated to America from Mexico when Jose was 1 year old. Jose, a sixth-grader, speaks English fluently. At home he speaks Spanish. The school psychologist reports that Jose has a low average IQ. Jose reads at a sixth-grade level, makes a few miscues when reading aloud, but most of his miscues make sense. Jose is neither popular nor unpopular with his classmates and hasn't much to say during class discussions. Jose's teacher notes that he has had thoughtful conversations with him about drawing, but when school subjects are discussed, he has little to say. He spends every spare minute drawing. His drawings are mature and exquisitely detailed, and they feature animals and nature subjects. Jose doesn't write much and shows little interest in writing.

1. Jose has a reported low average IQ. What might explain this relatively low IQ score? Does the IQ finding concern you? Explain.
2. How might you use Jose's strengths to advance his literacy skills?
3. What would you do to advance and encourage Jose's artistic interests?

# Revisit the Anticipation Guide

Return to the Anticipation Guide in the chapter opener, and review your original responses to the questions. Having finished the chapter, complete the guide again, and then consider these questions.

1. Did you change your mind about any items? Which ones? Why?
2. Which idea did you encounter with which you most strongly agree? Explain.
3. Which idea did you encounter with which you most strongly disagree? Explain.
4. Which chapter ideas did you find most useful? Least useful? Why?
5. If you had written this chapter, what would you have done differently? Explain.

## VideoWorkshop Extra!

If your instructor ordered a package including VideoWorkshop, go to Chapter 2 of the Companion Website (www.ablongman.com/cramer1e) and click on the VideoWorkshop button. Follow the instructions for viewing the appropriate video clip and completing the accompanying exercise. Watch the Companion Website for access to a new interactive teaching portal, My Lab School, currently under construction.

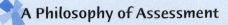

### A Philosophy of Assessment

*Steven Gould, an anthropologist, in a book called The MISmeasurement of Man (1996, 2nd Edition), shows that efforts at measuring human qualities reveal a history of mismeasurement brought about by prejudice, ignorance, and just plain foolishness. Do not think that such mismeasurement exists only in the past. Even today, we continue to mismeasure. Can any reasonable person believe that 30–40% of the children in a certain urban school district have learning disabilities? Are we, in these modern times, simply continuing a long disgraceful chapter in the history of the mismeasurement of human qualities? Will common sense come to our rescue before more harm is done?*

*Assessing children's knowledge of reading and writing requires, above all, that we do no harm. Therefore, we must know what is authentic, useful, and necessary; we must recognize what is inauthentic, useless, and unnecessary. We need a foundation of assessment values as well as knowledge, so that we can accurately and fairly assess the strengths and needs of the children we teach. MISmeasurement must be unacceptable because it does irreparable harm to the children whose lives are entrusted to our tender mercies.*

# 3 Assessing Writing and Reading

### Big Ideas for Chapter 3

1. The major purpose of assessment is to improve teaching and learning.
2. The most valid assessment occurs as you observe authentic literacy events.
3. Looking for children's strengths and needs is crucial to effective assessment.
4. Valid assessment is guided by principles and values that constitute the philosophical underpinnings of all assessment practices and procedures.
5. Writing assessment tools include checklists; conferences; portfolios; holistic, analytic, and primary trait scoring; self-assessment; and "kid watching."

6. Reading assessment tools include a reading performance checklist, an interest inventory, and administration and interpretation of an informal reading inventory (IRI). An IRI is used to assess comprehension and word recognition.
7. Two primary objectives of reading assessment are the determining of comprehension strengths and needs and word recognition strengths and needs.
8. Standards and high-stakes testing have become part of the educational landscape. Increase in their use raises many significant issues regarding teaching and learning.

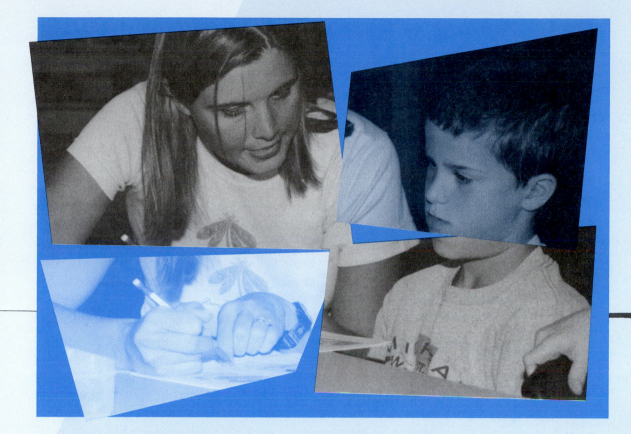

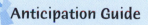 ## Anticipation Guide

*Consider each of the following statements, and determine whether you agree or disagree. Save your answers, and revisit this guide at the end of this chapter.*

1. Informal assessments are more useful than standardized tests.    agree    disagree
2. The best assessment stems from observing authentic literacy events.    agree    disagree
3. Philosophy influences assessment procedures and decisions.    agree    disagree
4. Analytic assessment gives a quick overall impression of writing.    agree    disagree
5. Holistic assessment provides a detailed analysis of writing.    agree    disagree
6. Informal inventories assess comprehension and word recognition.    agree    disagree
7. Placing children at their instructional level ensures success.    agree    disagree
8. Word recognition is the most important issue in reading assessment.    agree    disagree
9. Reading miscues help determine instructional levels.    agree    disagree
10. High-stakes standardized testing has improved achievement in schools.    agree    disagree

> *And the trouble is, if you don't risk anything, you risk even more.*
>
> —Erica Jong

## A Literacy Story

A young boy stands in the schoolmaster's office, about to receive a strapping: "You know it's coming to you?" "Yes sir," the boy replies. The boy takes his licks, as the schoolmaster insists, "like a man." Then a serendipity occurs. The schoolmaster takes the boy to his home, invites him into a study lined with more books than the boy had ever imagined existed, and says, "You do not behave yourself very well in school, but I do not know that it matters. It is possible that you have a mind. . . . It may be there are books here that will be of help. You are to come and go as you please. You are to take what books you want to read." The boy becomes a passionate reader.

The boy grew up, had a family, abandoned his conventional life as a manager of a paint factory, and headed for Chicago, a place of literary ferment in the early 20th century. He wanted to experience the literary renaissance of Midwestern America; he wanted Paris on Lakeshore Drive; he wanted to write. Over the next few decades he wrote short stories, novels, memoirs. His first collection of short stories, *Winesburg, Ohio*, became his most important work. His stories departed from the traditional emphasis of plot and action and blazed a new path—one of psychological insight into the thoughts and feelings of story characters.

He became friends with William Faulkner, not yet a successful writer but seeking a place in the literary world. Faulkner drew inspiration from his friend and wrote his first novel, *Soldier's Pay*. The friend recommended Faulkner's book to his publisher in return for the promise that he wouldn't have to read the manuscript.

The boy from a small town in Ohio grew into a highly respected writer and influenced the work of Hemingway and Faulkner, two Nobel Prize-winning authors. Do you know the name? Probably not, for even avid readers may not have heard the name, much less read the writing of, Sherwood Anderson, the boy who took his whipping "like a man."

Sherwood Anderson is an important writer, yet perhaps his contribution to other writers is even more important. Teachers, too, can make contributions to others. You don't have to win a Nobel Prize to have a hand in shaping those who do.

# A MATTER OF STANDARDS

## The Assessment of Reading and Writing

The International Reading Association and the National Council of Teachers of English have promulgated a separate set of standards for the assessment of reading and writing. An abbreviated description of assessment standards for reading and writing appears below.

Standard 1: The interests of the student are paramount in assessment.

Standard 2: The primary purpose of assessment is to improve teaching and learning.

Standard 3: Assessment must reflect and allow for critical inquiry into curriculum and instruction.

Standard 4: Assessment must recognize and reflect the intellectually and socially complex nature of reading and writing and the important roles of school, home, and society in literacy development.

Standard 5: Assessment must be fair and equitable.

Standard 6: The consequences of an assessment procedure are the first, and most important, consideration in establishing the validity of the assessment.

Standard 7: The teacher is the most important agent of assessment.

Standard 8: The assessment process should involve multiple perspectives and sources of data.

Standard 9: Assessment must be based in the school community.

Standard 10: All members of the education community—students, parents, teachers, administrators, policy makers—must have a voice in the development, interpretation, and reporting of assessment.

Standard 11: Parents must be involved as active essential participants in the assessment process.

Each of the assessment standards is important, but several deserve particular mention. Standards 1 and 2 stress the idea that assessment is intended to improve teaching and learning. This standard is foundational to all assessment because it is the single most important reason for assessing children's achievement. Yet much of the testing associated with state and federal standards violates this fundamental premise. Teachers are seldom privy to an item-by-item analysis of their children's performance on standardized tests, yet this information is vital to assessing children's strengths and needs. Instead of an item-by-item analysis of performance, teachers usually receive only the composite scores of their children's performance. But composite scores have little, if any, diagnostic value since teachers cannot deduce from composite scores precisely where children performed well or poorly. Standard 7 states that teachers are the key agent in assessment. This is true, but teachers cannot perform this key function unless they have access to all pertinent data, and they seldom do. Still, this does not leave teachers helpless because they can assess children's needs through informal instruments and observation. This chapter describes instruments, procedures, and observational methods for assessing and correcting reading and writing difficulties.

*Source:* From Task Force on Assessment (1994). *Standards for the Assessment of Reading and Writing.* National Council of Teachers of English and International Reading Association. Reprinted with permission of the International Reading Association. All rights reserved.

Every time I start a new chapter, I ask myself, "Where shall I begin? And then I remember what the King told the White Rabbit in Lewis Carroll's *Alice in Wonderland:* "Begin at the beginning and go on 'til you come to the end; then stop." So I begin with this definition: the Latin origin of assess means "to sit beside and assist." Metaphorically, this meaning suggests the value of assessing children by sitting

"Our mission as educators is to help every child become a more active, engaged, committed, and skillful learner, not just for a text but for a lifetime."

—James Bellanca

down beside them and observing what they are doing, and how they are doing it, in order to guide learning.

Assessment has two main branches: (1) gathering the information required to understand the strengths and needs of children, and (2) analyzing the information so it can be used to improve teaching and learning. Teachers are often more familiar with the first branch than the second. But the first branch has little relevance if the second is neglected. This chapter will keep both branches in mind, since learning how and what information to gather is only half the task—the other half is making effective use of it. Assessment is more art than science because it relies on teachers' intuitive good judgments about the *meaning* of what they see and hear as children go about their daily learning activities.

This chapter discusses types of assessment, principles that guide assessment, and ideas and techniques for assessing writing and reading.

## Three Types of Assessment

There are three types of assessment: *formative, summative,* and *research*. Each has a purpose and place in assessing elements of the educational enterprise. While each type has a specific focus, there is overlap among them.

### Formative Assessment

"We must constantly remind ourselves that the ultimate purpose of evaluation is to have students become self-evaluating."

—A. L. Costa and B. Kallick, "Reassessing Assessment," 1992.

Formative assessment is aimed at improving instruction and learning. Accurate and timely assessment enables teachers and children to make informed decisions regarding design of literacy programs and projects, delivery of instruction, and the environment needed to support teaching and learning. No outside agent can provide assessment that is more relevant, accurate, or useful than the assessment the teacher and her children can provide for themselves. Therefore, formative assessment is best carried out in the classroom by teachers and children.

### Summative Assessment

Assessment designed to assess the state or quality of an enterprise or institution, or to report on its progress to an outside audience, is called summative assessment. Its purpose is not improved instruction, yet it may indirectly bring about such a result. Summative assessment guides administrative decision making. A school district, a state, and even a nation needs to know whether its children are receiving effective instruction. Local, state, and national agencies need to know how reading and writing are progressing so that goals can be set, programs evaluated, and resources provided. Teachers and administrators need to know how children are progressing so that they can report progress to parents and the community. Such reports take many forms; the most common are report cards and standardized test results.

## Research Assessment

Assessment that inquires into the procedures, products, and processes of literacy is research oriented. Its purpose is to inform and reform instruction in valid and reliable ways and to determine the conditions under which literacy instruction works best. It can lead to new or improved ways of delivering instruction. Research can tell us how well children are reading and writing, how one aspect of literacy influences another, what strengths and needs students exhibit, which schools are doing well or poorly, what strategies and processes are most productive, and whether our resources are spent wisely or foolishly. Literacy research need not be limited in its methodology. No promising research paradigm need be excluded. Quantitative and qualitative procedures can and should be used.

## Section Summary: Three Types of Assessment

1. Formative assessment is aimed at improving instruction and learning in the classroom and is usually carried out by classroom teachers.
2. Summative assessment is aimed at reporting the state or quality of an enterprise or institution, often to a local, state, or national audience.
3. Research assessment inquires into the procedures, products, and processes of literacy with the intention of informing or reforming instruction.

## Principles of Assessment

Assessment is going in two directions today. There is a movement to rely more and more on standardized tests at the local, state, and national levels. The impetus for this movement comes from politicians seeking "accountability," and it receives some support from within the education profession, particularly those holding administrative or quasi-administrative positions. Teachers are less enthusiastic about the usefulness of standardized tests to assess how well children are learning. While there is a need for accountability, there is an overabundance of faith in the accuracy and adequacy of the instruments and procedures used. There is also reason to suspect that overreliance on standardized tests distorts instruction, forcing teachers to conform to a test curriculum. Assessment should not drive curriculum; curriculum should drive assessment. Standardized testing is most useful when it is combined with teacher's assessment of children's strengths and needs, which includes daily observations, informal testing, checklists, curricular adjustments, and other informal ways of understanding how children are learning, what their needs might be, and how instruction is progressing. A related emphasis is self-assessment, by which children are taught to assess their own performance. The principles described in this section offer guidelines for assessing teaching and learning through informal classroom observations.

> "The methods of assessment must align with the new goals and measure whether or not students have achieved them."
> —K. Burks, *The Mindful School: How to Assess Authentic Learning*, 1992.

## Authentic Assessment

The most valid assessment occurs in observing real-life literacy behaviors (Johnston, 1997; Leslie & Jett-Simpson, 1997). Informal tests, such as informal reading inventories (IRIs), are useful, but even informal tests create an artificial perspective from which to observe literacy. The most valid assessment comes from watching how children perform while engaged in activities that are authentic, not manufactured. For example, as children discuss a recently read book in a literacy circle, listen to their retellings and conversations and ask yourself: Are my children puzzled or articulate about the book they have read? Are their conversations thoughtful? Can they relate what they read to their personal experiences? Observations made on the spot may suggest the need for more appropriate books, minilessons on book discussions, or additional strategy instruction. No one is in a better position to make such judgments than the classroom teacher.

## Purposeful Assessment

Always assess performance with a purpose. Ask, Why am I assessing this? How will I use the information I gather? With these questions in mind, consider the types of assessment available and their relationship to your purpose. Think through what you need to know and what you will do with the information you obtain; once you have determined these purposes, you will be in a position to carry out meaningful assessment. This step is especially important when assessment involves testing, whether informal or standardized.

*Informal instructional sessions, as shown here, can provide teachers with valuable assessment information about children's listening and language needs and strengths.*

## Assessment and Curricular Goals

Match assessment to curricular goals. What do you expect *your children* to learn? If you can answer this question clearly, you have a good sense of your curricular goals. For instance, if revising is a goal in your writing program, have children keep drafts of writing in their portfolios. Scan drafts to see what aspects of revising reveal strengths or needs. If your children are good at adding strong details but need help deleting irrelevant information, address this problem directly. You have many choices: schedule a minilesson where you model deleting, organize group revision conferences, suggest a focused task for peer editing sessions, or discuss the problem during author's chair sessions. The first time you notice the beginnings of successful deletion, tell the class how pleased you are at their progress. Encouragement toward a goal is crucial to achieving it.

## Assessment and Instruction

Assessment does not occur at a given point and then cease; the best assessment extends into and through instructional time and space. For example, after having administered a comprehension check using an informal reading inventory, be cautious about interpreting the results. Use them as a tentative starting point. Then confirm your data and analysis as you direct daily comprehension sessions. Ask questions: Is Sally doing better or worse in this instructional situation than she did on the inventory? What is the quality of Sally's comments and conversations following a story or social studies lesson? Compare your instructional observations with IRI results. They are sometimes more valid and reliable than test performance. Inventory results are valuable, but they are not infallible. Observations derived from daily performance can be and often are more reliable and valid than test performance.

> "Assessment is trustworthy and authentic when it occurs as a regular part of classroom learning and instruction. Assessment helps teachers plan curriculum and instruction in order to meet the needs of every student."
>
> —B. Campbell-Hill and C. Ruptic, *Practical Aspects of Authentic Assessment,* 1992.

## Culture and Language

Children come to us with diverse cultural, linguistic, physical, mental, and gender experiences. Sensitivity to and awareness of these differences are crucial if we intend to help all children achieve their potential. Differences are not weaknesses; they are strengths that can enrich your classroom. How we assess skills and the conclusions derived from such assessment must be tailored to the special requirements of the children. For example, I had intended to administer an informal reading inventory to a 9-year-old Chinese girl who had enrolled in the University Reading Clinic. Yamin's parents had moved to Michigan within the past year. She spoke English haltingly and was quite shy. I soon realized that the IRI was inappropriate linguistically as well as culturally. So I put it aside, and we had a conversation. I made a *best guess* placement in one of our clinic groups because I knew her teacher would soon learn more about Yamin from daily clinic instruction than I could learn from an IRI. This turned out to be a good guess. Over the next several months, Yamin's reading and writing grew apace with her mastery of English.

## Field Notes
### Real-Life Experiences of a Classroom Teacher

When I taught fourth grade on the Navajo reservation, I was in the minority. All my students were Native Americans. I came to the classroom believing that my students spoke Navajo and knew the traditions of their tribe. I soon learned otherwise.

Once I started teaching, I realized that my children were as diverse as those of any other classroom in the United States. Yes, the students were all Native American, but still they were individuals and came from a variety of backgrounds. I wanted to learn about their culture, yet many of my students didn't appear to know much about their heritage. Many of the parents were not involved in school. Then, a serendipity occurred.

The tone of my classroom changed with one book, *Sing Down the Moon,* by Scott O'Dell. This

Jennifer Hill

book tells the story of a traditional Navajo girl who lived in Canyon de Chelly, located about 40 miles from our school. The story takes place during the time of the Long Walk, during which the tribe was forced off their land and moved to New Mexico. In one chapter, the protagonist goes through the ceremony of womanhood. Some of my children had been to such a ceremony, some had heard of it, and a few did not know what it was. Everyone went home and talked to their parents about it. I was amazed. Reading became exciting. Suddenly, my students were active participants in discussions; parents sent in notes with personal stories; we were becoming a community of learners. Literature awakened my understanding of the power of culture in teaching and learning.

It takes effort and thought to appreciate the language and culture of children and the role they play in teaching and learning. When Jennifer Hill first taught in a Native American school in Arizona, she had more to learn than her students did. She tells, in the Field Notes piece, how a single book became the catalyst for appreciating the role her children's cultural heritage could play in teaching and learning.

## A Philosophy of Assessment

Assessment provides information about how children perform; what you do in response does not follow automatically from your observations. Instructional decisions are influenced by beliefs as well as observations. What you believe determines what instruction you will provide. For instance, if assessment suggests the need for instruction in word recognition, how you provide it depends on what you believe about that type of instruction. Dozens of kits and workbooks purport to teach word recognition. Which one, if any, shall you use? You can choose a synthetic or analytic approach, but these two approaches operate on fundamentally different premises. The first starts with the parts and builds toward the whole; the other starts with the whole and works toward the parts. And, of course, there are other choices as well. Your instructional philosophy—what you believe—will determine your decision as much or more than the assessment you made.

## Children Are Partners in Assessment

Children sometimes know more about their strengths and needs than do the adults who work with them. Make children partners in assessing their strengths and needs. It is not a good idea to turn assessment over to children without adult monitoring, but it is a good idea to teach children to monitor their own learning processes. Self-assessment grows through work with peers, teacher modeling, and conversations that help children develop ways to critique their own performance. For example, show children how to ask questions about their learning: Why am I using this strategy? How does it help me? Am I using this strategy well? How can I improve my use of this strategy? As children become more aware of their ability to monitor and control their learning, they can help their teachers assess learning progress. This process is called metacognitive awareness, a way of understanding how we learn.

*Teaching Tip*

"The long-term goal is for students to practice enough self-assessment under the teacher's guidance to be able to create their own lists of expectations and to measure their own performance independently."
—Educators in Connecticut's Pomperaug Regional School District 15, *A Teacher's Guide to Performance-Based Learning and Assessment,* 1996.

## Looking for Strengths and Needs

Strengths tell you where to start and what to build on. Needs tell you where performance can be improved *Assessment is not a relentless search for weaknesses.* More often than not, weaknesses are readily apparent. Successful assessment should be a vigorous search for strengths, and strengths are not always academic. Tony, an eighth-grader, came to our reading and writing clinic with an attitude of indifference and many obvious instructional needs: he couldn't read, spell, or write anywhere near his potential. He had reason to dislike school, since everything he was expected to do there, he couldn't do well. His clinic teacher noticed two important strengths: (1) he possessed a high listening capacity—he could understand text read to him one level higher than his grade placement; this suggested more than adequate language and mental capability; and (2) he possessed highly developed drawing skills; his drawings suggested exceptional powers of observation.

These strengths were more than promising, so we used them to entice him into literacy, starting with language experience stories—a perfect forum for using his oral language. Tony used his artistic skills to illustrate his own stories, as well as those written by his peers. Of course, it took time to strengthen his reading and writing skills, but his teacher used his strengths to improve academic performance, which, incidentally, helped reshape his attitude.

Children have more than one face. The public face may feign indifference and dislike, but the private face is often quite different. Most children want to learn, but they cannot reveal their desires publicly; they need a private audience; they need someone who cares; they need assurance that they can learn. Then indifference turns to trust; dislike turns to earnest effort.

## The Tentative Nature of Assessment

Assessment is a best estimate, not a final answer. Estimates are sometimes wrong, but do not fear this; instead, recognize that you almost certainly will make such errors. Initial misjudgments can be corrected as you extend your observations into instructional time and space. Misjudgments typically result because of problems with the assessor, the assessed, the instruments of assessment, and the context of assessment.

- *The assessor.* Some days your observations will be on target, other days less so. The reason is that you are human. But as you become more experienced, your estimates will become more accurate.
- *The assessed.* Children have good and bad days. On any given day a child may be sharp, energetic, lethargic, hungry, tired, or unmotivated. If key assessments occur on a very good or very bad day, they may not represent typical performance.
- *Instruments of assessment.* No one has yet devised a completely valid and reliable instrument for assessing human behavior—no one ever will. Instruments sample behavior; they cannot assess the universe of behaviors. It is easy to get a nonrepresentative sample and make a misjudgment based on it.
- *The context of assessment.* The environment in which assessment occurs influences outcomes. Distractions and other environmental influences affect behavior and consequently influence results.

Awareness that misjudgment is possible is not a cause for alarm but simply a recognition of reality. It will help you avoid rushing to conclusions about students' performance. It will make you a better teacher and evaluator.

## Informal Instruments in Assessment

Informal instruments of assessment are preferable to standardized instruments. Much assessment today focuses on group behavior, group norms, group scores. But classroom assessment needs to be keyed to individuals, not to groups. Standardized tests have their uses, but they are not helpful in assessing day-to-day classroom performance. Standardized tests have established reliability (consistency in measurements) and validity (a truthful or factual condition) data. They typically involve time limits and scripted instructions—ignoring these features can result in faulty interpretation of data. In contrast, informal assessment tools offer a more flexible and personalized way of assessing children's strengths and needs. For example, informal reading inventories allow you to probe responses, restate questions, and take as much time as needed to assess comprehension and word recognition skills qualitatively.

> "Only by being true to the full growth of all individuals who make it up, can society . . . be true to itself."
>
> —John Dewey

## Assessment as Art and Science

Assessment is more art than science. Effective assessment relies on data, experience, and informed intuition. Many skills are involved: keen observation of children's behavior, knowing the value and limitations of test data, understanding the strengths and weaknesses of assessment tools, understanding the psychology of children's behavior, knowing how to analyze data, and knowing how to elicit information from children. Assessment judgments derive from experience, knowledge, and the art of combining what science may provide with thoughtful detection and analysis.

## Section Summary: Principles of Assessment

1. The most valid assessment occurs as you observe authentic literacy behaviors.
2. Assessment without purpose is useless. Know prior to assessment why you are assessing a behavior and how you will use the information obtained.
3. Match assessment to curricular goals so children will know what they are expected to learn and you will know what you need to teach.
4. The best assessment extends into and through instructional time and space.
5. Sensitivity to cultural and linguistic differences gives direction to assessment and is an asset to classroom ambience and achievement.
6. Philosophy influences assessment; your beliefs drive decisions about how to assess and what to do with assessment information.
7. Children's self-assessment can help them understand their literacy strengths and needs and can guide your assessment decisions.
8. Assessment should focus on strengths as well as needs. Strengths tell you where to start and what to build on; needs tell you where performance needs to improve.
9. Assessment is nearly always a best estimate. Misjudgments inevitably occur, but when assessment is linked to ongoing instruction, they can be readily corrected.
10. Informal assessment is more flexible and personalized than standardized assessment and therefore is better matched to classroom needs.
11. Effective assessment is more art than science, more creative than scientific.

# Assessment of Writing

The sportswriter Red Smith once said, "There's nothing to writing. All you do is sit down at the typewriter and open a vein." I'd like to paraphrase Mr. Smith: "There's nothing to teaching children; all you do is walk into a classroom and pour out your heart." Of course, I'm talking about the dedicated teacher, the hardworking teacher, the compassionate teacher. Among the hardest jobs a teacher has is the assessment of writing. Most teachers find it difficult. It's time consuming, and it's hard to assess fairly.

The characteristics of writing offer one challenge—some are more important than others. Then there is the personal factor—it is not just writing that teachers assess; it is the writer as well. This section suggests ideas about what to assess, how to go about it, and how to lighten the paper load. Even so, nothing will ever make the task of writing assessment easy.

> "Assessment includes systematic observations that will provide a continually updated profile of the child's current ways of responding."
> —I. Fountas and G. S. Pinnel, *Guided Reading,* 1996.

## Observing Children

One of the great psychologists of the 20th century, Jean Piaget, set forth a theory of children's intellectual development based on observations he had made. Some of his conclusions were based on observing his own children. His observations helped

Teaching Tip

## Electronic Portfolios

Connecting Technology to Teaching

Technology will probably have an important role to play in assessing your students. Technology as a tool for assessment is currently being used for a variety of purposes. Personal digital assistants (PDAs) make it very easy to record observations about students. Numerous programs can help you create your own assessment tools such as tests, checklists, and rubrics. The most significant assessment potential, however, is in the ability to create electronic portfolios.

Electronic portfolios offer many advantages over traditional ones. Because they take up "electronic space" and not physical space, electronic portfolios offer teachers an opportunity to keep a wide variety of student products. A variety of media can be stored within a child's file. Artwork can be scanned in; performances and presentations can be video-recorded and saved. Digital photographs can be used. In a small space you can easily record the entire school-year experience. Because they can be easily posted on the the World Wide Web, electronic portfolios can provide easy access by students, parents, administrators, and other stakeholders to student performance. Cross-referencing student work is easily accomplished through hyperlinks. A project that meets multiple objectives can be listed in the table of contents under multiple cat-

egories. By saving the portfolio to a floppy disk or CD-ROM, it can be easily transferred to another teacher or school. Because copies are easy and inexpensive to create, a record of an entire year's achievements can be given as a keepsake for each student.

In order to implement a successful portfolio project, it is not necessary to collect students' best works. Rather, a wide range of actual student products should be incorporated into the portfolio. By allowing a more complete representation, the portfolio is better able to provide accurate insight into the student's development. In order to give the student a sense of ownership, the selection of materials for inclusion should be a collaborative venture between the student and the teacher. Students should be allowed to review their portfolio and the portfolios of their peers. By placing "comment" buttons on each portfolio, anyone viewing the portfolio can provide feedback to the student, a useful tool in the student's self-reflection process. Because their work is displayed for others to examine, electronic portfolios motivate students and encourage them to effectively use technology for an authentic purpose. The advantages offered through a computer-based portfolio system should continue to make it a popular assessment tool for students and teachers.

Contributed by Lisa Kunkleman

him understand that surface behaviors had a deeper meaning than seemed apparent at first sight. Piaget's (1981) observations led to an influential theory of intellectual development in children. Some say his theories are sound; others disagree. But certainly this conclusion can be drawn from his experience: *careful observation of children yields important clues in understanding how they learn, what strengths they possess, what needs they have, what stage of learning they are in, and how we can best teach them.*

Jerome Wideman, author of *East Fourth Street*, made a lifelong practice of recording facts, events, conversations, and observations encountered in daily life. Later, he transformed his notes and observations into grist for the novels and stories he wrote. This practice, modified to fit the teaching profession, can help teachers just as it helps writers. Observing children is instructive and enjoyable. Recently I watched a very young child look around a room, spot a box about 6 inches high, pick it up, and place it in a strategic spot. Then she stood on it so that she could reach a toy previously beyond reach. What powers of insight and reason propelled this behavior? Observation. She'd seen others do something similar; she observed that it worked; she now employs it as her own strategy.

The premise for observing children is this: *children are purposeful and rational.* Rarely do they behave randomly or irrationally. Reason and purpose underlie their behavior, including their bad behavior. Discovering and understanding children's strengths and needs in the area of literacy are based on this premise. Suppose, for example, you hear this observation in the teacher's lounge: "Tangela hates writing." There must be reason and purpose behind Tangela's dislike. What are the reasons? How can they be changed? The observant teacher seeks answers to these questions. Tangela's perspective can be changed. Observant teachers seek out the reasons behind surface behaviors because they wish to understand the deeper meanings beneath them. When they succeed, teachers can engage or reengage children in doing what they do so well—*learn.*

## Standing on the Shoulders of Giants
## Historical Contributions to Literacy
### Bill Martin Jr.

There can't be many children in America who haven't heard or read Bill Martin's *Brown Bear, Brown Bear, What Do You See?* This book has sold in the high millions, and it set a pattern that has been imitated countless times in a genre now known as *predictable books.* Bill Martin Jr. wrote this book, and his good friend, Eric Carle, illustrated it. Bill Martin has written over 300 books, and he's been writing them since 1945, when he published his first book, *The Little Squeegy Bug: The Story of the Firefly.* But writing books only illustrates one aspect of Martin's creative genius.

As a speaker, he has no peers. I've seen him hold a thousand students spellbound while he recited stories and poems, sang songs, and preached the gospel of literature as a source of creativity and inspiration for teachers and children. Bill Martin Jr. spent many summers teaching courses at Oakland University, and it was here that I first met him. I never met a teacher who didn't love to listen to him talk about what it meant to be a teacher and how teachers could use literature to inspire children's creative spirit.

For all of the fine books Bill Martin has written, his *Sounds of Language* series may rank among his finest. These books provided an innovative substitute for the deadly dull basal readers that held sway in the 1950s and 1960s. While these books never quite reached the wide acceptance they deserved, they challenged the traditional format of basal readers. They contained excellent poetry, stories, and illustrations. They also introduced creative ways to design and present the printed word. I came to love these books, especially one called *Sounds of Home,* which contained my favorite story, "Daddy's Home." I read "Daddy's Home" to my children countless times. We had a ritual. I'd come home with peppermints in my pockets and sing the opening lines of Bill's story. My children always came running, eager to see what I had for them. It gave me an opportunity to steal a hug and a kiss. I loved that book!

The teaching profession is deeply indebted to Bill Martin Jr. His legacy as a teacher and writer is enduring. Some of my favorite books by Bill Martin Jr. include: *Knots on a Counting Rope, The Ghost-Eye Tree, Barn Dance,* and *Adam, Adam, What Do You See?*

## Writing Performance Checklist

There are many ways of assessing performance in writing: conferences, conversations, class assignments, holistic and analytic rubrics, grading, and daily participation in writing activities. An additional observational tool is the writing performance checklist (see Figure 3.1). This observational tool can be completed once every four weeks, more often if deemed necessary. Using this checklist, a teacher assesses the consistency of a student's performance on key indicators of writing performance. The behaviors described in the writing performance checklist cover issues relevant to writing process stages, writing skill, general writing knowledge, topic selection, and writing conventions. The checklist assesses performance on a 3-point scale—*usually, occasionally,* and *seldom.*

**Figure 3.1**

Writing
Performance
Checklist

Name _____ Grade _____ Age _____

*Instructions: For each behavior described below, circle the letter that best describes student performance over the past four weeks.*
*(U = Usually     O = Occasionally     S = Seldom)*

**Writing process stages**

| | | | |
|---|---|---|---|
| Plans and researches before writing | U | O | S |
| Drafts fluently | U | O | S |
| Revises and edits | U | O | S |
| Publishes and shares writing | U | O | S |

**Writing skill**

| | | | |
|---|---|---|---|
| Content writing contains good ideas and information | U | O | S |
| Story writing is believable and interesting | U | O | S |
| Uses and chooses words well | U | O | S |
| Sentences are well formed and varied | U | O | S |
| Organizes writing coherently | U | O | S |

**General writing knowledge**

| | | | |
|---|---|---|---|
| Conferences with peers and teacher are productive | U | O | S |
| Sensitive to audience for writing | U | O | S |
| Shares writing with classmates and others | U | O | S |
| Uses word processing when appropriate | U | O | S |

**Topic selection**

| | | | |
|---|---|---|---|
| Writes on a variety of self-selected topics | U | O | S |
| Writes on a variety of assigned topics | U | O | S |

**Writing conventions**

| | | | |
|---|---|---|---|
| Demonstrates functional knowledge of writing mechanics | U | O | S |
| Corrects spelling during revising and editing stage | U | O | S |
| Corrects mechanics during revising and editing stage | U | O | S |
| Handwriting is legible | U | O | S |

## Portfolio Assessment

Literacy instruction has changed dramatically in the past few decades. As new instructional strategies are developed, better assessment tools are needed. Teachers need assessment tools that reflect their practices and values. Traditional standardized tests will not do, as they seldom reflect modern teaching practices and are often based on flawed premises. Assessment procedures that reflect real-world performance and achievement are needed. Portfolio assessment enables teachers to document real-world reading and writing achievement.

> "Besides celebrating a student's polished pieces and range of work, portfolios can also document a student's learning process."
> —B. Campbell-Hill and C. Ruptic, *Practical Aspects of Authentic Assessment,* 1994.

Portfolios are organized collections of the products and processes of reading and writing chosen to represent the owner's best work. They provide source material for teacher assessment and self-assessment and document achievement, growth, effort, and interests over time. Portfolios usually reflect a collaborative effort between teachers and children. It is crucial for children to have a stake in selecting and reflecting on the contents of their portfolios. Ownership creates willingness to participate, independent work habits, and healthy attitudes toward learning. The more children participate in creating their portfolios, the more likely they are to use them as meaningful tools for assessment.

Purpose determines the kind of portfolio and the work products that go into it. Two models of portfolio assessment are common. The simplest model is a collection of best pieces chosen by the student and teacher. A more complex portfolio model includes not only finished pieces of work but the related pieces that preceded the final product. These pieces are used for sharing, assessing, and grading.

Table 3.1 suggests guidelines for starting a portfolio assessment plan. Modify these ideas to suit your circumstances and your children's needs.

## Holistic Assessment

Infrequent writing guarantees mediocre writing. On the other hand, frequent writing generates an endless stream of writing to assess. Is there a way to keep children writing steadily without creating an impossible paper load? Holistic assessment can lighten that load.

The term *holistic* derives from the word *whole*. In holistic assessment, writing is assessed as a whole rather than in detail. The details regarding writing strengths and needs are not counted, corrected, or commented upon, though notice may be taken to guide future decisions. Usually two to four minutes are devoted to each piece. The goal is to reach an overall impression as rapidly as is consistent with reliable and valid assessment. Holistic assessment works on the premise that the whole adds up to more than the sum of its parts.

Writing has many components: content, organization, sentence and paragraph structure, word selection, and mechanics, among others. In holistic assessment, a rater may recognize strengths or needs among these components but does not comment on them separately. According to the principles of holistic assessment, counting errors is, by itself, an insufficient means of judging writing competence. The holistic scorer ranks compositions on a 3-, 4-, or 5-point scale. Assessment is guided by a set of standards, or rubrics, called a scoring guide.

**Table 3.1**

**Working with Portfolios**

1. *Models of portfolios.* Introduce the portfolio concept by showing children how and why a professional photographer, model, or journalist creates a portfolio.
2. *Beginnings.* Ask students to contribute ideas for creating portfolios, and share your ideas. Discuss these questions: How can we get started? How will a portfolio improve my work? What should go into a portfolio?
3. *Portfolio containers.* Establish a place where portfolios may be kept, such as a cardboard folder with dividers, a large manila folder, or a plastic basket.
4. *Portfolio contents.* Children must have a role in selecting portfolio pieces. Show them that portfolio contents derive from ordinary classroom activities: writing, projects, subject matter assignments, and other classroom work.
5. *Learning self-assessment.* Model ways in which children can assess their work. For example, have them compare pieces of writing completed ten weeks apart. Examining changes over time documents progress.
6. *Reviewing portfolios.* Review portfolios periodically. This should paint a picture of the

student's efforts, achievement, and progress. Work with children to select a limited number of items appropriate for a joint review.

7. *Portfolio conferences.* Help children recognize the progress they have made. Ask them about the items they have included in their portfolios; convey compliments and suggestions. Each item should be there for a reason.
8. *Sharing portfolios.* Have children share their portfolios in forums such as the author's chair. Sharing helps children recognize which pieces to include or exclude from their portfolios.
9. *Involving parents.* Explain the portfolio concept; tell parents how it will be used and how it will benefit their children. Suggest ways they can participate. At parental conferences, use portfolios to document growth and achievement.
10. *Grading and portfolios.* If you are required to grade children's work, help them select the pieces you will grade. Portfolios provide a sounder instructional foundation for determining grades than does grading workbook pages and dittos.

A holistic scoring guide offers prototype compositions—examples of children's writing, ranging from the lowest to the highest competency level. In addition, it provides a description of writing features at each level, to guide the rater in making decisions. A rater reads a student composition and matches it with an approximately equivalent piece of writing in the ranked series of prototype compositions, keeping in mind the features of different levels of writing achievement.

Teachers can prepare their own holistic guides and select prototype compositions from writing produced by their children. A scoring guide should represent the standards and instructional practices of your school or classroom, and it must be appropriate for the children whose writing will be assessed. Through discussion and practice, consistency can be achieved by rating compositions together, discussing differences, and developing a consensus about writing assessment. Teachers working cooperatively can learn from one another and join forces in implementing a strong writing program.

Making your own holistic guide increases familiarity with the problems and pitfalls of assessment. But it is not necessary to start from scratch. You can use a ready-made guide, such as those shown in Tables 3.2, 3.3, and 3.4, as a starting point. However, relying on prepared guides may be less useful than making your own, since it may be better suited to the specific needs of your children. Whatever assessment guide is used should represent the standards, thinking, and experience of the teachers who use it. The prototype compositions, of course, must be drawn from the population of children being assessed.

Chapter 6 in *Windows into Literacy* provides a helpful description of analytic and holistic techniques as they are used for large-scale analysis of writing. See *Windows into Literacy: Assessing learners K–8,* by L. Rhodes and N. Shanklin, 1993.

## Analytic Assessment

Analytic scoring provides a more detail-oriented assessment option. Still, holistic and analytic scoring has similarities. For example, both consider similar writing

**Table 3.2**

### Standards for Evaluating Narrative Writing

**Structure: Does the story hang together?**

Low:     No identifiable beginning, middle, or end. Action and characters undeveloped. Details confusing. Story problem unresolved.

Middle:  Beginning, middle, end present but may be unclear. Some details given. Story problem present, resolution may be fuzzy.

High:    Clear beginning, middle, end. Action and characters well developed. Story problem resolved.

**Story Idea: Is the story idea interesting, and is there a story plot?**

Low:     Uninteresting, trite, or unclear. No identifiable plot.

Middle:  Interesting. Has a plot but inconsistent.

High:    Fresh or imaginative; plot well developed and executed. Has satisfying ending.

**Setting: Where and when does the story setting take place?**

Low:     No time or place identified. Details inappropriate or missing.

Middle:  Time or place suggested. May be uncertain or inconsistent.

High:    Time and place clearly identified. Stays consistent throughout.

**Character: Are the characters interesting and believable?**

Low:     Weak or absent. Unclear whom the story is about.

Middle:  Developed but not in detail. Not always consistent or appropriate. Action and speech present but inconsistent.

High:    Believable and well developed. Action and speech appropriate to characters.

**Dialogue: Does the conversation move the story forward?**

Low:     Muddled or missing. Does not develop character, action, or outcome.

Middle:  Works in some places, but not consistently. Dialogue has some influence on action and outcome.

High:    Develops personality and interaction among characters. Characters' words related to story action and outcome.

**Table 3.3**

### Standards for Evaluating Expository Writing

**Content: What is the quality of the content, ideas, and information?**

Low:      Ideas vague, incoherent. Details may be irrelevant, inaccurate, or undeveloped. Not imaginative or original.

Middle:   Ideas are sound but not imaginative. Presentation of ideas is uneven in completeness, logic, or relevance.

High:     Ideas are clearly presented, complete, relevant, accurate, logical. Rich in thought and imagination.

**Organization: Are ideas and information organized in an orderly way?**

Low:      Information incoherent, not well sequenced. Connections between ideas are absent or mishandled.

Middle:   Information usually coherent and sequential. Connections are made between ideas but not consistently.

High:     Information coherent and sequential. Connections signaled by transition words, phrases, or sentences.

**Words: Is word selection interesting, accurate, and appropriate?**

Low:      Word selection inexact, limited, or immature. Figurative language used sparingly or inappropriately, or not at all.

Middle:   Vocabulary usually suitable and accurate. Overuses some words. Uses some figurative language but may lack freshness.

High:     Shows flair for word choice. Uses words precisely. Figurative language used interestingly and accurately.

**Sentences: Are there a variety of well-formed sentences?**

Low:      Sentences poorly formed or awkward. Run-ons and fragments.

Middle:   Most sentences well formed, but some awkward or puzzling ones. A few run-ons or fragments.

High:     Sentences well formed, varied in length and structure. Smooth flow from sentence to sentence. Few, if any, run-ons or fragments.

**Paragraphs: Are paragraphs ordered and developed in an appropriate, interesting fashion?**

Low:      Topic difficult to discern. Few, if any, topic sentences. Details incomplete. Orders ideas incoherently.

Middle:   Usually sticks to topic. Uses topic sentences but inconsistently. Some awareness of paragraph types. Usually orders details well.

High:     Shows good control of paragraph topic and topic sentences; shows awareness of paragraph types; orders details well.

features, and both recognize that the whole is greater than the parts. But where holistic assessment is rapid and impressionistic, analytic assessment is deliberate and detailed. When teachers wish to focus closely on specific writing features, this deliberate and detailed approach is appropriate. Analytic assessment deals with specific writing features, analyzed in terms of their absence or presence, strength or needs,

**Table 3.4**

**Standards for Evaluating Mechanical Skills**

---

**Grammar and Usage**

   Low:      Conventions for inflections, modifiers, verbs, pronouns, and nouns seldom observed. Miscues frequent.

   Middle:  Conventions for inflections, modifiers, verbs, pronouns, and nouns usually observed. Some miscues.

   High:     Conventions for inflections, modifiers, verbs, pronouns, and nouns observed. Miscues infrequent.

**Punctuation**

   Low:      Ending punctuation often missing. Other punctuation infrequent or incorrect.

   Middle:  Ending punctuation usually correct. Other punctuation used, but inconsistently.

   High:     Ending punctuation nearly always correct. Other punctuation usually used correctly.

**Capitalization**

   Low:      Seldom capitalizes first word in sentences. Proper nouns and other conventions seldom observed. Capitals used incorrectly.

   Middle:  Usually capitalizes first word in sentences. Proper nouns usually correct. Uses other conventions, but inconsistently.

   High:     Always capitalizes first word in sentences. Proper nouns nearly always correct. Good command of other conventions.

**Handwriting**

   Low:      Handwriting difficult to read. Letter formation and spacing make handwriting nearly illegible.

   Middle:  Handwriting is readable. Letters usually clearly formed. Spacing may occasionally be crowded.

   High:     Handwriting easy to read. Letters clearly formed, spacing appropriate.

---

high or low quality. The number of features examined in analytical scoring varies based on purpose, the nature of the composition, and the level of the student.

The writing features differ according to the type of writing. For example, a narrative guide will assess different writing features than an expository guide. Features examined in expository writing normally include content, organization, sentence and paragraph features, word selection, and mechanics, as shown in Figure 3.2 on p. 108. Features examined in narrative writing normally include story idea, setting, development, characters, dialogue, and mechanics. Features can be added or deleted according to your purpose and writing philosophy. An example of an analytic scoring guide for narrative writing is shown in Figure 3.3 on p. 109. Writing features in both scales are rated on a scale of 1 to 5, and a place is provided for teacher comments; Figure 3.3 shows an example. Interpretative comments should be given to supplement the rating.

Analytic assessment enables teachers to give more detailed information to the writer than holistic assessment permits. On the other hand, it is more laborious

**Figure 3.2**

**Analytic Scoring Guide for Expository Writing**

| | Fair | | Good | | Excellent |
|---|---|---|---|---|---|
| **Content** | | | | | |
| Theme or controlling idea | 1 | 2 | 3 | 4 | 5 |
| Details | 1 | 2 | 3 | 4 | 5 |
| Originality | 1 | 2 | 3 | 4 | 5 |
| Examples and reasons | 1 | 2 | 3 | 4 | 5 |
| **Organization** | | | | | |
| Plan of organization | 1 | 2 | 3 | 4 | 5 |
| Introduction | 1 | 2 | 3 | 4 | 5 |
| Development | 1 | 2 | 3 | 4 | 5 |
| Conclusion | 1 | 2 | 3 | 4 | 5 |
| Information in sequence | 1 | 2 | 3 | 4 | 5 |
| Transitions | 1 | 2 | 3 | 4 | 5 |
| **Wording** | | | | | |
| Precise word choice | 1 | 2 | 3 | 4 | 5 |
| Concrete, specific language | 1 | 2 | 3 | 4 | 5 |
| Figurative language | 1 | 2 | 3 | 4 | 5 |
| **Sentences** | | | | | |
| Sentence variety | 1 | 2 | 3 | 4 | 5 |
| Well-formed sentences | 1 | 2 | 3 | 4 | 5 |
| Avoids fragments, run-ons | 1 | 2 | 3 | 4 | 5 |
| **Paragraphs** | | | | | |
| Main or controlling idea | 1 | 2 | 3 | 4 | 5 |
| Relevant supporting details | 1 | 2 | 3 | 4 | 5 |
| Appropriate sentence order | 1 | 2 | 3 | 4 | 5 |
| **Mechanics** | | | | | |
| Spelling | 1 | 2 | 3 | 4 | 5 |
| Punctuation | 1 | 2 | 3 | 4 | 5 |
| Capitalization | 1 | 2 | 3 | 4 | 5 |
| Form | 1 | 2 | 3 | 4 | 5 |

**Comments:**

and time consuming. Even so, analytic assessment is similar to the kind of analysis teachers have traditionally provided young writers. In analytic assessment, it is crucial to give children positive information about their writing. Bleeding red ink all over a child's writing is more than simply useless; it is destructive. Analytic assessment is formative and is best used for diagnostic purposes.

Figure 3.3

Analytic
Scoring Guide
for Narrative
Writing

Student Name _____

Composition _____

| Writing Features | Fair | | Good | | Excellent |
|---|---|---|---|---|---|
| | | | Rating Scale | | |
| 1. Story idea | 1 | 2 | 3 | 4 | 5 |
| 2. Story setting | 1 | 2 | 3 | 4 | 5 |
| 3. Story development | 1 | 2 | 3 | 4 | 5 |
| 4. Story characters | 1 | 2 | 3 | 4 | 5 |
| 5. Story conversation | 1 | 2 | 3 | 4 | 5 |
| 6. Mechanics (spelling, punctuation, etc.) | 1 | 2 | 3 | 4 | 5 |
| Points Scored | 0 | 4 | 3 | 8 | 5 |

Total Score: 20

**Comments:** Your lead caught my interest. You set the scene well, but I had trouble figuring out the order of events. When you revise, think about working on this. The conversations between Ellie and Terry helped me understand what was happening in your story. Ellie comes across as smart and funny. Terry seems shy and uncertain. Is that what you tried for? After you've revised your story, edit for mechanics and spelling. This is going to be a fine story when you're finished.

## Primary Trait Assessment

As its name implies, primary trait scoring assesses a single writing feature rather than the whole piece. Since it focuses on a specific trait or feature, the guide can be much simpler than scoring guides for analytic or holistic scoring. In primary trait scoring, for example, you might decide to assess a piece of writing on the trait of persuasiveness. If this were the case, all writing features not relevant to persuasiveness would, in theory, be ignored. But it is difficult to ignore all writing features but one, and that is one of the problems of primary trait scoring.

Nevertheless, primary trait scoring is useful for specific purposes. A teacher can, for instance, focus on a specific trait to see how effective instruction on that trait might have

*Blake is writing a story that his teacher can evaluate, using the scoring guides detailed in this chapter.*

been. Suppose you have been teaching persuasive writing, and you want to know whether your instruction is working. Using primary trait scoring, you could assess a set of compositions for the trait of persuasiveness. Valuable diagnostic information may result. You might discover how well your children have learned what you taught, or you might find they are not doing as well as expected. If they have done well, you might conclude that your instruction worked. If not, you can adjust instruction and try again. Primary trait scoring is sometimes used in district and state assessment protocols to discover how students measure up on a specific writing criterion.

*Writing Assessment: Issues and Answers* is a videotape on direct assessment of writing based on teacher evaluations of student writing samples. Holistic, analytic, and primary trait scoring is demonstrated. The package includes a user's guide, background reading, and handouts. Available from IOX, 5301 Beethoven St., Ste. 109, Los Angeles, CA 90066-7061.

Assessing one trait at a time has inherent problems. Raters have difficulty ignoring other important writing features while trying to focus exclusively on one. Furthermore, it is difficult to isolate certain writing traits. Punctuation, for instance, is easy to isolate as a primary trait; persuasiveness is more difficult because it is more global. How persuasive a piece of writing is depends on a complex set of factors: relevance and power of reasons cited, strategic order in which reasons are presented, subtle language clues, style, appeal to prejudice. Even grammar and spelling can have a negative or positive impact on persuasiveness. Thus, though focusing on one writing trait may seem simple enough, in practice, primary trait scoring turns out to be a challenge. Nevertheless, it can be useful in an appropriate context and for a specific purpose.

## Peer Assessment

Peer assessment allows children to work on writing in collaborative settings. It has many advantages: it helps children learn how their writing affects others; it helps them see how other writers approach writing; it confronts children with the need to revise and edit their drafts; it gives children a sympathetic audience. Most important, it helps children see how different individuals perceive the same piece of writing.

Peer assessment can be conducted in whole class settings, in small groups, or one on one. It works well where students have developed trusting, collaborative relationships. Initial peer assessment sessions should be short and well planned. It helps to start with a whole class activity. The first sessions should establish standards of respect and tact, develop guidelines for constructive feedback, and stress the importance of avoiding destructive criticism. Small group and one-on-one sessions can be planned after basic concepts have been learned in whole class settings.

Peer assessment benefits writing in three ways. First, as students help others, they help themselves become better writers. Peer assessment improves organization, sentence revision, theme writing, and critical thinking (Lagna, 1972). Second, peer assessment helps children develop standards for judging the quality of their own writing. Peer evaluators look for the presence or absence of specific writing features in the writing of their peers. As they do so, they gain greater understanding of what makes their own writing comprehensible to others. Third, peer assessment broadens the audience for writing. Since children relate well with their peers, it is reasonable that some writing be assessed by this sympathetic audience. Broadening the audience for writing may also stimulate children to select a wider range of writing topics.

## Self-Assessment

Johnston (1997) argues that self-evaluation is the most important form of assessment—undoubtedly correct. Self-assessment is akin to a take-out meal. It goes with you when you leave school behind and blend into the nonschool world. Self-assessment is the ability to improve one's own reading and writing through self-directed awareness of one's own learning. For example, revising is the ultimate writing skill. And though it can be taught, it can be learned only through personal application. Writers must become their own best critics.

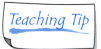

*Teaching Tip*

It is said that the fox knows many small things, but the hedgehog knows one big thing. Writers need to be both fox and hedgehog. Writers need to know which details need refining but must also know if the piece works as a whole—a fox-and-hedgehog set of skills. A writing teacher has no greater challenge than to start young writers on the road to self-assessment. This means gradually releasing to children the responsibility for learning. Table 3.5 suggests ideas for implementing self-assessment in your classroom.

## Grading Children's Writing

I know of a fifth-grade teacher who has worked hard to help her children improve in reading and writing. She is working with children who have few economic advantages in life. She has been succeeding, and her children have worked hard and

### Table 3.5

**Implementing Self-Assessment**

1. Good questions help students assess their writing. During conferences, ask questions that lead students to think about their ideas, organization, style, and mechanical skills.
2. Encourage students to listen to their own writing before revising it. This can be done with a partner, reading one's writing aloud, or recording writing and playing it back.
3. Have students wait a day or two before revising. Then have them reread their writing and imagine themselves as the audience. For example, ask students to imagine the piece they wrote was not theirs but a piece found in a magazine.
4. Show students contrasting sets of words that illustrate exact versus inexact word choice: *horse* versus *animal; pillows, blankets, and sheets* versus *stuff*. Then practice changing inexact for exact words.
5. Have children write questions about the important ideas in their writing. A partner reads the account and listens to the questions. Together they discuss problems they encountered. The discussion should lead to revising.
6. After children have gained experience in self-assessment and peer assessment, have them help younger children with their writing.
7. Teach revision and editing skills in revision workshops.
8. Place composition charts in key places around the room. The charts should cover composing strategies and writing mechanics.

successfully—but not enough, apparently, since her district requires that each of these children be given an *F*. They haven't met the new standard. Evidently, substantial improvement is not enough. Some people will call this tough love; I call it unfair.

> "Marking all the errors in a student paper is no more effective, in terms of future growth or improvement, than marking none of them. The only difference is the huge expenditure of teacher time and the student demoralization that accompany this practice."
> —S. Zemelman, H. Daniels, and A. Hyde, *Best Practice: New Standards for Teaching and Learning in America's Schools,* 1998.

Writing is not comparable with history, math, or science. It is more like music, drama, and art. If I get an *F* in math, I can say (and have), "I'm not mathematically inclined." But writing is different. An *F* in writing is personal, and I cannot shrug it off. So special consideration must be given to grading children's writing.

Teachers are often required to grade writing, whether they want to or not. They fear that grading will inhibit creativity and drive a wedge between teacher and child. Indeed, there is reason for concern, since insensitive grading inhibits writing and can seriously damage a writer's morale. When grades must be assigned, three issues need to be considered: (1) the purpose of grading, (2) understanding what is and is not good writing, and (3) what constitutes fair guidelines for grading.

**The Purpose of Grading.** While the values that grading implies are open to debate, grading can serve a useful purpose. For instance, grading is one way of conveying to parents a sense of how their children are progressing. But conferences and portfolios are probably better ways of helping children and parents understand how writing is progressing. Grading must be perceived as fair, accurate, and informative. When it fails in any of these aims, it can be destructive.

Grading practices often deserve the terrible reputation they have acquired. Grading can stifle creativity and advance questionable values. But it need not stifle creativity or unfairly compare children. Grading can be used intelligently and sensitively, though often it is not.

**What Is and Is Not Good Writing.** Grammar and mechanics are the handmaidens of good writing and must not be ignored. But writers can achieve mechanical

*Never underestimate the power of fun in teaching students to read and write. Fun is another way of saying "this interests me."*

CALVIN AND HOBBES © Watterson. Reprinted with permission of UNIVERSAL PRESS SYNDICATE. All rights reserved.

**Table 3.6**

**Guidelines for Grading Children's Writing**

1. Assess only students' best work. Professional writers are not judged by their drafts or unpublished failures but by their finished and refined writing.
2. Make grading philosophy consistent with instructional philosophy. For example, if you stress self-assessment, factor this into your grading criteria.
3. Writing selected for grading should have traversed the cycle of the writing process so that opportunities for improvement have been abundant.
4. Drafts and notes can be included in grading decisions. When this is done, process as well as product is given due consideration.
5. Grade as few pieces as possible. A large number of grades are not necessary in order to make fair judgments.
6. Take improvement into consideration in devising a grading scheme.
7. Delay grading as long as possible. The younger the child, the less necessary it is to grade. If possible, delay grading until middle school or later.

and grammatical excellence and still produce poor writing. Conversely, writers can violate mechanical and grammatical norms and produce good, though incomplete, writing. It is difficult to define good writing, but it is clear that *correct writing* is not synonymous with *good writing*.

*Teaching Tip*

We should pay attention to grammar and mechanics, but this should be done within the context of actual writing. A fundamental criterion of good writing is the quality of thinking that underlies its ideas. You can improve the quality of children's writing by enhancing the experiences that precede and follow writing. Good literature freshens the wellspring of creativity. Excellent examples of children's writing provide motive and models for writers. Children have an astonishing ability to think creatively. If you believe this, you can succeed in enticing the good ideas children possess out of the crevices of their fertile minds and onto paper. Although the guidelines in Table 3.6 do not resolve all of the philosophical issues involved in grading children's writing, they may be helpful.

## Section Summary: Assessment of Writing

1. Writing growth can be monitored through checklists that assess performance on writing process, skills, knowledge, topic selection, and conventions.
2. Writing portfolios are collections of the products and processes of reading and writing. They represent the owners' best works.
3. Holistic scoring assesses writing as a whole rather than its specific details.
4. Analytic scoring assesses specific writing details. Holistic and analytic scoring looks at similar writing features but from different perspectives.
5. Primary trait scoring assesses a single writing feature, such as persuasiveness.
6. Peer assessment envisions children working collaboratively by sharing, aiding, and advising one another on their writing.
7. Self-assessment helps children develop skill in evaluating their own writing through self-directed thinking, revising, and editing.

## Point ⟩⟩ Counterpoint

### A Debatable Issue
### Grading

**Background**

Grading is an issue in the teaching of writing. Clearly, overuse of the "red pencil" can be destructive to writers' morale. On the other hand, children need to learn the basics of writing etiquette—grammar, spelling, and mechanics. But does "red penciling" actually result in better writing?

**The Debatable Issue**

Teachers should grade writing mostly on content. Grammar, spelling, and mechanics should play a lesser role.

**Take a Stand**

Argue the case for or against the debatable issue. Do grading practices need to be reconsidered? What arguments might you propose for rethinking them? Marshal your arguments based on your philosophy, experience, relevant research, and expert opinion. After you have discussed the question among colleagues, debate the issue in your class.

## Assessment of Reading

Assessing writing is different from assessing reading. Writing makes thinking visible. In writing, a student's thinking appears on the page; it may be muddled, maddening, and meandering, but there it is. Once thinking is cast in writing, it is difficult but manageable to assess writing strengths and needs. Reading comprehension is less visible. It happens in the head and is accessible primarily through conversation and observation. The challenge of reading assessment is to find ways to keep track of reading achievement. This can be done through written notes, conferences, conversations, class assignments, and daily participation in reading activities. This section also considers what aspects of reading to assess, how to do it, and how to interpret and use what assessment has revealed.

"Successful early intervention programs include systematic, regular assessment in order to monitor progress and provide a basis for instructional planning."

—J. Pikulski, "Preventing Reading Failure: A Review of Five Effective Programs," 1994.

### Reading Performance Checklist

A useful observational tool is the reading performance checklist (see Figure 3.4). This checklist can be completed once every four weeks and more often if deemed necessary. The behaviors described in the reading performance checklist cover three areas: word recognition, comprehension, and strategy use. The checklist assesses performance on a 3-point scale—*usually*, *occasionally*, and *seldom*. These three categories allow a teacher to judge the consistency of a child's performance on key indicators of reading achievement.

**Figure 3.4**

**Reading
Performance
Checklist**

Name _____ Grade _____ Age _____

*Instructions: Circle the letter that best describes student performance over the past four weeks. (U = Usually    O = Occasionally    S = Seldom)*

### Monitoring word recognition

| | | | |
|---|---|---|---|
| Uses meaning to identify unknown words | U | O | S |
| Self-corrects miscues | U | O | S |
| Uses context to figure out words | U | O | S |
| Uses phonics to figure out words | U | O | S |
| Uses word structure to figure out words | U | O | S |
| Uses word recognition strategies in combination | U | O | S |

### Monitoring comprehension

| | | | |
|---|---|---|---|
| Asks thoughtful questions | U | O | S |
| Answers questions thoughtfully | U | O | S |
| Predicts based on text, reasoning, and prior knowledge | U | O | S |
| Changes predictions when evidence changes | U | O | S |
| Cites evidence from text to support ideas | U | O | S |
| Draws inferences from text | U | O | S |
| Reads fluently and confidently | U | O | S |
| Understands and uses text structure | U | O | S |
| Negotiates meaning with others | U | O | S |
| Reads flexibly, depending on purpose and nature of materials | U | O | S |
| Has wonderful ideas | U | O | S |

### Monitoring strategy use

| | | | |
|---|---|---|---|
| Metacognitively aware of comprehension strategies | U | O | S |
| Uses KWL, DRTA, QAR and other strategies appropriately | U | O | S |
| Incorporates strategies into independent reading | U | O | S |

## Interest Inventory

Interest influences comprehension. A systematic way of determining children's interests is through an interest inventory. A starting place for understanding children's interests, it can be followed up in less formal ways. For example, determining children's interests can be assessed through private and public conversations, books children select to read, what they talk about, and the activities they enjoy. The interest inventory shown in Figure 3.5 on p. 116 is an example of the kinds of information that can be gathered. You can use this interest inventory, though you may wish to modify it to more precisely meet your needs.

"Many children have a hobby or a passion for some topic about which they will willingly dig and devour information. As they learn about this topic, they not only increase their knowledge of this topic, but of their general knowledge as well."

—P. Cunningham and R. Allington, *Classrooms That Work: They Can All Read and Write,* 1999.

**Figure 3.5**

**Interest
Inventory**

Name _____ School _____

Age _____ Grade _____ Date _____

1. Name three things you enjoy doing at home.

    a. _____

    b. _____

    c. _____

2. Name three things you enjoy doing at school.

    a. _____

    b. _____

    c. _____

3. Name three places you have enjoyed visiting.

    a. _____

    b. _____

    c. _____

4. What do you like or dislike about reading?

    _____

    _____

5. What book or books have you read in the past month?

    _____

    _____

6. Which of these activities do you like best? Put 1 beside the one you like best, 2
   for next best, and so on through 8.

    ___ Watching TV              ___ Being with my friends
    ___ Reading a book           ___ Playing
    ___ Writing                  ___ Helping people
    ___ Going to movies          ___ Thinking about things

7. Tell me about the activity listed above that you liked best and least.

    a. I liked best _____

    b. I liked least _____

# Informal Reading Inventory (IRI) Assessment

Classroom teachers face a problem similar to the one Goldilocks faced. She found the bears' beds to be too hard, too soft, and just right. If reading materials are too hard, little progress will be made; if reading materials are too easy, there will pose an insufficient challenge; if reading materials are just right, children will progress according to their abilities. In a sense, teachers are in the business of seeking the *just right* bed for every child. Determining this requires assessing four levels of reading achievement: independent, instructional, frustration, and listening capacity.

**General Description**. An IRI consists of a series of narrative and expository reading passages representing different levels of difficulty. The passages, followed by comprehension questions, are designed to assess reading levels ranging from pre-primer through high school. There are three types of inventories: (1) freestanding commercially published inventories, (2) inventories based on specific basal reader programs, and (3) teacher-made inventories.

IRIs assess oral, silent, and listening comprehension by analyzing children's responses to three types of questions: explicit, implicit, and vocabulary. An inventory that fails to provide a balanced set of question types is deficient and should not be used. Some inventories assess comprehension by asking children to *retell* as much of a passage as they can. After retelling, the examiner continues assessing comprehension by using questions to cover information not mentioned in the retelling.

An IRI also assesses word recognition in context and in isolation. Miscues during oral reading are recorded as the child reads oral passages aloud. Most IRIs also assess word recognition in isolation by having children read lists of words graded by difficulty, ranging from pre-primer to high school levels. Word lists can be administered under timed and untimed conditions. While it is faster to administer the lists only under untimed conditions, useful diagnostic information can be gained by obtaining both timed and untimed scores.

**Purpose and Nature of IRIs**. Informal inventories are not standardized. At first, this may seem a weakness. But in fact, it is precisely the strength of an IRI. Standardized tests generally measure group performance. Standardized tests are administered according to the standards established in creating the test. Thus, the designated time limits and script must be followed. If they are not, the norms for achievement will be neither valid nor reliable.

IRIs are informal instruments; they do not typically have formal validity and reliability coefficients. If they did, much of their value would be lost since the most important consideration in using IRIs is not the instrument itself but the skill of the examiner. It takes experience to make effective use of an IRI. The skilled examiner takes advantage of the instrument's informality. For instance, an inventory question may be awkwardly worded; experienced examiners will reword the question if the child seems puzzled. If a child responds minimally, the experienced examiner will probe to discover what else the child knows but hasn't

> "Tests such as an Informal Reading Inventory and observational tools, like the keeping of anecdotal records involve the ability to be acutely aware of clues exhibited by the child of his or her needs as a reader and writer."
> —E. Jager, "The Reading Specialist as Collaborative Consultant," 1996.

|                              | Independent | Instruction | Frustration |
| ---------------------------- | :---------: | :---------: | :---------: |
| Oral, silent, and listening comprehension | 90–100 | 70–89 | 69 or less |
| Word recognition in isolation | 90–100 | 70–89 | 69 or less |
| Word recognition in context | 96–100 | 90–95 | 89 or less |

**Note:** Scores of 50–69% fall into a kind of gray area. Technically, these scores are in the frustration range. But gray-area scores are sometimes unreliable and must be interpreted carefully. For example, a score may slide into the gray area for reasons having little to do with a child's reading ability: uneven difficulty of the inventory, unskilled administration of the IRI, a confusing passage, weak questions, lack of experience with expository text, or momentary distraction. Such circumstances make it possible to unintentionally underestimate reading levels, which can lead to placing children at incorrect reading levels. And that is the reason why it is best to not stop testing until the reader is deep (50%) into the frustration range.

mentioned: "What else can you tell me?" If the child does not respond at all, the experienced examiner will say, "What's your best guess?" *The idea is to find out what a child knows, not what a child does not know.*

## Criteria for Levels of Performance

Inventories would be useless without criteria to define acceptable levels of performance. Over the years, such criteria have been established, though different IRIs may suggest slightly different ones. Criteria for inventories are designed to establish four levels of achievement: independent, instructional, frustration, and listening capacity. Criteria for acceptable levels of performance are given in Figure 3.6. Verbal explanations of these levels are given in Table 3.7.

## Administering the IRI

The IRI is an individually administered test, so the first requirement is sufficient time and an appropriate place. A quiet, nondistracting atmosphere is needed. It is unnecessary and overly time consuming to administer the full battery of an IRI to every child in your classroom. An IRI may take anywhere from 45 to 90 minutes. Administer the full battery only to children who need it. Choose certain subtests for other children, depending on what you need to know. For instance, a child who has no word recognition problems probably would not need to take the oral comprehension and word recognition portion of an IRI, and certainly will not need the test for word recognition in isolation. Steps in administering the IRI are described in Table 3.8 on p. 120.

**Word Recognition in Context**. Two scores for word recognition in context may be derived from the oral reading passage: (1) total miscues and (2) significant mis-

**Table 3.7**

**Descriptions of Reading Levels**

| | |
|---|---|
| **Independent level: I can do it on my own.** | **Frustration level: I cannot do it—too hard.** |
| Excellent comprehension<br>Can read text fluently<br>Understands text without help or instruction<br>Used to improve fluency, provide pleasure, increase knowledge<br>Normal to exceptional growth in comprehension and word recognition expected | Extremely weak comprehension<br>Miscues may overwhelm comprehension<br>Signs of physical and mental discomfort when reading<br>Instruction ineffective<br>Little or no growth in reading expected |
| **Instructional level: I can do it with my teacher's help.** | **Listening capacity level: I can comprehend it when read aloud to me.** |
| Comprehension and word recognition instruction provided as needed<br>Can read comfortably with satisfactory to good comprehension<br>Sufficient challenge present to maintain interest<br>Normal to strong growth in comprehension and word recognition expected | Used to determine reading potential when children cannot read text on their own<br>Comprehends ideas and words when text is read aloud<br>Comprehension consistent with general capacity expected |

cues. Total miscues are calculated by counting all recordable miscues (see Figure 3.7 on p. 121). The significant miscue score is derived by examining each recorded miscue qualitatively, asking, "Is this miscue likely to have caused a loss of meaning?" If you judge that a given miscue did not cause a loss of meaning, it is *not* counted as a miscue in the significant miscue column. While both total and significant miscues are taken into consideration in determining levels, the significant miscue score is the most reliable.

A more thorough analysis of miscues can be pursued by following the procedures outlined by Goodman, Watson, and Burke in their *Reading Miscue Inventory* (1987). Their analysis takes into account semantic, syntactic, auditory, and visual issues involved in miscue analysis, to give a more complete picture than the procedures typically used in *Running Records for Classroom Teachers* (Clay, 2000) and informal reading inventories. A more thorough analysis of miscues may be warranted in certain cases of reading difficulty but is not essential for typical classroom diagnosis. Nevertheless, miscue analysis is a window on the reading process. Consequently, understanding why and how miscue analysis is done will add substantially to a teacher's repertoire of reading knowledge.

**Word Recognition in Isolation**. A test of word recognition in isolation provides useful diagnostic information. By carefully examining miscues and scores across grade levels, the skilled examiner can discover (1) extent of sight vocabulary, (2) fluency of response, (3) patterns of word recognition errors, (4) self-correction capability, and (5) differences between timed and untimed scores.

**Table 3.8**

**Administering an Informal Reading Inventory**

1. *Establish rapport.* Get acquainted. Try to put the child at ease. Explain what you will be doing and why.

2. *Word recognition in isolation.* Start testing at an estimated independent level. Test until the student is missing about half of the words. Some IRIs suggest stopping after a child misses 5 or 6 words in a row. Use the coding system shown in Figure 3.8.

3. *Oral reading.* Start testing at the highest independent level achieved on the test for word recognition in isolation. Have children read the passage aloud, and tell them you will ask questions when they have finished (see note). Explain that you will be recording miscues. If it turns out that you have started at too difficult a level, move back a level or two.

4. *Silent reading.* Administer the silent reading passage, starting at the same level as the oral reading passage. Continue testing, alternating between oral and silent passages, until two scores in a row are at or near 50%.

5. *Listening or hearing comprehension.* When the frustration level is reached, begin administering the listening capacity passages. Tell children you want them to listen as you read aloud and that you will ask questions when you finish. Some IRIs do not have separate listening passages. However, you can use either the oral or silent passages to check listening capacity.

6. *Comprehension scoring.* Give full or half credit for each question. If you are uncertain about the acceptability of an answer, write down the answer and consider it after testing.

7. *Word recognition in context scoring.* As you administer the oral reading passages, mark each error as the passage is read aloud. Use the coding system shown in Figure 3.7.

Note: I recommend that children be allowed to look back at IRI passages when answering comprehension questions. This is controversial but is a fairer and more accurate measure of comprehension since it avoids overreliance on cognitive memory. Mature readers reread to comprehend, and we consider this appropriate and necessary. Looking back enables children to locate factual answers, which is more important than simply recalling them, and to scan context to determine word meaning, a skill we wish to inculcate. Looking back is not necessarily helpful in answering inference questions, since they are not directly answered in a text.

1. **Untimed**. The untimed test for word recognition in isolation assesses strength of sight vocabulary—words the reader knows immediately, readily, and automatically. A weak sight vocabulary interferes with reading fluency and comprehension. Of course, sight vocabulary is relative to one's age and reading experience. For example, a 5-year-old may know only 20 words at sight, but this would be a strong sight vocabulary given the age and reading experience of a 5-year-old. On the other hand, a 10-year-old with average capability who knows only 100 sight words can be said to have a weak sight vocabulary relative to presumed experience as a reader. When administering an untimed test, have the child read the list while you record the performance. Stop after five or six consecutive misses or after the reader has missed about half of the words.

2. **Timed–untimed**. If you need a more complete assessment of word recognition, administer the test of word recognition in isolation as a timed–untimed test. Both scores can be derived in a single administration. Here's how. Flash the words for the timed test using two index cards (alternatively, you can program your computer to

| Type of Miscue | How to Record | Example |
|---|---|---|
| **Omission:** Word(s) or punctuation left out | Circle omitted word. | The ⟨brown⟩ rabbit jumped over the garden fence and disappeared. |
| **Substitution:** Nontext word is substituted for text word | Draw a line through substituted word and write the substituted word above. | The ~~brown~~ *big* rabbit jumped over the garden fence and disappeared. |
| **Insertion:** Word(s) not in text is added | Use a caret to indicate the inserted word(s). | The ^*big* brown rabbit jumped over the garden fence and disappeared. |
| **Mispronunciation:** Word in text incorrectly pronounced | Phonetically spell the mispronounced word above the text word. | The brown *rub–uth* rabbit jumped over the garden fence and disappeared. |
| **Repetition:** One or more words are repeated | Draw a line under the repeated word(s). | <u>The brown rabbit</u> jumped over the garden fence and disappeared. |
| **Self-correction:** Incorrect response is corrected | Write *SC* above the miscue. | The brown rabbit jumped over the garden fence and dis*SC*appeared. |
| **Aided:** A word unknown by reader is given by examiner | Place an *A* for *aided* over the supplied word(s). | The brown rabbit jumped over the garden fence and dis*A*appeared. |
| **Transposition:** Word order is reversed | Draw a curving line over and under the transposition. | The brown rabbit jumped over the garden ⟨fence⟩ and disappeared. |

**Figure 3.7**

**Informal Reading Inventory: Miscue Notation System**

flash the words, using PowerPoint®). The reader is given about 1 second to respond to the timed flash of a word. After the child responds, code the timed response. If a child miscues on the timed exposure of a word, open the cards to give the reader an untimed opportunity to look at the word. Record the untimed response. The untimed exposure of the word usually takes 5 or 6 seconds. Keep in mind that when the timed response is correct, it is assumed that the untimed response would also be correct.

Coding timed and untimed responses takes longer but yields more diagnostic information, including (1) extent of gain from timed to untimed conditions—a large gain suggests stronger word recognition skill than a small gain, (2) opportunity to observe how the reader uses phonetic and structural information, (3) types of errors made in untimed responses, (4) strategies used to decode words in isolation, and (5) amount of time required to decode words in isolation—another indicator of fluency. Coded timed and untimed responses are shown in Figure 3.8.

**Figure 3.8**

**McCracken Test for Word Recognition in Isolation: Grade 5**

|  | Timed | Untimed |
|---|---|---|
| 1. bound | | |
| 2. embers | | |
| 3. yoke | SC | |
| 4. blinked | | |
| 5. fuel | fool | |
| 6. celebrate | | |
| 7. marvelous | | |
| 8. bullets | | |
| 9. mercy | | |
| 10. palms | | |
| 11. skirted | | |
| 12. rifle | | |
| 13. pouches | pooches | |
| 14. fortune | | |
| 15. increasing | | |
| 16. widow | | |
| 17. miracle | | |
| 18. shuddered | | |
| 19. shod | shoe-duh | |
| 20. equipment | | |
| 21. dynamite | | |
| 22. jagged | | |
| 23. erect | | |
| 24. occasion | | |
| 25. determined | 0 | |
| **Score** | | |

**Coding Symbols**

*Correct response* = Leave space blank
*Incorrect attempt* = Write all attempts phonetically
*Self-correction* = SC (Not counted as a miscue)
*No response* = 0

**Interpreting IRI Scores.** IRI scores are sometimes straightforward. In such cases, the inexperienced examiner can usually make sound appraisals of reading level. Often, however, IRI scores present an inconsistent, puzzling pattern. The more serious the reading problem, the more likely the scores will be difficult to interpret. Table 3.9 suggests guidelines for determining levels and interpreting IRI scores.

Figure 3.9 shows the scores derived from Greg's IRI performance. Greg is in fourth grade and is 9 years old. His teacher describes him as verbal and often thoughtful. He does best on activities that have a significant listening component. His oral reading lacks fluency, but his miscues often make sense. He doesn't like to read aloud. He's usually cooperative but sometimes gets angry and frustrated. Using

**Table 3.9**

**Guidelines for Determining Levels and Interpreting IRI Scores**

1. Comprehension scores have first priority in determining levels. Compare performance on each type of comprehension question—factual, inferential, and vocabulary. Teach to the strengths and needs this analysis suggests.
2. Word identification in context has second priority in determining levels. The adjusted score, which counts only *significant* word recognition miscues, is given more weight than the total miscue score. Analyze miscue types, and teach to the strengths and needs this analysis suggests.
3. There is often a significant difference between oral and silent comprehension scores. If silent comprehension is consistently weaker than oral, use comprehension strategies such as DRTA, KWL, and comprehension modeling.
4. The listening comprehension score indicates reading potential, which is often higher than actual reading achievement. This is a significant strength and often indicates that word recognition has not kept up with general capability.
5. Word recognition in isolation scores are not useful for determining level decisions. However, the types of miscues noted provide diagnostic information useful for guiding word recognition instruction.

| Grade Level | WRI-T | WRI-UT | WRC-T | WRC-S | Oral Comp. | Silent Comp. | Listening Comp. |
|---|---|---|---|---|---|---|---|
| PP | 100 | 100 | | | | | |
| P | 96 | 100 | | | | | |
| 1/2 | 92 | 100 | | | | | |
| 2/1 | 76 | 96 | 92 | 97 | 100 | 90 | |
| 2/2 | 60 | 84 | 91 | 96 | 70 | 80 | |
| 3/1 | 56 | 72 | 89 | 93 | 85 | 70 | |
| 3/2 | 40 | 48 | 88 | 90 | 55 | 40 | 100 |
| 4 | | | | | | | 80 |
| 5 | | | | | | | 80 |
| 6 | | | | | | | 40 |

WRI-T   = Word recognition in isolation—timed
WRI-UT = Word recognition in isolation—untimed
WRC-T  = Word recognition in context—total
WRC-S  = Word recognition in context—significant
Comp.  = Comprehension

**Figure 3.9**

**Greg's Informal Inventory Scores**

the criteria for determining levels shown in Figure 3.6 (p. 118) and the verbal descriptions of levels shown in Table 3.7 (p. 119), answer these questions:

1. What is Greg's independent level of reading?
2. What is Greg's instructional level of reading?
3. What is Greg's frustration level?
4. What is Greg's listening capacity level?

## Section Summary: Assessment of Reading

1. Reading achievement can be monitored with the reading performance checklist, which assesses word recognition, comprehension, and strategy use.
2. An inventory can be used to learn more about children's reading habits, general interests, and preferred activities.
3. Informal reading inventories (IRIs) assess oral, silent, and listening comprehension and word recognition in context and in isolation. Assessment is based on four levels of reading achievement.

# Standards, High-Stakes Testing, Accountability, and the Curriculum

Helen Keller, blind from the age of 6 months, was asked, "Is there anything worse than losing your eyesight?" She replied, "Yes, young man. Losing your vision." America is engaged in an effort to redefine its vision of an excellent public education system. Clearly, part of that vision is that every child must have an opportunity for an excellent educational experience. Most interested parties can agree on that part of the vision. What they cannot agree on is how to best achieve it. The debate is about means more than outcomes. The issues involved include (1) standards, accountability, and high-stakes testing; (2) standardized tests versus performance assessment; (3) curriculum and testing; and (4) preparing for high-stakes testing.

## Current Policies and Trends

Over the past decade, and more recently with the implementation of the "No child left behind" federal initiative, testing has significantly increased. This has enormous consequences for educators, children, parents, minorities, legislators, and the general public. Collectively, these groups are called *stakeholders*—people who have a significant investment in the quality of schools and schooling. How well children achieve in reading, writing, and content subjects raises the issue of accountability. Teachers and administrators are held responsible for implementing standards and achieving results as measured by children's performance on standardized tests or other approved measures.

The federal government, state governments, and school districts have promulgated standards and benchmarks by which they assess how well schools are achieving excellence in education, often without sufficient input from all stakeholders. These standards and benchmarks establish the goals and objectives for judging the quality of teaching and learning in reading, writing, and the content subjects. Doing well on tests is deemed to be proof that a quality educational experience has been provided. However, if a school district does well, even very well, there is no assurance that *all* children in the district have had a quality educational experience (Allington, 2002).

Standardized tests are most often used to determine the extent to which goals and objectives have been met. National standardized tests, such as the Iowa Test of Basic Skills, are commonly used. Other tests include state-sponsored tests. A standardized test has specified tasks and procedures so that comparisons can be made across different schools and communities. Such testing is referred to as high-stakes testing because passing or failing has enormous consequence for teachers, children, and all other stakeholders (Heubert & Hauser, 1999). High-stakes testing has become the roulette wheel of education. You can lose your stake in the American Dream if your number doesn't fall into a winning slot.

High-stakes tests are also used to determine graduation, retention, and tracking into academic or general school programs. About 20% of states now require an exit exam, and more are contemplating adding it as a requirement for high school graduation. Exit exams are controversial since failure can mean denial of a high school diploma or receiving a different type of diploma. Standardized tests are also used to decide whether children will be retained at their current grade level. Retention is expensive for schools and traumatic for children. Whether retention improves achievement is debatable, but it does seem to increase the dropout rate. Tracking influences children's educational experience. It may also determine access to higher education, which has implications for employment and the economic well-being of students once schooling is over. The stakes are truly high.

## Standardized Tests Versus Performance Assessment

Measurement of any sort is difficult and therefore often produces incorrect data. How we measure is extremely important since so much is riding on the outcome (Gold, 1996). Two types of measurement are typically used to determine graduation, retention, and tracking: (1) standardized tests and (2) performance assessment.

Standardized tests tend to have a high proportion of multiple-choice items and short passages. They are easy to administer and relatively inexpensive. Administrators and legislators tend to prefer them for these reasons. Standardized tests tend to have satisfactory reliability or consistency. Their validity, on the other hand, is questionable. Standardized tests do not necessarily accurately measure what they claim to measure. Validity is crucial, and if a test's validity is questionable, reliance on the results must also be questionable. Another related concern is whether standardized tests fairly and accurately measure the achievement of minority children. For these reasons, many educators prefer performance assessment (Allington, 2002; Graves, 2002).

Performance assessment looks at achievement in ways more closely aligned with real-life experience. For example, a student may be asked to write an essay or read a lengthy passage and respond in writing. Portfolios are another means of realistically assessing performance. Performance measures avoid overreliance on machine-scored, standardized tests, in which multiple-choice items are the coin of the realm.

Unfortunately, educators and legislators do not necessarily prefer performance measures since they are more expensive, more time consuming, and more difficult to assess. However, they have the virtue of creating a more complete and valid picture of a child's performance over the course of a semester or school year. Fortunately, some states and schools try to balance standardized testing with performance assessment, but most rely too heavily on standardized tests.

## Curriculum and Testing

High-stakes testing tends to narrow the curriculum, aligning instruction with what tests measure. When testing drives the curriculum, teaching and learning are distorted, important educational experiences get insufficient attention, and teachers direct their efforts toward helping children perform well on tests. Realistically, teachers and administrators may have no other reasonable option. Their jobs and reputations may be at stake. They are often pressured to spend significant time and effort on test preparation when they would prefer to direct their instruction to more worthy curricular objectives—a luxury they lack. Sometimes standardized tests are seriously misaligned with the school's actual curriculum. The preferable circumstance is to align assessment with curriculum, so that the contents and skills that teachers, administrators, and stakeholders have determined ought to be taught and learned is also what is assessed. Accountability would then be appropriate and fair. Ideally, testing and assessment should broaden and improve curriculum. It is doubly ironic that this narrowed curriculum can actually decrease, rather than increase, test scores (Yen & Ferrara, 1997).

## Preparing Children for High-Stakes Testing

Teachers are on the horns of a dilemma. On the one hand, they want to teach what they believe is the best curriculum for their children. On the other hand, they cannot ignore the reality of high-stakes testing. Can teachers have their cake and eat it, too? Not quite, but teachers can take certain measures that prepare children for high-stakes testing but also provide the essential skills for a curriculum not driven by such testing. For instance, every state and federal standards document recognizes the importance of oral language development, and a strong research base exists that demonstrates the interrelationship of the language arts. Consequently, activities such as reader's theater, storytelling, and writing poetry can actually help get children ready for high-stakes testing.

The following five strategies are helpful in getting children ready for high-stakes tests. These ideas are extrapolated from research reports, including analyses by Guthrie (2002) and Feuer and colleagues (1999).

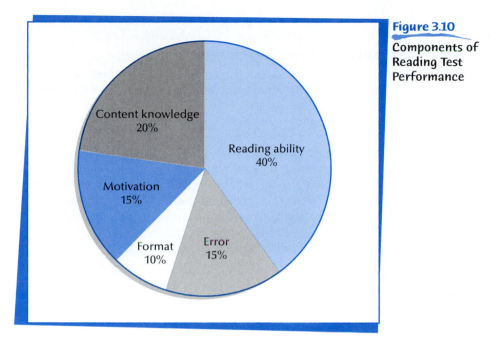

**Figure 3.10**

**Components of Reading Test Performance**

1. Reading comprehension accounts for about 40% of the difference among students in performance on high-stakes tests. Successful comprehension, in turn, depends on the effective use of comprehension strategies. Therefore, the best preparation for high-stakes testing is consistent, long-term emphasis on comprehension instruction (Feuer et al., 1999).

2. Work to alleviate the stress and worry that children feel as testing time approaches. Build children's self-confidence and prepare them for the tasks they will face on the tests they must take (Paris et al., 1991).

3. Motivate children to engage in independent reading many months prior to testing. Volume and frequency of reading have a significant impact on vocabulary development and general comprehension (Cunningham & Stanovich, 2003).

4. Practice activities that approximate the format of the test children will take. For instance, teach students to use time effectively, check their answers, and use deductive reasoning to discriminate among items on a multiple-choice test (Millman & Bishop, 1965).

5. Employ long- and short-term test-taking strategies. For instance, comprehension must be developed over the course of months rather than weeks. On the other hand, format preparation may require no more than a few weeks.

The pie chart in Figure 3.10 shows how much each of the five components contributes to reading test performance (Guthrie, 2002).

## Section Summary: Standards, High-Stakes Testing, Accountability, and the Curriculum

- Standards are usually written by the federal or state government and are *intended* to provide a quality education, though they do not necessarily do so.
- Educators are held accountable for implementing standards, though often they have little or no say in setting the standards.
- High-stakes tests are used to determine how children and schools are performing and also to determine retention, tracking, and graduation.
- Though standardized tests may be reliable, their validity is questionable. Performance measures, such as portfolios, maybe be a better alternative.
- High-stakes tests tend to narrow the curriculum and cause teachers to spend an inordinate amount of time preparing children for testing.
- Teachers can implement strategies to help students prepare for standardized tests.

## Practical Teaching Ideas and Activities

*Teaching Tip*

**1.** *Become an informed and active assessment expert.* Across the country, assessment and evaluation are becoming critical issues for politicians, parents, teachers, and students. An overreliance on standardized testing and quantifying these isolated scores overshadows the fundamental purpose of assessment—to guide instructional decision making based on students' strengths and needs. Teachers *must* take an active stance and voice their concerns about this issue. This does not mean rejecting standardized testing but rather exercising our professional judgment in choosing multiple authentic assessments that arise from day-to-day classroom literacy experiences; the data used to evaluate students' comprehensive literacy journey should be largely drawn fom these experiences. Keep informed about new assessment tools, and become involved with committees that determine curriculum and assessment practices in your district. Educate parents, administrators, community members, and politicians about the unbalanced profile of a student's learning that subtest scores can give; a discrete set of skills is valuable only to the extent that it can be strategically integrated into the context of real reading and writing. A passive attitude or complaints from the sidelines will not benefit our students!

**2.** *Manage ongoing assessment.* Managing ongoing assessment processes and organizing the data to be useful in planning for instruction are integral to effectively meeting the needs of a diverse group of learners. Numerous management techniques are suggested throughout professional literature; some have been included here. You will probably combine several organizational methods to develop a system that works best for you. Keep a three-ring binder with sections for each student. Each child's section may include multiple assessment measures and information on different content areas. Or keep separate binders for reading, writing, math, and other content areas, each with a section for each student. The key is to keep all of a student's assessment information in one place.

**3.** *Maintain student literacy portfolios.* As teachers, we must promote self-evaluation and encourage our students to take responsibility for their learning and growth. Student literacy portfolios foster shared responsibility in documenting and evaluating growth over time. For each piece students select to include in a portfolio, encourage them to think about why they selected it and what it shows about them as a reader or writer. Pizza boxes are ideal for storing portfolio materials because some items may be large or three-dimensional (such as cassette tapes and art projects). Assemble flat, unopened boxes "inside out" (with the pizza logo on the inside), leaving the outside plain to individualize with each child's name and personal artistic touch. A pizza place might donate a set of boxes. Include artifacts such as work samples with an attached self-reflection on each piece, learning logs, cassette tapes of recorded readings, photographs to preserve evidence of projects and group experiences, reading and writing logs, and videotaped literature responses, dramatic expressions, or interpretations. These literacy portfolios can be used in periodic, one-on-one evaluation conferences. Allow the students to spread out their work and guide them individually in reflecting on what they notice about themselves as readers and writers. Record information to include in written summaries titled "What I Noticed About Myself as a Reader" and "What I Noticed About Myself as a Writer." Depending on writing fluency and age, either the student can draft the summary or a dictation can be recorded. You can also extend the process by planning periodic portfolio evenings to allow students to share their work with family members and celebrate their progress.

See the Blue Pages at the back of the book and on the Companion Website for additional activities.

## ◄ Reflection and Summary ─────────────

### Reflection

Garrison Keillor hosts a radio show on National Public Radio called *A Prairie Home Companion,* featuring stories about folk from the mythical city of Lake Wobegon, where "all the children are above average." I love the image of this *abnormal* city because it brings to mind a question I have often wondered about: *What's normal?* For example, politicians want us to think that normal reading and writing achievement is synonymous with grade level. So, according to this standard, every child should be reading at grade level. I don't think so. According to my thinking, this is abnormal.

Much of what we understand about children and fail to understand comes from too narrow a view of what's normal. As I see it, normal achievement in reading and writing ought to mean that children read and write up to their potential—whatever that might be. It is not rational to believe that every child has the same reading and writing potential any more than it is rational to believe that every child has the same potential to play the violin like Isaac Stern, paint like Mondrian, or think like Einstein. Not everyone is destined to be an excellent writer or a keen reader. And neither is it necessary. It is normal for children to possess different gifts, capabilities, and interests. For some, the gift is academics; for others, athleticism; still others, the social graces. Good teachers honor and respect children for all they possess and can become; they work hard to help children achieve their potential, follow their interests, and exercise their capabilities. This is what is normal—not some daydream that every child must read and write at grade level. *That is abnormal.*

## Summary

Assessment is guided by principles that inform and direct the assessment process. Therefore, assessment focuses on real life literacy behaviors, has an explicit purpose, matches the curriculum, extends into instructional time and space, considers diverse cultural and linguistic circumstances, is influenced by instructional philosophy, makes use of student self-assessment, looks for strengths and needs, recognizes that assessment is a best estimate, prefers informal to standardized procedures, and recognizes assessment as more art than science. This chapter has presented the following main ideas:

- There are three types of assessment: (1) formative, aimed at improving instruction and learning; (2) summative, designed to assess the state or quality of an enterprise or institution; and (3) research, aimed at inquiring into procedures, products, and processes of literacy.
- Eleven assessment principles were described, each of which suggested a foundational perspective for assessing literacy.
- Procedures for assessing writing include observing children; using a writing performance checklist; building portfolios; using holistic, analytic, and primary trait scoring; peer assessment; and self-assessment. Grading of writing requires a purpose, criteria for good writing, and fair guidelines.
- Procedures for assessing reading include use of reading performance checklists, interest inventories, and informal reading inventories.
- Standards and high-stakes tests have narrowed the curriculum. Standardized tests are used to judge teaching and learning effectiveness as well as determining graduation, retention, and tracking. Questions have arisen as to whether high-stakes tests or performance measures are most useful in determining such matters.

## Questions to Challenge Your Thinking

1. Three types of assessment were discussed: summative, formative, and evaluative. Which of the three is most useful for classroom teachers? Why?
2. Why is observation so crucial to effective assessment?
3. Eleven principles of assessment were suggested. Which principle did you find most persuasive? Least persuasive? Why?
4. How can portfolios be useful in teaching writing?
5. Why is it crucial to teach children to assess their own work?
6. How can holistic assessment help lighten the teacher's paper load?
7. What additional guidelines would you suggest for grading writing?
8. In what ways are informal reading inventories

more comprehensive than most other reading assessment procedures?

9. What have you learned that you didn't know before you read this chapter?

## A Case Study

Look back at the IRI scores for Greg shown in Figure 3.9. You should have made these level decisions: the independent level is 2.1; the instructional level is 3.1; the frustration level is 4; the listening capacity level is 5. But level decisions are only the first step in analyzing data from an IRI. After level decisions are made, look for strengths and needs. Then decide on a tentative instructional program. Keep in mind that the IRI data are important, but so is your instructional philosophy. Use information in this chapter to help you answer these questions:

1. What strengths does Greg show?
2. What instructional needs does Greg have?
3. What instructional program would you recommend for Greg over the next few months?

## Revisit the Anticipation Guide

Return to the Anticipation Guide in the chapter opener, and review your original responses to the questions. Having finished the chapter, complete the guide again, and then consider these questions.

1. Did you change your mind about any items from the beginning to now? What did you change your mind about? Why?
2. Which assessment ideas did you find most useful? Why?
3. Which assessment idea did you most strongly agree or disagree with? Explain.
4. Which assessment idea did you encounter with which you most strongly disagree? Explain.
5. What assessment idea(s) would you propose as an alternative or addition to the ideas presented in this chapter?
6. If you had written this chapter, what would you have done differently? Explain.

 ## VideoWorkshop Extra!

If your instructor ordered a package including VideoWorkshop, go to Chapter 3 of the Companion Website (www.ablongman.com/cramer1e) and click on the VideoWorkshop button. Follow the instructions for viewing the appropriate video clip and completing the accompanying exercise. Watch the Companion Website for access to a new interactive teaching portal, My Lab School, currently under construction.

### A Philosophy of Listening and Speaking

*Listening and talking are given short measure in school curriculums, perhaps because we think of listening and talking as natural—something every child can do unless there is physical impairment. On the other hand, since many children come to school who can neither read nor write, we tend to devote precious instructional time to these areas, rather than listening and talking. There is some common sense in this view. But perhaps children would make better progress in reading and writing if we rebalanced the language arts equation and devoted more time and attention to listening and talking. This could prove effective, since listening comprehension strengthens reading comprehension. Likewise, more attention to talking strengthens writing. The language arts work best when they work together.*

# 4 Listening and Talking

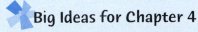

### Big Ideas for Chapter 4

1. Listening is often neglected in language arts instruction, even though most information conveyed in school is apprehended through listening.

2. Listening instruction is important since it improves poor listening habits and contributes to reading comprehension and learning.

3. The four types of listening are interrelational, aesthetic, efferent, and critical listening; these types overlap.

4. Talk at home that focuses on children's meaning helps prepare children for successful literacy experiences when they start school.

5. Talk between teachers and children is crucial in developing language and thought.

## Anticipation Guide

*Consider each of the following statements, and determine whether you agree or disagree with each. Save your answers, and revisit this guide at the end of this chapter.*

1. Listening in school consumes as much as half of instructional time.   agree   disagree
2. The cognitive skills required for listening are the same as those for reading.   agree   disagree
3. Listening is crucial to growth in word recognition and comprehension.   agree   disagree
4. Teachers spend as much time teaching listening as reading or writing.   agree   disagree
5. Children who hear well are the best listeners.   agree   disagree
6. Since talk is natural, children seldom need instruction in oral expression.   agree   disagree
7. Talk is a tool for learning and communicating.   agree   disagree
8. Talk that focuses on children's meaning has a good influence on literacy.   agree   disagree
9. Imitation has a negative influence on language growth.   agree   disagree
10. Talking ought to focus mostly on informal ways of communicating ideas.   agree   disagree

> **W**ithout sufficient money for a meal I have spent the few pence I possessed to obtain from a library one of Scott's novels, and reading it, forgot hunger and cold, and felt myself rich and happy.
>
> —*Hans Christian Andersen*

## A Literacy Story

I'm teaching my grandson to read; trouble is, he can't talk yet, so I haven't any benchmarks against which to mark his progress. He listens well enough, except on those occasions when he doesn't want to "hear" what I've said. He babbles a lot, too. I can figure out, with the aid of some imagination, about three or four of his words. It doesn't seem to bother him that most of what he says is beyond my poor powers of comprehension. He goes on without the least concern for my ignorance. His mother is worried about the slow progress of his speech. She desperately wants him to say "Mama." I understand her concern; new mothers have earned the right to hear that special word. But language has its own timetable. It can't be hurried—though perhaps it can be curried.

I'm doing those things that I know will get him ready for the more difficult task just over the horizon—learning written language. No, I haven't ordered a "Hooked on Phonics" kit; I haven't bought any "genius" kits either. I have better ideas. I have long conversations with him; he responds with conversations of his own. I read books to him. Lap time is sweet, as I get to hold him close. I've taught him how to scribble. He made a lovely scribble the other day. I told him I was proud of his first piece of "writing." Naturally, it's hanging on the refrigerator door. And just yesterday, we started a new game. I call it "Throw me a picture." I name the picture card and throw it to him. He loves the throwing part. Makes him laugh.

We're on the road to literacy. A combination of fun, love, and language. And don't imagine I'm doing this all by myself. Mother and Grandmother are doing even more than I am. This boy is going to learn to read, write, and love it. It's kind of a literacy family circus.

## A MATTER OF STANDARDS

### Listening and Talking

**Standard 12:** Students use spoken, written, and visual language to accomplish their own purposes (e.g., for learning, enjoyment, persuasion, and the exchange of information).

One major goal of schooling is to develop literacy skills that children can use to accomplish their own purposes now and throughout their lifetimes. Standard 12 emphasizes the link between school experience and lifelong appreciation and enjoyment of spoken, written, and visual language. The best way to meet this standard is to help children enjoy and appreciate the literate life while they are still students. Perhaps the most valuable trait we can instill in children is an appreciation of literature—a love for a life in books. Lifelong learning habits require instilling positive attitudes in children while they are young. Listening skill can help children accomplish their own purposes for learning. This chapter emphasizes five reasons for developing children's listening skills: to enhance human relationships, to strengthen academic knowledge, to improve critical thinking capability, to appreciate the value of the spoken word, and to provide pleasure.

Walter Loban, grand master of the language arts, estimated that we listen a book a day and speak a book a week. Can this be true? Probably, but there are many exceptions. For instance, I have an acquaintance who speaks a book a day and listens a book a month. He's a torrent of speech and a trickle of listening. Talking and listening are tightly connected. Speakers send messages, it is said, whereas listeners receive them. In this sense, talking is productive and listening is receptive. But this idea is seriously misleading, since listening is as productive as talking when it is active, imaginative, and meaningful—and it is all of that at its best.

Listening is the first language art children acquire. From a tender age, children make meaning from the sounds they hear. At 7 months, Ben has a repertoire of listening skills and the basic phonemes of speech. At 13 months, James Taylor songs elicit a huge smile, and he reaches out for his mother so they can dance. At 16 months, he *produces* only a few words, yet he *receives* language in abundance. "Get your tractor; hug the doggie; shall we go outside?" Understanding language before producing it continues throughout life. We add new words to our vocabularies by first comprehending them as listeners or readers. Later, we use them in speech or writing as a token of final ownership.

The early primacy of listening soon takes on the related dimension of speech. Somewhere around age 1 children may utter single words: *doggie*. Quickly one-word utterances blossom into telegraphic sentences: *all gone cookie*. We can easily identify four types of sentences in early telegraphic speech: statements, questions, commands, and negatives. These utterances serve functional purposes for children: labeling, describing, possessing, negating. *Language is a miracle of achievement.* Yet young children replicate this miracle as though there were no trick to it at all. Lis-

> "Instruction begins when you, the teacher, learn from the learner, put yourself in his place so that you may understand what he learns and the way he understands it."
> —Søren Kierkegaard, philosopher

tening and talking is the Rubicon that must be crossed before literacy can be fully acquired. Many children acquire listening and talking skill with an abundance of help from home and school. Other children face overwhelming odds, get little help at home or school, yet acquire language in abundance (Pinnell & Jaggar, 1991). Helen Keller, deaf, mute, and blind, is the supreme example of overcoming insurmountable odds. Sadly, some children who have all the language and intelligence needed to acquire literacy do not acquire it early or easily. Early positive experiences at home and in school with listening and talking improve the odds for acquiring literacy.

Listening, the neglected language art, and talking, the glorious language art, are defined, described, and debated in this chapter.

##  Listening

In a narrow sense, listening is the perception of sound, but in the fullest sense listening is, like reading, an active search for meaning. There is a tendency to think of listening as passive; teachers talk and students take it in. No doubt, a lot of listening is passive—listless listening to lullabies. But this is the opposite of what listening ought to be. Good listening is *active, imaginative, meaningful*. These traits constitute the AIM (active, imaginative, meaningful) of listening. When these traits are missing, listening is mood music for sleepy time.

There seem to be many good readers, writers, and speakers, but fewer good listeners. Good listeners cultivate specific listening skills. They do not dominate conversations. Instead, they ingest conversations and invest them with meaning. Good listeners respond to what they hear selectively, sensibly, and sensitively. They use their imaginations, seeing and sensing beyond the spoken words. Such listening is unusual, but it can be taught, at least to a degree, when time and attention are devoted to cultivating it.

Accomplishing such goals means treating listening more as we treat the other language arts—as a crucial skill. This requires employing strategies that will assist in its development. Such strategies are available but underused. It is true that we give lip service to listening; we talk about it as though it were an equal partner with the other language arts. But we often act as if listening should take care of itself. Fifty years ago listening was called the neglected language art. It still is. We assume listening and talking are natural capabilities and therefore require little, if any, direct instruction, as do reading and writing. So we make a choice. Society has its priorities, and teachers necessarily reflect them. But we add value to all of the language arts when we teach listening.

### Why Teaching Listening Is Crucial

My dog, Blackie, has the keenest hearing of any dog in my neighborhood. She can hear a footstep on the driveway before a foot hits the pavement. On the other hand, she doesn't listen as well as she hears. Blackie listens like the dog once pictured in Gary Larson's comic strip, *The Far Side*.

What I say: Bad dog, Blackie. Stay out of the trash, Blackie.
How Blackie listens: Blah blah, **Blackie.** Blah blah blah blah blah **Blackie.**

Blackie's listening faults can be traced to her owner. Pets aren't the only creatures with poor listening skills. They abound among people, too. Any spouse can tell
you that a *certain somebody* they know doesn't
listen well, as can any parent or child. So dogs,
spouses, parents, and children don't listen as
well as they should. There are reasons why this
is so, and they are described below.

**Poor Listening Habits Are Common**. Many
children have acquired poor listening habits
prior to coming to school. The manner in
which children have been listened and spoken
to predisposes them to learn what they have
been taught. Children respond, consciously or
unconsciously, to the models that surround
them. They respond to the behaviors of parents
and peers more than to their words. For example, Kathleen comes into the house with two
frogs she's caught at a nearby pond. Her shoes
are muddy and her clothing disheveled. She's
excited about her frog-catching adventure and
starts to tell Dad all about it. Five minutes of
listening to Kathleen's adventure with appro-

*Laurie Eckert is conversing with Adam and Emma. Their
topic is books, but it could well be something else. The
crucial point is focusing on what children find meaningful.*

priate questions, comments, and responses are in order. Instead, Dad's worried
about mud tracked into the house; he wants Kathleen to change her clothes; he
orders her to return the frogs to the pond, "where they belong." Dad didn't listen
actively; he failed to imagine Kathleen's adventure; he did not focus on Kathleen's
meaning. He modeled perfectly how *not* to listen. *Children learn what we teach them.*

**Listeners Get No Respect**. Society rewards good talking skills but seldom rewards good listening skills. The good listener is often the quiet
introvert, the good talker the outgoing extrovert. Good talkers are often
thought of as intelligent and are more likely to be popular with their
peers. You can imagine someone saying, "Joan is such a good talker, and
she is so intelligent." It is more difficult to imagine someone saying,
"Joan is such a good listener, and she is so intelligent." Good listeners,
while appreciated, are usually noticed only when we need someone to listen to our troubles. Like the comedian Rodney Dangerfield, good listeners get no respect.

"Listening also involves judgment making, with listeners
deciding about the rightness,
goodness, or harmfulness of
ideas and the manner in which
those ideas are being presented."
            —Dorothy Grant Hennings,
    *Communication in Action:
    Teaching Literature-Based
    Language Arts,* 2002.

**Listening Influences Comprehension**. Listening lays the foundation for comprehension. The cognitive skills required for listening are the same ones required for
reading comprehension (Stiht & James, 1984). Interaction between listening and

reading comprehension occurs throughout the reading process. For instance, any discussion that occurs before, during, or after reading depends as much on listening and talking as on the written text. Discussions focused on meaning cannot proceed without effective listening. A successful KWL (What do you KNOW? What do you WANT to know? What have you LEARNED?) or DRTA (directed reading thinking activity) depends on a good mix of listening, talking, and reading. The same is true of most reading strategies. Listening and talking are crucial to successful presentation and discussion of every comprehension skill or strategy teachers use.

**Listening Influences Word Recognition**. Listening is an indispensable tool for learning to decode and is connected to acquiring word recognition skills. In early reading, children acquire word recognition skills through listening to language. Listening enables them to gain phonemic and phonological awareness, prerequisites to reading. Children must also listen in order to associate letters with sounds, which aids word recognition and spelling (Cramer, B. B., 1985; Cramer, R. L., 2001). So listening plays a crucial role in learning to read.

## Four Types of Listening

While it is somewhat artificial to categorize listening by type, doing so highlights some important features of this skill. Though I have outlined four types of listening—interrelational, aesthetic, efferent, and critical—I recognize that these categories overlap. For instance, critical listening can have an aesthetic or informational component. Categorizing the types of listening is also useful in making instructional decisions. For example, it can help teachers structure listening instruction to include each of the types.

**Interrelational Listening**. The term *interrelational* describes the use of language in human relationships with students, friends, and others. We know there are those who listen well—who *really* hear us—and those who do not. Interrelational listening implies presence in the moment. It requires attention; it is an affirmation of worthiness; it is the listener's gift of himself. Interrelational listening has many practical uses. For instance, having a friend who truly listens may diminish the need for counseling and provide consolation in times of trouble and stress. The entire counseling enterprise is built on the assumption that thoughtful, compassionate listening is helpful to clients.

The manner in which a child has been listened and spoken to early in life establishes a pattern for listening and learning. I recently observed how poor listening skills may develop in young children. A family walked toward a department store with a chattering little girl of 5 or 6. Her dad paid no attention as he hurried toward the store entrance. The little girl stopped, stood still, and yelled, "I'm talking!" Dad turned and gave his attention, but note how his attention was acquired. *He had to be yelled at.* Dad heard but had not listened. If Dad's behavior represents a family pattern, then one might expect poor listening habits will be passed on from dad to daughter and taken to school.

Ginott (1965) found that poor communication between parents and children influences children's development. Generally, parents and children do not listen to one another. They converse in monologues—criticisms and instructions, denials and pleadings. Ginott sees this problem arising not from lack of love but lack of respect, not from lack of intelligence but lack of skill. Lack of skill suggests the possibility that instruction might change the equation.

Children come to school with unconscious but well-developed ideas about listening and talking. Before listening can be used effectively for learning, ineffective habits must be modified. Teachers can begin by being good listeners and models of the positive use of language in the classroom. For example, stooping down to children's level, looking into their eyes, and focusing fully on what children say are effective ways to positively influence children's listening and talking habits. Children need to know that their words and ideas are important and understood. Thoughtful comments send signals that children will perceive as models for their own behavior:

"I thought about what you said . . ."
"I remembered what you told me last week . . ."
"I really liked the way you said . . ."
"Janis feels better because your words to her were so kind."
"I'm so pleased that you thought to say . . ."

Such exchanges plant the seed for good listening and raise the prospect that unproductive habits may be diminished or replaced by better ones. Interrelational listening cannot occur without interrelational speech. The two go hand in hand in building or destroying human relationships. If we want children to use language as a tool for building good relationships, we must affirm and demonstrate good relationships. Being fully present in the moment with children as we speak and listen together helps establish positive listening–talking relationships.

"Students spend more time listening than they do reading, writing, or speaking, and as our society becomes increasingly media oriented, listening becomes more important as a language skill."
—H. Burz and K. Marshall, *Performance-Based Curriculum for Language Arts,* 2002.

Strategies are available to help you implement improvements in interrelational listening skills. First, evaluate yourself as a listener. Ask yourself these questions:

1. Do I maintain eye contact with the speaker?
2. Do I sometimes come down to the speaker's level?
3. Do I carefully focus on the speaker's meaning?
4. Do I perceive the significance of the speaker's meanings?
5. Do I remember and do what the speaker has asked of me?
6. Do I take the time for a thoughtfully considered response?
7. Do I reflect on how I feel when attention has not been paid?

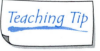

Being a good listener is the best beginning in teaching listening. It lends power and authority to teaching formal listening strategies and provides a foundation for other types of listening strategies.

You might also collect a file of poetry, prose, and activities useful for listening and talking. Short, powerful poems work well in initiating discussion. This poem by Emily Dickinson lends itself to thoughtful listening discussions.

A word is dead
When it is said,
Some say.
I say it just
Begins to live
That day.

Ask students to listen as you recite the poem a few times. Open the discussion by asking what they think the poem means. Follow up with questions: Do words have power? What kind of power? How does the poet feel about words? Ask the students to share words that have hurt or healed. How did those words make them feel? What sort of words do they want to use for others to hear? Words that hurt and words that heal live long in our memories.

There is no better strategy for developing interrelational listening skills than for teachers to develop good listening abilities themselves and to use them with children, giving them the power and attention they deserve. Take advantage of every opportunity to instruct students in the power of words to hurt or to heal. Encourage children to draw on their better instincts in their language choices. Language reflects who we are. Making positive language choices helps us become who we want to be and offers practice in making choices in life.

**Aesthetic Listening.** Aesthetic listening focuses on pleasure and appreciation. It conveys to children the sounds and sense of language they most enjoy, often through stories, poetry, nursery rhymes, and song. Many children have experienced aesthetic listening at home, and increasingly at school, though perhaps children do not get as much aesthetic listening as they should. The sounds and sense of written language, vastly different from spoken language, offer a rich pleasure that children must have. Listening to stories that are told and read brings children pleasure, but those that are read can be fully enjoyed only after an "ear" for written language is acquired.

Some teachers make a practice of reading aloud to their students. Not only does it have a calming influence on a classroom, but it makes children eager to read better themselves. Children who have listened to nursery rhymes at home have a head start on the enjoyment of stories and poetry in school. What delight to the ear are lines such as "Diddle-diddle, dumpling, my son John . . ," "Higgeldy, piggeldy, my black hen . . ," and "Wee Willie Winkie runs through the town." Frost, Yeats, and Shakespeare may come years later, but they will come more easily if children's appetites have been whetted early. The wise teacher learns early that children enjoy being read to. Children are exposed to rich new vocabulary and varied life experiences in the process.

Ask yourself the following questions as you plan aesthetic listening experiences:

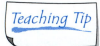

1. Is my class ready for this piece of literature? Does it suit their age and experience level? Many children can listen with understanding to material a level or two beyond the level at which they can operate instructionally.
2. Does the piece appeal to me in such a way that I can create a good listening experience?

3. Does this story, book, or poem appeal to children's better instincts?
4. What do I want my students to derive from hearing this piece?
5. Will this piece help my students deal with painful experiences they may have had? For example, *Ten Good Things About Barney* may help a child who has recently lost a pet.
6. Should I extend this experience with discussion, music, or art?

Of course, with these questions asked, the teacher will also consult lists of books that have received Newbery, Caldecott, and Coretta Scott King Awards and Honorable Mentions to gain even more ideas.

**Experiencing the Imaginary Life**. Listening to literature provokes deep emotional responses. Mark Jonathan Harris, documentary filmmaker and novelist, said, "The writer's art and the reader's imagination free children to rethink, reassess, and refeel their own attitudes about themselves, about others, and about the world in which they live." Once, as I finished reading a particularly vivid chapter from *Old Yeller* to fourth-graders, little Kathy fainted. She revived quickly, and with a broad smile said, "Oh, it was so scary; it was just like I was there."

Today's children are used to scary fare and may find it more difficult to create vivid pictures in their own imaginations, but they can be encouraged to do so. Carefully chosen books can deepen and enrich inner aesthetic experience and can create a desire to learn to read better and to read independently.

Many textbooks recommend preparation before reading aloud, such as predictions or discussion of characters or plot. But often a book chosen for the aesthetic experience will speak for itself. Discussion, in such instances, can follow rather than precede reading aloud. Of course, the teacher needs to have read the book in advance so as to recognize what areas may generate discussion.

**The Painted Word**. Reading experiences can be enriched by juxtaposing reading with art, music, or dance. For example, a group of fourth-graders had spent several sessions listening to Robert Frost's poetry. Their teacher brought in some prints by the artist Andrew Wyeth and displayed them around the room. The children were asked if Wyeth's work made them think of other work in other areas. One insightful student suggested that Wyeth seemed to do with paint what Frost did with words. (How often does such a teachable moment occur?) This comment initiated a high-level discussion of similar feelings evoked by artists and poets.

Part of the aesthetic experience of poetry is the delight of sounds. Reading poetry to children helps anchor the sounds of language in children's inner ears. Children enjoy rhyme, rhythm, alliteration, and nonsense. Playing with words and sounds is fun. For example, the sounds and the nonsense of "Apple Dapple," written by a fourth-grade teacher, appeal to children's sense of linguistic fun.

**Apple Dapple**

Apple dapple
Maple syrple
Licka pickle
Plumpa purple

Aubergini
Pumpernickel
Green zucchini
Okra doka
Artichoka
Gorgonzola &
Ricotta
Hotta, hotta
Chocolatta
Bravo, bravo
Avocado
Noodle
Strudel
Macaroni—
Aw, baloney!

—Barbara B. Wilson

It is good to have students listen for the sounds that delight them and for the way something is said. Shel Silverstein's anthologies, *Where the Sidewalk Ends* and *Light in the Attic,* are a delight to children for their sounds as well as their nonsense. Older children may enjoy comparing rhyme scheme patterns in poems they have heard or read. Frost's "Stopping by Woods on a Snowy Evening" has an easily determined rhyme scheme, the perusal of which may lead interested students to ask why the words, *deep, keep, sleep,* and *sleep,* ending the last four lines of the poem, *all* rhyme, and why the last two are the same. Aesthetic listening often stimulates a desire to write a story or poem. Encourage this.

**Efferent Listening.** Efferent listening implies getting the facts and understanding the ideas. Examples of efferent listening (also called informational listening) include following directions, grasping meaning, and recalling and understanding information from lectures, debates, presentations, and dramas. Efferent listening occurs throughout life in all types of circumstances. We listen to learn what products to buy, programs to view, movies to attend, doctors to choose.

Children can often set their own purposes for informational listening, but they need guidance. To guide an experience of efferent listening, you must know in advance what significant information students should derive it, and then help students set purposes for acquiring that information. Here are some strategies.

**Following Directions.** Listening to follow directions constitutes a large proportion of a school day, and every teacher ponders the enigma of how to get children to listen to directions. Children must learn that directions are not just to hear, but to heed. The linking step between hearing and heeding is remembering. Some teachers of very young children use a "pay attention puppet." The puppet directs them to look at the teacher, be quiet, close their eyes, and try to remember the directions by reciting them silently. The puppet later follows up to evaluate how well the directions were remembered and followed.

Some teachers have found music helpful to direct listening. They sing some lines of their own creation to gain and focus attention. A teacher I know sang these words to the melody of "Frère Jacques":

Are you listening,
Are you listening,
Boys and girls,
Girls and boys?

As the children settled into place and became quiet, ready to listen, they responded:

I am listening,
I am listening,
Yes I am,
Yes I can.

Older students may need a focusing strategy to call them to attention for listening to directions. When directions are given orally, use simple, clear, and concise language. This eases the burden on memory. Using transition words (*first, second, next, finally*) provides markers that enable listeners to follow more effectively.

**KWL**. Ogle (1986) first proposed KWL primarily as a reading strategy, but it doubles effectively as a listening strategy. The letters *K, W, L* stand for what do I *Know,* what do I *Want* to know, and what have I *Learned.* The strategy makes use of prior knowledge, prediction, and reasoning. KWL can help children get the information needed to perform the reading task that follows oral discussion.

**Directed Listening Thinking Activity**. Stauffer (1969) developed and refined the directed reading thinking activity (DRTA). Subsequently, Cramer and Hammond (1970) extended the DRTA as a strategy for directing listening activities—directed listening thinking activity (DLTA). This activity uses the same philosophy and procedures as a directed reading thinking activity *except that the teacher reads the material aloud.* DLTAs are appropriate for fiction or nonfiction materials, though the procedures are somewhat distinct (for more about DRTA and DLTA, see Chapter 8).

An important advantage of the directed listening thinking activity is that it can be used to direct comprehension among students who have not yet acquired sufficient word recognition skill to handle complex text. It is ideal for teaching content materials, such as social studies or science, when students have wide disparities in decoding capability but fewer disparities in oral language and thinking capability. For example, in a class of 30 children, large disparities in reading levels often exist. In this case, some children may be unable to read a text but can listen to it.

In a directed listening thinking activity, students use prior knowledge to make predictions, check on the accuracy of predictions, and confirm or modify their original ideas. Table 4.1 (p. 144) summarizes the steps for conducting a DLTA.

**Critical Listening**. Critical listeners weigh the merits of information, come to conclusions, and make inferences. Critical listening deals with thinking, especially the inferential thinking involved in forming opinions, making judgments, and

**Table 4.1**

**Steps in Conducting a DLTA**

*Teaching Tip*

**Before Listening**

*Establish purposes for listening.* Ask initiating questions requiring predictions. Follow these questions with probes keyed to children's responses. Initiating questions for an essay about wild horses might include questions such as these: Where in America might we still find wild horses? Where might wild horses have come from? What kinds of difficulties might wild horses encounter in today's world?

**During Listening**

*Develop comprehension.* The purpose of a DLTA is to develop habits of reasoning, applying prior knowledge, testing the validity of predictions, and citing supportive evidence. Teacher questions, comments, and probes are the key to reaching these goals. Questions are intended to help students cite supporting or contrary evidence concerning their predictions and to modify and extend their initial predictions.

**After Listening**

*Discuss, elaborate, clarify, and develop skills.* After the DLTA is concluded, direct follow-up activities dealing with vocabulary, comprehension, oral language, prediction effectiveness, and word recognition. There is usually not time to do all of these activities following a DLTA, but all are important concluding experiences.

Adapted from Stauffer, 1969.

"Adding movement to the music or rhyme provides an extra sensory input to the brain and probably enhances the learning."
                    —P. Wold, *Brain Matters*, 2001.

reaching conclusions. Critical listening moves beyond facts and information into judgments, analysis, and reasoning. Inference makers ask questions and seek answers: Why do some ranchers want to kill wild horses? Do wild horses damage the environment? What can be done to protect wild horses? Do I need more background information about wild horses or about protecting the environment to draw a conclusion?

Listening experiences at the critical level often deal with persuasive language. Children understand and use persuasive language before they come to school. Teachers help children extend and develop language so that it becomes a tool in personal decision making. Persuasive language operates on three levels: (1) appeals to intellect—eat your broccoli for its excellent nutritional value, (2) appeals to character—be a good boy and eat your broccoli—I know you always want to do the right thing, (3) appeals to emotion—Daddy loves you so much, so eat your broccoli and make Daddy happy. Listening activities will help students gain awareness of these techniques.

**Making Inferences.** This level of interpretation requires that listeners go beyond what is explicitly stated, relying on text, world knowledge, and reasoning to draw inferences. Children should often be asked what they infer from information sur-

## Using Multimedia

Technology can extend options for listening and talking in many ways. One is multimedia, a computer-based technology that integrates text, graphics, animation, audio, and video. Through this integration of textual, visual, and aural stimuli, students can construct meaning and develop new understandings.

Multimedia presentations can be used as a presentation tool by teachers or students. The most common classroom uses of this technology are presentation software and electronic books. Three popular multimedia presentation tools are Hyper-Studio® (http://www.hyperstudio.com), KidPix® (http://www. broderbund.com), and Microsoft's PowerPoint®. All allow users to create presentations incorporating text, sounds, pictures, and animation. Electronic books allow you to combine reading, writing, listening, and speaking as you develop children's literacy skills. Not only do they help in decoding by presenting written information and spoken words simultaneously, but electronic books and online texts are also often equipped with hypermedia—links to text, data, graphics, audio, or video. As students read, they can click on the links to access definitions of words, information on concepts, illustrations, animations, and video.

The aural and visual capabilities of multimedia support the development of literacy skills in a variety of ways:

1. When multimedia is presented by the teacher during whole class discussion, the visual images provoke and support dialogue about the text.
2. Since multimedia is multisensory, it supports different learning styles.
3. Text-to-speech capabilities provide scaffolding for young readers.
4. When children engage in multimedia activities, talk between and among students and teachers is increased.
5. The creation of multilayered compositions encourages self-expression and a sense of ownership.
6. Multimedia composing reinforces reading and writing skills and strategies.
7. Multimedia helps students make connections between facts, ideas, words, and pictures.
8. Multimedia helps create an active rather than passive learning environment.
9. The varied informational formats make presentations engaging and student centered.
10. Multiple informational formats allow students to go beyond text-based presentation.
11. Multimedia makes learning FUN.

Contributed by Lisa Kunkleman

rounding them. For example, when the weather reporter announces a fair Wednesday in February, children infer, "Good; we can have recess outdoors today." Previous experience in school has taught them that there is no outdoor recess if it is raining or snowing. They make these kinds of inferences often and automatically. To teach how to make more formal inferences, use written text read aloud. Short poems work well. Inferences can range from simple to complex, as demonstrated with the use of Frost's poem (Lathem, 1969):

### Stopping by Woods on a Snowy Evening

Whose woods these are I think I know.
His house is in the village, though;
He will not see me stopping here
To watch his woods fill up with snow.

My little horse must think it queer
To stop without a farmhouse near
Between the woods and frozen lake
The darkest evening of the year.

He gives his harness bells a shake
To ask if there is some mistake.
The only other sound's the sweep
Of easy wind and downy flake.

The woods are lovely, dark and deep,
But I have promises to keep,
And miles to go before I sleep,
And miles to go before I sleep.

—Robert Frost

A simple inference from Frost's poem is that the season is winter; a more complex one is that it takes place on December 21—the darkest evening of the year. Another simple inference is that the little horse is impatient to get home; a complex and debatable inference is that "Before I sleep" implies death. Many other inferences, simple or complex, can be drawn from Frost's poem: the horse may have been wearing bells on his harness due to the nearness of Christmas; the poet is drawn to the deep, quiet mystery of the woods; the poet has something on his mind, so he stops to think about it. Making inferences such as these empowers the listener to probe not only the text and the poet's mind but also the listener's own world of experience and mind. Students learn from one another by discussing their inferences. Because their backgrounds and interests vary, their inferences vary as well. Key discussion questions include these: Why do you think this is so? What makes you think so?

> "Listening skills are not automatic. They must be taught. Instruction in listening should assist students in listening critically and appreciatively in order to interpret, evaluate, and integrate what they hear."
> —H. Burz and K. Marshall,
> *Performance-Based Curriculum for Language Arts,* 1997.

An inference can be legitimately made even though a speaker or writer did not intend to imply it. Frost, for example, said that sometimes the word *sleep* just means sleep—not death. Making an inference where one is not implied adds to the dimension of the piece. *This is the prerogative of the listener and reader. We construct our own meanings.* The varying backlog of experiences and world knowledge we possess leads us to the "this is what it means to me" level of interpretation. However, both in responding to poetry and to life situations, students must learn to bring sound reasoning to their inference making and defend that reasoning. Sensitivity to one's own biases is also an important issue to discuss.

**Recognizing Opinion.** An opinion is a belief or conclusion held with confidence but may not be substantiated by proof. Listeners and readers must learn to distinguish opinion from fact, yet this is more complex than it appears. Opinions cannot be proved decisively; they inevitably reflect personal preferences, biases, and beliefs. Yet facts are not easily determined either. Furthermore, facts alone are seldom determinative, since they are open to interpretation. For example, nearly a century and a half have passed since Abraham Lincoln's assassination; yet the facts are often disputed and are subject to widely different interpretations. Such disputes lead to varying opinions about the assassination. The same is true of President Kennedy's assassination.

Facts are not as stable as they are often portrayed to be. It is important for children to understand that facts in one historical period may be understood in an entirely different light in another, or even determined to be inaccurate. The same is true in science. Thus, we must not give children an overly simplistic understanding of the task of determining facts or differentiating fact from opinion. The traditional presentation to children that facts represent truth and opinion does not cannot be sustained as a thoughtful way to deal with the complexities involved. It is seldom the case that facts inevitably lead to truth and opinions are mere personal views, lacking any claim on truth.

In this quotation from *Crazy English* by Richard Lederer (1989), we find a mix of fact and opinion: "English is the most widely used language in the history of our planet. One in every seven human beings can speak it. More than half of the world's books and three quarters of international mail are in English. Of all languages, English has the largest vocabulary—perhaps as many as two *million* words—and one of the noblest bodies of literature. Nonetheless, let's face it: English is a crazy language."

Five statements in Lederer's piece may possibly be factual: (1) English is the most widely used language in Earth's history, (2) one seventh of the world's population can speak English, (3) more than half the world's books are in English, (4) three fourths of the world's mail is in English, (5) and English has the largest vocabulary in the world. All five statements are presumably provable and may represent a limited version of the truth about the use of English in today's world. But none of these statements tells us much about English as literature. When Lederer says that English has one of the noblest bodies of literature in the world, he is expressing an opinion. One might adduce evidence in support of this opinion (Shakespeare, for instance), but this opinion could be vigorously contested by scholars with a contrary view.

Opinions are not to be taken lightly. We all have them. What is the quality of the information and reasoning that buttress our opinions? How are they arrived at? These are debatable issues. Listening to statements such as English has "one of the noblest bodies of literature" makes for interesting discussion. We want children to wrestle with the complexities of facts and opinions and to consider which statements may be factual, which opinions, and to understand the nature of opinions, the debatable nature of facts, and the need to assess the validity of opinions as well as facts.

**Forming Opinions**. Thoughtful persons form opinions based on facts and reasoning. They come to appreciate the complexity of dealing with facts and opinions. As they learn to identify facts and evaluate opinions, this ability grows. Listening to text and reading text require similar, if not precisely the same, cognitive capability. Thus helping children understand the nature of opinion through listening experiences helps prepare them to understand the nature of opinion when they are reading text. Hennings (1999) uses what she calls the O/P/O strategy for listeners as they evaluate the facts and opinions of others when forming their own opinions. They listen to ferret out the opinions of others (O), identify the facts or proofs (P) the speaker offers, and then formulate a personal opinion (O). As children learn to recognize biases or preferences, they come to understand that they have biases and preferences as well. Here are some questions teachers may employ to help students form and test their opinions:

1. Are my opinions based on credible facts?
2. What combination of facts and reasoning led to my opinion?
3. What personal beliefs and preferences influenced my opinion?
4. Are my facts valid and reliable? How do I know?
5. Is my opinion biased? How do I know?

Cultural, educational, and religious backgrounds play a role in the development of opinions. Strong cases can often be made on both sides of an issue: Should people eat meat? Is nuclear power good or bad for humanity? Is war ever just? We often become convinced that our own tightly held opinions are the correct ones, but we need to test them in the marketplace of ideas. Knowing what influences our opinions can help us understand and accept the differing opinions of others.

**Identifying Propaganda**. Propaganda is an attempt to persuade people to a particular view or belief about an idea, product, or even a system of government. Propaganda and persuasion are related but not synonymous. Persuasion attempts to convince through reasoning and logical argument. One might, for example, try to persuade people that socialism is a better system of government than communism, using reasoning, arguments, and information. Propaganda, on the other hand, often attempts to persuade through deceit, distortion, or exaggeration.

Propaganda techniques are often used to sell commecial products and by governments to sell policies or programs it wishes to implement. Identifying propaganda is not always easy, since propaganda often includes distortions and deceptions along with legitimate persuasive information and reasoning.

Certain characteristics of propaganda were described by the Institute for Propaganda Analysis at the beginning of World War II. The stated intent was to educate the public lest people be manipulated by propaganda. Of course, this effort had its own propaganda intent. Brown (1958) maintains that most people can detect propaganda techniques, such as those described below. While it is indeed useful to make children aware of propaganda techniques, we should not give students the idea that propaganda is easy to detect, since it is often a clever mixture of truth and faction. Six common propaganda techniques are described below.

1. *Card stacking.* This approach involves presenting only one side of an issue while deliberately ignoring or omitting the other. The positive side of the promoted viewpoint alone is presented; the negative or weak points are never mentioned.
2. *Bandwagon.* Bandwagon consists of psychological pressure to conform to group behavior—which may or may not actually exist. This technique

attempts to convince listeners that everyone else is doing it, so they should join in rather than be left out.

3. *Prestige suggestion.* There are two types of prestige suggestion—testimonial and transference. In a testimonial, a well-known or popular person speaks favorably on behalf of an issue or a product (usually for money) in order to convince others to buy into it or purchase it. Transference is more subtle—the persuader tries to transfer the prestige of a given person or product to the idea of the object being promoted.

4. *Name calling.* This technique involves an attempt to attach a bad name or label to something or someone the persuader wants a listener to dislike.

5. *Glittering generality.* These generalizations are statements so broad that they could not possibly be true yet are attractive to the audience. The persuader tries to associate an idea or product with such a generality, such as the American Dream.

6. *Plain folks.* This is a persuader's attempt to convince John Q. Public that a political candidate, for example, is just one of the regular folks—just like all the rest of us.

Have students listen to radio, television, and public speakers to see how many of the preceding propaganda techniques they can identify. For example, prepare a large poster board for each of the propaganda techniques. Have children find examples to list under the various categories.

Most critical listening and thinking involve a form of judgment, even in the aesthetic realm. Judgment must come into play when a speaker or writer has attempted to persuade us by subtle or direct means. Teach students not to give their consent without careful consideration. Forming opinions is an area in which they have choice. Teach them to appeal to reason, to character, and to emotion where that emotion is helpful and not debilitating. Above all, teach children to ask questions, such as the following.

- Does this make sense?
- Who is presenting this information and for what purpose?
- What persuasive techniques are used?
- Should another viewpoint be considered here?
- What references are used?
- Where can I go to check this information or find out more?
- What is this speaker trying to get me to do? What action is expected of me?
- Is this person qualified to present this information?
- Would accepting this viewpoint of product help me become who I want to be? Does it draw out the best that is in me?
- What judgments and feelings are developing inside me as I listen?

*Teaching Tip*

It is important for students to know about the different kinds of listening and to be reminded of their value. Table 4.2 on page 150 suggests questions teachers can ask and the desired response from students.

**Table 4.2**

**Listening Habits**: Questions and Desired Responses

| Teacher Question | Desired Response |
|---|---|
| Do you know how to be a good listener? | Look at the speaker. Think about what is said. Pay attention. |
| What can you do to become a better listener? | Figure out what the topic is. Ask what I already know about the topic. Make predictions. Pick out main idea and supporting points. |
| How does a good listener behave while listening? | Does not distract the speaker by talking, reading, shuffling around. |
| What does *attention* really mean? | It means thinking; keeping my mind on what I am hearing; interacting with the speaker inside my head; not missing the speaker's ideas as I think about my own ideas. |
| Why listen anyway? | I may learn something new. I may develop new understanding of something I already know. I may form new opinions. |
| How will you know if you are a good listener? | I will have new ideas; I will learn new things. I will agree or disagree with what has been said. |

## Section Summary: Listening

1. Teaching listening is important because many children have acquired poor listening habits prior to coming to school. Listening should be emphasized since society rewards good talking skills but seldom rewards good listening skills; listening lays the foundation for comprehension; and it is an indispensable tool for learning to decode.
2. The four types of listening include interrelational listening, aesthetic listening, efferent listening, and critical listening.

# Talking

We ask of politicians, "Do they walk the talk?" Do politicians actually do what their words promise? Talk is not enough, we say. Words are cheap. But serious talk is never cheap. We tend to exalt action over words, but talk necessarily precedes action. If we wish to see change in our schools, talk is the essential first step. Of course, talk without action will not lead to desirable change. But talk can change perceptions and lay the foundation for action; talk can determine what action is needed. It can bring teachers, parents, and children together so that action can follow. Talk can be hateful or healing, harsh or gentle, constructive or destructive. The right kind of talk—particular words and the manner of delivery—can contribute immeasurably to the literacy development of children. Silence isolates; talk reconciles.

## Standing on the Shoulders of Giants
### Historical Contributions to Literacy
### William Shakespeare

As I thought of candidates for historical perspectives on literacy, I went through a multitude of names, yet William Shakespeare never appeared on any of my early lists. He never wrote a textbook, taught a reading course, or conducted a research study. So, why Shakespeare? Literacy is embedded in a social context larger than the affairs of reading professionals. Literacy is connected to literature; literature is synonymous with the name William Shakespeare. Shakespeare contributed more words to the English language and is quoted more often than any other writer. His work represents the best of what a literate society is all about.

Shakespeare is sometimes thought of as a mysterious figure of whom little is known. But though parts of his biography are debated, a great deal is known, though there has always been some difficulty separating the facts from the myths. Yet myth has its own value, particularly concerning the author of the world's finest sonnets and plays. Scholars have argued over the authorship of Shakespeare's works—Christopher Marlowe is a favorite alternative. Controversies stir the imagination, and they have an undeniable appeal. But really, there's not much there. Shakespeare wrote Shakespeare.

Daniel Burt (2001) said, "Shakespeare's greatness rests not principally on either his daunting range or virtuosity, but instead in his power to communicate, to reveal our selves in the mirror of his art" (p. 5). Burt has nailed the reason for Shakespeare's staying power. He speaks to the heart as well as the head. We see ourselves in his sonnets and plays, and that is why his words and works have endured across the four centuries that have passed since he first put pen to paper.

"Stop talking!" How many times have you said that to your students? Well, if you've taught for any length of time, you have had to say it often enough. So it may sound strange to suggest that children need to learn how to talk. Don't they already know too much about talking? Not quite. Of course, children can talk. But can they carry on purposeful conversations connected to your curricular goals? Can they tell a story? Can they participate in spontaneous drama? Can they give an oral report? Can they talk thoughtfully about a book? Can they recite a poem? If not, they need opportunities to develop competence in these forms of talk. Purposeful oral presentations and discussions are among the kinds of talk that children need to learn in school. Many children are not prepared to engage effectively in purposeful oral expressive activities. It is necessary, therefore, to help children learn to express themselves effectively through talk that has academic and aesthetic value.

Talk may be formal or informal. Telephone and playground conversations are usually informal. Discussing literature and giving oral reports are formal. Another way of classifying talk is as aesthetic or efferent. Aesthetic talk is experienced when children respond to literature, as in literature circles and book talks. For example, one purpose of aesthetic talk is to interpret the meaning of a story. Another type of aesthetic talk is to engage in conversations about a book: What surprised or interested them? What did they think about the characters or plot? Did the book connect to their lives in some meaningful way? (Peterson & Eeds, 1990).

Efferent talk is different from aesthetic talk and is intended to inform or persuade. Oral reports and debates are examples of efferent talk. For instance, a debate has a formal structure and a persuasive intent. The participants engage in a conversation intended to inform and persuade the audience to accept a specific view. A group of children might work together to prepare and present an oral report on a social studies theme. As they engage in talk, they build content knowledge and share their ideas with an audience.

> "When discussions develop according to students' interactions with texts, a bond is formed with characters and themes, and that bond leads students to understand the consequences of human behavior and see connections to their own lives."
> —L. Yoder, "Benefits and Adaptations of Discussion Use in the Reading Classroom," 2001.

Classroom talk can, under guided language experiences, develop children's understanding of the conventions of conversations, strengthen their knowledge of content subjects, add to their vocabulary, and broaden their understanding of how language works in formal and informal settings. Good talk can strengthen the bonds that hold a classroom community together. It is necessary to see beyond the obvious fact that children already know how to talk. They do, but children also need to develop skills and come to understand that talking is a tool for learning, communicating, and enjoying the pleasure of thoughtful conversations.

This section has two broad themes: talk in the home and its consequences for literacy and talk in the classroom as a means of developing children's repertoire of oral expressive skills.

## Family Literacy: Talking at Home

Home experiences are an important reason why differences exist in children's oral language skills when they are old enough to be enrolled in school. It is normal, of course, for children to possess different social, emotional, and intellectual traits, so differences in language skills are also expected. But sometimes language differences result from unsatisfactory home contributions to language growth. Children who have many opportunities to talk in meaningful ways with their parents and peers at home are better prepared for the literacy tasks encountered in school (Tough, 1973).

It is sometimes said that children do not have enough opportunities to talk at home. But Tough (1973) found that it is not the amount but the quality of talk that counts. Specifically, she found that talk must focus on meaning. Failure to do so results in miscommunication. When this happens, parents and children talk past each other instead of with each other. Such miscommunication diminishes literacy prospects.

Tough (1973) recorded conversations between British preschool children and their mothers over the course of years. Her research has shown how damaging miscommunication can be. She concluded that miscommunication adversely affects oral language development and diminishes prospects for literacy. On the other hand, focusing on meaning strengthens children's oral language and improves prospects for learning to read and write. The conversation in Table 4.3 between Jimmie and his mother illustrates miscommunication between mother and son. Of course, this conversation could happen between any parent and child. But this conversation was not unusual; indeed, it represents the norm. Tough had recorded many such conversations between Jimmie and his mother.

**Table 4.3**

**Failure to Focus on Meaning in Conversation**

*Setting:* Jimmie, 5 years old, approaches his mother, hand clenched, and begins a conversation.

*Jimmie:* Look—look what I've found.
*Mother:* Just look at your hands—black bright aren't they?
*Jimmie:* Look at this thing—this ladybird—look it's right little.
*Mother:* Go wash your hands now—just look at the colour of them.
*Jimmie:* It's a ladybird. I want to keep it.
*Mother:* Go wash your hands now—do as I say—and put that thing down. Let it go—do you hear.
*Jimmie:* I want it—I want to keep it.
*Mother:* Whatever next. Go wash your hands and don't make a mess. You can have a biscuit [cookie] then.

From Tough, 1973, p. 33.

Consider the particulars. Notice that Jimmie's interests are ignored; notice that Mother's interests dominate the conversation. Mother insists on her meaning while Jimmie's questions and comments are ignored. The consequences of this kind of talk are significant. Jimmie's mother conveys many *unintended* messages about learning: don't be curious; don't inquire; don't make connections; don't ask questions; don't seek answers. On the other hand, Jimmie's mother is explicit about a set of social messages: be good, be quiet, be clean. Jimmie's mother cannot get outside of herself. She is wrapped up in her own meaning and is unable to focus on Jimmie's.

The conversation does not mean that Jimmie's mother lacks good intentions. On the contrary, she loves and cares for Jimmie. She wants the best for him. But still she is unable to focus on Jimmie's interest in the ladybird; she does not respond to his fascination and curiosity. Conversations of this sort, carried out over the course of years, diminish the qualitative aspects of talk between mother and son and have serious consequences for future learning. *Such talk diminishes prospects for literacy.* Tough's follow-up study found that, once enrolled in school, Jimmie had difficulty in learning to read, write, and behave. Literacy had been imperiled.

Now consider the conversation in Table 4.4 (p. 154) between Mark and his mother. This conversation is a typical example of how Mark's mother often conversed with her son and, incidentally, with Mark's little sister as well. Consider the particulars of this conversation. Mark's interests dominate the conversation. Mark's questions and comments are never ignored, but neither is his social behavior. Mother helps Mark recall past experience, defines words, adds pertinent details, and encourages thinking. She invites the use of past experience to understand language; she suggests appropriate social behavior; she enumerates options for consideration; she listens and responds, giving verbal reinforcement; she suggests

**Table 4.4**

## Successful Focus on Meaning in Conversation

*Setting:* Mark, a 5-year-old, and his sister, Julie, are playing on the floor. Mark is looking through a box of toy vehicles. He stops to examine a toy lorry [truck]. The mother is sitting on a chair beside them, knitting as she watches and talks.

*Mark:* What's this funny thing for?

*Mother:* Let me look—oh yes, see it's a hook. Can you find something that will fasten on behind the lorry?

*Mark:* Yes, I see—well it might be a breakdown one couldn't it?

*Mother:* Oh, do you think so? What are breakdown lorries like? Do you remember?

*Mark:* I know—you know—'cause I saw one. At Grannie's I saw one. It's not a breakdown thing—it hasn't got a big thing that pulls up.

*Mother:* A big thing? You mean the crane do you—that lifts the car up?

*Mark:* Yes, it lifts it up like this—off the ground to pull the car—the accident one you see.

*Mother:* And isn't this a breakdown lorry then?

*Mark:* No, no—it's only a hook. It's for pulling I think.

*Mother:* I wonder what it might pull.

*Mark:* I'm looking—perhaps a cart or a thing behind like this.

*Mother:* You mean a trailer.

*Mark:* Yes, Julie give me that—I want to fasten it on. (Mark pulls the trailer away from Julie who protests.)

*Mother:* Oh, that wasn't kind Mark, was it? Julie was playing with it. She doesn't like you taking it like that. You should have asked her if she would change for something else. Julie you have the fire engine instead.

*Mark:* She's a baby isn't she?

*Mother:* Would you like me to take your lorry now?

*Mark:* No, you can't.

*Mother:* No, well Julie doesn't like it either—but she's all right now. What does the fire engine say Julie? (Julie makes a noise and Mark joins in laughing with his baby sister.)

From Tough, 1973, pp. 35–36.

multiple solutions to problems; she helps Mark anticipate the future. Mark's mother is a superb language model, offering information, inviting discussion, and provoking thought. When Mark started school, his progress in literacy was rapid and successful. The quality of talk that preceded school undoubtedly played a role in his academic success.

There is much to be learned from these two conversations. Like parents, teachers can be good or bad role models for language learning. Many of the messages we send are unintended: don't inquire, don't be curious, don't make connections, don't explore, don't focus on meaning. Or we can send more positive messages: seek information, be curious, make connections, explore past experience, seek meaning. The following suggestions may help send positive messages in the conversations we have with children.

- Respond as fully and thoughtfully as possible to children's questions, observations, and comments. This requires focusing on children's meanings rather than your own.
- Try not to let your own agenda interfere with communication between you and your children. Of course, parents and teachers have an agenda that must be communicated. Even so, it is essential to listen to what children say and to focus on their meaning.
- Try to understand the world of children at their level rather than at an adult level. You don't have to be a child to perceive a child's world.
- Refer children back to their prior knowledge; help them connect what they know with what is happening in the present and what may happen in the future.
- Enrich children's language by providing labels, definitions, and details that clarify and extend language and thought—as Mark's mother did.
- Model the language and thought you wish to encourage. Jimmie's mother modeled the wrong kind of response, which sabotaged her good intentions. Mark's mother models effective intellectual and social engagement.

## Talking in the Classroom

Talk between teachers and children is crucial to the development of language and thought. A teacher may be the only person in some children's lives who can provide the language experiences needed to establish the skills that make literacy possible. Teachers who flood their classrooms with conversations, materials, and activities are the ones who enable language and thought to flourish. Tough (1973) describes such an environment:

> Children are essentially curious and want to explore materials, and use them to construct and represent. They are interested in a whole range of natural phenomena. They are interested in other people and their behavior. The enabling environment seems likely to be one that encompasses activities that are likely to gain the child's interest and so ensures motivation for thinking and understanding. Such activities provide a potential basis for meaning to be developed, provide the context in which dialogue can become rewarding to the child, because it brings new understanding and a new mastery of the world around them. (p. 178)

Teachers can do many things to help children communicate their ideas effectively. Focusing on children's meaning in conversations is crucial, and teachers should make every effort to develop children's listening and talking skills. Classrooms should be organized to promote activities and strategies involving group activities. Those suggested below are rich with possibilities for engaging children in organized and purposeful talk.

**Book Talks and Literature Circles**. Conversations about books are as good as conversation gets, or at least they can be. Talking about books excites children's imaginations and can integrate listening, talking, reading, writing, and critical thinking. Conversations about books in literature circles can alternate between talking and reading selected passages from a book. Teachers may participate in these conversations either as listeners or speakers. Of course, teachers must not take over the conversation, but they can be catalysts to stimulate and extend meaningful talk about books.

The Field Notes feature contains a recorded conversation among four of Jennifer Hill's students. Her students were discussing *Island of the Blue Dolphins* by Scott O'Dell (1960) and the movie that grew out of O'Dell's book. Ms. Hill tells what she learned as a teacher through book conversations and what she believes her children learned.

**Storytelling**. Max, nearing age 2, visited cousins Elise, 3, and Nicholas, 4. While the parents visited, the children went into the family room where Grandma suggested they act out the story "The Three Billy Goats Gruff." Nicholas protested: "But we don't know how." "Then first, you must hear the story," Grandma said. So she told them the story in her most dramatic voice. "Now let's play out the story. You be the billy goats and I'll be the troll. Nicholas, you're the biggest, so you be Big Billy Goat. Elise, you be Middle-Sized Goat, and Max can be Little Billy Goat."

> "Children learn not only by imitating grown-up behavior, but by taking an active part, constructing and testing hypotheses, and initiating action themselves."
> —S. Zemelman, H. Daniels, and A. Hyde, *Best Practice*, 1998.

Max didn't really understand the plan, but he was delighted just to be running around the sofa with the others. As the goats came over the bridge, Grandma called out in her scary troll voice, "Who comes trip-trapping over my bridge?" Nicholas helped Max with his responses, but Elise made her own: "It's me. Middle Billy Goat. Don't eat me!" Grandma's troll voice seemed so real to Elise that twice during the play, she asked for reassurance: "It's pretend, isn't it?" Reassured, she continued in her role. Nicholas played the Big Billy Goat part with gusto and delighted in butting the troll into the river. Finally, to Grandma's delight, Nicholas declared that he wanted to be the troll. Roles were reversed, and the play went on amid shouts and laughter.

This storytelling carried three young children into an imaginary land that delighted them. Children who have listened to stories told or read aloud are prepared to tell or retell these stories orally. Without such preparation, this ability is diminished. But effective classroom storytelling and reading can provide what some children may have missed at home. Children's storytelling tends to have three stages: closely imitated, loosely imitated, and original. Close imitation is essentially a summary of a story heard or read. It contains few, if any, original contributions. It follows the story plot and characters as closely as the child remembers them. Children who closely imitate stories may not be aware that they are using someone else's words and ideas. Close imitation should be accepted as a natural starting point. The story below is a close imitation of the original story of "Goldilocks and the Three Bears" as told by a first-grade child.

> The three bears lived in the woods. There was a father bear and mother bear and baby bear. Their house was made out of wood. And there was a girl named Goldilocks. She went to the three bears' house when the bears were away from the house because they were waiting for their porridge to cool.

## Field Notes
### Real-Life Experiences of a Classroom Teacher

Jennifer Hill discusses Scott O'Neill's Newbery award winning book, *Island of the Blue Dolphins,* with her students. The book is based on the true story of Karana, an American Indian girl stranded on the island for 18 years. The conversation among Ms. Hill's students fosters comprehension and appreciation of literature.

Prior to the conversation, I had all my children work in groups to discuss the book we had read. I asked them to respond, in writing, to four questions. After 15 minutes of writing, the students gathered in groups to discuss the book. I assured them their conversation could be wide open. They did not have to talk about the questions they had written about. Here is part of a conversation I recorded in the group made up of Molly, Nick, Nathan, and Emmy.

Jennifer Hill

**Molly:** Okay. Well, I like the movie because now I know what the island looked like.

**Nick:** Yeah, me too.

**Nathan:** I already knew what the island looked like. The book had a lot of description about it.

**Nick:** But I didn't know Rontu was brown until I saw him in the movie. I thought he looked different.

**Nathan:** He was different. He's not described that way in the book.

**Emmy:** Yeah, he had yellow eyes.

**Nick:** Well, he was brown.

**Molly:** But he looked friendlier in the movie.

**Nathan:** Don't you remember that Ms. Hill said there's a lot of imagery in this book?

**Nick:** Oh, yeah. What's imagery?

**Molly:** Lots of description.

**Nathan:** Things went faster in the book. Karana was never in the cave with the skeleton, and she never killed the devilfish. That was my favorite part of the book.

**Nick:** Me too. But I still liked the movie better.

**Emmy:** My turn. Yeah, the book has more description. Is this really a true story?

**Molly:** Yes. It says so at the end of the book, and it said that in the movie, too. Can you believe she lived so long on an island all alone?

**Nick:** I would not have liked that. I would need someone to talk to.

**Nathan:** I think that's why she kept Rontu for a pet—even though he might have killed her brother. At least she had a friend.

**Nick:** When my dog died, I was sad.

**Emmy:** I wouldn't have had a pet dog. I just would have had the birds for pets.

**Nick:** Maybe she would have just pretended to want to have Rontu for a pet but then killed him later on.

**Molly:** But then she REALLY would have been lonely.

**Nathan:** Maybe she decided that killing the dog wasn't as important as she thought it was.

After the groups had their discussions, I brought the whole class together to continue the discussion. I brought up some points that I had thought about while listening. We had a discussion about Nick's comment that the movie reflected what the dog looked like. Students discussed why they thought the movie was more truthful than the book. Some students said they knew that movies are not always true, but they can portray incidents that are close to the truth.

I've found these book conversations extremely valuable. I understand my children's thinking much better as a result of listening to them talk. It's valuable to have conversational interaction among my students, especially conversations centered on books.

Loose imitation is a transitional stage in storytelling. Loosely imitated stories have features not found in the original story, but the essential story elements of plot and character remain the same. Parody is an example of loose imitation; the storyteller deliberately imitates a literary work to produce a comic effect or ridicule. The characteristic style of the original is maintained, adding to the humor. Folk literature is often loosely imitated by children as well as adults. For example, many versions of "The Three Pigs" are told from the Wolf's perspective, and updated versions of "Cinderella" set the story in different times and places. These are loose imitations. Patterned or predictable stories are yet another example of loose imitation. Children may be encouraged to model their storytelling and writing on a predictable story. Amy's story, "David Was Mean," is a loose imitation of Bill Martin Jr's book *David Was Mad*.

### David Was Mean

David was mean.
MEAN MEAN BAD
He was so mean that he kicked the cat.
Mother and Father knew that David was mean.
They knew because David yelled at them.
Grandpa knew that David was mean.
He knew because David wouldn't get the paper for him.
The teacher knew that David was mean.
She knew because David was hitting the kids.
Big brother knew that David was mean.
He knew because David tore up his room.
Little sister knew that David was mean.
She knew because David spit on her.
Everybody hated it. Everybody got meaner and meaner.
They all began to get mean. They began to feel all
black inside. They were so mean they began to fight.
They fought and fought. Everyone had a terrible time.
It was one of the horriblest days they ever had.
"This was a terrible day," David said. And he
began to cry. He cried and cried.
"Yes, that's how it is," Mother said.
"Meanness is like the wind. It blows on everybody that's near."
Already David was feeling better. He was
beginning to feel all warm inside.
His meanness had passed.

—Amy, age 8

The third stage in storytelling and writing involves original work based on some of, but usually not all, the features found in traditional stories. Even original stories written by sophisticated writers contain imitative elements along with the authors' original contributions. For example, Western literature uses and reuses a dozen or so basic plots. Authors use basic plots over and over but add their own unique features. Steven Fry (2002) points out that the plot of his novel, *Revenge,* is based on Alexandre Dumas's *Count of Monte Cristo.* Dumas, he discovered, had taken his plot from a local legend about a sailor wrongly imprisoned. The movie *Shawshank Redemption,* based on a novel by Steven King, uses a similar plot. The originality lies not in the borrowed plot but in the unique treatment authors bring to their stories.

Character types are also frequently imitated. Edgar Allan Poe originated the mystery genre, which introduced the idea of the brilliant detective and his not-so-brilliant associate. Since Poe's original story "Murder in the Rue Morgue," mysteries have nearly always presented two major characters, the lead detective, often brilliant and eccentric, and the associate, a lesser light. Think Sherlock Holmes and Dr. Watson, or Nero Wolfe and Archie Goodwin. Still, regardless of certain imitative features, such literary works are regarded as original since authors add their own unique features to the stories. Children, too, may tell or write a story that can be regarded as original even though certain literary features are, to one degree or another, imitative. In the story "Autumn" a young English lad narrates a common occurrence in nature through the brilliant use of metaphor—a war among the forces of nature. This is an original story with all of the strengths and weaknesses one might expect of a young author.

### Autumn

The Autumn pays us a visit. It comes strongly like an army of ten million men. Each man of the ten million strikes a blow with his ax and each one kills a leaf. The birds zoom in like jet planes killing off the juicy red berries. The brilliant red apples fall and blow up the leaf's bases. The army of leaves are finished. They all lie on the ground like a corpse. The trees stand bare because of the battle. But the army of wind isn't satisfied. They keep on striking, killing off the petals on the last flowers. It just keeps on conquering. It knocks off the conkers so the little children can pick them up and the evil army faints, seeing they have for once helped someone so they become silent for a moment. Only one moment. They can't waste any time, they have to get on with their evil conquering. Then the leaves change colors on their carpet they become red and yellow and different golden colors as though they were turning into ghosts going to haunt the wind. The leaves call for reinforcements, the raindrops. The raindrops come and kill off the wind. The armies go away. The people pick the rosy red apples now because they dare not come out while the battle was on. The harvest starts and the stubble is burnt reminding children to get their bonfires ready and to be buying their rockets and bangers, airbomb repeaters and all the other fireworks. The children find the biggest potatoes and hide them so their mums don't find them and use them. Then on bonfire night they bring them out of their hiding places and roast them.

—Paul, age 10

Encourage children to tell or retell stories orally. Often it is helpful to write a story first, or its essential elements, and then practice telling it. Teacher modeling can help get children into the storytelling mode. Children can tell or retell stories only after they have acquired a sufficient background in reading and hearing stories. Until then, they will not

"Thou shalt not is soon forgotten, but 'once upon a time' lasts forever"
—Philip Pullman, 1996 Carnegie Medal acceptance speech

**Table 4.5**

**Ways to Encourage Storytelling**

*Teaching Tip*

1. Read stories with simple plots and themes, and discuss the stories with children. Later, as children come to understand the structure of simple stories, read more complex stories.
2. Tell stories orally. Start with simple accounts of life events. Move gradually to stories that have fictional parts along with real-life events.
3. Remember that young children move through levels of skill in telling and writing stories. Patience is, therefore, required.
4. Connect written storytelling with oral storytelling. Remind children that much of traditional literature derives from stories first told orally. It can work the other way around, as well. Children may write stories first and practice telling them orally.
5. Praise children for the success of their storytelling skill as well as for the effort they make in becoming storytellers.
6. Teach children to use vocal variations in telling their stories and to incorporate physical movement into their storytelling repertoire.
7. Invite local storytellers to your classroom so that children may experience a storyteller at work.

have acquired a sense of story structure, character, point of view, theme, and plot, which good storytellers need. Table 4.5 identifies some strategies for encouraging children to tell and write stories.

**Show and Tell**. Show and tell encourages children to bring objects and experiences to school so they can talk about them. It is an excellent way to bridge the gap between home and school. But children who are talkative on the playground may fall silent during show and tell, as in this first-grade conversation:

**Teacher:** Edie, do you have something to share?

**Edie:** Yes (whispered).

**Teacher:** Can you tell us about it?

**Edie:** Yes.

**Teacher:** I see you've brought your teddy bear. Is it new?

**Edie:** No.

**Teacher:** What do you and your teddy bear do together?

**Edie:** Sleep.

**Teacher:** I'm so glad you brought your bear to school. Maybe you can tell us about it later.

Edie is shy, and though she talks readily enough in many situations, her reluctance to talk during show and tell may be due to factors other than her natural shy-

## Point Counterpoint

### A Debatable Issue
### Imitation

#### Background
Imitation has a bad reputation but an honorable history. Artists and writers frequently speak of the value and necessity of the imitative stage in their own careers. Nevertheless, some educators fear that imitation in storytelling and writing will adversely influence children's creativity and originality.

#### The Debatable Issue
Encouraging imitation in storytelling and writing prevents children from developing their own creative and original ideas.

#### Take a Stand
Argue the case for or against the debatable issue. Is there a legitimate distinction between certain forms of imitation and plagiarism? Do our ideas about the role of imitation in learning need to be reconsidered? What arguments might you propose for or against the debatable issue? Marshal your arguments based on your philosophy, experience, relevant research, and expert opinion. After you have discussed these questions among colleagues, debate the issue in your class.

---

ness. It is often helpful for the teacher to drop into the background rather than direct the conversation. Encourage the listeners to become engaged in getting Edie to tell about her bear. This may result in more natural conversation and engage the audience as listeners and speakers. Teachers are the natural classroom leaders, but this does not mean that they must lead in every circumstance. Sharing control of the show-and-tell experience often produces livelier conversations—more listening and more talking. Speaking of robust conversation, a teacher told me how she increased the willingness of her children to talk in her classroom. She asked her husband for a birthday present—a portable microphone. Her children loved this device and vied for opportunities to give reports and participate in any activity that allowed them to use it.

> "By encountering and using language in the environment, children learn the rules they can then use to generate an infinite number of sentences."
> —I. Fountas and G. S. Pinnell, *Guided Reading,* 1996.

Show and tell is usually considered a primary-grade activity, but it can be extended into higher grades and may be especially useful for older children who lack oral language fluency. Of course, it may take a different form to accommodate the more mature interests of children in upper elementary school.

It is useful to have children create their own set of guidelines for conducting show and tell. Without guidelines, this activity can degenerate into unfocused talk and conversation. Here are a few guidelines that an elementary school teacher shared with me. Mrs. Edward's children wrote these rules with her help.

1. Rules for the speaker
   - Share something that you enjoy.
   - Share something that others might enjoy.
   - Think of what you want to say.
   - Talk loudly and clearly.

2. Rules for the audience
   - Listen carefully.
   - Ask questions or make comments.
   - Be courteous and kind.

**Panel Presentations.** Television news sometimes features investigative reporting in which teams or various individuals report or comment on a topic about which they have special knowledge. The acquisition of special knowledge usually requires research and experience, such as reading books and articles, searching the Internet, conducting interviews, and listening to conversations. Students can participate in a similar experience. Panel presentations can give children the opportunity to work in teams, provide opportunities for participants to present information orally, and involve the audience in listening, commenting, and asking questions. In such panels, information can be presented in a variety of formats, including discussions, charts, drawings, books, recordings, and electronic presentations using Power-Point® or other computer software formats. Panels work especially well with content subjects.

Children can experience the different roles normally assumed by panelists, such as moderator, expert witness, commentator, or proponent or opponent of a particular view. It is probably wise, especially for younger children, for the teacher to assume typical panel roles initially, especially the role of panel moderator. Gradually, children can be introduced to a variety of roles.

**Reader's Theater.** Reader's Theater is a dramatic interpretation of a prepared script derived from a literary work. Its many benefits include engagement in creative oral expression; comprehension and interpretation of literature; social inter-

*This Reader's Theater group is presenting a story. They are developing the oral reading skills of fluency, phrasing, and expression.*

action, improvement in listening, editing, and talking skills; engagement in purposeful reading and writing; and strengthening confidence in giving oral presentations. Reader's Theater effectively integrates reading, writing, listening, talking, and thinking. Few other dramatic activities work as well to accomplish these goals.

Reader's Theater does not require memorization of scripts, though this may be done. Essentially it is a dramatic reading of a rehearsed script. It is important for children to prepare and practice the reading thoroughly so that they are comfortable reading and interpreting their parts. Rehearsal, discussion, and interpretation of the text are crucial. Teacher modeling helps children understand how effective dramatic expression can breathe life into a text. Lesesne (1998) suggests these steps to achieving success with Reader's Theater: (1) choosing the literature, (2) choosing the scene, (3) editing the text and script, and (4) rehearsing. Pavonetti (2002) has suggested criteria for assessing Reader's Theater presentations: (1) comprehending, interpreting, and selecting the literature; (2) contributions to preparing the script; (3) staging the presentation; (4) dramatic effectiveness of the presentation; and (5) improvement in interpreting and reading the script.

> For a listing of websites highlighting storytelling, drama, creative dramatics, puppetry, choral speaking, and Reader's Theater for children and young adults, see http://falcon.jmu.edu/~ramseyil/drama.htm

**Creative Drama**. Informal creative drama can play a role in the development of oral language skills. Creative drama, sometimes called spontaneous drama, provides a forum for inventing and enacting an oral language experience without any special preparation or rehearsal. Creative drama is spontaneously generated under the direction of the teacher. Children participate in a dramatic activity by reading a character's line(s) in a story, or they compose lines related to an episode drawn from it. Creative drama is typically organized around literature, though it can also be based on ideas drawn from social studies and other content material.

A typical creative drama activity might start with a simple line from a story, such as the line spoken by the wolf in "The Three Little Pigs": "I'll huff and I'll puff and I'll blow your house down." Children are asked to dramatize the line in the way the wolf might have said it. They may also try different versions of how it might have been said—slyly, loudly, angrily. Later, they might compose their own line of dialogue, perhaps a more tactful or silly version of what the wolf said.

**Oral Reports**. What do you most fear? When adults are asked that question, they do not mention crime, death, or getting old. Most state that talking in front of a group tops their list of frightening experiences. Teachers who spend their lives speaking in front of children often fear speaking in front of their peers. This is natural, but experience in presenting oral or written reports can reduce, if not eliminate, anxiety.

> In surveys, people have ranked the fear of public speaking ahead of such things as financial ruin and even death. See http://resources@uen.org

Reports are stressed more in the middle and upper grades than in early elementary grades. Children need guidance about how to get ready for a report, and how to present it. Reports can be classified as subject matter reports, such as those concerning topics in science and social studies, and reports focusing on reviews and previews of stories, television shows, and movies.

The following steps will help children give effective oral reports. Figure 4.1 is a checklist to help speakers assess how well they prepared and presented a report.

*Teaching Tip*

1. *Choose a topic.* It is best for children to choose their own topics, since prior knowledge, interest, and experience are crucial to successful oral reporting.
2. *Collect information.* Access to readable and meaningful information is crucial. Sources include the Internet, books, reference materials, and interviews of people who have special knowledge of the chosen topic.
3. *Organize the information.* Once sufficient background information is obtained, it should be organized into a few main ideas—usually not more than three to five, with appropriate supporting detail.
4. *Prepare props.* Charts, maps, photographs, illustrations, or artifacts will make the report memorable. Such props reduce the need for long verbal explanations. They may be created or selected from available resources.
5. *Rehearse.* Encourage students to practice in front of a mirror or a sympathetic audience and to make sure they have a firm grasp of their subject matter. Preparing note cards will remind the speaker of key points.
6. *Present the report.* An interesting opening remark—a quotation, a surprising idea, or a brief story will draw interest. Appropriate volume and eye con-

**Figure 4.1**

**Assessing an Oral Report**

| Name _____ | | Date_____ |
| Topic _____ | | |

A = Excellent     B = Satisfactory    C = Needs improvement

| | A | B | C |
|---|---|---|---|
| 1. I chose a topic that interested me. | — | — | — |
| 2. I researched my topic for useful information. | — | — | — |
| 3. I organized my ideas for presentation. | — | — | — |
| 4. I limited the number of main ideas. | — | — | — |
| 5. I had supporting details for my main ideas. | — | — | — |
| 6. I prepared visual illustrations. | — | — | — |
| 7. I practiced before I presented. | — | — | — |
| 8. I spoke loudly and clearly. | — | — | — |
| 9. I used my note cards well. | — | — | — |
| 10. I prepared a good opening remark. | — | — | — |
| 11. The audience liked and understood my report. | — | — | — |

I can improve my next report by:

A. _____

B. _____

C. _____

**Figure 4.2**

**Audience Behaviors for Listening to Oral Reports**

Name _____ Date_____

Topic _____

Think about what you did as you listened to the report? What did you think, say, or do during the report? Did you behave in an excellent or satisfactory way? Or do you need to improve your behavior as a member of the audience? Grade yourself on each of the following statements, using the following grading system.

A = Excellent      B = Satisfactory      C = Needs improvement

|  | A | B | C |
|---|---|---|---|
| 1. I listened carefully to the report. | — | — | — |
| 2. I looked at the speaker as I listened. | — | — | — |
| 3. I thought of a compliment I could give the speaker. | — | — | — |
| 4. I thought of a question to ask the speaker. | — | — | — |
| 5. I thought of a comment for the speaker. | — | — | — |
| 6. I can recall the main points the speaker made. | — | — | — |

tact will engage the audience, but reading the report or staring at note cards will put listeners to sleep.

An audience can make or break a speaker. An audience that projects indifference, boredom, or hostility can have a devastating influence. A responsive audience motivates and reassures a speaker. Teach children to be attentive to speakers; suggest ways they can put the speaker at ease; show them how to ask thoughtful questions. Figure 4.2 offers a checklist of helpful audience behaviors.

*Calvin needs to upgrade his idea of research. Most children need help in locating sources of information as they prepare oral or written reports.*

CALVIN AND HOBBES © Watterson. Reprinted with permission of UNIVERSAL PRESS SYNDICATE. All rights reserved.

## Section Summary: Talk

1. Oral expression can be described as formal or informal, aesthetic or efferent. For example, aesthetic talk occurs when children respond to literature whereas efferent talk focuses on informing or persuading.
2. Home experiences influence language learning and literacy acquisition. Parents can provide good models of listening and talking by inviting discussion, answering questions, encouraging curiosity, and provoking thought.
3. Classroom instruction should provide opportunities for oral expression, such as: book talks and literature circles, storytelling, show and tell, panel presentations, Reader's Theater, creative drama, and reporting. Such experiences develop talking skills and strengthen prospects for literacy.

## Practical Teaching Ideas and Activities

*Teaching Tip*

**1.** *Develop listening and speaking standards collaboratively.* Collaborating as a learning community, develop a set of guidelines for participating as a respectful listening audience. Generate specific ideas for what respectful listening looks like and sounds like; record them on a chart. Collaborate on guidelines for participating as an effective speaker as well. Display this piece of shared writing in a prominent area of the classroom, adding to it when necessary. This collaborative process will foster students' independence in understanding the criteria for speaking and listening and encourage thoughtful self-evaluation.

**2.** *Respect the diverse experiences individuals bring into the learning community.* Consider beginning each school day with a morning meeting that opens with a prompt, such as "Good morning. Who has news they would like to share?" This oral language experience lets students share stories and special events in their lives, such as the arrival of a new sibling, a family outing, an accomplishment, or any other news from their individual experience outside of school. The entire community listens, respecting the diversity of experiences each individual brings. Establish this routine as a consistent way to talk together and listen, sharing stories from students' lives, setting a respectful tone for the day, and building a sense of community. (Adapted from the work of Frank Serafini, 2001.)

**3.** *Model active listening and response.* Gather students in a "fishbowl" to model how to actively listen and build upon others' responses in order to make thoughtful contributions to discussion.

**4.** *Encourage active listening in partner or group interactions.* Teachers can ask students to partner up or convene in small groups for a brief, 3- to 5-minute focused discussion on a particular topic. Prior to their discussions, explain that when everyone reconvenes as a whole group, paired individuals will share not their own thoughts but those of their buddy. Small groups will summarize the key ideas that surfaced during their discussion.

**5.** *Summarize presentations.* Prior to an oral language experience, ask students to listen carefully to the speaker, and explain that they will be asked to recall as many details as possible afterward. This activity is most effective if students share what they recall with a partner or in a small group. This gives all students the opportunity to develop their own oral language skills and to carry equal responsibility for listening.

**6.** *Use interactive read alouds.* Talking about reading encourages active participation in the reading process. Students' oral language strengths are emphasized through predicting, questioning, summarizing, and agreeing and disagreeing with others.

**7.** *Utilize think-pair-share.* During interactive read-aloud experiences, provide students consistent opportunities to turn to a partner and exchange thoughts, wonderings, and ideas for 1 to 2 minutes at strategic pausing points that you select beforehand.

**8.** *Encourage visualizing and creating images based on text.* Have students listen to a read aloud without viewing any story art. Encourage them to visualize and describe their personal interpretation of the story. Vary this experience by reading a segment of a story and having the students illustrate it and then write vivid words to describe their art.

See the Blue Pages at the back of the book and on the Companion Website for additional activities.

## ➤ Reflection and Summary

### Reflection

Good teachers have spiritual sons and daughters—students they've taught who will carry a part of them into places they will never reach. It might surprise us to know who among our students retains a residue of our influence. As for me, I like to imagine it might be one of my not-so-good students. Could it be Gary? I never succeeded in teaching Gary to read. I didn't know much about teaching reading at the time, but I tried most earnestly. Did you learn to read, Gary? Did you get on? If so, no thanks to me.

I'd like to think I influenced Kenny, who died in the Attica Prison riot not ten years gone from my fifth-grade classroom. Of all my students, I have most fervently hoped that I might have influenced him. In my dreams, I imagine that I did. Yet I shall never know, for I never saw Kenny again after that last sunny June day when he sauntered—Kenny never just walked—out of my fifth-grade classroom.

Am I alone? Or is it a common human trait to seek a small foothold on immortality? Teachers, more than any other professionals, have the opportunity to spawn spiritual sons and daughters who touch the future. I'm hoping for a small footnote in a future I shall never see. Are you hoping for one too?

## Summary

1. Teaching listening is crucial because many children have acquired poor listening habits prior to coming to school. Though society rewards good talking skills, it unfortunately seldom rewards good listening skills, which lay the foundation for comprehension and are an indispensable tool for learning to decode words.

2. Four types of listening are interrelational listening, concerning language in human relationships; aesthetic listening, focused on pleasure and appreciation; efferent listening, focused on getting information and understanding what has been heard; and critical listening, focused on making inferences, forming opinions, making judgments, and reaching conclusions.

3. Talking can be described as aesthetic (informal) and efferent (formal). Aesthetic talk occurs when children respond to literature, art, and music, for example. Efferent talk focuses on informing, as in giving reports, or persuading.

4. Home experiences influence language learning and literacy acquisition. Parents and peers can provide good models of listening and talking. Talk with children should focus on children's meaning by inviting discussion, encouraging curiosity, answering questions thoughtfully, and connecting prior knowledge with the present.

5. Talk in the classroom should provide many opportunities for oral expression. Activities such as book talks and literature circles, storytelling, show and tell, panel presentations, Reader's Theater, creative drama, and reporting can strengthen oral expressive skills. Effective classroom talk develops language and thought.

## Questions to Challenge Your Thinking

1. What do you think should be done to improve listening instruction in the literacy curriculum?

2. Listening comprehension is similar to reading comprehension. How might you take advantage of this similarity in teaching reading comprehension skills?

3. Some children come to school with an insufficient background in listening to stories and poetry at home. How can teachers help close this gap?

4. Give some examples of how teachers can focus on children's meaning when conversing with them.

5. How can talk within the classroom help children develop their literacy skills?

## A Case Study

Read the following true case study, and then discuss the questions below with your classmates or colleagues.

You are a fourth-grade teacher. One of your students, Emily, tells you she wants to be a beekeeper. She says to you, "My uncle Bill lives in North Dakota and has 1,000 beehives. Uncle Bill takes his beehives to farms and orchards all over the country, so his bees can pollinate the flowers. Farmers pay him to do this. Then he sells the honey. I'm not afraid of bees."

Given Emily's interest in bees and your desire to capitalize on her interest, consider these questions (Table 4.6 provides some beekeeping facts from Hesser [2002].):

1. What comments or questions would you use to continue the conversation Emily has initiated? Write an imaginary conversation you might have with her.

2. What materials, activities, and ideas would you suggest to help Emily follow up on her interest in bees?

3. What opportunities for listening and talking might Emily's interest in bees provide for the rest of the class?

**Table 4.6   Some Facts About Bees and Honey**

1. California and North Dakota produce more honey than any other states.

2. White honey is as pure and clear as water. Some honey is amber in color. Color depends on the flowers from which nectar is extracted.

3. Migratory beekeepers truck their beehives from state to state, following the seasons. For instance, the same hive of bees might spend winters in California and summers on the great Midwestern plains.

4. Some beekeepers have as many as 9,000 beehives. As many as 80,000 bees can inhabit a single hive.

5. The hum you hear around a beehive comes from worker bees flapping their wings to dry the honey.

6. Worker bees make honey by taking nectar from a flower and storing it internally. On returning to the hive, the bees inject the nectar with enzymes and place it into cells in the honeycomb.

7. National production of honey reached 186 million pounds in 2001.

## ◄ Revisit the Anticipation Guide

Return to the Anticipation Guide in the chapter opener, and review your original responses to the questions. Having finished the chapter, complete the guide again, and then consider these questions.

1. Did you change your mind about any items? Why?

2. Which chapter ideas did you find most useful? least useful? Why?

3. What did you read that most interested you? most surprised you?

4. Did any important ideas in this chapter need more discussion? Which ones?

5. Which chapter ideas would you like to know more about?

## VideoWorkshop Extra!

If your instructor ordered a package including VideoWorkshop, go to Chapter 4 of the Companion Website (www.ablongman.com/cramer1e) and click on the VideoWorkshop button. Follow the instructions for viewing the appropriate video clip and completing the accompanying exercise. Watch the Companion Website for access to a new interactive teaching portal, My Lab School, currently under construction.

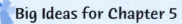

## A Philosophy of Emerging Literacy

**D**awn is a lovely time of day. The sun emerges over the horizon; life begins to stir. Scenes hidden by night's darkness spring into existence, as though by magic. But no magic is involved; dawn reveals what the shades of night had hidden. The emergence of life is so beautiful. Max emerged into this life just 2 years ago. He is experiencing the dawning of literacy long before he can read and write. He pages through his many books, holding the books right side up most of the time. Max knows these stories well. His mother reads five or six books to Max every day. And not just any book. Max has favorites; he likes rhyming books best. New books have to be introduced carefully. He's stingy about allowing them into his pantheon of acceptable bedtime stories. And just yesterday he placed his first scribble marks on the living room wall.

Literacy emerges out of the enlightenment of attentive parents, peers, grandparents. It is the harvest of many stories told, many books read, many songs sung, many hugs given, many kisses stolen. Max's mother began planting the seeds of literacy the day she brought Max home from the hospital.

# 5 Emerging Literacy

## Big Ideas for Chapter 5

1. Reading and writing behaviors emerge prior to conventional literacy.
2. Reading improves writing; writing improves reading.
3. A culture of home literacy improves children's reading and writing prospects.
4. Marie Clay identified seven principles of emergent writing.
5. Prerequisites for emergent writing include: writing the alphabet, phonemic awareness, and associating letters with sounds.
6. Four emergent writing stages are scribbling, drawing, letter strings, and invented spelling.
7. Principles of emergent reading include meaning, word recognition, phonemic awareness, oral and written language experiences, reading aloud, and reading fluency.
8. Five written language skills should be assessed: phonemic awareness, print concepts, writing vocabulary, spelling knowledge, and reading miscues.

## Anticipation Guide

*Consider each of the following statements, and determine whether you agree or disagree with each. Save your answers, and revisit this guide at the end of this chapter.*

1. Emerging literacy begins at birth and ends at about age 6.    agree    disagree
2. A literate home makes it easier to learn to read and write.    agree    disagree
3. Good conversations improve prospects for literacy.    agree    disagree
4. Teaching the alphabet early can delay learning to read.    agree    disagree
5. Invented spelling is harmful to later spelling success.    agree    disagree
6. The primary goal of reading is phonics.    agree    disagree
7. Surrounding children with oral and written language aids literacy.    agree    disagree
8. Reading fluency is aided by reading difficult material.    agree    disagree
9. Phonemic awareness is prerequisite knowledge for learning to read.    agree    disagree
10. Recording reading miscues is a good way to assess reading comprehension.    agree    disagree

*S*ome people there are who, being grown, forget the horrible task of learning to read. It is perhaps the greatest single effort that the human undertakes, and he must do it as a child.

*—John Steinbeck*

## A Literacy Story

Mary Frances Kennedy Fisher wrote short stories, novels, poetry, and books about food and travel. M. F. K. Fisher, as she is known, became famous for a fine prose style, an exceptional achievement, given the subject matter of much of her work.

M. F. K. Fisher learned to read before going to school. She grew up in a home culture that honored literacy. Her father read the newspaper headlines at breakfast; her mother read her recipes and pages from a novel. Mary Frances memorized some of the pieces read to her and then reread them to the cook. Her first book, she recalls, was *The Wizard of Oz*, which she read aloud in a high, keening shriek. This *noise* annoyed her grandmother, who said that Mary Frances had merely memorized the words and wasn't *really* reading. Thus challenged, Mary Frances determined to prove her grandmother wrong. At the suggestion of her mother, she read to her grandmother from the Old Testament, a book she had never previously read. Her performance convinced her grandmother that, indeed, Mary Frances could read. Thereafter, Mary Frances often read to her grandmother, who listened and provided correction—none too gently, one suspects.

Mary Frances walked through the door to literacy and never looked back. Her description of the wonder of reading for oneself is classic: "I lay voluptuously on my stomach on the big bed, blissfully alone, and I felt a thrill which has never left me as I realized that the words coming magically from my lips were mine to say or not say, read or not. It was one of the peaks of my whole life. Slowly my eyes rode across the lines of print, and the New World smiled. It was mine, not something to beg for, book in hand, from anyone who could read when I could not. The door opened, and without hesitation I walked through."

## A MATTER OF STANDARDS

### Emergent Literacy

**Standard:** The IRA/NCTE standards document does not list a specific standard for emerging literacy. However, the preamble to the standards document states that "literacy growth begins before children enter school as they experience and experiment with literacy activities—reading and writing, and associating spoken words with their graphic representation."

Emergent literacy is not one of the 12 official standards listed in the IRA/NCTE Standards for the English Language Arts. However, the introduction speaks to the issue of emergent literacy as quoted above. This statement implies that schools have a role to play in sponsoring and fostering emergent literacy. Literacy emerges in tiny bursts of enlightenment as parents read to young children, engage them in meaningful conversations, sing the alphabet with them, recite nursery rhymes, and encourage drawing and writing. While a culture of home and family literacy aids and abets emerging literacy, not all children receive a sufficient measure of home literacy experiences. Such children need emergent literacy experiences developed and sponsored by educational institutions such as Head Start as well as kindergarten and primary-grade instruction. When given rich emergent literacy experiences, children make the transition to conventional literacy much more successfully. This chapter describes ways in which this standard can be met.

The term *emergent literacy* is well known, but what does it mean? I came across one definition that extends emergent literacy from birth to death. This definition reminds me of Abraham Lincoln's favorite logic question: "If you count a dog's tail as a leg, how many legs does a dog have?" The logical answer, seldom given, is four, since the tail remains a tail no matter what you call it. So I discount this illogical and elongated definition of emergent literacy in favor of Teale and Sulzby's (1986) more parsimonious one. They define emergent literacy as the reading and writing behavior and development that precede conventional literacy.

> "When I look back, I am so impressed again with the life-giving power of literature. If I were a young person today, trying to gain a sense of myself in the world, I would do that again by reading, just as I did when I was young."
> —Maya Angelou, poet

Most early reading and writing behaviors are observable; others are hidden. Easily observable behaviors include the scribbling of a 1-year-old, the pretend reading of a 2-year-old, the alphabet writing of a 3-year-old. Other emergent literacy behaviors are hidden. For example, babbling infants utter sounds that are not relevant to their native language. But by 6 or 7 months, these irrelevant sounds have disappeared from infants' stock of sounds. Infants sort among the environment language sounds they hear, determine which ones are relevant to their native language, and eliminate the irrelevant sounds from their babbling. This linguistic behavior is hidden to all but the well-trained linguist. This sorting and classifying of sounds is an enormous intellectual feat and deeply relevant to learning to read and write. Thus emergent literacy begins at birth, but it is harder to determine exactly when it ends. A reasonable guess is that emergent literacy ends when children have become relatively fluent readers. But reading fluency is achieved at different rates and times for different children, depending on circumstances within and outside the child. For many children, fluency is observable as early as age 4, 5, 6, or 7.

Jerome Bruner said, "The kinds of make-believe writing and reading children bring into their play can tell us a great deal about how and when literacy begins." His remark appeared in *Acts of Meaning,* published in 1970, well before the emerging literacy movement got under way. Bruner's remarks seem exceptionally insightful, but actually they have historical precedent going back for centuries. Unfortunately, the principles of emerging literacy did not take root in school policy until recently. In some venues, they have not yet taken root.

Literacy is more likely to emerge in circumstances in which children experience a culture of literacy: meaningful conversations, storybooks read aloud, adults who model literacy, affectionate and meaningful connections established between children and literacy events. Like rain and sunshine on planted seeds, growth toward literacy awaits only the natural flowering toward maturity that favorable environmental conditions provide.

While it is reasonable to say that children construct their own literacy, they do so within a social environment. Vygotsky (1962, 1978) stressed the idea that literacy is facilitated by social interaction with peers and adults. Adults and peers facilitate children's emergence toward literacy by providing instructional support within the zone of proximal development (ZPD)—that space between independence and the need for instructional support. Bruner (1966) suggests that children's learning, including literacy, is aided by scaffolding, or instructional support provided at key times. Scaffolding, as conceived by Bruner, implies a gradual transference of responsibility for learning from adult to child. Vygotsky's idea of zone of proximal development and Bruner's scaffolding metaphor are consistent with Piaget's (1955) theory of how children learn.

> "It is not enough to simply teach children to read; we have to give them something worth reading. Something that will stretch their imaginations."
> —Katherine Paterson, author

## The Relationship Between Reading and Writing

Tierney and Shanahan (1991) conducted a thorough review of research on the reading–writing relationship. At the conclusion, they stated: "We believe strongly that in our society, at this point in history, reading and writing, to be understood and appreciated fully, should be viewed together, learned together, and used together." This is a ringing endorsement of the importance of the reading–writing relationship, notwithstanding the numerous caveats, qualifications, and reservations raised concerning what specific transferable knowledge processes and skills are involved.

Many researchers believe there is a strong case for the following proposition: reading improves writing; writing improves reading (Loban, 1963; Moffett & Wagner, 1983; Shanahan, 1980, 1988; Stauffer, 1970; Stotsky, 1983; Tierney and Leys, 1984). If reading improves writing and writing improves reading, then it follows that (1) reading and writing share underlying skills and cognitive processes that mutually reinforce each other, (2) there is a sound pedagogical rationale for integrating reading and writing instruction, and (3) integrated instruction is more efficient than teaching reading and writing separately.

While we know a lot about the reading–writing relationship, we do not yet understand some things. For example, further research is needed to answer the following questions more definitively: How does one process contribute to the other? What literacy activities and experiences are most likely to exploit the full potential of the relationship? Given what is presently known, we can safely endorse the following statements about the reading–writing relationship.

- Emergent writing provides information that enhances print awareness and word recognition (Chomsky, 1971a, 1971b; Juel, Griffith, & Gough, 1986; Shanahan, 1984).
- Knowledge gained through reading aids spelling, which influences writing (Cramer, 1970; Shanahan, 1984).
- A writing program emphasizing invented spelling aids reading achievement and word recognition (Clarke, 1988; Garcia, 1997).
- Reading provides models for writing stories, poems, characters, plots, and narrative events (Graves, 1983, 1994).
- Reading motivates writing; writing motivates reading. This is the testimony of writers, including James Baldwin, Eudora Welty, Truman Capote, Winston Churchill, William Faulkner, Frederick Douglass, Will Durant, Isaac Bashevis Singer, and Paule Marshall, among many others.

The fifth point is of special interest, as I trust in the testimony of writers. They know literacy and literature as few others do. Literature and literacy are their occupation, written language their passion. No profession, not even the teaching profession, has a greater need or opportunity to understand the connection between reading and writing. They know, from intimate experience, that reading and writing influence each other. Faulkner, in particular, pinpoints the importance of the reading–writing relationship dramatically: "Read, read, read. Read everything—trash, classics, good and bad, and see how they do it. Just like a carpenter who works as an apprentice and studies the master. Read! You'll absorb it. Then write."

> "What is reading, but silent conversation."
> —Walter Savage Landor, author

Wisdom is where it is found, and not all wisdom resides in our own profession. Research is an invaluable resource in understanding teaching and learning, but it is well to remember that research is also a cemetery of dead ideas. The slipperiness of research is well understood by scientists, especially medical scientists. They know you cannot go from ignorance to enlightenment in a straight line because today's truth will be tomorrow's ignorance. The history of scientific research is that one truth is thrown out in favor of another that better fits the latest research truth; this truth is later thrown out in favor of ever more recent research truth. It is no less so with pedagogical research.

This does not mean that research has no value; indeed, the contrary is true. Research proceeds forward and backward—never in a straight path to enlightenment. We must take what guidance we can from research without turning its findings into dogma—ideas considered to be absolutely true. We cannot limit teaching to those ideas sanctified by research. Research is a method of *searching* for truth; it must not become dogma that limits the free reign of examined experience and open minds.

## Section Summary: The Relationship Between Reading and Writing

1. Reading strengthens writing; writing strengthens reading. The two should be taught, learned, and understood as complementary processes of literacy.
2. Writers, nearly universally, insist that reading makes an enormous and essential contribution to writing.

# Literacy in the Home

## The Loving Connection

Love is that feeling of tender affection that arises out of kinship, attractive qualities, or a sense of oneness. Love, or something close to it, nurtures children's emergent literacy. The absence of affection does not inevitably lead to or even contribute to illiteracy; there is anecdotal evidence to the contrary. But an affectionate connection among parents, children, and literacy events contributes to children's interest and performance in reading and writing. Pat Conroy, novelist and poet, wrote these words, which convey beautifully the importance of the loving connection between parent, child, and literacy: "Each night of my boyhood, my mother read to me, and I still hear her voice, lovely beneath soft lamplight, whenever I sit down with a pen in my hand. It was my mother who told me she was raising me to be a 'southern writer,' though I have never been sure that she knew what that meant." Of course, whether she knew or not doesn't matter. Pat Conroy's prose seizes and shakes his readers—a gift bequeathed him by his mother through the loving connection.

Reflect on the following three literacy scenarios. Decide if you agree or disagree with the idea that an affectionate connection between parents and children can make a positive contribution to children's literacy prospects.

*Scenario 1:* Mrs. Goodheart sets Allison on her lap, gives her an affectionate hug and kiss, and says, "What book shall we read this evening?" Allison mentions several but settles on *The Three Bears*. Mrs. Goodheart reads the story, interprets the text with comments and questions, asks Allison's opinion about Baby Bear, follows the print with her finger, and invites Allison to turn the pages. Mrs. Goodheart listens and responds to Allison's questions and comments. She praises Allison's performance from time to time. Perhaps a second and third book are read, and the reading ends with a good-night hug and kiss, as Mrs. Goodheart puts Allison to bed.

*Scenario 2:* Mr. Efficiency sits on a chair and Casper sits alone on his bed. Without consulting Casper, Mr. Efficiency decides to read *The Three Bears.* He reads briskly, skipping pages 6 and 7. Casper says, "You left out Papa Bear." Paying no attention to Casper's complaint, Mr. Efficiency reads on. He asks no questions, makes no comments, and brushes aside Casper's request for a second book with the

> "Shared reading was developed by New Zealand educator Don Holdaway, who wanted to simulate for children in school the 'lap reading' experience that many are fortunate enough to also have had at home as they hear, read, and discuss stories with adults in emotionally comfortable, risk-free settings."
>
> —S. Taberski, *On Solid Ground,* 2000.

*Despite Calvin's remark, a "good night," a good story, and a smooch help associate literacy with love.*

comment, "It's bedtime, Casper. One book is enough for tonight." With a perfunctory good night, Mr. Efficiency walks out of the bedroom and back to his busy schedule, television program, or evening paper.

*Scenario 3:* Mrs. Busy hasn't time to read a book to Sharon tonight, nor last night, nor the night before. Besides, there are few books suitable for Sharon to hear, as she has few books of her own. It's near bedtime, and Mrs. Busy says, "Mama's busy tonight. You can watch *The Rug Rats,* and then you must go right to bed. Run along, be a good girl, and don't forget to brush your teeth."

Do such scenarios influence a child's view of literacy? I haven't a doubt that they do. And it is not necessarily a lack of love and affection that is involved in scenarios 2 and 3. Mrs. Goodheart, Mr. Efficiency, and Mrs. Busy

> "From your parents you learn love and laughter and how to put one foot in front of the other: but when books are opened you discover that you have wings."
>
> —Helen Hayes, actress

## Point ⟷ Counterpoint

### A Debatable Issue

### A Loving Connection

**Background**

I have presented three scenarios on the loving connection, featuring Mrs. Goodheart, Mr. Efficiency, and Mrs. Busy. Some might say the idea that a loving connection influences literacy prospects is sentimental nonsense with no research support. Others might say the idea makes sense, whether or not it is sentimental or supported by research.

**The Debatable Issue**

The absence of a loving connection between parent and child diminishes the prospects for literacy.

**Take a Stand**

Argue the case for or against the debatable issue. Does a loving connection add anything of value to a child's literacy prospects? Can young children succeed just as well whether or not parents take the time to connect literacy with affection? Marshal your arguments based on your philosophy, experience, research, and beliefs. After you have discussed these questions among colleagues, debate the issue in your class.

may all love their children with equal intensity. What is missing in scenarios 2 and 3 is the *loving connection* that brings parents, children, and literacy events together. *The absence of such a connection diminishes prospects for literacy.* That's my view. What do you think?

## A Culture of Family Literacy

Bruner (1970) said, "Literacy is a social and cultural achievement, as well as a cognitive one." A literate family life is the best assurance that literacy will be transmitted to children. A culture is the totality of socially transmitted thought and behavior. It includes art, beliefs, institutions, and patterns of interactions. Certain features of a culture may be shared by nearly everyone in a given nation, state, city, or family. Others may not be widely shared. For instance, a farm community may have certain cultural features not shared within a city culture; a single family may share certain cultural features with neighbors yet have its own distinct cultural features. There are many kinds of cultures: religious, secular, political; we can also speak of a *literacy culture.*

A literacy culture is one in which education is honored, learning is respected, and literacy is valued. Reading, writing, and thinking are its crucial components. Books, magazines, newspapers, and other symbols of literacy are present and appreciated in a literacy culture. There may be many books and publications or just a few, depending on economic and social circumstances. Abraham Lincoln grew up in a frontier culture where books were scarce. The Bible and a few other books made up the extent of Lincoln's library, enriched marginally by those he borrowed from neighbors. But he knew his few books well. His stepmother, Nancy Hanks, fostered Abe's desire to read and his dream to make progress in learning. Abraham Lincoln's literacy culture was circumscribed—meager, by today's standards—but it served him well.

Homes that share a literary heritage, no matter how humble, have the potential to magnify a child's prospects for literacy. A shared literacy culture increases a child's literacy quotient. In a multicultural world, it is essential for every child to experience what it means to live in a home where a literacy culture is embraced.

### Section Summary: Literacy in the Home

1. A loving connection among children, parents, and literacy events contributes to children's interest and performance in reading and writing.
2. A shared literacy culture can increase children's literacy quotient.

## Emergent Writing Concepts

Children can write at an early age, but they need models at home and at school. Children can ask for no greater gift than to have parents and teachers who encourage them to write, show them how it's done, and provide good models. A great movement is taking place in American schools, which encourages early reading and writing. Over the past two decades, I have seen more and more teachers sponsor writing and reading among kindergarten and first-grade children. This is the ideal age to instill a love for literacy in children.

Teachers work for modest pay, often under bitter criticism. Yet they care about their children and maintain a professional attitude. Lisa Rose Granitz Chottiner is one such teacher. She teaches first grade; she writes for and with her children. Many of her children lack the opportunities that encourage early literacy growth. Yet Ms. Granitz Chottiner believes she can make a difference. *And she does.* She's excited about the progress her children are making; she knows that she can make a difference, in part because she cares so much about her children and her profession. She recently completed her master's degree in reading and language arts—going to school nights and summers, paying high tuition bills to strengthen her professional knowledge base. She explains how personal writing adds to her teaching repertoire in the Field Notes feature.

Ms. Granitz Chottiner, like all good teachers, took ownership of her writing program, assumed responsibility for making it better, and succeeded. She still struggles sometimes, even though she knows many things about writing. It is only when you undertake to use what you know that you discover how to transform knowledge into performance. This is the hard work of becoming a good teacher. It doesn't come without cost in time and effort. As you read this section, you may gain *knowledge*, but you must work to transform knowledge acquired through reading into teaching performance in your classroom. *Transforming knowledge into performance is a lonely, difficult task, but it is the only way to become an effective teacher.*

*Teaching Tip*

## Field Notes
### Real–Life Experiences of a Classroom Teacher

I love stories. I remember sitting on the carpet in second grade, listening as the words flowed gracefully from my teacher's tongue. It was magic—entire worlds existed in those words. Authors were like gods. I knew I wanted to be one. I wanted to create that magic.

So, I began to write. I won a few school writing contests. This reaffirmed my heavenly potential. As I went through school, my writing changed from public to private. Yet I wanted to write for the world, have my voice heard. My parents encouraged me to pursue something more financially stable. Naturally, I selected the lucrative profession of teaching.

After college I was filled with hope. I diligently sent manuscripts to publishers and agents. Soon I had bags of rejections. But I did not stop writing. I had my own audience—my first-grade students. Some of my students can barely make scribble marks on paper, but they know the magic of stories. They know stories can take you places.

My students know I write stories. They know that when I'm stuck, I ask for their advice. My students know I appreciate and use their suggestions. This makes them more comfortable with their own writing. They know it is okay to ask for and accept help. I show my students it is okay to make mistakes, but it is not okay not to try. I used to think being a writer meant being shelved at Borders. Now I know the truth. True authors inspire others.

**Lisa Rose Granitz Chottiner**

## Clay's Principles of Emergent Writing

In every era, educators arise who see farther and understand more deeply than their colleagues. There is no shortage of such seers today. Marie Clay ranks among the most farsighted and influential educators of our time. Her work in reading led to Reading Recovery, a highly successful tutorial reading program for the lowest-achieving first-grade children. Perhaps less well known is the work Marie Clay has done in writing. Her book *What Did I Write?* has made an important contribution to our understanding of emergent writing. Clay (1975) identified principles which describe the nature of children's early writing and provide clues for nurturing it (see Table 5.1).

## Prerequisites for Independent Writing

Three skills are needed before children can write independently: writing letters of the alphabet, phonemic awareness, and associating letters with sounds. None of these prerequisite skills need be fully mastered. A moderate level of knowledge in each is sufficient. For example, children can write invented-spelling messages long

**Table 5.1**

**Clay's Principles of Emergent Writing**

| Principle | Explanation |
|---|---|
| Meaning principle | Children intend to convey meaning in their writing, and meaning is its most pervasive characteristic. |
| Exploration principle | Children examine and investigate the use of letters, words, and ideas in their early writing to understand how they work. |
| Sign principle | Children learn that their marks on paper stand for something beyond the symbol itself; they learn that symbols represent meaning. |
| Generative principle | Children discover that a few letters, used in varying combinations, can generate words and messages. For example, writing a string of letters is a child's way of generating a meaningful message in "words." |
| Directional principle | Children acquire directional orientation as they progress in reading and writing. The directional confusion they sometimes demonstrate is normal and developmental; it does not signal dyslexia or learning disability. |
| Inventory principle | Children assess their knowledge of letters and words by writing "inventories" of the letters and words they know. |
| Spacing principle | Initially, children may ignore word boundaries, or use periods or stars to represent spaces between words. Later, they use traditional spacing. |

before they have acquired a full command of all letter–sound connections or even all letters of the alphabet.

**Writing the Alphabet**. Learning to recite the alphabet can be tough. A kindergarten child came home and told his mom that he had learned to sing the alphabet song: "Let's hear it," Mom said. The child piped up with "A, B, C, D, E, F, G, H, I, J, K, N, L, M . . . N, O, L. M . . . [long pause] W. W. W. dot com." Writing the letters of the alphabet is even tougher than singing it, but it is prerequisite to independent writing. Even Joe, the unlettered blacksmith in Dickens's *Great Expectations*, understood this concept. Joe tells Pip, "The king upon his throne, with his crown upon his 'ed, can't sit and write his acts of Parliament in print, without having begun, when he were an unpromoted Prince, with the alphabet."

Alphabet knowledge, along with phonemic awareness, makes it possible for children to connect letters to sounds. When knowledge of sounds and letters is present, children can begin to invent the spelling of many words. Of course, children can copy words and names without knowledge of sounds and letters, but this is not the same as consciously making connections between letters and sounds. Fortunately, with patient instruction, most children can learn to write the letters well enough to begin writing within a few weeks of entering first grade, and many children bring this knowledge from home or kindergarten. Children can begin writing *before* they can form *all* the letters of the alphabet. Knowledge of a dozen or so consonant letters and a few vowel letters will suffice for a lot of invented spelling. But the more letters, the merrier the writing.

*Teaching Tip*

**Phonemic and Phonological Awareness**. Phonemic awareness is the ability to distinguish one speech sound from another and to segment sounds within words. (I have described phonemic and phonological awareness in detail elsewhere in this book.) Many children learn to do this on their own through exposure to literature and word play. But if not, children can be taught to distinguish and segment sounds within words. Reading stories, rhymes, and books is an excellent place to start: *The Three Pigs; Brown Bear, Brown Bear; Hickory Dickory Dock;* and hundreds of children's books present sounds and meaning that children love to hear. The repetition helps anchor the sounds of language in children's ears—part of the process of developing phonemic awareness. More direct activities are also useful. For example, "Listen to these three words: *pig, pat, cat*. Which word starts with a different sound?" Once children can isolate one sound from another within words, they can begin to associate speech sounds with the letters that represent them. This capability is crucial to learning to read and write (Adams, 1990; Ayres, 1993; Pressley, 1998; Yopp, 1992).

*Teaching Tip*

**Associating Letters with Sounds**. Young children are extraordinarily sensitive to the phonology of language. Children's knowledge of the phonology of their language can be put to use in writing sooner than has been generally understood. Many children of ages 3 to 5 have learned to do so (Read, 1971). Once children know some letters of the alphabet and possess phonemic awareness, they can usually associate letters with sounds, particularly consonants and long vowel sounds.

**Figure 5.1**

Lynn's "Big Ivs"

The Big Ivs
I like to pl with my ts wn day my ts
wt ta I as my mom af sy nw wa ty wa
tn I fa o. c. my cat wi my ts. I td my
mom tat I fd my ts. my mom sd gd I
am ga tat you fd your ts and sa gv me
a big hg the nx day I td my dad abt
the big ivs and ha liked ti I ct on ti pb
ab the big ivs sa I nva ft the big ivs
and I rmb it all my lfe.

**The Big Adventure**

I like to play with my toys. One day my toys weren't there. I asked my mom if she knew where they were. Then I found O.C. my cat with my toys. I told my mom that I found my toys. My mom said, "Good I am glad that you found your toys," and she gave me a big hug. The next day I told my dad about the big adventure and he liked it. I kept on telling people about the big adventure. So I never forgot the big adventure and I remember it all my life.

Of course, they need practice and encouragement as they take those early steps of writing with invented spelling. Figure 5.1 illustrates just how successful Lynn, a first-grader, was in using her knowledge of the phonology of English, even though she could not yet spell many words correctly.

## The Four Stages of Emergent Writing

Stages are a convenient way of discussing a continuous process in distinct terms. However, children do not move in a strictly linear fashion from one stage of emergent writing to another. For example, letter strings are most characteristic of the third stage of emergent writing, but that does not mean that scribbling, characteristic of the first stage, has been entirely abandoned. Furthermore, children move through stages at their own rate—fast, average, or slow.

Four stages can be observed among emerging writers: scribbling, drawing, letter strings, and invented spelling—some call this stage developmental. The first three stages are prephonetic, before alphabetic writing. Prephonetic writings include cursivelike lines, letters, and copied words, but they do not evidence systematic connections between letters and sounds. The last stage is phonetic; children produce conventional writing using invented spelling—the first appearance of systematic connections between letters and sounds. The following sections discuss each stage and ideas to encourage children as they navigate it.

**The Scribbling Stage.** Writing begins the moment a child reaches out, grasps a crayon, and scribbles. Between ages 3 and 5, many children believe that the marks they make on paper (or walls) have meaning. We call these marks scribbling, but it is scribbling with a purpose—a kind of childhood graffiti. For 1- and 2-year-olds, scribbling is initially a physical activity but doesn't remain so for long. They soon see that a pencil applied to paper is a way of conveying meaning.

Scribbling has features characteristic of conventional writing, such as a left-to-right and top-to-bottom orientation. Letters and cursivelike lines soon appear in children's writing and drawing (see Figure 5.2). A child may show you his "writing" and ask, "What does it say?" Parents can encourage scribbling by talking about letters, playing with magnetic letters and letter blocks, writing a child's name on her papers, and hanging her writing on the refrigerator door. Comments and activities that show children that their "writing" is valued will contribute to their future development as writers. If children's early writing is valued, they will soon begin alphabetic writing, in which systematic connections are made between letters and sounds—the invented spelling stage. You can promote this initial stage of writing through these actions:

- Encouraging early attempts to write (scribble)
- Providing crayons, paper, and other writing devices
- Reading books, playing with letter blocks, and talking about letters and words
- Writing children's names on their papers
- Taking dictation—a few words or a sentence will do
- Displaying their writing in conspicuous places

**Figure 5.2**

**The Scribble Stage**

*Teaching Tip*

**The Drawing Stage.** Picture writing is at least 30,000 years older than alphabetic writing. Drawings on ancient cave walls in Lascaux and Chauvet in France tell of the cultural life of the cave's former inhabitants. Early *Homo sapiens* drew animals, people, and objects that illustrated daily events in their lives. Some archaeologists believe these paintings express the creative and symbolic thinking of ancient humans. Children do something similar. Their drawings illustrate their daily experiences and express their creative and symbolic thinking. Figure 5.3 is an example of the drawing stage of writing.

Drawing plays a supportive role in writing long after children have learned its conventional forms. For young children, drawing and writing are ways of communicating meaning (Dyson, 1988). There are reasons why young children "write" with drawings. First, they may not have full command of the alphabetic system for representing meaning; drawing is an alternative. Second, since they can represent meaning through drawings, there is no pressing need for alphabetic writing. Third, drawing does not require the fine motor control needed for writing. Fourth, draw-

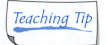
*Teaching Tip*

ing is itself a form of writing suitable for conveying meaning, as Dyson (1997) has documented. Fifth, drawing helps children recall the message they have represented. Encourage drawing by these actions:

- Commenting positively on the details within a drawing
- Commenting on letters, names, or words incorporated into drawings
- Reading children's writing back to the author if asked, "What did I write?"
- Praising and making specific observations about the piece
- Displaying drawings and writing prominently

**The Letter-String Stage.** English writing is produced by combining and recombining a limited set of letters (26) and numbers (10). Once children discover that writing can be generated by using only a few letters and numbers in varying combinations, they string letters together, which, they believe, convey messages. Children begin stringing letters and numbers together soon after they have learned to form them. This stage is prephonetic writing since it lacks a systematic connection between letters and sounds (see Figure 5.4). As in earlier stages of writing, features of conventional writing appear in the letter strings children produce. Features include

**Figure 5.3**

**The Drawing Stage**

letters, numbers, names, copied words, memorized words, punctuation, and directional orientation. Children explore the world of letters and words long before they have figured out the principles needed to generate phonetic writing. Marie Clay (1975) described how a child might view writing at this stage: "The child seems to say, 'I hope I've said something important. You must be able to understand what I've said. What did I write?'" (p. 24). You can encourage development in this stage by these actions:

- Encouraging the incorporation of environmental print into writing
- Suggesting ideas for inventorying letter and word knowledge
- Answering questions and making observations about words and letters
- Asking children to tell you about their writing and drawing
- Sharing writing within the learning community

**The Invented Spelling Stage.** I watched Angie, a first-grader, invent the spelling of *sand*. She hissed the /s/ several times, turned to her paper, and wrote a big curvy *S*. She looked pleased with herself. Then she continued. She exploded a "duh" a couple of times, turned to her paper, and drew a big, fat *D*. I said, "*SD* for *sand* is

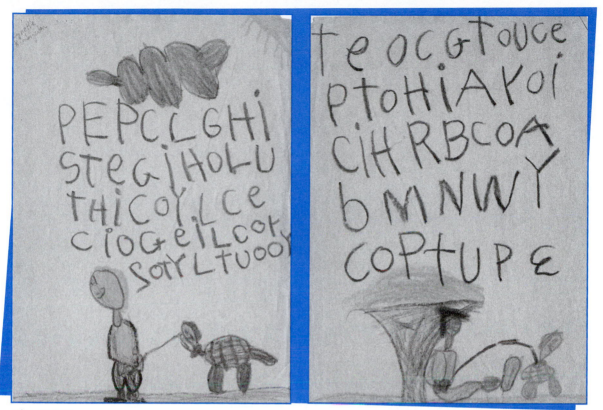

**Figure 5.4**

**The Letter-String Stage**

very good, Angie." She looked at me with a satisfied smile and said, "Thanks. I'm pretty good at it." I'd just watched an amateur linguist at work.

Invented spelling is a boon to emergent writing. It teaches children much of what they need to know about written language and contributes to learning to read and write (Chomsky, 1971a; Fresch, 2001). At this stage, a significant shift occurs. Children now make systematic connections between letters and sounds. It's a giant leap. Scribbling, drawing, and letter-string writing are prephonetic, but the invented spelling stage is phonetic. Writing now is alphabetic. Letters and sounds are connected.

Once children realize that letters stand for sounds, they need some explicit guidance; they need to know how to invent the spelling of the many words available in their oral language. I ask three questions, give guidance, and provide assurance as children take the giant leap into alphabetic writing.

1. "What do you hear first in *elephant?*" (I give the first consonant sound extra emphasis.) Often children answer *l.* If so, I say, "Good, write an *l.*"

*Teaching Tip*

2. "What do you hear *next* in ele**ph**ant?" (I emphasize the second consonant sound.) Sometimes children answer *f.* If so, I say, "That's good, write an *f.*"

3. "Now, what's the *last* sound you hear in elephan**t**?" (I give the last consonant sound extra emphasis.) Some children say they don't hear anything. In that case I repeat the word *elephant,* emphasizing the last sound again. If children respond with *t,* I say, "Wonderful. Write a *t.*" But some children may still not hear the ending sound. In this case I say, "Okay. You've done fine. Just keep writing, and try to spell words you don't know as best you can."

Each time I say the target word, I emphasize the sound I want children to hear. These procedures may elicit varied spellings for elephant: *lt, lft, elfnt.* It doesn't matter whether they get one, two, three, or more letters in the early going. I just want them to use what they know to invent the unknown, as best they can.

Research shows that children can invent spellings remarkably well at an early age—sometimes on their own, sometimes through instruction (Chomsky, 1971a, 1971b; Cramer, 1970; Fresch, 2001; Read, 1971). Many children have acquired some knowledge of phonemics, but they do not automatically understand how to put it to use. When children's knowledge of phonemics is joined with the understanding that letters stand for speech sounds, children are ready to put their knowledge to use. But patient instruction is required, along with a mix of reassurance that an approximate spelling is fine *for now.* Correct spelling, while important, can be attended to later. Consider the following suggestions for encouraging invented spelling:

- Encourage spelling inventions and provide help as needed.
- Encourage detailed illustrations.
- Have children read their writing aloud.
- Read good literature and talk about the authors.
- Share writing from the author's chair.

When first-grade teacher Ann Marie Laskowski writes the morning message on the board, she has her children participate with her, using invented spelling. After the children reread the message, Ms. Laskowski rewrites the message, using standard spelling and punctuation. Here is an example.

Children's invented spelling version: *Ye wnt to v zou. Ye sah anmls of awl cnds. Ye hd fun.*

Ms. Laskowski's rewrite, using standard spelling and punctuation: *We went to the zoo. We saw animals of all kinds. We had fun.*

Ms. Laskowski *shows* her children how to use invented spelling, how to stretch out the sounds, how to make best guesses, how their version compares to the standard version of written language. Like baby shampoo, Ms. Laskowski's method works well—*and without tears.*

Ms. Hamilton, also a first-grade teacher, reads a lot of books to her children and encourages them to write about what they hear. One day she read *In a Dark, Dark, Room and Other Scary Stories* by Alvin Schwartz to her class and then encouraged them to write about it. Anthony wrote the story shown in Figure 5.5. Although

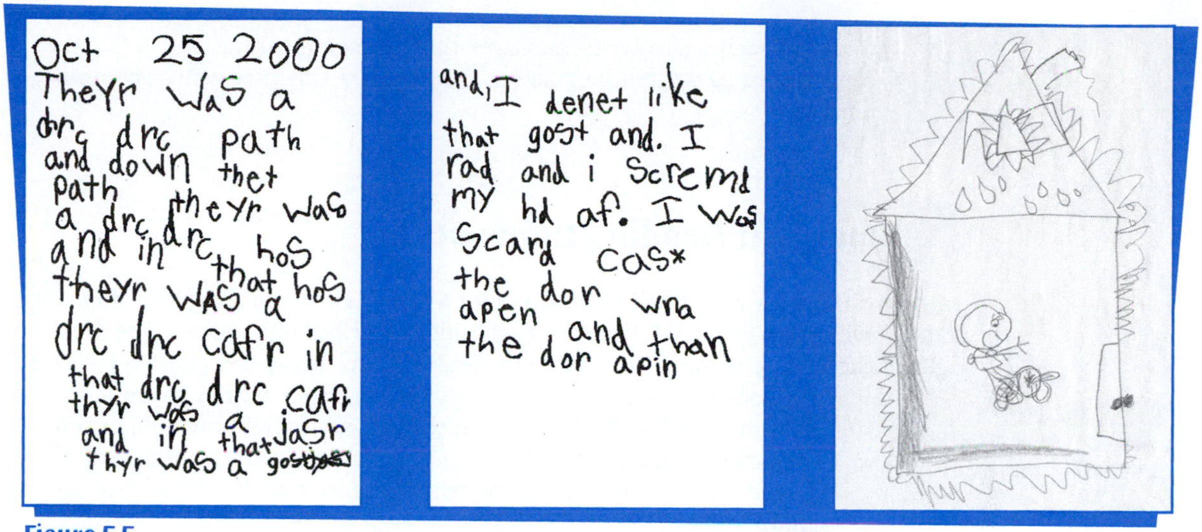

**Figure 5.5**

The Invented Spelling Stage

most of the words he wrote can be read easily, the following translation may be helpful:

There was a
dark dark path
and down that
path there was
a dark dark house.
And in that house there was a
dark dark coffin. In
that dark dark coffin
there was a jar
and in that jar
there was a ghost.

And I didn't like
that ghost and I
ranned and I screamed
my head off. I was
scared cause the door wouldn't
open and then the door closed.

## Section Summary: Emergent Writing Concepts

1. Clay's principles describe how children come to understand the conventions of written language.
2. Three skills are needed to begin independent writing: writing the alphabet, phonemic awareness, and associating letters with sounds.
3. There are four emergent writing stages: first, children make scribbles on paper or walls and often believe these marks convey meaning; next, they express their experiences and creative interests through drawings, which may include features of printed language; later, children write strings of letters that they believe stand for words and messages; and finally, they use

invented spelling to write messages that convey meaning and learn the conventions of written language as they explore this new way of communicating.

# Emergent Reading Concepts

Give a child a toy and it will be amusing for a time. Give a child the gift of reading and it will never grow old, never be cast aside, never become useless. The greatest gift is the love of reading. It fulfills our need for adventure, our quest for knowledge, our hope for companionship. It costs little and returns much. This investment will prevail over any recession, no matter how mild or severe. The earlier reading is established as a habit and a passion, the greater the chance that it will remain so when children make the transition to adulthood.

> "You cannot teach a man anything. You can only help him discover it within himself."
> —Galileo

## Technology for Emergent Literacy

Connecting Technology to Teaching

Observe the placement of technology in an average classroom of emerging readers, and you may find one or two computers placed on the periphery of the room. You might also notice that they are not integrated into the curriculum for all students. Technology's potential is stifled in such circumstances. However, when used appropriately, technologies such as electronic books, multimedia applications, and even tape recorders can support emerging literacy.

Electronic books are interactive and thus highly supportive of young children's needs. As children manipulate the content, they experience all facets of literacy: reading, writing, listening, and speaking. Even if they can't read, children can follow along as the text is highlighted. This feature also helps emerging readers develop decoding skills since they are able to view the text while hearing it spoken. Comprehension is also supported through the use of images and sounds. Electronic books give immediate feedback and help children monitor their own performance.

Multimedia applications also support literacy instruction. In simple terms, multimedia refers to any combination of sound, motion video, still pictures, animation, Clip Art, and/or text whose purpose is to relay information. Presentation programs such as Kid Pix® and Microsoft PowerPoint® are two of the most commonly used programs.

These types of applications draw upon children's multiple intelligences by allowing them to write, draw, paint, input video and pictures, create animations, and record sound. Ease of use makes these applications accessible to the youngest of students. For example, children can compose an ABC book or make word-family slide shows using a digital camera and later share their work with the class.

Although the tape recorder rarely comes to mind when thinking about technology, it is not outdated. Allowing students to tape-record themselves as they read can support literacy instruction. For example, children can dictate stories and reread them later with the teacher after they have been transcribed. Technology experiences should be developmentally appropriate and should engage students in meaningful literacy activities that connect to real reading and writing activities.

Contributed by Lisa Kunkleman

Reading and writing are obverse processes. Readers are given the text, but they supply the sounds. Writers possess the sounds, but supply the text. Readers construct their own meaning and compare it with what they think the writer may have intended. The reader-writer relationship is powerful. It enables the literate person to track back and forth between the two roles. One moment you are the writer creating the text and investing it with meaning; the next, you are the reader constructing the text. Alternating the two ways of engaging text creates a more powerful reader and a more perceptive writer. Emergent readers are strengthened when they learn both processes simultaneously rather than sequentially. When simultaneous instruction in reading and writing is neglected, something of value is lost.

Some principles of emergent reading are the same or similar to principles of emergent writing. You would expect this, given the reading–writing relationship. However, principles for emergent reading are more controversial than those for emergent writing. *Let the debate begin: the most crucial principal is that one reads for meaning from the beginning.* Let there be no delay in attending to meaning while decoding (*phonics* is the word for this that is often heard in public debate) proceeds. Consider the following seven principles of emergent reading.

## The Construction of Meaning

Reading is about meaning and how it is achieved. Meaning must be emphasized from the beginning. Psychologists and reading theorists use the word *construction* to denote how meaning is acquired. Here is how this builder's metaphor fits with reading. Thinking takes place through organized thought structures in the brain called schemata. Our schemata (plural of *schema*) represent our prior knowledge. You might call schemata our storehouse of world knowledge. Some storehouses are more robust than others, some more mature than others.

Schemata are instrumental in enabling readers to comprehend, to construct meaning. These bundles of gray matter organize what we know. They are modified each time new information lodges on a schema's sticky little pads. Comprehension, according to this theory, is a transaction between reader, text, and context. Meaning is enriched or diminished by the quality of a reader's schemata, the acuteness of the reader's reasoning, and the reader's use of prior knowledge. Theoretically, each successful comprehension experience extends the robustness and maturity of the schemata one possesses, though, in reality, it may not turn out that way.

## Phonemic and Phonological Awareness

Phonemic awareness and phonological awareness are related. Phonemic awareness is the ability to distinguish one speech sound from another within spoken words. A phoneme is the minimal sound unit of speech. There are 44 phonemes in English. Phonological awareness has a larger province; it describes three constituent sounds in words: (1) syllables, (2) onsets and rimes, and (3) phonemes. For example: *cat* has a syllable, /cat/; *cat* has an onset, /k/, and a rime, /at/; *cat* has three phonemes, /k/, /a/, and /t/.

Some children develop phonemic and phonological awareness as a result of emergent literacy experiences prior to school; others learn it in kindergarten and first grade; alas, some never learn it. While phonological awareness is not needed for children to learn to talk, it is a prerequisite for learning to read and write. Once children can distinguish one constituent sound from another within words, they can begin to associate speech sounds with a letter or letters. The two best ways to develop phonemic awareness are invented spelling and reading literature aloud. Cramer (1985) found that invented spelling aids the development of phonological awareness. As emergent writers, children usually spell only one or two sounds within a word, most often the first and last consonant sounds. Consonants are easier to spell than vowels because their letter–sound correspondences are more regular. Ayres (1993) found that reading literature aloud has a positive influence on the development of phonological awareness; in fact, literature with rhyme and alliteration is especially powerful in developing phonological awareness. Adams (1990), Yopp (1992), and Pressley (1998) claim that phonological awareness is not only a predictor of reading success but a prerequisite for it.

## Word Recognition

The goal of reading is meaning; the entrance fee is decoding, or *phonics,* as it is referred to in popular usage. Theoretically, there should be no argument about the necessity of word recognition. Nevertheless, there is, unfortunately, characterized by too much dogma and not enough reasoned discourse. Much of the disagreement about word recognition centers on methods of instruction rather than whether it should be taught. Few, if any, professionals in the field of literacy think word recognition is unnecessary. Disagreements almost exclusively concern how to teach it.

Word recognition refers to the skills needed to pronounce words. It is broader than the term *phonics,* which is often incorrectly used to describe the whole process of word recognition. There are four components to word recognition, and phonics is one of them.

1. *Contextual analysis.* This refers to using surrounding language as clues to the meaning or pronunciation of an unknown word.
2. *Phonetic or phonic analysis.* This involves associating speech sounds with letters and blending the sounds into syllables or words.
3. *Structural analysis.* This refers to identifying meaningful *chunks,* or units, within a word to aid in determining pronunciation or meaning; these units include roots, affixes, inflected and derived endings, compounds, and syllables.
4. *Sight words.* These words are recalled from memory and known instantly at sight; they do not require further analysis to determine their pronunciation.

The four word-recognition skills are normally used in combination to aid pronunciation or meaning. Word recognition and comprehension typically occur together; when they do not, word recognition may be inaccurate or some aspect of comprehension may go awry.

Emergent readers need word recognition skills. A goal of reading instruction is to simultaneously expand sight vocabulary and word meaning vocabulary. Effective word recognition can provide the approximate pronunciation of a word, but without a counterpart word in one's oral language lexicon, the reader is stranded without a meaning and remains uncertain of the word's pronunciation. This is especially true of emergent readers, but a mature adult reader could easily encounter the same problem reading an advanced medical textbook. Without corresponding oral language, successful pronunciation of an unknown word often ranges from difficult to impossible. Guidelines for teaching word recognition are suggested in Table 5.2.

**Table 5.2**

**Word Recognition Guidelines**

1. Meaning is the principal goal of reading; word recognition is the decryption system that breaks the code.
2. Phonemic and phonological awareness is prerequisite to more advanced word-recognition skills.
3. Teach strategies for sequential application of word recognition skills.
4. The components of word recognition are integrated, not independent.
5. Teach only those word recognition rules that have a high degree of utility.
6. Tie word recognition instruction to meaningful reading experiences.
7. Word recognition skills are reinforced through writing.
8. Word recognition instruction should proceed from whole to part, known to unknown.

*Teaching Tip*

## Language: Oral and Written

A mother told Hughes Mearns about something her son had said. Mearns thought the boy's words remarkable. He wanted Mother to appreciate just how special her son's words were. So he said to her, "It is poetry." Then Mearns cast the words into free verse lines and read them to her. Mother was surprised and pleased but still protested, "Poetry! But it doesn't rhyme." Mearns reminded her that the Psalms do not rhyme either and explained that rhyme is not a necessary adornment to poetry. Poetry existed in all its magnificence long before rhyme was invented, he explained. The words the boy said before going to bed went like this: "Do you know what the stars are, Mother? They're the lights God puts out so I won't be afraid of the dark." Mearns cast the words into four lines, like this:

> Do you know what the stars are, Mother?
> They're the lights God puts out
> So I won't be afraid
> Of the dark. (Mearns, 1929, p. 77)

Children—especially young children—often speak the language of literature. They use language magnificently, often poetically. They shape, construct, and reconstruct language to satisfy their needs, control their behavior, control others, tell their personal stories, discover insights, imagine possibilities, and communicate with the world—all in a few short years (Halliday, 1973).

Fortunate, indeed, are the children who are surrounded by oral and written language. It is their passport into literacy, a priceless legacy bequeathed by parents and peers that gives children an advantage in learning to read and write. I witnessed the passing on of the gift of language just yesterday as I walked toward my car in the parking lot. A young mother just ahead of me was reciting a poem to the little boy she held in her arms. He couldn't have been much more than a year old. Curious, I asked her what poem she was reciting: "Oh, it's not a poem. It's a book I've read to him so many times, I know it by heart."

What a lucky little guy. How delighted he appeared as he listened to his mother recite this now-familiar book—minus the book. Surround children with rich oral language; apprise them of the environmental print that exists around them. Help them understand the connection between oral and written language. Plant the seeds of language in the Spring of life; it will yield a child ready for all seasons.

## Dictated Stories

Dictated stories, or language experience stories, are effective for struggling readers as well as children progressing rapidly. Children who are unable to read prepared text are able to read dictated stories, often flawlessly, when systematic rereading procedures are followed. Once children discover they can read their own texts easily and fluently, they are motivated to learn. The idea is to make reading easy and successful and to follow up dictated stories with word recognition activities. Dictated stories are different from text written by someone else because they reflect children's own words and experiences. This permits children to recognize words they would otherwise be unable to decode or understand. Children are rarely unable to read their own dictated stories, which makes them an excellent starting point for advancing reading and writing skills.

> "Storytelling offers children a unique and thoroughly involving means to further explore the language and themes of literature, as well as the connections between literature and real-life experiences."
> —L. M. McGee and D. J. Richgels, *Literacy's Beginnings: Supporting Young Readers and Writers,* 1996.

These language experience stories begin with the teacher recording the account, reading it, and rereading it with the child; finally, the child reads the stories independently. (A complete account of language experience is recorded in Chapter 1.) Later, words are drawn from the stories to create word banks for teaching word recognition. Language experience stories may be taken from individual children or in small groups. Dictation is gradually phased out as children become fluent readers. Those who are progressing more slowly continue until they, too, can read fluently.

## Reading Aloud

What pleasures and treasures reading aloud bequeaths to children. The residue may be simultaneously delightful and scary. For instance, the poet E. E. Cummings recalled the aftermath of listening to *Treasure Island* read aloud: "the blind pirate Pew followed me upstairs for weeks; while for months, if not years, one-legged John Silver stood just behind me as my trembling fingers fumbled the electric light chain." But don't imagine for a moment that this deterred Cummings from wanting to hear more. Oh no! More was always welcomed. Reading aloud bequeaths to children man-eating tigers, adventures under the sea, nights in the wilderness sleeping in a tepee—imaginations on fire, lit by the language of literature.

> "Reading out loud to children helps them develop a love for good literature, motivation to pursue reading on their own, and familiarity with a variety of genres."
> —L. Lipton and D. Hubble, *More Than 50 Ways to Learner-Centered Literacy,* 1997.

Reading aloud has its more mundane, though crucial, benefits as well. It anchors the sounds of language in children's ears, which is essential to emergent reading and writing (see Chapter 6 for more details).

## Reading Fluency

Readers demonstrate fluency when they read smoothly and easily with little or no hesitation in identifying words or comprehending text. Readers who process print smoothly have acquired *automaticity*. Automaticity enables readers to direct attention to comprehension rather than decoding. A goal of reading is to develop a substantial sight vocabulary so that there is less need to devote attention to figuring out the pronunciation of words. The more words readers know automatically, the less often reading is interrupted to identify words.

Reading fluency is relative to a reader's level of instruction and background knowledge. A first-grader may read fluently in a first-grade text, but not in a second- or third-grade text. A mature adult reader may read complex novels fluently, but a specialist medical textbook might interrupt fluency, since the pronunciation and meaning of its words may be unfamiliar.

*Buddy reading gives children the chance to read together and share their thoughts about and reactions to what they read.*

Fluent readers spontaneously self-correct; nonfluent readers are far less likely to self-correct. To improve fluency follow these suggestions: (1) place children at their appropriate instructional level, (2) address any word recognition difficulties children may have, (3) build sight vocabulary through independent reading, frequent writing, and other meaningful activities such as reading familiar text, repeated readings, choral reading, and experience stories.

Reader's Theater "helps students' reading more if they don't memorize lines, but rather, read, and reread their parts until they can read them fluently."

—P. Cunningham and R. Allington, *Classrooms That Work*, 1999.

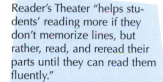

## Section Summary: Emergent Reading Concepts

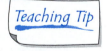

Teaching Tip

1. Schemata, thought structures representing prior knowledge, are instrumental in constructing meaning.
2. Phonemic and phonological awareness are prerequisite for learning to read.
3. Word recognition instruction is crucial, as it gives readers access to meaning.
4. Emergent reading is facilitated by access to rich oral and written language.
5. Dictated stories can ease children into successful early reading.

6. Reading aloud is the single most beneficial influence on emergent literacy.

7. Fluent reading enables readers to devote more attention to comprehension.

## Assessment of Emergent Reading and Writing

Assessment must be aligned with instruction. When we assess what children know, our purposes and procedures must be consistent with what we have taught or intend to teach. Assessment must have instructional value; without it, the effort is wasted. Instructional value is strengthened by teacher observations and informal measures made as children go about meaningful daily classroom reading and writing tasks. Standardized tests have their uses, but they cannot inform teachers about the instruction or strategies that Jake or Myrna needs here, in this classroom, at this teachable moment. That information can be made only by knowledgeable teachers who understand the reading and writing processes, who are ready and able to respond to what they see happening as the daily classroom routine progresses.

The assessment procedures described here focus on informal ways in which teachers can inform themselves about the needs of the young Jakes and Myrnas who populate their classrooms.

### Assessing Print Awareness

Exposure to environmental print helps children understand the form and function of letters and words. Print awareness comes about through exposure to print, but its quality is a function of how adults help children interact with print. Scout, the little girl in *To Kill a Mockingbird,* never watched a TV show, and she saw less environmental print than today's children. But Scout had sat on her daddy's lap, watching and listening to him read *The Mobile Register.* Scout's exposure to print at home got her into trouble. Miss Caroline, Scout's teacher, scolded her: "Now you tell your father not to teach you anymore. It's best to begin reading with a fresh mind. You tell him I'll take over from here and try to undo the damage." Some damage! Would that every child could be so damaged.

> "You don't have to burn books to destroy a culture. Just get people to stop reading them."
> —Ray Bradbury,
> science fiction author

Today's children are surrounded with print. This environmental fact can be an ally in leading children to literacy. You can construct an assessment tool to help you estimate children's print awareness. Clip and paste pieces of print and their logos (soft drink, soup, and fast-food labels) onto posterboard. Assemble 10 or 12 such pages in a three-ring binder so that the pages can be shown one at a time. Then assess children's print awareness through informal questions and probes as you expose them to the pages. For example, show a child a picture of the McDonald's logo. Ask, "Can you tell me what this says?" A child may answer with the word *restaurant* or *hamburger* or *McDonald's.* If a child points to the print rather than to the arches, you know the child has distinguished the print from the background. Some children will not distinguish print from the logo itself. For example, if a child has pointed to the arches, ask, "Which part says McDonald's?" Or point to the first letter and ask, "What letter is this?" Continue probing in this fashion, seeking to learn what the child understands about the forms and functions of print.

Assessment of print awareness reveals which children have a rich, moderate, or weak understanding of print. A child who cannot distinguish the print from the logo requires more emergent literacy experiences than the child who can. The child who recognizes a few letters and no words requires different initial experiences than the child who has a stronger grasp of the forms and functions of print. The more you learn about a child's print awareness, the easier it becomes to decide what literacy tasks to emphasize in the early weeks and months of reading and writing instruction. Language experience stories are the best way to orient children to the forms and functions of print since recording the child's own language and experience makes reading as easy and successful as it can possibly be.

## Assessing Phonemic and Phonological Awareness

Phonemic awareness is the ability to distinguish one speech sound from another and to segment sounds within words. Phonological awareness describes three constituent sounds in words: (1) syllables, (2) onsets and rimes, and (3) phonemes. Most children learn to segment sounds on their own, but those who do not can learn to segment sounds within words. Once children can segment, or isolate, one sound from another within words, they can begin to associate speech sounds with the letters that represent them. This capability is prerequisite to learning to read and write (Adams, 1990; Ayres, 1993; Busink, 1997). Children acquire phonemic and phonological awareness by listening to books read aloud, songs, and nursery rhymes. Mother Goose, folktales, and Dr. Seuss books make excellent reading for this purpose. Phonemic and phonological awareness is also aided by wordplay activities and invented spelling (Cramer, 1970, 1998, 2001). The following are brief descriptions of useful phonemic awareness tests.

1. *Yopp-Singer Phonemic Segmentation Test.* The examiner says a word and instructs the child to break the word apart. For example, the examiner says *old,* and the child's task is to make the three sounds /o/ /l/ /d/ (Yopp, 1988).
2. *Bradley and Bryant Oddity Task.* The examiner instructs the child to listen to the beginning sound of each of four words, for example, *bag, nine, beach, bike.* The child's task is to identify which of the four has a different beginning sound. Bradley and Bryant also have constructed tests to assess awareness of beginning, middle, and ending phonemes (Bradley & Bryant, 1983).
3. *Supply Initial Consonant Test.* The examiner instructs the child to listen to two words. For example, "Say *cat.* Now say *at.* What sound do you hear in *cat* that is missing from *at?*" (Stanovich, Cunningham, & Cramer, 1984).

## Assessing Writing Vocabulary

Robinson (1973) found that writing in the first 18 months of learning to read was an indicator of literacy progress. Her early work influenced the design of Reading Recovery instruction (Clay, 2001). Clay suggests inventorying children's writing vocabularies as an indicator of how they are progressing in their understanding of literacy concepts. This procedure is useful for reading and writing assessment. Writing is important in learning to read, since reading and writing are reciprocal activities. Writing should not follow reading; it should not precede reading; it should be taught side by side with reading. Writing is sometimes confused with handwriting, and it should not be. The term *writing* should be reserved for composition, and the term *handwriting* used to describe the forming of the script itself. Of course, children need to form the letters of the alphabet—and the earlier, the better.

The writing vocabulary inventory is simple to administer. Just say to children, "I want you to write as many words as you can in 10 minutes. I'll tell you when to stop." Be sure children are in a setting where they will not be tempted to copy words from a source, such as chalkboards and the signage available in most classrooms. Invented spelling of words is necessary and acceptable in this inventory procedure.

## Assessing Reading Miscues: Marie Clay's Running Record

Beginning readers must learn to attend to the visual and auditory features of words. Some children learn the features of written language—letters, sounds, spaces, sequence—before going to school. Such children may have listened to stories while sitting on Mom's or Dad's lap. Some children have had extensive exposure to environmental print along with crucial help from adults. Some children have not had much help in understanding the form and functions of print. These children may have missed some or all of the foundational knowledge about written language that is needed to read. Clay (2001) developed Reading Recovery for just such children. This program provides one-on-one tutoring for first-grade children who test in the bottom 20% of their classes. Reading Recovery's objective is to bring these children up to the average performance level of their classmates. Instruction generally continues until this objective is achieved.

Clay (2000) developed an assessment procedure for recording reading miscues to facilitate instruction. She called the procedure a running record. Running records of oral miscues help teachers understand what children know or do not know about printed words and the messages they convey and whether a text is too hard, too easy, or just right; this latter function of running records informs level decisions. Running record procedures are similar to those used for recording miscues during the oral reading of an informal reading inventory passage.

Clay (2000) believes that running records enable teachers to understand whether children are reading for meaning. They are also an excellent procedure for assessing decoding skills. Running records, or their equivalent, are a necessary but insufficient means of assessing comprehension. The focus on decoding text is necessary, but additional assessment is needed to adequately assess comprehension. That is why informal reading inventories are an essential adjunct to running records. Clay (2000) seems to disagree. She cites three reasons why it is not necessary to assess comprehension directly:

1. Because different teachers ask different questions, the assessment is weakened.
2. The answers to questions depend more upon the difficulty of the questions asked than on the child's reading.

3. Comprehension depends on the difficulty level of the text. It makes no sense to assess comprehension on a hard text, nor on an easy text. If the text level is instructional, then that tells the teacher to teach for understanding.

Clay's claims seem to assume that if children can decode text at an instructional level, comprehension at that level is assured. But this is not necessarily so. There are children who decode text fluently at levels beyond their capacity to comprehend that text. Furthermore, comprehension assessment must be addressed broadly so that explicit, implicit, and vocabulary assessment is included in the informal reading inventory. Running records alone cannot accomplish this kind of assessment. Without a broad measure of comprehension to accompany assessment of miscues, teachers cannot know which specific comprehension skills need attention. If assessment of comprehension strengths and needs is lacking, instruction is likely to be imprecise at best or neglected at worst.

The three reasons Clay cites as to why it is not necessary to assess comprehension are debatable. First, Clay is correct in asserting that different teachers asking different questions can yield different results. But any assessment instrument or procedure, including running records, can yield different results when administered by different teachers. Obviously, care must be taken. But teachers make informal comprehension assessments every time they teach a comprehension lesson. They can be trusted to make sensible judgments about comprehension. An abundance of help is available, including commercially prepared informal reading inventories: Qualitative Reading Inventory (2001); Reading Inventory for the Classroom (2001); Bader Reading and Language Inventory (2002); Classroom Reading Inventory (2001); Classroom Assessment of Reading Processes (2000); and Basic Reading Inventory (2001).

Second, Clay says that the answers to questions depend more on the difficulty of the questions than on the child's reading comprehension—another valid point. It is possible to ask difficult, even unanswerable, questions about any text. But the answer to this problem is to ask sensible, text-based questions that establish a balance among the major components of comprehension. This is not an exceedingly difficult task. Many teachers do this routinely; others can learn to do it.

Third, Clay's statement that it "makes no sense to assess comprehension on a hard text, nor on an easy text" ignores the importance of assessing comprehension across three levels: independent (easy), instructional (challenging), and frustration (hard). Knowing a child's independent level enables teachers to provide guidance for independent reading; knowing the highest levels at which children are instructional (many children have more than one instructional level) provides guidance for level decisions and daily instruction; knowing children's frustration level enables teachers to recognize when reading materials are too difficult and must be avoided. So, there is good reason to assess comprehension broadly across all three levels—independent, instructional, and frustration.

It is not my intention to diminish the value of running records, which are an excellent observational tool. But like any other assessment procedure or instrument, they are not useful for all seasons and all reasons. Analyzing miscues provides valuable insight about reading knowledge. Thoughtfully analyzed, running records can inform teaching and give insight about which print concepts a child has

## Standing on the Shoulders of Giants
## Historical Contributions to Literacy
### Marie Clay

She founded a literacy organization that has pro-vided tutorial help for more than a million first-grade American children, to say nothing of perhaps as many children in other countries. She was the first non-American president of the International Reading Association and the first woman professor at the University of Auckland. She is the founder and is the guiding light of Reading Recovery. Her name, of course, is Marie Clay.

Marie Clay was born in Wellington, New Zealand, in 1926. She earned her bachelor's and master's degrees from the University of New Zealand and received a Fulbright scholarship to study developmental child psychology at the University of Minnesota. She became the first woman professor at the University of Auckland in 1975. She has received honors throughout the English-speaking world for her work in Reading Recovery.

Some people may not realize that when Reading Recovery was still a concept in Marie Clay's fertile mind, she had already written a marvelous book about the writing of young children, called *What Did I Write?* She has also written thoughtfully on children's oral language development. But Marie Clay will forever be recognized for her extraordinary contribution to emergent reading development and the program she founded, called Reading Recovery.

As early as 1963, Clay had concluded that reading was going astray for many young children. She believed that something needed to be done to change this bleak picture. Starting in 1976, Clay worked with Barbara Watson and Sara Robinson to develop an intervention that would become known as Reading Recovery. It became a national education program in New Zealand in 1983. It now operates throughout the English-speaking world and is making a transition to Spanish- and French-speaking countries as well (Gaffney & Askew, 1999).

Marie Clay has written many books, articles, and chapters on a broad array of literacy topics. She has lectured throughout the world and has received many honors, including the title conferred by Queen Elizabeth II in recognition of her extraordinary service to the literacy profession: Dame Marie Clay.

learned or failed to learn. It is a mistake to think that time spent observing and analyzing reading behavior steals time from teaching. Quite the opposite. Observation makes teaching more efficient since it identifies the direction instruction ought to take.

Clay's notation system for recording miscues is precise and complex. For greater detail, I recommend Clay's book *Running Records for Classroom Teachers* (2001), a handbook on why and how miscues are recorded. Suggestions are made for scoring and using running records as an instructional tool. It is an excellent book for teachers interested in using running records in daily classroom situations.

## Section Summary: Assessment of Emergent Reading and Writing

1. Print awareness is a function of exposure to print and the qualitative nature of that exposure. Informal measures of print awareness can be easily constructed.

2. Phonemic and phonological awareness can be measured formally with a variety of available tests, including informal teacher-made measures.

3. Writing vocabulary can be assessed by asking children to write as many words as they can in a given period of time, usually 10 minutes.

4. Running records assess the qualitative nature of children's reading miscues and give insights into children's understanding of basic print concepts.

## Six Conclusions About Emergent Literacy

Teale and Sulzby (1986) have researched and written about emergent literacy more than any other professionals in the field. Their work has contributed substantially to what is known about the development of reading and writing during the early childhood years. They drew six conclusions regarding literacy development in early childhood.

1. Literacy development begins long before children start formal instruction. Children use legitimate reading and writing behaviors in the informal settings of home and community. The search for skills that predict subsequent behavior has been misguided because the onset of literacy has been misconceived.

2. Literacy development is the appropriate way to describe what was once called reading readiness: The child develops as a *writer–reader*. The notion of reading preceding writing, or vice versa, is a misconception. Listening, speaking, reading, and writing abilities (as aspects of language—both oral and written) develop concurrently and interrelatedly, rather than sequentially.

*Ariel is making words with magnetic letters and keeping track of her work in a notebook.*

3. Literacy develops in real-life settings for real-life activities in order to "get things done." Therefore, the functions of literacy are as integral a part of learning about writing and reading during early childhood as are the forms of literacy.

4. Children are doing critical cognitive work in literacy development during the years from birth to 6.

5. Children learn written language through active engagement with their world. They interact socially with adults in writing and reading situations; they explore print on their own, and they profit from modeling of literacy by significant adults, particularly their parents.

6. Although children's learning about literacy can be described in terms of generalized stages, children can pass through these stages in a variety of ways and at different ages. Any attempts to "scope and sequence" instruction should take this developmental variation into account. (Teale & Sulzby, 1986, p. xviii)

These conclusions are sound, though there is room for debate concerning the second half of the first one—that the search for predictors of reading has been misguided and misconceived. It is instead appropriate and has yielded useful information about emergent literacy.

## Practical Teaching Ideas and Activities

*Teaching Tip*

**1.** *Provide an environment that nurtures early literacy development.* The environment you establish plays a significant role in fostering young children's awareness of the purpose for reading and writing in their everyday lives. Nurture children's curiosity and their extraordinary ability to make sense of the world around them. Accept all approximations. Foster collaboration and a sense of community. Value children's language. A meaning-centered curriculum revolves around authentic literacy experiences.

**2.** *Develop phonemic and phonological awareness daily.* Many young children come to school without much exposure to or knowledge of children's rhymes, finger-plays or songs. Since these are an important foundation for the development of phonological awareness, it is important to include them on a daily basis. If you are uncomfortable as a singer yourself, you can buy wonderful tapes and CDs of children's songs and finger-plays. Throughout the day include these wordplay activities. Consider writing some favorites on chart paper to be used for shared reading. Also, many songs and finger-plays are great as a framework for creating your own verses or innovations, thus offering additional opportunities for shared writing.

**3.** *Surround children with environmental print.* Environmental print is the first context in which young children experience "reading." Children make associations and are able to point out and read words and labels on food containers, signs, stores, and restaurants. Through experiences with print young children learn that a group of letters makes up a word that can be read and provide information. Provide a rich array of environmental print in the classroom such as labels on objects in the classroom and environmental logos such as McDonald's arches and familiar food items.

**4.** *Use predictable and patterned books.* Predictable and patterned books are valuable for emergent readers because the predictability allows young children to "behave like a reader" from their very first encounters with printed materials. Participation is encouraged when children are able to predict what comes next. Motivation and self-concept are enhanced because predictable, repetitive language patterns make them easy to read as well. High-quality predictable texts encourage a constructive use based on a child's oral language, knowledge of the world, or familiarity with story structure.

**5.** *Arrange shared reading experiences.* In this approach, originated by Don Holdaway, big books are used for shared reading and form an essential part of the early literacy framework. These oversized books have print large enough for the entire group to see. The large print and pictures provide a valuable and enjoyable opportunity for children to actively engage in the pleasurable experience of the story, the meaning of the text, and the details of the print as the group reads the text together. Texts should be selected carefully. Emergent readers need stories with strong story lines, rich language, repetitive patterns and rhymes, and high-quality illustrations. A shared reading experience usually involves rereading familiar texts for enjoyment, modeling, and direct instruction in reading skills and strategies, followed by introduction of a new text. Big books can be reread by the teacher and children several times over the course of the year. In each rereading, the children should gain increased control over the reading.

**6.** *Integrate dramatic play and retellings.* After reading a folk or fairy tale several times, generate ideas with the students as to what materials they need to create the setting and costumes. Once these are gathered, the whole group can act out the story several times. After this group retelling, create the setting in the dramatic play area, and place costumes and props there for students to use during center time.

See the Blue Pages at the back of the book and on the Companion Website for additional activities.

## Reflection and Summary

### Reflection

Five-year-olds subject language to rigorous demands. If there is a word for it, there must be a "real" example. That's their logic. Literacy professionals sometimes fall into the same trap—naming concepts that may not have an independently verifiable existence in the real world.

Children are endowed with an extraordinary capacity for language learning. That they do learn it, twist it, turn it, demand it adhere to their logic is testimony to their creative genius. True north, for me, lies in the creative minds of young children. They activate my interior dowsing rod. Respect for children and their language is well deserved. Every teacher worthy of the name surely recognizes this. Language must be nurtured; language must be appreciated. It is, after all, the material from which children create their own literacy with the help of thoughtful parents and teachers.

## Summary

- Research supports the idea that reading strengthens writing and writing strengthens reading. They should be taught, learned, and understood as complementary literacy processes.
- Prospects for literacy are enhanced in homes where there is a loving connection and a shared literacy culture.
- Clay's principles of emergent writing describe its nature and provide clues for nurturing it. There are three prerequisites for emergent writing: writing the alphabet, phonemic and phonological awareness, and associating letters with sounds. The four stages of emergent writing are scribbling, drawing, letter strings, and invented spelling.
- Seven concepts related to emergent reading are the construction of meaning, phonemic and phonological awareness, word recognition, rich oral and written language experiences, dictated stories, reading aloud, and reading fluency.
- Ways to assess emergent literacy include assessment of print awareness, phonemic and phonological awareness, writing vocabulary, and running record miscue analysis procedures.
- Teale and Sulzby have suggested six conclusions about emergent literacy.

## ◄ Questions to Challenge Your Thinking

1. Do you think it is a good idea to encourage children to read and write prior to going to school? Why?
2. How would you define the concept of emerging literacy?
3. What advice would you give parents who want to foster their children's literacy?
4. Do you agree or disagree that invented spelling improves children's prospects for literacy? Explain.
5. Why might it be useful to provide toddlers with crayons and paper?
6. What distinction can be made between phonemic and phonological awareness?
7. What ideas can you propose for assessing emerging literacy?
8. Teale and Sulzby maintain that literacy development begins long before children start formal instruction. Do you agree or disagree? Why?
9. Choose one idea from this chapter with which you agree or disagree. Defend your view of that idea.
10. What have you learned that you didn't know before you read this chapter?

## ◄ A Case Study

Read the following true case study, and then discuss the following questions with your classmates or colleagues.

Surhin is in kindergarten. His teacher has encouraged the children to write. Surhin has made moderate progress over the 6 months he has been in

Mrs. Mongo's class. At the beginning of the year, he showed little or no phonemic awareness, could not write the letters of the alphabet, and could not connect letters with sounds. Mrs. Mongo read predictable books and folktales, encouraged drawing and writing, and played word games with the children. She taught her children the alphabet. Those who could not write drew pictures instead. Mrs. Mongo wrote whatever words the children wanted written on their drawings. She encouraged invented spelling for those who could write. Surhin's first invented spelling story is shown in Figure 5.6.

Study Surhin's story and then discuss the following questions with your classmates.

1. Can you read Surhin's story? What does it say?
2. What is Surhin's stage of writing development?
3. Why might Surhin have left out the vowel letters in the words *little* and *bird*?
4. Given that Surhin can write, do you think he can also read? Explain.
5. What would you say to Surhin about his writing?

**Figure 5.6**

**Surhin's First Story in Invented Spelling**

## Revisit the Anticipation Guide

Return to the Anticipation Guide in the chapter opener, and review your original responses to the questions. Complete the guide again, and then consider these questions.

1. Did you change your mind about any items? Why?
2. Which chapter ideas did you find most useful? least useful? Why?
3. Why would a literate home make learning to read and write easier?

4. Could an adult just learning to read show signs of emergent literacy? Explain.
5. Can invented spelling help a 5-year-old learn to read? Explain.
6. Give an example of focusing on meaning when talking to a child.
7. Do you think adults make reading miscues similar to the ones children make? Why or why not?
8. What might be a good way to help a preschooler learn the alphabet?

## VideoWorkshop Extra!

If your instructor ordered a package including VideoWorkshop, go to Chapter 5 of the Companion Website (www.ablongman.com/cramer1e) and click on the VideoWorkshop button. Follow the instructions for viewing the appropriate video clip and completing the accompanying exercise. Watch the Companion Website for access to a new interactive teaching portal, My Lab School, currently under construction.

### A Philosophy of Literature and Literacy

**W**hat would I take with me if I were condemned to live alone for the next ten years? Books! Loneliness would be a problem, but books can dispel loneliness. Mental stimulation would be a problem, but books contain the distilled knowledge and wisdom of the ages. No one to talk to would be a problem, but I could have an imaginary conversation with John Adams or get into an argument with John Dewey. Reading gives vicarious experience—living life mentally rather than physically. Some say reading is an escape from real life. If so, give me the vicarious life. Often it's better than real life. Books are not a way to escape life but a means of participating more fully in it. Through reading, I escape from my air-conditioned car into the heat of dust bowl America. Vicariously, I am driving with Joad and his family from Oklahoma to California in a rattletrap truck. Through reading I escape from my privileged life into one I have not actually lived.

# 6 Literature and Literacy

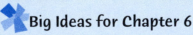

## Big Ideas for Chapter 6

1. Literature humanizes and promotes intellectual and emotional insight.
2. Children's literature is defined as literature intended for children, though some books not originally intended for children have become classics.
3. Literary elements include character, setting, point of view, plot, theme, and style.
4. Literature genres include picture books, traditional literature, poetry, realistic fiction, historical fiction, fantasy/science fiction, informational books, and biography.
5. Children can respond to literature through writing, reader's theater, and shared books, among other procedures.
6. School and classroom libraries are crucial to an effective literature-based literacy program.
7. Reading aloud is one of the best ways to hook children on books. It also stimulates language growth and develops an appreciation for literature.
8. Storytelling is an ancient art form, requiring an understanding of drama to be most effective. Its purpose is to give pleasure, but it also offers academic benefits.

## Anticipation Guide

*Consider the following statements, and determine whether you agree or disagree with each. Save your answers, and revisit this guide at the end of this chapter.*

1.  Reading series books, such as Nancy Drew stories, can be harmful.          agree    disagree
2.  "Melting pot" is a good metaphor to describe a diverse society.            agree    disagree
3.  Plot is more important to children than character.                         agree    disagree
4.  Point of view refers to where a story takes place.                         agree    disagree
5.  Picture books seldom include text with pictures.                           agree    disagree
6.  Traditional literature has its roots in an oral tradition.                 agree    disagree
7.  A work of fiction cannot convey truth.                                     agree    disagree
8.  A nonfiction book conveys true information.                                agree    disagree
9.  Response to literature is best done through writing.                       agree    disagree
10. Reading aloud is a waste of valuable instructional time.                   agree    disagree

> We read to find out more about what it is like to be a human being, not to be told how to be one.
>
> —*Penelope Lively*

## A Literacy Story

I have breakfast every morning in a Greek restaurant. One morning the man in an adjoining booth, pointing to his paper, asked, "What's this word?" I stopped to peruse the headline in which the offending word appeared. So began John's journey to literacy.

Over the course of many breakfasts, John told me his story. He had worked for his father, a contractor. He drilled wells, laid bricks, finished cement, wired houses, installed plumbing. Then his father died, and with him went the contractor's license. John couldn't read, so he couldn't pass the written exam required to get his own license. Life got more and more difficult. He got bilked out of his inheritance. He couldn't spell well enough to write his own checks. Merchants and relatives took advantage of John's illiteracy.

I began tutoring John every morning at breakfast. After several weeks John asked the big question, "I'm 50 years old. Is it too late to become a good reader?" Fortune smiled. I had just read, "It's a Beautiful Life," the story of a man who learned to read at age 98. I said to John, "You're only half the age of a man who learned to read at age 98." Later, I gave this book to John to read. He's finished it now, though he struggled some in the beginning.

I've arranged for John to have a regular tutor in addition to the breakfast sessions. One morning John said, "Yesterday, for the first time in my life, I wrote my own checks." I gave him a new book, *A Tree Grows in Brooklyn*. I worried that it might be too challenging, and he did struggle for a short while. Every morning he tells me something about Frances, the main character. Recently he said, "You know, Ron, at first I had a hard time with both books. But after a while, I found I could read almost every word I came across." Two books can be a challenging library for a man on his way to becoming literate. A year has passed since I first met John. He's studying to take the contractor's licensing test. His two-book library has expanded to many books, including books he reads to his grandchildren. This delights him. He's determined to "become a good reader." I'm certain he's going to do just that.

## A MATTER OF STANDARDS

### A Variety of Literary Texts

**Standard 2:** Students read a wide range of literature from many periods in many genres to build an understanding of the many dimensions (e.g., philosophical, ethical, aesthetic) of human experience.

Standard 2 focuses on literary texts that represent human culture across time and place. Literature is not only the foundation of literacy but also the foundation of ethical, aesthetic, and philosophical thought. A literature-based curriculum provides students with the richest possible medium for gaining an understanding of themselves and the world. Literature provides models for speaking and writing and the materials through which critical and creative thought is developed. Literature extends knowledge, promotes intellectual and emotional insight, and provides the humanizing themes that bind us together as a nation and global community. Literature opens the doors to lifelong literacy, offers escape from life's pressures and problems, and invites the reader into its pleasures and bounties.

Expose children to literary texts that relate to their own experiences as well as texts that contrast with their experiences and perspectives. Many genres are needed to provide a wide spectrum of possible worlds, both imaginary and real. This chapter insists on the importance of exposing children to prose, poetry, essays, biography, classic and contemporary literature, fiction and nonfiction, and literature that honors diversity of culture, belief, and values. Exposing children to the richest treasure that human culture has to offer is a standard that teachers can embrace with enthusiasm.

STANDARD

---

Literature carries us away on the wings of imagination like no other medium. As a child, Charles Dickens read as if his life depended on it. He read *Tom Jones, Don Quixote, Robinson Crusoe,* and many others. He said of his books, "They kept alive my fancy, and my hope of something beyond that place and time." Literature is many things to many people. It's an escape from despair, the path to knowledge, the stretcher of mind and imagination.

The Roman author Pliny said, "I find my joy and solace in literature." Many of us do. Try to imagine a day without reading. You're unable to read a newspaper column, a billboard, a street sign. Imagine a life without books. Oh, we could get by for a while without the intense pleasure they bring. In fact, on some days much of what we read is limited, mundane, uninspiring, tasteless, tedious. But a few days without good books puts the avid reader into a funk. Television may satisfy briefly, but the avid reader must have books. The mind must have its furnishing of knowledge, its burnishing of imagination.

Mark Twain said, "The man who does not read has no advantage over the man who cannot read." Those of us who *can* read and *do* read owe a debt to those who taught us or inspired us to read. And who might that have been? For some, the debt is owed to our families. For others, the debt is owed to a good teacher who made a difference. And let us not forget ourselves. We may owe a debt to our own internal need to seek the light. Dickens had such a need. His childhood filled him with grief and humiliation. He worked in a factory at age 12. Yet for him some internal urgency created a thirst for knowledge. Dickens found his consolation in literature. Even in the years of his fame and fortune, he often wandered back in his imagination to his years as a young reader, when literature lit the flame that burnished the mind which produced *Great Expectations, Bleak House, A Tale of Two Cities,* and *A Christmas Carol.* Some young reader, even now, may be finding inspiration in one of Dickens's books. Maybe that youngster will write books to be read by future generations.

# The Value of Literature

Aleksandr Solzhenitsyn, the great Russian novelist, described literature as "the living memory of a nation." Literature allows us to imagine ourselves as different persons than we are, to live different lives than we lead, to abide in different places than where we are stationed. Literature allows us to live in palaces or hovels, cabins or penthouses, wigwams or igloos. Through literature we imagine ourselves bolder and braver, richer or poorer, kinder or meaner than we may be in daily life. These riches are possible because we read. The value of literature is the subtext—that subterranian river of thought that flows beneath the surface—of this chapter.

## Literature Extends Knowledge

Through the language of literature children extend their understanding of the world. Consider the expression *David and Goliath.* Suppose you are a Detroit Tigers fan, and you say to a friend, "Last night David laid low the mighty Goliath," meaing that the Tigers (David) had beaten the mighty New York Yankees (Goliath). Those with a broad knowledge of literature would know exactly what you mean. The term

> "Wherever there are beginners and experts, old and young, there is some kind of learning going on, and some sort of teaching. We are all pupils and we are all teachers."
> —Gilbert Highet, author and critic

refers to a story from the Bible in which David, a man of ordinary stature, challenges a giant of a man with a reputation for fierceness in battle, Goliath. As if those odds aren't bad enough, David uses a measly weapon, a slingshot, to fight his enemy. And he wins. Thus the names David and Goliath have become a metaphor for unexpected strength or cunning of the weak against the mighty—the average consumer winning a dispute with a huge corporation, an underdog battling a favored opponent. Literary knowledge facilitates a mental shortcut; those who understand the metaphor get the message clearly. Shared literary knowledge instantly connects past with present and present with future. Similarly, a lack of familiarity with literature handicaps communication in a literate society.

Experience with literature increases and enriches cultural knowledge. Successful reading requires knowledge beyond the text we are reading—knowledge that already abides in the structures of the mind. We comprehend best when we connect new information with what we already know; what we already know determines, to a large degree, which new information and ideas will be assimilated into our mental schema of the world. The more children share of a broad literary heritage, the more likely they will attain a high literacy quotient. In a multicultural world, it is essential for people of all cultures and ethnic groups to know one another's literature because it connects us, enables us to understand our shared values, and fosters appreciation of our differences.

## Literature Promotes Intellectual and Emotional Insight

Literature gives emotional and intellectual insight to those who seek it. Langer (1995) maintains that: "Through literature, students learn to explore possibilities and consider options for themselves and humankind. They come to find themselves, imagine others, value differences, and search for justice. They gain connectedness and seek vision." If Langer's vision for literature were possible, how enriched would be the lives and minds of children. Literature shapes and reshapes thought. It empowers children to create their own texts. It can ennoble the aspirations of readers, though this is not an inevitable outcome.

Literature connects us to the minds of the past and reveals the history of humanity. It can reveal that which is good, bad, and even ugly. I do not expect miracles from literature; no one should. But a life without access to literature impoverishes children's possibilities. No one can say for certain that a life without literature imperils the intellectual and emotional lives of individuals. But one can say with some assurance that a life imbued with literature stretches the mind, enriches the soul, and elevates the spirit.

> "Drawings capitalize on the narrative impulse in young children. They can be revised, just as writing is revised. They provide lavish details. Art can expand awareness and reach beyond the traditional intelligences of verbal reasoning, math, and logic."
> —M. A. Sidelnick and M. L. Svoboda, "The Bridge Between Drawing and Writing: Hannah's Story," 2000.

## Literature Humanizes

The French writer André Maurois said, "The art of reading is in great part that of acquiring a better understanding of life from one's encounter with it in a book." Literature is not a movie screen flashing someone else's pictures. It is book after book, sentence after sentence, rubbing our little gray cells together until they spark their own pictures. Literature depicts the human condition in all of its beauty and tawdriness. Who has ever drawn a more vivid picture of depression America than John Steinbeck (1939) in *The Grapes of Wrath*? Steinbeck takes us on a journey across America, discovering again and again the naked realities of America divided along lines of class and wealth. As Steinbeck describes the hardships of the farm families migrating across the country during the Great Depression, readers generate their own images of rattletrap cars, evening campfires, hungry children, haunted men and women pursuing their unrealized dream of settling in the promised land—California.

Literature explores life's humanizing themes: love, bravery, sacrifice, friendship, loyalty, family, hardship, courage, coping, kindness, compassion. Literature also explores life's dehumanizing themes: poverty, cruelty, hate, prejudice, evil, dishonesty, cruelty. Children are exposed to all of these when they read literature, and they take away their own lessons. Identifying with literature's themes, characters, and circumstances sparks children's interest: Cinderella dressing for the ball, Peter Rabbit hiding from Mr. McGregor, Charlotte talking to Wilbur, Jack scampering down the beanstalk with the giant's gold, The Velveteen Rabbit long-

> For ideas on including hypertext elements and multiple perspectives in early writing instruction, read "Reading and Writing 'hypertextually': Children's Literature, Technology, and Early Writing Instruction" by Dawnene Hammerberg, 2001, *Language Arts,* 78(3).

ing to become real, Harry Potter boarding the secret train for Hogwarts School of Witchcraft and Wizardry, Alice's surprise at the strange world at the bottom of a rabbit's hole.

It is possible to overestimate the degree to which literature can have a humanizing influence. Great literature, accumulated over the centuries, did not prevent the Holocaust, has not eliminated wars, has had little ameliorating influence on the hatred that one ethnic group or nation harbors for another. Nevertheless, on an individual and personal level, literature has and will continue to have a humanizing influence.

## Section Summary: The Value of Literature

1. One of the most important values of literature is that it passes on its riches and wisdom from generation to generation.
2. Literature extends cognitive, cultural, and linguistic knowledge, enabling people to communicate more effectively with one another.
3. Literature promotes emotional insight, enabling readers to consider options for themselves and humankind that they might not otherwise consider.
4. Literature has a humanizing influence, though it is possible to overestimate its power and breadth.

## Connecting with Literature

Connecting Technology to Teaching

Technology can help reluctant readers make meaningful connections to books and encourage their growth as readers. Internet activities and technology-supported projects can motivate and support all types of readers. For example, online book clubs can help students explore their ideas through literary conversations. Many authors maintain websites. Students can learn about their favorite authors and even communicate with them through e-mail. Students can create a classroom website or an online literary newspaper. They can gather information about authors and review their books. Because students can follow their interest by using hyperlinks, online books provide students with a refreshing change from the linear process of reading traditional text. Virtual field trips can enrich their background knowledge. Such activities support readers as they make connections to the lives of literary characters. Here's how I helped my students do this.

I had my students prepare a talk show project based on a book we had read. I divided the class into groups. Group 1 selected a host and determined the talk show format. Another group chose a book character who would be a guest on the show and coached the character in how to respond to questions. Yet another group wrote questions for the audience to ask the character.

Prior to the show we wrote invitations, using a publishing program. Later we sent e-mail reminders to invited guests. As guests arrived, they were given cards with questions to ask the talk show guest. We produced the show in the school auditorium, and it was a great success. This project helped my students make emotional and intellectual connections to the book we had read. It helped my reluctant readers as well as my good readers. Technology can support literature in interesting and rewarding ways.

Contributed by Lisa Kunkleman

# Qualities, Quirks, and Issues in Children's Literature

## A Definition of Children's Literature

Children's literature is usually defined as literature specifically *intended* for children. However, through historical circumstances, certain books not originally intended for children have become classics of children's literature. For example, *Robinson Crusoe* is considered a classic piece of children's literature today, but it was not originally intended for children. Furthermore, traditional literature derives from an oral tradition of storytelling that did not *necessarily* have children in mind—at least not exclusively. Still, many oral tales, once written, become classics of children's literature—"Cinderella" and "Jack and the Beanstalk" come to mind.

Some experts believe that only quality literature should be considered literature for children. I understand the good intentions behind this notion, but it raises two questions: What is quality literature? Who makes that decision? Taste and preference must be considered when defining what deserves the label of quality literature. This issue is considered briefly in this section.

A renaissance of children's literature in America has taken place over the past few decades. Though once children's literature existed in the backwater of the publishing industry, it now has a most vibrant life. The astonishingly successful Harry Potter series by J. K. Rowling outsells most adult best-selling books. Where once successful authors of children's books seldom appeared as major speakers at professional conferences, today they are among the most sought-after speakers. There are more than 50,000 English-language titles for children and this body of work grows by about 5,000 books per year (Temple et al., 2002).

## The Love and Limits of Literature

There is something almost mystical about the way literature lovers believe in the inherent goodness of books. Maurice Sendak describes this feeling well: "As a child I felt that books were holy objects, to be caressed, rapturously sniffed, and devotedly provided for. I gave my life to them—I still do. I continue to do what I did as a child: dream of books, make books, and collect books." Book lovers believe that books will elevate children's intellectual, moral, and emotional quotient. They believe that literature will strengthen knowledge, convey an appreciation for words and ideas, make accessible the inner world of thought and feeling, provide shelter from loneliness, overcome emotional distress, and add meaning to our lives. They believe literature will make children's lives better and give them access to a magical world that they will surely miss without books.

These are powerful reasons to encourage the love of books among children. Naturally, lovers of literature overstate their case. Actually, literature is not an "open sesame" for everyone. Many fulfilled men and women have had little acquaintance with literature—either by choice or because they were denied access to it. These people sometimes find other means of succeeding in life. The ideals of literature lovers are sound, yet literature is not the only path to the good life. The

British essayist William Hazlitt expressed this idea better than I can when he said, "Books are a world in themselves, it is true, but they are not the only world. The world itself is a volume larger than all the libraries in it." We can extol the virtues associated with literacy and literature and still understand that not all of our hopes and dreams for children will be fulfilled because books have been read—or not read.

## A Good Word for "Trashy" Literature

Richard McKenna, novelist and short story writer, makes this argument for what some call "trashy" books: "I believe that any book, however trashy and ephemeral, is good for a child if he finds pleasure in reading it. Any book that helps him to form a habit of reading, that helps to make reading one of his deep and continuing needs, is good for him." *I couldn't agree more.* McKenna's ideas do not devalue quality literature. On the contrary, they increase the likelihood that children will one day read quality literature.

The argument in favor of so-called trashy literature is reminiscent of the story about a farmer and his mule, Bessy. A neighbor asked, "Why are you hitting Bessy with that two-by-four?" The man answered, "Because, first I have to get Bessy's attention." There are better ways to get attention than hitting someone with a two-by-four, but it is essential to get children to attend to literature. Children need to know that reading is pleasurable. For some children, getting attention may come through reading quality literature aloud. For other children, literature that lacks the finest qualities gets their attention. It's a place to start and often leads to better literature down the road.

The designation "trashy" is distasteful. Those inclined to label certain books in this way may have in mind Junie B. Jones, Nancy Drew, Goose Bumps, or Baby Sitters Club. Such books do not fit a stringent definition of quality literature and may be written to a formula by anonymous underpaid authors. Their plots may be thin and their linguistic style mundane. Still, their themes may be uplifting and their characters interesting to children. In spite of their perceived shortcomings, children often get hooked on them. Eudora Welty, the novelist, and H. L. Mencken, the critic and journalist, got hooked on literature through works that some call trashy. But literature that leads children to enjoy reading is valuable. Once a child is hooked on reading, the good things we wish to see happen can happen. If we cannot get children to enjoy reading, it's a foregone conclusion that quality literature will not be part of their future. But quality literature may be on tomorrow's agenda for children who find today's pleasure in reading so-called trashy literature.

## Multicultural Literature and Diverse Perspectives

Literature influences how we think, feel, and act toward one another. At issue is the fundamental fairness and freedom that Americans value. Literature with a diverse perspective can have a powerful influence on how children view themselves and one another. While literary experiences are vicarious, the depiction and interaction of diverse characters within literature can provide insight into how children understand their own culture and the cultures of others. As the world, and especially the United States, grows more diverse with each passing year, it is crucial for children to understand and appreciate racial, religious, gender, ethnic, economic, and linguistic differences and similarities. Informational and fiction accounts that deal accurately, honestly, and sensitively with diverse perspectives are available today as never before. Guiding children to develop the attitudes and skills necessary to live and participate in a just society is a worthy goal of teaching and learning.

For information on anything and everything about words, visit http://www.wordwizard.com

While there is consensus about the need for multicultural literature, agreement has not been reached on how broad or narrow its definition ought to be. Harris and Hodges (1995), editors of *The Literacy Dictionary,* define multicultural literature as "1. writing that reflects the customs, beliefs, and experience of people of different nationalities and races, 2. materials designed to reflect the interests, vocabulary, and experiences of students from various cultural or ethnic backgrounds." This definition is sufficient for our purposes, though some professionals prefer to emphasize or deemphasize one aspect or another of the many legitimate issues that arise when discussing multicultural literature.

Various metaphors have been used to represent multicultural issues. The melting pot has the longest history. This image suggests that different cultures flow together through assimilation over the course of time, creating a kind of uniform culture unique to America. Many object to this image as inadequate and inaccurate. They argue that the cultures, ethnic groups, and races did not, in fact, melt together, as the metaphor suggests. Historically, the melting pot metaphor applied primarily to European immigration to America, and certainly did not include African Americans, who were originally brought to America as slaves. Nor did it fit Asian immigrants or even Native Americans, the original inhabitants of America.

A more recent metaphor describes America as a salad bowl. This image suggests different vegetables mixed but not melted together. Each different cultural, racial, and ethnic group retains its individual identity, adding its own unique contribution of taste, texture, and color to the salad that is America. This is a more pleasing and accurate description of America's history and current diversity.

The mission of multicultural literature is to fairly and accurately depict people of different cultural, ethnic, social, economic, religious, gender, and physical identities. Has multicultural literature accomplished its mission? There have been successes and failures. One failure has been a tendency to substitute form for substance. For instance, some books present illustrations that are diverse but text that is not. This failure is often associated with a commercial motive—a desire to capitalize on a trend without troubling to understand the important issues involved. Sometimes shortcomings in multicultural literature come about in a more innocent way—good intentions gone awry. While counterfeit multicultural literature is damaging, authentic multicultural literature can be identified: when a literary work presents characters, concepts, facts, and illustrations that fairly and accurately represent a culture, the result is a literary work with an authentic perspective. Many books fit this definition; some are listed in Figure 6.1 (p. 214). A more extensive list appears in the Blue Pages at the back of this book.

**Figure 6.1**

**Multicultural Books**

Blanco, Alberto. *Angel's Kite/La Estrella de Angel*. Illustrated by Rodolfo Morales. Children's Book Press, 1994.

Brown, Vee. *Animal Lore and Legend: Owl*. Cartwheel, 1995.

Chan, Harvey. *Three Monks, No Water*. Annick Press, 1997.

Curtis, Christopher Paul. *The Watsons Go to Birmingham — 1963*. Delacorte, 1995.

Erdrich, Louise. *The Birchbark House*. Hyperion, 1999.

Garza, Carmen Lomas. *In My Family/En Mi Familia*. Children's Book Press, 1996.

King, Martin Luther, Jr. *I Have a Dream*. Illustrated by Ashley Bryan et al. Scholastic, 1997.

Martinez, Floyd. *Spirits of the High Mesa*. Piñata Books. 1997.

Nez, Redwing T. *Forbidden Talent*. Northland, 1995.

Say, Allen. *Grandfather's Journey*. Houghton Mifflin, 1993.

Taylor, Mildred D. *Let the Circle Be Unbroken*. Dial, 1981.

Whitethorne, Baje. *Sunpainters: Eclipse of the Navajo Sun*. Rising Moon, 1994.

## Section Summary: Qualities, Quirks, and Issues in Children's Literature

1. Children's literature is defined as literature intended for children, though some books not intended for children have become classics of children's literature.

2. Literature is an important contributor to a well-lived life, although many folks have lived successful, fulfilled lives without significant exposure to literature.

3. So-called trashy literature appeals to many children and has hooked many on reading. The word trashy is an unfair term and should be discontinued.

4. Literature defines and influences a culture. Consequently, literature ought to authentically reflect a diverse, multicultural perspective.

## Elements of Literature

Some writers say they do not know exactly how they create stories. Others have a well-thought-out plan. For instance, best-selling author John Chambers plans and researches each work meticulously: setting, plot, characters, theme, point of view. His planning may take as long as a year; then he writes the book in 3 or 4 months. The French novelist François Mauriac says that every novelist ought to "invent his own technique." Thus, how a writer creates and manipulates characters, plot, theme, setting, or point of view cannot and should not be reduced to formulas. So as I describe the literary elements typically found in works of fiction, I describe them only in general terms; I do not suggest that there is a particular way in which literary elements must be handled when one writes fiction.

The major elements of fiction writing include setting, character, plot, theme, point of view, and style. Listing six elements of literature may give the impression that a story consists of six separate and distinct parts. Not so. A fine story is blended into a seamless whole. Readers experience a story as viewers might experience Van Gogh's *Starry Night*—as a whole, not as paint, canvas, and brushstrokes. Every reader approaches the elements of literature from a different perspective. Some read to revisit beloved characters; others to follow plot; still others are attracted to style. What readers experience most viscerally, however, is the wholeness of a literary work.

> "Reading out loud to children helps them develop a love for good literature, motivation to pursue reading on their own, and familiarity with a variety of genres."
> —L. Lipton and D. Hubble, *More Than 50 Ways to Learner-Centered Literacy,* 1997.

## Character

"Bah, humbug!" Sound familiar? Charles Dickens intended Scrooge to be someone you loved to hate—so that you could love him again and maybe shed a tear or two at his transformation. The best writers create unforgettable characters. And who is more unforgettable than Scrooge in *A Christmas Carol?* Writers create a character through descriptions, actions, behaviors, reactions of others to the character, and the character's words, eccentricities, dress, habits, gestures, and thoughts. Stories are about characters and their choices, not about language. Language serves story, not the other way around. There is no end to the ways in which good writers make you love, hate, enjoy, or despise their characters. Though every reader reads for different purposes, many, perhaps most, read to identify with and vicariously become a character in a story.

François Mauriac speaks of the role of characters in fiction: "The invented characters of fiction, like recorded music, come to life through some element which we ourselves supply. It is we, the readers, who give these imaginary creatures a setting in time and space somewhere within ourselves, which enables them to move freely and suddenly, to impose their destinies." And they do impose their destinies upon us. Rex Stout, the creator of the Nero Wolfe mysteries, has two main characters, a traditional pattern in mystery novels. Nero Wolfe is an eccentric genius. He's a book-loving, erudite, lazy, orchid-growing detective who never leaves his brownstone house except under extreme duress or in greedy pursuit of orchids to add to the 10,000 he tends on a rooftop greenhouse. Archie Goodwin is all action. He's a suave lady's man with a sharp wit and a tart tongue. He is the antidote to Wolfe's laziness, the burr under his saddle. Rex Stout wrote 40 Nero Wolfe mysteries. I've read them all, but it is not the mystery itself I love. The mysteries are somewhat predictable and formulaic. It's the characters that pique my interest. I love Stout's characters. I am a visitor in Wolfe's magnificent office, a guest at his gourmet dinners, a witness to remark and retort between two charismatic characters.

## Setting

The time, place, and circumstances in which a narrative takes place is called the setting. Settings may be described directly or indirectly. There are two types: the backdrop and the integral setting (Anderson, 2002). The backdrop plays a less important role; it may be a palace, hut, or forest. Backdrop settings are most common in traditional literature, for instance, the forest in "Goldilocks and the Three Bears." This backdrop is not really essential to the tale—in fact, the story line can be reimagined in almost any setting where there are bears and little girls.

By contrast, the story line is strongly affected by an integral setting—time, place, or circumstances that influence characters and events. Historical fiction, for example, heavily depends on a particular time, place, and set of circumstances. The plot, characters, and action could not realistically take place in any other setting. For example, in Linda Sue Park's book *When My Name Was Keoko,* the setting is Korea just prior to World War II, when it was occupied by Japan. This story could not have realistically or historically taken place in any other setting.

## Point of View

Who's telling the story? How much does the storyteller know? If you can answer these two questions, you have an understanding of point of view—sometimes called perspective. For instance, Billy Jo tells the story in Karen Hesse's novel *Out of the Dust.* As you read the story, set in the Oklahoma dust bowl during the Great Depression, you find Billy Jo referring to herself as *I* and *me.* So we are told the story and know about the other characters through the eyes of Billy Jo. This is called first-person point of view. First-person point of view requires that the author tell only those things that Billy Jo can know. First-person narrative can also alternate between characters. For example, in *When My Name Was Keoko,* two parallel stories are interwoven in a narrative describing Sun-hee and Tae-yul's wartime experience in occupied Korea. Sun-hee, a girl, and Tae-yul, a boy, narrate alternating chapters, and the reader experiences the story from two different points of view.

There are other alternatives. In omniscient point of view, the narrator knows everything, a sort of literary all-knowing deity. This narrator stands outside the story and is not a character who takes part in it. This omniscient voice narrates the events that occur and can reveal what any character is doing and thinking, what has happened in the past, and what will happen in the future. In the omniscient point of view, the story is told in the third person, and characters are referred to as *he, she, it,* or *they*—pronouns indicative of the third person.

Rarely, the *you* of second-person point of view is used. Second person is used in *A Time of Wonder* by Robert McCloskey, where it creates a sense of urgency. More recently, Chris Lynch used this point of view in *Freewill;* the second-person point of view creates the sense that Will's brain is talking to him.

In the limited omniscient perspective, the story is revealed from the perspective of one character. The story is not told by that character, however, but by the omniscient narrator who enters the mind of the character and tells us what the character thinks, feels, and does, and the story is cast in the third person (characters referred to as *he, she,* etc.). In this perspective, the reader is told only what the chosen character can know and understand. An example of this perspective occurs in Mildred Taylor's *Roll of Thunder, Hear My Cry.*

Finally, there is the objective perspective. Here the narrator acts as a reporter, presenting only the facts without commenting on or interpreting the events of the story.

## Plot

Ray Bradbury (1996) said, "*Plot* is no more than footprints left in the snow *after* your characters have run by on their way to incredible destinations. *Plot* is observed after the fact rather than before. It cannot precede action. It is the chart that remains when an action is through. That is all *Plot* ever should be. It is human desire let run, running, and reaching a goal. It cannot be mechanical. It can only be dynamic" (p. 152).

At its simplest level, plot is what happens in the narrative. More formally, plot is the plan of events and action in a narrative: "A plot is a meaningful ordering of events with their consequences—a 'what happened to whom and why.' A plot is the conveyor belt that pulls a reader through the text, getting to know characters and scenes along the way, before arriving at a cumulative insight" (Temple et al., 2002, p. 38). For some readers, plot is *the* reason for a story's existence. Some writers pride themselves on the twists and turns their stories take before reaching an unexpected ending. This is particularly true in thriller mysteries. For some writers, it is plot above all else; for others, it is character. Readers divide in similar ways.

A major feature of plots is conflict. Eudora Welty referred to conflict as "trouble" and called trouble the "backbone of literature." Conflict comes in many colors. There are conflicts between characters (Harry Potter and Voldemort), conflict within a character (*Holes*), conflict with the environment (*Julie and the Wolves*), conflict between a character and society (*The Giver*).

My sense is that most young readers are more interested in character than plot, although conflict adds suspense and intrigue to the narrative, heightening interest. Plot readers want to know "What's it about?" My more knowledgeable children's literature colleagues tell me children prefer plot over character. Still, identification with characters explains children's insatiable appetite for reading book after book in popular series such as The Box Car Children. The plots are thin in some series books, lacking substantial structure or even surprise. But children visit them again and again, partly eager to find out what kind of trouble the characters will encounter this time, but mainly because they have come to identify with the characters. As one little girl explained to children's author Leland Jacobs, "I like Betsy

*When a plot works, the reader wants what the protagonist wants. When this doesn't happen, the plot "thins" rather than thickens.*

PEANUTS reprinted by permission of United Feature Syndicate, Inc.

Byars's family better than my own." Eudora Welty said that in her youthful reading she came across a series she called The Randy Books. She read *Randy's Spring, Randy's Summer, Randy's Fall,* and *Randy's Winter,* each book more disappointing than the previous one. Nevertheless, Welty said, "I was disappointed in her whole year as it turned out, but a thing like that didn't keep me from wanting to read every word of it." Welty had identified with the characters, and she needed the reassurance of a backlog of books to read.

Plots have many twists, turns, and features, but literary critics point out that the actual number of plots is small—perhaps not more than a score. Consequently, a plot based on a journey or a quest has been used thousands of times, but the means, events, episodes, and characters in a particular work, when well done, satisfy readers and may appear completely original, though it is actually a variation on an established plot structure. Though plots in children's literature are not generally complicated, those of science fiction and fantasy tend toward greater complexity.

## Theme

Theme is the central idea running through a work of literature. Put another way, theme deals with the question "What does this story mean?" Theme may be a lesson to be learned, such as a moral. For example, in the fable "Two Ducks and the Fox," the ducks have gotten into the routine of taking the same road to the pond. One day they meet Fox, who is most interested in their habitual travel of the same road. Next day they take the same road again and Fox tries, unsuccessfully, to kidnap them. Only then do the ducks decide to vary their routine. The moral: At times, a change of routine can be most healthful (Lobel, 1980). Theme may be an underlying message, intended or unintended, or a belief about a social issue, such as poverty or race. Theme may be stated explicitly, as in fables, but more often theme is implicit, not stated but implied through the behavior of characters or the outcome of plot. Sometimes theme imparts a clear message, but it may also be ambiguous, suggesting questions rather than answers.

Theme as an element of literature is somewhat controversial. For instance, some writers claim that their stories do not have a theme. Others make no claim one way or the other. Also, theme can be difficult to identify and may be open to substantially different interpretations. Another related issue is reader's purpose. Readers have different purposes for reading. Some readers have no interest in theme. Others do. For some readers, this interest may depend on genre. For instance, an avid reader of mysteries may not ask "What does this story mean?" Instead, the exploration and enjoyment of characters may be the reader's main purpose. On the other hand, a different literary genre may invoke in the same reader an intense interest in theme. "What does this story novel mean?" becomes an important question. The intellect is engaged at a different level based on purpose or preference.

Assuming theme exists in a literary work, how can it be identified? One way is to ask questions like these:

- What does this story mean?
- What big idea ties this story together?

- What big ideas does the author express about life, society, human nature?
- What beliefs do the main characters express about life?
- What values are stated or implied in this story?
- What message, if any, does the author convey in this story?

## Style

Why does a certain arrangement of musical notes haunt us? Why does a certain sentence or phrase resonate in our minds? These are high mysteries to which there is no clear answer. Consider how Dickens begins *The Tale of Two Cities*: "It was the best of times, it was the worst of times . . ." These two clauses resonate with style, and it is hard to imagine an acceptable alternative. But let's try:

> Times were both good and bad . . .
> Times were good and times were bad . . .
> Times were bad but not all bad . . .

What's wrong with these alternatives? They are grammatically acceptable; their meaning is clear; they are economical. But would they have withstood the test of time, as Dickens's original words have? No way. The original words have the mark of Dickens stamped upon them as clearly as if they contained his DNA. His distinctive use of rhythmic language, his assertive personality, his spirit are expressed in the opening sentence of *A Tale of Two Cities*.

Style exhibits a writer's distinctive voice, individuality, and imagination. After you have read a book, can you say, "I know something of this writer's personality, mind, or spirit"? If you can, the writer's style has captured your interest or imagination. Style has been revealed to you through the writer's distinctive use of language—word choice, pacing, voice, descriptive power, subtlety with emotion, and so on. Though an aura of mystery is associated with style, nevertheless, it can, to some extent, be analyzed—though mainly it is something to be enjoyed and appreciated. Style is the essence of a writer's personality splashed upon the page. And as we cannot precisely define personality, neither can we precisely define style.

Since style is elusive, can we teach it? Here there is no mystery. We can no more teach style than we can teach personality or imagination. But we can encourage children to write in their own natural voice; we can teach children to use, appreciate, and enjoy distinctive language; we can engage children in discussions focused on writers' use of language, plots, characters, themes, or settings. Questions such as the following may stimulate discussions of style.

- What did you think about the author's choice of words?
- Can you give an example of a distinctive word or phrase?
- Did the author use any unusual metaphors or images?
- What distinctive sounds or rhythms did you hear in this piece?
- Is the language appealing?
- Can you imagine knowing this writer after reading his writing?
- Is there something about the writer's language you find memorable?
- What is distinctive about this writer's characters, plots, themes, and settings?

*Teaching Tip*

## Section Summary: Elements of Literature

1. The elements of literature include these six features of fiction writing: character, setting, point of view, plot, theme, and style.
2. Character is defined by what characters do (people, usually), how they do it, and how others react. Conversations, actions, and reactions help define character.
3. Setting refers to the time, place, and circumstances in which a story takes place.
4. Point of view concerns who is telling the story. Stories often have a first-person or omniscient narrator, although other perspectives are possible.
5. Plot is what happens in a story. Plot includes the plan of events and actions in the narrative.
6. Theme is the central idea running through a work of literature. It deals with the question "What does this story mean?"
7. Style exhibits a writer's unique voice, individuality, imagination, and distinctive use of language.

## Genres of Children's Literature

Mother was in Arizona, 2,000 miles away from her son. Every day she called, hoping to "talk" to him, but Teddy never listened for more than a few seconds before running off to play. Then Mother had an idea. She had read his favorite books so many times that she had memorized many of them. So the next time she called, she began by reciting one of her son's favorite stories. Success! Teddy listened for 3 or 4 minutes before running off to play. Literature is a tie that binds mothers to their children and teachers to their students. This bond remains unbroken with the passing of the years.

As a tattoo leaves an indelible mark on the body, so does the written word leave an indelible mark on the minds of children. M. F. K. Fisher, poet and novelist, recalled her childhood experience with the written word: "Everybody in the house who could follow a printed sentence read aloud. Grandmother read the Bible to me. Mother read whatever she was reading. . . . Father read headlines at the breakfast table." Hearing literature sets the stage for reading literature on your own.

For information on providing a print-rich environment, see *Literacy Development in the Early Years: Helping Children Read and Write,* by L. Morrow, 2nd ed., 2001.

There are many types of children's literature, and fortunate are the children who are exposed to them: picture books, traditional literature, poetry, realistic fiction, historical fiction, fantasy and science fiction, informational books, and biography. All these genres are described in this section, along with a short list of books representative of each type.

### Picture Books

On first hearing about picture books, I imagined a book in which the pictures alone told the story. This sensible idea turns out to be only one kind of picture book. More common are picture books with a blend of picture and text. But wait, there's more.

**Figure 6.2**

**Picture Books**

Aardema, Verna. *Why Mosquitoes Buzz in People's Ears: A West African Tale.* Illustrated by Leo and Diane Dillon. Dial, 1987.

Brown, Margaret Wise. *Goodnight Moon.* Illustrated by Clement Hurd. Harper, 1947.

Carle, Eric. *The Very Hungry Caterpillar.* Philomel, 1984.

Christelow, Eileen. *Five Little Monkeys Jumping on the Bed.* Clarion, 1989.

Hyman, Trina Schart. *Little Red Riding Hood.* Holiday House, 1983.

Keats, Ezra Jack. *The Snowy Day.* Viking, 1962.

Kunhardt, Dorothy. *Pat the Bunny.* Western, 1940, 1968.

Martin, Bill, Jr. *Brown Bear, Brown Bear, What Do You See?* Illustrated by Eric Carle. Holt, 1967, 1983.

McCloskey, Robert. *Make Way for Ducklings.* Viking, 1941.

McMillan, Bruce. *Counting Wildflowers.* Lothrop, Lee & Shepard, 1986.

Perrault, Charles. *Cinderella.* Illustrated by Marcia Brown. Scribner's, 1954.

Potter, Beatrix. *The Tale of Peter Rabbit.* Warne, 1902, 1986.

Sendak, Maurice. *The Nutshell Library.* Harper & Row, 1962.

Seuss, Dr. *The Cat in the Hat.* Random House, 1957.

Steptoe, John. *Baby Says.* Lothrop, Lee & Shepard, 1988.

In some picture books, words carry the story more than the pictures. In others, pictures carry the story more than the words. The ideal picture book achieves a harmonious blend of text and illustration, where pictures enhance the contribution of the text, and the text enhances the contribution of the pictures, creating a coherent whole. The many kinds of picture books include: toy books, alphabet and counting books, concept books, books with only pictures, books with minimal text, predictable books, and picture storybooks.

Picture books have a long history. The first was published in 1658 by Johannes Amos Comenius. Comenius believed that illustrations would enhance comprehension and enjoyment of the text. Others followed Comenius's early example. John Newbery, Walter Crane, Randolph Caldecott, and Beatrix Potter contributed their talents to the concept of unifying text and pictures. When text and pictures work harmoniously, the result adds up to more than the sum of the parts. A few picture storybooks come close to achieving this goal. Beatrix Potter's *The Tale of Peter Rabbit* is an excellent early example, and Maurice Sendak's *Where the Wild Things Are* is a more recent one. The goal of perfection in harmonizing text and illustration is, of course, impossible. Still, the best authors and illustrators seek to do just that. The Caldecott Medal, awarded every year, honors those who have come closest to reaching this elusive goal.

## Traditional Literature

Literature implies the written word, yet traditional literature, also called folk literature, is based on the spoken word. Storytellers created what we now call traditional literature. Long before written language was invented, people passed on tales to the next generation to explain and instill their values, beliefs, history, religion, and customs. What motivated the first storytellers? Perhaps, like us, they wanted the next generation to remember who they were, where they came from, what they believed, why they existed. The oral tradition, also called folklore, arose in the mists of a bygone era. Of the many themes of traditional literature, perhaps the most common are the triumph of good over evil ("Hansel and Gretel"), reversal of fortune ("Cinderella"), and the small outwitting the big ("Jack and Giant Beanstalk").

Opinions differ as to which forms are properly included within the category of traditional literature. Temple and colleagues (2002) include myths, fables, epics, ballads, legends, folk rhymes, folk tales, fairy tales, apprenticeship stories, hero tales, numbskull tales, pourquoi tales, trickster tales, tall tales, and cumulative tales. For technical reasons Temple classifies certain forms under different genres. For instance, fairy tales are not always classified as traditional literature.

Guttenberg's invention of the printing press in the 1400s profoundly influenced traditional literature. Now the spoken word could be preserved in writing. In 1667, Charles Perrault recorded the tales told by his nursemaid and published them in a book entitled *Stories or Tales from Past Times with Morals,* which includes "Cinderella" and "Little Red Riding Hood." Antoine Galland in 1704 published *The Arabian Nights, or Tales Told by Sheherezade,* which includes "Ali Baba and the Forty Thieves." Jakob and Wilhelm Grimm in 1815 published *Nursery and Household Tales,* which includes "Hansel and Gretel," "Rumpelstiltskin," and "Snow White." Joel Chandler Harris collected African American folklore and in 1881 published *Uncle Remus: His Songs and Sayings.* Many other collections of folklore were published in countries throughout the world. Over the years, many were rewritten to

**Figure 6.3**

**Traditional Literature**

dePaola, Tomie. *The Legend of the Poinsettia.* Putnam, 1994.

Harris, Joel. *The Tales of Uncle Remus.* Adapted by Julius Lester and illustrated by Jerry Pinkney. Dial, 1987.

Hodges, Margaret. *St. George and the Dragon.* Illustrated by Trina Schart Hyman. Little Brown, 1984.

Kellogg, Steven. *Johnny Appleseed.* Morrow, 1988.

Lesson, Robert. *The Story of Robinhood.* Illustrated by Barbara Lofthouse. Larousse Kingfisher, 1994.

Mayer, Marianna. *Baba Yaga and Vasilisa the Brave.* Illustrated by K. Y. Craft. Morrow, 1994.

McDermott, Gerald. *Coyote: A Trickster Tale from the American Southwest.* Harcourt, 1994.

Rogarsky, Barbara. *Rapunzel: From the Brothers Grimm.* Illustrated by Trina Schart Hyman. Holiday House, 1982.

Singer, Isaac Bashevis. *Mazel and Shlimazel: Or the Milk of a Lioness.* Translated by Elizabeth Shub, photographs by Margot Zemach. Farrar, Straus & Giroux, 1995.

Steptoe, John. *Mufaso's Beautiful Daughters.* Lothrop, Lee & Shepard, 1987.

Yagawa, Sumiko. *The Crane Wife.* Translated by Katherine Paterson. Illustrated by Suekichi Akaba. Morrow, 1987.

Yolen, Jane. *Favorite Folk Tales from Around the World.* Pantheon, 1988.

modernize the language and moderate violence. Often different versions of a tale would appear in different countries, adapted to the language, values, morals, beliefs, and culture of its source. For instance, over 100 different versions of "Cinderella" have been identified.

Traditional literature has identifiable characteristics. Anderson (2002) suggests these characteristics: unknown authorship, conventional introductions and conclusions, vague settings, stereotyped characters, anthropomorphism, cause and effect, happy endings, magic, simple and direct plots, and repetition of actions and verbal patterns (pp. 78–80).

## Poetry

A. E. Houseman, the English poet, said, "I could no more define poetry than a terrier can define a rat." Now we all know that terriers cannot define rats. But I happen to own a terrier, and I can tell you that while Blackie cannot define a rat, she can *smell* a rat well enough. And if Blackie could talk, she might say, "Why define a rat? Just enjoy the rat." Maybe that's good advice, but unlike terriers, humans seem to want definitions. There are many definitions of poetry as well as claims that it cannot be defined. The Welsh poet Dylan Thomas defined it as "statements made on the way to the grave." On the other hand, he also said, "There is no such thing as poetry, there are only poems." My mind resonates with both comments. Poetry is venerated as humanity's finest literary achievement, the most beautiful, impressive form of language. The rhetoric surrounding poetry is impressive, yet there is no definition that will satisfy more than a dozen or so poets or lovers of poetry. So, let's forget definitions and get on with a discussion of poetry as a genre within children's literature. (Chapter 11 deals with poetry more broadly.)

For more information, read *On Solid Ground*, by S. Taberski, 2000.

Some literary critics make a distinction between verse and poetry. Poetry, these critics suggest, is more varied, sophisticated, and complex than verse, which deals mostly with rhythm, rhyme, and sound. In this classification scheme, Mother Goose rhymes are verse but not poetry. This scheme also suggests that Jack Prelutsky and Shel Silverstein wrote light verse, not poetry. Emily Dickinson and Myra Cohn Livingston, on the other hand, wrote poetry. This dustup may amount to a quarrel between the elites and the plebeians, *but it has serious implications for exposing children to poetry.*

There is no sound philosophical or practical reason to limit children's exposure to Mother Goose, Jack Prelutsky, or Shel Silverstein. Children love them. The first premise of exposing children to poetry is enjoyment. Enjoyment captures interest; interest motivates. Having laid the groundwork through these well-liked works, the teacher can move on to Langston Hughes or Robert Frost, free verse or narrative poetry.

Kutiper and Wilson (1993) found that elementary school children enjoy poems that contain humor, rhyme, rhythm, sound, animals, and familiar experiences. They like narrative poetry but dislike free verse, haiku, visual imagery, and figurative language. This study suggests that first you have to get children's attention; you have to understand where they are and what they enjoy. You do that

**Figure 6.4**

**Books on Poetry**

Adoff, Arnold. *All the Colors of the Race*. Illustrated by John Steptoe. Lothrop, Lee & Shepard, 1982.

Ciardi, John. *You Read to Me and I'll Read to You*. Harper Trophy, 1987.

Hopkins, Lee Bennett. *Pass the Poetry, Please*. HarperCollins, 1987.

Hughes, Langston. *The Dream Keeper and Other Poems*. Illustrated by Jerry Pinkney. Knopf, 1996.

Kennedy, X. J., and Dorothy Kennedy, eds. *Knock at a Star*, 2nd ed. Little, Brown, 1999.

Livingston, Myra Cohn. *There Was a Place and Other Poems*. Simon and Schuster/ McElderry, 1988.

Prelutsky, Jack. *The New Kid on the Block*. Illustrated by James Stevenson. Greenwillow, 1984.

Sandburg, Carl. *Good Morning, America*. Harcourt, 1928.

Silverstein, Shel. *Where the Sidewalk Ends*. HarperCollins, 1974.

Temple, Charles. *Trains*. Illustrated by Larry Johnson. Houghton Mifflin, 1996.

Viorst, Judith. *If I Were in Charge of the World and Other Worries*. Illustrated by Lynn Cherry. Atheneum, 1981.

Yolen, Jane. *Dinosaur Dances*. Illustrated by Bruce Degen. Putnam, 1990.

through poems that contain humor, rhyme, rhythm, and familiar experiences. Critics who plump for more sophisticated poetry will say that this is just the problem—you're bowing to children's worst instincts. I beg to differ. Every concept, like every building, stands on a foundation. A foundation is made of concrete and steel because it has to bear a lot of weight. Instruction must be built on the foundations of enjoyment and interest; they can bear a lot of weight. Teach poetry that children dislike, and you make poetry an enemy for life. Teach poetry that children love, and you have laid a strong foundation on which to erect the superstructure of more complex and sophisticated poetry. Figure 6.4 identifies some books on poetry. Lists of poets, poetry books, and other ideas for teaching and learning poetry can be found in Chapter 11.

## Realistic Fiction

Realistic fiction has a long and honorable history. Many famous books fall into this category: *Little Women, Huckleberry Finn,* and *Black Beauty* are examples. Many series books also fall into the realistic fiction category: Nancy Drew, Encyclopedia Brown, and The Hardy Boys, for example. Realistic fiction deals with real-life situations, takes place in real-world locations, and features realistic people as characters. Fantasy as a genre allows for unreal events and characters, such as a talking bear or a prince changed into a beast, whereas realistic fiction has no such events or characters. Realistic fiction deals with a vast array of real-life topics and themes: love, hate, death, divorce, illness, war, school, work, poverty, drugs, abuse, honor, family life, growing up, sexuality, nature, sports, survival, romance, morality, death, mysteries, multiculturalism, friendship, honesty, integrity, enemies, and much more. It may take place in the recent past or have a contemporary setting. The value of realistic fiction is inestimable. It enables children to vicariously participate in many experiences, meet characters similar or dissimilar to themselves, and identify with people and places they might never otherwise experience.

Realistic fiction is richly diverse. It may be humorous or serious or a combination of both. Problems and solutions in realistic fiction may be happy or sad, satisfying or disappointing. As in adult fiction, when a problem needs to be resolved, it may work out in a way that does not resemble the traditional happy ending. In realistic fiction the resolution will comport to life as actually lived.

Realistic fiction portrays life in ways that children will recognize. Temple and colleagues (2002) said, "Realistic fiction, then, offers readers the opportunity to see themselves reflected in the literature, as well as the opportunity to see the lives of people with very different lifestyles. It offers readers realistic views of the world in which they live" (p. 282).

The term *realistic fiction* conjures up the notion of truth, always a somewhat controversial issue in fiction. Every good reader must ask, "Whose truth is being told?" Every writer of fiction has an ax to grind, an idea or ideal to express. In fiction, the characters represent different versions of truth. Writers typically present their version through the protagonist (good guy or girl) or the antagonist (bad guy or girl). Realistic fiction tips the scales toward someone's version of what is good, desirable, best, moral, or right. This is not negative. On the contrary, various versions of the truth can be presented in fiction in entertaining ways, and thinking readers have the opportunity to decide for themselves what is true or untrue, good or bad, right or wrong, moral or immoral, wise or foolish. A reader has only to imagine the same issues and facts in a story as they might be viewed from another character's perspective to recognize that issues may be viewed differently by different people, given their background of experience, culture, beliefs, ethnicity, race, or creed.

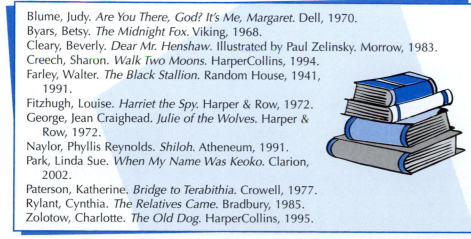

Blume, Judy. *Are You There, God? It's Me, Margaret.* Dell, 1970.
Byars, Betsy. *The Midnight Fox.* Viking, 1968.
Cleary, Beverly. *Dear Mr. Henshaw.* Illustrated by Paul Zelinsky. Morrow, 1983.
Creech, Sharon. *Walk Two Moons.* HarperCollins, 1994.
Farley, Walter. *The Black Stallion.* Random House, 1941, 1991.
Fitzhugh, Louise. *Harriet the Spy.* Harper & Row, 1972.
George, Jean Craighead. *Julie of the Wolves.* Harper & Row, 1972.
Naylor, Phyllis Reynolds. *Shiloh.* Atheneum, 1991.
Park, Linda Sue. *When My Name Was Keoko.* Clarion, 2002.
Paterson, Katherine. *Bridge to Terabithia.* Crowell, 1977.
Rylant, Cynthia. *The Relatives Came.* Bradbury, 1985.
Zolotow, Charlotte. *The Old Dog.* HarperCollins, 1995.

**Figure 6.5**

Realistic Fiction

## Historical Fiction

Historical fiction is usually defined as a story *set in the past*. The problem is that *every* event is set in the past; only the future fails to fall into it. How far into the past must a story be set before it can be considered historical fiction? Arbitrary benchmarks exist. Anderson (2002), for instance, sets 1964 as the benchmark date: "I selected 1964 because laws, attitudes, and opportunities concerning minorities in the United States were very different before that year; this fact needs to be kept in mind when we read and evaluate historical fiction" (p. 234). Other dividing lines could be set, but Anderson's choice is as good as any.

For an extensive listing of children's literature appropriate for various activities and grade levels, visit the Children's Literature Web Guide, located at http://www.acs.ucalgary.ca/~dkbrown/index.html

Another issue in historical fiction is a problem that arises due to the passage of time. Suppose an author publishes a novel in 2002 about events in Africa, America, or Asia. A hundred years from now that novel could reasonably be thought of as historical fiction. Children read books today that were contemporary novels when first published. *Little Women* and *Little House on the Prairie* are examples. Both books are considered historical fiction today because of the passing of time, not because the authors set out to write historical fiction.

Historical fiction is entertaining, but is it also enlightening? Can it supplement nonfiction history? Should social studies classes use more historical fiction and fewer social studies textbooks? One can argue for either position. I believe historical fiction can improve the learning of social studies concepts. Well-written historical fiction can present historical content more interestingly than can social studies texts. Historical fiction is seldom boring whereas social studies texts often are (though they need not be). Some may claim that using historical fiction will "water down" historical content. Others will say that fiction writers take poetic license with history: they make up the words their characters speak, inject drama where it may not have existed, get historical facts wrong, and interpret facts based on personal bias, values, and beliefs. *All this is true.* But these problems also exist in social studies texts. Even academic history, written by esteemed historians, is not immune

**Figure 6.6**

**Historical Fiction**

Alcott, Louisa May. *Little Women*. Scholastic, 1968, 1995.
Brink, Carol Ryne. *Caddie Woodlawn*. Macmillan, 1935.
Curtis, Christopher Paul. *The Watsons Go to Birmingham—1963*. Delacorte, 1995.
Cushman, Karen. *The Midwife's Apprentice*. Clarion, 1995.
de Angeli, Marguerite. *The Door in the Wall*. Doubleday, 1949, 1989.
Forbes, Esther. *Johnny Tremain*. Houghton Mifflin, 1943.
Hunt, Irene. *Across Five Aprils*. Scholastic, 1964, 1999.
MacLachlan, Patricia. *Sarah, Plain and Tall*. Harper & Row, 1985.
Paterson, Katherine. *Jacob Have I Loved*. Crowell, 1980.
Paulsen, Gary. *The Rifle*. Harcourt Brace, 1995.
Rylant, Cynthia. *When I Was Young in the Mountains*. Illustrated by Diane Goode. Dutton, 1982.
Speare, Elizabeth George. *The Witch of Blackbird Pond*. Houghton Mifflin, 1958.

to these problems. Every historian who ever put pen to paper gets facts wrong, interprets facts in light of personal biases and values, and may inject drama when little or none existed. Critics claim that social studies texts cover history broadly but thinly and tend to reduce history to focus on the trivial. Well-written historical fiction usually avoids these pitfalls. Figure 6.6 provides examples of wonderful historical fiction.

## Fantasy and Science Fiction

Fantasy literature creates a world in which magic happens. Readers of fantasy must suspend disbelief in order to appreciate the genre, and children are prepared to do so. When Alice tumbles down a rabbit hole and has a chat with an overgrown egg, Humpty Dumpty, the reader has to believe that such a story is plausible though not in keeping with the real world. Even adults can suspend disbelief and enjoy the magic of *Alice's Adventures in Wonderland*. The world of fantasy has its own plausibility when depicted well—when the characters are intriguing and the plots and events are well developed. The fantasy world seems a natural, even reasonable world for those who have not lost the capacity to imagine.

Fantasy has its roots in traditional literature and is generally divided into two branches, as Anderson (2002) explains: "Today, because both genres still share so many elements, we distinguish them by referring to them as traditional stories and modern fantasy stories" (p. 113). Folktales had their magical creatures—dragons, fairies, and leprechauns. Following the advent of printing, collections of folklore tales were published by Perrault and the Grimm brothers. Around 1835, Hans

Babbitt, Natalie. *Tuck Everlasting*. Farrar, 1975.
Dahl, Roald. *Charlie and the Chocolate Factory*. Illustrated by John Schindelman. Knopf, 1964.
Grahame, Kenneth. *The Wind in the Willows*. Illustrated by E. H. Shepard. Scribner's, 1908, 1933.
Hughes, Monica. *The Dream Catcher*. Macmillan, 1987.
Lewis, C. S. *The Lion, the Witch, and the Wardrobe*. Illustrated by Pauline Baynes. Macmillan, 1950.
L'Engle, Madeleine. *A Wrinkle in Time*. Farrar, 1962.
Lowry, Lois. *The Giver*. Houghton Mifflin, 1999.
O'Brien, Robert C. *Mrs. Frisby and the Rats of NIMH*. Illustrated by Zena Bernstein. Atheneum, 1971.
Potter, Beatrix. *The Tale of Peter Rabbit*. Warne, 1902.
Rowling, J. K. *Harry Potter and the Sorcerer's Stone*. Scholastic, 1998.
Tolkien, J. R. R. *The Fellowship of the Ring*. Houghton Mifflin, 1955, 1967.
White, E. B. *Charlotte's Web*. Illustrated by Garth Williams. Harper & Row, 1952.
Williams, Margery. *The Velveteen Rabbit*. Illustrated by Michael Hague. Holt, 1922, 1983.

**Figure 6.7**

**Fantasy Literature**

Christian Andersen began publishing fairy tales, which probably had their origin in folklore. But many of his stories were original—literary fairy tales, they are called. His best-known original creations include "The Emperor's New Clothes," "The Little Mermaid," and "The Ugly Duckling."

Science fiction is a branch of fantasy literature, though different in important respects from traditional and modern fantasy. Science fiction is based on extrapolations and projections from real science. The story events in science fiction usually have the *potential* of becoming reality at some future time. Whereas conversations with a cracked egg, such as Humpty Dumpty, can never be possible, a trip to another galaxy seems plausible, though not yet possible. Jules Verne imagined a submarine before submarines existed, in *Twenty Thousand Leagues Under the Sea.* Submarines were not yet reality in 1869, but one could imagine the concept as possible at some future time. While some elements of science fiction have scientific probability or possibility, others do not. For instance, the film *Star Wars* features characters and events that are scientifically imaginable but also some that are premised on magic. The mixing of magic and science is considered a hybrid type of science fiction.

## Informational Books

Informational books inform readers about a concept or idea, usually on a specific topic. They do not include textbooks, dictionaries, encyclopedias, or other books used primarily for instruction or reference. Informational books are meant to be read from cover to cover. Their language differs from that of fiction. Fiction writers use dialogue and narration whereas informational literature emphasizes exposition. Narration is used in some types of informational books, such as those describing events in history, but such narration typically includes a great deal of exposition. Informational books are often organized in logical or chronological order, though this is not always the case. They may include photographs, maps, or tables to convey supplemental information, whereas fiction is more apt to employ illustrations. Informational literature covers many subjects and exists in different formats: people and cultures, history, nature, art, music, dance, crafts, how-to, and concept books about the physical, natural, social, and educational world.

A well-written informational book not only informs and instructs but also uplifts readers by animating the subject matter. If it only informs and instructs, it may miss the mark by failing to draw and retain the reader's interest. Informational books build a repertoire of world knowledge for children, influence the development of knowledge structures, and satisfy children's curiosity about the natural, physical, and social world.

Informational books can dovetail well with fiction. Suppose, for instance, you have just read *Julie of the Wolves* to your class. Curiosity about wolves is at a natural peak, making this a good time to introduce a related informational book, such as Jim Brandenburg's *To the Top of the World: Adventures with Arctic Wolves.* Juxtaposing fiction with nonfiction develops a more nuanced understanding of fiction and nonfiction, not the false dichotomy that fiction is described as *not true* and nonfiction is *true.* Informational books cannot simply be called true; fiction can-

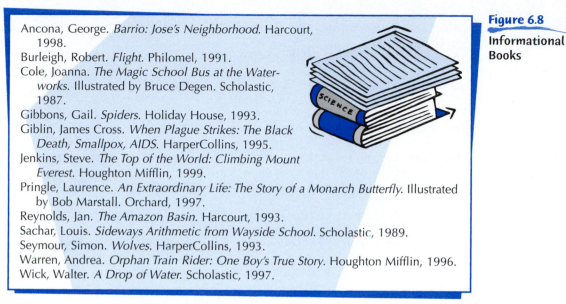

**Figure 6.8**

**Informational Books**

Ancona, George. *Barrio: Jose's Neighborhood.* Harcourt, 1998.

Burleigh, Robert. *Flight.* Philomel, 1991.

Cole, Joanna. *The Magic School Bus at the Waterworks.* Illustrated by Bruce Degen. Scholastic, 1987.

Gibbons, Gail. *Spiders.* Holiday House, 1993.

Giblin, James Cross. *When Plague Strikes: The Black Death, Smallpox, AIDS.* HarperCollins, 1995.

Jenkins, Steve. *The Top of the World: Climbing Mount Everest.* Houghton Mifflin, 1999.

Pringle, Laurence. *An Extraordinary Life: The Story of a Monarch Butterfly.* Illustrated by Bob Marstall. Orchard, 1997.

Reynolds, Jan. *The Amazon Basin.* Harcourt, 1993.

Sachar, Louis. *Sideways Arithmetic from Wayside School.* Scholastic, 1989.

Seymour, Simon. *Wolves.* HarperCollins, 1993.

Warren, Andrea. *Orphan Train Rider: One Boy's True Story.* Houghton Mifflin, 1996.

Wick, Walter. *A Drop of Water.* Scholastic, 1997.

not accurately be described as untrue. Books reveal truth and falsehood in far more complex ways. A work of nonfiction may be true, partly true, or wholly false. For example, Adolf Hitler wrote *Mein Kampf,* a work of nonfiction. Yet this book is not a revelation of truth simply because it is classified as nonfiction—quite the opposite. On the other hand, a book classified as fiction may illuminate important truths. Arthur Koestler's novel *Darkness at Noon* tells more truth about the nature of Communism under Josef Stalin than most nonfiction accounts are likely to reveal.

## Biography

Biographies are written histories of the life and times of people, most often people who are famous or infamous. Biographies usually depict historical figures such as presidents, politicians, soldiers, writers, celebrities, and cultural heroes. At one time intended to set a moral or heroic example of how life ought to be lived, biographies, either implicitly or explicitly, present their subjects as role models. Thus, there have been many biographies of presidents such as Abraham Lincoln and George Washington. More recently, this subject matter has broadened. Biographies of noteworthy individuals, seldom of the type celebrated in the past, have proliferated in recent decades. Biographies now deal with minority heroes such as Rosa Parks and Martin Luther King Jr., feminist heroes such as Elizabeth Cady Stanton and Rosie the Riveter, and social justice heroes such as Mother Jones and Jane Addams. Biography provides insight into how cultural experiences influence life's decisions. When biographies are well written and researched, they make excellent reading for children.

**Figure 6.9**

**Biography**

Alder, Davi. *Jackie Robinson: He Was the First.* Illustrated by Robert Casilla. Holiday House, 1989.

Aronson, Marc. *Sir Walter Raleigh and the Quest for El Dorado.* Houghton Mifflin, 2000.

Cooper, Floyd. *Coming Home: From the Life of Langston Hughes.* Philomel, 1994.

Fisher, Leonard Everett. *Gandhi.* Atheneum, 1995.

Freedman, Russell. *Eleanor Roosevelt: A Life of Discovery.* Clarion, 1993.

Fritz, Jean. *Bully for You, Teddy Roosevelt!* Illustrated by Mike Wimmer. Putnam, 1991.

Kraft, Betsy Harvey. *Mother Jones: One Woman's Fight for Labor.* Clarion, 1995.

Lyons, Mary E. *Sorrow's Kitchen: The Life and Folklore of Zora Neale Hurston.* Scribner's, 1990.

Martin, Albert. *Unconditional Surrender: U. S. Grant and the Civil War.* Atheneum, 1994.

Myers, Walter Dean. *Malcolm X: By Any Means Necessary.* Scholastic, 1993.

Stanley, Diane. *Leonardo da Vinci.* Morrow, 1996.

Towle, Wendy. *The Real McCoy: The Life of an African-American Inventor.* Illustrated by Wil Clay. Scholastic, 1993.

Uchida, Yoshiko. *The Invisible Thread.* Julian Messner, 1991.

Like informational books, good biography depends on factual accuracy, impartial interpretation of information, sound organization of content, format and design suitable for the intended audience, and a writing style that is lively and considerate of the intended reader.

Autobiography and memoir are related to biography, but with an important distinction. An autobiography is about the person who wrote it. The reader must keep in mind the temptation that authors face when writing about their own life and times; they are likely to put the best spin on their subject matter—themselves. This constraint should not deter readers from taking autobiography seriously. Biography faces a similar problem. Biographers, consciously or unconsciously, may also put the best or worst spin on the life of the person they write about. When critics review biography, they will often say that authors have been unduly friendly or unfriendly, or remarkably balanced, in the treatment of the life and times of their subjects.

## Section Summary: Genres of Children's Literature

1. Genres, or types, of children's literature include picture books, traditional literature, poetry, realistic fiction, historical fiction, fantasy and science fiction, informational books, and biography.

2. Picture books may have only pictures, but more often they combine illustrations and text.

3. Traditional literature is based on oral tradition. It includes folktales, fairy tales, myths, ballads, epics, legends, fables, hero tales, tall tales, pourquoi tales, trickster tales, and cumulative tales.

4. Poetry is a crucial genre of children's literature. It captures interest, imagination, and exposes children to one of the richest forms of written language.

5. Realistic fiction deals with real-life situations, takes place in real-world locations, and has realistic people as characters.

6. Historical fiction refers to stories set in the past. This definition raises the question of how far in the past is sufficient for a book to be classified as historical fiction.

7. Fantasy creates a magical world, as when Alice chats with Humpty Dumpty. Science fiction is based on projections from real science rather than magic, though some works mix these elements.

8. Informational books inform readers about a concept or idea, often on a specific topic such as dinosaurs. They are most often written in an expository style.

9. Biographies are histories of the lives and times of people, most often people who are famous or infamous.

## Response to Literature

Louise Rosenblatt (1978) explains her theory of literary response in *The Reader, the Text, the Poem.* According to Rosenblatt, when one reads, a *transaction* may occur between reader and writer—a coming together of *reader* and *text* to create a *poem*— a response to literature: "*The poem* comes into being in the live circuit set up between the reader and the text." (p. 14). A subjective, creative experience is said to result from that transaction: "A novel or poem or play remains merely ink spots on paper until a reader transforms them into a set of meaningful symbols" (p. 25). Sebesta suggests three outcomes of a literary transaction.

> First, the reader must be encouraged to surrender to the literary work, to "live through" the reading of it, to experience it fully without future purpose in mind. This is a stage of evocation, which avid readers will immediately recognize. Second, the reader broadens the transaction, examining alternatives based on other points of view suggested by the text, by other readers, and by comparison with other works. Third, the reader considers application of the experience to his or her own life: What is the ultimate effect of the transaction? This is the stage of reflective thinking and evaluation. The teacher's job, then, is to encourage and guide students through this model without imposing an interpretation or stock response on them. (Sebesta, 1995, p. 209)

Teachers can support response to literature through the instructional activities they sponsor. The teacher's role in applying reader-response theory is not that of grand inquisitor but of thoughtful guide, able to accept students' subjective

## Standing on the Shoulders of Giants
## Historical Contributions to Literacy
### Louise Rosenblatt

I never met Dr. Louise Rosenblatt, never heard her speak. Yet I feel I know her. Is it any wonder? You can't pick up a journal or textbook on literature and literacy without reference to her work. Peruse the reference section of any literature, reading, or language arts text, and you'll find references to her texts.

Louise Rosenblatt is known for what is now called reader-response theory. Her classic book, *The Reader, the Text, and the Poem* (1978) put forward the theory that a literary work is an experience shaped by the reader under the guidance of the text. Arguably, no other book in the past half-century has so profoundly influenced the thinking of literacy professionals. Louise Rosenblatt wrote yet another classic book, *Literature as Exploration*, way back in 1938. While it was well received among literary critics and has never gone out of print, literacy professionals took a long time to discover it. Her first important book wasn't quite like "dropping rose petals down the Grand Canyon and waiting for an echo," but it came close. Sometimes you wait a long time to get your due, but Louise Rosenblatt has finally gotten the recognition she has earned.

Louise Rosenblatt was educated at Columbia University, the University of Grenoble, and the University of Paris. She earned her doctorate in comparative literature from the Sorbonne. She has taught at New York University, Barnard College, Columbia University, and Northwestern University. Her list of awards and honors is long and prestigious: the International Reading Association's Reading Hall of Fame, Outstanding Educator in English Language Arts, Great Teacher Award from New York University, a Guggenheim fellowship, the Leland B. Jacobs Award for Literature, Lifetime Research Award, and several honorary doctorates. The list goes on, but you get the idea.

Louise Rosenblatt is an original thinker. She pursued her ideas, even though they did not receive the imprimatur of the literary critics in vogue when she published *Literature as Exploration.* It takes character to persevere in the face of long odds. She is a woman for all seasons. Her ideas have improved the teaching of literature in countless classrooms, and her theories have enriched literacy discourse.

interpretation of the text without imposing their own—an extension of the principle of ownership. Teachers can support responses to literature in many ways, including writing, shared reading, and reader's theater, which are discussed in this section. Other responses include literature circles, book clubs, and individualized reading, which are discussed elsewhere in this book. But children can respond to literature in their own ways. Sometimes it is best to let books teach their own lessons, fulfill their own destinies, and create their own memories as readers roll along on their own.

## Writing as Response to Literature

Teachers are models; literature is a model. Both play important roles in children's writing success. Modeling is based on the premise that exposure to literature is one of the best ways to teach and learn writing. For example, if you want to expose children to elegant sentence writing, E. B. White is one master. Read aloud or have children read *Trumpet of the Swan, Stuart Little,* or *Charlotte's Web.* White has set a standard worthy of imitation, or modeling, if you prefer.

Fortunately, children assimilate ideas and information as they read. They absorb words and phrases, content and mechanics, topics and techniques from the stories they hear and read. Later, these assimilated elements appear in their writing. Teachers sometimes admonish children to avoid imitating, but these admonitions are inappropriate and may do more harm than good. Imitation and modeling are not plagiarism (the deliberate or careless appropriation of someone else's writing or ideas to pass them off as your own). The key is intent. Sometimes children retell familiar stories as if these stories were their own inventions. A child may turn in a composition, for instance, that closely resembles "Goldilocks and The Three Bears." This is especially likely if the child has recently read or heard the story. Young children are not necessarily aware of the closeness of their retelling to the original story. From their perspective, they are simply *telling a story.* In effect, they say to themselves, "Well, here is a story I know. I'll tell this one." Retelling is common in the writing and storytelling of young children. This need not worry teachers, and it must not be punished. Rather, regard it as a natural starting point for writing and storytelling—a legitimate response to literature. Children soon move beyond retellings to creating stories of their own making.

**Writing Literature in Response to Reading.** Modeling a story or poem can be done with the whole class or a smaller group (Cramer, 2002). The following guidelines can be used to stimulate writing as a response to literature.

*Teacher Erin Caldwell is talking with Joe and Amanda about extending a book they have read into a writing project.*

1. Select a story or poem with content and a linguistic pattern that will interest your children.
2. Read the piece aloud. Invite children to describe the images and ideas the selection arouses. Point out specific words, images, and patterns not mentioned by children.
3. Write a class story or poem. Start by inviting children to offer the first line. If they hesitate, offer the first line yourself.
4. Record the composition on a large piece of paper or on the board.
5. Refine the draft. Add or delete lines, improve word selection or story line, or rearrange lines and verses as needed.
6. Make copies for each child, and have them illustrate the composition.
7. Have children write their own stories or poems.

As noted earlier, many children think that fiction is writing that is untrue, but most fiction, and certainly the best fiction, is about real life, and it has more than a dollop of truth. Even popular genres such as mystery, science fiction, and romance deal with real-life issues. In fact, writing fiction starts with observation and diligent research.

Fiction deals with representational truth, just as art does. Picasso painted his great masterpiece *Guernica* to protest the Nazis' bombing of a Spanish town. *Guernica* is not a photograph of Nazi atrocities, but it represents the truth of atrocities as well as or better than any photograph could. *Guernica* is a symbolic representation of truth. Fiction writers also represent truth symbolically. The plots, settings, characters, events, and resolutions of fiction are of the same genre of truth as that of art. Norman Mailer makes this point explicitly in the epilogue to his novel about the CIA, *Harlot's Ghost*.

> My hope is that the imaginary world of *Harlot's Ghost* will bear more relation to the reality of these historical events than the spectrum of facts and often calculated misinformation that still surrounds them. It is a sizable claim, but then I have the advantage of believing that novelists have a unique opportunity—they can create superior histories out of an enhancement of the real, the unverified, and the wholly fictional. (p. 1288)

Encourage your children to read and write fiction. They can do it. You need only show them the pathway: share literature with them, suggest a few ideas, and get out of their way. They have experiences and they can use them in their writing.

**Engaging in Dialogue to Facilitate Writing**. I've always loved the term Nancie Atwell (1987) coined to describe talk about literature. She called it "literary gossip." She could as well have called it "response to literature."

> I've learned the value and necessity of allowing children to read as real readers do, choosing, skimming, skipping, and abandoning. Maybe the hardest lesson of all, I've learned how to respond authoritatively to what readers are trying to do without coming across like a teacher's guide or a test. Instead, I can affirm, challenge, gossip, joke, argue, recommend, and provide information to reader needs. I can also offer some well-placed "nudges." (p. 170)

The fiction children write will be anemic unless they understand what writers do, how they do it, and why. "Gossip" with your children about the books they have heard or read. Talk about fictional characters. Get children's views on what makes a good story. Use selected fiction to show students that stories can be partially based on real people, their problems and feelings, and events that actually took place. This can be done through informal discussions or response journals. The possibilities are legion. For example, children will enjoy gossiping about *Nettie's Trip South* by Ann Turner, *Walk Two Moons* by Sharon Creech (1995 Newbery Medal winner), *Dicey's Song* by Cynthia Voigt (1983 Newbery Medal winner), *Dear Mr. Henshaw* by Beverly Cleary (1984 Newbery Medal winner), *Nobody Listens to Andrew* by Elizabeth Guilfoile, *Tom and the Two Handles* by Russell Hoban, Tomie dePaola's semi-autobiographical book *The Art Lesson,* and Steven Kellogg's book about friendship and imagination, *Best Friends*.

It is amazing how quickly and easily children understand the connection between literature and writing. Ms. Stanley (1988) discovered this while conducting a revision study with third-grade children. Early in the study she observed, "My students, particularly the more fluent writers, began fictionalizing their pieces early in the study. I could not discover why, I could only guess and wonder if it had to do with the fiction I was reading to them" (p. 26). As time went on, however, Ms. Stanley discovered that her children were linking literature with writing. The more she engaged them in conversations about literature, writers, and writing, the more the children applied this knowledge to their writing. For instance, one day she noticed a few children rather furtively reading books during the writing period. She wanted them to know this was all right. So she asked the children a few questions: Would it be all right to read a book during writing time? Could this help you with your writing? How might it help? she asked. Here are her children's responses:

I could get an idea for a topic.
I could check out how to write quotes.
If I'm publishing, I could see how the author puts the dedication down.
I might get ideas on how long to make my chapters.
I could see how the characters act.

Ms. Stanley discovered that her third-graders were capable of writing fiction. She never underestimated what they could do. The more you "gossip" with children about literature, writers, and writing, the more they will apply this knowledge to their writing. As you discuss literature with your students, and as they retell stories they've read, discuss the components of a story: characters, settings, conflicts, events, resolutions. Familiarity with these components enables children to anticipate the problems, events, and resolutions of stories they are reading, and it will help them create their own stories. Books that may prove useful are *The Sign in Mendel's Window* by Mildred Phillips, *Sarah, Plain and Tall* by Patricia MacLachlan, *Are You There, God? It's Me, Margaret* by Judy Blume, and *A Gathering of Days: A New England Girl's Journal* by Joan W. Blos. Table 6.1 on page 236 suggests ideas for using literature for writing fiction.

**Table 6.1**

**Using Literature for Writing Fiction**

1. The best fiction for this purpose is about real people, problems, and events.
2. Writing fiction is not simply thinking up imaginary events and people that never existed anywhere in the world before. Once children understand this, they can see that their own experiences are a resource for their own fiction.
3. Teach children the value and use of research in writing fiction.
4. Engage children in literary dialogue about the fiction they are reading, so that they will understand what writers do, how they do it, and why.

*Teaching Tip*

Engaging in dialogue about literature benefits all children, including struggling readers. Read the conversation in the Field Notes feature between Michelle Krzeminski, a ninth-grade teacher of English and literature, and Ashley, a third-grader, which took place at a clinic for struggling readers. Ashley has gotten off to a slow start in reading and has had few opportunities to respond to what she has read, as her comments clearly suggest. The conversation reveals that Ashley feels neglected, perhaps resentful, at this slight. When struggling readers aren't called on for a response to what they have read, they realize that their ideas aren't valued as highly as those of the better readers. This can only add to the struggling readers' problems.

## Field Notes
### Real-Life Experiences of a Classroom Teacher

**Ms. K:** Ashley, do you like to read?

**Ashley:** I like to read, but if my friends want to play, I'll go outside and play instead.

**Ms. K:** When do you usually like to read?

**Ashley:** When it's rainy outside—then I'll stay home and read.

**Ms. K:** Where do you like to read?

**Ashley:** On my bed or at my desk.

**Ms. K:** What are your favorite things to read?

**Ashley:** Mysteries and funny books—because these are the most interesting.

**Ms. K:** How often do you read?

**Ashley:** Once a week.

**Ms. K:** What do you expect from your teachers in your reading assignments?

**Ashley:** I would like for my teacher to call on me more. I think she doesn't think I read fast

**Michelle Krzeminski**

enough or good enough, so she just skips right over me.

**Ms. K:** What do you think you most need to work on in your reading?

**Ashley:** Sounding out words and reading the letters that are there.

**Ms. K:** What books are you reading now?

**Ashley:** *Ramona the Brave.*

**Ms. K:** Are you enjoying *Ramona the Brave*?

**Ashley:** Yeah, because Ramona is silly. She tried to scare off the boys by sticking her fingers in her ears.

**Ms. K:** Does Ramona remind you of anybody you know?

**Ashley:** Me! But I'm not as silly as she is.

**Ms. K:** How do you think the book will end?

**Ashley:** I know it will have a silly, funny ending.

## Reader's Theater as Response to Literature

Reader's Theater is a forum for responding to literature as well as creative engagement in a dramatization activity. Reader's Theater fosters comprehension, since it puts children in the position of reader and writer—they are involved in preparing the script. It allows students to engage in oral reading with a purpose while gaining confidence in their oral reading ability.

There are various ways to conduct Reader's Theater. For instance, children can read narration chorally, and individuals can read the parts of story characters. After the teacher has modeled this procedure, children can adapt their own scripts from the literature they are reading or create their own. Books that have extensive dialogue and a minimum of narration work especially well. Some books, such as *Tiger Soup* by Frances Temple, offer a scripted version. Figure 6.10 identifies other books especially useful for reader's theater.

Reader's Theater does not require children to memorize scripts. On the contrary, they read from a rehearsed script. Children should practice until they can read their parts confidently. Reader's Theater provides an opportunity to interpret the mood, tone, and rhythms of a piece of literature. It is important, therefore, for the teacher to help children understand the text. Practice helps accomplish this, along with discussion and modeling by the teacher.

## Shared Reading as Response to Literature

The purpose of shared reading from big books is to help children respond to literature and develop a sense of how print works. Among the most popular big books is the classic by Bill Martin Jr. and Eric Carle, *Brown Bear, Brown Bear, What Do You See?* This predictable book has a rhythmic repetition of lines, which enables children to chant the predictable lines as the teacher reads aloud. Later, children will be able to read much of the book themselves because of the predictable refrains. Other types of books also work well, including nonfiction books. The key to

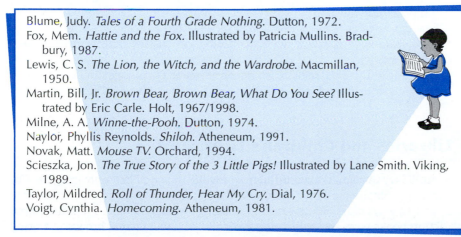

Blume, Judy. *Tales of a Fourth Grade Nothing.* Dutton, 1972.
Fox, Mem. *Hattie and the Fox.* Illustrated by Patricia Mullins. Bradbury, 1987.
Lewis, C. S. *The Lion, the Witch, and the Wardrobe.* Macmillan, 1950.
Martin, Bill, Jr. *Brown Bear, Brown Bear, What Do You See?* Illustrated by Eric Carle. Holt, 1967/1998.
Milne, A. A. *Winne-the-Pooh.* Dutton, 1974.
Naylor, Phyllis Reynolds. *Shiloh.* Atheneum, 1991.
Novak, Matt. *Mouse TV.* Orchard, 1994.
Scieszka, Jon. *The True Story of the 3 Little Pigs!* Illustrated by Lane Smith. Viking, 1989.
Taylor, Mildred. *Roll of Thunder, Hear My Cry.* Dial, 1976.
Voigt, Cynthia. *Homecoming.* Atheneum, 1981.

**Figure 6.10**

**Books for Reader's Theater**

effective use of big books is the interaction generated among the children as they discuss the ideas presented in the book.

While shared reading provides a forum for response to literature, it also helps develop print awareness. As children learn to match spoken words with print, they acquire an understanding of what constitutes a printed word—often referred to as *concept of word* (Morris, 1980). Concept of word is prerequisite knowledge for learning to read fluently. Shared reading is normally conducted using big books so that children can sit in a circle and still see the print and illustrations clearly from a distance.

Barr and Johnson (1997) trace the roots of shared reading to Stauffer (1969) and Holdaway (1979). Stauffer (1969) pioneered the language experience approach and Holdaway, the shared book experience. Reading a big book with children is similar to how a group- or individual-dictated story is read and reread. The procedures for sharing a book are as follows:

*Teaching Tip*

1. *First reading, teacher only.* Select a big book, such as *Polar Bear, Polar Bear, What Do You Hear?* Read the story aloud, pointing to the words as you read. Read slowly, but avoid reading choppily.
2. *Second reading, teacher and children.* After reading the story aloud, invite children to read with you. Continue pointing and sweeping from line to line.
3. *Third reading, children only.* Invite individual children to read lines, providing immediate help when a child has difficulty recalling a word.
4. *Follow-up.* Ask questions designed to encourage discussion of the story. Later, do some print awareness activities. For example, point to the word *Polar* and ask, "Can someone find the same word elsewhere in the story?"

## Section Summary: Response to Literature

1. Rosenblatt proposed a theory of response to reading, suggesting that when one reads, a *transaction* may occur between reader and writer—a coming together of *reader* and *text* to create a *poem*.
2. Writing is one of the most productive ways to encourage children's response to literature.
3. Reader's Theater is an excellent way for children to respond to literature. Furthermore, it provides an opportunity for creative engagement in a drama activity.
4. Shared reading of big books is an effective way to encourage discussion and response to reading. It also helps develop a sense of how print works.

## Libraries and Children's Literature

A modest library in a small town influenced my life in ways I can only imagine. On my first visit I obtained a library card and the librarian pointed to the fiction section. I was 12 years old and knew next to nothing about libraries. I soon discovered that fiction books were shelved in alphabetical order, so I started browsing among the *A*'s. Unlike Frances in *A Tree Grows in Brooklyn,* who had determined to start with the *A*'s and read on through to *Z,* I started with the *A*'s with no plan at all. But soon I came upon a book by Joseph Altsheler, *The Riflemen of the Ohio.* The title interested me, so I checked it out. *What good fortune smiled down upon me that day.* I had discovered an author whom I would not abandon until I had read every book in the library he had written. His books got me seriously interested in reading.

"All beginnings are hard," Chaim Potok tells us in *In the Beginning.* But not in my case. My beginnings were easy. I gobbled that first book and returned, hoping for more. And there were seven more books in Altsheler's series, The Young Trailers. Of course, I read them all. But now what? Panic. I had fallen in love with five characters: Henry, Paul, Shiftless Sol, Long Jim, and Silent Ross. I did not want to move on. I wasn't ready to move on. I discovered endings can be harder than beginnings. I solved the problem easily enough: I read them all again. Finally, I was ready to seek other books of similar genre. I chose Zane Grey, as there seemed to be an ample supply in our library. And then eventually I tired of Grey and was ready to seek a wider variety of fiction. But all this took a while—perhaps a year. But in the meanwhile I had become an avid reader.

So I have an affection for libraries and am interested in the role they play in the lives of writers. Isaac Bashevis Singer, an observant Jew, entered a small library in Poland and shyly told the librarian, "I want to know the secret of life. I want to read a book on philosophy." The kindly librarian accommodated him. Singer fondly recalled the kindness of this person. Sherwood Anderson's first library was the home office of the school superintendent. Anderson compared this tiny library, in his imagination, to Emperor Napoleon's palace library at Fontainebleau. Paule Marshall's first library was the imposing edifice on Macon Street in Brooklyn. Here she discovered black writers she did not know existed: Paul Lawrence Dunbar, Langston Hughes, and Zora Neale Hurston. Soon she began harboring the "dangerous thought" that someday she could become a writer, too.

Two great stone lions flank the entrance. An inscription at the entrance reads, "But of all things, truth beareth away the victory." How perfectly these words represent the mission of one of the great public institutions in this country—the New York Public Library. How right that people from every state and nation have passed through its doors. Public libraries were once, and often still are, the only place where poor folks have had free access to books. Untold numbers of immigrants found their way to that library. Often their hopes for an education rested solely on access to such a place. They believed that books could deliver them from their difficult circumstances. Often they were right. They longed for a foothold on the ladder of learning. There, in that great library, they filled the reading rooms, read the books, and started their journeys to fulfill the American dream.

## Classroom Libraries

If teachers had to choose between furniture for a library or books, most would choose books. It shouldn't come down to such a stark choice, but there are schools in this country where library shelves are empty. If you were to visit schools in desperately poor countries and ask the teachers to choose between books and furni-

**Table 6.2**

**Characteristics of a Classroom Library**

*Teaching Tip*

| Physical accommodations | Locate the library in an area of the room where it will be noticed but will not be intrusive. The eye should take notice of this space upon entering the room. Partition off this area from the rest of the room by using bookshelves and furniture. It should be large enough for half a dozen students. Decorate the library with posters of authors, illustrators, medal winners, and children's posters advertising their favorite books and poems. Encourage children to participate in making the library attractive. Accommodations can include rugs, cushions, or chairs. |
|---|---|
| Books | A classroom library needs at least six or seven times as many books as students. Books should span three or four levels of readability. There should be fiction, nonfiction, poetry, picture books, and multicultural books. Select high-quality literature, books recommended by children, and books of many genres. Start a collection of books written by students. |
| Organization of books | An organizational system is essential so that children can locate books appropriate to their interests and reading level. |

ture, they would not hesitate—they would always choose books. Some school districts seem to have funds to buy basal textbooks but will not buy books for classroom libraries. In some schools, even central libraries are neglected—they do not exist or are poorly stocked. Even if there is a decent central school library, it is still crucial to have a classroom library. Bissett (1969) found that children in classrooms with good libraries read 50% more than children in classrooms without them. But even if this were not so, classroom libraries are an invaluable adjunct to effective literacy instruction. There is no substitute for the immediacy and the ambience of a well-stocked, well-used classroom library. A minimum ratio of books to children is about seven books to each student. Table 6.2 suggests essential characteristics of a classroom library.

## Censorship

An official censor is a person authorized to examine books, films, or other material and to remove or suppress what is considered morally, politically, or otherwise objectionable. Ancient Rome had official censors who were responsible for taking the public census and supervising public behavior and morals. Today we have unofficial censors, often parents, who want to deny children access to books and ideas they regard as morally, politically, or otherwise objectionable. Figure 6.11 lists the

20 most challenged books from 1990 to 2000 (you can view the complete list of 100 banned books at http://www.ala.org/bbooks/top100bannedbooks.html). Pressure to censor books and other materials is increasingly common. Occasionally, a timid school administrator complies with such censorship. Denying access to books and ideas is not a good idea. Yet the pressure generated by unofficial censors can make life miserable for teachers and librarians.

Organization A says, "We object to *Huckleberry Finn* because it is racist." Group B says "We object to *Harry Potter and the Sorcerer's Stone* because it fosters witchcraft." Each group denies the validity of the other's concerns. Each believes it holds the high moral ground. *Each group sponsors censorship.* If the individual members of these groups wish to control the reading material of their own children in their own homes, that's their right. But since both groups attempt to impose their moral objections on public institutions, such as libraries and schools, there is reason to oppose their goals.

"Children have a lot more to worry about from the parents who raised them than from the books they read," said novelist E. L. Doctorow. How true. *What* children read is less important than *that* they read. Reading abets thinking, and children can learn to sort out the toxic from the tonic only if we empower them to make thoughtful judgments about the goodness, the badness, and the ugliness they will surely encounter throughout their lives. When my daughter was in fifth grade, she wanted to read Judy Blume's book, *Wifey*. Unknown to me, Jen's mother had already forbade the book. Playing both sides against the middle, as children will do, she asked me if she could read it, and I said yes. I knew it was too mature for her, but I also knew Jen. A few days later she said to me, "Maybe I'll read this book when I'm older." She censored herself: the best possible outcome. This was a home, not a school, matter. But I can imagine the fuss that would have arisen had the issue come up in school.

Censorship is harmful because it denies children access to ideas. Schools should not be party to denial of access to ideas since the purpose of schooling is to expose children to all manner of ideas. Of course, ideas may be encountered in

1. Scary Stories (series) by Alvin Schwartz
2. *Daddy's Roommate* by Michael Willhoite
3. *I Know Why the Caged Bird Sings* by Maya Angelou
4. *The Chocolate War* by Robert Cormier
5. *The Adventures of Huckleberry Finn* by Mark Twain
6. *Of Mice and Men* by John Steinbeck
7. Harry Potter (series) by J. K. Rowling
8. *Forever* by Judy Blume
9. *Bridge to Terabithia* by Katherine Paterson
10. *Alice* (series) by Phyllis Reynolds Naylor
11. *Heather Has Two Mommies* by Leslea Newman
12. *My Brother Sam Is Dead* by James Lincoln Collier and Christopher Collier
13. *The Catcher in the Rye* by J. D. Salinger
14. *The Giver* by Lois Lowry
15. *It's Perfectly Normal* by Robie Harris
16. Goosebumps (series) by R. L. Stine
17. *A Day No Pigs Would Die* by Robert Newton Peck
18. *The Color Purple* by Alice Walker
19. *Sex* by Madonna
20. Earth's Children (series) by Jean M. Auel

*Source:* http://www.ala.org/bbooks/top100bannedbooks.html

**Figure 6.11**

**The 20 Most Challenged Books, 1990–2000**

**Table 6.3**

**Dealing with Censorship**

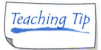

*Teaching Tip*

1. Be respectful to the complaining party. Try to cooperate within reasonable parameters without yielding your principles.
2. Establish guidelines for choosing good literature. The National Council of Teachers of English has such guidelines, and they can be obtained by writing to NCTE, 111 Kenyon Road, Urbana, Illinois, 61801. You can also look them up online: www.ncte.org/censorship
3. If you are in danger of serious consequences for standing on your principles, contact your local American Civil Liberties Union. They can give you good advice and in some instances may provide legal advice and counsel.
4. The American Library Association has an Office of Intellectual Freedom. Their Internet address is www.ala.org

places other than schools, but the principle that schools should provide access to ideas is crucial. Parents have a legitimate role in educating their children, but their role should not be to control access to controversial ideas. Table 6.3 suggests ideas for dealing with censorship when the issue arises.

## Section Summary: Libraries and Children's Literature

1. Libraries have played a crucial role in the lives of many individuals. They are especially important to the literacy prospects of the poor and disenfranchised.
2. Classroom libraries are crucial to a successful literature-based curriculum. A minimal ratio of books to children is about seven books to each student.
3. Censorship is the suppression or removal of books and materials considered morally, politically, or otherwise objectionable. Censorship is harmful because it denies children access to ideas.

## Reading Literature to Children

I recall sitting under an apricot tree, chores completed, with nothing but pleasure stretching ahead of me. I have been to the library, and I have a new book. I have graduated from Joseph Altsheler to Zane Grey. I have read other books by this most famous of all western writers. I know I am about to encounter good and bad guys. I am ready for the journey. Perhaps I'll travel into the Badlands of the Dakotas or onto the High Plains of Montana. Avid readers can recall a time when words from a book engrossed them completely. Every child deserves to experience the same pleasure when reading on their own or being read to.

## Point ≡ Counterpoint

### A Debatable Issue
### Censorship

**Background**

Teachers sometimes face censorship issues. Books such as the *Harry Potter* series and *Huckleberry Finn* have been objected to by parents and community groups. Some folks argue that censorship is never acceptable. Others say it depends on the issues involved in a particular case.

**The Debatable Issue**

Teachers should take a stand against removing books from their classroom libraries based on objections made by parents or community groups.

**Take a Stand**

Argue the case for or against the debatable issue. Might some circumstances persuade you to remove a book from your classroom library? How about pressure from a parent or the community? Marshal your arguments based on your philosophy, experience, and beliefs. After you have discussed these questions among colleagues, consider debating the issue in your class.

Reading aloud is an adventure, and you are the guide, leading children into exciting new places, times, and adventures. It is well established that reading to children supports learning to read. It is less well recognized that reading aloud supports writing; enriches the store of language available for speaking, listening, and writing; and develops cognitive structures that enable children to relate new information to established schemata.

Brown et al. (1972) found that children who were read many linguistically complex books developed greater linguistic capabilities than children who were not read to. Trelease (1995) cites dozens of highly successful read-aloud school and community programs organized throughout the United States. As mentioned earlier, after a review of the literature, Anderson, Hiebert, Scott, and Wilkinson (1985) concluded that reading aloud to children constituted the single most important experience for reading success. Elley (1992) collected data from 32 countries and found that factors which differentiated high- from low-scoring countries included "large school libraries, large classroom libraries, regular book borrowing, frequent silent reading in class, *frequent story reading aloud by teachers* [italics added], and more scheduled hours spent teaching the language" (p. xii). Light (1991) found that parents who regularly read aloud had a significant positive effect on their children's attitude toward reading. The common denominator in all these programs and experiments is the beneficial influence that reading aloud exerts on literacy and learning. The evidence is solid. *Reading aloud ranks among the most valuable of all educational experiences.* Having books read to us when we are young has a lasting influence. Ms. Brown, a history teacher, always started her class by reading aloud. The storyteller's art drew her students into its sticky web. Ms. Brown's teaching instincts were golden. She must have sensed that history is a story to be heard, which can awaken an interest in reading about history on one's own.

## Creating Receptivity

Reading to children requires a climate of receptivity. Every farmer knows that seeds thrive in well-prepared soil. Just as a farmer prepares the ground for planting, so teachers prepare children's minds to absorb the spoken word. The following four suggestions can enhance children's receptivity to the read-aloud experience.

1. *Make reading aloud a time for enjoyment and relaxation.* If children are more comfortable resting their heads on their desks, encourage this. If cushions and rugs are available, younger children may wish to sit or lie on them. Textbooks and other working materials should be kept in desks so as not to distract. Set the stage for pleasure.

2. *Schedule time for reading aloud.* Some teachers schedule reading aloud just before writing time to make the literature–writing connection more direct. But there are other options. Reading aloud during the last 20 or 30 minutes of the day sends children home with a pleasant conclusion to the day's activities. The beginning of the day, on the other hand, has the advantage of getting the children off to a good start. A teacher friend of mine, however, insists that after lunch is the best time for reading aloud to children.

3. *Jointly establish a few rules.* Only a few rules are needed, and they are intended to create a relaxed and pleasant atmosphere. Have your children participate in making the rules, as this gives them a sense of ownership, and they are more likely to comply with rules they helped create.

4. *Do not withdraw reading aloud as a punishment.* When children misbehave, it is reasonable to discipline them, but reading aloud should seldom, if ever, be withdrawn. No one withdraws math because children have misbehaved. Rightly so, because math is important. And reading aloud is the single most important adjunct to learning to read, write, and enjoy literature.

## What to Read

There are more excellent books for children today than there have ever been. Recent data indicate that more children's books were sold in 2002 than in any preceding year. This is good news for teachers and children. Taking advantage of the growing abundance of children's literature requires planning. The following guidelines can help you select books to read aloud in your classroom.

- *Age and interest levels are pertinent guidelines in selecting literature to read aloud.* But, nobody knows your children as well as you do, so trust your judgment in selecting read-aloud literature.

- *Read from any genre your children enjoy.* Traditional or folk literature links the present generation with its cultural heritage. Justice, equality, courage, honesty, and a sense of humor are values revealed in traditional literature, and these concepts remain important in modern times. At the same time, modern literature and fantasy provide language, settings, and situations that delight and enlighten children.

- *Read fiction and nonfiction.* The balance of reading selections should tip in the direction of fiction. Children identify with the characters and situations portrayed in fiction. It gives them an opportunity to be someone else, to imagine and to fantasize. On the other hand, children need to build a store of information from nonfiction works. The information thus obtained helps children formulate new ideas and expands their world knowledge.
- *Read prose and poetry.* Most children read prose; fewer read poetry. Reading poetry aloud provides the exposure that develops understanding and appreciation of poetry. Ms. Jonella Mongo teaches in Detroit. Since most of her children are African American, she reads poems by Langston Hughes, Nikki Giovanni, Paul Lawrence Dunbar, and other gifted African Americans. She tells her children about the lives of these writers. Then she invites them to read and write, and they do.
- *Read multicultural literature.* Children need to known about their own heritage. Children need to know about the heritage of their classmates. This

*After studying books on the life of Martin Luther King Jr., students used chart paper to write about what they learned.*

chapter has listed some fine multicultural books. The Internet provides another rich resource. Read books that represent the cultural and ethnic heritage of your children. The past several decades have seen an increase in the publication of books written by and about African, Asian, Latino, and Native Americans. Walters, Webster, and Cramer (1998) have compiled an extensive bibliography of multicultural literature for younger and older children containing over 700 listings.

- *Select some challenging readings.* Some read-aloud books should extend children's literary experience beyond their independent reading capability. For instance, many Newbery Award–winning books fall in this category. Keep the challenge you present within an acceptable interest and listening range. Fortunately, when we go beyond an acceptable level, children usually let us know. Some of the books you read aloud may be appropriate for children to read independently. Encourage this, since hearing a book read aloud makes independent reading more manageable.

- *Study bibliographies of children's literature, and choose those books that seem best suited to fulfill the needs of your children.* Children love stories in which the characters' emotions and problems parallel their own. They enjoy literature that tells of the human struggle against the forces of nature and the confrontation of good with evil. They especially like stories that enable them to imagine and dream of their future, as Paule Marshall did. Bibliographies for reading aloud can be found in *The Read-Aloud Handbook* by Jim Trelease (1995), *Best Books for Children: Fourth Edition* by Gillespie and Naden (1990), and "Children's Choices," which appears annually in *The Reading Teacher*. Most bibliographies of children's literature are revised every few years, so it is best to seek out the latest edition.

## Reading the Selection

*Teaching Tip*

Select appropriate materials and read them well. Plan each day's selection in advance: certain days can be reserved for reading continuing books such as *Charlotte's Web*, *The Secret Garden*, or *James and the Giant Peach*. It is also useful to reserve some time for special selections, such as poetry or readings intended to mesh with classroom projects. Interpret the mood, tone, and action of the passage being read. I once heard Bill Martin Jr., a consummate teacher–actor, say that teachers would benefit by taking a course in acting. I've often regretted that I never took his advice. I see now how acting can serve a teacher. Reading aloud is a good time to do a little acting. Younger children will appreciate "Jack and the Beanstalk" all the more if you let your voice rise and fall with the natural rhythms and emotions evoked by the story. Older children will also enjoy the extra dimension that dramatic interpretation adds to books such as *Harriet the Spy* by Louise Fitzhugh or *A Wrinkle in Time* by Madeleine L'Engle. Self-consciousness sometimes makes us hesitant to dramatize stories as we read. However, children are a generous audience. They will appreciate your efforts to dramatize literature.

Distinguish between reading aloud and directed reading instruction. It is neither necessary nor desirable to turn reading aloud into a directed reading lesson, unless that is the specific purpose of a read-aloud session. Enjoyment is the major and distinctive purpose of reading aloud. When enjoyment is paramount, other important purposes are also accomplished. For example, reading aloud often leads to sharing the special passages that literature inevitably contains. Sharing literary gems makes literature special. If a sentence is especially well written, point it out; if a paragraph gives a marvelous vignette, mention it; if a passage has special meaning to you, tell about it. Encourage your students to reciprocate. Ask them to share favorite passages with you and their fellow students. The pleasures of literature are always sweeter when you have someone to share them with. Perhaps the most important result of your efforts will be to bequeath an enduring love for literature. No gift could be more precious, no legacy of greater value.

Choose strategic stopping points. When reading a continuing narrative, stop at a point that will build anticipation for the next episode. Avid readers know the pleasure of anticipation when they have a good book awaiting them at home in the evening. Anticipation is one of the great pleasures of life, and this doubly applies to reading. Anticipating the next day's reading can have a positive affect on attendance, although its primary benefit is to sustain interest in the selection.

## Section Summary: Reading Literature to Children

1. Reading aloud supports learning to read, writing, and language growth.
2. Create a climate of receptivity for reading aloud. Make the experience enjoyable and regularly scheduled, with a few rules jointly established.
3. Select books that are suitable to children's age and interests. Choose a balance of books from among the many genres of children's literature.
4. Reading the selection well requires planning and the interpretation of mood, tone, and action.
5. Do not confuse reading aloud for pleasure with directed reading instruction, which has a different purpose.
6. Choose strategic stopping points so as to build anticipation for the next episode.
7. Do not punish children by threatening withdrawal of the read-aloud experience, since reading aloud has an essential strategic purpose in literacy instruction.

## The Storyteller's Art

I grew up in the storytelling tradition of the hills and hollows of West Virginia and Pennsylvania. Everyone in these communities had heard stories told by their parents, grandparents, aunts, uncles, and neighbors. Storytelling usually started after supper or on a social occasion. As darkness gathered around the cabin, the old folks, as we little ones called them, visited, laughed, and drank coffee—sometimes something a little stronger. The storytelling setting might be the front porch or the kitchen, sometimes by the light of a fire or a kerosene lamp.

After mild coaxing, Uncle Charlie was usually the first to tell a story because he was known far and wide for his storytelling skill. In our community this skill was regarded as high art. Everyone grew quiet as Uncle Charlie started. Even when we had heard the story before, we knew it might take a different turn tonight. As the evening wore on, other storytellers followed. We children listened quietly, not wanting to hear that terrible word, *bedtime*. We'd get sleepier and sleepier, propping our eyes open with our fingers, dreading what we knew was coming: "Time you kids went to bed." We'd beg to stay up, and often we were granted a reprieve and carried to bed later in the evening.

Many of the stories I heard had a supernatural element. They often featured hunting dogs and haunts—*ghosts*. How we loved those stories, and how we shivered at the haunting call of the fierce ghost dog. On dark nights we shunned the graveyard where Old Mr. Buswell had been buried. We dreaded his reappearance, lamp in hand, searching, searching for his lost sons and daughters.

Every culture has its stories, and these stories are passed from generation to generation. Hirsch, Kett, and Trefil (1988) make an interesting observation about such stories: "The tales we tell our children define what kind of people we shall be" (p. 27). Stories define us in more ways than we might expect. They tell of our fears and frivolities, values and traditions, prejudices and ideals. *Story* is an upbeat word. Its synonyms include *tale, yarn, anecdote, narrative,* and *history*. In other contexts it can mean falsehood, exaggeration, or lie. Stories may be written or oral, factual or fiction, prose or verse. In a more literary sense, *story* suggests characters, settings, plots, events, and resolutions.

Stories are as old as human history, and storytellers have always held an honored place in human affairs. Stories constitute an important part of the collective memory of a culture. The fabled mountain men of American frontier folklore were great story tellers. A mountain man wore his reputation as a storyteller as a badge of honor. Once a year, these rough-and-tumble men traveled hundreds of miles across mountains and plains to gather at their annual roundup. They traded skins, fought, drank, and swapped stories. The stories they told were a duke's mixture of fact and fiction, exaggerated accounts of dangers faced, deeds done, victories won. If they bragged too much and misrepresented the truth more than just a little, well, that was part of the storyteller's art. Storytelling filled a need that lonely men have for narrative, a need common among adults and children at all times and in all places.

Stories have a transforming, almost magical effect on children. Stories have a practical academic purpose as well. They are a powerful way of conveying information to children. Flood (1986) found that stories are one of the best ways to convey historical and cultural information to children. Throughout history and prehistory this has been so. During the 15th and 16th centuries, stories from the oral tradition began to find their way into print, thanks to Guttenberg's invention of movable type. Traditional literature arose out of the oral storytelling tradition.

In a literate culture, such as ours, literature has become the repository of the tales our children need to hear. Listening to oral stories, reading story text, and telling stories develops a cognitive map for how a story is structured. Virtually all stories have certain components in common: settings, characters, problems, events, and resolutions. Researchers call this story grammar (Applebee, 1978; Mandler and Johnson, 1987; Stein, 1979). Having these cognitive maps enables children to anticipate problems, events, and resolutions in stories they have not yet encountered. Repeated exposure to oral storytelling and story text helps children's sense of story grow.

Oral storytelling is a dramatic art form and should be approached with drama in mind. As a classroom activity it can take the form of preparing a story derived from a written source, such as traditional literature. Stories may also derive from personal experience or an oral tradition in a family or community. In any case, preparation for telling the story is crucial. A written source has the advantage of providing the novice storyteller with content and structure already established. Personal stories may tell about family, friends, ghosts, riddles, jokes, and tall tales. Regardless, the storyteller needs to pull listeners into the experience. A good story requires excitement and drama. The content and structure are important, but bodily movements, voice, cadence, rhythm, and even props contribute a lot to the experience. Table 6.4 suggests ideas for presenting a story to a listening group.

*Teaching Tip*

**Table 6.4**

**Steps in Telling a Story**

1. *Choose.* Decide which story you will tell. Choose one that you like and enjoy telling to others. It can come from a book or other written source. It can also come from personal experience, such as a family tall tale or a ghost story you have heard at home or in your community.

2. *Learn.* Know your story well enough to feel comfortable telling it to others. Do not memorize it word for word. Memorizing can interfere with spontaneity. You don't want to forget the story sequence at a vital point, and rote memory can fail you at a critical point. Good storytellers suggest that you know how the story starts, the important events, the story characters, and the story ending. You can summarize the vital parts on index cards. Go over your cards until you know each part well. A basic and familiar story structure makes it easier to invent interesting phrasing and develop ideas as you tell your story.

3. *Rehearse.* Once you know your story, rehearse it. Practice telling your story to an imaginary audience, or perhaps your dog. Then practice telling it to friends, parents, or a small group of students. If you know your story well, you may never need to look at your index cards.

4. *Revise and refine.* If you have followed steps 1, 2, and 3, you have a rough draft of your story. But just as good writing requires revising and refining, so does oral storytelling. For instance, think about different ways to start your story. How can you hook your audience's interest right away? Ask yourself what your characters are like. Are they sneaky, brave, dumb? Your answers will tell you how you want to use your voice or body movements when you talk about your characters. Think about your story ending. Is it scary? sad? funny? Good endings are crucial to storytelling success. Your words and gestures here are especially important since the ending is the dramatic high point of your story.

*Good luck!*

## Section Summary: The Storyteller's Art

1. Storytelling is an ancient art form. Effective storytelling requires an understanding of story elements and drama.

2. Storytelling has an aesthetic purpose. It also has an academic purpose—the transmission of values, information, culture, and linguistic and dramatic skill.

3. There are four preparatory steps for storytelling: choose a story you are comfortable with; learn the elements of the story well; rehearse telling the story; revise and refine the story in final preparation for telling it.

## Practical Teaching Ideas and Activities

*Teaching Tip*

**1.** *Provide access to an extensive library collection.* Together with the students, arrange the classroom library. At the beginning of the school year, unpack a box or two of books at a time, allowing the children ample opportunity to explore them, sharing favorites and investigating new titles, authors, or themes. Involve the students in sorting classroom books, and collaborating on establishing categories by which to organize them, such as genre, theme, author, illustrator, or series. Display the categories of books in tubs or baskets that are clearly labeled and easily accessible. This process gives students a sense of ownership and a sense of the variety of books available to them. It also stimulates rich dialogue about genres, authors, illustrators, and collections of books.

**2.** *Make literature connections in all areas of the curriculum.* Reading aloud, accompanied by interactive discussion of picture books, poetry, chapter books, and expository text, should occur multiple times a day, every day. Literature is a means to pass on culture and wisdom from generation to generation. As such, many literary works can be used to enrich understanding in the content areas. Children's literature can provide powerful models in writing workshops, to introduce aspects of writing craft, to share information for topic exploration in science or social studies, or to explain mathematical concepts. For example, when learning about the civil rights movement, students could read the short novel *Well* by Mildred Taylor, to better understand the suffering of black Americans in the South. Or when studying the Holocaust, reading *Daniel's Story* by Carol Matas would help students connect in a personal way to the children who experienced the inhumanity of those times and places. These experiences with literature deepen understanding of history in ways that textbook accounts can't accomplish.

**3.** *Teach students to make connections.* Because good readers connect new information with what they already know, it is essential to help them recognize when they are making connections between themselves and the text, between the world and the text, or between a previous textual experience and this new text. Choose literature that will clearly demonstrate these connections. Newspaper articles or other informational resources are a good place to start because they often offer all three types of reader–text connections. Once students become comfortable making and recognizing these connections, move on to other genres. Teach students that good readers make connections between familiar and new text and use this process to better comprehend and appreciate what they are reading. In addition, it is wonderful when students realize that each reader makes unique connections; in a way, each person who reads a given story gets his or her own special version of it.

**4.** *Conduct buddy book swaps.* Set aside a specific time every few weeks for students to chose a buddy (perhaps match up those who share an interest in a particular genre or author), and have them do a brief book talk and book swap of a favorite, recently read piece of literature.

**5.** *Utilize a reading workshop—a literature-based, child-centered approach to reading instruction.* Provide students with a full hour to engage in meaningful reading, collaboratively sharing with others about the books they are reading. They also need to participate in direct reading instruction, receive guidance, and have frequent contact with you, the teacher, to address individual reading needs and receive feedback.

## ◄ Reflection and Summary

### Reflection

The Persian poet Omar Khayyam wrote an oft-quoted line of verse: "A Jug of Wine, a Loaf of Bread—and Thou . . ." What's missing from Omar's list? Did Omar neglect to mention literature? No. The line that precedes the famous one; it says, "A book of Verses underneath the Bough."

Who could not live joyously on these four good things: literature, food, drink, and companionship? Who could not feast on this heavenly bounty? Shakespeare's character Prospero in *The Tempest* highly values his books: "mine own library with volumes that / I prize above my dukedom." Literature is highly democratic; you don't have to be a duke to feast on its bounty. Willie Sutton, bank robber, was famous for his answer to the question "Why do you rob banks?" His answer was simplicity itself: "Because that's where the money is." Willie is less well known for how he spent his years in prison: "I'll spend the rest of my life reading, and because I'd rather read than do anything else, I don't look forward to years of hopeless, black despair." Literature intensifies life yet slows it down so that reflection is possible. It opens doors to different ways of imagining and thinking. It offers escape from life's events; it offers entrance into life's events. Those who refuse or are refused its bounties are missing out on life's greatest pleasure. Those who accept its bounties are fortunate above all others.

### Summary

1. Literature passes on its values, riches, and wisdom from generation to generation; extends cognitive, cultural, and linguistic knowledge; promotes emotional insight; and has a humanizing influence.

2. Current issues in children's literature include how to define children's literature, how it contributes to a well-lived life, how so-called trashy literature has

its own redeeming features, and how authentic multicultural literature helps define and influence culture.

3. The elements of literature include these six features of fiction: character, setting, point of view, plot, theme, and style.

4. Genres, or types, of children's literature, include picture books, traditional literature, poetry, realistic fiction, historical fiction, fantasy and science fiction, informational books, and biography.

5. Rosenblatt proposed a theory of response to reading, which suggests that when one reads, a transaction occurs between reader and writer. Ways of responding to literature include writing, reader's theater, and shared reading.

6. Classroom libraries are crucial to a successful literature-based curriculum. A minimal ratio of books to children is about seven books to each student. Censorship of children's books is harmful because it denies children access to ideas.

7. Reading aloud is a crucial adjunct to literacy instruction because it supports reading, writing, and language growth. Effective reading aloud requires a climate of receptivity, selecting books appropriate to children's age and interests, planning the reading, and interpreting the selection.

8. Effective storytelling requires an understanding of the dramatic effects. Its purpose is to provide pleasure and academic knowledge. Four steps involved in storytelling are choosing the story, learning its components, rehearsing the telling, and revising and refining the selection for final presentation.

## ◀━ Questions to Challenge Your Thinking ━━━━━

1. Do you agree with the idea that literature humanizes? Explain.

2. As a child, did you read books that might, by some standards, be considered trashy? What is your view of literature that might fall into such a category?

3. What is your favorite literary element? Explain why you prefer it.

4. What genre of literature do you read most often? Why are you attracted to it?

5. Do you think children should read more informational books? Why or why not?

6. How does writing benefit when used as a response to literature?

7. Can reading aloud instill a love of literature in children? Explain.

8. What is the best way to prepare children for the read-aloud experience?

9. How can storytelling benefit literacy instruction?

10. What have you learned that you didn't know before you read this chapter?

## ◀━ A Case Study ━━━━━━━━━━━━━━━━━━━━━━━

Read the following true case study, and then discuss the questions below with your classmates or colleagues.

Megan is a third-grader who will be going into fourth grade in 4 months. She has become an avid reader after going through some difficult times in second grade. She has definite ideas about teachers. For instance, she said to me, "I'm hoping to get Mrs. Roeper for fourth grade because she's a good teacher." I asked Megan, "How do you know she's a good teacher?" Megan said, "She teaches her lessons for an hour—*till you get it.* Also, if you've been good all day, you get an extra recess."

1. Would you be willing to spend an hour five days a week, teaching literature-based language arts? Explain.
2. What connection might there be between effective teaching, good behavior among children, and rewards, such as an extra recess?

3. Assume that you are going to teach fourth grade in an urban school. Most of your children are members of minority groups. One of your goals is to help them write fiction. Suggest an instructional plan that will help you accomplish this goal.

## Revisit the Anticipation Guide

Return to the Anticipation Guide in the chapter opener, and review your original responses to the questions. Complete the guide again, and then consider these questions.

1. Did you change your mind about any items? Why?
2. Which chapter ideas did you most strongly agree with? Why?

3. Which chapter ideas did you most strongly disagree with? Why?
4. Do you think the author of this text is too opinionated? Explain.
5. Suggest some ideas that would make you a better teacher of children's literature.

## VideoWorkshop Extra!

If your instructor ordered a package including VideoWorkshop, go to Chapter 6 of the Companion Website (www.ablongman.com/cramer1e) and click on the VideoWorkshop button. Follow the instructions for viewing the appropriate video clip and completing the accompanying exercise. Watch the Companion Website for access to a new interactive teaching portal, My Lab School, currently under construction.

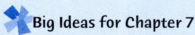

### A Philosophy of Content Area Literacy

*Content teachers often say they haven't time to teach reading and writing. They argue that they have enough to do teaching their subject matter. If you teach science, history, or math, you are right to regard yourself as a science, history, or math teacher. But attention to content literacy can and often does result in more effective learning of content. This chapter considers issues and strategies that will improve performance in your subject area. In the end, that is exactly what content teachers want. But it would be a travesty to foist upon subject matter teachers additional responsibilities if they detract from content teachers' primary mission: to convey concepts, information, and ways of thinking about subject matter. On the other hand, children who do not read and write effectively cannot benefit from subject matter instruction; they need instruction in content literacy. Probably most subject matter teachers would agree with that idea.*

# 7 Content Literacy: Reading and Writing in the Content Areas

### Big Ideas for Chapter 7

1. Readers construct meaning using prior knowledge, reasoning, and information from the text.
2. Learning content is enhanced through engagement and interest.
3. Purpose determines reading rate, and there are four ways to adjust it: skimming, scanning, studying, and surveying.
4. Four important content reading strategies are: directed reading thinking activities,

question/answer relationships, anticipation guides, and modeling.
5. Writing process applies to content writing, but it is also essential to emphasize the importance of the written product.
6. Ten content writing strategies are: learning journals, double-entry journals, essays, literary gossip and dialogue journaling, note taking, summaries, reports, poetry, letters, and freewrites.

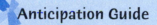
## Anticipation Guide

*Consider the following statements and determine whether you agree or disagree with each. Save your answers, and revisit this guide at the end of this chapter.*

| | | |
|---|---|---|
| 1. Readers get meaning directly from text. | agree | disagree |
| 2. The more information available, the more learning occurs. | agree | disagree |
| 3. Knowing word meanings guarantees comprehension. | agree | disagree |
| 4. The faster you read, the more you comprehend. | agree | disagree |
| 5. Questioning strategies seldom enhance comprehension. | agree | disagree |
| 6. Writing creates new knowledge while using prior knowledge. | agree | disagree |
| 7. Writing should always proceed through the four stages of the writing process. | agree | disagree |
| 8. The written product is not as important as the writing process. | agree | disagree |
| 9. Content writing should include some poetry. | agree | disagree |
| 10. Essays are seldom used in content writing. | agree | disagree |

*If children are apparently unable to learn, we should assume that we have not yet found the right way to teach them.*

—*Marie M. Clay*

## A Literacy Story

I learned one big thing in my first year of teaching, and I made one big commitment. I learned that I knew nothing about teaching reading, and I decided to remedy my ignorance. Years later I wrote a poem that tells of my ignorance and my decision to remedy it.

**Did You Get On, Gary?**

Today my thoughts drifted back to
The classroom where we first met,
My first year of teaching,
Your fifth year in school.

You couldn't read;
I couldn't teach you to read.
I was impatient and frustrated
First with you, later with myself.

Yet you repaid impatience and ignorance
With trust and affection.
Three decades have not erased memories
Of your smiling face, your puzzling difficulties.

The fault was mine, not yours,
Though I didn't know that at the time.
Thanks to you, I know now
What I didn't know then.

Can you read today, Gary?
Has your life been harsh?
How many doors did I nail shut?
Did you get on?

Rosemary and Stephen Vincent Benét
Wrote a poem called *Nancy Hanks,*

I've asked the same questions about you, Gary,
That Nancy Hanks asked about her son, Abe.

"You wouldn't know
About my son?
Did he grow tall?
Did he have fun?
Did he learn to read?
Did he get to town?
Do you know his name?
Did he get on?"

Reading and writing are not identical twins but fraternal twins. Reading and writing are alike, yet different. It is almost impossible to speak of one without referencing the other. If you love reading, you depend on writers to supply your needs. If you love writing, you depend on readers to consume your wares. Readers and writers are lovers, but they are also competitors. Good readers can become good writers, but this is not automatic; they have to work at it. Good writers can become good readers, but this also is not automatic; they have to work at it. Finding ways to bring the fraternal twins together to enhance the learning of subject matter is

## A MATTER OF STANDARDS

### Content Area Literacy

**Standard 1:** Students read a wide range of print and nonprint texts to build an understanding of texts, of themselves, and the culture of the United States and the world; to acquire new information to respond to the needs and demands of society and the workplace and for personal fulfillment. Among these texts are fiction and nonfiction, classic and contemporary works.

**Comment:** Students read more traditional than nontraditional texts, though the balance is shifting toward texts that mix print, nonprint, and graphics. The Internet is a good example of this shifting balance, and it has presented a new challenge in the teaching of reading. We do not yet know much about how reading

and readability works on the Internet, since researchers have only recently started to examine the implications of new text formats presented there and in newspapers and magazines as well. Whether traditional or nontraditional text formats predominate, reading instruction must stress the importance of helping children build their understanding of how the texts they read relate to their own lives, how one text relates to another, and how texts relate to the world. Increasingly, new demands are placed on readers as they go about their responsibilities to society, the workplace, and themselves.

All text types can contribute to the realization of these essential goals. This chapter focuses on content reading and writing and provides ideas and strategies for helping children read and write traditional and nontraditional texts.

the greatest challenge facing content teachers. This chapter suggests ways to meet that challenge.

# Reading in the Content Areas

Content teachers are frequently accused of not caring about reading and writing because of their focus on content. But what kind of content teachers would fail to focus on content? Of course they do. Nevertheless, the more content teachers know about reading and writing, the better they can be at teaching content. Content courses and materials are challenging even for good students; for marginal students, content courses and materials are extremely difficult. Students need to learn to adjust reading rate to purpose, construct meaning, pronounce technical words, and comprehend specialized vocabulary. This section deals with the challenges students face when reading in the content areas and how content teachers can help students achieve content literacy.

## Concepts for Content Reading

**Making Meaning**. Readers do not *get* meaning from text; they *make* meaning through a combination of reasoning, prior knowledge, and text. Readers, consciously or unconsciously, adopt a stance toward the texts they read. According to Rosenblatt (1978), a reader's stance may be efferent (to carry away text information) or aesthetic (to live through text events). But, you may ask, isn't it the reader's job to *get* what the text explicitly states or implicitly suggests? Don't writers expect readers to *get* what they have written? Yes, but readers and authors have different purposes, backgrounds, and beliefs. What readers carry away from a text is influenced by what they bring to the text—their reasoning, and prior knowledge and the social context in which the text is read. And that is why you will agree with, disagree with, amend, supplement, or negotiate what I say here. You will make your own meaning from the words I write, and they may be different from what I intend to convey.

**Schema Theory**. A schema (the plural is *schemata*) is a mental structure that enables us to comprehend text. Schemata represent our organized knowledge of the world. Schemata are abstract concepts postulated to describe how we learn, how we accommodate new knowledge, how we interpret text, and how we understand new experiences. Schemata organize knowledge, memories, and experiences. As new knowledge is acquired, existing mental schemata are modified to accommodate it. Readers possess different quantitative and qualitative amounts of prior knowledge, and they have different ways of organizing and accessing their mental schemata. Read the following passage, and see if you have enough prior knowledge to comprehend it.

> Richmond was in dire straits against St. Kilda. The opening pair who had been stroking the ball with beautiful fluency on past occasions were both out for ducks. Once again the new ball pair had broken through. Then Smith turned

on surprising pace and moving the ball off the seam, beat Mazar twice in one over. Inverarity viciously pulled Brown into the gully but was sent retiring to the pavilion by a shooter from Cox.

Jones in the slips and Chappell at silly mid-on were superb, and Daniel bowled a maiden over in his first spell. Yallop took his toll with three towering sixes, but Thompson had little to do in the covers.

Grant was dismissed with a beautiful yorker, and Jones went for a brute of a ball. Wood was disappointing, the way he hung his bat out to the lean-gutted Croft was a nasty shock. The rout ended when McArdle dived at silly leg and the cry "'Ow's that!" echoed across the pitch.

If you had difficulty interpreting the passage, it is because you lack sufficient prior knowledge of the game of cricket—your existing schema for games does not include it. You may have thought that the passage reminded you a bit of American baseball, but even with this analogy, it is difficult to construct meaning for this passage. Notice that you are perfectly capable of pronouncing the words in this passage, and most likely you know some meanings for most of the words. But certain words have cricket-specific meanings, and the absence of prior knowledge makes it difficult to assign meaning to them within the context of this passage. Your schema for cricket is missing key vocabulary, concepts, and the rules of the game.

Cricket is played in England and most of its former colonies. The culture of these countries includes cricket, whereas American society does not. How we think about ideas and information is determined, to some degree, by the society that surrounds us. The cricket passage is incomprehensible to an American audience but less troublesome for an English audience. A transaction between an American reader and this text is less likely to occur in American society than in a British or Australian society. When children read content material for which they lack key vocabulary and concepts, they are unable to construct meaning—their prior knowledge is insufficient. The more prior knowledge readers possess, the greater the likelihood that they will construct meaning from written text.

**Transmission Model of Learning**. The transmission model of learning can be called the empty jug theory of learning. According to this analogy, writers and teachers transmit ideas and information from their heads into the heads of readers and listeners. Eventually, the empty head (jug) gets full of someone else's ideas and information. Contrast the transmission model with the making-meaning model of learning, and you have a different perspective. The former implies no use of prior knowledge and reasoning when learning something new. The latter implies the definitive of prior knowledge and reasoning when learning something new. If content cannot be directly transferred from one head to another, content teachers must consider instructional strategies based on a different model of learning—the making-meaning theory, in which students use prior knowledge to construct new knowledge. The connecting link is reasoning.

> "The aim should be to teach us rather how to think, than what to think."
>
> —James Beattie, professor and poet

**Information Isn't Learning**. Students have access to more information now than ever before. While access to information is good, information by the ton guarantees nothing. You cannot become educated by knowing more than everyone else. Information is merely raw material; it can be used wisely or foolishly. We cannot educate children by simply giving them more information. Unfortunately, teachers are often coerced into substituting coverage for instruction. Cover this material; make sure children know this so they can do well on a standardized test. If access to information were learning, this would be the smartest generation the world has ever produced. As a profession, we must fight against the pernicious notion that education is about coverage of content. Education is about reasoning, reflecting, and understanding. *I most emphatically am not saying that information per se is bad.* On the contrary, information is good. But teachers must have a significant voice in what information is covered and how it is to be conveyed.

**Engagement**. Learning cannot occur without engagement. Watch children at play, and you will see engagement; watch teenagers in conversation, and you will see engagement personified. Why do social events engage children's attention but learning environments often do not? Partly, it is because social settings are more natural and thus more engaging. Since schools are not natural social settings, they lack this ambience. Effective teaching, therefore, seeks to create informal, engaging learning environments. Authentic tasks ground learning in the real world.

**Interest**. Interest influences learning and comprehension. Reading and writing instruction that provides no pleasure is unlikely to succeed. Effective instruction seeks to heighten interest in learning tasks that might otherwise appear unappealing. When interest is present, learning and comprehension proceed smoothly, though not without challenges. When it is absent, learning and comprehension are likely to take a vacation. It is as important to work on student interest as it is to work on learning content. A student who is interested in art is likely to give it top priority, but if you want that same student to learn science, you need a hook. You might try to establish a bridge between science and art, perhaps through the work of Leonardo da Vinci, an artist who had a dual interest in science and art. Exploring his dual interests can be the bridge to heightened engagement.

## Content Reading Strategies

**Rate and Purpose**. Interest in rate, or speed, of reading has waxed and waned in reading instruction over the decades. Reports of reading rates faster than a speeding bullet have surfaced from time to time. But reading rate should be considered only in relation to comprehension. Nothing is gained by reading 1,000 words per minute if comprehension is imperiled. Indeed, such "reading" cannot reasonably be considered reading at all, since comprehension is the gold standard of reading. On the other hand, much is gained if one reads at 100 words per minute and comprehends thoroughly. Rate is governed by purpose, and accomplishing one's reading purpose is the measure of successful reading.

The issue is not how fast but how effectively readers achieve their purpose. Purpose guides the reader's choice of rate as well as other decisions about how to approach a particular reading task. Purpose supplies the reason for reading and determines what is read, how it is read, and what is accomplished by it. Children can be taught to adjust the rate at which they read and how their choice of rate is connected to purpose. There are four ways to adjust rate to purpose: skimming, scanning, study reading, and surveying. Each implies a matching of reading rate to purpose.

**Skimming**. Skimming means to read quickly but selectively for a given purpose, usually to locate very specific information. It may mean seeking answers to questions concerning *who, what, when,* or *where.* Looking for key words or phrases makes this task simpler. For example, if a social studies student needs answers to the following questions, skimming would be an appropriate strategy.

- Who signed the Declaration of Independence? (look for names)
- When did they sign the Declaration of Independence? (look for date)
- Where did the signing take place? (look for a place—city, state, building)

Skimming is less effective in locating answers to *why* and *how* questions, since more complex issues are typically involved—although this depends on how a question is framed. Sometimes a reader has a dual purpose and may need to combine skimming with scanning or study-type reading. For instance, I might skim a chapter to locate the name of a specific reading strategy, say, the KWL strategy. But upon locating the term *KWL,* I may want to reflect upon *why* it works or *how* it is done. In such a case, I would move from skimming to more detailed scanning or studying to accomplish my dual purpose.

*Chad sits beside two semantic maps that represent ideas that he and his classmates have brainstormed about reptiles and the sea.*

**Scanning**. Scanning describes the normal rate at which most of us read most of the time. We scan from sentence to sentence, paragraph to paragraph, taking in all of the information in the text, making inferences, and comprehending as we proceed. Scanning has a more general purpose than skimming. Skimmers have an explicit and limited mission. Scanners have a broader one. Readers scan to answer questions focused on *how* and *why.* For example, if I asked, "How and why has the Mississippi River influenced the development of cities along its banks?" I would need to examine all relevant text that might provide an answer. Skimming won't work with such a purpose. Answering this question will require a careful reading, mentally noting appropriate information as I proceed.

**Study Reading**. Study reading differs from scanning in that it requires a deliberate pace, allowing time for reflective thinking and rereading. Words per minute are not relevant in study-type reading. Critical or creative thought will be needed, prior knowledge will be crucial, and reasoning will be the main activity. Study reading means comparing text concepts with prior knowledge. It may require seeking information outside of the text. Outcome is far more important than speed. Study reading seeks a deep understanding of text ideas and weighs them against other standards. A reader studying for an essay examination will be interested in explicit information primarily for the purpose of interpreting it and drawing inferences from it. The emphasis will be upon evaluating, comparing, and contrasting information rather than simply recalling facts or locating information.

**Surveying**. The purpose of surveying is to examine or preview a large piece of text to get a general sense of its contents. A chapter or book, for example, ought to be surveyed before it is read. As a surveyor of land seeks to establish the boundaries of a tract of land, so the surveyor of a chapter or book seeks to grasp the outlines of the material to be read. The reader wants to know what a chapter contains before reading it in detail. Thus, the reader peruses the introduction, headings, graphs, tables, figures, and summary. Surveying a book requires a broad preview and might include an examination of the table of contents, preface, and index. A quick view of a few chapters may also be useful, but a survey does not require any detailed reading. The idea is to get a general impression rather than a detailed understanding. A textbook is surveyed differently than a novel is, since a novel has a narrative structure. A survey of a novel might include perusing the dust jacket, which may include a summary of the story or a sketch about the author, or even reading a few pages to get a sense of voice and style. How one surveys a text depends on the type of text and the purpose for eventually reading it.

**Content DRTA**. Stauffer (1969) developed and refined the directed reading thinking activity (DRTA). DRTAs create a forum for activating prior knowledge, confirming or modifying predictions during reading, checking the accuracy of predictions during reading, and general discussion and prediction assessment after reading. Chapter 8 outlines Stauffer's steps in directing a DRTA for narrative text. This section discusses how a DRTA is used to stimulate thinking about content materials. A DRTA has these objectives:

1. *To establish purposes for reading by asking questions requiring predictions.* Initial questions are followed up with deeper questions and comments intended to help readers elaborate and refine their predictions.
2. *To guide readers through text by choosing strategic stopping points for reconsidering and resetting predictions and to cite evidence supporting or failing to support original predictions.* Evaluating and adjusting predictions increases reader interest and enhances comprehension.
3. *To observe the needs readers reveal as they read.* Readers may experience certain difficulties as they proceed through text. Make note of these issues and deal with them—immediately, if necessary, or as a follow-up to the DRTA.

4. *To develop comprehension of subject matter text.* Effective use of the DRTA helps develop skills of reasoning, evaluation of evidence, and use of prior knowledge. Teachers' questions, comments, and probes are the keys to achieving these goals. Three question types are typically used: prediction, citing supportive evidence, and thoughtful discussion of text ideas and information.

5. *To discuss, elaborate, clarify, and develop general reading skills.* After the DRTA is concluded, follow-up activities focus on one or two of the following skills: vocabulary, word recognition, comprehension, prediction effectiveness, evaluation of evidence, and writing.

Table 7.1 provides an example of the type of questions a teacher might prepare for discussions before and after reading. These questions are based on an article about crocodiles. Notice how the before-reading questions differ from the after-reading questions. Before reading you want to encourage students to make best guesses based on reasoning and prior knowledge. When students make prereading predictions, they are more apt to notice and recall information that connects to their predictions. The purpose of predicting is not simply to be right, although students enjoy being right. Instead, the purpose is to use prior knowledge and encourage logical and creative thinking about *possibilities* and *probabilities* relevant to the upcoming reading task. The teacher's job is not to reward accurate prediction any more than it is to punish inaccurate ones. *The teacher's job is to direct, stimulate, and*

*Teaching Tip*

**Table 7.1**

**Discussion Questions for a Content DRTA**

| Questions Before Reading | Questions After Reading |
|---|---|
| 1. Crocodiles have a bad reputation. Do you think this reputation is deserved? | 1. How good were your predictions? |
| 2. Some people think crocodiles eat people. Do you agree? Is this a myth? | 2. What did you learn about crocodiles that you didn't know before? |
| 3. Do you think crocodiles are in danger of extinction? Why or why not? | 3. What was the most surprising fact you learned about crocodiles? What was the most interesting? |
| 4. How big do crocodiles grow? How long? How heavy? | 4. What questions did you have that were not answered in this article? |
| 5. Do crocodiles live and hunt in social groups or alone? | 5. Do you think it is okay to use crocodile skins to make shoes and purses? |
| 6. Are baby crocodiles born live, or are they hatched from eggs? | 6. Why do you suppose some people consider crocodiles evil? |
| 7. Would you guess that crocodiles are attentive or inattentive parents? Why? | 7. What did the author not discuss that you want to know about? |
| 8. Do crocodiles hunt on land or only in the water? | 8. If you had written this article, what might you have done differently? |
| 9. How long ago do you suppose crocodiles first made their appearance on earth? | 9. Do you think it is okay to raise crocodiles for their hides? |
| 10. What differences, if any, might there be between alligators and crocodiles? | 10. What was the most interesting word or phrase you encountered in this article? |

"Open questions, which have many possible answers, lead to richer language interactions and higher levels of thinking than closed questions, which have simple, often one-word answers."

—P. Barnes, *From Communication to Curriculum,* 1992.

*choreograph thinking.* Comment favorably on logical and creative thinking, even if the prediction is unverified in the text.

Questions that follow reading are substantially different from pre-reading questions. After-reading questions are intended to stimulate thoughtful discussion of information and ideas revealed in the text. To discuss these facts and ideas, avoid the traditional mode of asking explicit factual questions. Rather, focus on extending text ideas, reflecting on reading performance, and evaluating the worth of text ideas. Discussions that arise from this type of questioning inevitably highlight text ideas and information while simultaneously moving students into the realm of critical and creative thinking (Rapp-Ruddell, 1993; Ruddell, 1999; Stauffer, 1969).

**Question/Answer Relationship (QAR).** Raphael (1986) developed a strategy for helping students understand how questions and answers are related (QAR). She divides question/answer relationships into four categories.

1. *Right there question.* The answer is located in one specific place within the text—a literal, factual answer to a question.
2. *Think and search question.* The answer is located within the text but in more than one place. While the answer may be literal or factual, putting together information drawn from more than one place requires reasoning.
3. *Author and you question.* The answer is determined by combining reasoning and prior knowledge with information in the text. Since an inference is required, thinking is paramount in this question type.
4. *On my own question.* The answer is not in the text but is derived from the reader's experience and judgment. Thinking is essential here as well, though text information may not be required.

Raphael (1986) recommends teaching children these question/answer relationships. When given guidance, children can learn what they are looking for within a text, how extensively they must search within the text, when they must combine reasoning and prior knowledge with text to make inferences, and when they must reason on their own without direct reference to a text.

**Anticipation Guides.** Anticipation guides raise questions that help students make predictions about content-relevant statements. They can be used before and after reading. Most often anticipation guides use a true–false or an agree–disagree format. Students' responses to the questions provide a purpose for reading and an opportunity to think about the content they will encounter in the reading material. Their responses are based on prior knowledge, personal experience, and best guesses.

Predictions made prior to reading heighten awareness of the content to be read. After reading, students return to the anticipation guide and complete it again, based on what they have learned. This provides an opportunity to revisit original predictions, consider whether the new information confirmed or debunked their predictions, discuss what students learned as well as any changes in their think-

## Visual Learning Programs

Reading and writing across the curriculum can be supported with technology. Interactive software and the Internet provide ways to support student learning. Because of the interactive nature of electronic environments, students are usually motivated to use them. But with the abundance of software available, it is hard to decide what to invest in.

One of the most useful tools is a visual learning program. Currently the most commonly used visual learning program in schools is Inspiration®. Although Inspiration® is targeted for grades 6–12, elementary students can also use it. It is a user-friendly program that assists students in clarifying thinking, understanding concepts, and integrating new information. This tool offers a range of visual learning techniques: concept mapping, planning, outlining, graphic organizing, webbing, brainstorming, and creative thinking. This tool allows students to graphically represent ideas and use information aids to clarify, organize, and recognize patterns and relationships.

Even if your school does not have the resources to provide this type of electronic tool, consider investing in a visual learning program for yourself. You can use it to create learning aids for your students. And by connecting a laptop computer to a television, you can use it as a teaching tool in front of the class. To download a free, full-version 30-day trial of Inspiration® software, visit www.inspiration.com.

The Internet enables students to engage in a variety of communication and information and retrieval activities. WebQuests are problem-based/inquiry learning experiences that are available on the Web. A basic Internet search will reveal numerous WebQuests in every content area. Created by teachers, they are available for anyone. If you have a specific set of objectives to meet, you might consider creating your own WebQuest. They are fun and easy to create. There are two excellent resources for information and templates: www.ozline.com and http://edweb.sdsu.edu/webquest/webquest.html.

By creating an itinerary for students to follow and developing support material, students can use the Internet to take a virtual field trip. E-mail and discussion groups allow students to engage in authentic conversations and share their learning with others. Internet search engines promote research and investigation skills and enable students to locate online information on any topic. Whether students are using innovative software programs or navigating the Internet, all of these activities can extend and enrich your content curriculum.

For a variety of lesson plans and instructions on designing WebQuests, visit Bernie Dodges's homepage: http://berniedodge.com

Contributed by Lisa Kunkleman

ing, and consider which questions remain unanswered. The sample anticipation guide questions in Table 7.2 (p. 266) use a true–false format. They are based on a social studies chapter called "Africans in the American Colonies." This anticipation guide has only five questions, but ten or more questions may be used.

It is easy to construct an anticipation guide. The following guidelines can be modified to suit your needs.

1. Write questions based on the important facts and ideas in the reading material. Base your questions on an estimate of what students might already know or are able to make reasonable guesses about.
2. Include one or two questions not directly answered in the text. This provides a rationale for additional research and discussion after reading.

*Teaching Tip*

## Table 7.2

### Anticipation Guide for Studying Africans in the American Colonies

Read the questions, and make your best guess by marking *T* if you believe the statement is true or *F* if you believe the statement is false. Save your answers. After reading the chapter, "Africans in the American Colonies," we will revisit this guide and discuss your best guesses.

_____ 1. African Americans established a settlement in America before European whites.

_____ 2. The first African Americans in America were slaves.

_____ 3. The first Africans in America could own property and vote.

_____ 4. By 1700 African slaves in Virginia outnumbered free people.

_____ 5. The founders of Georgia pictured a colony without slaves.

3. Administer the anticipation guide, and discuss answers.
4. Assign the reading on which the questions were based.
5. After reading, return to their anticipation guides. Have students compare their before-reading answers with their after-reading answers. Discuss whether they changed their minds, and why or why not.
6. If students disagree with the answers, have them cite evidence to support their views. Such discussions stimulate critical thinking and should be encouraged.

**Think-Aloud Comprehension Modeling.** As teachers, we are models, whether we acknowledge it or not. A model serves as an example to be imitated. Teachers can be models of how a mature reader comprehends text. You can deliberately and systematically serve as a model comprehender of text and gradually move your students toward a more mature understanding of how to comprehend text, particularly by making inferences. Inference is a sophisticated thinking skill that often gives readers difficulty.

Thinking is "the magic of the mind."

—Lord Byron

The absence of direct instruction partially accounts for the comprehension difficulties children exhibit (Durkin, 1979). Some children have never experienced direct instruction in comprehension; others have experienced it only rarely. Modeling corrects this omission. For example, the master carpenter shows the apprentice how to make a tight joint, and then coaches as the apprentice tries to follow the example. Many children have never heard a mature reader explain how inferences are drawn. You can demonstrate this through think-aloud modeling. Then coach the apprentices as they practice implementing the skill you have demonstrated. Gradually release responsibility to your apprentices, just as the master carpenter does.

Table 7.3 suggests six steps in conducting a process lesson on comprehension modeling. These steps start with teacher modeling and end with responsibility handed over to students (Schwartz and Cramer, 1988).

**Table 7.3**

## Six Steps in Modeling a Process Lesson on Inferential Reasoning

1. *Decide what process changes would improve student performance.* Good readers construct meaning from text-based information, reasoning, and prior knowledge. Less skilled readers approach reading as a task of selecting information, usually literal, rather than one of constructing meaning. This leads to difficulty in responding to inference questions, since answers cannot be directly identified in the text.

2. *Help students understand the purpose of the lesson through analogy.* For example, stride into the classroom, slap a book on the desk, and feign anger. Then ask, What did I throw on the desk? Next, ask, Would this be a good time to ask me for a favor? Finally, ask, How was answering the second question different from answering the first? Point out that they made inferences to answer the second question by using prior knowledge and reasoning.

3. *Help students connect prior knowledge to new process information.* Extend the analogy by linking it to the process good readers use to make inferences. Point out that they use inferential reasoning in everyday situations, but they need to learn ways of applying their inferential capabilities to reading. Focus on the importance of providing support for answers by citing facts, prior knowledge, and reasoning.

4. *Break instruction into four incremental steps, over the course of several lessons, to help students develop their performance theory.*
   a. *Teacher modeling.* Using materials jointly read, draw an inference: "I think the butler killed Mrs. Pepper." Then explain how you used text, reasoning, and prior knowledge to draw your conclusion.
   b. *Joint teacher–student modeling.* State an inference and then invite children to partici-

pate. "I think this story proves that Sherlock Holmes was an outstanding detective. What information and reasoning supports my idea or proves me wrong?"
   c. *Student application.* Identify text-based information, and ask students to decide what this information implies: "I think this story suggests that the even the smallest clue can help catch a murderer. What information and reasoning do you think I used to come to this conclusion?"
   d. *Independent practice and assessment.* Provide independent practice by posing questions that require students to draw inferences. For example, following an independent reading about dolphins, ask, Are dolphins able to communicate with one another? How do you know? Encourage students to consider multiple answers and to cite the information, prior knowledge, and reasoning they used to support their answers.

5. *Provide meaningful practice in the new process.* Give students a set of inference questions with answers that include supporting information and reasoning. Then have students write inference questions based on a different passage and answer them. Group students and have them share their work and discuss the supporting evidence, prior knowledge, and the reasoning required to answer their questions.

6. *Extend the process lesson by making applications to other areas.* Discuss the types of inferences appropriate for different kinds of texts or subject areas. For example, a mystery requires inferences about motive, means, and opportunity, whereas content areas rely heavily on prior knowledge of basic concepts and vocabulary.

*Teaching Tip*

> ## Section Summary: Reading in the Content Areas
> 1. Readers *construct* meaning from text; they do not simply *get* meaning.
> 2. Engagement and interest favorably influence content comprehension.
> 3. Schemata, mental structures in the brain, enable readers to comprehend text.
> 4. Rate of reading is relevant only as it relates to the purpose for reading.
> 5. Types of rate adjustment include skimming, scanning, studying, and surveying.
> 6. Strategies for comprehending content materials include content DRTAs, QARs, anticipation guides, and think-aloud comprehension modeling, among others.

# Writing in the Content Areas

Writing makes effective use of prior knowledge, creates new knowledge, and stabilizes concepts currently under study. Yet writing in the content areas is underused as an adjunct for learning content concepts. There are reasons for this circumstance. Content teachers in middle school and high shcool must focus on covering the materials they are responsible for teaching. In addition, they may think that writing will only add to the heavy paper load they already bear. Finally, content teachers have less access to in-service instruction in the writing process. Knowledge of the writing process is widespread among primary and intermediate grade teachers, and it has altered the role of writing in these grades. We have yet to see such a writing revolution among content teachers in middle schools and, particularly, high schools. But it is not too late. I hope to persuade content teachers of the value of applying the principles of the writing process and its significant contribution to learning content concepts.

Content teachers are rightly concerned about children's reading skill. They understand that content materials require higher-order thinking. They are aware that content materials put a heavy vocabulary burden on students. They recognize that a huge proportion of content reading is expository and, therefore, presents a challenge for many students. These things are true and all the more reason to understand how writing connects to these reading issues. Writing strengthens thinking and builds vocabulary. Content reading materials are usually expository, and the best way to understand expository materials is to create them (Camborne, 1995; Graves, 1994).

## The Writing Process and the Written Product

**The Writing Process.** The writing process emphasizes theories and procedures about how writing is accomplished; it is organized in stages; prewriting, drafting, revising, and sharing or publishing. Prewriting focuses on tasks such as collecting and organizing information; drafting involves putting initial ideas on paper with the understanding that a draft requires substantive changes; revising involves making the changes so that ideas and information are added, deleted, and rearranged; eventually, after editing and proofreading, the written product is shared or published. This outlines the theory of writing process, but in practice, writing doesn't always fit the theory quite so neatly. Here's why. Not every piece of writing goes through the stages described; every writer's process is unique and does not necessarily follow, in a linear fashion, the stages described.

> "If writing is thinking and discovery and selection and order and meaning, it is also awe and reverence and mystery and magic."
> —Toni Morrison, novelist

Every writer is unique, and every writing task has different requirements. Writers develop habits and procedures that do not conform to an idealized version of the writing process. Every writing task has its own imperatives. For instance, suppose you're e-mailing a brief note to a friend. You may skip prewriting completely, miscues may abound, and yet you send it off into the world without a qualm. On the other hand, if you're writing a poem, you may take a different approach. *Different audiences and purposes require different procedures.*

Writing a poem may mean jotting down a few words or a random line or two. If things go well, you may write 10 or 15 lines and trash all but 1 or 2. What now? It depends on the writer. You may retreat to the prewriting stage, seeking fresh ideas. Or you may work with the line or two you salvaged from the first draft and continue from there. You are working, in other words, in a recursive fashion, moving back and forth from one stage of the process to another. Your writing is folding back upon itself through the writing stages in an unpredictable fashion—but a fashion that suits your style and the task. The writing process is messier, looser, and more idiosyncratic than the theory seems to suggest. And this is exactly as it ought to be, since we do not need to and should not want to impose a rigid process on writers, young or old. We should make children aware of the stages of the writing process but implement the process in a flexible manner.

**The Written Product.** The ultimate goal of writing is the product, not the process. The process is the business of the writer; the product is the interest of the reader. The reader doesn't need to know, and couldn't care less, what process the writer went through to create the written product. The test of the writing process is the worthiness of the product, not the convolutions of the creative work itself. Those of us who teach writing process must ask, *Does the process make a better written product?* If it does not, then the process is flawed; if it does, then the process is valuable. A sound theory of the writing process will produce better writers and better written products. Balance must be maintained between process issues and writing outcomes.

> "What is written without effort is in general read without pleasure."
> —Samuel Johnson, British writer and lexicographer

Traditional approaches to writing overemphasized the written product, and this resulted in emphasizing correctness at the expense of good writing. The writing process movement restored the emphasis on good writing but tended to pay insufficient attention to correct writing. There need not be a trade-off between the two. Correct writing enhances good writing. We can value the writing process and still maintain a focus on correctness. It is simply a matter of getting priorities straight. Correct writing is not automatically good writing. Good writing is incomplete without correctness. Process and product are not in competition. Rather, they are contributing partners in the writing enterprise.

*Fancy words are not the key to fine writing. Having something to say and saying it clearly and simply make for compelling text.*

## Content Writing Strategies

**Learning Journals.** A learning journal is an excellent device for developing ideas for content writing. Learning journals can be used in many ways specifically related to your teaching objectives the content issues. The following list identifies five ways in which learning journals can be used.

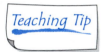

1. *What I learned.* Reading, listening to lectures, and participating in discussions often have the objective of conveying new information and ideas. An excellent question to prompt student writing about after such experiences is this: What do you know now that you didn't know before reading this chapter? listening to this lecture? participating in this discussion?
2. *Agree-disagree.* If you're studying an issue that is controversial, have students make a list of ideas they agree with and a list with which they disagree. These lists can then be used in class to discuss reasons why students agree or disagree with certain ideas.
3. *Observing and hypothesizing.* Science is a discipline wherein careful recording of observations and measurements is crucial. Suggest one or more topics that require careful observations. Have students record their observations in journals. Then ask them to hypothesize as to the meaning of their observations.
4. *Making lists.* Make lists of words and phrases related to a specific content topic; vocabulary is central to comprehension of any specialized area or topic. If you are studying rain forests, for example, a chapter on this topic will contain many content-related terms. You might suggest that students list words in this pattern: five words you understand, five words you find difficult, five words you've never encountered before, and so on.
5. *Predicting.* A thoughtful prediction uses prior knowledge to predict how the past will influence the future. Prediction reaches into the past to forecast the future. Christopher Columbus predicted discoveries based on incomplete knowledge of the geography of the world. Scientists predict the outcome of their experiments based on what is known and what they think might happen under given conditions. Predication is an excellent way to stimulate thinking. It is engaging because it requires intellectual risk taking.

## Standing on the Shoulders of Giants
## Historical Contributions to Literacy
### Donald Graves and Donald Murray

A quiet revolution occurred in American schools in the 1980s and 1990s. Not in whole language, as you may think, but in *writing*. Revolutions are often difficult to trace, but in the case of the writing revolution, tracing its origins is not difficult. Two Donalds are at the heart of the writing revolution—Donald Graves and Donald Murray. Revolutions don't happen without forerunners, people who laid the foundation. There are many unsung heroes in this story, and I shall acknowledge only a few. In 1929, Hughes Mearns wrote *Creative Power: The Education of Youth in the Arts*. I consider it among the best books on children's writing ever written. In 1939, Alvina Treut Burrows and her colleagues, Doris Jackson and Dorothy Saunders, wrote *They All Want to Write*. These two books were straws in the writing winds of what was to come a half-century or so later.

Once the revolution got under way, Lucy Calkins (*The Art of Teaching Writing*) and Nancie Atwell (*In the Middle*) added their unique voices to the movement. And there are many others: James Britton, Janet Emig, Carol Chomsky, Russell Stauffer, Regie Routman, Ken and Yetta Goodman, Dorothy Grant Hennings, and Kenneth Koch, among others. Surely I've left deserving individuals off of this list, but I'm not writing a history of writing, just a tiny footnote of appreciation. Now comes the revolution led by the two Donalds—the fulfillment of Mearns's dream: children are creative artists, and writing is a primary outlet for that creativity.

Donald Murray started as a journalist. He won a Pulitzer Prize in 1954, the highest award a journalist can receive. But he wanted to write books about writing and teaching writing, so he became a pro-

fessor at the University of New Hampshire. And he did write books—17 at last count. He has written poetry, novels, articles, and columns, but perhaps his finest contribution has been that of teacher and mentor. The measure of great teachers resides in the quality and contribution of their students. Murray taught and mentored Donald Graves. He's taught many others as well, including those of us who have read his books—among my favorites are *Shoptalk, Learning by Teaching, A Writer Teaches Writing,* and *Expecting the Unexpected*.

Donald Graves was a teacher, principal, and language supervisor before joining the faculty at the University of New Hampshire. His classic book, *Writing: Teachers and Children at Work,* published in 1983, changed the world of children's writing. This book, more than any other publication, fired the shot heard round the world. Graves's writing and travels throughout the English-speaking world planted and nourished the writing process movement through its early years. His cogent writing showed teachers what they could *do,* but more important, suggested what they ought to *be* as teachers of writing. Graves wrote many other books, but his 1983 book remains the classic, a standard against which other books on children's writing will be measured. Donald Graves influenced a generation of teachers, stimulated a flood of publications, and introduced millions of children to the pleasures of writing.

Who would have thought that two good and gentle men, who simply loved to teach and write, would become the revolutionaries who changed the world of children's writing?

**Double-Entry Journal**. As the name implies, a double-entry journal contains two-column entries on a topic. Divide a journal page into two columns. The first column has questions, comments, words, ideas, and facts. The second column asks the question "What does it mean to me?" Thus, the second column responds to items

**Table 7.4**

**Double-Entry Journal**

| Column 1 | Column 2 |
| --- | --- |
| Why so many gods and goddesses? | There were many kinds of gods and goddesses in Egyptian life. People tried to please them. I'm surprised at how many different gods and goddesses there were. |
| Did Egyptians believe in life after death? | They believed you had to be good in this life to get into the next life. They expected it would be beautiful. I think their view is not so much different from my own. Most religions believe in an afterlife. |
| No one knows for sure how the pyramids were built. What do you think? | The pyramids are a mystery to me. I've read different accounts about how the pyramids were built. The Egyptians must have been very smart to figure out how to do it. Each stone weighs tons. I think they were built by slaves. |

in the first and includes responses, interpretations, speculations, and opinions. The entries in Table 7.4 illustrate the concept.

**Essays**. An essay is a short piece of writing, usually limited to one topic. The Latin word for essay, *exagium,* meant "a weight or weighing," which captures perfectly the point of an essay—to present the author's point of view on a topic. Francis Bacon was a famous essayist in his time. E. B. White, author of *Charlotte's Web,* ranked among America's finest essayists in more recent times.

Writing essays ranks among the most frequent writing tasks assigned by content teachers. Content courses, by their very nature, present an abundance of topics for essays. Essays provide fertile grounds for analyzing, synthesizing, and interpreting content ideas and information. An advantage of essay writing is that it requires writers to seek sources of information in order to inform the writing. While English teachers are most likely to assign essays, there is no reason why essays should be limited to literature. Science, for instance, presents an enormous number of issues and problems that lend themselves to essay writing. Newell's research (1984) suggests that essay writing has a positive influence on content knowledge. Langer and Applebee (1987) found that analytic writing, when combined with reading, enables students to think more deeply about ideas and information encountered in reading. These conclusions fit the wider literature, which makes the case that combining reading and writing has a positive influence on learning in general (Langer, 1986).

There are traditional ways of teaching the essay format. The five-paragraph essay, for instance, is often recommended in English textbooks. English teachers would be well advised to take William Carlos Williams's advice: "I have never been one to write by rule, not even my own rules." The five-paragraph essay sets up a rule-governed way to write essays, but these rules do not conform to anything an experienced essay writer would recognize. You will search in vain among the works of competent essayists to find such a sterile formula used to create actual essays. There is a better way to teach essay writing. Create a file of short but well-written essays on a variety of topics. Look for ones that illustrate humor, whimsy, argument, or analytic approaches to a topic. You can find excellent short essays in local and national newspapers and magazines. Editorial and opinion pages are full of examples. While topics are often political, there is no shortage of other topics: gardening, cooking, schooling, finance, environment, humor, sports, shopping. And remember Friedrich Nietzsche's advice: "A man has no ears for that to which experience has given him no access." Young people cannot write essays on topics of which they have no experience. This is the best reason for allowing freedom of topic selection when directing children to write essays.

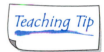

*Teacher Stephanie Tracy helps Samantha, who is creating a book about frogs.*

### "Literary Gossip" and Dialogue Journaling.

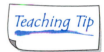
Teaching Tip

Gossip is generally defined as idle chatter among friends. Its content is usually negative, dealing as it does with rumors, half-truths, and lies. Yet adults and teenagers love to gossip. Why not rescue this negative forum from its naughty reputation and turn it into a force for good? Perhaps Nancie Atwell (1998) had this in mind when she invented the term that describes a journaling technique for getting students to "gossip" about literature.

"You write to me, and I'll write back." That's dialogue journaling; that's also literary gossip. A dialogue is a conversation between and among friends or acquaintances. Dialogue journaling is a conversation between teachers and their students, using journals as the medium. Like oral conversations, literary gossip or dialogue journaling has guidelines, described in Table 7.5 (p. 274). Observing these practices enriches the experience.

### Learning Logs.

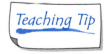
Teaching Tip

A learning log is a journal used for subject area learning. Learning logs have a natural connection with expository writing, but they can also stimulate expressive writing when a writing prompt lends itself more to expressive than expository writing. Learning logs are used to record notes, respond to teacher-generated questions and requests, and pose or answer self-generated questions. Teachers can provide prompts to motivate students to respond in their learning logs or guide students to develop their own. Effective prompts, closely connected to subject matter interests, are the key to effective use of learning logs.

**Table 7.5**

**Guidelines for Literary Gossip and Dialogue Journaling**

1. The dialogue must be mutual. Both parties have a responsibility to sustain it. When one party lets the other down, the conversation is over. As one student wrote to his teacher, "I'm not going to write until you write back."

2. Conversations flag when boredom sets in. Try to get journalers and gossipers focused on what's important or interesting for them. Then the conversation is likely to continue.

3. Don't correct grammar and mechanical errors in journals. Such matters, while important, are best attended to in other writing forums such as minilessons. A teacher should, however, keep track of writing needs so that instruction can be provided in the appropriate forum.

4. Don't restrict gossip and dialogue journaling to written conversations between teacher and students. Encourage students to have dialogue among themselves. This increases opportunities for students to write while easing the paper load. Dialogue partners and dialogue groups work well.

5. Listen to entries with your head and your heart. Your head will tell you about instructional needs your students may have; your heart will tell you about their emotional needs. Reach out to satisfy both.

*Teaching Tip*

Writing in a learning log can be a powerful tool for assimilating content-related ideas and information. Possibilities for stimulating subject matter writing are enhanced when teachers elevate a basic idea beyond its obvious uses. Imaginative teachers, of whom there are many, will undoubtedly do so when using learning logs. Some learning log prompts may include leading questions or direct requests, such as the following:

| Leading Questions | Direct Requests |
|---|---|
| What do I already know? | List five things you learned about . . . |
| What do I want to know? | List one thing that confused you. |
| What did I learn today? | Write a paragraph about . . . |
| What new idea did I learn? | What was life like during . . . |
| How can I apply what I learned? | Describe why you think . . . |
| What questions did I ask today? | Take notes in your learning log on . . . |
| What problems did I identify? | |
| What might you say if you met . . . ? | |

**Note Taking**. Walters (1990) notes that note taking has four important learning functions: (1) encourages organization of information, (2) focuses thinking and attention on comprehension, (3) aids memory of information, and (4) provides reviewable materials for discussions, tests, and quizzes. She suggests four note-taking alternatives to outlining and in-text notations: "There are four notetaking variations: (1) make use of bold headings; (2) turn bold headings into questions; (3) organize and clarify written responses to teacher-made or textbook questions; and (4) organize vocabulary words" (p. 34).

One of the biggest problems in note taking is that students tend to copy directly from sources, often word for word. This problem can be overcome only by focused instruction. Students need to learn how to appropriately use sources and cite them correctly. Few students learn to do these things on their own. Most students use sources inappropriately because they have not learned the correct procedure. Instruction designed to replace bad habits can help solve this problem. The skills needed are complex and cannot be learned in a few brief exposures. However, patient instruction paced over time works. Suggestions that will lead students in the right direction are listed in Table 7.6.

**Summaries**.  A summary is a condensed version of a larger whole, a brief statement that covers the main points. Writing a summary is a challenge and requires much practice. Knowing the steps that lead to effective summarization helps. Work through a large piece of text with the whole class to produce a summary; model the steps from start to finish. Use the following ideas to help students proceed when writing a summary.

1. Identify important main ideas by asking and answering these two related questions: What's important here? What's redundant, minor, trivial, or less essential to the author's main concerns? Text structure (main headings, subordinate headings, transition words) are clues to help separate main ideas from less essential ones.
2. Once a main idea is identified, write a sentence expressing its essence. Sometimes main ideas are stated explicitly in the text, sometimes not. In either case, it is best to paraphrase main ideas in your own words.
3. Write an integrated summary, using the main ideas you have identified. The number of basic main ideas in a text varies, depending on its length and

*Teaching Tip*

**Table 7.6**

**Practical Ideas for Teaching Note Taking**

1. Decide where you want your students to record their notes. A learning log is a good place for certain projects. For more extensive research reports, it may be best to use note cards.
2. Show students that expository text is usually organized through the use of bold and italicized titles along with graphs, tables, and boxed materials. Point out what information is contained in each element.
3. Select statements from texts, and model how you would restate an author's words, using your own phrasing. This is called paraphrasing, and few students know how to do it. After modeling, provide practice exercises.
4. Emphasize that notes don't contain every detail contained in a text. They don't need to be written in compete sentences. They record brief, essential facts and ideas.
5. With large chunks of text, such as chapters, model how chapter titles and headings can be used to make predictions and set purposes for note taking.
6. Model how notes can be used to create outlines or maps for writing. The task is to identify main ideas and place supporting details in subordinate relationship to them. Mapping, because of its visual nature, is ideal for helping students understand the relationships within text structure.
7. Show students when and how to cite reference sources. A written guide with examples is essential.

structure. Putting main ideas together in an integrated manner is the most challenging of all summarization tasks. Key words, transition words, and sequence of content are crucial.

4. Revise, edit, and proofread the integrated summary. This means you may need to add, delete, or rearrange the draft text. Once these major revision tasks are finished, polish the draft by refining the wording and proofreading for mechanical and spelling errors.

**Reports.** Children should be involved in reporting from the earliest ages. Initially, reports should be oral and informal, such as share-and-tell sessions and talking about a book. As children move through the grades and as content subjects become increasingly common, children need to begin writing reports. Initially these reports should take the form of a collaborative group or class report. Later, they take the form of individual reports. The procedures are similar.

1. *Choose a topic.* This step is more important and more difficult than it may appear. Of the several things to keep in mind, the most important is interest. If students are not interested, shoddy work may result. The best topics are ones for which students have background knowledge. This may mean choosing a topic currently being studied, for which some background knowledge has been established. A major misstep is to choose too broad a topic; help children narrow a topic to manageable proportions. For instance, the topic of Egyptian culture is too broad. The importance of cats in Egyptian culture is narrower and more manageable.

2. *Ask questions that can guide preliminary inquiry.* Usually the questions to be asked and answered center on: *who, what, when, where, why,* and *how.* Questions can emerge from a brainstorming session. If the topic is pyramids, these questions might arise: What is a pyramid? Are pyramids found in places other than Egypt? Who built the pyramids? Why were they built? How big are they? How old? Brainstorming stimulates all sorts of questions, some less useful than others. Cull the list of questions to manageable proportions and pursue the most interesting.

3. *Gather and organize information.* This step includes information obtained from the Internet, books, and oral sources. Printed information is easier to obtain than a reliable oral source. But if someone who can provide authentic information lives in the community, this good source is likely to enhance interest in the topic as well. Gathering information requires note taking. If notes are kept in a journal or on note cards, the following information is usually needed: subject of the card, bibliographic information (author, title, publisher, date, and page numbers), and summary of main ideas gathered from the source. A second step is to organize the information into a cluster map or an outline. The purpose of outlining is to sort main ideas from subtopics and subordinate details.

4. *Make a rough draft.* For a written report, this step is essential. For an oral report, talking points (main ideas) may be sufficient. In a collaborative effort, students share responsibilities for writing different parts of the report.

5. *Revise, edit, and proofread the report.* Use the steps in the writing process.
6. *Share or publish the report.* This crucial step is the most rewarding part of the work.

Teacher Kristin Wilson wanted her students to research a topic, write a script, and present an oral report in a talk show format. She explains how she went about this task in the Field Notes feature.

**Poetry.** Many teachers think of poetry as unrelated or only marginally related to content writing. For instance, science teachers might not immediately think that poetry fits their discipline. Yet Einstein said that the most important qualification

## Field Notes
### Real-Life Experiences of a Classroom Teacher

I have 24 students in my class. I wanted to find a way for students to "want" to research a topic of interest. I found a way that couldn't fail: a talk show.

I introduced the project by forming groups to put together a talk show of their own. This excited them. I suggested the following guidelines.

1. Select a debatable issue to be discussed on the show.
2. Choose "experts" to represent each angle of the issue.
3. Create an active part for everyone in the script.
4. Only the show's host may read from cards.
5. Research must be used in creating the script.
6. Factual data must be included in the script.
7. Use appropriate language and behavior on the show.
8. Meet established due dates.
9. Strive for creativity and organization.

Kristin Wilson

It seemed as if I had not mentioned the dirty word *research*. Students didn't mind that they would be spending days in the media center and evenings in the library. Each group selected its topic quickly.

I provided a "Timeline and Due Dates" sheet for them to follow. This information helped them pace themselves and helped me to organize and control the flow of work. To stay organized, I listed each group on a clipboard, visited each group, and recorded what each member was doing and what research they were using. I provided materials, advice, and guidance. The class almost ran itself once I set up the schedule.

I also distributed in advance, the evaluation form I would be using. It included two areas of evaluation: (1) presentation: knowledge of material and ability to answer questions from the audience, organization, creativity, effort and enthusiasm, and overall flow of the show; and (2) criteria met: host/hostess, experts representing each side, guests with clear understanding of roles, and an issue that could be debated. Knowing evaluation guidelines in advance eliminated a lot of questions and directed students' attention to the appropriate aspects of the show.

Everyone got into character when they presented the show, and they used their research well. If I had given each student a test on his or her topic, all would have passed with flying colors. This was an enjoyable way to use research and writing in my classroom, and it was meaningful to my students.

of a scientist is imagination. Poetry lends itself to imagination—the wonders of stars, dinosaurs, and synergy. Synergy is the topic of the poem written by a high school student.

### The Miracle of Synergy

The sun streams down
Its pure white light
The beautiful spectrum
Colors so right.


Both long and short, the wavelengths fly
With frequencies both fast and slow
Molecules vibrate
And the prism will show.


With the molecules defracting
There's much scattering to do
The colors are dispersed
But the blue shows through.

—Anonymous


**Letters**. Letters can be sent or not sent, though we seldom think of the unsent letter. Unsent letters can be just as interesting as ones we actually send. Most of us

---

## Point ≡ Counterpoint

### A Debatable Issue
### Using Poetry in Content Learning

**Background**

Writing and reading poetry are common in English and literature courses. But poetry may seem an odd forum for learning in content areas such as social studies, science, or math. But is this so, or is this just a stereotype?

"What is poetry? Why, Sir, it is much easier to say what it is not. We all know what light is, but it is not easy to tell what it is."

—Samuel Johnson

**The Debatable Issue**

Poetry is an excellent forum for developing reading and writing knowledge in content areas such as social studies, science, or math.

**Take a Stand**

Argue the case for or against the debatable issue. Marshal your arguments based on research, experience, and your teaching philosophy. After you have discussed the issue among colleagues, consider debating it in your class.

have written letters that were composed in the heat of anger. Sometimes we send these letters; sometimes they are unsent. Anger can overwhelm good sense and polite dialogue, though an unsent letter need not take an angry tone.

Unsent letters can be tied to topics studied in class. For example, an assignment for an English class reading a Shakespeare play might be to write an unsent letter to Shakespeare. A social studies class studying local, state, or national politics might write to a local, state, or national politician—the letter could be sent or unsent. Closer to home, school governance is a topic students might find interesting, since issues related to school governance influence students' daily lives. The letter in Figure 7.1 was written by a high school student to his school principal. The student, Jason, attempts to persuade his principal to act on an issue important to today's high school students—parking. (The letter was sent, though not without reservations.)

Dear Ms. Smith,

I'm not sure you will read this letter, but I hope you do. I think our school needs to add spaces in our parking lot. You probably think parking is not so important, because our school needs other things. But I hope to convince you that my idea is important.

Right now there are very few places to park your car unless you happen to get to school early. You can drive around the parking lot for ten minutes and if you find a spot you're lucky. I know what you're thinking. Why don't I take the bus to school? I have a reason. I need my car to get to work after school. Here's another reason why more parking is a good idea. If we had more parking places, fewer students would be late for class. Thanks for listening to my problem.

Sincerely,

Jason

**Figure 7.1**
Jason's Persuasive Letter

**Freewrite.** The idea of freewriting is to let thoughts flow freely without regard for mechanics, sequence, relevance, or ultimate worth of the ideas. Freewriting helps develop fluency and can provide a start on a topic that may be developed later. The freewrite does not have to meet traditional standards, though there is no intent to disregard standards. The procedure includes these steps: (1) choose a topic and write for 5 to 10 minutes without stopping; (2) do not worry about mechanics or the worth of the ideas you are recording; (3) when you cannot think of anything to say, write, "I can't think of anything to say"; (4) reread your freewrite, and circle any ideas that can be expanded later. If the freewrite is well developed, treat it as a first draft.

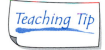

*Teaching Tip*

To the novelist William Faulkner, writing is "a voyage of discovery."

Freewriting is adaptable to content writing and is especially useful for students who are uncomfortable with writing. The guidelines for a freewrite provide the freedom to write without the usual constraints, and students find this condition attractive. Freewriting can provide the raw material from which more sophisticated pieces of writing can be harvested. Of course, freewriting may turn up little that is worth further development, but even in this case it aids writing fluency. On the other hand, a freewrite may stimulate thinking that will prove useful at some future time.

## Section Summary: Writing in the Content Areas

1. Writing generates new knowledge and reinforces prior knowledge.
2. The writing process emphasizes procedures for organizing writing in four stages: prewriting, drafting, revising, and sharing or publishing.
3. Every writer is unique, and every writing task has different requirements. Consequently, it is useful to think of *a* writing process rather than *the* writing process.
4. The goal of writing is the written product, not the process. Process is the business of the writer; product, the interest of the reader.
5. Content writing strategies include learning journals, double-entry journals, essays, literary gossip and dialogue journaling, learning logs, summaries, reports, poetry, letters, and freewrites.

## Practical Teaching Ideas and Activities

*Teaching Tip*

**1.** *Plan and organize integrated units.* Integrated units of study maximize higher-level thinking skills, make connections to the outside world, create links among content areas, generate meaningful and authentic experiences, and foster active engagement among the learning community. There are three levels of planning and instructional decision making: first, *the year-long focus,* which includes the major understandings, strategies, and values you want your students to achieve; second, *the units of study,* which include blocks of focused study (or thematic units) into which the year-long curriculum is divided; and third, *the lessons,* which include the learning experiences in which the students will engage. Integrated units combine multiple modes of instruction and learning, a thematic focus, and connecting ideas and activities. They emphasize all of the language arts: reading, writing, listening, speaking, and visual representation.

**2.** *Consider the following steps when planning a thematic unit.* First, identify an inquiry question, event, or piece of literature to connect all ideas and activities. Second, outline unit objectives, or the outcomes students should be able to demonstrate as a result of their inquiry. Third, obtain a multitude of print resources as well as other related materials to enhance the experience. Fourth, organize specific instructional and learning experiences. Finally, determine evaluation criteria and techniques.

**3.** *Use picture book read-alouds to prepare for forthcoming events and experiences.* Children's literature provides valuable opportunities for students to learn about themselves, life experiences, and topics of study. Prior to a content-related experience, read aloud and discuss related picture books. Writing extensions can be included as well.

**4.** *Use writing to explore and clarify meaning.* Writing becomes a very valuable learning tool as students read content area and thematic text. Writing fosters learning through note taking, exploring ideas, recording learning processes, and organizing information. This is a meaningful, purposeful use for writing—to understand and sort out what was just read, or as a prereading strategy to think about what is about to be read. There is a reciprocal relationship between writing and reading. Writers are concerned with communicating meaning through the use of the same print conventions used in the reading process. As teachers, we must make the clear link between reading and writing evident to the students.

**5.** *Incorporate learning logs.* Writing can be used as a reflective learning tool through the use of content area journals or learning logs. Students regularly keep records of their learning through reflections, observations, questioning, inquiring, and making charts and diagrams. This provides the opportunity to reflect on insights, questions, confusions, or disagreements about a topic. Entries can be *open-ended,* in which the students choose what to write about, or *closed,* in which the teacher selects specific ideas to explore or prompts to respond to. Students write in these logs regularly, for a brief period of time (10 to 15 minutes) to sort through their thinking and learning.

**6.** *Use one-minute reporting.* To develop oral language skills connected to the content area at any grade level, ask students from time to time to give a quick one-minute rundown on a given topic you have been studying together. Tell reluctant speakers a day in advance that they will be giving a one-minute report the following day.

See the Blue Pages at the back of the book and on the Companion Website for additional activities.

## ◄ Reflection and Summary

### Reflection

"Papa, monsters," my grandson said as he pointed to an advertisement for a movie he loves—*Monsters, Inc.* That single telegraphic sentence, uttered out of the depths of his tiny repertoire of language, thrilled me. You could say I'm easily thrilled. Or, less cynically, you could say I'm aware that mighty oaks grow from tiny acorns. Language is the key to growth in content reading and writing. Children's language progresses from acorns to mighty oaks before our very eyes. But sometimes we do not appreciate the beauty, magnificence, and potential that children's language represents. Pessimists tend to see the language glass as half empty. Optimists see it as half full. And what is it full of? *Potential for growth.* Pessimists, they say, are never disappointed because they do not expect good things to happen. Optimists are different; they expect good things to happen; they make good things happen. Optimists view the present and imagine a promising future for even the least promising child. Optimists look at a weak piece of writing and see its strengths. Pessimists look at a good piece of writing and see its weaknesses. Children who do not look promising in the present moment will not disappoint the pessimists. They expect to be disappointed. But the optimists—well, it wouldn't surprise them if some of their least promising acorns grow into mighty oaks.

## Summary

1. Readers construct meaning from text, using prior knowledge and reasoning. The concept of constructing knowledge is distinct from the idea of passively absorbing meaning from the written page.

2. The more interesting and engaging instruction and materials are, the greater the influence on comprehension of content concepts.

3. Learning results in the growth and development of mental structures called schemata. New information modifies and extends schemata.

4. How fast one reads is irrelevant without considering the purpose for reading. Purpose controls the rate and manner of reading. Good readers adjust their rate of reading by choosing an appropriate procedure such as skimming, scanning, studying, or surveying.

5. Strategies for comprehending content materials include content DRTAs , QARs, anticipation guides, and think aloud modeling.

6. Writing process emphasizes procedures for organizing writing around stages: prewriting, drafting, revising, and sharing/publishing. Nevertheless, the goal of writing is to produce a good written product, not process itself. Process is the business of the writer; product the interest of the reader.

7. A variety of content writing strategies were described including: learning journals, double-entry journals, essays, literary gossip, dialogue journaling, learning logs, summaries, reports, poetry, letters, and freewrites.

## ◀ Questions to Challenge Your Thinking

1. Do you think content teachers have time to concern themselves with reading and writing? Why or why not?

2. Do you think it's important for a scientist or mathematician to learn to read and write well in their discipline? Explain.

3. How important is it to read rapidly? What should readers keep in mind about reading rate?

4. Do you think comprehension modeling can really work? Explain.

5. Explain how prior knowledge aids in reading comprehension.

6. Should all writing go through the stages of the writing process? Explain.

7. The writing process is the business of writers; the written product is the business of readers. Explain what you think these two statements mean.

8. How can poetry be useful for content reading and writing?

9. Suppose you want your children to write essays. How would you go about preparing them for this type of writing?

10. In the reflection piece, I make a case for being an optimist. Do you agree or disagree with my argument? Why?

## ◀ A Case Study

Reading strategies can heighten engagement and interest among students as they prepare to read content materials. For instance, if you're teaching science and are about to read an article or chapter on black holes, two strategies discussed in this chapter would be particularly useful: (1) you could conduct a DRTA, and prepare questions to use before and after reading, or (2) you could construct an anticipation guide (containing agree–disagree or true–false questions) and administer the guide before and after students read the text.

Select an article or chapter dealing with any content subject. Prepare an anticipation guide or a set of prediction questions to be asked before students read your selection. Follow the guidelines suggested in this text as you construct your guide or DRTA questions. Locate a group of students and try out your strategy to see how it works. If you do not have access to children, ask your university colleagues to participate. If the materials are level appropriate, the anticipation guide or prediction questions are likely to work as well with them as with children. Write a report describing and analyzing how your strategy worked.

## ◄— Revisit the Anticipation Guide

Return to the Anticipation Guide in the chapter opener, and review your original responses to the questions. Complete the guide again, and then consider these questions.

1. Did you change your mind about any items? Why or why not?

2. Which major idea in this chapter do you disagree with? Why?
3. Which major idea do you agree with? Why?
4. How might you use an anticipation strategy with young children?

## VideoWorkshop Extra!

If your instructor ordered a package including VideoWorkshop, go to Chapter 7 of the Companion Website (www.ablongman.com/cramer1e) and click on the VideoWorkshop button. Follow the instructions for viewing the appropriate video clip and completing the accompanying exercise. Watch the Companion Website for access to a new interactive teaching portal, My Lab School, currently under construction.

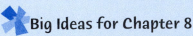

### A Philosophy of Reading Comprehension

*Reading is a partnership of mind, text, and context. The mind contributes its existing knowledge, the text offers the stimulus, and the setting provides the context. Each plays a role in determining comprehension— the goal of reading. Reading is said to be reasoning, an active search for meaning, the construction of meaning. Still, I cannot but wonder if our theory of reading is similar to the mythic tale of seven blind men. Each man touched a different part of an elephant and then described a vastly different beast. None had captured the essence of the living, breathing elephant. Had the men been able to see, ride, and observe the living, breathing beast, surely their explanations would have been more accurate. Yet even then their explanations could not have been fully accurate. Because complex phenomena can be appreciated more readily than they can be explained. Such is the case with reading.*

*Reading is complex. Its activity takes place in the brain. Its deepest secrets are invisible. Technology can reveal some of the brain's secrets, but we are far from understanding this inner sanctum. So we are left with theory: occasionally brilliant, sometimes mistaken, always ambiguous.*

# 8 Teaching Children to Comprehend Written Text

### Big Ideas for Chapter 8

1. Reading is an active search for meaning. The more prior knowledge readers have, the greater the likelihood they will construct meaning from text.

2. Factors that influence comprehension include the reader, the text, the quality of instruction, purpose, independent practice, and interest.

3. Four underlying comprehension components are explicit meaning, implicit meaning, word meaning, and evaluative–appreciative meaning.

4. The literature suggests the existence of 40 or more comprehension skills. This number is misleading, since many of the skills may not exist as independent entities.

5. Useful comprehension strategies include DRTA, KWL, mapping, retelling, and independent reading—among others.

6. Asking questions is an art that, when effectively executed, has a positive influence on comprehension.

7. Guided reading is close instruction in small group settings. Teachers observe, monitor, and provide scaffolding to children as they develop comprehension and other skills.

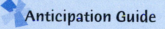
## Anticipation Guide

*Consider the following statements, and determine whether you agree or disagree with each. Save your answers, and revisit this guide at the end of this chapter.*

| | | |
|---|---|---|
| 1. Prior knowledge has a significant influence on comprehension. | agree | disagree |
| 2. Cognitive psychology has had a major influence on current views of comprehension. | agree | disagree |
| 3. It is best for teachers to set purposes for reading. | agree | disagree |
| 4. Excellent reading strategies can overcome weak teaching. | agree | disagree |
| 5. Questioning techniques have little influence on comprehension. | agree | disagree |
| 6. There are 20 or more measurable comprehension skills. | agree | disagree |
| 7. Independent reading practice is as important as reading instruction. | agree | disagree |
| 8. A major need of struggling readers is more help in phonics. | agree | disagree |
| 9. First children must learn to read; then they can read to learn. | agree | disagree |
| 10. A philosophy of teaching has little relevance in teaching reading. | agree | disagree |

It is not true that we have only one life to live; if we can read, we can live as many more lives and as many kinds of lives as we wish.

—S. I. Hayakawa

Every man who knows how to read has it in his power to magnify himself, to multiply the ways in which he exists, to make his life full, significant, and interesting.

—Aldous Huxley

## A Literacy Story

Slaves were forbidden to read and write; despite this injunction, fate intervened and a miracle, of sorts, enabled Frederick Douglass to become a writer, journalist, and leader of the abolitionist movement in America. Frederick frequently heard his "mistress" reading aloud from the Bible, so he asked her to teach him to read. She consented and took great pride in his rapid progress. Soon, however, Frederick's "master," Mr. Ault, discovered his wife's secret and forbade further instruction. Ault believed that if you teach a slave to read, he will soon want freedom. In this conviction, he was of course right.

The reading lessons stopped, but Ault's harsh words lit a fire of rebellion. As Frederick recalled years later: "In learning to read, therefore, I am not sure that I do not owe quite as much to the opposition of my master as to the kindly assistance of my amiable mistress." Frederick's initial tutoring served as the foundation on which he built his edifice of literacy. He taught himself the rest of what he needed to know and soon ran away to the North, where later he purchased his freedom.

Frederick's natural oratorical and literary brilliance catapulted him into the public limelight, where he fought for civil rights, women's rights, and freedom for slaves. He started his own antislavery newspaper, *North Star*, and wrote an autobiography with a familiar title: *The Life and Times of Frederick Douglass*. It remains a classic of American literature. Evil sometimes works to the benefit of those who perpetrate it, but often a determined individual overcomes evil. Frederick's long life and fight for literacy enriched the world and serve as a model for all those who seek the enlightenment that literacy can bring.

## A MATTER OF STANDARDS

### Comprehending Written Text

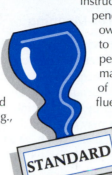

**Standard 3:** Students apply a wide range of strategies to comprehend, interpret, evaluate, and appreciate texts. They draw on their prior knowledge, their interactions with the readers and writers, their knowledge of word meaning and of other texts, their word identification strategies, and their understanding of textual features (e.g., sound–letter correspondences, sentence structure, context, graphics).

Standard 3 implies that reading is intended to provide pleasure, to enlighten the mind, and to acquire knowledge. Comprehension instruction must develop readers capable of comprehending a wide range of texts for multiple purposes. The goal of comprehension instruction is to enable children to become independent readers and thinkers who can set their own purposes for reading. We want children to read fiction and nonfiction with equal competence; we want children to acquire information as well as to experience the pleasures of the reading life; we want children to read fluently, widely, and flexibly. This chapter focuses on such outcomes. It discusses factors that influence comprehension, suggests strategies for developing comprehension, emphasizes the importance of purpose setting, and presents theories and practices that foster comprehension, interpretation, evaluation, flexibility, and appreciation of texts of every genre.

---

Reading is *an active search for meaning,* but this description does not address the aesthetic purpose of reading. For Isaac Bashevis Singer, reading embodied a search for the secret of life; for William Gladstone, reading was a sensuous warm bath; for Ross McDonald, reading was insulation against the world and its disasters. Every avid reader searches for meaning, but its grander purpose cannot be encapsulated in the prosaic phrase "an active search for meaning." Reading is also an entrance into the imaginative, creative, and aesthetic realms. Reading has pragmatic functions in the commercial, academic, and quotidian realm, but the best part of the reading life is lived on a higher plain. Reading is more than a theory purporting to account for how we *construct meaning* from text; it is also a portrait of Mona Lisa— a classical symbol of beauty and mystery that lies beyond and above all attempts to know it completely. Still, we can appreciate its magnificence, even though our knowledge is limited by the complexity of the subject we seek to understand.

##  Defining Comprehension

I've always enjoyed watching the comedy team of Laurel and Hardy, also known as Stanley and Ollie. After a typical disastrous adventure, Ollie often complained, "Another fine mess you've gotten us into, Stanley." Like Stanley, I've gotten myself into a mess. I've implied that a complete definition of comprehension lies beyond current knowledge, but a definition *is* necessary. Perhaps I can wiggle out of my predicament by explaining that the definition I propose represents the best of current reading research and theory. A definition of reading, as currently understood, comes in three parts: (1) an active search for meaning, (2) the cognitive connection, and (3) prior knowledge, schemata, and the construction of meaning.

## An Active Search for Meaning

Reading is an active search for meaning, but this is like saying that the sea consists largely of water. What does it mean to *actively search for meaning?* Suppose your faucet is leaking and you have acquired the materials to fix it at the hardware store. Directions are included with your faucet—in English and in the indecipherable language of "how to." So you have a text (but it may be confusing), you have a bit of prior knowledge about leaky faucets, and you have a context within which to work. Your task is to actively search for meaning from that set of directions—academics call it a *text*.

To search for meaning, one must "know how to navigate in a forest of facts, ideas, and theories."
—Raymond Queneau, French poet and novelist

To fix your faucet, you'll have to activate the dusty chamber where prior knowledge of faucet repair is stored and organized into interrelated networks called schemata—cognitive structures stored in memory. Your prior knowledge will help you connect text with task, but there is no guarantee that your chamber is well stocked in the area of faucet repair. As you search your network of schemata for relevant information, you must also consider how different kinds of text are structured. Directions for how to do home repair tasks are usually sequential, although there is no guarantee that they will be logical. As you read the text, you must apply reasoning skills to understand the relationship between text and task. If all goes well, you complete the task correctly by using prior knowledge, reasoning, and context. If your attempts at actively constructing meaning go badly, you probably don't have hot and cold running water yet. On the other hand, if fortune smiled, your neighbor showed up and installed the faucet for you.

## The Cognitive Connection

According to the cognitivist view, readers actively construct meaning as they read. Rather than respond passively to text, they construct meaning, using reasoning, prior knowledge, and text. Your job, as reader, is to actively construct meaning from the explanations that follow, so that a transaction can occur between you and this text. The more prior knowledge you bring to the explanations that follow, the better chance you have of understanding them.

Cognition is the process of knowing. Cognitive psychology is the study of the process by which we know, reason, recognize, and interpret our world. It is the dominant school of psychology today, having replaced the now moribund behaviorist theory, which emphasized a stimulus–response framework for learning. The bold new world of cognitive psychology raised the revolutionary idea that something important was going on in the mind that ought to be studied, and a more robust understanding of learning began to evolve. Behaviorists had paid little attention to that "little black box" and for that poor decision are now consigned to history. But weep not for the behaviorists; academic fashion will surely resurrect it, give it a new smile and stylish clothing, and proclaim another "bold new world." Déjà vu all over again, as Yogi Berra would say.

## Prior Knowledge, Schemata, and the Construction of Meaning

The search for meaning is immeasurably aided by the reader's existing store of knowledge. The more prior knowledge readers possess, the greater the likelihood that readers will *construct* meaning from written text. Further, the society in which we live also influences comprehension. This idea is referred to as social construction of knowledge. How we think about ideas and information is determined, to some degree, by the society that surrounds us.

For more information on schema theory, see "Understanding Understanding," by D. Rumelhart, 1984, in *Understanding Reading Comprehension,* edited by J. Flood. Newark, DE: International Reading Association.

Consider, for example, this sentence: "On the third night of hunger, Noni thought of the dog." I've directed reading–thinking activities with adults and children starting with this, the first sentence of a story entitled "Two Were Left." Here is what I often hear. Adult readers typically construct a setting located in polar regions, often Alaska; they nearly always conclude that Noni is an Eskimo; they expect a disaster to unfold. Children construct meaning for this text as sophisticated as adult constructions: Noni is usually constructed as an Eskimo boy; Noni is worried about the safety of his dog; Noni is thinking his dog might attack him.

Where do these constructions come from? Readers have organized schemata, a system of cognitive structures stored in memory about events, objects, and social relationships that represent an individual's world knowledge. More specifically, in this case, readers have a store of knowledge about names, hunger, dogs, and polar weather, which enables them to construct meaning for the sentence. As the story unfolds, readers elaborate on and refine their initial ideas. For instance, Noni, an Eskimo lad, is aware that his hungry dog might attack him. Noni also knows that the men of his village wouldn't hesitate to eat their dogs in an emergency, a societal norm. Here is where personal schemata come into play. Readers personalize their construction of meaning, and their constructions are often deeply subjective. For instance, avid pet lovers usually reject the possibility that Noni will eat the dog, or vice versa. Pet lovers have a vastly different schema for dogs than readers who have no sentimental attachment to them. Those who don't love dogs seem to have less trouble imagining Noni eating the dog or vice versa.

Readers construct their own meanings through a mental process that connects information encountered in a text with their knowledge of the world, their knowledge of how texts are structured, and their knowledge of specific content subjects. For example, the content of this textbook revolves around language arts; it anticipates familiarity with how textbooks are typically structured; it presumes a modicum of knowledge about teaching and children; it conceptualizes language arts within a particular philosophical framework; it assumes knowledge of certain vocabulary. Each of these knowledge domains is vast; it also overlaps with the others. Readers not only possess differing quantitative and qualitative amounts of knowledge but presumably have different ways of organizing and accessing these domains. All of these issues, and more, influence the meaning you will construct from this text and the success of the transaction between the reader of the text, the text itself, and the intent of the writer of this text.

## Section Summary: Defining Comprehension

1. Readers actively search for meaning. This is accomplished by activating prior knowledge structures in the brain, called schemata.
2. The cognitivist view of comprehension suggests that meaning is constructed interactively through the use of reasoning, prior knowledge, text, and context.

### Evaluating Reading Software

*Connecting Technology to Teaching*

Teachers need access to technology that's user-friendly, has pedagogical integrity, and extends the literacy program beyond what teachers are already providing. Sound criteria for evaluating reading software are crucial; without them you may end up with digitized books that add little to your literacy program. Consider the following criteria as you select software.

1. *User-friendliness.* Is the presentation clear and simple? Is it easy for the child to navigate? Are directions available in both written and auditory formats?
2. *Instructional integrity.* Does it activate prior knowledge? Is it engaging? Are the activities meaningful? Does it support the learner? Does it allow for multiple learning styles? Is the child provided with relevant, positive feedback? Does the software come with support materials? Can the child control the pace of learning? Does the program provide opportunities for applying new skills?
3. *Literacy instruction.* Does it offer explicit instruction of reading comprehension skills? Does it model comprehension skills? Does it encourage the student to think about reading strategies? Does it promote fluency? Do the questions move beyond the text? Does it utilize opportunities to show reading as a real-life activity? Is adequate

demonstration provided for the student? Does it prompt children to extend their reading?

When carefully selected, multimedia programs support literacy instruction. Excellent software can provide direct, individualized instruction and immediate feedback. The four programs listed below, although not perfect, are worth exploring.

Arthur's Reading Race
    Ages 3–7
    Brøderbund (The Learning Company)
    http://www.learningcompanyschool.com

Living Books Library I
    Ages 3–8
    Brøderbund (The Learning Company)
    http://www.learningcompanyschool.com

Reading Explorer Series
    4 levels are currently offered
    Gamco Education Materials/Siboney Learning
        Group
    http://www.gamco.com

CornerStone Reading Comprehension
    Levels A and B address the needs of students in
        grades 3–6.
    Hart, Inc.
    http://www.hart-inc.com/csrdg.htm

Contributed by Lisa Kunkleman

# Factors Influencing Comprehension

Many factors influence reading comprehension. Some are obvious, others less so. A complete accounting is impossible, since our knowledge of how the brain functions and how individual readers perform is limited. Research and expert opinion provide some likely candidates. It is reasonable to presume that this section presents the most relevant factors influencing comprehension. Nevertheless, other factors undoubtedly affect comprehension, some specific to the individual reader, others simply unknown. This section describes six factors: (1) the reader, (2) the text, (3) quality of instruction, (4) purpose, (5) independent practice, and (6) interest.

## The Reader

Learning occurs in social–cultural contexts through social interaction with adults and peers and, once learned, becomes internalized (Vygotsky, 1978). This statement suggests the value of strategies modeled by the teacher and reinforced through work with peers. As growth in reading and writing occurs, independence develops, and teachers can gradually pass responsibility on to the learner. This progression is one of the outcomes of scaffolding—offering a level of support to the student that decreases over time, as the student becomes more proficient in the task.

Children bring a wealth of knowledge to the classroom. It is important, therefore, that instructional strategies be designed to help children integrate new information with prior knowledge. Sensitivity to what children know is crucial since their prior knowledge will determine, to a large degree, what they will learn. When instruction is directed in ways that take advantage of prior knowledge and the social–cultural learning environment, the possibilities for successful comprehension increase. One thing children do not always bring with them is skilled decoding of text. The more skilled children are at decoding, the more attention is available for comprehending text (Pressley, 2000).

## The Text

The type of text children read influences comprehension. Children who have had broad exposure to stories are familiar with story grammar and are thus able to comprehend stories with less difficulty than children with little exposure to story texts. But children who comprehend story text readily may have difficulty with informational texts. Children need to be introduced to expository writing early, and they need sustained exposure to such texts over time.

Expository texts usually present information in non-story form, though some parts of such texts may be expressed in narrative form. Expository prose differs from text to text, depending on the content and the choices writers make. Vocabulary, organizational structures, and concepts in expository text differ from those of fiction. Complex vocabulary adds to the reader's burden; organizational structure may obscure meaning; concepts may be densely packed. The less familiar readers are with the structure of expository text, the vocabulary it contains, and the concepts it presents, the more difficult it will be for children to comprehend.

## The Quality of Instruction

Quality of instruction influences comprehension. Quality instruction, in turn, is influenced by teachers' personalities, the characteristics of their instruction, and the competence with which they implement it. Personality is reflected in temperament, intellect, and affect. The elements of instruction and the manner in which they are executed influence instructional outcomes. Competence is demonstrated by depth of literacy knowledge and classroom management. There is no single teaching personality—teachers are as diverse as the rest of the universe—but there are qualities and characteristics that determine teaching success. Researchers at the Center for English Language Arts at the State University of New York, Albany (1998) identified nine characteristics of effective literacy instruction (see Table 8.1).

## Purpose

The goal of reading is comprehension; reaching that goal is augmented by purpose. Purpose focuses the reader's attention. Teachers can set purposes for their students, and often do. A teacher may say, for example, "Read Chapter 2 to learn what caused the Civil War." But teacher-dictated purposes do not work as well as empowering

### Table 8.1

**Characteristics of Effective Literacy Instruction**

1. *Engagement.* Engages students productively in literacy activities and keeps them on task about 90% of the time.
2. *Management.* Manages all aspects of classroom learning, including student behavior, instructional aids, instructional planning, implementation, and scheduling of activities and events.
3. *Environment.* Creates and maintains an inviting, cooperative classroom environment including clear rules, high expectations, fair and constructive discipline, a pleasing physical environment, and a challenging learning atmosphere.
4. *Explicit skill instruction.* Teaches skills explicitly and in context, including word recognition, comprehension, vocabulary, spelling, and writing. Provides review, reteaching, and sufficient practice as part of the daily routine.
5. *Literature.* Emphasizes literature, reads literature aloud, conducts author studies, discusses

books, maintains a classroom library from which children self-select reading materials.
6. *Frequent reading and writing.* Schedules blocks of time for reading and writing. Sees that children read and write with someone every day: teacher, visitor, buddy, aide. Plans at least 45 minutes of reading and 45 minutes of writing every day.
7. *Supportive instructional context.* Establishes challenging but realistic expectations. Monitors student accomplishments and expects accuracy within realistic parameters. Matches learning demands to student competence.
8. *Self-monitored learning.* Shows students how to use their time productively, organize their work habits, check their writing for meaning and correct conventions.
9. *Integrated curriculum.* Makes explicit connections between reading, writing, and content subjects.

children to set their own purposes. Self-declared purposes stimulate the desire to read, direct the quest for information, certify the reader's sense of competence, and most important, *simulate the conditions that must prevail in independent reading.* Thus, a better way to introduce a chapter on the Civil War would be to ask, "What do you think might have caused the Civil War?" Then have students read to find out how their predictions stack up in reference to the author's perspective.

> "Students will best develop their knowledge, skills, and competencies through meaningful experiences and instruction that recognizes purpose."
> —National Council of Teachers of English and the International Reading Association, *Standards for the English Language Arts,* 1996.

The key to self-declared purposes is prediction. Predictions made by readers become their purpose for reading. Prior to and during reading, therefore, use a prediction strategy, such as those that follow, to help readers set their own purposes for reading.

- *Direct readers to set their own purposes.* Readers make their own predictions in response to teachers' questions. In fiction materials, the questions might focus on possible events and outcomes (What do you think this story might be about?). In nonfiction, questions might connect what readers already know with what will be revealed in the text (Do alligators really eat people, or is this a myth?).
- *Provide opportunities for refining, modifying, or rejecting initial purposes at strategic stopping points in the reading.* For example, after students have read a title, the first paragraph, or the first page, you may wish to stop for predictions. Early stopping points provide opportunities for divergent and creative ideas. Later stopping points often lead readers to modify or reject early divergent hypotheses in favor of more convergent possibilities.
- *Become familiar with the content of the reading materials students are about to read.* Teachers' foreknowledge of content enables them to direct the reading lesson consistent with text content and desired outcomes.
- *Employ a variety of purpose-setting strategies.* Several excellent prediction strategies enable readers to set their own purposes. For example, the directed reading thinking activity (DRTA), the directed listening thinking activity (DLTA), anticipation guides, and KWL are prediction-based strategies. Descriptions and procedures for using these strategies are discussed later in this chapter.

## Independent Practice

Good luck is invoked in show business with the words "Break a leg." That's the good luck H. G. Wells, a British author, had as a young lad—a broken leg. With no place to go and nothing to do, Wells began to read—a duke's mixture of books and magazines: "My world began to expand very rapidly, and when presently I could put my foot to the ground, the reading habit had got me securely" (Gilbar, 1989, p. 31). A long convalescence can be a burden or a blessing. For Wells, convalescence became an extended period of practice that led to a love of the written word. Now I'm not recommending that you break children's legs to induce an extended period of reading practice. But I do believe that the sharpest saw in the tool box of practice strategies is independent reading. Practice does not make perfect, but it does make better when supportive instruction has preceded practice.

It is best for children to choose their own books for independent reading. While other materials may supplement independent reading, an abundance of books is crucial to success. It is also important for children to practice reading books that match or approximate their independent reading level. Except in special circumstances, do not encourage children to read books that are too hard—materials that are beyond a child's instructional level due to difficulties with comprehension, word recognition, vocabulary, or insufficient prior knowledge.

Teachers often ask, "Is it a waste of instructional time to have children read independently in class?" Definitely not, for several reasons. First, independent reading in school may be the *only* sustained reading some children will experience. Second, instruction works best when it is followed by meaningful practice of what has been taught. Independent reading provides such practice. Third, independent reading can lead to a love of reading. Reading instruction is necessary, but independent practice produces avid readers. Fourth, the pleasure of reading can be discovered only by reading—*not by reading instruction, but by reading.*

## Interest

Interest it is often the catalyst for reading. William Corbett, a British journalist and politician, was but a lad when he left home and journeyed to the city. On passing a bookseller's window, his eye fell on a little book an the odd title, *Tale of a Tub.* Unable to pass it up, he spent his last pennies for the book, even though the expenditure meant no supper that evening. Never mind. On finding a convenient haystack, young Corbett sat down to read and read until dark. Has a book ever so interested you that you went hungry to read it? If so, you've known the power of interest.

Interest in reading a specific author influenced Will Durant's career as an historian. As a young boy, he had an avid interest in Dickens's book *The Pickwick Papers.* He wanted more of Dickens and found a cheap edition of David Copperfield in a bookstore. Unfortunately, he had only 14 cents but needed 25. The store owner, unmoved by Will's plight, was about to return the book to the shelves when fate intervened. A gentleman, whom Will conceived to be a millionaire, made up the difference, remarking in jest, "When you get rich you can pay me back." So Will got his book and walked home in ecstasy, thanking Providence for his good fortune. That day marked a milestone in Durant's reading life. Durant and his wife, Ariel, became famous historians, writing the mammoth multivolume *History of Civilization.* Incidentally, the "millionaire" turned out to be a goodhearted plumber.

What makes the written word so interesting, so consuming, so engrossing that we will, in desperation, read matchbook covers if nothing else is within reach? It is curiosity, engagement, fascination, titillation, attraction, absorption, thirst,—in short, *interest.* Some of us are hyperlexic—we can't stop reading. Lynn Sharon Schwartz (1996), author of *Ruined by Reading,* is one such person. She said, "We read to seek the answer, and the search itself—the task of a lifetime—becomes the answer."

The world exists to be read. *Have you read it?* This is a good question to ask ourselves and our children. What makes us want to read the world? What makes some readers hyperlexic? Perhaps it comes down to sheer pleasure and insatiable,

*Poor Calvin—if something doesn't interest him, forget it. If you can pique children's interests, they can comprehend surprisingly difficult material.*

unquenchable curiosity. Once we discover that some books pose provocative questions and others provide plausible answers, we're off to feed that internal fire, that insatiable curiosity, that unscratchable itch, that thirst for answers, that need to read.

## Section Summary: Factors Influencing Comprehension

1. The following six factors have a significant influence on comprehension: the reader, the text, the quality of instruction, self-declared purposes, independent practice, and interest.
2. Reading itself, not reading instruction, produces avid readers.

## Four Basic Components of Comprehension

Over the years, an extensive list of comprehension skills has developed, naming 40 or more skills. But are there as many comprehension skills as there are names? Are there 40 or more measurable and distinct ones? Research points to a more limited set (Davis, 1944; Hunt, 1957). Actually, four major components are sufficient to encompass all the various comprehension skills. These components are (1) explicit meaning, (2) implicit meaning, (3) word meaning, and (4) evaluative–appreciative meaning.

### Comprehension of Explicit Meaning

The comprehension of explicit meaning requires readers to recall or recognize literal information stated in a text. This is sometimes referred to as "getting the facts." Explicit comprehension requires locating information, following directions, identifying supporting detail, recognizing a sequence, and other such literal reading tasks. Explicit comprehension overlaps a category called cognitive memory—

the understanding and retention of information. Cognitive memory, like explicit comprehension, provides essential background information and is needed to operate effectively at all levels of comprehension.

Explicit comprehension is the most frequently taught and tested comprehension component. Perhaps because it is relatively easy to teach and test, there is a tendency to overemphasize it (Durkin, 1979). Though important, it should not be emphasized out of proportion to its contribution to thinking. Regarded as the lowest skill in the comprehension hierarchy, it should nonetheless not be neglected—meaningful transactions with text are impossible in the absence of comprehension of explicit meaning.

Two concerns are prominent in teaching explicit comprehension. First, a disproportionate amount of time is devoted to it. Estimates suggest that as much as 80% of instructional time is allotted to explicit comprehension. Teachers and instructional materials focus too much attention on it. Second, the thinking connection between explicit and implicit comprehension is often neglected. The regurgitation of literal information has limited relevance, but the *application* of literal information to stimulate thinking is more nourishing to readers' minds.

## Comprehension of Implicit Meaning

Implicit meaning involves behaviors commonly associated with critical thinking (Pearson & Johnson, 1978). The ability to read effectively at an implicit level distinguishes the active from the passive reader. Many, if not most, of the important ideas gained from reading fall into this category. Implicit meaning is achieved when readers make an inference—they comprehend a concept that is not explicitly stated in a text. Nevertheless, explicit information is the linguistic resource on which inference is predicated.

> "Reading furnishes the mind only with the materials of knowledge; it is thinking makes what we read ours."
> —John Locke, British economist

Inference runs the gamut from simple to complex. Two simple linguistic inferences can be drawn from these two sentences: "John ate a pie. Later he ate two more."

Inference 1: *He* refers to *John*.
Inference 2: *More* refers to *pies*.

This type of linguistic inference is common. We make them automatically, with little conscious thought. They are so basic that you may not even credit them as inferences. Yet they are.

Two or more inferences may be drawn from the following statement: "Teachers who expect children to write poetry must have the courage to write poetry themselves."

Inference 3: Teachers who write poetry are better able to inspire students to do the same.
Inference 4: Teachers who do not write poetry, but require children to, may expect less success.

Inferences 3 and 4 are complex, controversial, and contradictory. They require serious thought. Drawing one or the other depends on readers' beliefs about teaching poetry to children. Readers will differ regarding which of these inferences is credible, since personal and professional values are at stake. But disagreement should not be considered a problem—it is an opportunity. Thoughtful discussion thrives on intellectual struggle; it is how we come to understand what is true, good, and right.

Implicit comprehension requires teacher involvement. Thoughtful discussion among students and teacher is needed if inferential thinking is to occur. A provocative text and thought-provoking questions can stimulate such freewheeling classroom discussion. Agreements and disagreements about the implied meaning of an interesting text give life to discussion, and the wise teacher expects and accommodates these differences. They are signs of reasoning and maturity in the reading skill of your students.

## Comprehension of Word Meaning

Words are subtle, supple, and slippery. Take the word *Hollywood*. Obviously, it denotes a city in California. Less obviously, it carries connotations of glamour, since Hollywood is where films are made, stars reside, and dreams of stardom are focused. It may also be associated with decadence, depending on the reader's perspective. Our depth and breadth of word knowledge depend largely on the quality and extent of our world experience, particularly our reading experience. A rich level of word knowledge is prerequisite for efficient and effective comprehension. Words are the symbols of our thinking, the bearers of our concepts, the conveyors of our knowledge. At its simplest level, comprehension of word meaning requires an accurate translation and explanation of words. At its more challenging levels, comprehension involves layers of complexity.

A grasp of word meaning is prerequisite to every level of reading comprehension. As early as the 1940s and 1950s, studies by Davis (1944) and Hunt (1957) identified a general verbal factor related to word meaning. Children acquire their reading vocabularies primarily through reading. Nagy, Herman, and Anderson (1987) estimated that the number of words learned from incidental contextual reading ranges from 750 to 8,250 per year. The more children read, the more words they are likely to learn.

> "Words are like bodies, and meanings like souls."
> —Abraham Ibn Ezra, rabbi, scholar, and poet

## Comprehension of Evaluative-Appreciative Meaning

Imagine that you've just read a story and you say to yourself, "What a lousy ending to a good story." You've quickly calculated the qualities that, in your judgment, make for a good story and a good ending. Your critique is based on your prior knowledge of stories and your personal criteria. You may have judged harshly, wisely, fairly, or foolishly. Your judgments may be well informed or ill informed. None of this matters. This is your evaluation of a story, perhaps primarily an affective response. Evaluative–appreciative comprehension extends reading beyond the text, generating a reader response that does not necessarily depend on the text for substantiation, evidence, or worth.

Comprehension at this level operates beyond the bounds of traditional assessment. It is based on personal criteria regarding meaning. Here the reader's judgment reigns supreme. Some readers may appreciate a poem because they find it sublime; others may consider the same poem silly, but appreciate it all the same. While comprehension on this level is personal and often affective, it is not divorced from cognitive processes. Evaluative–appreciative meaning requires reasoning. It differs from the other comprehension components in emphasis and outcome, not in process.

Logical analysis also suggests evaluative–appreciative meaning is a component of comprehension. While we cannot reliably measure comprehension of beauty, for instance, it would be myopic to think, therefore, that it does not exist. Beauty lies in the eye of the beholder. In the summer, I enjoy watching the sun set over Lake Leelanau. I cannot numerically rate the extent of my appreciation for the beauty of this scene. I see no reason to do so. I could describe it, I suppose, but what puny words would suffice? What works better is to sit with a friend and enjoy the sunset. The evaluative–appreciative dimension of comprehension may be something like watching the sun set over a lake. It enriches mind, soul, and intellect. We can talk about it, appreciate it, evaluate it, but in the end no instrument can measure its boundaries. It is simply there to be felt and enjoyed.

## The Proliferation of Comprehension Skills

The philosopher John Stuart Mill said, "The tendency has always been strong to believe that whatever received a name must be an entity or being, having an independent existence of its own. And if no real entity answering to the name could be found, men did not for that reason suppose that none existed." Professions of every sort invent names to describe ideas and activities in their field. Many named entities have a verifiable existence, some are simply redundant, others duplicate existing names.

Though the literature on reading instruction suggests the existence of 40 or more comprehension skills, there is little empirical evidence that each is an independent entity. The number of comprehension components that can be reliably and validly measured is small (Davis, 1944; Hunt, 1957). The four we have discussed are sufficient to describe most, if not all, of what is important to teach children about understanding text. The three measurable comprehension components are explicit meaning, implicit meaning, and word meaning. Evaluative–appreciative meaning cannot be reliably or validly measured.

From an instructional perspective, how should we deal with the 40 or more named skills that are not independently measurable? They have a place in our instructional traditions, with the understanding that they consist of *reading activities with a particular instructional emphasis*. Such activities may contribute to attaining skill in the four underlying comprehension components described earlier. For example, think of the comprehension skill of determining the main idea. Such a reading activity may foster growth in explicit or implicit meaning. In one instance a main-idea reading activity may require locating an explicitly stated piece of information. Another activity may require implicit comprehension. Table 8.2 contains a list of common names of reading skills and classifies them according to the four main comprehension components. But a warning is in order. This classification scheme is merely one way of conceptualizing and classifying the commonly named skills. It is not based on empirical evidence—none exists.

**Table 8.2**

**Classifying Commonly Named Comprehension Skills**

| Explicit (literal) | Implicit (reasoning) | Word Meaning (vocabulary) | Evaluative–Appreciative (affective, judgment) |
|---|---|---|---|
| Main idea—stated | Inference | Denotation | Mood |
| Sequence | Prediction | Connotation | Tone |
| Following directions | Application | Multiple meanings | Characterization |
| Restating | Cause/effect | Contextual meanings | Beauty |
| Finding proof | Interpretation | Compounds | Evaluation |
| Factual details | Contrast | Synonyms | Value judgments |
| Locating information | Comparison | Antonyms | Feelings |
| | Extrapolation | Homonyms | Opinions |
| | Drawing conclusions | Word roots | Humor |
| | Generalization | Figures of speech | |
| | Main idea—implied | Word origins | |
| | | Idioms | |
| | | Metaphors | |
| | | Similes | |

## Section Summary: Four Components of Comprehension

1. The four basic components of comprehension are (1) comprehension of explicit meaning, (2) comprehension of implicit meaning, (3) comprehension of word meaning, and (4) comprehension of evaluative–appreciative meaning.

2. The reading literature abounds in names of skills that may not, in fact, exist as measurable independent entities. We should think of these as activities focusing on a particular instructional emphasis. Such activities may contribute to growth within one or more of the four underlying comprehension components. The precise number of comprehension skills is probably unknowable.

## Comprehension Strategies: Before, During, and After Reading

Strategies are instructional tools. But it is the manipulator of the tools, not the tools themselves, that determines success. For example, a carpenter's tools do not guarantee quality workmanship; the carpenter's skill does. Strategies do not guarantee effective instruction, but they make effective instruction more likely when used skillfully. Two different teachers may use the same strategy and implement it in a seemingly similar manner—yet one may fail and the other succeed. This is because a strategy is an inert set of procedures; it has no life of its own, no magic automatically released upon its implementation. It awaits the teacher to transform its potential into actuality. The craft, competence, and personality of the teacher make or break a strategy. Teachers succeed who skillfully engage children in thoughtful discussions that challenge thinking, arouse interest, and engage prior knowledge. The art and craft of the teacher transform strategic procedures into productive learning.

There are many reading strategies, but one need not use all of them to become an effective reading teacher. A relatively modest set of strategies, deeply understood and effectively implemented, will provide teachers with a sufficient repertoire, providing other crucial elements of effective teaching are present. This section describes a select number of strategies: (1) the directed reading thinking activity and its listening counterpart, the directed listening thinking activity, (2) anticipation guides, (3) KWL, (4) mapping, (5) reader's theater, (6) shared reading, (7) reading aloud, (8) uninterrupted sustained silent reading, (9) retelling.

## DRTA and DLTA

Stauffer (1969) developed and refined the directed reading thinking activity (DRTA) because he believed that the directed reading activity (DRA) placed insufficient emphasis on thinking as part of the reading process. The directed reading activity had been developed by Betts (1946), Stauffer's mentor. For decades, the DRA was widely used in basal reader instruction. Whether Stauffer's criticism of the DRA was valid is arguable. Nevertheless, it provoked him to develop his alternative. For a long time, the directed reading thinking activity was known only within the relatively small coterie of Stauffer's students. However, in recent decades it has been broadly recognized as a highly effective strategy for directing group reading comprehension (May and Rizzardi, 2002; Rapp-Russell, 1993; Ruddell, 1999).

Stauffer conceived the directed reading thinking activity as a teacher-directed comprehension activity to be used with small groups of readers able to read at approximately the same level. Subsequently, Cramer & Hammond (1970) amplified the DRTA process as a tool useful for directing listening activities—directed listening thinking activity (DLTA). The DLTA operates with the same philosophy and procedures as a directed reading thinking activity except that the teacher reads the material aloud. An advantage of the DLTA is that it can be used to direct comprehension of written material with students who haven't yet acquired sufficient word recognition skill to handle a complex text. Thus, it is an ideal procedure for teaching content materials, such as social studies or science, where wide disparities exist in decoding capabilities but there are fewer, if any, disparities in oral language and thinking capability.

In a DRTA, students use prior knowledge to make predictions about content, check the accuracy of their predictions, and confirm or modify their original ideas as the reading proceeds. Stauffer outlined, in detail, five steps in a DRTA.

**Before Reading**

1. *Establish purposes for reading.* Ask an initiating question requiring predictions: What might this story be about? Follow this question with probes keyed to children's responses: Can you add to that idea? What makes you think that is so? Interesting idea, Tim. Ann, do you agree with Tim, or do you have a different idea?

2. *Adjust reading to purposes and nature of the material.* Determine the rate of movement through the text by choosing strategic stopping points. In story material, stopping points follow plot so that key events may be predicted prior to their revelation. For nonfiction material, stops are keyed to text structure and content. The number of stopping points varies with the time available and the content. For instance, an essay on crocodiles might start with these questions: Do crocodiles really eat people? Where might crocodiles live? How are alligators different from crocodiles?

*Teaching Tip*

**During Reading**

3. *Observe the reading.* As students read, be alert to needs. For example, a student may need help pronouncing a word or determining meaning. If so, provide immediate help. Avoid lingering, and do not divert attention from the comprehension purpose of the DRTA. For example, this is not a time for teaching word recognition. But make notes, mental or written, about instructional needs and tend to them during follow-up.

4. *Develop comprehension.* The purpose of using DRTAs is to develop habits of reasoning, applying prior knowledge, testing the validity of predictions, and citing supportive evidence. Teacher questions, comments, and probes are the key to reaching these goals. Three question types are especially useful: (1) prediction: What do you think will happen? (2) citing supportive evidence: What information supports your idea? and (3) thoughtful discussion: Why do you suppose the author said that?

**After Reading**

5. *Discuss, elaborate, clarify, and develop skills.* After the DRTA is concluded, begin follow-up activities such as vocabulary development, word recognition, comprehension, oral language, reviewing prediction effectiveness, and writing. Usually there will be time for only one or two such activities.

## Anticipation Guides

Anticipation guides help students use their existing knowledge through prediction. Students use them to predict ideas and content likely to be encountered in a passage. Anticipation guides take many forms, including true–false questions, agree–disagree formats, and categorizing key words and concepts from the text. Students consider the accuracy of their predictions as they read. After reading, students evaluate their performance and discuss what they have read. For instance, this chapter begins with an anticipation guide with an agree–disagree format. This

## Standing on the Shoulders of Giants
### Historical Contributions to Literacy
### Russell Stauffer

The first time I presented a paper at a literacy conference, I spoke on the topic of dialect and its connection to issues then current in literacy instruction. My mentor, Russell Stauffer, attended as a courtesy to his graduate student. Just before I started my presentation, Dr. Emmet Betts walked into the room, and in his usual bluff manner, shouted across the room, "Well, Russ, I see you're in the right place. You could use a little help with your dialect."

Russell G. Stauffer was born and reared in what was then known as Pennsylvania Dutch country. The Pennsylvania Dutch, as they were then called, were of Germanic origin. As a result, Russ Stauffer had a slight but noticeable accent. Stauffer served in the U.S. Army during World War II. After the war, he earned a Ph.D. at Temple University, where he studied under Professor Betts, a pioneer in literacy who developed the widely used directed reading activity and the informal reading inventory.

Few have served the literacy profession as well as Russell Stauffer. He developed the directed read-ing thinking activity, expounded and elaborated the language experience approach, served for eight years as editor of *The Reading Teacher*, and helped found the International Reading Association. He directed one of the federally funded first-grade reading studies in the 1960s. When additional funding was not forthcoming, he continued his study for five more years without it. A prolific writer, he produced numerous articles and editorials and three major books, *Thinking as a Reading Process*, *Directing Reading Maturity as a Cognitive Process*, and *The Language Experience Approach to Reading Instruction*.

Russell Stauffer directed the Reading Study Center at the University of Delaware for two decades, where he held a prestigious endowed professorship. His many students and friends remember him with affection and respect for his personal and professional contributions to their lives.

strategy gets readers to use prior knowledge to make educated guesses about chapter content, develop purposes for reading, and heighten awareness of chapter content.

Suppose your students are about to read an essay about fruit bats. Write a series of questions based on the content of the essay, including a question or two that is not answered in the essay so that a reason for further research is established. Here is an example:

1. Fruit bats have a wingspread of 5 feet or more.          agree     disagree
2. Fruit bats live in caves.                                agree     disagree
3. Fruit bats are carriers of rabies.                       agree     disagree
4. Fruit bats often destroy farmers' crops.                 agree     disagree
5. Fruit bats live only in tropical climates.               agree     disagree

Students form predictions by agreeing or disagreeing with the statements you have prepared. After reading, students return to their anticipation guide and complete it again, based on what they have learned. Discuss whether all questions were answered in the text. If not, suggest additional research. Talk about what was learned, what new information has been acquired, what questions remain, what changes in thinking about fruit bats may now exist.

## KWL

The letters *KWL* stand for what I **k**now; what I **w**ant to know; and what I **l**earned. Through teacher guidance, students are led to tell what they already know about a topic and this information is recorded on the board or on a large piece of paper. After the K part is completed, students are guided to suggest what they WANT to know or expect to find when they read the selection. After reading the selection, the teacher directs students as they discuss the L part—what they have learned from the selection.

This strategy, developed by Donna Ogle (1989), is an excellent method for involving readers in the comprehension process. It is popular with students and teachers because it stimulates prior knowledge, requires making educated guesses, and reveals what children have gotten from their reading experience. Table 8.3 shows a KWL chart produced by Ms. Jacobson's third-grade children, who were learning about frogs.

## Mapping

Mapping is an outline in graphic form, which depicts how topics are related to subtopics and how subtopics are related to subordinate details. Picturing ideas graphically appeals to children, and they usually enjoy doing it. Mapping can be done as early as kindergarten and is easy to learn because of its concrete, pictorial

**Table 8.3**

**KWL Chart: Frogs**

| What Do We Know? | What Do We Want to Know? | What Did We Learn? |
|---|---|---|
| 1. They jump. | 1. Where do they live? | 1. They have sharp teeth, lay eggs, and live in ponds and grass. |
| 2. They swim on top of the water. | 2. What do they eat? | 2. They begin life as tadpoles. |
| 3. They have a little brain. | 3. Where can you find frogs? | 3. Later tadpoles grow legs and turn into regular frogs. |
| 4. They eat weeds. | 4. How little or big are they? | 4. They eat bugs, butterflies, and insects. |
| | | 5. They have long legs for jumping. |
| | | 6. They can't live around garbage and junk. |
| | | 7. Snakes eat frogs. |
| | | 8. Tree frogs are tiny; bullfrogs are huge. |

*Keith and Brianna are working on a KWL about sharks.*

format. Outlining is more difficult than mapping because it is more abstract. An effective way of teaching outlining, which is quite useful for older students, is to start with mapping and convert the map into an outline. This enables children to compare the visually obvious relationships to their outlined counterparts. Teaching mapping and outlining concurrently makes outlining more understandable than when it is taught alone.

Mapping can take different forms, depending on the type of work envisioned. A map for story writing, for example, can be a simple affair, representing only a topic and three subtopics: beginning, middle, and ending. Or a story map can be more complex, dealing with narrative structures such as story problem, setting, characters, events, and resolution. While visual maps are usually arranged in a hierarchical structure showing logical connections among topic, subtopic, and subordinate details, they can also be organized nonhierarchically. Such maps are useful during brainstorming, when logical structure is not yet apparent. Such maps can later be reorganized in a hierarchy.

## Reading Aloud

Having books read to us when we are young has a lasting and profound influence. Research has established that reading to children supports learning to read. And practical experience with children supports its value as well. Andy is 3 years old. Already he has a library of over 200 books, and all have been read to him—no book has lacked opportunity. But Andy has his own ideas. He has books he wants to hear over and over. He also has books he won't listen to—gives them a little shove with his tiny but forceful hand. He has books he won't go to bed without. He has books he doesn't want in his bed. Consider how powerful reading aloud must be. Andy has already heard a couple of hundred or more books read aloud—his favorites repeated dozens of times. He loves the sounds of certain books; rhyme makes him laugh out loud. Certain songs bring a smile to his face and a wiggle to his body. Bill Martin Jr. called this *anchoring the sounds of language in children's ears.* Reading aloud does the anchoring, putting the child in the safe harbor of the love of language. Of course, mothers have known this since that most famous of mothers—Mother Goose. Research has caught up with mothers' intuition.

## Independent Reading, Self-Selection, and USSR

Instruction is important, but it is equally important to provide opportunities to practice reading so that skills may be practiced in a realistic context. Occasionally, teachers feel guilty about having children *just read,* fearing that it uses up valuable instructional time. But skill of any sort is learned well only when sufficient practice is provided. Consider, for instance, a sport such as swimming. Instruction in technique is essential, and the better the coach, the more likely important swimming techniques will be learned. But every coach knows that instruction must yield to practice. Consequently, swimmers spend far more time practicing swimming than they spend learning the techniques of swimming. So it is in reading.

Independent reading of self-selected books is a good way to move children into authentic literature. This can be done in a variety of ways, including introducing it through uninterrupted sustained silent reading (USSR), wherein students and teachers spend a period of time, usually 20 to 30 minutes, reading silently from books or other materials they have self-selected. During this time, *everyone reads without interruption.* Once independent reading is under way, it is necessary to broaden the scope of USSR and establish procedures for sharing and exchanging ideas and information about the books children are reading. One way to do this is through book talks. Usually done in small groups, book talks can also involve the entire class. Book talks have a history in literacy instruction. Jeannette Veatch (1959) and Lyman Hunt (1966) were advocates of individualized reading. Each developed procedures for directing conversations about books children had read. More recently, Raphael and McMahon (1994), Routman (1991, 2000), and Pressley, (2002), among others, have proposed procedures for using authentic literature to stimulate independent reading of materials that are at a comfortable independent or instructional level.

## Retelling

After reading or listening to a story or other account, students are asked to recall and retell as much as possible of what they have read. Comprehension is judged on the thoroughness of the retelling. Retellings may be done with pictures as well as text. Brown and Camborne (1989) found that retelling enhances comprehension and improves children's sense of story. In addition, Morrow (1986) has shown that retelling improves the language complexity of stories that children orally dictate. Before asking children to retell a story, it is a good idea to model the process. While retelling is not a drama activity, it enhances skills that will prepare students for drama activities.

## Section Summary: Comprehension Strategies: Before, During, and After Reading

1. The directed reading thinking activity influences growth in comprehension through prediction, verification, and follow-up discussion.
2. Anticipation guides help students use prior knowledge to predict probable outcomes prior to reading.
3. KWLs pose three questions which help direct readers' comprehension: What do I know? What do I want to know? What have I learned?

4. Mapping is a graphic form of depicting relationships among topics, subtopics, and subordinate detail.
5. Reading aloud builds vocabulary, general knowledge, knowledge of text structure, appreciation of literature, and other comprehension skills.
6. The more independent reading practice children have, the greater the likelihood they will become good readers.

# The Role of Asking Questions

Excellent comprehension questions stimulate higher-level thinking. Weak questions do little more than stimulate the recall of information, often trivial information. The former are highly desirable, the latter border on useless. Asking questions is an art. In the hands of a thoughtful practitioner, questions elicit information and ideas that enhance comprehension. Good questions stimulate productive discussion. Bad questions puzzle and frustrate readers and dampen discussion.

Asking questions contributes to assessment and instruction. The purpose of assessment is to determine how well children are performing, and when used properly, it enables teachers to adjust instruction to meet the needs they have observed. So assessment is an important but limited way to use questioning. Beyond assessment, questioning plays a major role in developing children's comprehension skills, and this is its primary role in reading instruction. When skillfully formed, questions lead to thoughtful discussion, establish purposes for reading, and stimulate thinking. The more astute the teacher is in asking strategic questions, the more

## Point ≣ Counterpoint

### A Debatable Issue
### Phonics versus Comprehension

**Background**
Decades ago, Jeanne Chall wrote *Learning to Read: The Great Debate.* It is about the role of phonics in reading instruction. The debate continues today. Some argue that initially, reading is made up of decoding. Once children can decode, there will be time enough to learn to comprehend. In other words, first children must *learn to read*—phonics. Then they can *read to learn*—comprehension.

**The Debatable Issue**
Should phonics take precedence over comprehension in early reading instruction?

**Take a Stand**
Argue the case for or against the debatable issue. Marshal your arguments based on your philosophy, experience, relevant research, and expert opinion. After you have discussed the issue among colleagues, consider debating it in your class.

likely comprehension instruction will achieve its purposes. Six issues related to asking questions are outlined in this section: initiating questions, text-based questions, questions not based on text, probing questions, four question types, and wait time.

## Initiating Questions

The first questions asked before, during, or after reading should initiate thinking about what will be read, what is being read, or what has been read. Different types of questions are required for each stage. Table 8.4 suggests possibilities.

Good questions help set purposes and require reflective reasoning. More factual information is retained when facts are used as a fulcrum to leverage thinking rather than as an excuse to test memory.

## Text-Based Questions

A text-based question can be answered using information explicitly or implicitly supplied in the text. Explicit information refers to literal information clearly stated and easily located. Implicit information refers to ideas or information not directly stated in the text that can be deduced through inference.

Every effort should be made to avoid trivial literal questions. Literal information is most useful when it lays a foundation for higher-level thinking. Consequently, explicit questions should focus on the most important or interesting literal information, and these explicit questions should then be used to support thinking. Some answers to explicit questions are easily found because they are located in a single place. But some answers require gathering information together located throughout a text. Knowledge of text structure and skimming are needed to answer

> "Students' critical skills are nurtured in classrooms where questioning is encouraged and rewarded."
> —National Council of Teachers of English and the International Reading Association, *Standards for the English Language Arts,* 1996.

### Table 8.4

**Initiating Questions: Before, During, and After Reading**

| | |
|---|---|
| Before reading | "The story we are about to read is entitled *Two Were Left.* What possibilities does this title suggest?" Divergent thinking is encouraged and inevitable, given the nature of the title and the limited amount of information available. |
| During reading | After reading the first page, more convergent predictions will be forthcoming. Hence, the question now might be, "Do you think the dog will attack Noni?" This question, while still providing possibilities for divergent responses, now focuses more closely on how the story plot will play out. |
| After reading | "Do you think Noni did the right thing by trusting that he and his dog would be rescued?" This is an evaluative question, opening the way for discussion of issues such as loyalty, trust, and risk taking. |

*Teaching Tip*

such questions. Putting pieces of information together usually requires making inferences about relationships and relevance.

Implicit questions stimulate thinking. Answers to implicit text-based questions are not directly stated in text, but they can be logically deduced from it. Prior knowledge, reasoning, and information from the text are all required to answer implicit questions. Four ways to ask them, in order of preference, are as follows: (1) provide the necessary explicit information in the stem of the question; (2) state the relevant explicit information, and ask a related implicit question; (3) ask an explicit question and, having gotten an answer, follow immediately with a related implicit question; and (4) ask the inference question directly, trusting that readers will recall the related literal information necessary for a thoughtful answer.

Imagine that you have asked an explicit question that is answered in the text: If whales continue to be overused for food and oil, what will happen to the whale population? (Answer: Many whale species will become extinct). Follow the explicit question with an implicit question: What might happen to whalers if many whale species become extinct? (Possible Answer: They will be out of work). Answering the implicit question not only makes use of literal facts (given in the stem of the question), but also it helps students apply literal information for a thinking purpose. An additional benefit is that you have increased the likelihood that students will remember the facts and may begin to understand that facts are important because they aid and abet thinking.

## Questions Not Based on Text

We want children to think beyond the text itself. To make this happen, we can ask questions that address ideas not directly alluded to in the text. Such questions are appropriate for either fiction or nonfiction. Some questions that go beyond the text have an indirect relationship to ideas and information in the text. If your students have just read a piece about Chicago, for instance, they may have learned that Lake Michigan played a key role in the city's growth. You can ask questions that go beyond the text:

1. Why do you think so many large cities are located near water?
2. How might water have contributed to the growth of New York City?
3. Can you think of any big cities that are not located near water? What might have helped them grow in the absence of a nearby river, lake, or ocean?

## Probing Questions

Teaching Tip

The word *probe* derives from a Latin word meaning "proof." Probing questions elicit consideration beyond initially offered responses. An effective probe ferrets out additional ideas, information, or reasoning that may extend or clarify. For example, suppose that during a directed reading thinking activity you have asked, "Lucy, what do you think will happen next?" If Lucy replies thoughtfully to this initiating question, you may wish to probe further. You might say, "I like that idea, Lucy. But what makes you think that will happen?" Your comment and question do two important

**Table 8.5**

**Ideas for Probing for Additional Response**

1. Sometimes a probe can be simple: "And?" "What else?" "Tell me more."
2. After a response, ask, "What's another possibility?" This question tends to elicit divergent responses.
3. After eliciting predictions that are imaginative but far out, ask, "What is most likely?" This question tends to elicit convergent responses.
4. When you want to redirect or refocus thinking, say, "Think about this." Then state an idea that focuses attention on an important idea that may have been missed.
5. Since children often generalize, a probe can help elicit greater specificity. Here are some examples:

   *Student response:* I think they will read *a lot* of books.
   *Teacher probe:* How much is *a lot? Three? Ten? Twenty? What's your guess?*

   *Student response:* I think they're going to get into *big* trouble.
   *Teacher response:* How *big*? Can you think of an example?

   *Student response:* They're going to find a lot of *stuff* in the cave.
   *Teacher probe:* What kind of *stuff* do you think they might find?

things: (1) Lucy receives an encouraging remark, and (2) you have implied that she had sound reasons for her prediction. Lucy may now explain her reasoning and cite evidence for her initial prediction.

Professor Dorsey Hammond, a masterful teacher, recently asked his graduate students what class discussion had been most helpful. The near unanimous response was "When you demonstrated how to probe student responses." Professor Hammond's ideas are listed in Table 8.5.

Children can think, but they must be given a forum for doing so. Probing provides that forum. Children need an intellectual and emotional atmosphere in which risk taking is honored. Intellect flourishes in a comfortable give-and-take atmosphere, where fear of ridicule is absent, where ideas are respected. The cure for silence is not noise but intellectual forums where everyone's ideas can be spoken without reluctance and with the expectation that ideas will be welcomed, especially those with which others may disagree.

## Questions Related to the Basic Components of Comprehension

Four basic comprehension components were described earlier in this chapter. This section suggests questions associated with each. Questions for explicit, implicit, and word meaning comprehension are based on an excerpt from a Sherlock Holmes story entitled, "The Blue Carbuncle." Questions for evaluative–appreciative comprehension are based on a short story.

> I took the tattered object in my hands, and turned it over rather ruefully. It was
> a very ordinary black hat of the usual round shape, hard and much the worse
> for wear. The lining had been of red silk, but was a good deal discoloured. There

*Asking the right questions of students can stimulate higher level thinking about literature and informational texts.*

was no maker's name; but, as Holmes had remarked, the initials "H. B." were scrawled upon one side. It was pierced in the brim for a hat securer, but the elastic was missing. For the rest, it was cracked, exceedingly dusty, and spotted in several places, although there seemed to have been some attempt to hide the discoloured patches by smearing them with ink.

"I can see nothing," said I, handing it back to my friend.

"On the contrary, Watson, you can see everything. You fail, however, to reason from what you see. You are too timid in drawing your inferences." (Doyle, 1905, p. 246)

### Explicit Questions

1. What is the object that Watson has been examining? (Answer: a black hat)
2. Give three facts that describe the condition of the hat. (Answer: It is: cracked, dusty, and spotted.)

These two questions require that the reader locate, recognize, or recall literal information. Learning to do this quickly and accurately is useful since grasping relevant literal information is prerequisite to higher levels of comprehension. Still, both questions border on the trivial. But they need not remain so if subsequent implicit questions are framed to generate thinking. Without such follow-up, the questions do not foster a useful comprehension purpose.

## Implicit Questions

1. What does the cracked, dusty, and spotted hat suggest about the sort of person the owner may have been? (Possible answer: The owner may have been a person of foresight and self-respect, but is perhaps less so now than in the past.)
2. Why does Holmes think that Watson has been too timid in drawing inferences? (Possible answer: Though Watson has observed a number of relevant facts about the hat, he ends up saying, "I can see nothing." Actually, he has seen everything but fails to use the information he has observed.)

Notice that both implicit questions require the use, but not the recall, of explicit information. Both require an interpretation of literal information to derive meaning not directly stated—an inference. Effective comprehension at the implicit level requires that the reader point to information that may logically support an answer. Arriving at correct answers is only part of the goal of implicit comprehension instruction—another important purpose is to challenge readers to use information in thinking. Disagreement as to what constitutes correct answers is inevitable and intellectually healthy. Good readers often form different conclusions and construct different meaning from the same literal information. The goal of implicit comprehension is to help readers learn how to construct probable and possible meaning from what has been literally stated. They need frequent and balanced instruction across the four basic components of comprehension.

## Word-Meaning Questions

1. What is meant when the lining of the hat is said to be discolored? (Answer: The original color of the lining had faded or been stained through use.)
2. What is meant by the expression "too timid in drawing your inferences"? (Possible answer: It means that Watson lacks the confidence or boldness to make guesses about the meaning of the facts he had observed.)

The first question deals with a specific word to which there is a denotatively correct answer. The second question focuses on a lengthier expression, to which the answer is open to interpretation. In teaching word meaning, primary stress should be placed on meaning in context. The contextual use of a word often conveys a subtle nuance or implication that goes beyond the definition given in a dictionary. The expression "too timid in drawing inferences" could be regarded as either a word meaning question or an implicit comprehension question. An inference question would focus on whether Holmes was expressing an implied criticism of Watson's power of intellect. The difference between a word meaning question and an inference question may be small or great, depending on the form the question takes. This further illustrates that the four basic components of comprehension are overlapping and interrelated.

**Evaluative–Appreciative Questions**. Enjoyment and appreciation are the principal outcomes of evaluative–appreciative comprehension. The emphasis is on the affective rather than the cognitive side of the intellect, though intellect is by no means absent. An example of evaluative–appreciative comprehension is illustrated in the following brief excerpt from a story entitled "Wild Dog."

> He stroked the dog's velvet ears and cupped the dog's muzzle between his hands, shaking it in rough tenderness. He stroked the dog's body and then, very carefully, so that the dog might not know any moment of fright, he drew his revolver from his belt and pressed it to the trusting head. (Cottrell, 1953, p. 69)

After the children had read the story, the following two questions were asked:

1. Do you think the boy should kill his dog? One child responded, "No, the dog trusted him and it would be cruel and disloyal to kill the dog." However, another child disagreed, saying, "Yes, I think he should have shot the dog. He loved the dog and knew that what he was doing was best for the dog." Both responses depend on personal judgments but are nonetheless valid. At the evaluative–appreciative level, responses are not right or wrong in the conventional sense. Thinking is required, but answers are based on personal values, judgments, and social norms.

2. What might you have done if you had been in the boy's situation? One child suggested that a veterinarian should have been called. Another felt that this would have been a waste of time. Others sympathized with the boy, feeling he had loved the dog and did the best he could. Most children recognized that there was no single correct answer to this question. Instead, they felt many choices were possible and reasonable.

## Wait Time

Sometimes we ask a question but fail to wait long enough to get a reflective response. When we do not get an immediate response, we are tempted to ask another question or turn to another student. How long should we wait? Ruddell (1999) suggests waiting 3 to 5 seconds. He found that a brief period of silence increases the likelihood of getting a response. Likewise, after a response is given, it helps to wait 3 to 3 seconds to provide time for additional response. Silence, it seems, stimulates additional response. When wait time doesn't work, and sometimes it does not, try a probing question or comment along the lines described earlier.

## Section Summary: The Role of Asking Questions

1. The first questions asked before, during, or after reading help initiate thinking about what will be read, what is being read, and what has been read.
2. Text-based questions can be answered using explicit or implicit information in the text.
3. Questions not based on the text help children think beyond the text itself.

4. Probing questions are follow-up questions designed to elicit consideration beyond initially offered responses.
5. Types of questions include: explicit, implicit, word-meaning, and evaluative-appreciative.
6. After asking a question, it is important to wait 3 to 5 seconds to give sufficient time for a considered response.

## Guided Reading

Small group instruction has a long history in reading. Round robin reading was one derisive name associated with such instruction. Children were assigned to groups by presumed ability—Robins to Buzzards, best to worst. Once assigned to a group, movement upward or downward seldom occurred—*birds of a feather flock together*. Typically, children read aloud from basal reader selections, answered questions, received corrective instruction, usually in word recognition, and discussed the selection.

For deeper background knowledge about guided reading, see *Guided Reading: Good First Teaching for All Children* by I. C. Fountas and G. S. Pinnell, 1996.

I'm hopeful that guided reading will not fall into this trap, and certainly its intentions and philosophy are different.

Wiencek (2001) describes guided reading as close instruction in small group settings, where teachers observe and monitor children, provide scaffolding in comprehension and other skills associated with reading. Guided reading is, indeed, a return to small group instruction, a welcome idea. The intention is to organize children into flexible groups to receive instruction as determined by the teacher's observation of needs. A teacher may, for instance, determine that five children have a particular need for supportive instruction in fluency. If so, she chooses a selection and strategy suitable for the occasion and provides 20 minutes of supportive instruction in fluency. The five do not constitute a permanent group. Grouping for guided reading is not a permanent condition but a response to specific needs the teacher has observed. Any one or more of the five members may participate in other groups with different instructional purposes, or not, depending on need. Further, members of the fluency group will be involved in other reading and writing experiences throughout the day, such as reading aloud, shared reading, independent reading, writing, and so on. Key characteristics of guided reading include the following:

- Instruction is organized around small groups of five to eight children reading at about the same level and having similar needs. Children often read from texts leveled in gradually increasing increments of difficulty.
- Grouping is flexible. Children work in one group for one reason and in another for a different reason.
- Explicit instructional support, often referred to as scaffolding, is crucial to guided reading instruction.
- The teacher observes and monitors student performance so that instruction may be adjusted to changing needs.
- Time devoted to guided instruction typically ranges from 15 to 25 minutes.

## Field Notes
### Real-Life Experiences of a Classroom Teacher

I'm getting ready to work with a small group of kindergartners. I know I won't succeed unless the rest of my children know what to do while I'm working with the small group. I start by modeling a writing assignment for the class. I talk about activities they can work on while I'm busy with the small group. I explain an oral language game; I set out some books for them to peruse; I describe a rhyming and letter-matching activity; I set up a listening station. I tell them they may choose to work on any of these activities *after* they finish their writing assignment. They know what I expect of them. A parent volunteer is here this morning, so I ask her to answer questions and monitor students' behavior. Incidentally, I don't often have a parent volunteer to help out. My students have learned what I expect of them, and they are beginning to learn independence. Things don't always work out perfectly, but I do have my instruction organized and under control.

Anne Marie Laskowski

- Effective classroom management is crucial since the other children must have independent work while the teacher works with small groups. For example, journal writing, independent reading, and peer partnership work might be assigned.
- Guided reading is only one among many reading and writing experiences provided in a rich literacy environment.

Successful guided reading depends on successful classroom management. What will the children *not* in the small group do while the teacher works with the small group? Ann Marie Lasdowski, a veteran teacher, explains in the Field Notes feature how she faces this issue.

## Section Summary: Guided Reading

1. Guided reading is instruction focused on small groups of children reading at the same level and having similar needs.
2. Instruction is typically limited to short sessions of 15 to 20 minutes. Grouping in guided reading is flexible and supports instruction.

## Help for Struggling Readers

What really matters for struggling readers? Allington (2001) provides excellent ideas and advice on this issue. His book *What Matters for Struggling Readers: Designing Research-Based Programs* is a must-read for those who need a detailed roadmap for helping struggling readers. He suggests they need to read a lot, to read good books, to set instruction that fosters thinking, and to engage in thought-ful conversations about books. What they do not need is an overempha-sis on skill and drill—a prescription that not only takes the pleasure out of reading but is of questionable efficacy.

Skill and drill have a place in reading instruction, but much depends on what is meant by *skill* and what constitutes useful *drill*. Skill is profi-ciency acquired through instruction and practice. For struggling readers, this means instruction and practice in comprehending text, reading for pleasure, thoughtful discussions, and independent reading. Drill means opportunities to experience and reexperience skills in meaningful contexts. But too often skill and drill turn out to be highly repetitive work on phonics, memorizing rules, tedious workbook pages, and answering low-level comprehension questions. Conversely, there is too little emphasis on thoughtful conversations about text, too few oppor-tunities for independent reading, not enough literature and writing, and an insuf-ficient emphasis on reading for pleasure.

*Struggling readers need reading—not just reading instruction and not completing workbook pages, but reading.* Skills must be taught and practiced, but much thought must be given to make this work productive. Six productive ideas for helping strug-gling readers are described in this section: (1) language experience stories, (2) time spent reading and volume of reading, (3) good books independently read, (4) flu-ency, (5) thoughtful engagement in discussions before, during, and after reading, and (6) skill instruction in meaningful and contextual situations.

> For information and resources regarding students with special needs, visit the website for the Council for Exceptional Chil-dren: http://www.cec.sped.org

## Language Experience Stories

I often ask my undergraduate students to find a child who can't read or whose reading is weak and so lacking in fluency as to be nearly incom-prehensible. Talk to that child, I say, about things that interest him or her. Then take a dictated story. If you follow the recording and rereading procedures outlined earlier in this book, you will be pleased at how well children can read their own texts.

> "What we have to learn to do, we learn by doing."
> —Aristotle

Children who are unable to read a text written by someone else can nearly always read their own experience stories fluently. Nothing empowers struggling readers faster or better than discovering they have read well and easily. Everyone loves to repeat successful experiences. Struggling readers are no exception. Often children ask, "Can we do this again tomorrow?" For struggling readers, a dictated story is profoundly different from text written by someone else because it is *their* oral language written down and *their* personal experiences that provide the content. They are accustomed to a struggle with reading and frequent failure. Failure rarely happens with dictated stories, and when followed up with appropriate procedures, dictated stories can be the starting point for developing independent writing, word recognition, and comprehension. Try language experience stories with your strug-gling readers. You will find they make for an excellent start on reading fluency, though of course they must be followed up with additional experiences such as writing, comprehension, discussion, and independent reading.

## Time Spent Reading and Volume of Reading

There is a relationship between how much children read and reading success. Children who don't read much lag behind their counterparts who read a lot. Therefore, time spent reading and volume of reading are crucial (Allington & Johnson, 2000; Pressley, 2000). Struggling readers do little reading. There is no pleasure; there is only frustration. So, what can be done? There are three impediments to securing more reading time for struggling readers. First, there is too much time devoted to unproductive reading activities such as completing workbook pages. Reduce some of this time and replace it with independent reading. Second, there may not be enough time scheduled into the day's activities for actual reading as opposed to reading instruction. Make sure there is ample time to just read, along with instructional time. Third, school organization may not allow sufficient *continuous* time for reading. Interruptions and the breaking up of the instructional day steal time from teachers' allotment of instructional time. This issue is almost exclusively administrative, and its solution must therefore be administrative. These impediments can be ameliorated if not removed, though it will require the combined efforts of teachers and administrators. Teachers cannot make all of these changes without administrative help.

## Good Books Independently Read

A fisherman needs a lure, a hook, and skill to reel in a catch. Good books read aloud are the lure; thoughtful discussions the hook, and independent reading the catch. But good books must be available. A classroom without a supply of good books is like a restaurant without food. You must have a classroom library of books, suitably leveled. But before independent reading there must be a starting point. You can't place books in children's hands until they are capable of reading. Reading aloud, language experience stories, and shared reading are starting points that can provide the initial skill needed to read books independently.

Struggling readers want to read, but they do not know that it can be pleasurable. They lack interest, and this must be reversed. Since interest usually precedes reading, start by reading good books to struggling readers to activate interest. Thoughtful talk about books read aloud stimulates reading interest. And remember, a struggling reader does not mean a struggling talker or thinker. Struggling readers are sometimes the best talkers and thinkers in the room—they have lots of spare time to hone the oral arts. They can contribute thoughtfully to book discussions.

We must also consider the concept load and word recognition challenge a book may present. Thus, we need to know the relative word recognition skill and prior knowledge any given reader possesses. Such awareness comes through diagnostic testing and classroom observation of readers' repertoire of knowledge and skills.

Once struggling readers are ready for independent reading, start with brief uninterrupted sustained silent reading (USSR) sessions. Start slowly—5 or 10 minutes in the beginning. Gradually increase the minutes read until you reach a goal—perhaps 20 to 30 minutes.

**Table 8.6**

**Ideas for Increasing Reading Fluency**

1. *Repeated readings.* Model fluent reading from passages within the struggling readers' word recognition and comprehension capability. Then have the child read the passage, imitating your model. Repeat this process several times, using the same passage, until the struggling reader comes closer and closer to the model you have provided. Struggling readers are interrupted for correction more often than their counterparts. Consequently, it is important to avoid interrupting their read-aloud efforts. If they are hesitating over a word, supply it and move on.

2. *Rereading language experience stories.* Reread language experience stories, using the rereading techniques described in Chapter 1. Word recognition problems are less likely to interfere with this than with other materials.

3. *Choral reading.* Select a passage for choral reading, and model reading it aloud. Then lead a small group of children as you chorally reread the selected passage. Practice the passage a number of times. Then seek volunteers to read the passage singly or in pairs.

4. *Echo reading.* Select a story you intend to teach. Read a couple of paragraphs or a single page aloud, using appropriate intonation and phrasing. Then have the children echo the passage or page. This introduces new words and concepts, and it tends to makes subsequent elements of the story easier for struggling readers.

*Teaching Tip*

## Fluency

It is not difficult to distinguish fluent from nonfluent readers. Fluent readers read faster and more accurately than struggling readers. Fluent readers read in 5- to 7-word segments; nonfluent readers read in 1- or 2-word segments. Fluent readers spontaneously self-correct; readers who lack fluency do not. Fluent readers use appropriate intonation and stress; readers who lack fluency do not (Allington, 2001). Struggling readers read slowly, stopping frequently to figure out word meaning or pronunciation. They may even read slowly from materials that match their word recognition and vocabulary skills.

Physical signs often accompany nonfluent reading, such as finger pointing, excessive lip movement, inability to sit still, and other signs of anxiety. When such problems overwhelm struggling readers, they stop reading, and it is hard to get them back on track. The medicine needed is reading fluency, but it doesn't come in pill form, and it doesn't yield to overnight recovery—it takes time and hard work. Table 8.6 suggests four ideas for increasing reading fluency.

## Engagement in Thoughtful Discussions

Reading is not a memory task; it is a thinking task. Good talk about ideas is the key to thinking and, therefore, the key to thoughtful literacy. If we expect to engage children in books and ideas, we must have thoughtful conversations with them about the books they read. Atwell (1998) calls this kind of talk literary gossip. She applies it to writing, but it can just as easily be applied to reading.

My colleague Dorsey Hammond and I often gossip about books we have read or are reading. He has a special interest in nonfiction, often Civil War books; I love novels by Robertson Davies and Rex Stout. We seldom read the same books, but we gossip about each other's books as though we had. I may describe Davies's grand plot for the Deptford trilogy; Dorsey may tell me about the Battle of Gettysburg. I do not quiz him to discover holes in his memory of details. If I ask questions, and often I do not, they are likely to be about important events, characters, or the author: How important was Gettysburg in the outcome of the Civil War? What did you like about the author's writing style?

Our book talks do not center on evaluation of each other's reading skill or a recitation of facts and information derived from the books. Most often our talk arises out of mutual interest in books, authors, and ideas. We do not try to trip each other up with questions intended to reveal ignorance. Rather, we are intent on expanding our camaraderie and interest in reading books. We do not make comments that might damage our regard for each other, rather our book conversations often entail laughter at ourselves and the human condition.

What kind of conversations do you have with your children? Is laughter present? Are your children having fun while engaging in friendly book gossip? Are you asking too many trivial questions, leading nowhere? Big ideas, personal reflections, and humor excite interest and ignite imagination. Trivial information bores and seldom leads to thoughtful conversation.

Sometimes conversations with children are adversarial, seemingly bent on revealing ignorance rather than enticing thoughtful ideas from children's minds. An adversarial stance is likely to promote silence rather than thoughtful conversation. Conversations with children should look to children's strengths rather than weaknesses. Conversations about books and ideas should celebrate originality and honor diversity of viewpoint and boldness of stance. Participation is much more likely when we exchange ideas in a friendly, informal atmosphere.

## Explicit Skill Instruction, When and Where Needed

There are two major aspects to reading: word recognition and comprehension. Word recognition is a means to an end, not an end in itself. The end, of course, is comprehension. Simple, no? But somehow this simple concept has gotten turned on its head. Word recognition (phonics, in its popular usage) is treated by the public, the press, and even educators as the goal rather than the means of reading. Word recognition is important, for without it readers cannot decode written language and hence cannot construct meaning. But skill in recognizing words must be understood as subsidiary and salutary to comprehension.

> "There is all the difference in the world between having something to say, and having to say something."
> —John Dewey, U.S. philosopher and educator

An associated problem is a tendency to shortchange comprehension, a kind of naive assumption that if children can decode words, comprehension will automatically follow. *Au contraire*. Comprehension, like word recognition,

**Table 8.7**

**What Teachers Need to Know About Struggling Readers' Skill Levels**

| Word Recognition | Comprehension |
|---|---|
| 1. Extent of sight vocabulary in and out of context | 1. Use of prior knowledge and reasoning |
| 2. Application of word recognition skills to unknown words in and out of context | 2. Relative ability to comprehend explicit and implicit information |
| 3. Level of accuracy when reading in context | 3. Word meaning knowledge |
| 4. Reading rate and its connection to word accuracy and comprehension | 4. Ability to think beyond the text |
| 5. Ratio of meaning-loss errors to no-meaning-loss errors | 5. Silent comprehension level and oral comprehension level |
| 6. Strategies for applying knowledge of word recognition | 6. Ability to locate and synthesize explicit information |
| | 7. Ability to apply literal information in order to make inferences |

requires thoughtful practice in appropriate contexts. Consequently, assessment of struggling readers is crucial to teaching them. You need to know something about their word recognition and comprehension strengths and weaknesses. Table 8.7 lists word recognition and comprehension capabilities that diagnosis and observation can reveal.

## Section Summary: Help for Struggling Readers

1. Struggling readers need good instruction and lots of it. Instruction must be provided over a sustained period of time.
2. Language experience stories, time and volume of reading, good books read independently, fluency, engagement in thoughtful discussions, and explicit skill instruction are essential goals and activities for struggling readers.

## Practical Teaching Ideas and Activities

**1.** *Build anticipation prior to, as well as during, the reading process.* Skillful readers are always anticipating what will come next, based on semantic, syntactic, and visual information. This may include anticipating the next event in a story or the next word in a sentence. To support children in the meaning-making process, the teacher must be familiar with the text structure and content. In a prereading discussion, talk about any unfamiliar vocabulary or concepts. This provides the

*Teaching Tip*

opportunity to deepen and refine students' prior experiences and background knowledge so they can more effectively meet the ideas of the author in the meaning-making process. Throughout the reading process, anticipation can be maintained through pausing, questioning, and discussing at strategic points in the text. Encourage the use of prior knowledge through modeling, specific feedback, and praise, even when predictions are inaccurate ("I wonder what could happen next"). Through shared reading experiences with repetitive structure and rhyme, students can learn to anticipate words.

**2.** *Support students in their integration of all three cuing systems.* If children rely too much on sounding out rather than reading for meaning, do an oral cloze activity. This procedure removes the sound-symbol cue to focus on other strategies. Cover up a select number of words and have the children predict words that would make sense (use of semantics) and sound right (use of syntax). To confirm or reject predictions, start to uncover the word, letter by letter, to cross-check it with beginning sounds.

**3.** *Encourage student-generated questions.* Once a routine of open-ended questioning and rich dialogue has been established in a community of readers, teachers can guide students toward generating their own questions. Discuss what makes questions thought-provoking or open-ended. Prior to reading, show a picture, and have students generate their own questions based on what they would like to know; help them question to establish a purpose for reading. Or read the opening of a selection, and have students generate questions prior to reading the remainder of the text. Support children in generating questions about the text after reading as well. Provide opportunities for small groups of students to ask one another questions about text.

**4.** *Make bookmarks.* Cut construction paper or tagboard into blank strips for bookmarks. Give each student a supply of bookmarks to use during independent reading, to note points of difficulty or to record responses, thoughts, and questions that arise. These bookmarks are shared during group discussion and ensure the student will contribute to the conversation. You might instead provide each student with a supply of self-adhesive notes to use in similar fashion while reading.

**5.** *Use "What's on your mind?"* Students write about or discuss what a poem or another text made them think about after listening to it. Encouraging personal responses with this open-ended prompt provides students flexibility. Students may choose to respond to the text with thoughts, insights, and wonderings; or they may prefer to reflect upon connections related to their experiences (adapted from Wilson, *Reading To Live,* 2001).

See the Blue Pages at the back of the book and on the Companion Website for additional activities.

# Reflection and Summary

## Reflection

I once knew a professor who claimed he had not read a book in years. Quite different from the Dutch scholar Desiderius Erasmus, who said, "When I get a little money, I buy books; and if any is left, I buy food and clothes." Then there is the Buddhist Chinese scholar who claims to have found independence of mind by giving up the reading of books: "It is better to keep your own mind free and to not let the thinking of others interfere with your own free thinking." Support for the lazy professor, I suppose. As for me, I will never voluntarily give up reading—not even if it actually creates independence of mind, which I doubt. I read to extend my thinking; I read to expand my imagination; I read to experience pleasure; I read to seek wisdom; I read to laugh. I appreciate the answer the French philosopher Descartes rendered to skepticism: "I think, therefore I am." It reminds me of my own raison d'être: "I read, therefore I am."

## Summary

This chapter has presented the following main ideas:
1. Reading can be defined as constructing meaning from text, using reasoning and prior knowledge. Further, comprehension is influenced by the society in which it takes place. This is referred to as the social construction of knowledge.
2. Additional factors that influence comprehension include the reader, the text, purpose, quality of instruction, independent practice, and interest.
3. There are four basic components of comprehension: explicit meaning, implicit meaning, word meaning, and evaluative–appreciative meaning. These components adequately describe what is independently measurable or distinct in comprehension.
4. Not every comprehension skill that has a name actually exists as an independent, measurable entity. The commonly named skills, perhaps 40 or more, are better thought of as reading activities emphasizing a useful comprehension objective.
5. There are many strategies for teaching comprehension before, during, or after reading. Eleven are described in this chapter: DRTA and DLTA, anticipation guides, KWL, modeling, mapping, reader's theater, shared reading, reading aloud, independent reading, and retelling.
6. The asking of pertinent questions plays a key role in comprehension. Questioning techniques include initiating questions, text-based questions, questions not based on text, probing questions, questions based on the major components of comprehension, and wait time.
7. Guided reading is a procedure for organizing children into flexible groups to receive instruction in reading or writing. Decisions about what to teach are determined by the teacher's observation of needs.
8. Ways to help struggling readers include language experience stories, adequate time spent reading and adequate volume of reading, good books independently

read, fluency practice, thoughtful engagement in discussions before, during, and after reading, and skill instruction where and when needed.

## ◄ Questions to Challenge Your Thinking

1. Reading is said to be an active search for meaning. What does this mean?
2. Why is prior knowledge a crucial issue in comprehension?
3. Make a case for or against the idea of four basic components of comprehension.
4. How would you teach making inferences to children whose inference skills are weak?
5. Why is independent reading important to growth in reading capability?
6. What is the distinction between questions based on text and not based on text?

7. What are some of the important goals of guided reading?
8. Why can a child read a language experience story and yet have difficulty reading seemingly easier text written by someone else?
9. Why is it important to engage struggling readers in thoughtful discussions?
10. Is skill instruction important? When, why, and under what circumstances?

## ◄ A Case Study

Read the following true case study, and then discuss the questions below with your classmates or colleagues.

Teddy is 10 years old and in fifth grade. Diagnostic testing and teacher observation confirm that he reads at a second-grade level. Yet he can comprehend ideas and information at a seventh-grade level when text is read aloud to him. He has excellent oral language skills; his behavior is exemplary; he has friends and is well liked. Teddy has a small number of sight words he recognizes immediately. When given time, he can accurately decode other words—but very slowly. When reading in context, Teddy reads choppily, often pausing to figure out words; he makes many miscues, yet most do not cause a loss of meaning.

1. Does Teddy have a reading problem? Explain.
2. What strengths do you recognize in Teddy's reading profile?
3. What weaknesses do you recognize in Teddy's reading profile?
4. Do you think Teddy needs help in word recognition? If so, what help would you recommend?
5. What benefit might Teddy receive from help with reading fluency?
6. Do you think Teddy needs help in comprehension? If so, what help would you recommend?
7. What is the prognosis for Teddy's reading future, assuming he receives appropriate help soon?

## ◄ Revisit the Anticipation Guide

Return to the Anticipation Guide in the chapter opener, and review your original responses to the questions. Complete the guide again, and then consider these questions.

1. Did you change your mind about any items? Why or why not?
2. What was the most surprising idea you encountered? In what way did it surprise you?

3. What ideas do you have for thinking about comprehension that you didn't have before reading this chapter?

4. What information or ideas did you encounter with which you disagree? Explain why you dis-agree and what you would propose as an alternative.

5. If you were writing this chapter, what would you have done differently? Why?

 ## VideoWorkshop Extra!

If your instructor ordered a package including VideoWorkshop, go to Chapter 8 of the Companion Website (www.ablongman.com/cramer1e) and click on the VideoWorkshop button. Follow the instructions for viewing the appropriate video clip and completing the accompanying exercise. Watch the Companion Website for access to a new interactive teaching portal, My Lab School, currently under construction.

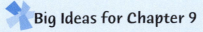

### A Philosophy of Word Study

I recently sat in a restaurant alongside four teenagers. Words tumbled out of their mouths with astonishing vigor and invective. But it wouldn't surprise me to hear from parents and teachers that these same children have little to say at home and school. How is it that the language power displayed among peers goes underground in the very places intended to cultivate language growth? I don't know, but here's my guess: most children are unaware of the language power they possess. Teachers and parents are more likely to focus on the banalities of "child-speak": Like, he goes like this; It's like, well, you know. This is not the language I overheard in the restaurant. Yes, I heard some of that language, but more often I heard words bordering on the poetic, metaphors and figures of speech; innovative teenage "secret-speak." Our job, as teachers and parents, is to apprise children of their linguistic strengths rather than focus on their linguistic weaknesses. Let children know that they have word power. Help them see that their words are precious and powerful.

# 9 Word Study: Word Recognition, Dictionary Skills, and Vocabulary Skills

### Big Ideas for Chapter 9

1. The debate over phonics versus no phonics is phony. The real question is not whether phonics should be taught; obviously, it should. There is disagreement as to how it should be taught.

2. Word recognition instruction has four components: phonetic, contextual, structural analysis, and sight words.

3. Children need strategies for decoding words, and teachers need strategies to help them apply their word recognition knowledge.

4. Word recognition is best assessed in context, using two types of analysis: total miscue count and a qualitatively adjusted miscue count connected to meaning.

5. Dictionaries have three major purposes: to determine word meaning, to check spelling, and to verify pronunciation.

6. Children need basic dictionary skills, but first they must have sufficient word recognition and spelling skills to use dictionaries effectively.

7. Children's vocabularies grow through volume of reading and direct instruction.

8. Direct vocabulary instruction includes activities such as concept of definition, brainstorming, mapping, and graphic organizers, among others.

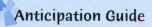 **Anticipation Guide**

*Consider the following statements, and determine whether you agree or disagree with each. Save your answers, and revisit this guide at the end of this chapter.*

1. The ultimate goal of phonics is not pronunciation but meaning.     agree    disagree
2. Frequent reading aids growth in word recognition.     agree    disagree
3. If a phonics rule works 50% of the time, teach it.     agree    disagree
4. Word recognition instruction should go from part to whole.     agree    disagree
5. Learning words by sight prevents children from learning phonics.     agree    disagree
6. Structural analysis deals with understanding words in context.     agree    disagree
7. First-graders should look up their misspelled words in a dictionary.     agree    disagree
8. The best way to foster children's vocabulary growth is through reading.     agree    disagree
9. Writing vocabulary words in sentences successfully builds vocabulary.     agree    disagree
10. Direct instruction of vocabulary is a waste of instructional time.     agree    disagree

> **W**ords are the legs of the mind; they bear it about, carry it from point to point, bed it down at night, and keep it off the ground and out of the marsh and mists.
>
> —*Richard Eder*

> **W**ords are as recalcitrant as circus animals, and the unskilled trainer can crack his whip at them in vain.
>
> —*Gerald Brenan*

## A Literacy Story

**E**very avid reader travels a different path to literacy. Every journey offers a different map. C. S. Lewis's father loved books. He collected them as a packrat hoards shiny objects and scattered them about the house. As C. S. Lewis grew up, books became his passion as well. Lewis said of his access to his father's books, "Nothing was forbidden me." How different from the journey to literacy Richard Wright, author of *Native Son*, traveled; no books were available to be forbidden him. Still, a passion to read books consumed him. He had no books of his own, so he forged notes, suggesting to the librarian that he was merely a messenger boy sent to pick up books for someone else. He carried the books he had obtained by stealth to work, where he read a few pages at every spare moment. His coworkers teased him, but this only fed his determination. Evenings, he ate his meager meals and read late into the night. He knew the hunger for knowledge that only those deprived of opportunity can know. Isaac Bashevis Singer, Nobel laureate for literature, had an entirely different story. His father, an Orthodox rabbi, banned all secular books from the household, though religious texts were plentiful. As a young man, Singer developed a deep curiosity about what might be in those forbidden books. He harbored the notion that they might contain "the secret of life." Curiosity is a powerful force, and Singer had to slake his curiosity. Fortune smiled on him the first day he entered a public library. A friendly librarian handed him two books on philosophy and said, "If a boy wants to know the secret of life, you have to accommodate him."

These famous writers, along with countless others, read whatever books piqued their interest, read passionately, read as though their lives depended on it. Many readers have endured insults and foolish admonitions as they pursued

**this passion. Jean Rhys's nurse told her, "Your eyes will drop out and they will look at you from the page." Rhys half-believed her nurse but not enough to give up her eye-popping habit. Determined readers endure admonitions, insults, and social slights. They are like bears after honey, enduring hundreds of stings from angry bees because the reward is so sweet.**

A Chinese proverb says, "The strongest memory is weaker than the palest ink." Books live. Memory fades. Writers die. But their words are their eternal testimony. A writer's words may sit on a library shelf for decades, unseen by human eye. Then one day a reader, wandering the stacks, plucks an obscure book from the shelf, unread for decades, and instantly a writer's words live again. Written words are forever. Books take us on journeys where no plane or ship can carry us. Emily Dickinson said it best: "There is no Frigate like a Book / to take us Lands away." Dead these many years, Emily Dickinson's words live again. They remind us that words and ideas remain powerful over the decades and centuries. No power on earth can cancel the words she penned. They live on forever in the minds of her readers.

"For one who reads, there is no limit to the number of lives that may be lived, for fiction, biography, and history offer an inexhaustible number of lives in many parts of the world in all periods of time."
—Louis L'Amour, writer

The philosopher Bertrand Russell loved words, and few deployed them more skillfully. He reminds us that words are the special province of humankind: "No matter how eloquently a dog may bark, he cannot tell you that his parents were

## A MATTER OF STANDARDS

### Word Study

**Standard 7:** Students conduct research on issues and interests by generating ideas and questions, and by posing problems. They gather, evaluate, and synthesize data from a variety of sources (e.g., print and nonprint texts, artifacts, people) to communicate their discoveries in ways that suit their purpose and audience.

**Comment:** An inquiry approach to learning provides the best opportunity for students to exercise their creative and critical faculties. Reading, writing, viewing, talking, and listening skill can be increased when children have opportunities to identify interesting topics for writing, are encouraged to read lit-

erature with creative and critical intent, to search out sources of information and inspiration, to interpret and apply what they have learned by writing, speaking, and constructing visual representations of their ideas. Children need to learn to ask interesting questions, evaluate and synthesize information from diverse sources, and interpret and apply what they have learned. They need to experience all types of texts, written, spoken, visual, and tactile. Words are the primary linguistic tool needed to formulate interesting questions, conduct inquiry, and seek answers to life's persistent issues.

This chapter focuses on ways in which word study contributes to the accomplishment of standard 7.

poor but honest." Words enable us to record and preserve the past, endure or enjoy the present, and predict and plan the future. Words are the most obvious feature of language. Scholars study words; writers splash them onto blank pages; politicians abuse them. Everyone depends on them. Words are innocent and innocuous in the abstract, but range from gentle to vicious in the concrete. Whatever one's station in life, rich or poor, wise or foolish, adult or child, words connect us with the social, spiritual, educational, and economic worlds.

> "We learn language not simply for the sake of learning language; we learn it to make sense of the world around us and to communicate our understandings with others." —National Council of Teachers of English and the International Reading Association, *Standards for the English Language Arts,* 1996.

Children have three main word-study tasks: they must learn to pronounce words, understand their meanings, and comprehend and compose words in written and oral discourse. Teachers have the same tasks, but their job is the mirror image of children's work. Teachers are mature readers; they often fall in love with words and find the study of them fascinating. Children do not always start with such an advantage. They do come to school with an astounding meaning vocabulary, ranging in the neighborhood of 5,000 to 15,000 words. A few children come to school with decoding skills as well, but their decoding knowledge ranges from zero to perhaps a few hundred words. Their oral discourse capabilities range from weak to extraordinary, but seldom do they possess strong capabilities in comprehending and composing written language. Teachers have the challenging job of aiding and abetting children's progress in word study. While this chapter is concerned with word recognition, vocabulary knowledge, and dictionary skills, success in these tasks opens the door to comprehending and composing written language.

## Word Recognition

The Punic Wars between Rome and Carthage lasted for over a hundred years, with periods of respite between battles. The Phonics Wars may already have exceeded the Punic Wars in length, if not ferocity. Educators, politicians, and the public have battled and battered one another over the question "Should phonics be taught?" The straw man of phonics versus no phonics gets propped up and knocked down regularly and vigorously. There is, however, a more important question to be debated: how should phonics be taught? Not *if*. I believe word recognition must be taught. And, it must be taught well, thoroughly, and early.

Word recognition (often referred to as phonics) is the process of determining the pronunciation of words, so that their meanings can be accessed. Word recognition has four components: phonetic analysis, structural analysis, contextual analysis, and sight word knowledge. Each component may be applied separately, but more often they work simultaneously or in a combination appropriate to the reader's needs.

Mature readers have a large set of words they can pronounce accurately, fluently, and automatically. These are called sight words. A major goal of word recognition is to build an extensive sight vocabulary so that phonetic, contextual, and structural analysis skills are seldom necessary but can be applied when needed. The four components of word recognition are often lumped together in public discourse under the umbrella term *phonics*. Technically, this designation is inaccurate, and some confusion may result from failing to distinguish phonics from word recognition, which is a broader concept. But rolling a big stone up a steep hill should only be undertaken if there is a compelling reason to get the rock to the top of the hill. In this instance, there is no compelling reason to disabuse the public of their preferred term. Let the public have its terminology, and let's get on with the peace process—educating teachers, politicians, and the public about the real dimensions of the great phonics debate: how, not whether, phonics should be taught.

## Principles for Teaching Word Recognition

Principles are sometimes thought of as an academic throwaway. They can be, but need not be. Principles are statements of philosophy and guides to practice. If understood and used in this spirit, they are valuable. The principles described here are culled from the philosophy and practice of good teachers, expert opinion, and research.

**1.** *Word recognition is crucial to effective reading.* If word recognition is neglected, in the hope that children will learn it "naturally," an unconscionable disservice will be done to children. Serious attention must be given to how, when, and why word recognition should be taught. But it would also be an unforgivable mistake to think that learning to sound out letters and acquire sight words is all there is to reading. Word recognition is the key that unlocks the linguistic code, so possessing the key is crucial. But we give this key to children for a higher purpose: to access the meaning that words convey.

**2.** *Word recognition practices that hinder the attainment of meaning or pronunciation should be avoided.* Choose word recognition activities carefully, so that meaning and pronunciation are facilitated, not hindered. For instance, looking for small words within big words can misdirect pronunciation and hinder understanding of meaning if precautions are not taken. The word *thinking* has two structural parts: *think* and *-ing,*—root word and inflected ending. These are the chunks we should teach children to look for. But we do not want children looking for the small words: *thin, in, ink, kin,* and *king,* though their letter combinations reside within the word *thinking*. The words *kin* and *king* do not have ties to the structure or meaning of *think* and *-ing*. Likewise, pointing out *thin* in *thinking* misdirects any study of meaning and pronunciation. As do *in* and *kin*. When teaching word recognition, choose strategies that do not distort meaning or pronunciation.

**3.** *Distinguishing one speech sound from another and one letter from another lays the foundation for word recognition.* Phonemic awareness—the ability to recognize, segment, and manipulate the phonemes or sounds in spoken words—enables children to distinguish one speech sound from another. (Phonemic awareness is distinct from phonetic analysis.) Visual discrimination is the ability to distinguish one letter from another. Phonemic awareness and visual discrimination develop in tandem, as students listen to literature read aloud, participate in rhyming activities, grow familiar with environmental print, use invented spelling, dictate and reread language experience stories, and share in other emergent literacy experiences.

See *Oo-ples and Boo-noonoos: Songs and Activities for Phonemic Awareness,* by H. K. Yopp and R. H. Yopp, 1996.

**4.** *Word recognition rules that have a high degree of usefulness should be the focus.* Two premises guide the choice of rules. First, a rule must apply to a substantial number of common words. A rule that works 95% of the time but is useful for only ten English words is not worth the effort required to teach and learn it. Better to learn the ten words by sight. Second, a rule that applies to many words should hold true about 70% of the time. For example, suppose you teach this rule: when two vowels go walking the first one does the talking. How often does this rule work? About 30% of the time. Even though it applies to many words, it is an unreliable rule and will mislead children 7 times out of 10.

**5.** *Application, not memorization, of rules should inform practice.* Children often recite rules they cannot apply. This means the rule has not been learned, merely memorized. There are two ways to teach a rule—through inductive and deductive reasoning. The inductive approach helps children discover a rule from an examination of relevant example words—going from the particular to the general. For instance, take a set of words that exemplify a useful rule, and lead children to search for the common element in the words through questioning: how are these ten words alike? Once children have discovered the common element, help them state the general rule in their own words. Then have them search for examples and exceptions to the rule they have formulated. In the deductive method, the teacher states the general rule and provides words that exemplify it—going from the general to the particular. The children do not discover the general rule on their own. Sometimes this is the more efficient means of teaching a rule. Balance the two methods. But if a rule is not reliable about 70% of the time, and if it does not apply to a significant number of words, neither approach will make it useful.

For a listing of children's books for developing phonemic awareness, read Helen Yopp's article "Read-Aloud Books for Developing Phonemic Awareness: An Annotated Bibliography." 1995, *The Reading Teacher,* 48.

**6.** *Instruction in word recognition should be tied to meaningful reading experiences.* After a word recognition lesson, reading meaningful text should follow. Everyone understands that after receiving a tennis lesson, actual game experience must follow. The same concept applies to reading.

**7.** *Writing develops, refines, and reinforces word recognition.* Writing contributes to word recognition, especially during the primary grades. Frequent writing, using invented spelling when necessary, contributes to word recognition knowledge (see Chapter 13). Writing and reading are obverse processes. Readers have the letters, but must produce the sounds; writers have the sounds, but must produce the letters. Alternating these related tasks builds word knowledge.

**8.** *Balanced and integrated instruction aids learning.* There are four components to word recognition: phonetic, structural, contextual analysis, and sight word—all are defined in this chapter. These four components are interrelated. Thus, when a word is unknown at sight and cannot be pronounced using contextual analysis, then phonetic and or structural analysis must be used to identify the word. The components of word recognition need to be taught and applied as an integrated set of skills. This may seem to imply a preferred sequence for using these components of word recognition, but in practice their application should be seamless and integrated.

**9.** *Word recognition should proceed from whole to part.* The sounds and structural patterns within words should be taught in the context of the words that exemplify them. For instance, teaching the isolated speech sounds *kuh-ah-tuh* to pronounce *cat* adds extraneous sounds. Isolating sounds and patterns from their sensible context makes pronunciation more difficult than it needs to be. Better to learn the word *cat* as a sight word and teach its sounds and patterns within the context of the known word. There may, of course, be exceptions to this generalization, but it is particularly appropriate in teaching phonics to young children. This whole-to-part approach to phonics has its naysayers; they subscribe to the part-to-whole approach, discussed in detail later in the chapter.

**10.** *Diagnosis directs instruction in word recognition.* Diagnosis can be formal or informal. Formal diagnosis involves assessing word recognition in context and in isolation. Informal diagnosis comes through monitoring problems and progress as children read and write. For instance, assessment of invented spelling provides clues about progress in spelling and word recognition. Miscue analysis and running records also help guide decisions about needed instruction.

## The Four Components of Word Recognition

**Phonetic Analysis**. Phonetic analysis is more popularly known as *phonics,* a term that has come to encompass all aspects of word recognition, though this is a misuse of the term. Phonetic analysis is the process of associating speech sounds with the letters that represent them and the blending of these sounds to pronounce words not known at sight. Phonetic analysis is one component of word recognition, used along with contextual and structural analysis. The term *phonetic analysis* derives from the broader term *phonetics,* a specialized branch of linguistics dealing with the scientific investigation of all aspects of producing and using speech sounds.

**Analytic and Synthetic Phonics**. There are two major approaches to teaching phonetic analysis: analytic and synthetic. Analytic phonics starts with sight words and proceeds to an analysis of their parts—*whole to part.* Synthetic phonics starts with word parts and proceeds to synthesize word parts to pronounce whole words—*part to whole.* Much of the phonics debate is characterized by disagreements between the advocates of these two approaches.

Advocates of synthetic phonics dismiss analytic phonics as a sight word approach. Some have claimed that analytic phonics does not teach phonics at all. Instead, they say, it teaches children to memorize whole words. *This is not true now and never has been.* On the other hand, advocates of analytic phonics often claim that the synthetic approach teaches phonics in isolation, distorts the pronunciation of words, and does not emphasize the role of meaning in reading. Synthetic phonics, it is said, produces readers who may learn to pronounce words but are unable to get meaning from text. The claims each side makes for itself and against the other are worse-case scenarios, which sometimes rely on questionable appeals to research, unsubstantiated claims of success, overstating the opponent's weaknesses,

## Point ≡ Counterpoint

### A Debatable Issue
### Analytic Instruction versus Synthetic Instruction

**Background**
Nearly everyone agrees that instruction in phonics is necessary and important. The real issue is *how* phonics should be taught.

**The Debatable Issue**
The analytic (whole to part) approach to phonics instruction is more compatible with how children learn than the synthetic approach (part to whole).

**Take a Stand**
Argue the case for or against the debatable issue. Marshal your arguments based on research, experience, and your teaching philosophy. After you have discussed it among colleagues, consider debating the issue in your class.

and exaggerating one's own strengths. The phonics debate has quasi-religious overtones; those who fail to accept the *one* correct doctrine shall be cast into outer darkness. It is time to acknowledge that while our differences are significant, there is no need for exaggerated claims and misrepresentations. Toning down the rhetoric might make room for a reasoned debate on the merits of each approach, and if not that, at least introduce an element of civility.

I prefer analytic phonics because there is merit in starting with sight words and approaching phonics from whole to part. I also prefer analytic phonics because it avoids, in part, isolating sounds within words. But, at least in theory, either approach could connect phonics instruction with reading meaningful text, or not. Nothing inherent in either approach precludes an emphasis on meaning. Practitioners of both approaches have undertaken just such an emphasis.

**Prerequisites for Phonics Instruction**. The first prerequisite for learning to read is phonemic awareness, the ability to identify and manipulate phonemes, the smallest units of sound in the language. Phonemic awareness does not require that printed words be used, since instruction is provided through oral language experiences.

For information on the Yopp-Singer Test of Phoneme Segmentation, see "A Test for Assessing Phonemic Awareness in Young Children," by H. K. Yopp, 1995, *The Reading Teacher*, 49.

Linguists typically identify 44 English phonemes, whereas there are only 26 alphabet letters. Since there are more speech sounds in English than alphabet letters, there can be no one-to-one correspondence between speech sounds and their representation in written language. This circumstance accounts for some of the irregularity of the English spelling system, though the irregularity is not as significant as popularly believed (Hanna, Hanna, Hodges, & Rudorf, 1966; Venezky, 1999). Irregularity of English spelling has led to many attempts to reform the English spelling system, including the initial teaching alphabet (ITA) devised by Sir James Pitman in the 1950s. Pitman created an alphabet with 44 distinct letters, one letter to match each English phoneme. ITA flourished briefly in America and England during the 1960s but failed because its linguistic premises were flawed and its practical consequences unacceptable. All other attempts to reform the English spelling system also failed for a variety of theoretical and practical reasons.

A second prerequisite for learning to read is visual discrimination, which Harris and Hodges (1995) define as "The process of perceiving similarities and differences in stimuli by sight" (p. 273). More specifically, visual discrimination is the ability to distinguish the features of letters and words from one another. For example, *b, d, q,* and *p* are distinguished by their position in space. Rotating these letters shows that their identification depends on their placement. The actual features that form these letters are nearly identical, an unfortunate circumstance for some children who reverse them, especially during the early years of learning to read. However, reversal of letters is much less a problem than it has been made out to be. Reversals are seldom an indicator of a serious reading deficiency (Cramer, 1998). More often they are simply a developmental phenomenon that disappears spontaneously as children grow in their ability to process print.

Phonemic awareness and visual discrimination develop prior to and along with learning to read. There is no set amount of phonemic awareness and visual discrimination that must be acquired before reading instruction can begin. We know that writing with invented spelling advances phonemic awareness (Stanovich, Cunningham, & Cramer, 1984) while simultaneously advancing reading and writing knowledge. We also know that children can write with invented spelling before they have acquired a full complement of phonemic awareness and visual discrimination skills (Stanovich et al., 1984).

**Sequence of Phonics Instruction.** Decisions about sequencing phonics instruction are based on research, logic, teacher experience, and linguistic clues. But some complicating factors make sequencing phonics instruction an uncertain enterprise. First, research evidence is available, but incomplete. Second, each child is an independent variable in the process of learning to read. An optimal sequence for one child may not be optimal for another. Third, the English spelling system complicates sequence decisions. For instance, we know that consonant letters are relatively stable, and therefore a promising place to start phonics instruction. Still, most consonant letters have two or three common spellings (/k/: *c, k, ck*; /s/ *s, c, ss*) and two or three less common spellings (/k/: *ch, cc, cq*; /s/: *z, se, ps*). We know that children find beginning and ending consonant spellings easiest to represent when they invent their own spellings (Cramer & Cipielewski, 1995). We also know that vowel spelling patterns are much more irregular than consonant patterns (Hanna et al., 1966; Venezky, 1999). Logically, therefore, starting with consonants, especially single beginning and ending consonants, seems sensible and is supported by research and experience (Hurst, Wilson, Camp, & Cramer, 2002). This doesn't resolve the rest of the sequencing issue, however. Some informed guessing is necessary. The sequence outlined in Table 9.1 on page 334 represents one sequence of phonics instruction; others may well exist.

I do not suggest that the sequence outlined in Table 9.1 supports a lockstep order of instruction. Children learn elements of phonics knowledge independent of any stipulated sequence. Phonemic awareness, visual discrimination, and elements

**Table 9.1**

**A Logical Sequence for Teaching Phonics**

1. Visual discrimination of words and letters
2. Phonemic awareness—discrimination of speech sounds
   Rhyming words
   Beginning single-letter consonant sounds
   Ending single-letter consonant sounds
   Consonant digraphs and blends
   Long vowels
   Short vowels
3. Letter–sound relationships
   Single beginning and ending consonants
   Consonant digraphs and blends
   Consonant substitution
   Phonograms
   Single-letter short vowels
   Single-letter long vowels
   Vowel digraphs
   Vowel diphthongs
   Double consonants
   *R*-controlled vowels
   Silent *e*
   Silent letter combinations
   Unusual consonant spellings
   Unusual vowel spellings

of phonics knowledge grow concurrently for many children. Writing with invented spelling enables children to develop their own sequence. It is, therefore, a good idea to begin writing within the first few days of first grade or during kindergarten.

**Teaching Phonics**. The major task in phonetic analysis is to determine the sounds that letters represent and to blend them to achieve conventional pronunciation of words. In order to pronounce a word using phonetic analysis, the separate parts of a word must be sounded and then blended. Sounding and blending are taught in different ways.

Perhaps the oldest technique is letter-by-letter sounding and blending. According to this procedure, the word *rat* would be pronounced in three parts. A reader would be taught to pronounced the *r*, *a*, and *t* sequentially and separately. A major difficulty with this technique is that extraneous sounds are often attached to each letter. The resulting pronunciation is often grossly distorted, sounding like: *ruh, ah, tuh*. Sounding and blending are difficult for many young readers, especially struggling readers. Adding extraneous sounds only adds to the difficulty and is likely to make meaning less accessible.

Another technique for sounding and blending is to combine the initial consonant and the following vowel as a unit and then blend this unit with the following consonant, as in *ra-t*. This makes it slightly easier to avoid extraneous sounds during blending, and it may prepare the way for analysis of syllables in multisyllabic words. Its limitation is that it is difficult to know which sound to give the initial vowel, since the sound of a vowel often depends on the letters that follow it, as in *ca-k(e)*.

Still another technique combines initial consonants with phonograms. A phonogram is a word part consisting of a vowel and an ending consonant: *ar* in *car*, *far*, *bar*, *tar*, *star* or *ake* as in *make*, *shake*, *lake*, *take*. Using the substitution technique, the phonogram is blended with different consonants. For example, the phonogram *ent* when combined with *b*, *c*, *d*, *l*, *p*, *r*, *s*, *t*, *v*, and *w*, produces the following set of related words: *bent*, *cent*, *dent*, *lent*, *pent*, *rent*, *sent*, *tent*, *vent*, and *went*. Substitution simplifies the blending and sounding task because it reduces the number of parts. It is also a good way to deal with vowel variation since it takes into account the entire vowel phonogram, rather than the separate vowel sound. When phonograms are taught, a vowel is always combined with one or two consonants or a consonant digraph. Using substitution and phonograms is a good alternative for children who have difficulty with vowel sounds—particularly those having problems distinguishing them. Its limitation is that it applies mainly to one-syllable words. However, it can also apply to many syllables within multisyllabic words.

**Contextual Analysis**. Contextual analysis is the search for the pronunciation and meaning of an unknown word by examining its linguistic and visual context. The richer the context, the more likely readers will determine the pronunciation and meaning of an unknown word. Contextual analysis is similar to the cloze procedure, taking advantage of the tendency to fill in a missing part to make a meaningful whole. Closure occurs when a reader uses context to determine pronunciation and meaning. The reader fills in the missing word(s) by making predictions derived from semantics, syntax, phonics, and structure. Some or all of these linguistic features are present to some degree in all written language. For example, the missing word is easy to predict in this sentence: "The cowboy jumped on his _____ and rode away." Even readers who do not have *horse* in their sight vocabulary are likely to correctly pronounce the missing word if they know the other words in the sentence. If a reader says *house* instead of *horse,* the teacher immediately knows that the reader is not using meaning as a word recognition strategy.

Context can be topographical as well as linguistic. Environmental print often has a topographical or visual context, particularly in environmental print. The symbol for *stop* is topographical, since the word *stop* appears within the context of a six-sided red sign, or symbol for *stop*. The visual shape provides the context and immediately suggests the word *stop*.

Ames (1966) listed ways in which context provides clues to word recognition and meaning: pictorial illustration, experience, comparison and contrast, synonyms, summary, mood, definition, familiar expressions, modifying phrases and clauses, description, words connected in a series, time, setting, reference or antecedents, association, main idea and supporting details, question–answer patterns, preposition, nonrestrictive clauses or appositive phrases, cause–effect patterns. Rankin and Overholzer (1969) found that the easiest context clues for intermediate-grade children were words connected in a series, modifying phrases and clauses, experience with language, familiar expressions, cause–effect patterns, and association clues. The most difficult were nonrestrictive clauses or appositive phrases, main idea and supporting details, comparison or contrast, and question–answer pattern of a paragraph.

While context is an important feature in word recognition, three circumstances may prevent readers from using it effectively. First, children may not have learned to use context as a word recognition strategy. Second, the surrounding linguistic and visual context may be weak, making context virtually useless. Third, the reading material may be too difficult for the reader, making context extremely difficult to use. Reading material must be at an independent or instructional level before readers can make effective use of context.

The closer the linguistic context is to children's own language, the easier it is to use context clues. The natural patterns of language must be present in instructional materials if contextual analysis is to succeed. Otherwise, beginning readers will be unable to use their language and meaning skills to best advantage. An advantage of the language experience approach is that dictated language ensures a perfect match between oral and written language.

**Structural Analysis**. English has conventions for word formation. Thus, we can have *happy* and *unhappy,* but we do not have *crazy* and *uncrazy*. We have *beautification* but we don't have *uglification*—or do we? Lewis Carroll challenged the rules of word formation and word meaning in *Alice's Adventures in Wonderland*. He invented new words and new meanings for words. Alice's trip down the rabbit hole introduced her to a whole new world of words. For example, prior to her tumble into the rabbit hole, Alice had not heard the word *uglification* or the expression *curiouser and curiouser*.

Few writers had more fun with words than Lewis Carroll. He invented *unbirthday*; a century later, *uncola* appears in a soft drink commercial. Carroll's poem *Jabberwocky* tells us of the *slithy toves* who did *gyre and gimble*; we are introduced to the *mimsy borogoves*; we learn that the *mome raths outgrabe*. This eccentric, creative man loved words, and his stories profoundly influenced our sense of the possibilities of the English language. His stories promoted the idea that nonsense can be profound, meaning can be invented, language can be playful, and word structure can be created—or even *uncreated*.

Structural analysis is the visual examination of words to discover component parts that can facilitate pronunciation and lead to a word's meaning. Structural analysis involves the identification of roots, affixes, compounds, inflected and derived endings, syllables, and contractions. Recently, chunking words into parts has become popular as a synonym for structural analysis. The term *chunking* has the virtue of simplifying the instructional vocabulary we use with children.

Word recognition is facilitated when children can identify and pronounce word parts. Using structural analysis, children can divide a word, such as *unkind,* into its two structural parts, the prefix *un-* and the root word *kind*—which also correspond to its two syllables. Once a structural element has been identified, the reader may combine contextual, phonetic, and structural information to pronounce the word and understand its meaning. As word recognition skill increases, reliance on breaking words into their structural parts and blending word parts into whole words is done rapidly and smoothly. Eventually, the word is recognized at sight.

**Inflected Forms**. Words are the major meaning-bearing units (morphemes, or forms) in English. Affixes (suffixes and prefixes) change meaning when they are added. Other forms, called inflections, change the form of a word to indicate differences in tense, number, person, degree, or ownership. There are eight inflectional forms in English. Some create difficulty for those learning to speak the language, although they seldom hinder communication when misused. Several pose difficulty to one who is learning to write English. Children need to know what happens to a root word when it is inflected and how to write using the inflections correctly. Some examples follow.

### Noun Inflections

Plurals (*-s*, *-es*, or irregular forms): dog/dogs, witch/witches, child/children
Possessives (singular: -'s, plural: -s'): cat's dish, cats' dishes

### Verb Inflections

Present tense, third person singular (*-s* or *-es*): he looks, she runs, it goes
Past tense (*-d*, *-ed*, or irregular forms): ogle/ogled, wish/wished, see/saw
Past participle and auxiliaries (*have, has, had*): have looked, has spoken, had gone
Present participle (verb + *-ing*) and auxiliaries (*am, is, are*): am looking, is singing, are thinking

### Adjective Inflections

Comparative (*-er*): big truck/bigger truck, long walk/longer walk
Superlative (*-est*): biggest truck, longest walk

The correct form of a possessive is perhaps the most difficult inflection for children to master. The context of one's own writing is the best forum for learning the inflections.

**Derived Forms**. A derived word is formed when a prefix, suffix, or both are added to a root word. Words such as *unkind, kindness, unkindly* are derivatives of the word *kind*. Root words form the foundation of a vocabulary, the language component to which other word parts are affixed. A prefix is a word part attached to the beginning of a root word to produce a derivative word. A prefix normally forms one syllable or more by itself and always modifies the meaning of the root word to which it is attached. A suffix is a word part attached at the end of a root word to produce a derivative word. A suffix usually forms one syllable or more by itself and always modifies the meaning of the root word to which it is attached.

Meaning is central in the analysis of derived words. Teach children that the meaning of a root word remains stable. However, the addition of an affix (prefix or suffix) modifies it to create a meaning distinct from that of the root word. Knowing the meaning of some common prefixes and suffixes expands vocabulary. A relatively small number of prefixes and suffixes help children recognize the meaning of many additional words. Learning key word parts comes about mostly through reading and writing. While direct instruction is valuable, vocabulary-building exercises are seldom mastered until words and their structures are encountered in reading and used in speaking, listening, and writing. Table 9.2 on page 338 lists common prefixes and suffixes.

**Compound Words**. Compound words are formed when two or more words are combined. Each part of a compound retains its original spelling. The individual parts are pronounceable units and an aid to meaning. While a compound word has its own meaning, the compound form retains elements of meaning from each component. Thus, both *basket* and *ball* are partly descriptive of the meaning of the compound word *basketball*. They contribute to, but do not fully define, the compound form.

**Table 9.2**

**Common Prefixes and Suffixes**

| Common Prefixes | | |
|---|---|---|
| **Prefix** | **Meaning** | **Example** |
| ab- | off from, away | absent |
| anti- | against | antibiotic |
| co-, con-, com-, col-, cor- | together, with | cooperate, content |
| de- | away, down, out of | depart |
| dis- | not, opposite | disclaim |
| en- | in | enclose |
| ex- | formerly, out of, from | ex-president, explain |
| in-, im-, il- | not, opposite | insane, impatient, illegal |
| non- | opposite | nonsense |
| pre- | before | prescribe |
| pro- | in favor of, for | proclaim |
| re- | back, again | return |
| trans- | across | transportation |
| un- | not, opposite | untrue |

| Common Suffixes | | |
|---|---|---|
| **Suffix** | **Meaning** | **Example** |
| -able | capable of, worthy | valuable |
| -ance, -ence, -ancy, -ency | act or fact of doing, state, quality, condition | emergency |
| -er, -or | person or thing, connected with, agent | worker, doctor |
| -ful | full of, abounding in | thoughtful |
| -less | without, free from | hopeless |
| -ly | like, characteristic of | friendly |
| -ment | state or quality of | argument |
| -tion, -sion, -xion | action, state, result | attention, invasion |

**Syllabication**. A syllable is a unit of speech containing one vowel or vowel-like sound, forming either a whole word or a word part. The role of syllabication in structural analysis is somewhat controversial. Much of the controversy centers on the teaching of syllabication rules. Many rules for syllabication are either too complex or do not work often enough to be useful. Studies by Clymer (1963) and Emans (1967) show that a few syllabication rules meet the test of usefulness. If taught, they should be simply stated and taught inductively and deductively. The following rules meet the criteria of simplicity and usefulness:

1. Every single vowel or vowel combination indicates a syllable except for final *e*: (de/mon/stra/tion).
2. Divide between the prefix and a root word: (re/gain).

3. Divide between the suffix and the root word: (help/ful).
4. Divide before the consonant in a consonant -le pattern (pad/dle, lit/tle).

**Sight Words**. Words recognized instantly are called sight words, since there is no need to analyze them phonetically, structurally, or contextually. Sight words are stored in memory, learned from repeated exposure, and identified by visual clues such as shape, length, unique features, and letter combinations—though these patterns are different for each child. Beginning readers have a small sight vocabulary or none at all. A small sight vocabulary is needed to teach analytic phonics, the whole-to-part approach to phonics.

Critics of analytic phonics sometimes claim that teaching sight words requires memorizing rather than learning words. This is a strange criticism indeed, since the goal of word recognition is to know as many words by sight as possible. Actually, the ideal reader would know every word in the English lexicon by sight and would seldom resort to phonetic, structural, or contextual analysis except when a reading miscue might require a reexamination of context. A sight vocabulary is not acquired through rote memorization. Rather, it is acquired through extensive reading in meaningful contexts.

Since beginning readers have small sight vocabularies, they must use contextual, phonetic, or structural analysis more often than mature readers do. The more children read, the more rapidly they build a sight vocabulary. The goal of word recognition instruction is instantaneous recognition of the maximum number of words. English has too many words in too many specialized knowledge domains for anyone to know every word by sight. Therefore, word recognition skills are needed throughout a reader's lifetime. Mature readers use phonetic, structural, or contextual analysis only when an unfamiliar word is encountered or when an unusual arrangement of words causes momentary confusion.

There are many ways to reinforce sight words. One of the most common is to associate words with pictures. Picture word cards can help beginning readers develop a small sight vocabulary, as can illustrations in storybooks. When children read and reread the same story, they often develop a sight vocabulary from the repeated exposure. Most children love having the same story read and reread to them, and they enjoy reading and rereading the same story on their own. Children enjoy repeating successful experiences, so rereading stories should be encouraged.

Flash cards are often used to build sight vocabulary. While this method is popular, most experts agree that it is a questionable practice and unnecessary, since more meaningful activities are available. One objection to isolated drill is that it provides little opportunity to connect words with meaning. Another problem is that words may be associated with irrelevant clues such as an ink stain on the flash card. Word cards are better used *after* words have been learned. Children can sort words based on phonetic, structural, or meaning features. After a few words have accumulated in word banks, children can work individually or in groups to construct and exchange short messages using those words.

Language experience provides an effective way to develop a sight vocabulary. The sight words learned from dictated stories are recorded on small cards and kept in a container, alphabetized, and used for word study. As words are learned, word sort activities are used to categorize words by meaning and by phonetic and structural patterns. Words learned from dictated stories differ from those learned in basal materials, which present a common core vocabulary that all students are expected to learn. While a common core vocabulary is not taught in the language experience approach, a common set of words is learned anyway due to the natural redundancy of the language. Table 9.3 suggests ways to teach and reinforce sight words.

*Teaching Tip*

## Strategies for Teaching Word Recognition

Word recognition lessons can be taught inductively or deductively. The following steps have proved effective in teaching a deductive phonics lesson.

1. *Modeling and illustrating.* The teacher models and illustrates the skill directly; children listen and observe. It might go like this, though it is not necessary to follow a precise script.
   - "Listen to these two words: *star, stone. Star* and *stone* begin with these two letters." Write *star* and *stone* on the board and underline the *st* blend in each word.
   - "Now listen to these two words: *stick, store. Stick* and *store* begin with the sound you hear in these two letters." Write *stick* and *store* on the board, and underline the *st* blend.
2. *Identification and recognition.* Step 2 extends step 1. The teacher discovers whether the learners have understood step 1. Children are asked to identify and recognize what has been taught in step 1.
   - "I'm going to say two words. Listen to these two words: *stop, black.* Which word begins like *star?*" If children respond correctly, write the two words on the board and say, "Yes, *stop* begins like *star, stone, stick,* and *store.*"
   - If children respond incorrectly, say, "Listen again: *stop, black. Stop* begins like *star.*" Write *start* and *stop* on the board, and underline the *st* blend. Then repeat step 1.

## Table 9.3

### Ways to Reinforce Known Sight Words

- Alphabetize known sight words.
- Classify words by phonetic, structural, or meaning features.
- Work in pairs to teach words to each other.
- Work in pairs to write phrases, sentences, or stories with sight words.
- Tell a story about a word from the word bank.
- Paint, illustrate, or dramatize a word.
- Trace words on sand, textured paper, or with a crayon.
- Locate known sight words in other sources such as magazines and trade books.
- Make a dictionary illustrating sight words.
- Make a spelling dictionary.
- Write words in a special script.

3. *Application and production.* Children demonstrate and apply what has been learned in steps 1 and 2 by producing a relevant example(s) of what has been taught.

- "Give me some words that begin like *star, stamp, stone,* or *stick.*" Write responses on the board. If the examples are correct, you can assume that children have learned what has been taught. The lesson should be followed up in context and taught again later for reinforcement.
- If children cannot produce correct examples, return to step 1 or 2, as you judge necessary.

**Helping Children Decode Unknown Words.** Some children have no strategy for decoding a word not recognized in text, though they may have the word in their oral vocabularies. Others may have a single strategy: sounding it out. Though useful, this strategy works best in conjunction with other equally important strategies. Children should be taught to use a series of strategies to decode an unknown word. The following strategies should be applied simultaneously rather than sequentially.

- Ask, "What makes sense?" Teach students that context helps, though not always. Still, readers need to ask this meaning-loaded question.
- Ask, "What's the sound of the first consonant(s) or vowel(s)? What other sounds in this word do I know?"

*Having previously relied only on a sound-it-out strategy, Anna now uses a combination of word recognition strategies, thanks to the help of Ms. Tippins.*

- Ask, "What word part(s) do I know in this word?"
- Then, "Try putting these clues together to pronounce the word."
- Finally, "Where can I get help?" Usually this means consulting the teacher or another student. Rarely would this mean going to the dictionary, for young readers.

Of course, children need strategies for decoding unknown words, but teachers also need strategies for helping children decode them. The following ideas are meant for teachers:

- Teach specific strategies for decoding unknown words (discussed earlier in this section).
- When helping children with an unknown word, start by asking, "What have you tried so far?" You want children to articulate their strategies and take personal responsibility for applying them.
- Observe any confusions or uncertainties children have as they attempt to apply strategies you have taught. Remind children of the correct procedures on the spot.
- Schedule a reteaching session for those who need additional instruction.

As word recognition skills develop, children must use them as they read materials at an instructional level. At this level, some unknown words should be encountered, but not more than 6 or 7 per 100 words. Materials with few or no unknown words lack opportunities for students to apply their growing skills in an appropriate context. On the other hand, children must not be put in circumstances where frustration overwhelms their attempts to decode unknown words.

Children can be readied to decode text even before they come to school. What parents do at home influences how children progress at school. I was reminded of this recently when a mother and her son visited my office. Liz Molnar, teacher and mother, told me she had been reading chapter books to her son, T.J. Having written a short paragraph about Ms. Molnar and T.J. for an earlier literacy story, I showed her what I had written. A few days later I received an e-mail from Ms. Molnar. (See the Field Notes feature.)

**Activities That Build Word Recognition Skills.** Five activities are described here; additional ones are suggested in the Blue Pages at the end of this book.

**Frequent Reading.** Simple as it seems, the most important word recognition activity is to have children read at their independent and instructional levels. The more they read, the more their sight and meaning vocabulary will grow. Good readers read more than poor readers; they are more likely to have strong sight vocabularies; they are more likely to interrupt their reading to figure out unknown words (Samuels, 1988; Stanovich & West, 1989). Frequent reading is what makes good readers good. But poor readers are less motivated and have fewer skills. Getting them to read more is a challenge. Poor readers are on the horns of a dilemma; what they need to do to improve is exactly what they cannot do well. But we must face this tremendous challenge. A

For more activities, see *Word Play and Language Learning for Children,* by L. Geller, 1985.

## Field Notes
### Real-Life Experiences of a Parent

Dear Dr. Cramer,

I was very flattered that you wrote about T.J.'s love of chapter books. Some may think that I've pushed reading chapter books on him, since I'm a teacher and will soon have my master's in reading. But honestly, he's asked to have these read to him because he simply loves hearing stories. He's beginning to read simple sight words and is intrigued with letters and sounds, though he's not any more advanced than most of his peers. Yet he's captivated and moved when I read passages telling how Henry Huggins found his dog, Ribsy, or when Charlotte dies and leaves Wilbur all alone. T.J. smiles, he laughs, he cheers, and he cries for characters that are alive in his mind and in his heart. I know we are experiencing a treasured time together that will last a lifetime. Thanks for letting me empty my heart.

**Liz Molnar**

significant strategy to improve poor readers' performances is to expose them to familiar text, which they have heard or read previously. Therefore they need books read aloud to them often enough so they can read those books on their own; they need exposure to previously read dictated stories so they can practice fluency in this highly familiar text environment; they need to read good literature at their independent level (Cunningham, 2000). No matter how difficult this challenge may be, it beats every other word recognition activity that even the finest teacher can devise.

**Making Words**. Starting from a bank of known words, students build additional words with similar spelling and rhyming patterns. For example, starting with a known word such as *like*, students can build words such as *bike, hike, mike, strike*.

You can also help children create new words by manipulating letters and word parts (Cunningham & Hall, 1994). For example, give children the letters *d, i, l, m,* and *e*. Then have them make a one-letter word (*I*), a two-letter word (*me*), a three-letter word (*lid*), and a four-letter word (*dime*). Other combinations are possible, so accept any appropriate words children build. This game can be played with word parts as well as letters—for example, give the phonogram *ore*, and have children make ten words that include this pattern: *bore, core, fore, gore, lore, more, pore, sore, store, shore*. Of course, children will make some nonwords, opportunity for further discussion of how words are made, spelled, and given meaning.

**Word Sorts**. Collections of known words can be sorted into categories according to their features. Features related to meaning, structure, and phonetic properties are appropriate categories. It is important to work with known, not unknown, words. The activity works best, but is not always necessary, to have children choose their own categories. And teachers must first demonstrate ways in which words can be sorted. Words drawn from children's language experience stories, writing, and topics of study are appropriate for this activity.

Have children write their words on small cards so that they can be easily placed according to category. Albert, a second-grader with significant reading difficulties, sorted some of the words from his language-experience word bank into the three categories shown in Table 9.4. This was one of Albert's first sorts and it worked well because he used about 30% of the words in his bank. He had a problem with *Saturday,* classifying it as a two-syllable word. His teacher, Ms. Goetz, said two things: "That's a good sort, Albert." Then she said, "Check your two-syllable words again." He did and found his mistake.

**Table 9.4**    Albert's Word Sort

| Family Words | Two-Syllable Words | Animals |
|---|---|---|
| and | table | groundhog |
| hand | reading | foxes |
| sand | mother | dog |
| sat | riding | horses |
| fat | going | |
| lake | Monday | |
| take | Sunday | |

**Word Walls**. Word walls can be used effectively, though often they are not. Too often they end up as wall decorations, which soon cease to register with children as useful. There are four ways to make word walls more effective. First, put only known words on the wall. Second, create procedures and activities that keep the wall in use. Third, do not require children to get spelling from a *general* word wall. Fourth, organize word walls into categories useful for your purposes and activities. For example, you might have categories such as weird words, social studies words, math words, hard-to-spell words, or animal words.

**Invented Spelling**. We want young children to write, but a massive obstacle stands in their way. Spelling! When children do not know how to spell a word, we must teach them to spell as much of it as their encoding knowledge permits (see Chapter 13). This may mean that Anne can spell *cat* with the single consonant letter *k*; DeJaun can spell *cat* with two consonant letters, *kt*; and Joan can spell *cat* with three letters, *kat* or *cat*. Anne, DeJaun, and Joan will learn something important about decoding (reading) by practicing encoding (writing).

Invented spelling plays a crucial role in learning to read as well as learning to write (Cramer, 2001). Invented spelling shapes children's knowledge of English spelling patterns. Spelling knowledge is acquired much like any other type of knowledge. Every relevant experience contributes; every opportunity to practice strengthens performance. Every instance of invented spelling is a relevant experience, an opportunity to practice phonetic or structural concepts. Every writing experience moves children closer to the goal of reading the language as well as writing it. Children go through a long process of understanding how words work. Letter by letter, word by word, concept by concept, children forge their knowledge of how to decode and encode the English language. The writing road to reading is just as royal as the reading road to writing.

## Assessing Word Recognition in Context

Word recognition can be assessed in isolation and in context. Both ways have value, although miscue analysis in context yields more useful information. For example, word recognition in isolation provides no information about comprehension and is not useful for placing children in reading materials. Word recognition in isolation (pronouncing words from a list) reveals extent of sight vocabulary, fluency in recognizing known words, and ability to decode by applying phonetic and structural analysis skills in the absence of context. *But that is all, and that is not sufficient.* By contrast, word recognition in context tells us how children process text, revealing strengths and weaknesses. Goodman, Watson, and Burke (1987) describe how to analyze reading miscues in their Reading Miscue Inventory. Their procedures take into account semantic, syntactic, auditory, and visual issues. But a quicker, simpler procedure can be used for classroom diagnosis.

Two miscue scores can be derived by having children read in context: total miscue score and adjusted miscue score. The total miscue score consists of all miscues, whether surface or meaning. It is calculated by counting all recordable miscues. A miscue occurs when the reader (1) substitutes one word for another, (2) mispronounces a word, (3) deletes a word, (4) inserts a word, or (5) rearranges words. Therefore, the total miscue score is quantitative, simply a count of all miscues.

The purpose of the adjusted miscue score is to consider miscues qualitatively. It is calculated by examining every miscue *qualitatively,* and answering this question: is it likely that this miscue caused a loss of meaning? Adjusted miscue analysis intends to distinguish between miscues that are surface errors, unlikely to influence the reader's building of meaning, and miscues that are likely to have a deeper effect on comprehension. An adjusted, or meaning, miscue makes meaning difficult or unlikely to be recovered through inference. Teachers make this qualitative judgment as they examine each miscue and compare it with the original text. While qualitative judgments can be wrong, so can every possible means of assessing performance. But teachers are well qualified to make sound judgments. After all, their entire life's work is predicated on making instructional judgments moment to moment, day to day, year to year. Table 9.5 on page 346 describes how to derive two miscue scores using the five miscue categories suggested above.

## Section Summary: Word Recognition

1. Principles of word recognition instruction are statements of philosophy to guide instruction. Some are controversial.
2. The four main components of word recognition are phonetic analysis, contextual analysis, structural analysis, and sight words. Phonetic analysis associates speech sounds with letters and word parts and blends them to

**Table 9.5**

**Determining Two Miscue Counts**

### Step 1: Count the total number of miscues.

The total miscue count is arrived at by coding major miscues: substitutions, omissions, mispronunciations, insertions, reversals, and aided miscues. Assume that you have scored an oral reading performance and have counted 10 miscues distributed as follows:

| | |
|---|---|
| Substitution errors | 3 |
| Omission miscues | 2 |
| Mispronunciation miscues | 2 |
| Insertion miscues | 3 |
| Reversal miscues | 0 |
| Aided miscues | 0 |
| Total miscue count | 10 |

Total miscue score would then be:

| | |
|---|---|
| Total possible score: | 100% (where each word in a 100-word passage equals 1%) |
| Total number of miscues | 10 |
| Total miscue score | 90% (where 10% is subtracted from the possible score of 100%) |

### Step 2: Count the adjusted miscues.

Assume you have recorded 10 total miscues. Now look at each miscue qualitatively and ask, *Did this miscue likely cause a loss of meaning?* Assume you decided that of the 10 total miscues, only 3 were likely to have caused a loss of meaning. In that case, the adjusted miscue score would be:

| | |
|---|---|
| Total possible score: | 100%  (where each word in a 100-word passage equals 1%). |
| Total number of miscues | 10 |
| Number of adjusted miscues | 3 |
| Adjusted miscue score | 97% (where 3% is subtracted from the possible score of 100%) |

### Step 3: Arrive at two scores for understanding miscues.

You now know the total miscue score is 90% and the adjusted miscue score is 97%. You have accounted for surface miscues, ones that do not substantially influence meaning, and meaning miscues, ones that likely cause a loss of meaning. In other words, you have a quantitative score—90%, and a qualitative score—97%. You now have a better understanding of the influence miscues have on comprehension. Even so, miscue information must be augmented by directly assessing comprehension through questioning. (Chapter 3 describes how an informal reading inventory is used to test comprehension.)

pronounce unknown words. Contextual analysis involves the examination of the surrounding linguistic and illustrative environment for clues to pronunciation and meaning. Structural analysis is the visual examination of words to discover component parts that lead to pronunciation and meaning. Words stored in memory are called sight words and, once firmly established, are recognized instantly.

3. Three steps for teaching a word recognition lesson are modeling and illustrating, identification and recognition, and application and production.

4. Students need strategies for decoding unknown words, and teachers need strategies for helping them.

5. Activities for building word recognition skills include frequent reading in level-appropriate text, making words, using word sorts, setting up word walls, and using invented spelling.

6. Word recognition can be assessed in isolation and in context. Context assessment is more useful for understanding comprehension of text.

7. Two miscue scores can be used to assess students' instructional needs: total number of miscues, regardless of the significance of the miscue, and adjusted miscues, in which meaning-related miscues are counted.

## Dictionary Skills

Misunderstanding the meaning of a word can be catastrophic. Richard Lederer (1991) reports that a misunderstanding of the Japanese word *mokusatsu,* may have led to the bombing of Hiroshima and Nagasaki, which resulted in the death of at least 150,000 Japanese citizens. Near the end of World War II, the Japanese government had been ordered to surrender unconditionally. The reply contained the word *mokusatsu,* which Lederer reports can be translated in two distinct ways: "we are considering it" or "we are ignoring it." The translator chose the second option. Some historians believe the Japanese government may have meant the other. Whether this is true or not will be debated for centuries. But there is no doubt that many world events, as well as countless personal ones, have turned on a single word or phrase.

A wonderful introductory dictionary for young children is *The Scott Foresman Beginning Dictionary.* It is written around the themes of ecology and zoo animals.

Most word meanings we know did not come about from reading dictionary definitions. Dictionaries have an ancient history, but early ones were modest affairs, valuable mostly to scholars and the educated class—a tiny proportion of the population. The first English dictionary, *A Table Alphabeticall,* by Robert Cawdrey, was published in 1604, and contained 2,500 words (Blachowicz & Fisher, 2002). Dictionary usage, even today, is most often associated with academic pursuits; far less often is it associated with daily language usage.

Nevertheless, dictionaries are a valuable resource, and children need to know how and when to use them. The three most important uses of general English language dictionaries are to determine word meaning, to check spelling, and to verify pronunciation. Dictionaries have other uses, but these three are the most pertinent here. Table 9.6 (p. 349) lists major features of dictionary knowledge.

# Standing on the Shoulders of Giants
## Historical Contributions to Literacy
### Edmund Burke Huey

Consider the following four ideas about current reading topics.

1. *Literature-based language arts.* "The home is the natural place for learning to read, in connection with the child's introduction to literature through story-telling." "The learning to read real literature should begin in the home and in the very first days of school." "The reading and hearing of literature is to be depended upon to impregnate the soul with the race's highest ideals and tastes."
2. *Reading exercises.* "The reading should always be for the intrinsic interest or value of what is read, reading never being done or thought of as an *exercise*."
3. *Grammar for young children.* "Grammar and other analytical study of language should play little part in training to the correct use of the mother-tongue."
4. *Readers' purposes.* "Most of the time usually given to *exercises* in reading aloud, etc., will be far more productive if spent in learning the effective use of the library, of indexes, books of reference . . . and to make effective use of these for the reader's purposes."*

A man once said, "The ancients have stolen all of my best ideas." Whoever said it must have known the history of his profession. There is a tendency to think our pedagogy is fresh, that we have invented wonderful new ideas. How wrong we often are about our predecessors. In 1908, Edmund Burke Huey wrote *The Psychology and Pedagogy of Reading*. Nearly a century later, reading educators can pick up Huey's book and discover ideas about the psychology and pedagogy of reading that are still sound—like the four ideas described above—all quotes from Huey's book.

*Source: The Psychology and Pedagogy of Reading, by E. B. Huey, 1908, 1968. Cambridge, MA: MIT Press, pp. 379–382.

---

A dictionary cannot be used effectively until the basics of word recognition and spelling have been acquired. Finding a word in a dictionary requires the use of contextual, phonetic, and structural analysis skills. Dictionary skills are not synonymous with word recognition. Rather, word recognition skills are used to check the meaning, spelling, pronunciation, usage, or etymology of words by using this resource.

Though children need to know how to use a dictionary, unrealistic expectations hinder growth in dictionary skills. It is naive to expect young readers to make frequent use of the dictionary. Even mature readers infrequently resort to them. Still, one cannot find treasure without the tools for recovering it, so acquaint children with a dictionary's treasures and equip them with the tools needed to search them out. Blachowicz and Fisher (2002) suggest five ideas essential for effective dictionary use:

Three excellent picture dictionaries for young children are *My First Picture Dictionary* (Lothrop/Scott, Foresman), *The Cat in the Hat Beginner Dictionary* (Random House), and *The Golden Picture Dictionary* (Western).

1. Knowing when to use a dictionary
2. Knowing how to locate a word
3. Knowing the parts of a dictionary entry
4. Choosing among multiple meanings
5. Applying the meaning

**Table 9.6**

**Basic Dictionary Skills**

1. Locating words
   a. Knowledge of alphabetical order by first, second, and third letters
   b. Dividing the dictionary into thirds (front, middle, and back)
   c. Guide words
2. Understanding entry words
   a. Regular entry words
   b. Special entry types (different spellings, cross-referenced entries, entries that are word parts, entries spelled alike, run-in entries, and run-on entries)
3. Pronunciation
   a. Pronunciation key
   b. Consonant symbols
   c. Vowel symbols
   d. Stress (primary, secondary, weak)
   e. Variant pronunciations
   f. Homographs
4. Meaning
   a. Order of definitions
   b. Finding the right meaning
   c. Using the context
   d. Understanding illustrative material
   e. Informal slang and idiomatic usage
   f. Synonyms
   g. Special circumstances (capitalized words, special plurals)
5. Spelling
   a. Finding a word you can't spell
   b. Variant spellings
   c. Spelling inflected forms
   d. Using a spelling chart
   e. Breaking a word at the end of line for writing (syllabication)
6. Abbreviations
   a. Common abbreviations
   b. Specialized abbreviations
7. Word histories (etymologies)
   a. How and where to locate them
   b. How to read them
   c. Abbreviations used in word histories

## Using Dictionaries to Determine Word Meaning

On July 17, 1938, Douglas Corrigan filed a flight plan for California, took off from Brooklyn in a single-engine plane, and landed in Ireland 29 hours later. His mistake almost certainly was a ruse to get around authorities' refusal to grant him permission to cross the Atlantic, although Corrigan never admitted to this. His humorous nickname has entered the lexicon: Wrong-Way Corrigan. Schools, too, come up with flight plans that lead children in the wrong direction. A common assignment given to children is to look up words in a dictionary and then write the words in sentences. Words are sometimes assigned without accompanying context. Even when a context exists, such as a social studies lesson, children are seldom given a procedure that ensures a match between the contextual use of the assigned words and the dictionary definitions. The sentences children typically produce for these assignments reveal shallow, incorrect, or almost meaningless definitions. They may avoid engaging a word's meaning but still manage to use it in a legitimate way. Here are two examples:

*global*: We live in a global world.
*prime minister*: The prime minister ate dinner alone.

Have you heard this one? One teacher got this sentence from a student: "Our family erodes a lot." Where did that sentence come from? Straight from a dictionary definition. One meaning of *erode* is to "eat away," as when water eats away the soil on a hill. If you have no schema for erosion, but you do have a schema for eating away from home at restaurants, then you have to admit, the kid had a point—he made a reasonable guess about how the word *erode* might be used in a sentence. Most teachers have encountered similar misunderstandings when children look up words in a dictionary and then use them in sentences. This kind of vocabulary assignment does not build word power, and there are reasons why writing isolated sentences is often counterproductive.

First, a grasp of a word's meaning depends on prior exposure in a variety of oral or written contexts. Insufficient background knowledge makes it difficult to connect definitions to real-life experiences. Second, dictionary definitions are often terse and lacking in context. This makes comprehension of definitions difficult for unsophisticated readers, who often have no strategy for checking the sense of a definition. Third, even when a definition is understood, it can be retained only through subsequent encounters in oral and written language. Many, if not most, of our meanings for words come from and are reinforced through reading and engaging in conversations with knowledgeable people. Fourth, since dictionary entries have multiple meanings, it is essential to choose the one that applies to the context at hand. Choosing the right meaning from a set of possibilities is the most challenging problem in teaching dictionary skills. Children need strategies for understanding and applying dictionary definitions.

Corrigan had intended to cross the Atlantic in a single-engine plane, and he had a strategy to achieve his objective—*better to ask forgiveness than permission*. Children, too, need strategies for choosing the appropriate meaning for a word from among multiple definitions. Bannon, Fisher, Pozzi, and Wessel (1990) have suggested a strategy. Their idea is to teach children to cross-check the probable contextual meaning of words with dictionary definitions. Their strategy involves prediction, verification, evaluation, and association. First, students *predict* meaning based on the context in which the word appears. Second, students verify the word's meaning in a dictionary. Third, students evaluate their prediction by cross-checking their prediction with the dictionary definition. Fourth, students associate the meaning of the word with an image to aid later recall. This strategy works best when first demonstrated by the teacher, using think-aloud modeling. While the procedure is time consuming, it works. It is best used by children working in small groups, though it can be done individually as well.

## Using Dictionaries to Check Spelling

Commercial spelling programs offer core and supplementary spelling words. The two categories account for 7,000 to 8,000 words for children to study in grades 1–8. Along with the words, children also study spelling concepts intended to expand the core spelling vocabulary well beyond the spelling lists. Yet it is easy to see that spelling study, even for those who are most successful, will not result in learning most English vocabulary. English is a word-rich language. An unabridged dictionary may have 600,000–700,000 entries, and some experts estimate that there are over 1 million English words. Even an abridged dictionary may have 200,000–300,000 words. And this does not count inflected and derived forms not listed as entry words, certain slang terms, or the thousands of recently invented words that have to be around for a while before they are given status as an entry word.

When the spelling of a word must be checked, where does one go? A decade ago, most of us would have said, "Look it up in the dictionary." Today we might say, "Use your spell checker." Sophisticated adult readers use dictionaries, but many adults, even writers, use spell checkers. For instance, a while back I wanted to use the word *amanuensis,* an archaic word for *secretary.* I could not remember the first two or three letters. After a frustrating dictionary search, I gave up because it occurred to me that if I made a couple of close guesses at the correct spelling, my spell checker might supply the correct spelling. It did. I should learn to spell *amanuensis,* but I rarely use it, so I'd probably soon forget it. Yet spell checkers cannot check errors with homophones, as the anonymous poem "Owed to a Spell Checker" suggests.

Eye halve a spelling checker
It came with my pea sea
It plainly marcs four my revue
Miss steaks eye kin Knot Sea.
Eye strikes a key and type a word
And weight four it two say
Whether eye is wrong oar write
It shows me strait a weigh.

As soon as a mist ache is made
It nose bee fore too long
And eye can put the error rite
Its rare lea ever wrong.
Eye has run this poem threw it
I am shore your pleased two no
Its letter perfect awl the weigh
My check tolled me sew.

Asking children to check the spelling of a word in the dictionary is useful only after children have acquired a substantial set of word recognition and spelling skills. Even then, it may be a fruitless search. Before sending children to the dictionary to check the spelling of a word, teach them strategies that will make a successful search more likely.

- Invent several alternative spellings for the word you want to spell. For example, if you want to spell *crazy,* try several logical possibilities: *krase, crasy, krazy.* Then use a spell checker or a dictionary to find the correct spelling.
- Try alternative spelling options. For example, if a word starts with an /f/ sound, try f (*fone*) and ph (*phone*). If a word ends with an /f/ sound, try gh (*laugh*) or ff (*stuff*). Then use a dictionary or a spell checker.
- Letters are often dropped, doubled, or changed when endings are added to words. Try different options: *begining* and *beginning; loveing* and *loving; easyest* and *easiest.* Then use a spell checker or a dictionary.

*Teaching Tip*

- Words related in meaning are often related in spelling in spite of changes in sounds. For example, if you can spell *marine,* you can probably spell *mariner;* if you can spell *compose,* you can probably spell *composition.*
- When writing, draft without concern for correct spelling. Then proofread for spelling errors. When in doubt, circle the suspect word and check it. Use a spell checker or dictionary, or consult a better speller.

## Using Guide Words

Two guide words appear at the top of every dictionary page, usually in bold print. Guide words make it easier to locate entry words. The first guide word (on the left) is also the first entry word on the page and the second guide word (on the right) is the last entry word on a dictionary page. Help children determine whether the word they are trying to locate can be found between the first and last entry words on a given dictionary page.

Beginning readers can start with picture dictionaries and learn to alphabetize, perhaps by alphabetizing their sight words as they place them in their word banks or by creating their own journal of words organized alphabetically. From this modest beginning, introduce children to more sophisticated dictionaries, and teach them to estimate the approximate location of a word by using guide words. It is probably not necessary to teach children to go beyond the two or three letters in guide words. For instance, Blachowicz, Fisher, Wohlreich, and Guastafeste (1990) report that fourth-graders found it easier to look across the middle of a dictionary page to get a sense of what words might be on that page. This research is reporting something teachers that ought to consider when teaching guide words. Children often figure out strategies on their own.

## Using a Dictionary to Check Pronunciation

It is hard to know which is more difficult for dictionary users: checking for spelling or checking for pronunciation. Yes, all dictionaries have a pronunciation guide, but it is highly dependent on phonetic knowledge that many children do not possess. Even children who have sufficient phonics knowledge may experience uncertainty about how to use pronunciation keys. It is difficult to feel certain that you have figured out the pronunciation of a word that you have never heard in oral discourse. In addition, pronunciation may differ due to dialect and regional differences. For instance, pronounce these three words: *Mary, merry, marry.* In certain regions of this country, these three words are pronounced alike; in other regions, each is pronounced differently.

I have never felt certainty as to how to pronounce the word *forte.* I have heard it pronounced both *fort* (as in an army fort) and *for-tay* (rhymes with *play*). It gets even more complicated. There are two entry words for *forte.* One is something a person does especially well, and the other pertains to music. I solve my problem the cowardly way. I avoid uttering the word in public. But sometimes the word slips out, and I immediately wonder if I have pronounced it correctly. But help is available—the electronic dictionary pronounces entry words for you.

Every dictionary has a pronunciation key, usually at the beginning of the dictionary. This key tells the user what sound each pronunciation symbol stands for. A pronunciation key provides illustrative words for each symbol. For instance, the sound /ă/ may have the key words *hat* and *cap*. This tells you that whenever you see the symbol ă in the pronunciation of an entry, you say the same vowel sound that you would say in *hat* and *cap*. This sounds simple enough, but children may find pronunciation keys difficult to use. They need to hear words uttered in oral speech to reassure them that they used the pronunciation key correctly. Provide oral reinforcement to help demystify the mysterious symbols of the pronunciation key.

## Section Summary: Dictionary Skills

1. A dictionary is a resource for checking meaning, spelling, pronunciation, usage, and word history. Its most important uses are determining word meaning, checking spelling, and verifying pronunciation.
2. Choosing the right meaning from multiple definitions is the most challenging problem in teaching dictionary skills.
3. Asking children to check the spelling of a word in the dictionary is useful only after children have acquired word recognition and spelling skills.
4. Guide words help children estimate whether the word they are trying to locate can be found on a given dictionary page.
5. The pronunciation key tells what sound each symbol stands for. Since they are difficult for children to use, oral reinforcement of how words are pronounced is helpful.

## Vocabulary

I'm walking in the woods with my 5-year-old. It's twilight time, and I say to Amy, "Isn't twilight lovely." She asks, "What's twilight?" Like the teacher I am, I give an explanation. "It's the time between sunset and dark when the light is sort of subdued." "Oh," she says, "you mean dark light."

I wish I had said that. My 5-year-old's poetic description of twilight outranked my formal definition. Words can wear coats of many colors. Poets' words conjure colorful images; children's language is often poetic. Most adults have a more difficult time dressing up their words in such lovely colors. Young children are often artists with words.

Words are tools, toys, and weapons. As tools, they help us acquire and manipulate ideas and information. As toys, they are the vehicles of jokes, puns, and other amusements. As weapons, words further our ambitions, increase our status, and punish our enemies. There are more uses for words than these three metaphors convey. Learning a new word is more complex than it may seem. Words seldom have a single stable meaning. Once we introduce a new word into our vocabulary, it gradually accumulates additional meanings, associations, and figurative possibilities. New words must be tamed and curried before we can ride them. The writer H. G. Wells said, "A new word is like a wild animal you have caught. You must learn its ways and break it before you can use it." The purpose of vocabulary instruction is help children learn the ways of words so that they can use them to enrich their academic, economic, social, spiritual, and aesthetic lives.

The Literacy Dictionary (Harris & Hodges, 1995) lists 11 types of vocabularies: controlled, core, expressive, listening, meaning, reading, receptive, sight, simplified, oral, and writing. This list does not exhaust the possibilities, however. This section focuses on meaning vocabulary (understanding the intent, significance, or sense of words) associated with listening, reading, speaking, and writing.

On first consideration, one might think that these four vocabularies are one and the same, but this is not the case. Generally, hearing vocabularies are larger than speaking vocabularies and reading vocabularies larger than writing vocabularies. One can observe these distinctions most easily among children, but they also exist among adults. Obviously, very young children's listening vocabularies exceed their speaking vocabularies, and they may have no reading or writing vocabularies at all. Eventually, the various meaning vocabularies come closer together, but they are never exactly proportional.

Increasing children's meaning vocabularies is a major instructional objective. An extensive vocabulary is an asset to learning and a boon to life in general. As children's vocabularies expand, their learning and social horizons also grow. Though we know how children's vocabularies grow, we are less adroit at making it happen. The task is fraught with challenges. For example, the most effective way to increase vocabulary is through reading. The more widely and deeply children read, the more vocabulary they acquire. So why not just have children read more? Well, getting children to read beyond classroom boundaries is difficult. Teachers must compete with society's attractive diversions: television, computer games, busy schedules, malling—you name it. The diversions are not going away. So the task of increasing children's vocabularies is ours, and we must do what we can to increase the volume and quality of children's reading and writing and develop more effective direct instructional strategies that influence vocabulary growth.

## How Vocabulary Grows

By age 6 or 7, children have acquired the phonology and grammar of their language. While refinements continue for a time thereafter, these two major features of language are acquired early. This does not mean that young children have acquired traditional school grammar nor the phonetic knowledge required to decode written language. Rather, they have gained speakers' knowledge of the grammar and phonology of their language. Thereafter, children need to acquire language skills associated with reading and writing. Vocabulary, or semantic knowledge, is different from syntactic and phonological knowledge of the language. It is the one major feature of language that continues to grow throughout life.

Children cannot learn new subject matter without a substantial general vocabulary and the specialized vocabularies crucial to every specialized field of knowledge.

Helping children acquire vocabulary is a major issue for teachers at every level and in every field. There are two major ways to increase children's vocabularies: reading and direct instruction. All other ways are associated, directly or indirectly, with these two instructional activities.

**Estimating Vocabulary Size.** The question of vocabulary size is fraught with difficulties. Researchers cannot follow people and record all of their conversations; they cannot read every word people have written; they cannot know every word understood through listening; they cannot monitor every printed word people know. Instead, researchers sample vocabulary knowledge, since actual vocabulary size cannot be measured. Through statistical techniques they analyze these samples. Researchers face three problems as they conduct this type of study: (1) what counts as a word, (2) what is the quality of word knowledge, and (3) what type of vocabulary is being estimated.

What counts as a word? For instance, do *run, runs, ran,* and *running* count as one word or four? This problem gets more complicated when considering root words or families of words. The roots *ann* and *enn* are used to form words such as *annual, biannual, biennial, anniversary, semiannual, perennial, millennium, centennial.* Should they count as one word (a word family) or eight separate words?

A second issue is the quality and depth of meaning associated with a word. How many meanings of a word has a person mastered? Are its subtleties and shades of meaning grasped? Depth of word knowledge is at least as important, if not more so, than breadth. For instance, *run* has over 100 definitions, and *set* has over 200. Nearly everyone has these two words in their vocabulary, but one person may know dozens of meanings for each word, whereas another may have a much smaller set. Qualitatively, such differences constitute vastly different vocabularies.

A third issue concerns reading, speaking, writing, and listening. Which type of vocabulary is best used to estimate one's store of known words? How are these different vocabularies related? Each type of vocabulary may be different in size and quality, each may play a different role in literacy, and this has implications for literacy instruction.

There are no definitive answers to these three issues. Still, recent studies of vocabulary show evidence of refined measuring techniques. Consequently, current estimates of vocabulary knowledge are reasonably accurate. Educators can assume that this information about vocabulary size and how it grows is sufficiently valid and reliable.

**Reading.** The best way to increase vocabulary is through reading (Mason, Stahl, Au, & Herman, 2003). Written language is rich in vocabulary—much richer than speech. This means, for instance, that a child who reads Rowling's first five Harry Potter novels, but sees none of the movies, will encounter a vastly richer vocabulary than a child who sees all five movies but does not read the books. Cunningham and Stanovich (2003) show that written text is lexically richer than oral language across almost any type of written text one can imagine. This is especially true of children's books. Children will encounter more high-quality words in literature, and with greater frequency, than they are ever likely to encounter in conversation, television, film, or other visual media.

Nagy and Anderson (1984) estimate that high school seniors know about 45,000 words and that children learn as many as 3,000 words per school year. This suggests that most words are learned through exposure to words in a variety of contexts, especially reading. Direct instruction cannot account for this learning rate, since it would require successfully teaching 166 words per school day, assuming a 180-day school year. Thus, as Laudner's research (1998) has shown, vocabulary growth occurs because of concentrated exposure to print. Cunningham and Stanovich (2003, 1997, 1990) conclude that print exposure is the most likely critical mechanism for vocabulary growth in school-age children. Other studies substantiate this conclusion (Miller and Gildea, 1987; Nagy & Anderson, 1984; Sternberg, 1985).

Therefore, reading is crucial in building vocabulary, and the more reading one does, the greater the growth. But what mechanisms promote vocabulary growth through reading? Part of the answer is volume of reading (Stanovich, 2000). Volume not only accounts for much vocabulary growth but is also a potential independent source of other cognitive differences among children. According to Cunningham and Stanovich, "exposure to print is efficacious regardless of the level of the child's cognitive and reading abilities" (2003, p. 671). They believe that even students with limited reading skills build vocabulary and cognitive structures through immersion in literacy activities. Stanovich (1986) has also shown that an early start in reading is an important predictor of lifetime literacy experience, regardless of the level of reading comprehension that an individual eventually attains. Taken together, these studies make a strong case for the importance of volume and variety of reading.

**Direct Instruction.** While most words are learned in oral and written language contexts, words are also learned through direct instruction (Stahl & Fairbanks, 1986). How is this to be done, given the large number of English words and uncertainty as to which ones are crucial? One answer is emphasis on word families. Nagy and Anderson (1984) estimate that 88,700 word families are discussed in chil-

*Though Calvin is working in a math context, Hobbes provides a social definition of the word* peck. *This mismatch confuses Calvin.*

dren's elementary and secondary textbooks. This is far too many to teach directly, since it would mean teaching nearly 7,000 words per school year, over 13 years. Nevertheless, since word families are created through word roots and prefixes, suffixes, and combining forms, it seems particularly valuable to teach structural analysis of words and to acquaint children with Greek and Latin word roots.

It is also clear that words must be encountered in the natural contexts of oral and written language. Direct instruction and encountering words in their natural written and oral context combine to enrich the acquisition of vocabulary. Cunningham and Stanovich (2003) agree with this conclusion in their survey of the literature on developing children's word knowledge. They suggest that direct vocabulary instruction and print exposure combine to create the best environment for maximizing the learning of new vocabulary.

## Strategies for Teaching Vocabulary

For an excellent source of activities with words, visit:
http://www.wordwizard.com

Though reading is the best indirect way to acquire vocabulary, direct instruction is also very useful. Five instructional strategies for developing children's vocabularies are described here: concept of definition, brainstorming, word maps, word histories, and graphic organizers. Additional suggestions are available in the Blue Pages at the end of this book.

**Concept of Definition**. Schwartz (1988) proposed a procedure for developing vocabulary through a process called concept of definition (CD). His strategy addresses the need for increasing word learning efficiency and provides a process that, once learned, can be applied independently. Such a strategy is crucial since context is often insufficient to reveal a word's meaning, as Schatz and Baldwin (1986) have shown. Concept of definition teaches children to map words by answering three questions: What is it? What is it like? What are some examples? The intent is not to determine the exact meaning of any particular word but to provide strategies, such as context or morphological analysis, to help in the process (Schwartz, 1988). The concept map in Figure 9.1 on page 358 illustrates how concept of definition works when mapping the word *dinosaur*.

**Brainstorming**. Brainstorming helps children reflect on a word, topic, or idea in an atmosphere that encourages all contributions, regardless of relevance. It facilitates divergent as well as convergent responses and can be adapted to many activities, such as reading, writing, or a vocabulary activity centering on a single word. Brainstorming also provides a forum for oral expression and oral language development. Children learn to verbalize their ideas in a friendly and respectful manner.

The teacher's role in brainstorming is to solicit contributions from children. This is done through questioning and through probing responses to questions: Do you have a favorite monster? What books have you read that have a friendly monster? Are all monsters friendly? What books or movies have you seen that have monsters? Are monsters real or imaginary? In the Field Notes feature on page 359, teacher Kelly Emmer tells how she used art and brainstorming prior to a descriptive writing experience. Figure 9.2 shows the descriptive words Jenny brainstormed for

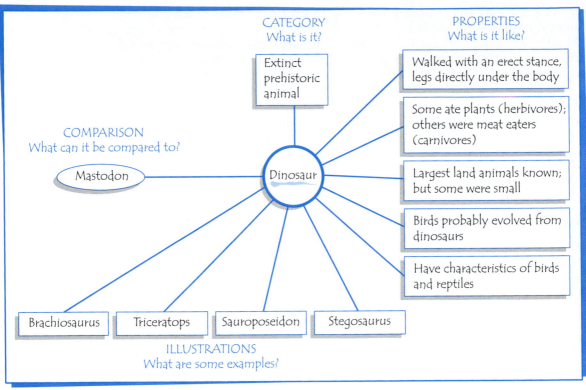

**Figure 9.1**

**Completed Concept Map for Dinosaurs**

her first draft—some of which are misspelled. Figure 9.3 shows the finished draft of her monster story. Notice that the words in her finished draft are now correctly spelled.

**Word Maps**. Mapping or webbing based on a word helps readers and writers explore and organize information and concepts associated with it. The resulting visual display shows how the various words are related. The first step is to choose a word connected to a topic or book with associated meanings that would be beneficial for students to study. Once a word has been chosen, have the children jot down all the words and ideas they know of that are related to the target word. After writing these on the board, group them into categories. Students may also choose to prepare their own word map. In some instances, young children simply write associated words or ideas without organizing them into categories—it is best to start with a simple concept map. The map in Figure 9.4 on page 360 resulted when third-grade children reflected on their study of cats.

**Word Histories**. Where do words come from? How do they acquire their meanings? Words have histories—etymologies, if you want a fancier word. Words aren't

## Field Notes
### Real-Life Experiences of a Classroom Teacher

**Kelly Emmer**

Children love writing and reading about monsters. This fall I read the book *Go Away, Big Green Monster!* to my students. We focused on ways authors describe monsters. After I had read the story, I had my students make up their own monsters. First, I modeled the making of my own. This encouraged my students to add ideas and details to their monsters. Once the monsters were finished, we moved into brainstorming for descriptive words, using a cluster map. While the brainstorming took place, I continuously brought the children back to the point of the activity—descriptive writing.

I read three excerpts from books with interesting descriptions. We discussed why authors use descriptive words and how their writing "shows" rather than just "tells" a story. These activities formed the prewriting part of the writing process. Following the brainstorming for descriptive words, we drafted our monster stories. Later, we worked on revising our drafts. Finally, I had my children talk about the monsters they made and the stories they wrote during our author's chair activity.

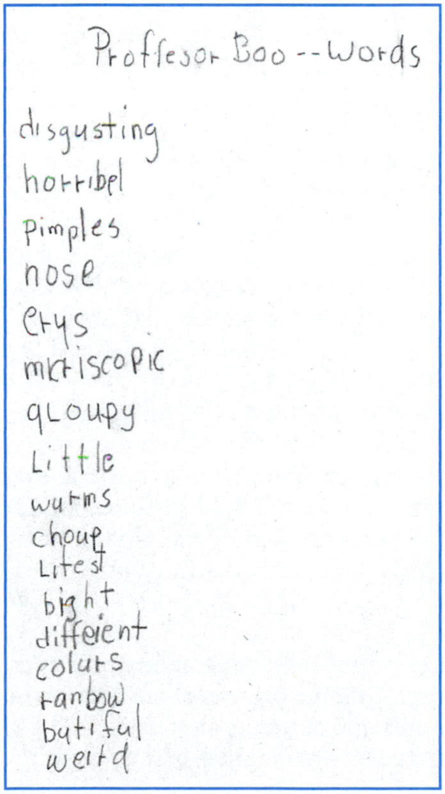

Proffesor Boo --Words

disgusting
horribel
pimples
nose
erys
mkriscopic
qloupy
Little
wurms
choup
Litest
bight
different
colurs
ranbow
butiful
weird

**Figure 9.2**

**Jenny's Brainstormed Words**

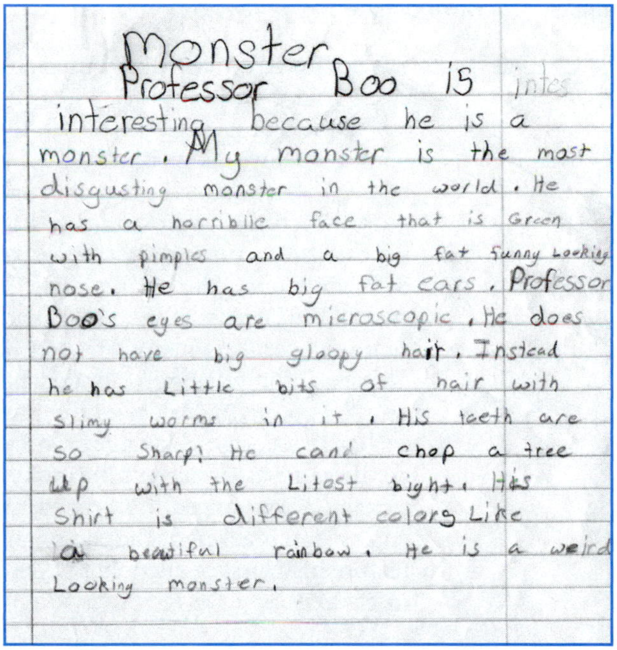

Monster

Professor Boo is intes interesting because he is a monster. My monster is the most disgusting monster in the world. He has a horrible face that is Green with pimples and a big fat funny Looking nose. He has big fat ears. Professor Boo's eyes are microscopic. He does not have big gloopy hair. Instead he has Little bits of hair with slimy worms in it. His teeth are so sharp! He cand chop a tree up with the Litest bight. His shirt is different colors Like a beautiful rainbow. He is a weird Looking monster.

**Figure 9.3**

**Final Draft of Jenny's Story**

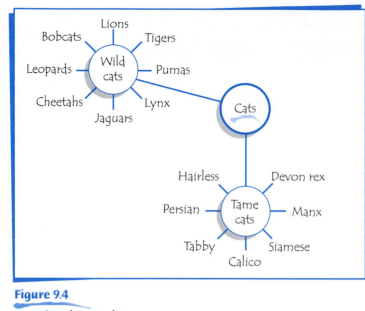

**Figure 9.4**

**Mapping the Word Cats**

discovered, like diamonds or gold; they're invented. William Shakespeare is undoubtedly the world's foremost inventor of words. The Oxford English dictionary attributes over 500 new words to Shakespeare's creative mind: *rival, countless, lackluster, honey-tongued, madcap, addiction, besmirch,* and *amazement,* to name a few. Writers sometimes invent words for their stories. Dr. Seuss invented the word *nerd.* Joseph Heller invented the term *catch-22* to describe predicaments in which things turn out badly no matter what you do. The original title of Heller's book was *Catch-18,* but he changed the title to *Catch-22* to avoid confusion with Leon Uris's recently published book, *Mila 18.* The term *catch-22* has become the most widely used allusion in American literature, according to Lederer (1991).

Some words originate to describe a behavior. *Phony* is one such word. In Ireland a con artist sometimes placed a *fawney ring,* or finger ring, in a public place, and waited for someone to pick it up. The ring had an imitation stone of little value, but the victim who picked it up thought otherwise. Suddenly, the con man would appear and persuade the victim to pay him to keep quiet about the find. Making off with the money, the con man left the sucker holding a fawney of little value. Garrison (1992) tells us that, "So many persons were defrauded that anything fake came to be called *fawney.* The original Irish word was *fainne,* in England it became *fawney,* and it was finally Americanized to *phony*" (p. 149).

A dictionary entry gives the history of a word—where it came from, how it is spelled in its original language, and what it originally meant, which may or may not be the same as its current meaning. If a word started out with a meaning that has remained unchanged, no original meaning is needed. Word histories are usually enclosed in brackets at the end of an entry. However, some dictionaries for children feature histories, or etymologies, set in special print with graphics, as in the entries in Figure 9.5.

**Graphic Organizers.** A graphic organizer can be used to arrange words and concepts in relation to the main ideas of a text. Graphic organizers are often used as a device for anticipating how vocabulary words and concepts are related. A list of key terms is presented prior to reading, and students make their best guess as to how the terms are related to the main idea of the text. This type of graphic organizer serves as a prediction activity. Graphic organizers can also be used during postreading activities to summarize and reinforce important concepts.

To create a graphic organizer for vocabulary, first, preview the text to identify new terms. If the text is long or complex, the number of terms can be overwhelming. In such cases, break the text into manageable sections, and identify relevant vocabulary one section at a time. The second step is to pare down the list so that it contains only the most essential terms. You should end up with main terms and subordinate terms. Set up the graphic organizer to reflect this hierarchy. For instance, you are now reading Chapter 9: "Word Study: Word Recognition, Dictionary Skills, and Vocabulary Knowledge." *Word study* is the main term discussed in this chapter, and the three subordinate ones are *word recognition, dictionary,* and *vocabulary.* Actually, each of these terms has associated subordinate terms as well, as shown in Figure 9.6 on page 362.

**were wolf** (wir´wŭlf´), (in folklore) a person who changes into a wolf at certain times. *n., pl.* **were wolves** (wir´wŭlvz´). Also, **werwolf**.

### WORD HISTORY

**werewolf**

*Werewolf* is from Old English *werwulf*, which comes from *wer,* meaning "man," and *wulf,* meaning "wolf."

**aghast** (ə gast´), struck with horror; filled with terror: *I was aghast when I saw the destruction caused by the earthquake. adj.*

### WORD HISTORY

**aghast**

*Aghast* comes from Middle English *agasten,* meaning "to frighten," and can be traced back to Old English *gāst,* meaning "ghost, spirit."

**Figure 9.5**

Sample Word Histories

## Section Summary: Vocabulary

1. Children's vocabularies grow in two major ways: through reading and direct instruction. All other ways are associated, directly or indirectly, with these two activities.

2. Strategies for teaching vocabulary include use of concept of definition, brainstorming, word maps, word histories, and graphic organizers. Concept of definition teaches children to map words by answering three questions: What is it? What is it like? What are some examples? Brainstorming helps children reflect on a word or topic and provides an atmosphere that encourages all contributions. Word maps help readers and writers organize information and ideas associated with the chosen word. The visual display shows how words are related. Dictionaries give word histories, telling

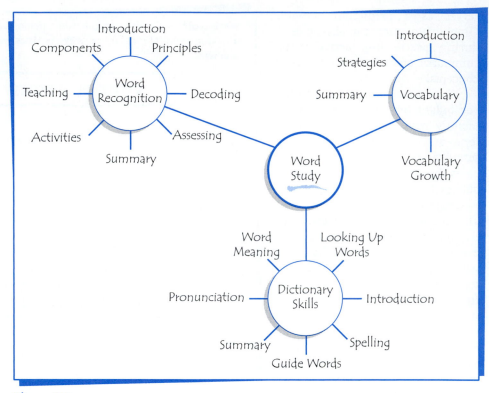

**Figure 9.6**

**Graphic Organizer for Word Study and Its Three Subordinate Topics**

where a word came from, how it is spelled in its original language, and what it originally meant. A graphic organizer arranges words and concepts in relation to the main idea of a text. It is often used with content materials before or after reading.

## Practical Teaching Ideas and Activities

*Teaching Tip*

**1.** *Put skills instruction in context.* Readers learn more about integrating multiple sources of information when skills and strategies are pointed out during purposeful, authentic reading and writing experiences. For example, a skills lesson on word ending chunks (rimes), can be demonstrated in a shared writing experience or pointed out in a shared reading text. Keep a portable wipe-off board handy in order to spontaneously respond to such teachable moments. Following the mini-lesson, this new learning needs to be applied to the original reading–writing context as well as other contexts.

## Technology for Vocabulary Instruction

There are many software packages on the market for vocabulary instruction. BEWARE! Many are nothing more than electronic versions of seat work that fail to provide any connection to real text. Much of what technology offers in vocabulary instruction imitates what teachers have done for a hundred years. Even so, technology combined with teacher expertise can produce well-developed activities for improving students' vocabularies.

Using commercial software, such as Crossword Weaver™, students can create crossword puzzles. They can then post their puzzles online at Vocabulary University (www.vocabulary.com) for students around the world to play. Students can use graphic organizer programs such as Inspiration® to analyze words in a variety of ways. An Internet search engine can facilitate a key word search of target words. Working in small groups and using the thesaurus of a word-processing program, students could rewrite a passage, collaboratively selecting synonyms to substitute for the original words. Then they can rewrite the passage. Students can also create poetry based on explorations in a thesaurus.

Though many websites provide lesson plans, worksheets, and suggestions, I recommend these two as exemplary models of what technology can provide:

1. *Merriam-Webster*® (http://www. merriamwebster.com/promos/ button/button.htm). This site provides a dictionary lookup button—for free. By following the simple directions at this website, you can add this helpful tool to the toolbar of your Internet browser. Whenever your students encounter an unfamiliar word at a website, they simply highlight the word and click the button. A dictionary entry for the word will appear.

2. *Visual Thesaurus by Plumb Design* (http:// thesaurus.plumbdesign.com/index.jsp). This is the place to visit if you need to understand a word. Users can type in any word and get a graphic representation of it. In addition to synonyms, this tool also provides the relationships between meanings. Fourteen categories of relationships (antonyms, synonyms, derivation, etc.) can be displayed. To fully understand the potential of this thesaurus, I suggest that you take the guided tour prior to your first use. This tool is a wonderful resource that can be used with students in upper elementary grades and higher.

Contributed by Lisa Kunkleman

**2.** *Search for letters, sounds, patterns, and words.* Provide interactive experiences of searching for particular print features. Students search their word wall for particular letters, sounds, spelling patterns, or high-frequency words. Read each word, and listen or look for the particular print feature. Write the words that apply to initiate a sort group. Develop a collaborative chart with examples taken from the word wall, shared reading and writing, and independent reading and writing experiences.

**3.** *Make picture sorts.* Make your own picture cards by pasting pictures from magazines, old worksheets, clip art, or other sources on index cards and laminating them. Children can attend to phonetic sounds through picture cards before they can actually read print. They may sort the cards based on beginning sound associations, word endings, vowels, rhyming, and syllables.

**4.** *Make a student-created ABC display.* Early elementary classrooms often display ABC bulletin boards for students to use as a resource when reading and writing. Rather than purchase a commercially produced one, consider creating one with students. On pieces of tagboard, print neatly or use the computer to create a display of the capital and lowercase form of each letter. Display these cards on a low bulletin board, or hang them around the perimeter of the room where students can easily see them. Invite children to cut out magazine pictures that correspond with the sound of each letter. Glue several pictures on each card.

**5.** *Create interactive word study charts.* The charts developed in word study minilessons should be displayed on the walls as a reference for use during reading and writing and as a connection to additional word study principles. These charts should outline specific principles and include several words demonstrating them. Revisit the charts regularly, adding additional examples and making further connections in word study. When students are engaged in independent reading and writing, encourage them to record applicable findings on self-adhesive notes. They can share them during sharing sessions.

**6.** *Teach decoding by analogy.* Teach students that when they come to a word they don't know, they can use known words or word parts to decode it. Show students that if they recognize a certain word or word part, they can use this knowledge to decode other words. For example, "If you you know how to read the word look, you can read the words book, took, and shook." Demonstrate this regularly with known words, and provide opportunities for students to apply this strategy in word study sessions.

**7.** *Make a decoding strategies bookmark.* Photocopy lists of decoding strategies onto tagboard. Cut out individual strips and laminate one for each student. Encourage independence by having students keep this bookmark in sight while reading to serve as a visual prompt. Send a bookmark home as well to support families as they discuss or reinforce the strategies.

See the Blue Pages at the back of the book and on the Companion Website for additional activities.

## ◄ Reflection and Summary

### Reflection

What an inheritance, the English language. Words are our army and navy, our suit of armor for debate. Words are the peacemakers that restore trust. Words display our wit and wisdom, foolishness and frivolity, decency and decadence. Words carry the colors of our character: red-hot ones for anger; vivid green ones for life; deep purple words for mood. A word for every color; a color for every word.

"Words, words, words." I wrote this recently, and a few days later learned that Shakespeare had written it centuries ago in a play. The more I read and think about words, the more I sense their power and glory. Sure enough: that's the title of a novel by Graham Greene: *The Power and the Glory*. It seems that every word, phrase, or sentence that might tumble from our tongues has had a previous life. Is there anything left to say or write that has not already been said or written? Perhaps not much. Yet we cannot cease speaking and writing because someone got there first. Readers and writers must have, use, and love words. They are our milk and honey in a sometimes barren land.

## Summary

1. Ten principles of word recognition instruction form the underlying philosophy of practice.
2. The components of word recognition include phonetic analysis, contextual analysis, structural analysis, and sight words.
3. A word recognition lesson can be planned in three steps: modeling and illustrating, identifying and recognizing, and applying and producing.
4. Just as children need strategies for decoding unknown words, teachers need strategies to help children in this task.
5. Activities for building word recognition skills include frequent reading in level-appropriate text, making words, using word sorts, creating word walls, and using invented spelling.
6. The three most important uses of general English language dictionaries are to determine word meaning, check spelling, and verify pronunciation.
7. Children need strategies for using dictionary definitions, since sorting out multiple meanings is especially difficult.
8. Asking children to check the spelling of a word in the dictionary is useful only after children have acquired basic word recognition and spelling skills.
9. Guide words help children discover whether the word they are trying to locate can be found on a given dictionary page.
10. Dictionaries have a pronunciation key that tells what sound each pronunciation symbol stands for. Children may need help in confirming the pronunciation of a word that is new to them.
11. Children's vocabularies grow in two major ways: through reading and direct instruction. All other ways are associated, directly or indirectly, with these two activities.
12. Strategies for teaching vocabulary include use of concept of definition, brainstorming, word maps, word histories, and graphic organizers.

## ◄ Questions to Challenge Your Thinking

1. What is the distinction between phonics and word recognition?
2. What is analytic phonics, and how is it different from synthetic phonics?
3. Why connect word recognition instruction to meaningful reading experiences?
4. What is structural analysis? How is it different from phonics?
5. What are sight words? How are they used in early reading instruction?
6. How can invented spelling help develop word recognition skills?
7. What must a child already know in order to use a dictionary effectively?
8. How does volume of reading influence the growth of vocabulary?
9. How is direct vocabulary instruction different from indirect instruction?
10. Why is it so difficult to measure vocabulary size?

# A Case Study

Read the passage in Figure 9.7, and examine each miscue. There are 100 words in this passage; thus each miscue is equal to 1% out of a possible 100%. Refer to the section on assessment of word recognition in context for help (page 335). When you have read the passage, complete the exercise and then answer the questions that follow.

## Examine the Miscues

1. Decide how many miscues fall into each category: substitution, omission, mispronunciation, insertion, reversal, or aided.
2. Examine each miscue qualitatively, and decide whether it is a surface or meaning miscue.
3. Calculate the two scores: total miscue score and adjusted miscue score.

## Categories of Miscues

1. Substitution miscue _____
2. Omission miscues _____
3. Mispronunciation miscues _____
4. Insertion miscues _____
5. Reversal _____
6. Aided _____

## Surface Miscues and Meaning Miscues

The miscues are numbered from 1 to 10. Classify each miscue as either a surface miscue or a meaning miscue and explain the reason for your decision.

---

(1) *screams*
The sun streams in the large kitchen window, as I sit drinking coffee and eating (2) scrambled eggs and toast. The wind is kicking up, and leaves are tumbling across (3) *clouds* (4) my lawn. I look out the window and see a dark cloud approaching, perhaps a thunderstorm later this morning. Morning is a blessing to me. I love the dark (5) green forest that looms in the distance. I feel snug and safe in my own (6) little house. But (7) I keep a careful eye out for the enemy. I know they can appear at any (8) *minute* and (9) (10) moment, but I am ready to do battle.

### Coding Symbols

| | | |
|---|---|---|
| 1. Substitution | Write the substituted word above the text word. *test* | |
| 2. Omission | Circle the omitted word. | |
| 3. Mispronunciation | Write the word phonetically above the text word. *ā bōv* | |
| 4. Insertion | Use the caret and write the inserted word. *a* | |
| 5. Reversal | Use a wavy line to show the reversal of word order. | |
| 6. Aided | Write the letter *A* above the word you supplied. *A* | |

**Figure 9.7**

**Case Study Passage: Ten Miscues**

| | Surface Miscue | Meaning Miscue | Reason |
|---|---|---|---|
| 1. | _____ | _____ | _____ |
| 2. | _____ | _____ | _____ |
| 3. | _____ | _____ | _____ |
| 4. | _____ | _____ | _____ |
| 5. | _____ | _____ | _____ |
| 6. | _____ | _____ | _____ |
| 7. | _____ | _____ | _____ |
| 8. | _____ | _____ | _____ |
| 9. | _____ | _____ | _____ |
| 10. | _____ | _____ | _____ |

### Final Scores for Word Recognition in Context

1. Total miscue score     100% minus _____     equals _____
2. Adjusted miscue score     100% minus _____     equals _____

1. How might this information be useful in understanding a child's strengths and weaknesses in word recognition?

2. What additional information is needed that miscue analysis does not provide?

## ◄Revisit the Anticipation Guide

Return to the Anticipation Guide in the chapter opener, and review your original responses to the questions. Complete the guide again, and then consider these questions.

1. Did you change your mind about any items? Why or why not?
2. Think of one major idea in this chapter with which you disagree. Explain why, and suggest alternative ideas.
3. Think of one major idea with which you agree. Explain why, and suggest alternative ways of thinking about it.
4. This chapter has stressed the importance of teaching word recognition. Do you agree or disagree with this emphasis? Why?

## VideoWorkshop Extra!

If your instructor ordered a package including VideoWorkshop, go to Chapter 9 of the Companion Website (www.ablongman.com/cramer1e) and click on the VideoWorkshop button. Follow the instructions for viewing the appropriate video clip and completing the accompanying exercise. Watch the Companion Website for access to a new interactive teaching portal, My Lab School, currently under construction.

## A Philosophy of Writing Process

**I**n the movie *Casablanca, Claude Rains, playing the prefect of police, is "shocked, shocked" to learn of corruption in Casablanca. I hope you will not be shocked to know that I sometimes ignore the precepts of the writing process. For instance, sometimes I start with drafting and do the planning later. Writing process stages (prewriting, drafting, revision, publishing or sharing) are a sensible and valid way to conceptualize the operations and activities of writers, but they were never meant to suggest that all writing moves in a straight line from prewriting to publishing. Actually, there is no such thing as a single writing process, except in a rhetorical sense. Among writers, one can observe similarities of process: operations and activities that are recursive; continuous development that involves change. Writers also have their own writing process, procedures peculiar to their purpose, style, and habits. No lockstep set of procedures must be applied to all writing all the time. True process writing honors, even encourages, individual differences.*

# 10 The Writing Process in a Workshop Environment

## Big Ideas for Chapter 10

1. Graves suggests six principles for effective writing: writing time, modeling, ownership, conferencing, revising, and sharing or publishing.

2. There are four writing process stages: prewriting, drafting, revising, and sharing or publishing: Prewriting is the mental and physical preparation prior to drafting. Drafting is getting ideas on paper quickly and effi-

ciently. Revising covers any changes in written text, large or small. There are four revision operations: adding, deleting, rearranging, and substituting. Publishing and sharing provide incentive and audience for writing.

3. A writing workshop is a community of writers (teacher and children) working together in an informal work environment to produce written texts using the writing process.

## ❖ Anticipation Guide

*Consider the following statements, and determine whether you agree or disagree with each. Save your answers, and revisit this guide at the end of this chapter.*

1. Children should write at least 40 minutes, four times a week.              agree   disagree
2. Teachers should not assign writing topics.                                  agree   disagree
3. Writing starts with planning and ends with publishing.                      agree   disagree
4. Good teaching is crucial for developing good writers.                       agree   disagree
5. Instruction in writing seldom works.                                        agree   disagree
6. Teachers should model writing for their children.                           agree   disagree
7. Revision is the most crucial writing skill.                                 agree   disagree
8. First-graders can learn the fundamentals of revision.                       agree   disagree
9. The writing workshop works best in an informal environment.                 agree   disagree
10. Instructional response is crucial for successful writing.                  agree   disagree

A writer needs three things, experience, observation, and imagination, any two of which, at times any one of which, can supply the lack of the others.

—*William Faulkner*

## A Literacy Story

The librarian accepted the library card from the man standing at the circulation desk and read the accompanying note: "Dear Madam: Will you please let this n—— boy have some books by H. L. Mencken?" The note was forged by Richard Wright, a young black man on a mission to obtain books from a library he knew would not lend books to a black man. Wright had borrowed a library card from a fellow worker, hoping by this subterfuge to obtain more of Mencken's works. Wright had read *A Book of Prefaces* by Mencken and was astounded to discover that "yes, this man was fighting, fighting with words. He was using words as a weapon, using them as one would use a club. Could words be weapons? Well, yes, for here they were. Then, maybe, perhaps, I could use them as a weapon?"

Wright forged more notes; his trips to the library became more frequent. Reading had grown into an insatiable appetite, more essential to nourishing his mind than food had become to nourishing his body. He carried books to his job, wrapped in newspaper. He endured the teasing that came from fellow workers.

"Boy, what are you reading those books for?"

"Oh, I don't know, sir."

"That's deep stuff you're reading, boy."

"I'm just killing time, sir."

"You'll addle your brains if you don't watch out."

Wright was born in 1908. His grandparents had been slaves. A novelist and short story writer, he often protested white people's treatment of blacks in his writing. Wright came to writing through reading. Reading fueled his passion to fight with words, helped him see what was possible, and opened new avenues of feeling and thought. Reading provided the fuel that lit the fire of Wright's need to use words as weapons against the injustice of racism.

## A MATTER OF STANDARDS

### Writing

**Standard 5:** Students employ a wide range of strategies as they write and use different writing process elements appropriately to communicate with different audiences for a variety of purposes.

Standard 5 emphasizes the importance of the writing process. Children need strategies to comprehend texts produced by others; likewise they need strategies to produce their own texts. A fundamental tenet of writing is that substantial practice is essential. Writing models are also needed, and they are provided through teacher modeling and

access to literature. Children need to know the stages of the writing process. Equally important, they must learn to value the importance of the written product. Through the writing process, children learn to plan, draft, revise, and share their writing with audiences inside and outside of their classrooms. Writing skill evolves from scribbling to the complex processes involved in creative and critical writing. As children mature, they need to learn the conventions of writing within the context of meaningful writing. This chapter describes how Standard 5 can be implemented for children from kindergarten through high school.

There are two important terms in the title of this chapter: *writing process* and *workshop environment*. Writing process suggests three things: a particular method, certain operations, and a continuing development of writing that involves change (Kane, 1988). Writing process emphasizes the operations by which writing is accomplished, not just the product. Sometimes children have their own sense of writing process. A fourth-grader offered this definition: "It's like you take a piece of your brain out and put it on paper."

Writing process is organized in recursive stages through which writing typically progresses: prewriting, drafting, revising, and publishing. A recursive task does not occur in a straightforward linear fashion, but moves back and forth among stages in whatever sequence suits the writer's needs. A writer may begin by choosing a topic and researching it (prewriting), draft a few pages while simultaneously revising elements of the draft (drafting and revising), and then return to collecting and organizing information and ideas (prewriting). This back-and-forth movement is natural.

> Thomas Kane (1988) describes the writing process in these words: "Writing in its broad sense—as distinct from simply putting words on paper—has three steps: thinking about it, doing it, and doing it again (and again and again, as often as time will allow and patience will endure)."

The term *workshop environment* conveys the idea that writing takes place in an informal working atmosphere. All participants pursue the same broad objective—learning to write. At the same time, individual participants pursue more narrow objectives related to personal writing projects. The workshop is led and organized by the teacher. Part of the teacher's workshop time is devoted to specific teaching objectives, such as minilessons, but most time is devoted to actual writing—participants cycling their writing projects through the stages of prewriting, drafting, revising, and publishing. No two writing workshops are likely to look exactly the same, nor should they. Throughout the workshop, the teacher is the indispensable listener, modeler, coach, and choreographer as children dance to the music of their writing muse. Teachers develop their own workshop plans, organize their own activities, evolve their own styles. But in broad outline, they share similar ideas of how to implement a particular theory or writing development in their classrooms.

## Graves's Writing Principles

Graves (1983) brought about a dramatic change in writing instruction by emphasizing not the product, but the process by which writing competence is acquired. Traditionalists, on the other hand, value correctness of the product while undervaluing the process needed to create it. The differences between process and product approaches to writing are real, but they should not be overstated. Traditionalists want a quality product, but they lack a theory of writing capable of accomplishing their goal. They stress correctness without a theory for achieving it. Graves supplied the theory, but it does not automatically lead to quality writing. Effective implementation of writing process is crucial; if this fails, the result is not appreciably better than the outcomes of the traditional approach.

A quality product—not process—is the goal of writing. Process is the business of writers; product is the business of readers. Process should lead to a better product; if it does not, it has failed. A sound theory of writing should promote procedures that lead to the best possible product. The traditional approach overstressed correctness, and this led to insufficient attention to content. The process approach can, if attention is not paid, lead to insufficient attention to correctness. Overemphasis on product can destroy good writing; so can overemphasis on process. This chapter discusses how the writing process can be implemented so that the product is not shortchanged.

Donald Graves, in my view, has done more than anyone to popularize process writing. Murray (1985), Calkins (1994), Atwell (1998), and others have also been influential. Key principles were first articulated as a coherent system in Graves's classic book, *Writing: Teachers and Children at Work* (1983). Here are six principles of process writing that Graves describes in his books and other writings.

### Writing Time

According to Graves (1994), children should write for at least 40 minutes a day, four times a week. "If students are not engaged in writing at least four days out of five, and for a period of thirty-five to forty minutes, beginning in first grade, they will have little opportunity to learn to think through the medium of writing. Three days a week are not sufficient" (p. 104). Graves believes that those who do not write daily cannot get into the rhythm of writing since writing rehearsal, thinking about writing, and actual writing will be diminished when writing time is insufficient.

### Modeling

Models have a powerful influence on writing. Teachers should talk about writing, be a primary audience, read books aloud, talk about authors, suggest strategies, and

PEANUTS reprinted by permission of United Feature Syndicate, Inc.

*Snoopy's idea is good. He'll model his story on Laura Numeroff's lovely book* If You Give a Mouse a Cookie.

establish a writing atmosphere. But nothing beats the simple device of writing with children. Writing a story or poem and sharing it marks you as a participant, not merely a spectator. No other idea, strategy, or device can beat writing with children.

I ask my graduate students to write, and I write with them. Initially, they do not want to do this. But when I write with them, their reluctance evaporates. Teachers who begin to write with their children will be surprised and pleased when they discover its power. There are many ways to model writing: write at your desk now and then while children are writing; write on chart paper, transparencies, or the board to illustrate writing skills; bring in a poem you have started but not finished and ask children's advice; write a lead for a story and have your children finish the story; write a line or two of a poem and ask for contributions. No other strategy builds credibility more effectively than teachers writing with children.

## Ownership

Graves (1983, 1994) believes that children must own their writing. Encouraging children to choose their own topics and pursue their own ideas places ownership in their hands. "When children write every day they don't find it as difficult to choose topics. If a child knows she will write again tomorrow, her mind can go to work pondering her writing topics. Choosing a topic once a week is difficult. The moment for writing suddenly arrives and the mind is caught unprepared" (Graves, 1994, p. 106).

To read about a mother's successful effort to instill independence and a sense of ownership in a reluctant young writer, her son, using word processing, see "Talking to Write: A Mother and Son at Home," by E. B. Kelso, 2000, *Language Arts, 77*(5), 414–419.

While it is important to allow as much topic choice as possible, it is desirable for teachers to retain co-ownership over topic selection, as long as children are allowed some choices. Co-ownership balances the teacher's responsibility to achieve instructional goals with children's need to own their writing. Allowing students choice within assigned genres, goals, and subject matter honors these two principles. Graves has modified his earlier views on topic choice, allowing for more assigned writing than he had earlier recommended. He now believes

## Writing and the Computer

The writing workshop approach provides many possibilities for teachers to use technology. With careful planning, technology can help teachers provide students with a supportive environment for developing the skills needed to become effective, confident writers. Although the most commonly used technology in writing process is word processing, over the past decade computer programs have become much more advanced and can provide other excellent opportunities to support and enhance student writing. For example, graphic organizer programs like Inspiration® and Kidspiration® can help students with brainstorming and organizing ideas. Additionally, they can be used for identifying main ideas and supporting details, retelling a story, sequencing, outlining, identifying story elements, creating cause and effect, comparing and contrasting, and word recognition. Here are some ways the computer can aid the student writer when teacher guidance is available.

- Students can easily utilize the Internet as a research tool.
- By having students turn off their monitors and freewrite, they are able to focus on thoughts, not errors.
- Grammar and spell checks can reinforce learning of grammatical concepts by alerting students to mistakes and then providing a list of possible solutions.
  - The ease of cut and paste functions makes students more likely to rewrite and edit their work.
  - Teachers can extend word-processing skills by going beyond simple text and including functions such as graphics and the formatting and styling of text.
- Publishing programs allow students to compose in a variety of formats, such as greeting cards, newsletters, brochures, business cards, faxes, flyers, memos, invitations, and letters on stationery.
- A computer makes writing look neat and professional.
- The possibility for students to communicate with an authentic audience through class webpages, e-mail, or publishing their work online can motivate them to write more and take more interest in improving their written work.

Potential obstacles such as student competency and availability of computers will determine how you use technology in the writing workshop. The thoughtful integration of these tools can motivate students to write and revise more. Although technology does not guarantee better student writing, it has the potential to enhance its quality.

Contributed by Lisa Kunkleman

that "Sometimes topic assignments are helpful and even necessary. Students do make bad choices and experience writer's block, or they need to shift to new topics after exhausting their usual few" (p. 108). Integration of writing time with subject matter (science, social studies, math) helps relieve the time crunch most teachers feel as they work to cover the full curriculum.

## Conferencing

Children know things about their writing that teachers cannot know until conversations take place: "The purpose of the writing conference is to help children teach you about what they know so that you can help them more effectively with their writing" (Graves, 1994, p. 59). Conferences are dynamic, according to Graves's model. Some are formally scheduled and pertain to predetermined objectives; others are roving and spontaneous, providing on-the-spot guidance. Whether teacher-directed or peer-directed, conferences provide an outside audience for writing, and this is crucial. Most conferences should be held while writing is in progress; Graves calls conferencing when writing is finished "an autopsy."

See "Conversations Among Writers in Author's Circles," by S. K. Villaume and E. G. Brabham, 2001, *Reading Teacher,* 54(5).

## Revising

Writers are seldom able to produce their best writing without creating successive drafts. They help writers discover *what* they have to say and *how* to say it. Graves says, "Children don't suddenly begin to revise during writing time. They need guidance" (1994, p. 226). Skill in revising is achieved through instruction and practice. The goal is to get children to understand that the most important revision question is this: How can I make my writing better? This question must replace the destructive one that children are often implicitly taught: What's wrong with my writing? This approach leads to correcting minor faults; it does not encourage discovery of what to say or how to say it. Negative thinking about writing puts an unhealthy spin on revision and encourages a focus on surface errors rather than reconsideration of meaning.

## Postwriting: Sharing and Publishing

Sharing and publishing writing are central to Graves's philosophy: "What authors of any age need most is attentive listeners" (1994, p. 133). Sharing and publishing can take many forms. They can occur in small groups or whole class sessions; they can involve posting writing on a bulletin board; they can mean publishing books, newsletters, or magazines; they can take the form of communication on the Internet. There are many ways to share and publish writing; teachers and students should try out many alternatives.

## Section Summary: Graves's Writing Principles

1. Children should write at least 40 minutes a day four times a week.
2. Writing models are crucial, and teachers and literature are the main models.
3. Self-selected topics help provide writers with a sense of ownership of their work.
4. Conferences help writers understand their writing strengths and weaknesses.
5. Revision is central to effective writing.
6. Audience for writing is a motivator. Author's chair and publishing centers are effective ways to give writers access to audiences.

# The Stages of the Writing Process

Typically, four stages of writing are identified: prewriting, drafting, revising, and sharing or publishing. And a case can be made that polished pieces of writing have moved through stages approximately consistent with the designated names. But something has gone wrong with our thinking about this. We have come to think of the stages inflexibly, as a straight-line process, moving invariably from prewriting to publication. It's time for a careful reality check. It is inaccurate and inflexible to think that all writing must move through the four stages. Lots of writing doesn't fit this mold; the most obvious example is informal writing, such as e-mail. Millions of e-mail messages are sent every day, with no serious concern for stage theory. Furthermore, plenty of formal writing does not fit stage theory. Children and adults write poems every day that do not, and often need not, move through the traditional stages. Stages of writing should match the author and the author's purpose, not some inflexible notion of how writing *must* be done.

A second notion that deserves reinforcement is the recursive nature of the writing process, as noted earlier. Writers plan and draft; writers draft and then plan; writers draft, revise, and then plan. In other words, writers write the Frank Sinatra way—*they do it their way.*

Nevertheless, it is instructive to understand the tasks that take place at the various stages of the writing process and helpful activities and operations to support certain pieces of writing at each stage. The order the stages occur in is up to the writer.

## Prewriting

Prewriting describes the mental preparation and the physical activities involved in planning a piece of writing. Prewriting involves brainstorming, laying plans, and collecting and organizing ideas and information prior to and sometimes during drafting. This section describes concepts, activities, and strategies that are crucial to planning effective prewriting experiences.

**Rehearsal.** Writing rehearsal is the mental preparation for writing and may occur at any time prior to actually writing. Of course, it occurs in the spaces and pauses between sentences or paragraphs or sections. Rehearsal is unlikely to occur, however, unless certain conditions prevail, especially frequency of writing scheduled in a predictable fashion—every day at a particular time, for example.

Much prewriting is invisible because it transpires in the writer's head. Rehearsal takes place during moments or months, for hours or even for years before writers put a word on paper. They refine and reject, nurse and nudge their topics until they are ready to write. Rehearsal sometimes involves broad issues such as choosing a topic or plot. More often it deals with narrower issues such as rehearsing a lead or planning a story event. It may involve making notes or doodling. Once writing has commenced, rehearsal of characters, conversation, ideas, or persuasive arguments continues throughout the construction of a piece. Rehearsal is a habit that evolves as one gains experience in writing. You can support its development by talking about your own rehearsal habits and by encouraging children to talk about their rehearsal experiences.

**Research and Information**. Research is crucial to prewriting. Writers conduct research in libraries or on the Internet, by searching through books, journals, and magazines, or by talking to people until they have located useful sources. They may make notes and organize them into maps or outlines to guide their writing. There is constant interaction between mental rehearsal for writing and physical preparation for it. Children need time to grow into these skills. But it is seldom too early for writers to learn about research.

Interesting information is the straw that binds the mortar of writing. As writers engage with it, interest in the topic accelerates during prewriting. When the mind is saturated with information on a topic, drafting also flows. Gathering information is necessary for both fiction and expository writing, though there is a tendency to think that it is relevant only for the latter. Books such as *Sarah, Plain and Tall* nicely illustrate how writers research and use information about historical context in fiction. Literature-based reading provides authentic literary models that can help generate ideas during prewriting.

**Thinking Time**. Just as a field produces better crops when it lies fallow for a season, so writing may be enriched by allowing time for an idea to lie fallow before it is developed into a story, poem, or essay. It takes judgment to recognize when a writing idea needs time to ripen, when it is simply unfruitful and should be abandoned for a new topic, or when a writer is simply stalling. Delay can sometimes be an excuse for not writing at all, but good writing is seldom produced on command. Teachers can help students use thinking time wisely.

**Choosing Interesting Topics**. Most writing topics should be self-selected. Powerful writing does not stem from a teacher's bag of motivating topics, even if they are innovative and interesting. Powerful writing stems from a desire to make a personal statement. Children's best writing deals with what they know and what they care about. Encouraging children to make their own choices results in more and better writing. Forcing topics on children without considering interest, knowledge, or personal commitment is unlikely to elicit the best they have to offer (Graves, 1983, 1994). Still, at early stages of writing, children need help in choosing topics. Brainstorming sessions to produce a list of topics on the board are a good way to begin. Have children choose topics from the list to add to their own topic lists.

Interest in a given topic is the key to generating good writing. It is sparked by an interaction between curiosity and growing knowledge. Just as gas fuels an engine, so interest fuels the writer. Interest may not arise spontaneously, so teachers must find ways to pique curiosity, such as discussion, reading aloud, independent reading, films, plays, music, drama, dance, and art. These activities can lay the groundwork for other prewriting activities.

**Writer's Journal**. A writer's journal is a notebook for recording ideas, observations, and information. A journal can be a gold mine. During prewriting, one can enter the mine looking for nuggets: topics, scraps of conversation, ideas for stories. A journal can be informal, simply a place where dated notes are kept. More formal journals are useful but more difficult to manage.

**Audience.** Some writers write to please themselves; William Faulkner is an example. Others imagine a broader audience. Children can learn to please their teacher, but their sense of audience may not expand unless they have additional readers. Children learn to write for others when writing is shared within a writing community. Peer conferences help writers learn how others perceive their work. The following suggestions can help develop audience awareness.

- Teach children how to ask audience-centered questions of their writing, such as these: Who is going to read my story? What will they find interesting? Are my ideas clear? Have I chosen the right words?
- Have children work in small groups to listen to one another's writing.
- Have children write the same story for two different audiences. Fifth-graders might write a story for their classmates and then rewrite it for kindergarten children.
- Have children imagine they are writing a description of the fall colors for a sighted and unsighted audience.
- Have children write separate persuasive letters to Mom and Dad or Grandmother and Grandfather. Children know well that what appeals to one parent or grandparent does not work with another.

**Choosing a Writing Form.** Form influences content and organization. Third-grade children include different kinds of information and present it differently when asked to write about the same topic in a story versus a report (Langer, 1985). Exposure to different forms adds variety and gives children opportunities to see how purpose and audience are related to form. For example, if a rap is used to present a message about peace, writers will have to consider that this form may appeal differently to teenagers than to adults. Table 10.1 lists traditional writing forms as well as less common ones.

**Strategies to Facilitate Prewriting.** Prewriting strategies should stimulate ideas and motivate writing. They should expand knowledge and develop thinking. They should give access to knowledge stored in memory and add new knowledge. Strategies should fit children's age, writing experience, purpose, and the demands of the form. Here are some possibilities.

- Have students use art to tap into ideas. Drawing makes ideas flow. It is a valuable prewriting activity for primary as well as older children.
- Organize opportunities for peer talk, and encourage children to talk to themselves as they plan writing—a barely audible whispering.
- Use books or other texts to stimulate thinking. Reading, aloud or independently, piques interest and provides authentic information about writing in general as well as particular subject matter.
- Read excerpts from literature to help children understand how writers make observations about their subjects. Accurate observation improves writing. Urge children to include such details in prewriting activities.

**Table 10.1**

**Traditional and Nontraditional Writing Forms**

**Traditional Forms**

| | | | |
|---|---|---|---|
| autobiographies | invitations | plays | biographies |
| poems | book reports | letters | reports |
| mysteries | reviews | essays | myths |
| fables | news stories | skits | fairy tales |
| stories | folktales | interviews | tall tales |
| personal narratives | journals | books | speeches |

**Less Common Forms**

| | | | |
|---|---|---|---|
| advertisements | greeting cards | proverbs | recipes |
| jokes | raps | bumper stickers | maps |
| cartoons | menus | riddles | comic strips |
| obituaries | song lyrics | editorials | posters |

- Urge students to do some preliminary research. The mecca of the intellectual life is the library, though the Internet is catching up with it. It is not a waste of writing time to teach children to use research resources.
- Have students map their ideas. Mapping illustrates pictorially how topics and subtopics are related. For example, a story map shows how story problem, setting, characters, events, and resolution are related.
- Interviewing provides information and ideas that can jump start writing. Older children can work in pairs. Show children how to prepare questions; then write about the experience.
- Use brainstorming, which allows a range of creative ideas to emerge, to generate topics and details. Remember the rule that no idea will be rejected or criticized.
- Use factstorming, the quick calling out of facts related to a topic, to produce an array of subtopics and details that could be used in a piece of writing. Unlike brainstorming, this process elicits factual information only.

## Drafting

Frank O'Connor said, "I don't give a hoot what the writing's like, I write any sort of rubbish which will cover the main outlines of the story; then I can begin to see it." Drafting is getting black on white as rapidly and as fluently as possible. Unlike revising, it is not concerned with precision. Drafters splash words across the page as boldly as an abstract expressionist splashes paint on a canvas. Drafting must be free of constraints. Freedom to draft means not worrying about spelling, punctuation, or grammar—or even content and meaning. This may seem counterproductive, but it is not. Drafting involves a search for meaning, not a guarantee of it. A writer may only vaguely sense the outlines of a topic, and this is what Frank

*Evan writes in his journal every day. He's developing a chapter book about wolves.*

O'Connor meant when he spoke of putting down "any sort of rubbish." The idea is to get something tangible on the page and work from that concrete beginning.

Many writers find drafting more difficult than revising. This is not surprising. Beginnings are hard. But writers have discovered ways to facilitate drafting, although it may never be easy. Children draft more easily when they have spent time getting ready to write. But then, like all writers, they must face the blank page and start. You can help children do this with confidence by cultivating conditions to facilitate fluency in drafting.

**Classroom Libraries.** When you're ready to write a first draft, you must have information in your head and at your fingertips. Sources of information should be available in the classroom as well as in the school and community. There is no substitute for a classroom library, modest though it may be. My first classroom library, when I taught fifth-grade in a rural community in upstate New York, came from many sources: parents and children donated books and magazines; I found books at garage sales and in used book stores; I joined book clubs to keep our library current. We cut up old textbooks and put the stories and articles in folders. Most important, the school library allowed each teacher to borrow books for classroom use. We appreciated our own library because we had cobbled it together through our own efforts.

**Modeling**. Show me and I'll remember. Tell me and I'll forget. Children can learn best by seeing how it's done. Model ways of obtaining information from print and interviews. Present simulated interviews before sending children off to do the real thing. Take a book and show children how to use the index, table of contents, headings, pictures, or graphs. Explain how and why you skim before you read closely. Take a few notes and explain how to translate notes into written text as paraphrases or quotes. After modeling, let children practice the skills you have demonstrated.

**Individual Styles**. Writers often stop during drafting to revise. Others stop only after they have completed a draft. Either approach can work well. It is sometimes recommended that a draft be completed without interruption, and this is a good idea for some writers, but others cannot write this way. They have more success drafting a little, revising a little, drafting some more, revising some more.

**Use of Time**. Simone de Beauvoir once lamented, "A day in which I don't write leaves a taste of ashes." Certainly this is an appropriate standard for a professional writer, but should children learn a similar one? Not quite. But children must write often if they are to develop writing skill. Pliny's advice to writers was "Never a day without a line." Of course, teaching circumstances do not always permit realizing this ideal. Still, teachers should strive to have children write every day for 40 to 60 minutes, particularly if they are conducting writing workshops.

**Drafting Leads**. Creating a strong beginning for a story can be quite challenging. Ms. Elson, a fifth-grade teacher, suggested to Mark that he might try *several* leads to his story "Nikki and Me." Mark returned a half hour later and said, "Ms. Elson, here are the *seven* leads you wanted me to write." The leads Mark wrote are a superb example of the flexibility and imagination children possess, as well as the benefits of creating more than one draft of part of a piece of writing. Like most drafts, they have minor errors that can be fixed later.

To read about teaching students to write strong leads, see *Teaching Writing with Picture Books as Models,* by R. Jursted and M. Koutras, 2000.

1. One bright, sunny day I walked into my mom's room and asked her, "Mom, did I ever do something funny as a baby?"
2. "Mom, did I ever do something, that was real funny, as a baby?" I asked curiously. "Why yes. Two things pop up from the top of my head."
3. There are two stories about me as a baby that are real funny.
4. One morning I crawled up to my dog's food, grasped as much as I could, and ate it.
5. I was sitting next to our big recliner resting. After awhile, I wanted to go somewhere else in the house. I tried to get up, but I couldn't. I struggled and struggled.
6. Ellerey and I were in my room shooting at the basket hooked up on my closet. "Say El, do you know anything you did, as a baby, that was funny?" "No," he replied. "Well I do. You want me to tell you about them?" "Sure," he said anxiously.
7. I was lying in bed trying to go to sleep. "I'll never be able to fall asleep!" I

whispered. I rested for awhile and then said to myself: "I might as well try what mom said to do. She always said, "If you can't fall asleep, think of something funny or happy." So I started to think about two funny things I did when I was a baby.

**Using Notes**. Writing often requires note taking. When children are writing book reports, articles, and essays based on research, remind them to review their notes just prior to starting a draft. An opening sentence can often be taken from information contained in notes. Quotations, examples, or arresting facts are excellent ways to begin a draft. You can illustrate how this works by taking a student's notes, sorting through them, and finding an interesting fact or quotation with which to begin a report. Then have children sort their notes into several categories for possible leads. Well-organized notes can also form a map for writing the body of a report, story, or other piece.

**Discovery Drafts**. Drafting can be difficult, even scary. Starting with a discovery draft can ease the writer into the process. Also called a test draft, zero draft, and practice draft, this step involves plunging ahead no matter what gaps are left when it is done. Exploration is the goal; staggering and stumbling are allowed. Discovery

"All my life I've been frightened at the moment I sit down to write."

—Gabriel García Marquez, Colombian novelist

drafts help writers uncover what they know or do not know, find out whether the topic is too broad or too narrow, encounter a surprise or two (pleasant or unpleasant) that may inform further writing. Most young writers do not think of first drafts as experimental but rather as permanent and complete. You might entice young writers into the arena of continuing discovery through this type of drafting.

**Getting Psyched**. Prior to a big game, many athletes use rituals and routines to get themselves mentally prepared to compete. Such rituals and routines are called psyching up. Many writers have similar rituals and routines. For example, George Steiner, author and critic, has a rather excellent ritual prior to writing: "Before I start a new book or a long essay, I will take a page of top prose in the relevant language and read it quietly before I start to write" (Steiner, 1995, p. 80).

Psyching up for writing is a comfort and a confidence builder. Some writers set goals: "I'm going to write for 30 minutes without stopping; I'm going to write 500 words this morning." Tell children of your writing rituals and routines. Explain the purpose they serve. Encourage children to develop their own.

**Rereading**. Writers often find that the initial rush of ideas slows to a trickle at some point during drafting. After a few sentences or paragraphs, they may say, in the words of a song made famous by Peggy Lee, "Is that all there is?" Perhaps the most universal strategy for getting the stream of ideas moving again is to stop and reread what has been written.

Rereading is like pole vaulting. You can't vault high if you start your run too near the takeoff point. Rereading sends the writer back to get a running start. It stimulates reflection, revisits the road already traveled, and offers fresh ideas for the road ahead. Fifth-grader Mercedes tells how rereading works for her: "Well, as I reread it, it helps me think about the story more. If I get stuck, I always reread my story and that always gets me going again" (Elson, p. 78).

**Talking**. Talk with a good listener when you are about ready to write a draft. In classrooms, that good listener may be the teacher or a classmate. At home the good listener might be Mom, Dad, or a friend. If you talk through your writing, you may find yourself drafting aloud. Once you've talked through a draft, the written draft seems easier.

**Walking Away**. Do teachers dare tell children to walk away from a draft? Won't they take advantage of this freedom? Yes, some will. But when we treat children like real writers, something wonderful happens: they begin to behave like real writers. They'll walk back. Of course, you will have to deal with those who take license, but solving big and little problems is what teaching is all about.

## Standing on the Shoulders of Giants
### Historical Contributions to Literacy
#### Hughes Mearns

The year is 1929. Herbert Hoover is president of the United States; the Great Depression is looming; the stock market is about to crash. In that same year, Hughes Mearns publishes *Creative Power: The Education of Youth in the Creative Arts*. Mearns believed that children possess latent powers of creativity and that insightful teachers could entice creative ideas from the minds of children. He had a special interest in writing, and his ideas and methods were far ahead of his time. In that era the left-handed child was taught right-handedness with the paddle, handwriting prevailed over content, and correctly spelled words and properly placed punctuation marks were honored more than creative ideas.

Mearns was influenced by his colleague, John Dewey, one of the great educational philosophers of the 20th century. Mearns wrote many books and articles, all of them stressing the message that children are intelligent, creative beings who need teachers who trust and respect their creative potential. As you read the quotations from his book, consider the tenor of the times in which Mearns wrote, and you will appreciate all the more the revolutionary quality of his ideas. His book *Creative Power:*

*The Education of Youth in the Creative Arts* is as relevant today as it was three quarters of a century ago.

- Children are creative persons, not scholiasts. They use language as the artist the world over and in all ages has used his medium, not as an end in itself but as a means for the expression of thought and feeling. (p. 11)
- . . . fact education has always insisted upon drill; education in feeling comes through experience. One appeals mainly to memory; *creative education demands an exposure to an influence*. (p. 46)
- What hounds they were on the scent of misspellings and wrong capitalizations! (p. 62)
- Don't bother for a minute about spelling, capitals, or commas and semicolons. Get that stuff out and down on paper while it is still hot! Scribble! Say everything, whether it belongs or not. Don't stop to think even. We'll fix all that up afterwards. (p. 257)
- The creative school cares not how inept and slovenly a lad may be this whole term if it sees something personal and fine taking slow possession of him. (p. 37)

**Writing Inside Out**. For Katherine Anne Porter, author of *Ship of Fools,* starting at the end was an article of faith: "If I didn't know the ending of a story, I wouldn't begin. I always write my last line, my last paragraphs, my last page first." Other writers start in the middle and work inside out. I often start at a place where I feel the greatest confidence or comfort, perhaps at a point where I feel my knowledge or experience is strongest. Children need to know about this trick as they approach drafting.

**Strategies to Facilitate Drafting**. Ideally, drafting should flow easily, though often it does not. As words hit the page, writers must constantly make decisions about sequence, meaning, audience, what to leave in, what to leave out. If too much thought is given to a first draft, fluency may be slowed, perhaps crippled. Yet fluency without deliberation is also less than satisfactory. Learning to draft fluently means balancing competing demands. Teachers can use these strategies to support students as they draft:

"Have a Speed Writing Party" by Hasty, Beasley, and Flourio-Ruane, April 1999, stresses keeping your eyes and pencil on the paper and writing without stopping for help with ideas or spelling.

*Teaching Tip*

1. *Write with children.* When teachers write, children notice. Melissa, a first-grader, asked, "Ms. Dalmage, did you really write that story for *us*?" Ms. Dalmage's answer reinforced what Melissa already suspected: "Yes, Melissa, I wrote that story just for you." Melissa returned to her seat with a pleased look on her face. This impressed her mightily.

2. *Confer with children.* Help those who have stalled, and encourage those who are drafting freely. Listen as they describe their problems. Ask questions that will get the words and ideas flowing again. A writer who has reached an impasse may need a specific suggestion. Do not allow concerns about student ownership of writing to keep you from giving advice and counsel when it is desperately needed. Young writers, like professional writers, benefit from the suggestions of a good editor, which is what a teacher must sometimes be.

3. *Manage the writing experience.* Determine goals, and try to achieve them within the framework of what seems possible. Plan short- and long-term writing goals. Develop a plan for evaluating writing performance over the course of the entire year. Remember, increments of writing growth are not easily detectable over short periods of time. Helping children maintain writing portfolios and writing folders is an effective way of assessing progress over longer spans of time. You are the ringmaster of your own three-ring circus. Keeping this enterprise operating smoothly requires the touch of the magician, the talent of the juggler.

4. *Listen when children talk.* Be the first audience for your children. Writers need constructive criticism, but much more they need encouragement and praise. An appreciative audience celebrates writing. Consequently, the teacher's first role is appreciative listener; the teacher's second role is constructive critic. Both are important, though listening may be the more important of the two.

5. *Teach directly to children's needs.* As you observe individual and class needs, consider ways to provide explicit instruction to meet them. When you spot a number of children with a specific writing need, teach to that need. You are in the best position to decide whether the instruction should be given to the

entire class, a subgroup, or an individual. Longer, formal lessons are sometimes needed, but it is better, in most instances, to teach 5-minute informal lessons to the class or to give brief personal suggestions to an individual. If you notice a tendency, for example, to choose vague rather than specific words, take 5 minutes to discuss precise word selection. Table 10.2 summarizes eight more ideas for facilitating drafting.

**Table 10.2**

**Practical Tips for Teachers to Facilitate Drafting**

1. Encourage mental and physical rehearsal for writing.
2. Make community and print resources available for writing.
3. Model drafting, using your writing as well as student writing.
4. Practice writing leads for narrative and expository writing.
5. Teach note taking, and show children how to organize notes for writing.
6. Encourage the writing of discovery or experimental drafts.
7. Practice freewriting to increase writing fluency.
8. Encourage the use of rituals and routines as a way of psyching up for writing.

*Teaching Tip*

## Revising

I like to think of revision in metaphorical terms: ship, anvil, and microscope. Revision is the ship on which writers set sail to discover what they have to say. Writers voyage into a sea of uncertainty, searching for meaning and a message only dimly perceived during drafting. Uncharted waters and dangerous shoals may surprise the writer, but eventually the compass of revision guides the writer into the safe harbor of meaning discovered.

Revision is the anvil on which writers shape their writing style and skill. Ben Jonson, the English poet and playwright, advised writers to "Strike the second heat / Upon the Muse's anvil." Writers seldom select their best words and thoughts in first drafts; the exact wording or the best arrangement of ideas must be shaped and hammered on the anvil of revision. The writer's unique style and skill emerges in the shower of sparks produced by constant hammering on the Muse's anvil.

Revision is the microscope that magnifies those craters, large and small, present in our writing that go unrecognized in our early drafts. Saul Bellow, a Nobel laureate, loved discovering large craters in his writing: "I'm happy when the revisions are big. I'm not speaking of stylistic revisions, but of revision in my own understanding." Writing is rarely a steady flow of words and thoughts. More often it is a halting dribble. We accumulate words and thoughts, piled one upon the other, as they tumble from our minds. First drafts corral our untamed words and thoughts. Revision tames and curries them.

**Definitions of Revision.** A crucial criterion in defining revision is this: *revision deals only with changes in written text; if no change occurs in written text, no revision has taken place.* Thus, rehearsal does not produce revision until it results in changes in the written text. Any change in a written text constitutes revision, whether it be large or small, formal or substantial, minor or major. Hence, editing and proofreading are revisions of a specific sort, occurring and recurring at unpredictable times during writing.

**Table 10.3**

**The Three Faces of Revision**

| Activity | Main Goal | Question the Writer Asks |
|---|---|---|
| Revising | Improve content | What do I have to say? |
| Editing | Refine language | How can I best say it? |
| Proofreading | Correct mechanics, grammar, and spelling | What needs final correction? |

Annette Osbourne of Oakland University uses "paper surgery" as a fun way for young writers to revise. Students cut their papers when deleting and staple or paste small pieces of paper to the existing piece when adding information during the revision process.

Revision has three faces: revising, editing, and proofreading. Revising deals with broad organic changes primarily affecting content; editing focuses on language refinement; proofreading concentrates on mechanical correctness. This sounds like a sequence: first revise, then edit, and then proofread. But writers seldom follow a strict revision sequence. While it is not possible to specify exactly where revising ends and editing or proofreading begins, nevertheless, the need for changes typically dwindles over succeeding drafts. Only in this sense can one think of moving from revising, to editing, to proofreading. It is a question of which activity dominates in a given draft. Table 10.3 describes the three faces of revision: revising, editing, and proofreading.

Faigley and Witte (1983) developed a somewhat different taxonomy, or classification system of revision, based on two major types of changes: (1) changes in form—mechanics mostly, and (2) changes in substance—content primarily. Changes in form typically involve the kind of corrections that a copy editor might make in preparing a piece just before publication. Changes in substance are more likely to alter meaning—although changes in form can also do this. Changes in either form or substance are brought about by completing any of four revision operations: adding, deleting, substituting, and rearranging (see Table 10.4). Each operation requires different considerations. For young writers, adding is the easiest operation, and rearranging text the most difficult. Substituting and deleting fall somewhere in between.

**Professional Writers' Revision Principles.** Some of the most important things we know about writing are derived from the knowledge of those who make their living by writing. For example, professional writers tell us that revision is fundamental to effective writing. Vladimir Nabokov, novelist and critic, said, "I have rewritten—often several times—every word I have ever published." James Dickey, novelist and poet, said, "I work on the process of refining low-grade ore. I get maybe a couple of nuggets of gold out of 50 tons of dirt." Theodor Geisel, otherwise known as Dr. Seuss, said, "To produce a 60-page book, I may easily write 1,000 pages before I'm satisfied." Joan Didion, novelist and essayist, said, "My writing is a process of rewriting, of going back and changing and filling in." Many professional writers follow these principles:

## Table 10.4

**Four Revision Operations**

| | |
|---|---|
| Adding | Good writing is complete without being too repetitive. Adding information is the easiest operation for introducing children to revision. |
| Deleting | Good writing is concise. Sentences need no extra words; paragraphs, no redundant sentences; compositions, no irrelevant information. Deleting is a challenging task for young writers, but a beginning can be managed fairly early. |
| Rearranging | Good writing is orderly. Writers must learn to arrange and rearrange words, sentences, and paragraphs with care. A paragraph's punch can be damaged by a misplaced sentence, a plot ruined by premature disclosure of a detail. Rearranging is the most difficult revision skill to master. |
| Substituting | Substituting is the simultaneous act of deleting and adding. It is challenging for young writers but can be managed. Older children substitute readily—usually at a surface level, unfortunately. |

- Revising enables you to discover your best ideas.
- Revising helps you understand what's going on in your work.
- Revising enables writers to discover meaning.
- Revising makes writing clear, true, and graceful.
- Revising consumes a substantial share of a writer's time.
- Revise until you are entirely satisfied; don't be easily satisfied.

**Research on Revision.** There is a long history of revision research, though the emphasis has shifted from mechanics to substantive changes in writing. Emig (1971) found that 12th-graders viewed revision as the correction of minor faults in punctuation, spelling, and grammar. Elson (1990) found that students with "low revision profiles" revise in smaller linguistic units, focus mainly on form, view revising as achieving correctness, and seldom aim at improving writing quality; subsequent drafts closely resemble previous ones. Students with "high revision profiles" think of revision as making changes in content, revise in larger linguistic units, exhibit a sense of ownership and control over their writing, see themselves as part of a writing community, and have confidence in themselves as writers. Some important research findings on revision include the following:

- Research has long found that revision has a positive influence on writing (Braddock, Lloyd-Jones, & Schoer, 1963), and more recent research concurs (Lane, 1993).
- Student writers often view revision as minor rewording and the correction of grammar, punctuation, and spelling (Cramer, 2000).
- Mature writers view revision broadly. They think of revision as discovery, rethinking, and making substantive changes (Elson, 1990).

- Topic selection and writing leads signal strong capacity for revising (Graves, 1994).
- Teacher intervention can sharpen revision skills (Graves, 1994).

*Teaching Tip*

**Philosophy of Revision**. A philosophy is a star by which to steer, a compass on a dark night. Your philosophy for teaching revision might include one or more of the following:

1. Set fair and reasonable standards for good writing and prepare your students to meet them. Challenges are necessary, but they must be attainable.
2. Focus on content. Correctness is important, but the first premise of revision is to rethink one's ideas and strive for simple, clear, and precise use of language.
3. Revision requires a heavy investment of the writer's time, and instruction must be organized to accommodate this requirement.
4. Teachers are models and must set an example by revising their own writing.
5. Children must feel they are part of a community of writers. Access to peers, instruction, audience, and writing camaraderie during revision are essential.
6. Collect and study children's writing. Awareness of the writing power children possess will help you set attainable standards for revision to strive toward.
7. Any piece of writing may be revised, but not all writing should be revised. Purpose and audience guide revision decisions.
8. Apprise children of their best ideas, and help them understand the distinctions that exist between good and mediocre ideas.
9. Writers need sincere praise, constant encouragement, especially during the difficult process of revision. Help them to strive for high ideals and achievement in their writing.

As you consider these principles and practices, decide whether they reflect your values and are compatible with your aspirations as a writer. Whatever you take from these ideas you must make your own before they can be of maximum value to you.

**Strategies to Facilitate Revision**. Teach revision. Some revision skills are relatively easy to teach at an introductory level, but they require constant monitoring and instruction as students develop more complex layers of revision knowledge. Occasional episodes of revision will not develop the skills. Children need instruction and meaningful practice in revising throughout their school careers. The six revision strategies described in Table 10.5 are among the most powerful ways to help children learn to revise.

For more information on the role of technology in the revision process, read "Revising Online: Computer Technologies and the Revising Process," by C. A. Hill et al., 1991, *Computers and Composition, 9*(1), 83–109.

**Revising and Technology**. *The New York Times Book Review* once featured a poet who claimed that poetry cannot be written on a computer. Poets must feel their pencils in their hands and experience the rhythm of the words flowing from the tips of their fingers, he claimed. A few weeks later, in the same publication, another poet ridiculed this notion as nostalgic nonsense. Research is still uncertain concerning the influence of computers on writing. Head (2000) found that students who

## Table 10.5

**Six Powerful Strategies for *Teaching* Revision**

1. *Conference.* Revision conferences help children reconsider their words and ideas. Focus on meaning, sufficiency and clarity of content, language, and final corrections, depending on where children have progressed through their revised drafts.
2. *Reread.* Rereading generates new ideas and reveals the need for change. Kate, a third-grader, said, "I like to stop every now and then to read my piece to see how it's going" (Stanley, 1988, p. 21).
3. *Read aloud.* Reading writing aloud helps writers *hear* their words and ideas. Martha, a fourth-grader, told her teacher, "I can hear myself better when I read it out loud than when I read it to myself."
4. *Model.* Demonstrate revision on an overhead projector or on a computer, using your own writing. As you revise, talk about the decisions and considerations that come to mind as you make changes in your writing.
5. *Direct instruction.* Teach children the operations of revision: how they work, when they are necessary, and how to do them (Table 10.8, p. 397). Use mini-lessons, maxi-lessons, and on-the-spot instruction.
6. *Practice.* Nothing worthwhile is learned well without constant practice. Provide the time needed to perfect skills and stimulate the interest and motivation needed to persevere.

revised on computers produced more and better revisions than students who used pen and pencil. She concluded that "students instructed to utilize revision strategies or manipulate text on a computer produce a higher quality of writing and an increase in the number of micro and macro revision changes" (p. vi). But other researchers have found that though word processing tends to produce more revisions, it does not necessarily result in an improvement of writing quality over pen-and-paper writing (Daiute, 1985; Owston, Murphy, & Wideman, 1992).

A computer does not make writing decisions less complex, but once a decision has been made, the computer makes the execution of that decision simpler. Moving text, for example, is a difficult chore to manage with pencil and paper, and it is not any easier on a typewriter. But the computer makes moving text simple. It is an ideal tool for learning to organize and reorganize text since it provides the means by which it can be easily practiced.

Computers make it easier to experiment with writing ideas. Visualization of thought is enhanced because computers make the manipulation of written text simpler. The novelist E. M. Forster spoke of visualization when he said, "How can I know what I think until I see what I say?" Computers make "seeing what you say" easier. Young writers get discouraged when they have to spend too much time recopying written work. Unless a piece is to be published or displayed, recopying wastes children's time. But revision changes are easily made on a computer. After rewriting, you are only a click away from producing a hard copy. Computers have influenced the quantity of writing students produce (e-mail, for example) and ease of executing certain writing operations. The next and more difficult step is finding ways that computers can help improve the quality of writing.

**A Final Word on Revision.** Like Tolstoy, most writers find it difficult to imagine writing without revising. The novelist John Irving said simply, "Half my life is an act of revision." Writers must learn to revise, but in their own idiosyncratic style. Children need the same freedoms so they can develop their own style of revising. Yes, children must learn the basics: why revising is important, how to go about it. But even though revising is complex, children can learn to do it. Move them beyond a surface view of revision. Let them experience its pleasures and its tedium. Teach them that revision is the heart and soul of writing. In the Field Notes feature, Peggy

## Field Notes
### Real-Life Experiences of a Classroom Teacher

Successful writers view themselves as an integral part of a writing community. They describe school-sponsored writing as occurring in an atmosphere conducive to writing and exploring ideas. Their attitude conveys the sense that "I'm a writer. My friends are also writers." Successful writers feel comfortable seeking support from peers and teachers alike. Ideas and learning spread quickly in a writing community. Lisa shares a lead, and similar interesting leads appear in other compositions. Mark shares a catchy title, and the quality of titles throughout the class improves. In a writing community, feedback and response are highly valued. Students' sense of a writing community mirrors what professional writers experience in a writing group or in a writer–editor relationship.

**Peggy Elson**

The following interview with Billy provides an example of how a writing community can aid writing. Billy sees it as a place to work out problems and seek advice from classmates when he gets stuck on a writing problem. Billy's fifth-grade writing community contrasts sharply with his previous classroom experience, where a focus on verbs and nouns and occasional writing episodes prevailed.

**Teacher:** Sometimes I see you sitting there, looking like you're deep in thought. What are you doing when you're doing that?

**Billy:** Well, I'm sitting there thinking about, like, what I should write about, what a character should do, or what a better word is, so I usually sit there and think about it. Or sometimes when I get stuck and I'm really stuck, then I have to go and see Robbie or Ryan or a couple more people.

**Teacher:** Did you do that in the past? Talk with your friends or have conferences about your writing?

**Billy:** I did that pretty much because sometimes I just go over to Robbie's or Ryan's desk and ask 'em what a better title would be or I read it to them, and I conference with them, and then we decide if this sounds right or not.

**Teacher:** You work pretty much like a team?

**Billy:** Yes.

**Teacher:** And did you do that in fourth grade or this year?

**Billy:** Mostly this year I learned to do that . . . 'cause last year we didn't write that much.

**Teacher:** What other kinds of things did you do in English?

**Billy:** Well, sometimes we did write, but that was personal narrative. Mostly we studied about verbs and nouns.

Elson, a fifth-grade teacher, discusses her success in establishing a writing community within her classroom.

## Postwriting: Sharing and Publishing

Charles Dickens, author of *David Copperfield, The Pickwick Papers,* and *A Christmas Carol,* had an unhappy childhood. Economic circumstances forced him to work in a factory at age twelve. The characters in Dickens's novels often face adversities similar to the ones Dickens himself faced. He also experienced good fortune from time to time.

What makes writers grow strong? Adversity contributes. If a tree is to grow strong, it must survive terrible storms while it struggles upward toward the light. But adversity destroys if not balanced by good fortune. A tree needs soil to nourish its roots, moisture to sustain its vitality, and a climate suitable to its nature. Writers have similar needs. Effective postwriting experiences nurture writers when they are most vulnerable, when personal adversity threatens to overwhelm, when confidence is shaken. The community that sustains, the nurturing environment that provides, the teachers who pull young writers upward toward the light are the blessings that build and sustain strong writers. Reasons for sharing and publishing writing are suggested in this section, followed by implementation strategies that make postwriting effective.

**Reasons for Sharing and Publishing Writing.** The final stage of the writing process is sharing and publishing. In a sense it is a crucible, a time and place to submit one's work to the trial of public acceptance or rejection. Writing moves onto the public stage and, for the first time, is beyond the author's control. It is a frightening as well as a joyful time. Writers fear rejection and ridicule, yet they yearn for acceptance and applause. Sharing and publishing are the reward for writing.

**1.** *Postwriting experiences integrate writing with broader curricular goals.* Sharing and publishing writing is one of several places within the writing process where integrating writing with reading, speaking, listening, viewing, and content subjects occurs naturally. Writing influences the development of a broad range of skills. It improves comprehension, word knowledge, and spelling. It provides a meaningful context for improving handwriting, grammar, and mechanics, as well as talking with assurance and listening with a purpose. Sharing and publishing move children naturally into research, note taking, organizing information, discussing, and collaborative learning situations. The interrelationships and interdependence of the skills of literacy reinforce one another when the language arts function as one entity with a common goal: communication of one's ideas.

**2.** *Postwriting experiences foster acceptance and acknowledgment of children's writing.* Professional writers yearn for public acceptance and acknowledgment of their work. Young writers need the same, though on a different scale. Broad public recognition for young writers is not necessary, nor is it likely. But it is important to acknowledge young writers' work to encourage a healthy view of their worth as writers and a belief in their writing and themselves.

**3.** *Postwriting experiences improve the written product.* Motivation for producing one's best work is inherent in the publishing and sharing process. Publicly presented writing, under most circumstances, passes through the recursive stages of planning, drafting, and revising. When this happens, writing moves closer to acceptable standards of substance and form. Peer review, for instance, gives writers an opportunity to monitor their own writing through the eyes and perspective of a valid audience. Of course, for beginning writers, standards must be flexible enough to accommodate invented spelling and an imperfect adherence to mechanics. But even beginning writers can be motivated to put their best foot forward when their writing reaches a public audience.

**4.** *Postwriting experiences strengthen writers' understanding of their capabilities.* Confidence grows when writing is acknowledged by others. Experiences that make children aware of their growing skill at telling stories, choosing words, and organizing ideas strengthen the emerging writer's command of the writer's craft. And writing is a craft, as Katherine Ann Porter informs us: "Most people don't realize that writing is a craft. You have to take an apprenticeship in it like anything else." Apprenticeship can be difficult. It certainly requires an expert mentor; it absolutely requires a motivated apprentice. But when these things are in place, writers can grow from their apprenticeship into journeymen and eventually masters of their craft.

**Strategies to Facilitate Sharing and Publishing.** Sharing can start as early as the prewriting stage or as late as reading a published book aloud. Nonetheless, publication is often a culminating experience that occurs after a work has been revised. This section describes ways to share or publish children's writing.

**1.** *Publish books.* "Books are a delightful society. If you go into a room filled with books, even without taking them down from their shelves, they seem to speak to you, to welcome you," William Gladstone said. Books symbolize the human desire to place our footprints in the sands of time, a hope that our words and ideas may have some permanence amidst the flux of human events. Children who are not acquainted with the delightful society of books can be ushered into their presence. Helping children publish their writing plants the seeds of authorship in fertile ground that may yield an abundant harvest in years to come. Simple books suffice most of the time; more elaborate bookmaking can be reserved for special purposes. Parents and volunteers can help in making them. Table 10.6 suggests six kinds of books that children can make themselves.

**2.** *Sponsor a young authors' conference.* A young authors' conference is a special celebration of writers and writing. The first was held at Oakland University decades ago, under the direction of Professor Harry Hahn. Today, young authors' conferences are held in school districts, schools, and classrooms all over the world. They differ as widely as teachers and schools differ, but they retain one common characteristic: they celebrate young writers and their writing.

**3.** *Establish an author's chair and a publishing center.* Establishing an author's chair within your classroom is easy enough. Get a chair, stool, podium, or platform.

**Table 10.6**

**Ways to Make Books**

| | |
|---|---|
| Cardboard books | A simple book cover can be made from pieces of cardboard cut to the same size as the pages on which a story, poem, or report has been written. |
| Shape books | Cut cardboard or construction paper into shapes that symbolize a book's content or theme. For example, if you've written about pyramids, cut pieces into the shape of a pyramid. |
| Folded paper books | Take six or so sheets of paper, and place a piece of colored construction paper the same size on top. Fold the stack of paper in half, and staple the pages together along the fold. |
| Accordion books | Cut strips of paper to a desired width and length. Fold the pages accordion fashion to make a book. Accordion books are excellent for writing long narrative stories and chapter books. |
| Canned books | Write stories on adding machine tape, roll up the tape and insert it into an orange juice can. Decorate the can with an appropriate illustration and title. Arrange the "canned" books on a shelf. |
| Scrapbooks | A scrapbook includes items that help you recall special occasions. A scrapbook can contain photographs, ticket stubs, report cards—anything that helps you remember events. |

Explain the idea of the author's chair to your children. Establish rules for sharing that serve your teaching goals. They can be made jointly by the teacher and the children. Model sharing techniques by reading your writing to children. When teachers take the first risk, children willingly follow. Set an example for critical listening by giving respectful and thoughtful attention to the writing children share. A writing center is also needed. Essentials include writing and drawing materials, table and chairs, books, computers, and perhaps a place for peer conferencing.

**4.** *Share writing with classmates.* There are excellent reasons for sharing writing among classmates. Initial reluctance gradually melts as group cohesion increases. It is important, therefore, to build cohesion within your classroom. Children work well within a classroom that has the comfortable feeling of family—a place where intimacy is possible, even though perfect harmony does not always prevail. Sharing writing with classmates will accomplish five writing goals:

- Sharing in peer conferences improves writing. Conference partners help each other gain awareness of their writing that is difficult to learn independently.
- Sharing gives writers a sense of how others react to what they write.
- Sharing writing fosters pride. Conference partners learn to evaluate each other's writing within a positive framework.

- Children need to share their writing with the outside world, but before this happens, it is instructive to be exposed to "friendly fire" within the family.
- Believing you have something worth saying is a basic motive for writing. Sharing helps convince children that their ideas are worthy of sharing with the world outside of the classroom.

**5.** *Publish writing in newspapers, magazines, and on the Internet.* There are newspapers and magazines which publish children's writing and an increasing number of Internet possibilities as well. Your local librarian can help you locate names and addresses of organizations that publish children's writing. A teacher I know went to the local newspaper and asked if they would publish her children's writing. To her surprise, they said yes and did so for most of the school year. Newspaper publication gave her a reason for stressing the need for correct mechanics and grammar. Perhaps not many newspapers are likely to publish children's writing, but you may live in a neighborhood where something of this sort is possible.

**6.** *Create interested audiences within schools.* Seek out interested audiences for children's writing within your school district or building. Audiences may include classmates, principals, school administrators, or children in nearby classrooms—even the custodian can be an audience for children's writing. Ms. Smith, a high school creative writing teacher, encouraged her students to write books for kindergarten children. First, she provided them with books appropriate for kindergarten children and helped her students develop a list of audience characteristics. Then book writing began. It was wonderful to see 12th-grade students writing and illustrating children's books. They asked questions of one another and read drafts aloud to get reactions to their words and ideas: they had a real purpose. When their books were finished and bound, the day came when the 12th-graders descended upon the kindergarten classes of a nearby school and read their books to a fascinated audience of 5-year-olds.

### Section Summary: The Stages of the Writing Process

1. *Prewriting.* Getting ready to write is aided by rehearsal, research, time for planning, gathering information, interest, choosing topics, keeping a journal, and choosing a writing form.
2. *Drafting.* Getting initial ideas on paper is aided by having access to a classroom library, modeling, time to write, writing leads, reviewing notes, discovery drafts, freewriting, rereading, talking, walking away, and writing inside out.
3. *Revising.* Making changes in written text requires four operations: adding, deleting, rearranging, and substituting. Revising is aided by opportunities to conference, reread, reading drafts aloud, instruction, practice, and modeling.
4. *Sharing and publishing.* Incentive to write is aided by having an audience for writing. Author's chair, publishing books, and publishing in newspapers and magazines are some of the options.

## Point ≡ Counterpoint

### A Debatable Issue
### Merits of the Writing Process

**Background**

Arthur Applebee, a noted researcher and writer, claims that the research base supporting the writing process is weak and needs to be augmented. He wonders if we have become too slavish in adhering to the stages of the writing process.

**The Debatable Issue**

Teachers should reconsider what it means to apply the writing process in their classrooms.

**Take a Stand**

Argue the case for or against the debatable issue. What arguments might you propose for rethinking aspects of the writing process? Does it need rethinking? Marshal your arguments based on your philosophy, experience, relevant research, and expert opinion. After you have discussed the issue among colleagues, debate it in your class.

# The Writing Workshop

A writing workshop is a community of writers working together in an informal work environment. The organizational structure varies according to the philosophy of the teacher and the circumstances under which a teacher works. Typically, writing workshops include three interrelated activities: instruction, writing, and response. The time devoted to writing workshops varies as a function of constraints imposed by school schedules, curriculum, and a teacher's priorities. Ideally, all members of the workshop community perceive themselves as writers, including the teacher. Achieving this ideal is an important goal of the writing workshop.

## Workshop Structure

Predictability is crucial for effective writing workshops—predictable time, activities, and expectations. Unfortunately, school schedules can make predictability difficult. Teachers cannot always operate a writing workshop in the manner they might prefer. Still, an effort must be made to avoid the chaos that can accompany an unpredictably scheduled writing workshop.

Generous amounts of time are needed for the workshop, usually 45 to 60 minutes, four or five times a week. Workshop activity can be divided into three parts: instruction, writing, and response. Each component imposes different time allotments and responsibilities on workshop participants. Table 10.7 on page 396 suggests a possible workshop structure with estimated time allotments.

## Workshop Instruction

Children learn to write by writing. There must be ample time to write so that vital practice is not shortchanged, but practice alone is not enough. Instruction is essen-

**Table 10.7**

**Workshop Structure and Time Allotments**

| Instruction (20%) | Writing (60%) | Response (20%) |
|---|---|---|
| Planning | Individual writing | Author's chair |
| Organizing | On-the-spot instruction | Discussing writing plans |
| Minilessons | Teacher conferencing | Talking about literature |
| Maxi-lessons | Peer work | Teacher modeling response to writing |

tial. Bruner, one of the outstanding psychologists of the 20th century, said, "any subject can be taught effectively in some intellectually honest form to any child at any stage of development" (Bruner, 1966, p. 33). Bruner's idea can be applied to teaching writing: *any writing skill can be taught effectively in some intellectually honest form to any child in any stage of writing development.* For example, revision is probably the most complex of all writing skills, yet very young children can learn its basic elements. Revision instruction works best when we familiarize children with three basic operations of revision—adding, deleting, and rearranging. Focusing on these operations makes instruction concrete, specific, and manageable. If we start with the broad concept of revision, instruction can become too abstract.

Instruction that is too abstract may explain why so many children have acquired the idea that revision consists of *substituting* one word or phrase for another and seldom go beyond this limiting idea. Superficial understanding of revision is harmful because it gives children the idea that they have revised when they have merely made minor surface changes. When children come to think of revision as proofreading for minor faults, they are unlikely to ask themselves the central question that true revision implies: how can I make my writing better? This section describes how workshop teachers can offer three types of workshop instruction: minilessons, maxi-lessons, and spontaneous instruction.

**Minilessons.** Raymond Carver, short story writer par excellence, is often cited as a writer who believed that *less is more.* Carver was associated with a writing movement known as minimalism. The idea of minimalism is to use the fewest and barest elements necessary to convey one's ideas in art, music, or writing. A minilesson embraces this philosophy: *teach the most essential elements of a writing skill in the shortest possible time, usually 3 to 10 minutes.* Table 10.8 provides an example of a five-step minilesson that might be planned or arise spontaneously as a result of teacher–student conferences.

For detailed examples of mini-lessons for upper elementary through high school writing, check out pages 148–216 in Nancie Atwell's *In the Middle: New Understandings About Writing, Reading, and Learning* (2nd ed.). Portsmouth, NH: Heinemann.

**Maxi-lessons.** If the minilesson embodies a minimalist approach to teaching writing, the maxi-lesson is designed to teach writing skills that require more time, demand a more comprehensive presentation, present a more formidable challenge, or are introduced for the first time. Maxi-lessons may last 10 to 20 minutes, occasionally longer. When more than

## Table 10.8

### Steps in Teaching a Minilesson on Revision

1. *Read* a child's writing, or ask the child to read it to you.
2. *Comment* on the piece the child has written: "I like your story about visiting your grandfather. The two of you must have had a good time."
3. *Ask* a story-related question: "What *else* can you tell me about your grandfather?"
4. *Wait* for a response. When the child responds say, "You can add that idea to your story if you wish. Adding information to your story helps me understand more about your visit with your grandfather."
5. *Reinforce* the concept of adding information as a revision skill: "When you add information to your story, it revises or changes the meaning. And it helps me understand more of what your piece is all about."

*Teaching Tip*

20 minutes is required, consider spreading the instruction over several sessions. The following maxi-lesson illustrates a revision lesson. Ms. Anderson chose a longer session because her sixth-graders hadn't much revision experience. She used a piece entitled "If I Were Rich" to start.

### If I Were Rich

If I had a lot of money I would be rich I would not buy a car motrsikl house and all the candy I could eat. My mom and dad woulnt have to work any more either they would have their own house and all they needed to live. I would give money to poor people to I would not waste the money like some people. going to coledg is what I want to do with some of the money. That is what I would do if I were rich

*First question:* Ms. Anderson projected the story on a screen and asked, "What do you like about this piece?" She wrote students' responses on the board and commented briefly on each. Student comments included these: *Words in the title are capitalized; The word "I" is always capitalized; Paragraphs are indented; Most sentences start with a capital letter; Several sentences have a period after them.*

*Second question:* Ms. Anderson asked, "How can we make this piece better?" Notice

Patterned writing based on a familiar book can be used to create group stories. This provides exposure to the conventions of written language and story ideas.

that student responses continue to focus on mechanics: *There should be a period after* rich *in the first sentence; I don't think* motorcycle *and* college *are spelled right; The word* going *should have a capital; There should be commas after* car *and* motorcycle; *There could be a period after* either. They *should be capitalized; It should be* t-o-o, *not* t-o, *and it should have a period after it.*

*Third question:* Ms. Anderson asked, "What did you think about the ideas in this piece?" This elicited the following responses: *I like the things the writer wants to do with the money; I think it's a good idea to share the money; I thought the last sentence was good; Sharing with Mom and Dad was the right thing to do; The writer does not want to use the money foolishly; Saving for college is a good idea.*

*Fourth question:* Ms. Anderson asked, "What sentence could we rewrite to get across the same idea differently?" One student suggested: *going to coledg is what I want to do with some of the money.* Five rewrites were suggested: *I want to go to college with the money; I'll use some of the money to go to college; A good way to use some of the money would be going to college; Since I want to go to college, I'll use some of the money for that; I want go to college. I'll use some of the money for that.*

*Application to personal writing:* Ms. Anderson said, "Let's apply one of these ideas to our personal writing. Get out the draft you wrote yesterday. Rewrite the first sentence as many ways as you can. I'll be around to help as you *revise.*"

Ms. Anderson had no illusions about the task ahead. Initially, her students focused on mechanical faults, a common pattern among weak revisers. Later, she got them to rewrite a sentence. Finally, she had them apply revision to their personal writing. Ms. Anderson knew she had a long way to go before she could move her students from surface revision to substantive revision. Her long-term goal was to move students away from asking, "What's wrong with what I wrote?" and toward asking, "How can I make my writing better?" Table 10.9 illustrates a five-step maxi-lesson on revision.

**Table 10.9**

**Steps in Teaching a Maxi-Lesson on Revision**

*Teaching Tip*

1. *Assemble* the resources you will need: overhead projector, marker, chalkboard. Your children will need a recently written piece of their own writing.
2. *Project* a draft of your writing or a draft solicited from a student. Ask, "What do you like about this piece?" List responses on the board. Then have students reread the draft, and ask, "What improvements can you suggest?" List suggestions on the board.
3. *Comment* on suggestions and offer instructional advice. Initially, children may focus on minor writing faults, but as they gain experience, their focus will shift to more substantive issues.
4. *Select* one item from student suggestions, and ask them to apply it to their own writing. For example, "Read through your draft. Choose a sentence and write it several different ways."
5. *Circulate* among the children, offering help. As revision skill grows, increase the number of revision tasks assigned.

**Spontaneous Instruction**. During a visit to a school for the creative arts, I observed the following spontaneous instruction by an art teacher. The teacher came and stood behind a student laboring over a painting. She observed for a minute or two, reached for the student's brush, and altered a single line. Then she asked, "Can you see how my line improves the perspective of your drawing?" The student produced an uncertain response, and the teacher briefly explained the distinction between her line and the student's and went on to the next student. Six instructional ideas can be derived from the art teacher's spontaneous instruction.

- *Model* what you want your students to understand.
- *Explain* why you've made a particular suggestion.
- *Seek* the student's response to your suggestion.
- *Make* only one instructional point at a time.
- *Conference* quickly and move on.
- *Recognize* that you have valuable ideas and information to convey.

Spontaneous writing instruction works well when these six points are followed. These ideas can work in many instructional settings. Comments a writing teacher might make in a spontaneous instructional setting include these:

> "Adnan, we put quotation marks around conversation. Try it like this. Can you see how quotation marks help the reader know exactly what your character said in this story?"
>
> "Mary Ann, it's a good idea to use exact words when you describe Anna's room. Instead of saying, 'Anna had lots of stuff in her room,' give a few examples. Perhaps Anna had a teddy bear or a rag doll on her desk. Or maybe clothing littered the floor. Do you see why this might give your readers a better picture of Anna's room?"
>
> "Toni, sometimes a good way to start an essay is with a quotation or an interesting fact that will grab the reader's attention. Did you run across any interesting quotes or facts in your research? Check to see if you might have something like that in your notes."

> "What I notice the most about using writer's workshop is the positive attitude the students show toward writing. They are engaged and interested. Sharing with one another gives the students pride in their efforts."
>
> —Meghan Hussain, third-grade teacher

## Individual Writing Time

As much as 60% of workshop time can be devoted to individual writing. This includes planning, drafting, revising, peer collaboration, reading, thinking, topic generation, and on-the-spot instruction. Third-grade teacher Kelly Emmer invited her students to come up with ideas of things to do during individual writing time, and they came up with the 18 ideas shown in Table 10.10 on page 400. Ms. Emmer directs an excellent writing workshop, beginning on the first day of school. She uses journals as a feature in her writing workshop, which she discusses in the Field Notes feature.

## Response to Writing

There are at least two types of responses to writing. The most obvious one, the one most often discussed, is instructional response to writing. Often there are a variety of strategies associated with instructional response. Author's chair, teacher–student

**Table 10.10**

**Things to Do During a Writing Workshop**

- Read a book to get ideas.
- Write a story with a friend.
- Read your work to a friend.
- Write a poem.
- Illustrate your story.
- Write a list of ideas.
- Write a letter.
- E-mail your e-pal.

- Edit with your teacher.
- Look out the window and write about what you see.
- Look at more than one book by the same author for ideas.
- Write to a friend.
- Write a piece on the computer.

- Listen to a friend's writing.
- Look at poetry books for ideas.
- Make a book.
- Walk around the school and look for ideas.
- Edit with a friend.
- Brainstorm new writing topics.

*Teaching Tip*

conferencing, and peer partnerships are typical examples of instructional response. A second type of response is less often discussed, and I don't know that it even has a name. I call it *attitude response*—the attitude we convey when we make comments to children about their writing. Effective response requires both types: instructional response and attitude response. One without the other leaves a black hole in the writing program.

Many instructional strategies can convey response to children before they write, as they write, and after they have written. Perhaps the best-known one is the author's chair, thanks to the advocacy of Donald Graves. It is the simple idea of

## Field Notes
### Real-Life Experiences of a Classroom Teacher

Writing is a crucial part of the curriculum, and therefore I introduce the writing workshop right away. My students begin writing on the first day of school. I was not always as enthusiastic about writing. Over the past four years, I have learned how to teach writing in a workshop environment. I now look forward to it every day of the week.

I introduce writing by showing my students journals I have kept from time I spent in Israel and Europe. My students love hearing about my journeys and experiences. I show them how journals are perfect for reflecting on trips, sharing feelings, writing stories and poems, and even writing about the history of places visited.

Keeping a personal journal has made our writing workshop better. On the first day of school, I

**Kelly Emmer**

give each student a pocket journal filled with lined paper. I show them how I have personalized my journals with pictures of family and friends, mementos, and other items. I encourage my students to decorate their journals, as I did, with pictures, drawings, fabric, glitter, stickers, and other materials.

Once the journals are decorated, students use them for most of their writing activities. I see the enthusiasm on their faces and hear the excitement in their voices when it is time to take out their journals and write. At the end of the year, their journals contain memories of their year in third grade, which they can reflect on for the rest of their lives.

gathering children together during writing workshop to share prospective ideas for writing, writing in progress, and writing completed. But Graves (1994) cautions that much of what passes for sharing in classrooms lacks vitality. He recommends rethinking the goals and procedures of the author's chair, though he retains his belief in its importance. When this activity becomes routine, it loses its vitality. Praise is essential, but unearned praise can be as corrosive as undeserved criticism. Teachers must model careful listening and thoughtful response so that children can learn to listen and respond appropriately.

Yet another powerful instructional strategy for responding to writing is conferencing. There are two major branches: teacher–student conferences and peer partnerships. Teachers are the indispensable audience for writing, but others are also needed: peers within the classroom and interested parties outside of the classroom. But for lasting impact, nothing can replace the influence of teachers as they confer with children, reflecting back to them a sense of how writing is proceeding, how to think about writing, how to improve it.

For more information on the role of conferencing with students during the writing process, see pages 308–322 in *Conversations,* by Regie Routman, 2000, Portsmouth, NH: Heinemann.

Peer partnerships are also crucial, and they can be powerful when children have had good models of how conferencing ought to proceed. Successful conferencing requires a repertoire of questions, comments, and attitudes to guide the conference. Table 10.11 suggests questions and comments to help guide peer partnerships as well as teacher–student writing conferences.

## Section Summary: The Writing Workshop

1. A writing workshop is a community of writers working together in an informal work environment.
2. Flexibility is necessary in allotting time for the writing workshop, but structure is also important; consider allotting 60% to writing, 20% to instruction, and 20% to response to writing.

**Table 10.11**

### Guidance for Writing Conferences

*Teaching Tip*

**Questions**

1. What are you writing about?
2. What have you written so far?
3. What will you write next?
4. What are you trying to say in this piece?
5. I see you have got a good start; where will you go from here?
6. What does your story say?
7. Will your first sentence capture your reader's attention?
8. Are you satisfied with what you've written so far?
9. Why did you choose this topic?
10. What word or line do you like best in your piece?
11. What did you learn from writing this piece that will help you with the next one?

**Comments**

12. Tell me about your writing.
13. Read your first paragraph to me.
14. I like your first sentence. Keep going.
15. This is *my* favorite line in your poem.
16. You seem to know a lot about . . . ?

3. Instruction in writing workshop includes minilessons, maxi-lessons, and spontaneous on-the-spot instruction.

4. Two types of response include the attitude teachers adopt toward writing and writers and responses intended to provide instructional guidance.

## Practical Teaching Ideas and Activities

*Teaching Tip*

**1.** *Consider ambience.* Is the environment conducive to writing? It is important to think about the physical writing environment we establish for students. Is the area well lit? Are writing materials accessible so students can get what they need quickly and independently? Are seating and table areas comfortable? Is the writing area relatively distraction-free? Consider having students write silently for the first 10 to 15 minutes (after the prewriting discussions) in order to meet the needs of highly distractible students. Consider playing soft, lyric-free music as a background.

**2.** *Help students give positive feedback.* After a student shares writing, the rest of the class may not know how to provide useful feedback. Model how to use statements that begin, "I wonder . . ." and "I notice . . ." These are more tactful than "I don't get it." "I wonder" tells the writer that the reader is curious about something or may not have understood something—signs that more details or description may be necessary. "I notice" lets the listener point out the great things the author has done. After modeling these statements, have a student or two try using them. Remind students that the purpose is to comment on the writer's ideas and decision making rather than grammar and punctuation. Thus the writer will gain ideas on ways to strengthen his or her piece.

**3.** *Write frequently during student writing time.* When adults engage in an activity themselves, a powerful message is sent to the children. Just as our reading during silent reading time shows how much we value it, so too does our own willingness to write alongside our students. If your students write in notebooks, keep your own writing notebook as well! This experience will make you a better writer, model good writing behavior for the students, and help you understand in an authentic way some of the obstacles your students face. Commit to writing yourself for the first 5 to 10 minutes of the writer's workshop. Share your own writing regularly with your students.

**4.** *Develop appropriate checklists for students and teacher to use to mark growth in writing.* Checklists can be developed to address the mechanics of writing as well as aspects of content or composition. Brainstorm with students an exhaustive list of things that make for good written pieces. These could be typed up and kept in each student's writing portfolio for independent use or for teacher–student conferencing. Students should be taught to use these in a self-evaluative way as they learn to judge and modify their own work and to monitor their growth as a writer. These checklists also help students and teachers identify areas of strength and target areas that need to be developed.

**5.** *Conference with students weekly.* In order for students to quickly and effectively develop writing skills, they need frequent coaching and feedback. Structure your writing workshop so that each day you meet with a small group to conference about their writing. In the early grades, consider grouping children heterogeneously so that they can support one another. Committing to daily conferencing with a different group ensures that all students are guided regularly in their growth as writers.

**6.** *Use children's literature as models.* Using literature as models for writing increases children's awareness of diverse writing styles and techniques. Examine interesting phrases and words, how the author begins or ends a story, use of punctuation and spelling, and how the book is formatted.

See the Blue Pages at the back of the book and on the Companion Website for additional activities.

## ◂ Reflection and Summary

### Reflection

Walking into a classroom where a writing workshop is in full bloom is pure pleasure. There sits Elizabeth reading her draft to Paul; Paul looks a little bored. Elmer's pawing through his writing folder, looking for the piece he started two weeks ago; he can't find it. Evangeline has a pile of books on her desk; she's searching for an idea for her next writing project; Ms. Elson is listening to Jody read Chapter 10 of her novel; each chapter is one page long. Ms. Elson makes a suggestion as Jody gets ready to move on to Chapter 11. Anthony asks the visitor if he'd like to hear his story.

The room is humming with purposeful noise. I've been here before; it's always exciting and a little disconcerting. How does Ms. Elson get such good writing from her children? Her children can work for an hour or more every day and never seem to tire of their writing workshop. Sometimes I imagine that Ms. Elson is doing black magic, but I know better. She is simply a fine teacher, well organized, engaging children in work they enjoy in an atmosphere pulsating with purpose and pleasure. *An excellent writing teacher is a treasure forever.*

### Summary

This chapter has presented the following main ideas:

1. Donald Graves developed and promulgated much of the theory and practice associated with the writing process. He suggested six principles: write frequently, model writing, conference with children, encourage ownership of writing, teach revision, and share and publish writing.
2. The writing process implies four stages: prewriting—the mental and physical preparation for writing; drafting—getting one's initial ideas on paper; revising—improving writing through adding, deleting, rearranging, and substituting; and postwriting—sharing and publishing writing.

3. A writing workshop is a community of writers working together to produce and share writing, receive and share instruction, and encourage one another as writers.

## Questions to Challenge Your Thinking

1. What is the writing process? How is it different from traditional approaches to writing instruction?
2. Graves suggested six principles for process writing. Choose one of his principles, and evaluate its usefulness in teaching children to write.
3. What activities might you expect a writer to engage in during the prewriting stage?
4. How do the goals of revision change as writers move from revision to editing to proofreading?

5. What might be the first and easiest step in getting first-grade children to revise? Explain.
6. Immature revisers ask, "What's wrong with my writing?" What is a better question for revisers to ask? Why is it better?
7. Describe three types of instruction that might occur during a writing workshop. How are they alike? How are they different?
8. What did you learn that you didn't know before reading this chapter?

## A Case Study

Collin is a first-grader. Study his writing shown in Figure 10.1, and read his story and its translation. Then answer the questions that follow.

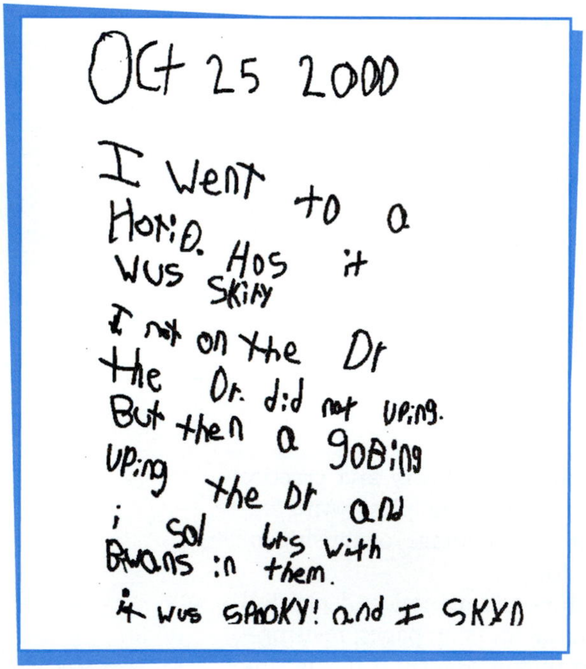

**Translation of Collin's Writing**

October 25, 2000

I went to a

haunted house it
was scary

I knocked on the door

the door did not open.

but then a goblin

opened the door and

i saw jars with
brains in them.

it was spooky! and I screamed

**Figure 10.1**

**Collin's Story**

1. What writing stage does Collin's piece represent? What evidence reveals this?
2. Examine Collin's spelling. What kind of words does he tend to spell correctly? What kind of words does he tend to misspell? What letter–sound relationships does he spell most accurately? What letter–sound relationships does he most often misspell?
3. What phonics skills do Collin's spellings reveal?
4. Is it likely that Collin is a good first-grade reader? Give evidence to support your answer.
5. What strengths can you detect in Collin's performance?
6. What instructional support should you provide over the next few months?

## Revisit the Anticipation Guide

Return to the Anticipation Guide in the chapter opener, and review your original responses to the questions. Complete the guide again, and then consider these questions.

1. How accurate were your predictions? Did you change your mind about any of your predictions as a result of reading and reflecting?
2. Did you change your mind about any items that you agreed or disagreed with? Which ones? Why?

3. Have reading and reflecting on ideas in this chapter changed any of your beliefs or practices about teaching writing? Explain.
4. Write a brief statement of belief or philosophy concerning the teaching of writing.

## VideoWorkshop Extra!

If your instructor ordered a package including VideoWorkshop, go to Chapter 10 of the Companion Website (www.ablongman.com/cramer1e) and click on the VideoWorkshop button. Follow the instructions for viewing the appropriate video clip and completing the accompanying exercise. Watch the Companion Website for access to a new interactive teaching portal, My Lab School, currently under construction.

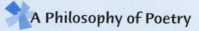

### A Philosophy of Poetry

**P**oetry exists within every child, but how do we call it forth? Maybe calling forth the poetry within children is easier than one might suppose. The key is believing that every child has poetic potential. And teachers can call forth that poetry. Teachers have chosen to live their lives among children because they believe *they can touch children's lives, develop the potential children possess, and unleash the power inherent in every child. Freeing the poetic spirit within children is perhaps the best opportunity to realize the dream we all held when we first decided to dedicate our lives to teaching children—the dream that we could make a difference. Teachers can make children's lives better through poetry. Not coincidentally, they can make their own lives better through poetry as well.*

# 11 Poetry for Children

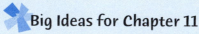

### Big Ideas for Chapter 11

1. You can prepare children for poetry by helping them develop an appreciation for poetry, reading poetry aloud, and by discussing poems and poets with them.
2. Teachers can write and share their poetry with children, nurture their natural creative capabilities, provide praise and instructional criticism, and help compose group poetry.
3. Writing poetry can be inspired through the arts and tapping into children's emotions, dreams, observations, journals, and memory.
4. Poetry makes use of special language and technical devices such as words, rhyme, rhythm, use of lines, punctuation, stanza, onomatopoeia, alliteration, repetition, imagery, simile, and metaphor.
5. There are over a hundred poetic forms. Forms often suggest guidelines such as number and length of lines, rhyme scheme, and traditional subject matter.

## Anticipation Guide

*Consider each of the following statements and determine whether you agree or disagree. Save your answers and revisit this anticipation guide in the last section of this chapter.*

1. Poetry's value is aesthetic, not academic.       agree    disagree
2. Poetry is rooted in the emotional side of our nature.       agree    disagree
3. Poetry is rooted in an oral tradition.       agree    disagree
4. Free verse is a better starting place for young children than rhyming poetry.       agree    disagree
5. Praise and instructional criticism can help young writers grow.       agree    disagree
6. There is an important connection between observation and imagination.       agree    disagree
7. Traditional punctuation should always be used in writing poetry.       agree    disagree
8. Words like *onomatopoeia* and *alliteration* are too difficult for first-grade children. They should, therefore, be avoided at this level.       agree    disagree
9. Do not introduce new poetic forms until earlier ones have been mastered.       agree    disagree
10. Poetry is too abstract for elementary school children.       agree    disagree

*P*oetry is an impish attempt to paint the color of the wind.

—*Maxwell Bodenheim*

## A Literacy Story

I recently received a nice letter, written on a computer, from a young friend who wished to share her reading experiences.

Dear Dr. Cramer,

When I was in kindergrdin I lernd how to srech out werds. I allsow lond how to look at the pechers. I have a jernel I right in every day. I lernd how to read chapter books. I read books to my brother. I read Go tran Go. It is a good book. It is about a trane that desids that he dos'nt want (to stop) at the stops anymore. All the pepple are angery at him everything is flying everyware. He dos'nt think it was a good ideia after-all. From that day on he allwas stoped at evry stashin.

At school I am in a reading grop. We read good books like Cam Jansen books. I aloso read at home wen I go to bed. My mom is reading Charlie and the choclite Factry to me. I read A to Z mysteries to myself. I some-times read so late my mom and dad tel me to go to bed.

Love, Allyson

Allyson's letter reveals a thoughtful young reader and writer, but I didn't know just how thoughtful until her mother told me this literacy story. Allyson had traveled with her parents and grandparents on a holiday trip. Mom had packed plenty of books. As they neared the end of the trip, Allyson assessed the state of reading knowledge in her family: "Grandma doesn't have a clue about reading. She doesn't understand text to text, text to self, or text to world." After a brief pause, she added, "Papa doesn't either." Luckily, Mom, a university reading professor, was exempt from Allyson's analysis of the woeful state of reading theory in her family.

Allyson actually knows what text to text, text to self, and text to world means. That would not have surprised Jerome Bruner (1966), who said, "We begin with the hypothesis that any subject can be taught effectively in some intellectually honest form to any child at any stage of development" (p. 33). Allyson reminded me of something I sometimes forget: *never underestimate what children can learn.*

## A MATTER OF STANDARDS

### Poetry

**Standard 11:** Students participate as knowledgeable, reflective, creative, and critical members of a variety of literacy communities.

Children need to see themselves as active members of different literacy communities. As students recognize their connections to a given literacy community, they learn to think and participate within it as knowledgeable and respected members, able to raise questions and investigate problems. Literacy communities emphasize the importance of collaborative learning experiences. For instance, children can join the Internet community of poets by sharing their poetry with e-pals or discover electronic sites where they can publish their poetry. They may be members of a creative writing community in which they read and write poems and stories; they may be members of an academic writing community in which they read and write essays and reports. This chapter focuses on reading and writing poetry. Poetry is typically associated with the creative side of the language arts, whereas academic writing is often associated with the critical side. This distinction is somewhat overdrawn, but it has some basis of reality. Still, it must be remembered that poetry has its critical side and academic writing its creative side.

Now and then a line or two of poetry takes root in the mind and will not be dislodged. Such happened a year or so ago when I read a poem by Robert Hayden (1997), "Those Winter Sundays." He tells of a working-class man who steadfastly performed his fatherly duties. No one thanked him nor thought overly much about his quiet devotion. Here are the two lines that I cannot dislodge from my memory:

What did I know, what did I know
of love's austere and lonely offices?

I associate the lines with my own father, a coal miner, whose life was much harsher than mine. The poet's words resonate within me. It has taken decades and a poet's poignant lines to bring me to an appreciation of my father's quiet devotion to the austere and lonely offices of fatherhood. Hayden's poem did what poetry is supposed to do. It made me think, made me remember, made me feel, made me understand something of the human condition. And while Hayden's poem recalled a sorrowful memory, poetry can have the opposite effect—joy.

Poetry can add a smile to our lives as well as a tear. In either case, it adds a thread to the short tapestry of our lives—that's how Giacomo Leopardi described the value of poetry. The smile that I recall from poetic expression came not from a mature poet but from a 3-year-old child resting in the play area of a nursery. She described herself as being "quiet as smoke." That's poetic, and I smile as I contemplate the perfection of a child's simile. Poetry is democratic. It is not the sole province of the intellectual, the gifted, or the mature. Poetry is the distilled essence of language, thought, and feeling—gifts we all possess.

Poetry is an emotional experience more than an intellectual one, and that is why children of all ages are capable of reading and writing poetry. Children's poems

"When relating unfamiliar text to prior world knowledge and our personal experience—those connections generally take three forms: text-to-text, text-to-self, and text-to-world connections."

—E. O. Keene and S. Zimmermann, *Mosaic of Thought*, 1997.

For detailed information about Robert Hayden, visit http://www.english.uiuc.edu/maps/poets/g_1/hayden/life

do not always achieve excellence, but sometimes they do. Still, successful children's poetry ought not be measured against adult standards. Rather, it should be measured by the opportunity it affords for discovery of interests, exploration of feelings, and exercise of the creative impulse.

## Preparing Children for Poetry

Fortunately, many children come to school with a background in poetry, though it may be limited to Mother Goose and Dr. Seuss. But Mother Goose and Dr. Seuss provide just the right sort of verse for phonemic awareness and enjoyment of poetry for young children. More serious poetry is welcome as well. But some children may have had little exposure to poetry of any sort. Whatever the case, there are ways to build on what exists and ways to introduce children who have missed out on poetry prior to schooling. This section suggests the need for developing an appreciation of poetry by reading it aloud and talking about poems and poets.

### Appreciating Poetry

*"Poetry is an orphan of silence. The words never quite equal the experience behind them."*
—Charles Simic, poet

Poetry is rooted in the emotional side of our natures rather than the intellectual. Poetry emerged among our ancestors as an expression of their emotions, not their intellects. Students who major in English may experience only the intellectual side of poetry if they are taught to dissect it line by line, much as a medical student might dissect a cadaver. Dissection alone cannot lead to a deeper understanding of a poem's personal meaning, an appreciation of its beauty, or an emotional response in our inner spirit.

An emotional response to poetry does not require an emotional outburst. Children recognize and reject unwarranted gushing over poetry. What is needed is a favorable response, and this begins with the teacher's response to poetry. If you harbor indifference to poetry, then the right place to start is with yourself. You can encourage children's appreciation for poetry in a number of ways.

*Teaching Tip*

For an alphabetical index of Mother Goose rhymes, see http://www.personal.umich.edu/pfa/dreamhouse/nursery/rhymes

- *Start with the known.* Most children have heard some poetry, though they might not have thought of it as poetry. Share the familiar, then introduce the unfamiliar. Mother Goose rhymes, poetic songs, and jump rope rhymes may serve as an introduction. Young children are especially attracted to songs or humorous and nonsense poetry. Read aloud examples such as "Blowing in the Wind," by Bob Dylan; "Puff the Magic Dragon," by Shel Silverstein; and "Little Abigail and the Beautiful Pony," by Shel Silverstein.
- *Associate poetry with pleasure.* Choose your favorite poems and read them aloud. Invite children to recite poems in chorus. Encourage them to choose a poem and illustrate it. Urge children to bring poems from home that they have clipped from newspapers or magazines. Offer opportunities to memorize and recite a poem or a verse from a poem. Have children copy favorite poems into their writing journals.

- *Start where children are, and broaden their poetic horizons gradually.* Nonsense and forbidden topics may partly account for the extraordinary popularity of Shel Silverstein's poems. Some will argue that such poems are unsuitable for young children. Others may insist that such poems are not poetry at all, merely light verse. But whether verse or poetry, the idea is to get children interested. Taste can be elevated, but first prepare an inviting table.

## Reading Poetry Aloud

Poetry is rooted in an oral tradition. Therefore, it is important for children to hear poetry read aloud. Select poetry that matches children's capacity to respond. The relevant factors include language, length, theme, interest, and relevance. When selecting poems to read aloud, choose poetry you enjoy, that touches on life in some special way, that incorporates the many moods of children's lives. Here are three issues to consider when selecting poetry for children.

Children enjoy humor, nonsense, and serious poetry. Read humorous poems from Shel Silverstein's books *Where the Sidewalk Ends* (1974) and *A Light in the Attic* (1981). Jack Prelutsky's *The New Kid on the Block* (1984) is also highly popular with children. Javaka Steptoe's *In Daddy's Arms I Am Tall: African Americans Celebrating Fathers* (1997) has many thoughtful poems children will enjoy. Eloise Greenfield's *Honey I Love and Other Love Poems* (1978) is also an excellent choice.

Children need poems that deal with both the tender and ragged parts of life. Read poetry that deals with death and disaster, sorrow and suffering, triumph and tragedy, love and loneliness. Select from among the best classic poets and children's poets. These include but are not limited to Edgar Allan Poe, Robert Frost, William Shakespeare, John Ciardi, Elizabeth Barrett Browning, Mother Goose, William Wordsworth, Lewis Carroll, Robert Browning, Arnold Adoff, Emily Dickinson, A. A. Milne, Barbara Esbensen, William Carlos Williams, Nikki Giovanni, Mary O'Neill, Langston Hughes, Theodor Seuss Geisel, Maurice Sendak, Margaret Wise Brown, David McCord, Karla Kuskin, Henry Dumas, Eve Merriam, Myra Cohn Livingston, Valerie Worth, Lillian Moore, and Aileen Fisher.

Children appreciate poetry that other children have written. While reading poetry written by children to a group of children, one child said, "Someone my age wrote that poem?" Hearing poems other children have written generates confidence that "I can do that, too." Collect copies of the poems your children write for use with future classes. Some schools publish collections of poems written for young authors' conferences. Newspapers sometimes publish collections of children's poetry. Two marvelous collections of children's poems and drawings are *Miracles: Poems by Children of the English-Speaking World,* edited by Richard Lewis (1966), and *I Never Saw Another Butterfly: Children's Drawings and Poems from Terezin Concentration Camp, 1942–1944,* edited by Hana Volavkova (1993).

Children respect the poems their teachers write. My undergraduates share the poetry they have written with children. Children offer encouragement and ask

"It is said that in many early and oral tradition-based cultures, the poet was the most important member of the community, since he or she knew all of the words, and all of the stories which the words made, and therefore they knew the order in which the society existed."

—http://cadre. sjsu.edu/switch/sound/articles/wendt/foldero/ngo1.htm

To read and learn more about poets from Angelou to Yeats, visit http://www.webenglishteacher.com

Visit http://www.dreampad.org to enjoy poetry and artwork by kids and for kids.

*First-graders collaborated to make this "wall rhyme" based on the familiar nursery rhyme "Hickory Dickory Dock." The teacher used it to teach minilessons about a variety of skills and strategies, and the children reread it throughout the week.*

questions: Did your teacher like your poems? Were you scared when you read your poems in class? Do you like writing poems? Children's interest in their teachers' writing experience, provides many opportunities for teaching poetry to children. Write an occasional poem for your children. You will rarely be disappointed by their response.

## Talking About Poems

Poetry may be an acquired taste. Therefore, children need exposure to it so they can come to understand and appreciate it. Start by reading poetry that represents different authors, cultures, genres, and traditions. Most children enjoy nonsense poems, and they can come to appreciate serious poems, as well. Children's experience with poetry can be broadened and should be. Seek out books and anthologies that have a broad range of uses: poems to be read aloud, children's favorite poems, humorous poems, tragic poems, poems suitable for modeling, poems about death and loss, and how to write poetry. Teachers who are interested in acquiring their own library of such books can do so readily enough at book stores, book sales, flea markets, and local libraries. The bibliography in Figure 11.1 is a good place to start.

## Talking About Poets

The value of poetry is enhanced when we consider the poet and poetry in close proximity. The first time I heard a poet tell why he had written a certain poem, I understood the connection between his words and the experience that led to his poems. Like adults, children know little about poets. We have all heard of the starving artist, mostly as a metaphor. Even America's finest poets seldom make a living

David Booth. (Ed.). (1989). *'Til All the Stars Have Fallen: A Collection of Poems for Children.* London: Viking.

John Ciardi. (1963). *You Read to Me, I'll Read to You.* New York: Lippincott.

John Drury. (1991). *Creating Poetry.* Cincinnati, OH: Writer's Digest Books.

Carol An Duffy (Ed.). (1996). *Stopping for Death: Poems of Death and Loss.* New York: Holt.

Eloise Greenfield. (1978). *Honey I Love and Other Love Poems.* New York: HarperCollins.

Paul B. Janeczko. (1999). *How to Write Poetry: Tips and Writing Exercises for Fun and Serious Poems.* New York: Scholastic.

Paul B. Janeczko. (2002). *Seeing the Blue Between: Advice and Inspiration for Young Poets.* Cambridge, MA: Candlewick.

X. J. Kennedy & Dorothy M. Kennedy. (Eds.). (1982). *Knock at a Star: A Child's Introduction to Poetry.* Boston: Little, Brown.

X. J. Kennedy & Dorothy M. Kennedy. (Eds.). (1992). *Talking Like the Rain: A Read-to-Me Book of Poems.* Canada: Little, Brown.

Amy A. McClure. (1990). *Sunrise and Songs.* Portsmouth, NH: Heinemann.

Javaka Steptoe. (Ed.). (1997). *In Daddy's Arms I Am Tall: African Americans Celebrating Fathers.* New York: Lee and Low Books.

Joseph I. Tsujimoto. (1988). *Teaching Poetry Writing to Adolescents.* Urbana, IL: National Council of Teachers of English.

Hana Volavkova. (Ed.). (1993). *I Never Saw Another Butterfly: Children's Drawings and Poems from Terezin Concentration Camp, 1942–1944.* New York: Schocken.

Susan Goldsmith Wooldridge. (1996). *Poemcrazy: Freeing Your Life with Words.* New York: Three Rivers Press.

**Figure 11.1**

**A Bibliography of Poetry for Children**

entirely from their published poems. Most poets make a living teaching, editing, driving a truck—whatever it takes. They live next door, teach down the hall, check out your library books. There is a pool of poetic talent in every community. They may not be professional poets; few people are. They may not be widely published; few attain this distinction. Nevertheless, they are a resource for stimulating interest in poetry among children.

For information on how to get a poet to visit your school, visit www.poetry4kids.com

Most children have never seen or heard poets recite their poems. Children need to know about poets—personal stories that show the human dimension and professional experiences that illustrate the poet at work. Information about poets is useful and often fascinating to amateur poets. If you can locate a local poet, invite him or her into your classroom to read poems and talk about writing poetry. If you can't find a poet, perhaps the next best thing is to read aloud brief biographical sketches of poets as you read their poetry to children.

## Reading Poetry

The place to start teaching poetry to children is by reading poetry yourself. Soon you may want to read your favorite poems to them. The next step is to write a few poems—but you have to read poetry if you want to write. You'll probably find you like to read poetry, although you won't necessarily like every poem. When this hap-

"I don't tell them poetry is important because I don't want them to shut off. I don't want them to think I'm trying to teach them something. I want to get them hooked on poetry because of the poetry itself."

—Ken Nesbitt, poet

pens, ask yourself, "Why don't I like this poem?" Of course, you should also ask the opposite question: "Why do I like this poem?" You can learn from those you like and those you don't like. Maybe you'll learn "Here's something I don't want to do when I write poems." More likely you'll learn "Here's something I'd like to try." This shows you're thinking about what you've read. Reading widely and deeply is essential. Faulkner had some advice for those who want to write. He said read everything, good and bad, and then something will happen: ". . . you'll get it. Then write."

## Memorizing Poetry

Memorized poetry leaves a legacy of literature that can be carried throughout life to great benefit. Bill Martin Jr. is one of the great orators in the field of literacy. One of his skills as a speaker and teacher is an abundance of memorized poems. He has delighted audiences of children and adults for six decades with his marvelous repertoire of memorized literature. He has these poems at his command for any relevant occasion. Many of us have wished we had a repertoire of memorized poems to enliven our teaching and enlighten our daily lives. Mr. Martin learned many of his poems as a child in school—a practice more common decades ago than today. Still, an old idea can be a good one.

"Memorization . . . builds into children's minds an ability to understand and use complex English syntax. The student who memorized poetry will internalize rhythmic, beautiful patterns of English language. These patterns have become part of the student's 'language store,' those wells of language that we all use every day in writing and speaking."

—J. Wise and S. W. Bauer, "Poetry Memorization: Methods and Resources," *The Well-Trained Mind Newsletter*

Memorized poetry works well for dramatic occasions such as reader's theater or choral readings. Children often need ideas for sharing with the class, and a memorized poem can be effective here as well. Memorized poems can be recited as a group or individual project. If you try this in your class, it is a good idea to give students a choice of poems to memorize.

## Revising Poetry

Writing poetry is not just a matter of spontaneously putting down any words that come to mind, though such brainstorming is important. After a first draft, it is nearly always a good idea to reconsider the word choices you have made. Not only is it appropriate to revise soon after a first draft, but also a good idea to rewrite your poems years after they were initially written. Consider the practice of William Butler Yeats, the great Irish poet who won the Nobel Prize for literature. He revised his poetry after initial drafts and even decades after a poem had been published. His friends questioned why he rewrote his poems. This was his answer:

> My friends who have it I do wrong
> Whenever I remake a song
> Must know what issue is at stake
> It is myself that I remake.

Yeats believed that revision not only changed his songs (his poems); revision also changed him. Revision alters thinking, changing us as well as our songs. It helps

**Table 11.1**

**Revising Poetry**

1. Let your poem sit for a while before you revise it. But think about it in the mean-while.
2. Don't settle for the first words you have chosen. Try different words at key places in your poem.
3. Ask yourself questions that might stimulate revision: Are my key verbs vivid and precise? Are there any surprises in my choice of words?
4. Compare your revised poem with your earlier version. Then read your revised poem aloud. What changes do you like? Are there changes you've made that you don't like as well as the earlier version?
5. Read your original and revised versions to a friend—it must be a good friend who is not too critical. Consider your friend's reactions, but in the end you must satisfy yourself.

writers reflect upon their thoughts and extends writers' ability to convey the meaning they intended but may not have achieved in early drafts. Table 11.1 suggests ideas for revising poetry.

## Section Summary: Preparing Children for Poetry

1. Develop an appreciation for poetry by appealing to children's emotional nature. Later, the intellectual nature of poetry can be explored.
2. Since poetry is rooted in the oral tradition, it is important to read good poetry aloud to children.
3. Discuss poetry that represents many different authors, genres, cultures, and traditions.
4. Children generally know little about poets. Discuss the lives and works of poets with them.
5. Encourage children to read poetry since this makes the writing of poetry easier.
6. Encourage children to commit some poems to memory.
7. Like other types of writing, poetry ought to be revised on most occasions.

## Responding to Children's Poetry

The creative impulse is fragile. It is often hidden and brought forth only in an environment that favors its unveiling. But once the creative impulse has found its voice, shyness and uncertainty disappear. Children possess powerful creative impulses. When this impulse is suppressed, it may find unhealthy outlets; when the creative impulse is encouraged, it flourishes. Writing poetry is an ideal way to nourish the creative impulse. Eddie, a seventh-grader, read like a second-grader. His teachers considered him hostile, a juvenile delinquent in the making. He dressed and groomed himself to cultivate the image of a rebel. Outwardly, he appeared sullen and uncommunicative. Fortunately, one teacher, Ms. Morgan, saw beneath his façade. She discovered he had a talent for drawing and a curiously gentle side that belied his outward demeanor. Ms. Morgan, imitating the *Little Engine That Could,* taught Eddie to read and write. She described her strategy this way: "I used art as

> "It is the supreme art of the teacher to awaken joy in creative expression and knowledge."
>
> —Albert Einstein

an entry to Eddie's mind and kindness to restore his damaged self-image." There is no simple formula for awakening the creative impulse within children, but there is always a place to start. Success is never ensured, but the only true failure is not to try. Consider the following ideas for nurturing the creative impulse slumbering beneath the surface of youthful insecurity.

*Teaching Tip*

- The early stages of creative endeavor are sometimes chaotic and uncertain. During these times, children need approval from people they respect—parents, teachers, peers. When they get it, they will work hard to continue meriting approval.
- Cultivate an openness of mind and spirit. Openness is not flabby and vacuous, and it does not require the uncritical acceptance of bad ideas as the equal of good ones. Openness is a vigorous state of mind characterized by the presence of one's own ideas and opinions but receptive to children's ideas and opinions.
- Place your highest value on ideas, and allow the mechanics of writing to take their rightful place as the handmaiden of good writing. Grammar and mechanics must be taught, should be taught, but they are best acquired within the context of meaningful writing. No amount of grammatical or mechanical sophistication can turn a poor idea into a good one.
- Steadfastly maintain faith in the creativity of children; remain calm and self-assured when your faith is tested. Patience is needed to receive the uninspired products that inevitably precede the inspired. Patience is also needed to wait through the long periods when little is produced to reward your faith in the creativity of children.

## Praise Thoughtfully

The writer Gertrude Stein said, "No artist needs criticism, he only needs praise." The validity of this remark depends of what Stein means by criticism. Criticism has two distinct meanings: (1) to find fault and (2) to render judgment regarding quality or worth. Writers need the latter type of criticism—thoughtful analysis regarding the quality or worth of their work. Writers do not need the former—fault finding. The first is positive and useful, the other, negative and useless. Criticism is an academic guidance system for improving writing when it is thoughtfully presented. Praise is also needed because it motivates. Intellectual and psychological insights are needed to use praise and criticism well. If they are used well, the intellectual, social, and emotional growth of children will follow. If they are used insensitively, growth will be hindered. Since everyone reacts differently to praise and criticism, no single approach, no single piece of advice, is likely to work for all children.

Writing is like the geography of a mountain range—a succession of valleys and peaks. When good work is produced, recognition must be forthcoming regardless of whether it meets the usual conventions. Extravagant praise is seldom warranted or even wanted. But recognition and appreciation are always warranted and desperately wanted. Reserve your highest praise for work that shows a personal touch, bears the mark of original invention, or delights in a particular way.

> "When educators have ulterior motives for supplying praise, children will surely pick up on it. Students quickly become suspicious of the motivation behind those who deliver praise, and thus the value of praise, and when it is selfishly delivered, is also suspect."
> —Sharon Tabor, educator

## Criticize Thoughtfully

Instructional criticism promotes writing growth when it is delivered in the right tone at the right time. Criticism must be focused and relevant to a writer's ability to make use of the instructional support provided. Criticism must have a positive intent and a proper tone. Otherwise it will do more harm than good. Criticism should support growth in writing knowledge. Negative feedback more often than not impedes growth. By tone, I mean that both what you say and how you say it are crucial. Criticism can be conveyed directly and indirectly. An indirect way is through asking questions. The right questions can help writers discover what they know but didn't know they knew, rethink their work, or adopt a new perspective. But just as important as the right question is the right manner. An instructional conference is as delicate as a

> "Good criticism is very rare and always precious."
> —Ralph Waldo Emerson

rose. The slightest inflection of voice or touch of hand sends subtle signals. The following questions may guide you. However, only you can determine the right questions for your students and sense the right tone and timing to summon the young writer to further reflection:

What were you trying to say in your poem?

Are you satisfied with the way your poem ends?

Walt, what's the main thing you're getting at in your poem?

How's your work going? Tell me about it.

What do you like best about your poem? Why?

Did anything you wrote surprise you? What?

*Good criticism helps writers improve their work; inappropriate criticism makes writers want to abandon their work.*

Ann, what did you learn about your writing this time?
What idea do you like best in your poem?
Do you like your poem? Talk to me about it.
 As you read your poem aloud, listen for the sounds you like best.
Have you listened to your poem read aloud? May I read it for you?

Instructional criticism can also take the form of qualified praise. For example, imagine a teacher saying: "I love the first line of your poem, 'Wispy cobwebs strung the fences.' The words *wispy* and *strung* create a vivid picture of how the cobwebs must have looked that day." Praise for precise word choice will lodge in the writer's mind. Sometimes instructional criticism requires more direct help than a question or an approving comment can provide. In such cases, give direct instructional suggestions such as the following: "You seem to be having difficulty with the rhyme in the first stanza, Joan. First, think of what you want to say. Get your ideas on paper. *Then* work on the rhyme. Later you can use the rhyming dictionary to help you make lists of rhyming words." Here's another example: "Dorsey, the first stanza of your poem is wonderful. Every line is compact and beautifully written. However, I'm not sure the last stanza works as well as the first. What do you think?"

> "When students feel valued by classmates and teacher, when a kind, caring community has been established, students appreciate constructive criticism."
>
> —Regie Routman,
> *Conversations,* 2000.

## Section Summary: Responding to Children's Poetry

1. Praise is essential to writing growth. Children need it, but it must be sincere, specific, and distinct from mere flattery.
2. Instructional criticism promotes writing growth when it is delivered in the right tone at the right time. It must be focused and relevant to each writer's ability to make use of the instructional support suggested.

## Sources of Inspiration for Writing Poetry

Walter (1962) said, "All true poetry is motivated by emotion. A poem does not come into being until an inner emotional compulsion moves a poet to put his thoughts and feelings into words" (p. 56). This does not mean that the intellect takes a leave of absence when the poet puts pen to paper. Rather, it means that emotion is the dominating force that brings poetry into existence.

For lesson plans that explore poetic devices through lyrics, see http://www.rockhall.com/programs/plans.asp

Poetry may have originated in ancient tribal rituals in which people expressed their feelings in the rhythms of dance and song. These feelings might include fear, anger, courage, love, hatred, triumph, and many more. The emotions that stirred our ancestors have not disappeared with the passage of time. The forces that guide poetic creation are alive and well, the very stuff of life. This section explores the feelings and thoughts that inspire poetry and also provides examples of how children and adults have expressed the rhythms of their own experiences in poetry.

## The Arts

The arts put children in touch with their inner world of thought and feeling, and helps children appreciate the richness of the outer world as well. Every human being has an inward and outward world. Art enriches and speaks to both. And while poetry can be about everyday topics—fishing, washing dishes, gardening—it can also be about the arts, such as music, painting, and photography.

**Music**. Writing poetry to music is inspiring. Music can clash, clang, whisper, and strum. So can poetry. Langston Hughes adapted some of his poetry to jazz music. Every type of music has its own rhythms, words, and sounds. Choose different types of music, and let children write to each: symphonic, rap, rock and roll, ballads, jazz, country. The poetry generated under the influence of music can be astounding in its diversity of thought and feeling.

> This is a good resource book for ideas on writing poetry with children. E. Kovacs, *Writing Across Cultures: A Handbook on Writing Poetry and Lyrical Prose,* 1994.

**Painting**. Painting is a natural source of inspiration for writing. Poet Terry Blackhawk teaches a poetry writing class at the Detroit Institute of Arts. She chose an art museum for the ambience of the setting and because the museum's collections provide inspiration for writing poetry. Teachers, of course, may not have regular access to a museum, yet reproductions of fine art can be found in books and magazines. After viewing a painting, lead a discussion. Ask children to imagine themselves within the painting, creating the painting, or watching the painter. Write to different styles of art, such as impressionism, realism, modern art, and pop art. For example, the lovely popular song "Starry, Starry Night" commemorates Van Gogh's famous painting *Starry Night*. Show children a reproduction of Van Gogh's work, tell a little about his tragic life, and play the song. Children's response to this inspiring combination of art, song, and biography can be remarkable.

**Photography**. Photography can be a source of inspiration for writing poetry. For instance, have children write a poem about a Civil War photograph, a family snapshot, or a Polaroid photo. Ask questions: What is this photograph about? What may have happened just before or after this photograph was taken? How did you think this photograph came to be taken? Who were the people in the photograph? What might they have been saying to one another? Not all photography includes people. Many photographic shots depict nature. Such photographs are also inspirational. *The National Geographic* is an especially excellent source of culturally diverse photography. Also, the nature photography of Ansel Adams, one of America's greatest photographers, can be a highly inspirational source for writing poetry.

> For more information on using poetry and photography, read *Haiku-Vision: In Poetry and Photography,* by A. Atwood (ages 9 and up). The author uses the camera as an aid in developing a sense of oneness with nature and of poetry as an experience of the spirit.

## Love and Anger

Love is a dominating emotion in poetry, but its expression is varied, subtle, and often mixed with competing emotions such as anger. The manner in which love or anger is expressed depends, to some degree, on the sophistication of the poet and the experience the poetry explores. The two poems below, "Anger" and "Love," were

## Field Notes
### Real-Life Experiences of a Classroom Teacher

I found poetry with my second-graders challenging but rewarding. The first time I taught poetry, I wasn't sure how to approach it. I thought that if I began with an acrostic poem, it would be easy and would require limited teacher assistance. Wrong. The challenge was greater than I expected. This is what happened.

First, I read several acrostic poems. I suggested some ideas, and then we brainstormed topics and words for the poems. I suggested some guidelines for writing acrostics, and we were ready to go—I thought. But soon I found myself surrounded with children needing my total attention. I wondered what I had done wrong. Nothing, it turned out. They just wanted help. When we were finished, we read our poems aloud and made a class book of poems. The children were proud. So was I. The book of poems became a class favorite. The

**Gail Pottinger**

big bonus was still to come. Over the next few weeks, I found my children creating their own poems. The second time we wrote acrostics, we all approached with confidence. Soon after we wrote the poems I learned of a publishing opportunity for young poets. My children submitted their poems to *Kaleidoscope Magazine* published by the Michigan Reading Association. My class entered many wonderful poems. But Molly's poem stood out, and it was chosen for publication. This was a dramatic experience for everyone in my class. Molly was invited to a young authors' conference in Grand Rapids where she met Mike Thaler, a popular children's author. The entire class found new enthusiasm for writing. They did not really believe that children's writing could be respected enough to be published. Publication was a powerful experience for all of us.

written by Brianna, a fourth-grader who had good reason for anger yet retained the hope that love might one day be possible.

**Anger**

Anger is red
Anger smells like firecrackers
Angers tastes like jalapeño peppers
Anger looks like a fire truck
Anger feels like hurt.

**Love**

Love is yellow
Love sounds like birds singing
Love smells like daisies
Love tastes like bubble gum
Love looks like peace
Love feels like the warm sun.

—Brianna

## Sorrow

When Robert Frost said, "No tears in the writer, no tears in the reader," he did not mean that the poet strives to make readers weep but that the poet reaches deep into mind and soul to express the innermost emotions. The result may be tears in the writer, and often tears in the reader as well. Perhaps this is because sorrow is the pathway to the mind's most potent words and ideas. Feelings of sorrow are complex and often mixed with feelings of anger and hurt. Sorrow's topics may include death, disappointment, and divorce, among others. When children write about their feelings, they may gain access to their best words and ideas. Read poems to children that express the range of emotions children are likely to experience. Then let them write their poems on topics of their own choosing. The poem "joyful noise" expresses complex emotions and has a title with an ironic twist.

### joyful noise

A shotgun blast
screams through the night
    echoing death,
echoing tears and loss,
    then dies on the wind.

children swallow ecstasy
    in search of paradise
and die in the crusty beds
    of dealers and pedophiles
who have learned to substitute
    cruelty for kindness
        and hatred for companionship.

old woman moves slowly
    down the street
eyes turn and follow
    as her rusty cart squeaks by,
        piled high with empty cans
    and filthy ragged clothes.
she hums softly to herself as she goes . . .
    Oh, make a joyful noise!

tiny flares of red
    in the dark
sounds like thunderclaps
    rip the silence
gangly adolescent boys,
    lonely boys,
    their blood running like water
        into the gutters
whisper for their mothers.
    Oh joyful noise!

young girl screams out
    silently for love,
her story on the walls
    in tiny spatters
        and long wavering smears
painted in blood red.
    make a joyful noise.

bombs shriek through the sky
    fall exploding on playgrounds
       and churches
parents sell their children
    for the cause of a "holy" war
    innocent sacrifices sent to die
their tears falling on stone hearts.

hear the voices, tens of millions,
    pleading in the void
    echoing fear and hunger,
      rage and loss
    echoing death
hear them fading on the wind
    joyful noise.

hear the voices, tens of millions,
    shattered spirits of the world's night.
see them gliding past
    silent shadows seeking shelter in the cracks
      of dying dreams. . .

God must have sad eyes.

—Kris Allen

## Dreams

Dreams are rich with images and provide material for the young poet. Milan Kundera, author of *The Unbearable Lightness of Being,* said, "Dreaming is not merely an act of communication (or coded communication, if you like); it is also an aesthetic activity, a game of the imagination, a game that is of value in itself." Dreams are of two major sorts: dreams that come with sleep and dreams that represent our purpose in life. Martin Luther King Jr. spoke of the latter kind in his historic speech "I Have A Dream." His purpose in life and in his speech was to make his dream of a just society a reality. Whether dreams are sleep-induced or our purpose in life, they make excellent material for poetry. Children may not, of their own accord, think of dreams as source material. It is useful, therefore, to read aloud poems that represent dreams and help children consider them as a topic for their poetry. Dana, a high school student, evokes the image of a dream in "Like a Dream."

**Like a Dream**

She comes with the mist, making her presence known.
Her existence only a dream, just a brush of reality.
The lights glimmer over her gorgeous dress,
Silhouetting her lovely appearance.
Her honeysuckle complexion captures many eyes
Like honey attracts bees.
Her silky straight hair reminds one of an ebony panther
Just stepping out of its morning bath.
similar to a graceful swan, she glides so elegantly.
Moving harmoniously with the sound of music
Her body flows like an ocean wave; she twirls, she spins,
She bends as she turns.
The crowd is pleased like children
Enjoying candy they just received,
Begging for an encore, wanting more of this enticing pleasure,
Knowing it will soon be over.
For the time has come to an end, she gracefully bows
And she disappears as she entered, accompanied by mist.

—Dana Moore

## Journals and Jottings

Keep a journal of your thoughts and observations. Journal entries can become source material for poems. Not everything recorded in a journal is likely to be used for poetry, but sometimes a word, thought, or observation can begin one. Try journaling with your children, and once they have gotten a good start, encourage them to comb their journals for ideas that could blossom into poetry. One way to encourage effective use of journals is to use yourself as an example. Take out your own journal and show your children how to do a purposeful search for a topic, line, or word. Explain what you did, how you did it, and the results of your efforts. Table 11.2 suggests different ideas for using journals in writing poetry.

*Teaching Tip*

**Table 11.2**

**Using a Journal for Poetry**

1. Record information and ideas about your family and friends.
2. Collect words, phrases, and sentences that interest you.
3. Write some sentences or paragraphs about yourself.
4. Experiment with words and ideas. Don't be afraid to draw in your journal.
5. Write a letter to yourself—or someone else.
6. Write quotations from books you've read. Note the sources.
7. Read a book or article about journals kept by other people.
8. Tell a story about yourself.
9. Record jokes and riddles you've heard or made up.
10. Write a poem.

## Memory Poems

Memory is a precious gift. One way to get children writing about their memories is to read poems with a memory theme. It is also helpful to provide structure lines or titles that invoke the memory theme. Two useful structure lines are *Moments from My Childhood* and *I Remember*. Even a 6-year-old can write about memories, and sometimes they write about "When I Was Young." A strategy for writing a poem based on the memory of someone other than yourself is to write as though you were speaking directly with the person you are recalling— "Dad, I remember the time . . ." Krystle's poem "I Will Always Remember You" recalls memories associated with her grandmother's funeral. She starts her poem with the line, "I remember Nana's funeral . . ." Writing from the personal point of view seems to make writing a memory poem easier for children.

### I Will Always Remember You

I remember Nana's funeral
Her favorite hymn, # 183 from the green book is playing softly.
Everyone showed up in dreaded black garb.
Tears coming from four walls.
It was family hour.
Mom held my little hand.
Her hand was cold like a bucket of ice.
As we got closer tears started to roll off her caramel face.
I tugged on her silk blouse.
"Lina Beana, now now," she yelled.
"Mama, look it's Nana!"
"Now now, Lina Beana, not now."

Nana was pretty.
With her hands crossed on her chest and eyes closed.
She wore her white suit that looks like the mother's board uniforms at
    church.
Her salt and pepper hair in tight curls,
Her long and natural fingernails were painted a solid beige,
The makeup she wore was all earth tones.
It all matched perfectly with the cream colored casket with golden bars.

I remember after the funeral.
We were all at Grandma's house.
Talking, Eating, Laughing, and Crying.
Emotions from every corner.
In the end all was happy.
Nana was gone from us,
But now living in a warm, beautiful, and loving place
with the man of her dreams.

I remember Nana's funeral.

—Krystle Hunter

## Literature

Literature is an excellent source of inspiration for writing poetry. It has probably inspired more poetry than any other resource. Fairy tales and folktales are especially useful. The young poet who wrote the following poem was so inspired. She brings Rapunzel into the modern age with her poem "RAP-unzel in the Year 2002."

### RAP-unzel in the Year 2002

My name is Rap-unzel and I'm here to stay,
My mama put me here and threw da key away.

She's the Queen of da castle and she rulez da throne,
But I've got a turntable and a microphone.

I'll hip and I'll hop till da break of dawn,
'Til I get enough homies gathered on da lawn.

So climb up da braids,
Come on give 'em a whirl,

Cause if you make it to the top,
I'll be your homegirl!

—Rebeca Valentin

## Collaborative Writing

When introducing a new poetic idea or a new poem, it is helpful to start with a collaborative class effort. Collaborative composition has many benefits, one of which is that it enables teachers to model writing. It also gives children experience in cooperative learning and builds confidence for independent composition. When initiating collaborative composition, keep the following guidelines in mind.

*Teaching Tip*

1. Choose a poem or topic and discuss it. Make notes or a web on the board when ideas are suggested.
2. Ask for lines to initiate the poem. If none are forthcoming, suggest a line of your own to get things started. Record suggestions on the board or on chart paper.
3. Encourage everyone to contribute. When suggestions slow down, add a line or an idea of your own.
4. Help children feel the rhythm of the lines by clapping, tapping, or chanting. This gives children a feeling for the rhythm or meter in their contributions.
5. Make one or more poems from the suggested lines. Have children select the lines they want for the first draft of the poem.
6. When the first draft is finished, revise the poem together. Take suggestions for improvements, and contribute some of your own.

7. Make a final copy of the poem. Send home copies; display the poems in the classroom; share them with the principal and students from other classes.

## Observing and Imagining

There is value in keenly observing the world that surrounds us—*not merely seeing, but observing.* Observation gives writers raw material for the imagination to work with. Imagination gives poetry its wings, its special distinctiveness. Imagination is not a magic carpet, an ethereal, otherworldly concept. It, too, is grounded in reality. Robertson Davies said imagination is "A good horse to carry you over the ground—not a flying carpet to set you free from probability." Walter (1962, p. 29) distinguishes between imagination and observation in the following example.

> Suppose you look out the window and say, "Oh, I see a butterfly!" Have you used imagination? Not if the butterfly is really there. Suppose you say, "I see a pretty yellow butterfly on the purple flowers." Have you used imagination? Not yet. The butterfly is there and the flowers are there, and they really are a butterfly and flowers. But suppose you think about the butterfly for a while and then say, "The butterfly is a fairy's golden airplane sailing over the purple flowers." Have you used imagination? Yes, because you have been able to see how an ordinary object is like something very different. Your statement has gone through three stages. The first stage is obviously not poetry. The second stage makes the picture come alive by the addition of color words and is often mistaken for poetry. But it is still just a picture. The third stage satisfies the first qualification for poetry—imagination—and is therefore a little poem. You might write it like this:

The butterfly
Is a fairy's golden airplane
Sailing over the purple flowers.

## Writing and Sharing Your Poetry

Children need sources of inspiration for writing, and teachers are in the best position to provide it. Teachers are the burr under the young writer's saddle; they can inspire children by example. If teachers want to awaken the slumbering imaginations of children, they must first awaken their own; if teachers want children to appreciate beauty, they must convey to children their own feeling for the beautiful; if teachers want children to write poetry, they must first write their own.

You may sincerely believe that you cannot write poetry. You may have heard that writing poetry requires special talent. Well, yes and no; partly true, partly false. Indeed, some writers are highly gifted, and great poets are certainly rare. But most writers have mastered their craft in much the same way that fine stonecutters master theirs. Work as a poet apprentice; learn the craft to the level that interests you. Perhaps you will never publish your poems. On the other hand, you may find that your poems are publishable. There is no need to rule out this possibility in advance, nor any reason for disappointment should it not occur.

## Section Summary: Sources of Inspiration for Writing Poetry

1. The arts, such as music, art, and photography, are an important inspirational source for poetry.

2. Love and anger are dominating emotions, and poetic expression often springs from a mixture of these two competitors.

3. Sorrow is a deeply felt emotion and can enrich the selection of words and thoughts. The poetic expression arising from sorrow is often powerful and poignant.

4. Dreams are rich with images and can provide inspiring material for the young poet. Dreams include the kind that come with sleep as well as dreams that express aspirations.

5. Journals and the jottings they contain can become a source for poetic ideas, including specific words, phrases, and even sentences.

6. Memory is a precious gift and can be used effectively to stimulate poetic writing. Help children write poems with a memory theme by providing structures that help them recall specific memories.

7. Literature, especially fairytales and folktales, is an excellent resource for writing poetry with children.

8. Careful observation gives writers raw material for poetic expression.

9. Teachers can inspire children to write poetry by writing and sharing their own poetic work with them.

10. A collaborative class effort is a good way to introduce a new poetic idea or a new poem.

# The Language and Technical Devices of Poetry

Music and poetry have much in common. Like music, poetry must be heard to be fully appreciated. No other use of language can match poetry for beauty, power, and technical brilliance. Poetry is unrivaled as a medium for verbal expression, the music of language. Children are natural poets. They are closer to the nuances of language than adults. Adults take language for granted; children do not. When children write poetry, they speak quietly of the joy that poetry brings them. This section discusses the language of poetry. Some poetic devices, such as rhyme and rhythm, are a natural part of language learning. Others, such as line and stanza, need only be discussed as children need to know about them. Still others, such as the concepts of onomatopoeia, alliteration, repetition, and imagery, should be discussed from time to time to help children understand more fully the sounds and sense of poetic language.

## Words

Kennedy (1986) tells a story about the painter, Edgar Degas, who complained to the poet Stéphane Mallarmé that he had lots of ideas for poems but selecting the right words frustrated him. Mallarmé replied, "But Degas, you can't make a poem with ideas—you make it with words." Had the situation been reversed, I imagine Degas might have said to the poet, "But Mallarmé, you can't make a picture with ideas, you make it with paint." Gerald Brenan would have sympathized with Degas's struggle. Brenan said, "Words are as recalcitrant as circus animals, and the unskilled trainer can crack his whip at them in vain."

Ideas are important, but words are the instruments that make the music; it is not the other way around. The choice and placement of words make poetry sing. Thus, any word can be the right word if it represents the right choice and is placed where it makes the right sense and sound. None of this is easy; no formula will produce good poetry.

Words have dictionary meanings, or denotative meanings; they also have positive or negative associations, or connotative meanings. For instance, the denotative meaning of *accountant* is a person who is skillful in financial matters. This is a positive, even flattering, description. On the other hand, *bean counter* is a synonym for *accountant,* but with entirely different connotative associations—it has a negative cast.

Teach children to respect words, the coin of the linguistic realm. Words are powerful when used precisely; they are flabby when used carelessly. The best way to teach children to respect words is to be a good example. Select words with care and use them intelligently, since children learn words and the concepts associated with them by hearing and reading them in meaningful contexts. The more children come to know and enjoy words, the more likely they are to use them effectively in poetry.

## Rhyme

Rhyme is an important poetic device, used at the ends of lines in some traditional forms but also in other ways. Undoubtedly the most universally recognized element in poetry, rhyme is a form of sound repetition that adds a pleasant quality

*Even Snoopy experiences the agony of choosing the perfect word—though his results are not spectacular!*

PEANUTS reprinted by permission of United Feature Syndicate, Inc.

to poetry. Three types of rhyme are near, internal, and end rhyme. In near rhyme, words share similar but not identical ending sounds. For example, *toast* and *fist* are examples of near rhyme, whereas *toast* and *roast* are examples of full rhyme. Internal rhyme occurs not at the ends of lines but in different places, such as beginnings or middles or ends of lines. End rhyme is the most familiar type, occurring at line endings.

Rhyme adds to the pleasant sound of the poem but can detract from meaning; if rhyme is forced, it can commandeer the poem. "The Remain" exemplifies this principle. The rhyme in the first stanza is natural, and the young poet does not strain to achieve rhyme. However, the second stanza is less effective than the first because meaning has been sacrificed to rhyme, which has become an end in itself.

**The Remain**

On Wednesday a fire came,
A big fire.
On Wednesday a fire came,
A jig fire
It came and went and saw
and spent
The value of the building.

But now it is a ghost
Because it took the most.
It was a century old
But now it is very cold.
It will never work again
And so it is a remain.

—Anonymous

The poet of "The Remain" is 7 years old. Viewed from that perspective, the poem is a success, and the first stanza is excellent. Nevertheless, the second stanza illustrates a typical problem: *children may focus on rhyme to the detriment of meaning.* This can hamper the natural beauty and rhythm of children's language. Rhyming is easily misused. The idea that poetry must rhyme is false and misleading. Children's poems should project sincere feelings cast in their natural but carefully chosen language. They need a significant period of time to write poetry unencumbered by technical demands such as those that rhyming presents. This delay gives them an opportunity to compose poetry without feeling constained by techniques that even mature poets find demanding. It releases them into enjoyment of the genre.

The following poems illustrate these points. In the poem "The Sky" we see a good poetic idea fail because the young writer felt obligated to use rhyme. Thus, we get an insincere poem which also lacks effective rhyming. In the poem "Cobwebs on a Foggy Day" no attempt has been made to use rhyme. The poem is written in the natural language of the child. Both poets are 10 years old; both have something to contribute. But the child who wrote "The Sky" might have written a much better poem if rhyme had not been forced on it.

### The Sky

The sky is as blue
As your baby blue eyes.
The sky is a place
That you dream of with sighs.
The sky is a place
To go when you're low.
The sky is a beautiful place,
You know.

—Anonymous

### Cobwebs on a Foggy Day

Wispy cobwebs strung the fences
Loosely drooping everywhere,
Like pearl beads.
They fade away if you touch them.
They hide in every crack;
They veil the trees
And carpet the grass.
Cold and grey
They blanket the world
Patching up holes.

—Anonymous

Children need to know when and how to use rhyme. Rhyme is a delightful, important poetic device, but it should not be stressed in early stages of poetic composition. When it is introduced or when children choose to use it on their own, they should be shown how it can both enhance and detract from the beauty of their poems.

## Rhythm

Rhythm in poetry is like the beat in music. In the rhythmic beat of poetry certain words receive more emphasis than others or are held for a longer duration. Words and their sounds  constitute an ordered, recurrent pattern of sound and silence. The rhythm of poetry underlies the music of the words. Watch a child sway to the music of a song, and you cannot doubt that a sense of rhythm is as natural as breathing. Swaying to the beat of music, following the flow of words, tapping a foot—all come without effort to children and adults. Poetry is simply a more ordered and deliberate realization of the rhythmic possibilities of words. Rhythm is a natural outcome of exposure to reading, writing, and listening to poetry. Children can write poems that embody their own music, their own rhythms, in their own words.

## Standing on the Shoulders of Giants
## Historical Contributions to Literacy
### Zena Sutherland

Imagine reading and writing a review of three books every single day for 27 years! That's how many books Zena Sutherland read and reviewed for *The Bulletin of the Center for Children's Books,* mostly a one-woman operation for most of those 27 years. And it's not as though she hadn't anything else to do. She reviewed books for the *Saturday Review* and *The Chicago Tribune,* taught at the Library School, and served on professional committees, including the Newbery and Caldecott Award Committees. Among her greatest accomplishments, however, must be listed the five editions of *Children and Books.* This classic textbook ruled and defined the field of children's literature for decades—and it's still in print.

Zena Sutherland is known for her pioneering critical reviews of children's books. Eden Ross Lipson said, "She accepted children as real and aware individuals and their books as real literature, and she was a stalwart sup-

For more information on Zena Sutherland, see http://www.news.uchicago.edu/relases/02/020614.sutherland.shtml

porter of books that addressed a range of problems and issues that some still find shocking" (Lipson, 2002, p. A27). Lipson cites as examples of enlightened reviewing Sutherland's reviews of Maurice Sendak's *Where the Wild Things Are* and *In the Night Kitchen.* Sendak's books were controversial when first published and are still controversial in a few circles today. Zena Sutherland found *Where the Wild Things Are* imaginative; she expressed no concern about Mickey's nudity in Sendak's *In the Night Kitchen.* All this sounds reasonable today, but her views were bold and controversial at the time Sendak's books were published. She was a pioneer, far ahead of many of her contemporaries in understanding what literature appealed to children and teachers.

She delighted in her work, loved receiving and opening the many books sent to her. Every book was like a present; every opening of a new package of books like a child opening a Christmas present. The body of work she left behind and her influence on children's literature will always be remembered. She died on June 12, 2002, at the age of 86.

## Use of Lines

The most obvious visual distinction between prose and poetry is the look of the line. Prose extends from margin to margin. Lines of poetry do not—with the exception of prose poems. Poetry simply looks different from prose.

How is line length determined in poetry? In free verse, the poet's personal inclination dictates it. Of course, the rhythm of the language guides the poet's decisions, but no formal rules tell the poet what constitutes an appropriate line of free verse poetry (see Table 11.3, p. 432). Poets sometimes rely on measures of beats or syllables per line, which characterize certain verse forms. The length of a cinquain or haiku line, for example, is determined by syllable or word counts. Poets can also choose their own patterns of lines. Clara established short line lengths for the following poem, to suit the rhythms of her language and thoughts. She preferred not to punctuate or capitalize in the traditional way, which adds to the flowing effect.

**Table 11.3**

**Making Line Breaks in a Poem**

*Teaching Tip*

1. Read your poem aloud. Make slash marks at each point where there is a natural pause for breath or emphasis. These pauses signal the rhythmic pattern of your language. Do not worry about getting the slash marks in exactly the right place. Close is good enough.
2. Add double slash marks at points where a new subtopic is introduced. The double slash marks indicate the stanza breaks in the poem.
3. Choose among these possible line breaks as you work on your poem.
4. Decide what visual effect you want your poem to have. Revise the way you've arranged the lines, if necessary.
5. Remember, you're the poet, and you have poetic license. If you like doing it a certain way, *do it*. Sometimes it's fun to create your own rules.

**Unsettled**

Long as the river flows
I will go
go to the end
the end where it bends
around and around
maybe even underground
as the river slows
I begin to know
that the river will end
end where it bends
I will see all around me
what's needed to be found
is the ground.

                        —Clara

## Punctuation and Capitalization

Punctuation and capitalization of poetry vary widely. For instance, Nikki Giovanni (1987) usually does not use punctuation, nor does she capitalize words in her poems. Her style is reminiscent of the work of E. E. Cummings. On the other hand, Langston Hughes and Robert Frost typically punctuate their poems based on the traditions of prose. They also capitalize words in the traditional way. The two poems below illustrate the traditional and nontraditional ways of punctuating and capitalizing poetry; both paths are fine. Children may want to experiment with both approaches.

**Circle**

Ask questions,
And you are thereby empowered to search for answers.

Search for answers,
And you may just find them.
Find them,
And you have learned.
Learn,
And you have grown.
Grow,
And you will find more questions to ask.

—Dan McCully


a snake
that glides
        across the dark
waters
        of faith

—Lyndonna Freeman


## Stanzas

A stanza is a group of lines in a poem. There are traditional stanza arrangements, such as quatrains (four lines) and tercets (three lines). Writers of free verse determine their own stanza groupings. Some poems are not broken into stanzas. Making stanzas for poems can be similar to paragraphing in prose, revealing subtopic breaks. Some traditional stanzaic patterns reveal the historical connection between music and poetry, as Padgett's (1987) account indicates:

> Back when poems were set to music, the stanza conformed to the tune. To coincide with the musical line, the stanzas were of equal length and hewed closely in measure and beat. They followed strict patterns. As now, the song often had a stanza that served as refrain (a stanza that would be repeated at intervals throughout the song).
>
> Even after poets no longer wrote for music, they continued to write poems that looked like those their predecessors set to music. Some poets didn't realize that the earlier poems had been written for music. And habit has its own force. But others just liked the way those songs looked. Since most people meet a poem first on the page, poets are very concerned with the way the poems look. For some poets, strict stanzaic patterns represent a challenge, for others the stanza is just an instruction to readers to pause. Some poets even use stanza breaks so the reader won't get confused or bored. (p. 194)

Give students freedom to experiment with stanzas. Literature models can reveal the possibilities.


## Onomatopoeia

The lovely Greek word *onomatopoeia* describes words that imitate their natural sounds. Words such as *buzz, growl, sizzle, hiss,* and *hum* are onomatopoeic. When they are pronounced, they sound like what they represent. *Hum,* for example, sounds like someone humming. Onomatopoeia can enhance the sound of a poem. Children like exotic words like *onomatopoeia,* and they enjoy working with onomatopoeic words. After reading poems with interesting sounds, encourage children to invent their own onomatopoeic words. Make up a few examples such as *bzitt:* the sound of a mosquito taking a bite; *zott:* the sound of a mosquito being swatted; *sqit:* the sound of a mosquito being squashed. Then have children work in pairs to create lists of real onomatopoeic words: *sizzle, purr, whir, pop, whoosh, screech, roar, ding-dong, jingle, bang, clang, growl, crack, bong, chug.*

## Alliteration

Alliteration is the repetition of initial consonant sounds of words placed in close proximity. Children can use alliteration in their writing and will enjoy doing so. Alliteration is used to good effect in Craig's poem.

Rabbits
Fuzzy, furry
Flipping, flapping, wiggling
Happy, gay, glad, funny
Bunnies

—Craig, age 9

*Teaching Tip*

The following suggestions will help children use alliteration in their poems.

1. Read several poems containing examples of alliteration. Point out alliterative phrases. Have children listen and identify phrases in the poems.
2. Write alliterative phrases on the board such as: *big bony bunnies, friendly freckled frogs, slithery slippery snakes.* Then have children write similar phrases of their own.
3. Choose a topic and write a collaborative poem. Ask children to contribute their own lines. Some of the phrases recorded on the board may become lines for the poem.
4. Have children write their own poems in which they use alliteration. Then have them read their poems from the author's chair.

## Repetition

Few things sound quite so lovely as the perfect achievement of repetition in poetry. Repetition of words, phrases, and sentences helps the poet achieve a desired effect in sound, meaning, or mood. Poe, for example, used repetition to create an ominous mood in "The Raven." The repetition of "Quoth the Raven, 'Nevermore,'" establishes the poem's mood of foreboding. Repetition reaches its zenith in the last two lines of Robert Frost's "Stopping by Woods on a Snowy Evening." The repetition of "And miles to go before I sleep, / And miles to go before I sleep" is a classic.

It's a long way from Frost to a first-grader, but even first-grade children can understand and use repetition effectively. The guidelines in Table 11.4 on page 436 will assist you in teaching children to use repetition in poetry. Mrs. Farah intro-

## Technology Tools

As I have written about connecting technology to the language arts, each step of my own writing has been supported with technology. I have used everything from the basic tools that were once technological breakthroughs—pencils and self-adhesive notes, for example, to the most savvy applications modern technology offers—a laptop computer with wireless Internet connection. These tools, combined with effective teacher instruction, can provide students with authentic audiences, purposes, and publication opportunities. I have used the following ideas with my students:

- E-mail and websites that give students authentic purposes and audiences for writing
- Publishing programs that provide students with tools to compose in a variety of genres for different purposes: greeting cards, invitations, brochures, certificates, booklets, and newsletters
- Story-composing programs, such as Storybook Weaver® DELUXE, and the Amazing Writing Machine® (by the Learning Company) to provide students with a range of writing prompts and projects
- Prentice Hall School's The Writer's Solution®, which familiarizes students with the process approach to writing as authors tell about the writing process
  - Word-processing software that helps students with their writing and reinforces grammar and spelling skills
  - Written interactions between students that can be supported with "musical computers" (Within a specified time, students compose one or two paragraphs. Then they switch computers and read the first author's text. They respond in different fonts and colors with their own paragraph. This cycle can be repeated as desired.)
- Graphic organizer programs such as Inspiration® and Kidspiration®, that help students brainstorm ideas and organize their thoughts

Technology provides a vehicle to help children develop writing ideas. Nevertheless, instruction in the elements of good writing is critical. Poor writing is poor writing, and no amount of electronic wizardry will transform it without teacher guidance. Glitzy animations, cool clip art, and funky fonts cannot hide poor writing. With teacher guidance, however, technology applied to the writing process in new and fresh contexts supports the development of writing skills.

Contributed by Lisa Kunkleman

---

duced the idea to her first-graders. She read poems with a repeated line and then suggested they try their hand at it. The results were mixed, as you might expect, but she got some lovely surprises. The first poem below was written by Eric, a fan of the Detroit Red Wings hockey team. As Eric wrote his poem, the Red Wings were in contention for the Stanley Cup, the top prize in ice hockey. This is what Eric wrote about the goalie, Dominik Hasek. The young author of the second poem, "The Fox," does an especially effective job of repetition of the line "The fox is on the run."

### Red Wings

Hasek got an assist
Last night
In the net
Last night

—Eric, age 6

**Table 11.4**

**Using Repetition in Poetry**

*Teaching Tip*

1. Read "Stopping by Woods on a Snowy Evening" by Robert Frost or "The Raven" by Edgar Allan Poe. Comment on the effect of the repeated line and how it adds to the poem. Invite children to comment as well.
2. Read "Red Wings" by Eric. Have children identify the repeated lines. Point out that this poem is a good example of effective repetition and that it was written by a 6-year-old first-grader.
3. Ask children to look for repeated words, phrases, and sentences in poems and songs they encounter. Comment on the examples they bring to you.
4. Have your children try repetition in their poetry. Their first efforts may prove clumsy. But continue to encourage their experiments and gradually your children's use of repetition will improve.

**The Fox**

Sleek, sly and sharp,
The fox is on the run,
The hens are wary,
The moonlight strong,
The fox is on the run.
The hens shivering,
The dogs trembling,
It is midnight,
The fox is getting nearer,
It prowls around the hen hut,
It creeps through the entrance,
Then a scream, squawk, and shuffle,
Then all goes quiet,
The fox comes out
With a hen in its mouth
And then goes off in the dark to
devour its prey.

—Anonymous

## Imagery

An image is a vivid mental picture that appeals to the senses and to the imagination. Poetry is filled with such images. Imagery achieves the unique, picturelike quality which distinguishes poetry from ordinary language. The raw material for imagery enters the bloodstream of the writer through the senses: taste, sight, smell, touch, hearing. Writers transform their experiences into images to capture the uniqueness of the person, place, or thing described. This requires thought, imagination, and hard work.

Even though our senses are constantly at work, it is possible to block out what they tell us. The closer writers are to their senses, the better chance they have of casting their experiences in strong, vivid images. We can become insensitive to the message of our senses, though this is more likely to happen to adults than to children. Sensory awareness is essential to creating fresh images. The guidelines suggested in Table 11.5 can help children develop powerful imagery. Quincy Vanderbilt, a high school student, created strong, vivid images in the poem "Jailbreak."

### Jailbreak

*(after Tyree Guyton's "Caged Brain")*

Detroit is a city
of caged brains,
of fogged eyes
that refuse to see
through a wall
where we want to go:
of singing mouths
that want to cry out to the world about
the talents inside
our bodies, bodies
Like wild horses
trying to be broken:
of muscled arms
that want to wrap up entire Libraries,
museums & history.
Detroit is a city
of skilled fingers
that manipulate

### Table 11.5

**Creating Imagery**

1. Pose a question such as What is fog? Urge children to "think wild." Tell them you want their most unusual, colorful, and even zany ways of describing how they feel, smell, taste, touch, or see fog.
2. Set a time limit, say 5 minutes. Record their words, phrases, and sentences on the board. Accept all contributions. Comment on those contributions that are most unique and apt. Then read Carl Sandburg's poem "Fog."
3. Put small groups of children together to organize the words, phrases, and sentences into a poem. Move about the class, assisting and encouraging each group in their work.
4. When the poems are complete, have each group present their composition. Lead a discussion on the imagery they have created.

*Teaching Tip*

our imaginations
like we're puppets:
of rooted legs
that refuse to uproot
so we can climb
over hot iron walls
of hearts that pump
oxygen to those brains
so that if they get
big enough maybe,
just maybe, we can
bust out of that cage
and grow to become
beautiful flowers

—Quincy Vanderbilt

## Simile and Metaphor

Simile and metaphor are figurative expressions and are especially useful for creating poetic images. A simile is a figure of speech comparing two unlike things, using the word *like* or *as*. Metaphor is also a figure of speech in which two unlike things are brought into even closer comparison—one is said to *be* the other, as in *bridges are iron lace.* Children are quite good at creating similes and metaphors naturally in everyday language. However, if you assign children to list five similes and five metaphors, they might ponder over the formal assignment all day with little success. Below are examples of similes and metaphors taken from children's conversations.

**Simile**

—my heart is like a wounded bird
—the road is like corduroy
—smelly as a sow's foot
—soft as a deer's face
—savage as a starved dog

**Metaphor**

—death is a twisted tongue
—the essay was a wasp that kept stinging me
—that boy is dog's breath
—the road is a black ribbon

Gather examples of figurative language by listening to children's conversations and searching their writings. Show them that they have a knack for this literary device. Then they can try introducing them into poems.

## Section Summary: The Language and Technical Devices of Poetry

1. Ideas are important, but words are the instruments that make the music of poetry. Choice and Placement of words make poetry sing.

2. Rhyme is the most universally recognized poetic device. It adds a pleasant quality to poetry. Three types of rhyme include near, internal, and end rhyme.

3. Rhythm in poetry is like the beat in music. Certain words receive more emphasis than others or are held for a longer duration.

4. The major visual distinction between prose and poetry is the look of the line. Some forms, such as haiku, limit line by syllable or word count. Poets are free to use established forms or make their own choices about line length.

5. Poets make their own rules for punctuating and capitalizing poetry. Some follow traditional rules; others do not.

6. A stanza is a group of lines in a poem. Traditional stanza arrangements exist, but poets can also make up their own stanza forms or avoid breaking the poem into stanzas.

7. Onomatopoeia describes words that imitate their natural sounds, such as *buzz, growl,* and *sizzle.* These words add a pleasant sound quality to poetry when used well.

8. Alliteration is the repetition of initial consonant sounds of words standing in close proximity.

9. Repetition of words, phrases, and sentences helps the poet achieve different effects in sound, meaning or mood.

10. Imagery achieves the unique picturelike quality that distinguishes poetry from ordinary language. It has a special appeal to the senses and the imagination.

11. Simile and metaphor are figurative expressions that draw comparisons between dissimilar things.

## Forms of Poetry

A poetic form is a structure incorporating set features such as number of lines, line length, rhyme scheme, and traditional subject matter. Traditional Japanese haiku, for example, is a poetic form with the following features: three lines, the first with 5 syllables, the second with 7 syllables, and the third with 5 syllables.

There are many poetic forms, and each has its traditional guidelines. Padgett (1987) lists 74 entries in his book on poetic forms and claims not to have exhausted the subject. The guidelines for poetic forms are seldom slavishly observed. Poets are an independent lot. They take liberties with poetic forms and write poetry in ways that satisfy their own creative instincts. In fact, poets continue to invent new forms. The very expression *poetic license* suggests independence. Children, likewise, are entitled to poetic license when working with a new form. Introduce children to a variety of poetic forms. They will add to children's poetic repertoire, challenge their imaginations, and expand their writing experience.

It is easy enough to make poetry dull. When introducing a poetic form, therefore, do not concentrate on its technical components. Rather, stress its purpose,

> "An image, like a paint stroke, means little alone but becomes a memory associated with a text in the mind of a reader."
> —E. O. Keene and
> S. Zimmermann,
> *Mosaic of Thought,* 1997.

## Point ≡ Counterpoint

### A Debatable Issue
### Nurturing the Poet

**Background**

Some teachers believe that children are natural poets. They feel that children's natural language is filled with meaningful poetic images, even though they may be unaware of it. They believe that an *early* emphasis on rhyming may lead children to produce poetry that neglects meaning because they are striving for rhyme. What do you think?

**The Debatable Issue**

It is best for children to begin writing free verse and other non-rhyming poetic forms rather than starting with rhyming poetry.

**Take a Stand**

Argue the case for or against the debatable issue. Marshal your arguments based on your philosophy, experience, and beliefs. After you have discussed the debatable issue among colleagues, consider debating the issue in your class.

---

pleasure, and challenge. Fill children's minds with the sounds and sense of a poetic form by reading poems that illustrate it. Then engage them in writing, with enjoyment as the primary goal. Guidelines for poetic forms can be bent or even ignored, but children should be aware of them. The springboard of creativity has more bounce when children are first fortified with knowledge of the new poetic form. Each form has its advantages, limitations, and challenges. Table 11.6 suggests guidelines for introducing a new poetic form. Poetic forms ranging from acrostics to tanka are described below in alphabetic order.

## Acrostic

An acrostic poem is one in which the first letter of each line forms a word, phrase, or sentence when read downwards. For example, in Amy's acrostic poem the vertical word is *dog*.

### Table 11.6

**Introducing New Poetic Forms**

*Teaching Tip*

1. Familiarity should first come through the ear and then the eye. Therefore, read aloud poems that exemplify the form. This will help children discover its structure.
2. Provide poems that illustrate the form for children to read. Discuss the form, emphasizing how it conveys feelings and thoughts. Talk about its technical guidelines: number of lines, line length, and related details.
3. Write a poem in the new form, and share it. Writing familiarizes you with the form and gives you confidence as you teach it.
4. Help children learn the purpose and structure of each new form.

Darn pest
Or lovable rascal
God when spelled backwards

—Amy

There are also double and triple acrostic poems. A double acrostic has a word or phrase at the line beginnings and ends. A triple acrostic has a word or phrase at the beginning, middle, and end. These forms are quite challenging, but some children may want to try them.

Simple acrostic poems are easy to write. First, choose a word or phrase for your acrostic poem. Next, write the word or phrase vertically down the page. Finally, write the lines that complete the poem. The acrostic form is well suited to writing Valentine poems. The poem below spells out the name *Ben*.

Beam me up, Scotty.
Earth is no place for me.
Need rest in eternity.

—Ben, age 16

## Alphabet

Letters of the alphabet are an excellent point of departure for creating poems. Alphabet poems can be written in many different ways. For example, an *a-to-z* poem starts with a word beginning with *a* and proceeds thus through the alphabet to *z*. Or the alphabet poem can be reversed and written from *z* to *a*. Another alphabet poem uses only words beginning with a single letter, such as *p* (Peter Piper picked a peck of pickled peppers). Of course, a few departures from the chosen letter are permitted. A simple alphabet poem is the LMNO poem. Instead of using the entire alphabet, have children choose three, four, or five letters as a basis for their alphabet poems.

"Always Bantering Couple" is an example of an alphabet poem in which all letters of the alphabet are used in order, starting with *a* and ending with *z*. It was written by Peggy Elson, a fifth-grade teacher, and used as an example prior to having her children try alphabet poems on their own.

### Always Bantering Couple

Alexandra bantered coolly,
Discussing epiphanies, fielding gossip,
Honing idle jabberwocky.
Kenneth listened, momentarily noticing
Other people quixotically responding;
Speculating together, unleashing vacuous words.
Xeroxing yesterday's zenith.

—Peggy Elson

## Cinquain

Cinquains are five-line poems with lines of two, four, six, eight, and two syllables, in that order. Adelaide Crapsey, an American poet, invented the form. A modified cinquain (pronounced SIN-kane), counting words rather than syllables, is frequently used. In this modified form, the five-line cinquain has one, two, three, four, and one word(s) per line, respectively. An example follows.

Seagull
Speckled motion
Graceful wings dipping
Distance in your heart
Fisherman

—Anonymous

## Clerihew

Got an idea for a new poetic form? Name if after yourself. That's what E. C. Bentley did. Bentley's middle name was Clerihew. This form consists of two couplets. Usually humorous or satirical in nature, clerihews often take the form of a biographical sketch. Clerihew is an interesting form to use with the study of historical figures, as the two examples below illustrate.

Benjamin Franklin
Deserves a thanking.
Because he flew a kite
We have light at night.

—Edgar, age 10

Abraham Lincoln
Started thinking
I'll free the slaves
From southern knaves

—Colin, age 13

## Diamante

The diamante is a seven-line contrast poem originated by Iris Tiedt. It takes its name from the arrangement of its lines and words into the shape of a diamond. The diamante is called a contrast poem because the first three lines contrast with the last three. This feature is well illustrated in "War." The contrast feature and the unusual shape snag children's interest. Diamante is especially suitable for children in intermediate grades and above. A diamante poem is arranged in the following way:

**Line Structure**

1  One subject noun
2  Two adjectives
3  Three words ending in -ed or -ing
4  Four-word summary sentence
5  Three *-ed* or *-ing* words, opposites of line 3
6  Two adjectives, opposites of line 2
7  One noun (opposite of subject noun in line 1)

> War
> death, sorrow
> fighting, killing, hating
> Nightmare of all nations
> helping, healing, loving
> life, joy
> Peace
>
> —David, age 13

## Free Verse

Free verse is unrhymed poetry, unrestricted in line length or rhythmic pattern. In short, there are no rules for writing free verse—the very essence of poetic license. Writers are free to determine their own rhythm or meter, where one line or stanza ends and another begins, which content and imagery to develop, how to end the poem.

Free verse is a natural form of poetry for children. Many children speak poetically; therefore they can write poetically. Free verse at this level requires no formal knowledge of poetry. Another significant advantage is that it does not have to rhyme. Rhyme has the unintended consequence of interfering with meaning when used by the inexperienced writer; free verse removes this constraint.

Encourage children to write free verse poetry about their daily experiences. Start by having children select a topic and discuss it. Write the ideas and images on the board. Mapping ideas in diagrammatic form may help children organize and visualize their ideas. Then the teacher and children can work together to shape ideas and images into a poem. The untitled poem below is an example of free verse written by a teacher.

> seeing with saddened night eyes
> i wander the empty streets . . .
>
> damp beneath my feet
> they reek of tears . . .
> the keeper of sorrow is near.
>
> through the muteness of the void
> his footsteps echo,

carried on the soft strands of night
they reach my ears . . .
    notes from his flute-like mouth
    playing tunes of death. . .
       the keeper of sorrow is near.

                —Kristine Allen

## Haiku

Writing haiku is a national pastime in Japan. Japanese poetry, of which haiku is the best-known form, emphasizes the wonders and beauty of nature, traditionally mentioning or referring to a season. Since it is strongly influenced by Buddhism, it also stresses the oneness of all creatures with the universe. The individual who understands one thing at one moment in time is better prepared to understand all moments and all things.

Content and linguistic style are important characteristics of haiku. Traditionally, there are three criteria for haiku. It is free of opinion; it alludes to a specific moment in time; it links nature and human nature. The language of haiku is uncomplicated and often free of metaphor or simile. The Japanese haiku is a three-line, seventeen-syllable poem. The first line has 5 syllables; the second 7; and the third, 5.

An English adaptation of haiku consists of three lines in which the first and third lines are slightly shorter than the middle line. This simpler form avoids the syllable count, a challenging discipline. Padgett (1987) maintains that there is no point in counting syllables in writing English haiku, since the English and Japanese languages do not share the same language rhythms. While Padgett makes an interesting point, the traditional syllable count can produce good poetry. Teach children the traditional guidelines. If your children find this too restrictive or too difficult, another form of Japanese poetry, senryu, provides a less demanding alternative. Naturally, children's haiku will sometimes depart from the traditional criteria. Nevertheless, their efforts should be recognized and appreciated. Here are two student examples.

In a huge meadow
A fawn leaps across the land
To its mother deer

          —Brittany

He is my daddy
Holder of my hand and heart
The one who loves me

          —Amy

## List

A list poem consists of a listing of items about people, places, events, and things. It can be rhymed or unrhymed. At first glance, one might wonder if it is actually a poetic form, but it has an honorable history. For instance, Allen Ginsberg's famous poem "Howl" starts out with a list, and Homer's *Iliad* lists the Greek heroes come to fight the Trojan War (Padgett, 2000, p. 100). The following poem, written by a former fifth-grade teacher, illustrates one type of list poem. It is followed by a student poem.

**Teach Long Enough, And. . .**

I Taught Them All:
Wayne, who made me laugh
Brian, who loved to read
George, who runs a junkyard
Elaine, who became a teacher
Kay, who writes poetry
Jim, who hated school
Kathleen, who often cried
Gary, who couldn't read
Kenny, who killed a man.
My kids, who grew up and left memories
As indelible as a tattoo on my mind.

—Nor Remarc

**Things That Make My Dog Happy**

Blowing leaves
Smells
People
Old bones
New bones
Buried bones
Squirrels
Birds
Even skunks
But mostly me.

—Jennifer, age 10

## Nonsense Verse

As the name implies, nonsense verse isn't supposed to make sense in the normal meaning of the word. Nonsense verse may mean nothing more than pure fun, as it turns logic on its head. Still, it appeals to children and to the hidden child that resides within every adult. Perhaps the best nonsense poem ever written is "Jabberwocky," which appears in Lewis Carroll's masterpiece, *Through the Looking Glass*. Lewis Carroll, an Oxford don whose real name was Charles Lutwidge Dodgson, wrote *Through the Looking Glass* because 10-year-old Alice Liddell asked him to write out Alice's adventures after he had told Alice and her sisters some stories orally.

For those who insist on making sense out of nonsense, "Jabberwocky" offers a challenge, particularly in its marvelously invented words. Words such as *frumious* are called *portmanteau words*. A portmanteau is a traveling bag, and just as one might jam many items of clothing into a portmanteau, Lewis Carroll enjoyed packing two or three words into one. Humpty Dumpty tells Alice that he can explain all the poems ever invented—and many that haven't yet been invented. Humpty says *slithy* means *lithe* and *slimy*. And it seems that *frumious* packs together *fretful, fuming, furious*. If you haven't read "Jabberwocky" before, you'll enjoy its nonsense, and your children will too. After reading the poem to your children and telling them about the portmanteau words, make up some words together. Later, have children make up their own portmanteau words. Enjoy nonsense.

### Jabberwocky

'Twas brillig, and the slithy toves
    Did gyre and gimble in the wabe;
All mimsy were the borogoves,
    And the mome raths outgrabe.

"Beware the Jabberwock, my son!
    The jaws that bite, the claws that catch!
Beware the jubjub bird, and shun
    The frumious Bandersnatch!"

He took his vorpal sword in hand:
    Long time the manxome foe he sought—
So rested he by the Tumtum tree,
    And stood awhile in thought.

And as in uffish thought he stood,
    The Jabberwock, with eyes of flame,
Came whiffling through the tulgey wood,
    And burbled as it came!

One, two! One, two! And through and through
    The vorpal blade went snicker-snack!
He left it dead, and with its head
    He went galumphing back.

"And hast thou slain the Jabberwock?
    Come to my arms, my beamish boy!
      O frabjous day! Callooh! Callay!"
    He chortled in his joy.

'Twas brillig, and the slithy toves
    Did gyre and gimble in the wabe;
All mimsy were the borogoves,
    And the mome raths outgrabe.

—Lewis Carroll

## Prose Poem

Prose poems are a cross between traditional poetic verse and prose. This form does not use rhyme, nor does it have a specified rhythm. It does make use of strong imagery and the freshness of language associated with traditional poetry. Padgett (1987) has given this description of prose poetry:

> You may find yourself writing a poem whose lines don't seem to have any natural breaking points; try recopying it as prose. Or you might find yourself trying to write a short story, when all you really want to do is to capture a moment or series of moments; try leaving out the characterization and plot. In both these cases, you can rework your piece a little and perhaps turn it into a prose poem, which might be the form it ought to have been in all along. (p. 152)

Jeni's poem fits Padgett's description of a prose poem. "My Chariot" has strong images but no plot or characterization. Originally, Jeni set this poem in traditional lines. Later, she experimented with the idea of writing it as a prose poem.

### My Chariot

Sometimes I sit alone at night. Loneliness paws at me, asking for my virginity. I feel God at the windowsill, knocking, asking, ready—waiting to take me there. I waited for my chariot at the river of unforgotten dreams. I hear a tinkling of bells and down Eternity Road comes my chariot. It is white and pillowed with cushions. Three others are seated there. One, a red brilliant light enclosed his head. This man is on his way to hell. Another, a woman, is on her way to her second life—reincarnation. And someone else, on his way to eternity. When I reached heaven, I lived again, happy, loved, and cared for once again.

—Jeni, age 13

## Quatrain

The quatrain is a four-line poem or stanza. It is one of the most common of all verse forms. Most often the quatrain is part of a longer poem organized into four-line stanzas. Songs and ballads are often written in quatrains, which can employ numerous rhyme schemes. A quatrain may be combined with a couplet to produce a six-line poem and, of course, there may be any number of four-line stanzas. Ben's "Three Sides of a Square" illustrates a mixture. The first two stanzas are quatrains with an *aabb* rhyme scheme. The last stanza is a combination of a tercet and a couplet.

**Three Sides of a Square**

Mulling around inside of me,
There are my selves, we number three.
They are not animate for eyes to see,
Meet emotional, physical, and rational me.

Emotional expresses my love or hate,
And conveys my opinion when someone's late.
Physical watches my body's well being,
And assures me of what I'm seeing.

When rational appears there will be no fight.
This side of me has true insight.
On matters concerning wrong or right,
Which of these appeals most to me?
The question's been answered; the number's three.

—Ben, age 16

## Rap

Rap derives from an African American oral tradition called signifying, a kind of word-magic contest in which participants insult one another as they rap in a rhyming, rhythmic chant. Early versions of signifying traveled from Africa to the antebellum South. Rap is now a major musical phenomenon, embraced not only by African Americans who have led the movement but also by the larger American community. Rap is especially popular among young people and is one of the most popular musical forms of our times.

Writing rap requires familiarity with the form. The best way to acquaint yourself with it is to listen to rap. Then think of something you want to say or a specific point you wish to make. Practice rapping in front of a mirror or with a friend. Tape-record your rap and listen to it. Compare your rap with your favorite rapper's music. Once you have a rhythmic feel for the music and the culture that rap implies, rework your rap until you are satisfied that you have made your point and remained true to the form. William, a high school student, wrote the following rap.

**Da Hood**

My boyz talkin' loud like true Dexter
boyz
I see my closest friends sellin' weed and
crack and becoming real drug boyz
I hear nothing but fast cars—
Regals, Cutlasses, Monte Carlos
purchased from Mel Farr.
I see nothing but vacant lots and
at the same time I hear gun shots.
I never see white people

unless they're cops.
I never see crackheads come out
until they're high off the rock.

But this is my hood.
When i step outside i feel cold
air in the winter but warmer air
in the summer and I know this
is my hood because seeing the worst
gives me strength.
I never see pretty girls, just
hoodrats, I never see taken care of
pets, just alley cats.
I don't think I've ever seen any other
bird except flying rats
I never hear any other music besides
rap. I never hear less than one
ambulance
a day. I guess somebody
somewhere
is peeling caps.

My hood may be hell
But my hood I love

—William Hector

## Senryu

When children write haiku, they may unintentionally produce a poem more accurately called senryu. Senryu is a three-line Japanese poetic form. Unlike haiku, it is not restricted to seventeen syllables, does not require the capturing of one moment, and need not refer to a specific time or season. Senryu can be introduced before haiku since it is easier for young children to manage. Group composition is a good way to start. Here is Andy's senryu.

My dog is a mutt
But he is a hero to me.
We sleep in the same bed.

—Andy, age 8

## Tanka

This ancient Japanese poetic form resembles an extended haiku. Tanka adds 2 lines of 7 syllables each to the basic haiku pattern of 5–7–5, giving a 31-syllable, 5-line composition structure of 5–7–5–7–7. This elaborate syllabic pattern makes writing tanka a challenge. An alternative form ignores the syllable count. Padgett (1987) suggests making the first and third lines short and the second, fourth, and fifth slightly longer. Either type may be used. The traditional form is more challenging, but Padgett's alternative may prove more manageable for some children. Tanka is not restricted by the traditional criteria that guide haiku. It can more easily accommodate a continuing theme or a progression of ideas and events.

> Some kids like to read
> Some like to play basketball
> Me, I like to write.
> When I write I feel special,
> Especially writing poems.
>
> —Manuel, age 13

## Section Summary: Forms of Poetry

1. A poetic form is a structure for creating a poem. Forms usually set features such as number of lines, line length, rhyme scheme, and traditional subject matter, though free verse has no such guidelines.
2. There are over a hundred poetic forms, and only 15 are described in this chapter. Ron Padgett's *Handbook of Poetic Forms* (1987, 2000) and John Drury's *Creating Poetry* (1991) describe many additional ones.

## Practical Teaching Ideas and Activities

*Teaching Tip*

**1.** *Foster a verse-rich learning environment.* Make poetry an integral part of all curricular areas rather than saving it for one focused unit of study. Link poetry to authentic, meaningful experiences for your community of learners, such as an apple poem prior to a field trip to the apple orchard or a poem about loss if a student loses a pet or family member. Link poetry to other reading and topics of focus that the class is engaged in. Numerous poems provide valuable enrichment and possibly present new information for your science, social studies, or math topics. When students have been exposed to a wide variety of poetry, they can even write poems to focus topics, present information, or demonstrate understanding. Read poetry aloud, and share in the joy of hearing language at its best!

**2.** *Put poetry in the classroom library.* Designate a poetry section in your classroom library. Make available a rich array of poetry for students to explore. You might even consider providing periodic opportunities for students to share and recite newly discovered poems with the class in a poetry circle. The children sit in a circle, and one student at a time expressively reads a favorite poem he or she has discovered. Be sure to give them time to rehearse first.

**3.** *Keep poetry journals or notebooks.* Students can use them not only to write their own poetry but also to copy favorite poems to read, illustrate, and enjoy.

**4.** *Create a young poets' word book.* Keep a class notebook available in your writing center as a place for students to write any word they find interesting, descriptive, silly, funny, or sad that they would like to share (such as *ironic, creepy, bashing-lashing-dashing, pouncing*). Encourage students to both contribute to the collaborative word collection and to look through it to find a word to add to a personal list. Allot several blank pages in students' writing notebooks or personal dictionaries for word collections. Organize words into categories. (Adapted from Janeczko, *Favorite Poetry Lessons: Grades 4–8*, 1997).

**5.** *Teach students to see the ordinary as extraordinary.* Part of the beauty of poetry is that it takes ordinary experience and turns it into the extraordinary. Poetry often awakens all of our senses, and that is one of the things that makes it so powerful. To get students to become more aware of their senses and how this awareness enriches our encounters in the world, ask them to "collect ten observations a day." In this activity, for a week they carry a small notebook in which to record things they observe with any of their senses. To get them started, together generate a list of the sights, smells, tastes, sounds, and textures in the classroom. Show the students how to use clear descriptive language, not necessarily in complete sentences. Later they can use these ordinary experiences as inspiration for poetry writing.

**6.** *Make a word box.* Fill a small box with numerous evocative words and phrases printed on slips of paper. Introduce the box by shaking it so the papers rattle but students have no idea what's inside. Give them some time to guess. Carefully open the lid and, as they peek in, they are hooked. Tell them that you are going to give each of them a "sprinkle of words." Let them play with them and make interesting combinations: things that sound nice or scary, that make you feel happy or sad. They can share with the class any combination they particularly liked after this exploration period. They can keep a list of "best phrases" to tap into later when looking for something to write a poem about. The objective here is to help young writers understand that poetry is comprised of words that have sound, meaning, and feeling. This word box is a starter; it helps the ideas for poems grow!

See the Blue Pages at the back of the book and on the Companion Website for additional activities.

## Reflection and Summary

### Reflection

An English teacher told me, "I don't have time for poetry. I have to get my children ready for the MEAP." Every Michigan child must take the Michigan Education Assessment of Progress for reading during fourth, seventh, and tenth grades. Failure to do well on this examination has serious consequences for Michigan teachers and schools. Nearly every state has similar examinations. I take seriously teachers' concerns about the use of instructional time. Teachers are the ones who bear the burden, pay the price, take the criticism when test scores disappoint. They have the right to guard their instructional time jealously. Yet I hope to persuade teachers that poetry is not a waste of time; it can yield short- and long-term benefits. Poetry teaches children to use language with precision; it uncovers latent talent and heightens self-awareness; it burnishes the intellect and exercises the imagination. Do not let concerns about exams, standards, and accountability crowd poetry out of your curriculum. It can elevate and enlighten the standards we seek to achieve in teaching literacy to children.

## Summary

This chapter has presented the following main ideas.

1. To prepare children to write poetry, develop an appreciation for it, read poetry aloud, talk about poems and poetry, talk about poets and their work, and read, memorize, and revise poetry.
2. Respond to children's poetry by nurturing the creative spirit, praising their efforts, and providing thoughtful instructional criticism.
3. Sources for inspiring poetry include writing about the arts, love and anger, sorrow, and dreams; memorizing poems; using literature to inspire; collaborative writing; observing and imagining; and writing and sharing your own poetry.
4. Poetry employs special language and technical devices. These include but are not limited to careful word selections, rhyme, rhythm, use of lines, punctuation and capitalization, use of stanza, onomatopoeia, alliteration, repetition, imagery, and simile and metaphor.
5. There are over a hundred poetic forms, many with set guidelines for number and length of line, rhyme scheme, and subject matter. Even so, poets tend to modify these guidelines to suit their own interests and convenience, a form of poetic license. Poetic forms include acrostic, alphabet, cinquain, clerihew, diamante, free verse, haiku, list, nonsense verse, prose poem, quatrain, rap, senryu, and tanka.

## ◀ Questions to Challenge Your Thinking

1. There are many ways of preparing children for poetry. Of the ones suggested in this chapter, which one do you favor most? Why?
2. This chapter suggests the value of teachers writing and sharing their own poetry with children. Make a rational argument for or against this idea.
3. Several ideas for inspiring children to write poetry were suggested in this chapter. What additional ideas would you suggest?
4. What is onomatopoeia? Make up some words that have onomatopoeic qualities.
5. Think of a poetic form not described in this chapter. How might you make this form accessible to children?
6. How is free verse different from haiku or cinquain?
7. When was the first time you wrote a poem? The last time? Choose one of the forms described in this chapter and write a poem.
8. Imagine that you have agreed to read poems to a class of third-graders. Which poet would you choose? What specific poems might you read aloud to the children?
9. What problem might an overemphasis on rhyme cause young poets?
10. Do you agree or disagree with the idea that children have creative potential? Defend the position you take.

## ◀ A Case Study

Read the following case study, and then discuss the questions below with your classmates or colleagues. (Reread the section in this chapter on praise and criticism.)

Michele Farah wanted her first-graders to write poetry. She read poems aloud, shared her own poetry, discussed poets, and generally developed an appreciation of poetry among her first-graders. After writing some early poems, she gradually introduced a few simple poetic devices. For instance, near the end of the year she introduced the poetic device of repetition of a line. Eric is one of Mrs. Farah's students. His reading has been coming along slowly, but he is enthusiastic about writing; he has an engaging personality, works hard, and loves sports. When Mrs. Farah introduced the idea of repetition in poetry, Eric jumped right in and wrote a poem,

which he entitled "Red Wings." Eric's poem also appears in the section of this chapter on repetition in poetry.

**Red Wings**

Hasek got an assist
Last night
In the net
Last night

—Eric

1. What would you say to Eric in praise of his poem?
2. Do you think there is value in providing instructional criticism in this instance? If no, explain why. If yes, what instructional criticism would you suggest, and why?

## ◀ Revisit the Anticipation Guide

Return to the Anticipation Guide in the chapter opener and review your original responses to the questions. Complete the anticipation guide again, then consider these questions.

1. Did you change your mind about any items? Which ones? Why?
2. What idea did you encounter with which you most strongly agree? Explain.

3. What idea did you encounter with which you most strongly disagree? Explain.
4. What chapter ideas did you find most useful? least useful? Why?
5. What's missing or incomplete in this chapter that you'd like to know more about?

## VideoWorkshop Extra!

If your instructor ordered a package including VideoWorkshop, go to Chapter 8 of the Companion Website (www.ablongman.com/cramer1e) and click on the VideoWorkshop button. Follow the instructions for viewing the appropriate video clip and completing the accompanying exercise. Watch the Companion Website for access to a new interactive teaching portal, My Lab School, currently under construction.

### A Philosophy for Teaching the Mechanics of Writing

The rules and styles of grammar and the mechanics of written language change over time. Some have their origin in Latin and Greek. Some are arbitrary and violate common sense—the double negative rule is an example. Styles of written and oral language also influence how we write and speak. Ordinary speakers of English influence rules and styles of expression, although writers, educators, and intellectuals may have the greater influence. For instance, Hemingway tended to write short sentences. Other writers imitated his style, and as a consequence, long, complicated sentences became less common among influential writers. We need rules to guide oral and written expression, but they are subject to reasonable change as language and culture changes.

# 12 The Mechanics of Writing: Grammar, Punctuation, Capitalization, and Handwriting

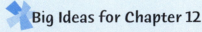

### Big Ideas for Chapter 12

1. While grammar has many definitions, grammar as a description of the language patterns which native speakers use automatically is of special interest.

2. Research, extending back 100 years, does not support the belief that the study of traditional school grammar improves writing.

3. Three reasons are often cited for studying grammar: it makes better writers, it enriches knowledge of the language, and it helps in learning a foreign language. However, these ideas have no substantial support in the research literature.

4. Relevant grammatical concepts should be taught within the context of writing.

5. There are four sentence types and three sentence structures. Sentences can be combined for economy, interest, and clarity.

6. Punctuation and capitalization are conventions needed for effective English writing. These skills are best taught and learned within the context of writing.

7. Teaching the mechanics of written language requires careful pacing, minilessons, and teacher modeling.

8. The major objective of handwriting instruction is legibility.

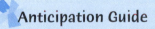 **Anticipation Guide**

*Consider the following statements, and determine whether you agree or disagree with each. Save your answers, and revisit this guide at the end of this chapter.*

1. Grammar instruction helps children enjoy and appreciate language.　　agree　disagree
2. Traditional school grammar is easily learned by most children.　　agree　disagree
3. Dialect speakers are in special need of grammar instruction.　　agree　disagree
4. A 6-year-old knows more grammar than a linguist can accurately describe.　　agree　disagree
5. Teach the rules of grammar and children will write better.　　agree　disagree
6. The rules for punctuation and capitalization are of little use to writers.　　agree　disagree
7. The mechanics of writing are best taught within the context of writing.　　agree　disagree
8. Young children have little need to learn the mechanics of writing.　　agree　disagree
9. Technology has made legible handwriting unnecessary.　　agree　disagree
10. Handwriting is a lost art.　　agree　disagree

I know grammar by ear only, not by note, not by rules. A generation ago I knew the rules—knew them by heart, word for word, though not their meanings—and I still know one of them: the one which says—which says—but never mind, it will come back to me presently.

—*Mark Twain*

Today I worked very hard. This morning I put in a comma. This afternoon I took it out.

—*Oscar Wilde*

## A Literacy Story

Anna Quindlen, author and columnist, wrote a fine book called *How Reading Changed my Life*. As a child, she read voraciously. She knew the characters in her books as real people. She won a scholarship to a private school because she remembered a passage from *A Tale of Two Cities*. She said of this book, "Like so many of the other books I read, it never seemed to me like a book, but like a place I had lived in, had visited and would visit again, just as all the people in them, every blessed one—Anne of Green Gables, Heidi, Jay Gatsby, Elizabeth Bennet, Scarlett O'Hara, Dill and Scout, Miss Marple, and Hercule Poirot—were more real than the real people I knew." Like many great readers, Anna Quindlen lived within the covers of the books she read. She knew the places and the characters as real life, *not as a reflection of life but life itself.*

This fascination, this identification, this obsession with books captivated Anna Quindlen. Great readers and writers do not spring from the excellence of our instructional strategies; they spring from our ability to involve children in books so that they open their own doors to the literate life. I doubt anyone ever became a great reader because they learned a great strategy; I know of many people who became great readers because they read a great book. We can teach grammar, the mechanics of writing, and fine penmanship, and these skills will have their useful place in life. But until we entice children into books, we will succeed only in creating semiliterate technocrats, which is a long way from a life steeped in books.

Angus Wilson said, "A child's story reading, if it is rich, lays open a world that lasts a lifetime; an impoverished, banal story world dulls the spirit forever." A rich story world is crucial to a life in literature and literacy. Reading aloud to children is the place to start. Just today a 4-year-old visited my office with his mother, a teacher. "I'm reading a chapter book," he proudly informed me. Actually his mother was reading a chapter book to him, but by his lights, who did the reading was irrelevant. He said to me, "Mom reads chapter books, so I wanted to read one, too." Way to go, Mom!

Early language educators created grammatical rules based on Latin, Greek, and other more dubious sources, including math. The famous double negative rule has its roots in math, not English grammar. Latin was thought to be the most eloquent of languages, but Latin is an inadequate model on which to base English grammar. Latin grammar depends substantially on inflected word endings for meaning; English grammar depends largely on word order. Some traditional school grammars are still based on Latin, but English grammar should be based on English as it is spoken and written today. Modern English grammar must depend on continuously updated linguistic descriptions of English, with a nod to social and educational acceptability. This means we must be open to modern usage, new vocabulary, and changing sentence structures.

> "While thought exists, words are alive and literature becomes an escape, not from, but into living."
> —Cyril Connolly

English is the language of world commerce and cultural interchange. For instance, English is the official language of aviation. Pilots from every nation use it. Few Americans realize that when they order a CD, check on their credit card account, or register a complaint about a faulty computer, they are often talking to

## A MATTER OF STANDARDS

### Language Conventions

**Standard 6:** Students apply knowledge of language structure, language conventions (e.g., spelling and punctuation), media techniques, figurative language, and genre to critique and discuss print and nonprint texts.

Standard 6 speaks of students' need to understand and appreciate the structures and functions of the English language. Consequently, they must become familiar with its conventions, grammar, punctuation, and spelling. There is no question of the appropriateness of this standard, but educators differ as to how it is best accomplished. The context of meaningful reading and writing pro-

vides the right setting for this instruction. Students need opportunities to plan, draft, and revise their own compositions. Children gain skill in understanding and responding to the need to improve their own texts, including the conventions, as peers and teachers respond to their writing. They need opportunities to critique the work of their peers through peer editing and conferencing. Standard 6 can be met when children have access to a variety of audiences and collaborators inside and outside of their classrooms. Publishing opportunities, author's chair experiences, peer editing, the Internet, and writing partnerships can provide the needed audiences and collaborators for readers and writers of all ages. This chapter suggests ways in which standard 6 can be met.

a citizen of India—living in India. English is no longer the exclusive cultural property of America or England. English belongs to the world; it belongs to immigrants. It belongs to ethnic groups; it belongs to the poor as well as to the rich; it belongs to the well educated as well as the undereducated. We must, in short, accept an expanded understanding of the role and function of English grammar in American society. We need not mourn this change. On the contrary, we should celebrate the extraordinary flexibility and expansiveness of the English language. It is no less ours because the world has adopted it.

 # Grammar

The purpose of grammar instruction is to improve children's written and oral expression. But often it does not achieve this purpose. One reason grammar instruction does not take hold is that it is often taught in isolation from the context in which it is used. For instance, isolated grammatical exercises have little impact on writing. On the other hand, grammatical concepts taught within the context of writing tend to improve writing. There is another reason why grammar instruction often fails. The most useful concepts are undertaught while the less useful ones are overtaught. For instance, learning to combine sentences improves writing, whereas learning the parts of speech does not. Until we learn which grammatical concepts to teach, how to teach them, when to teach them, and in what context to teach them, we will have difficulty helping children apply grammatical concepts to their oral and written language.

## Defining Grammar

There are many definitions of grammar. During the Middle Ages, grammar referred to Latin grammar and came to mean learning in general. Hartwell (1985) gives five definitions for grammar: (1) formal patterns that speakers of a language use automatically to convey meaning, (2) the scientific study of language, (3) rules governing how one ought to speak or write, (4) the grammar taught in schools, and (5) grammatical terms and concepts used to teach prose style. There are prescriptive grammars, the kind that appear in traditional grammar books. There are descriptive grammars, the kind linguists develop. No single definition can be all-inclusive. Perhaps the truest definition is this one: *grammar is a description of the language patterns that native speakers use automatically.* This restates the first definition above. This definition democratizes grammar; it reminds us that all speakers of a language know the grammar of their language, even though they cannot define it with the precision of a linguist. Grammar, in this sense, belongs to the people who speak a language.

How grammatical rules are established, taught, and learned is of concern to teachers and students who seek to understand and use them. Knowing grammar is useful to all who seek to speak and write within established traditions. Observing the grammatical conventions makes writing more easily understood. However, this says nothing about how knowledge of these conventions is acquired. The conventions of grammar are derived through linguistic analysis, but tradition plays a role as well, particularly in matters of usage and mechanics. Kane (1988) gives this explanation of what is grammatical:

> The sentence *"She dresses beautifully"* is grammatical. These variations are not: *Her dresses beautifully. Dresses beautifully she.* The first breaks the rule that a pronoun must be in the subjective case when it is the subject of a verb. The second violates the conventional order of the English sentence: subject–verb–object. (That order is not invariable and may be altered, subject to other rules, but none of these permits the pattern: "Dresses beautifully she.")
>
> Grammatical rules are *not* the pronouncements of teachers, editors, or other authorities. They are simply the way people speak and write, and if enough people begin to speak and write differently, the rules change. (p. 11)

## Research on Grammar and Writing

Traditional school grammar (TSG) has been taught in American schools for centuries. Many people believe that studying TSG improves writing. Little or no evidence supports this belief. After an extensive review of research, Braddock, Lloyd-Jones, and Schoer (1963) concluded, "The teaching of formal grammar has a negligible or, because it usually displaces some instruction and practice in actual composition, even a harmful effect on the improvement of writing" (pp. 37–38). Hillocks (1986) conducted a meta-analysis (a study of several studies) on grammar, usage, and mechanics to determine its influence on writing. He concluded, "School boards, administrators, and teachers who impose the systematic study of traditional school grammar on their students over lengthy periods of time in the name of teaching writing do them a gross disservice which should not be tolerated by anyone concerned with the effective teaching of good writing" (p. 248). Hillocks and Smith (2003) reported that when three of the best studies in Hillock's meta-analysis were examined separately, the case against grammar grew even stronger. They concluded that any focus on instruction is more effective in improving the quality of writing than grammar and mechanics.

Elley, Barham, Lamb, and Wyllie (1976) conducted a study that is considered by many to be one of the most carefully conducted studies on the topic of grammar and the improvement of writing. They found that studying grammar, usage, and mechanics had no beneficial influence on writing. Harris (1962) conducted a well-controlled two-year study in which one group received grammar instruction and the other group spent an equal amount of time reading and writing. He found that the non-grammar group wrote more complex sentences with fewer errors and scored higher on a number of other criteria. Smith and Elley (1997) concluded that while some exposure to the rules of grammar may be useful, it is not a prerequisite for learning to write effectively.

Part of the clash between research findings and teachers' beliefs is that research studies do not always differentiate among the factors that are often included under the general heading of grammar. Do some elements of grammar aid writing while others do not? Very likely, but this question is not fully answered either, although Shaughnessy (1977) suggested that four grammatical concepts may be useful:

sentence structures, inflection, tense, and agreement. Studying punctuation and capitalization, often included under a broad definition of grammar, aids writing. Unfortunately, few research studies separate strictly grammatical issues from mechanical skills, such as punctuation and capitalization.

An important issue is how, when, and in what context grammar should be taught. If taught within the context of writing, does it prove more beneficial than when it is taught in isolation? Yes. Grammar, punctuation, and capitalization are best studied within the context of actual writing (Calkins, 1980; Weaver, 1998) because in that meaningful context writers can see the need for appropriate grammar and mechanics. But research and experience give little reason to expect that traditional grammar improves writing when taught in isolation from writing.

## Typical Reasons for Teaching Grammar

Grammar instruction has a long tradition in American schools. It has never gone out of fashion, though its strength has waxed and waned. Various versions of grammar have been tried—traditional, structural, transformational. Arguments can be made for each type, but there is little evidence to recommend one over the other. Three reasons are often cited for teaching grammar: (1) it makes better writers, (2) it enriches knowledge of the language, and (3) it helps in learning foreign languages.

**Grammar Makes Better Writers**. Research tells us that teaching grammar in the traditional isolated manner has little or no appreciable influence on writing. The alternative is to teach the most relevant grammatical concepts within the context of writing. Thus, if five hours a week are available for teaching English, decisions must be made about how to best use the available time. We can teach writing for five hours, grammar for five hours, or divide the time equally between writing and grammar. If the objective is to develop better writers, using most of the five hours teaching writing is the better alternative since relevant grammatical concepts can be taught and learned within the context of meaningful writing. Teaching grammar within the context of writing means stressing revision and editing, teacher modeling of relevant grammatical concepts, and teaching minilessons on grammar and mechanical topics drawn from an analysis of student weaknesses and strengths.

Figure 12.1 on pages 461–462 includes several pages taken from a book written by Ali, a third-grader. The full piece is 18 pages long. In Ali's class children write for an hour every day. Visitors to Ali's room are always greeted with enthusiasm. The children are excited to have a visitor. They crowd around, begging the visitor to listen to their pieces. Everyone wants an opportunity to read. Their teacher, Ms. Monas, is an exemplary writing teacher. She teaches in a working-class neighborhood. All of her children write and all are excited about writing. While Ali may be the best writer in the class, many others write nearly as well. As you read Ali's piece, notice how easily he uses the conventions of written language. Notice too that most of the time he uses the conventions correctly, though sometimes he slips up. His illustrations are expressive and often humorous, although you would need the entire 18-page book to fully appreciate his sense of humor and creativity.

**Figure 12.1**

**Traveling Around the Planets** (continues on next page)

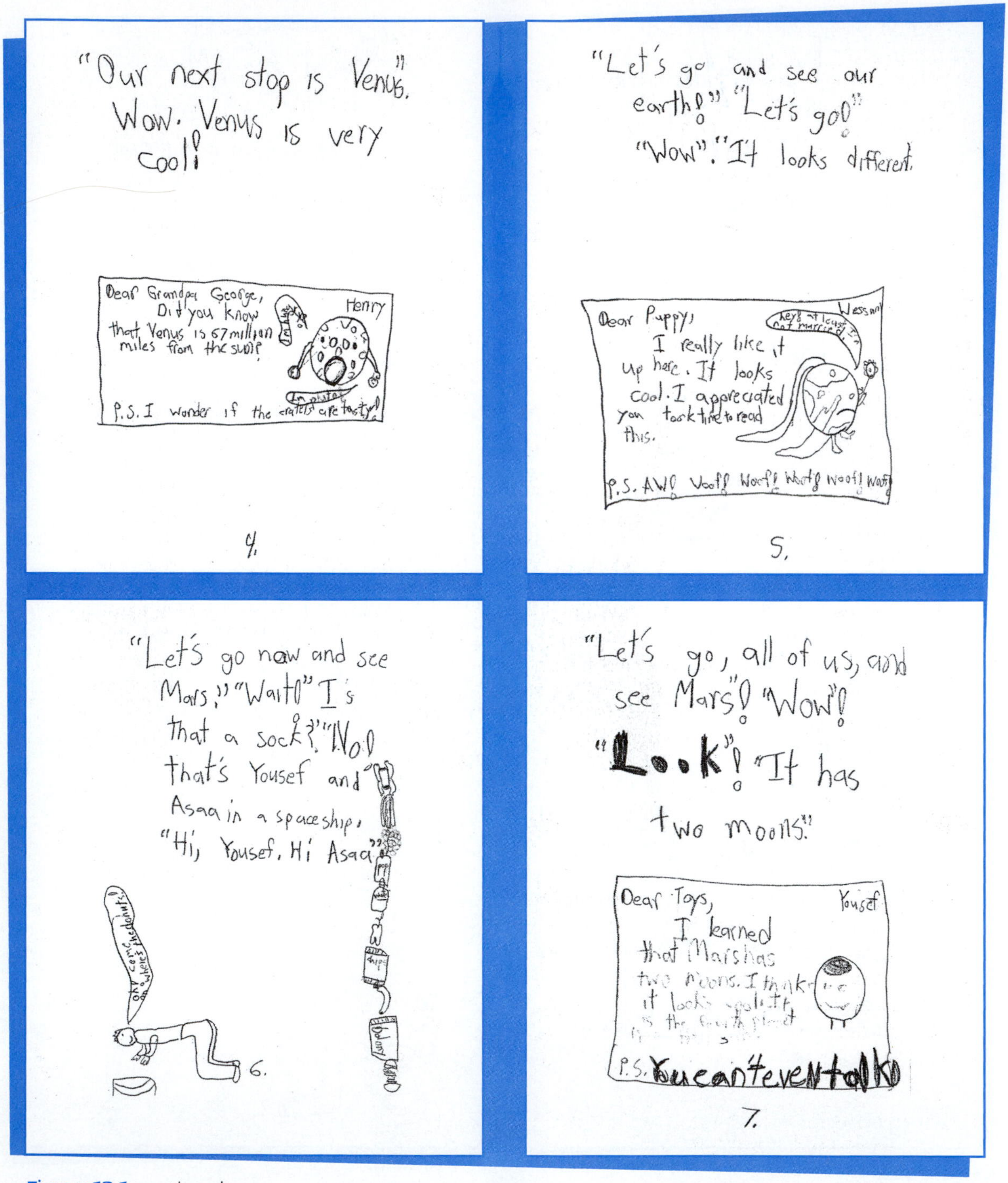

"Our next stop is Venus."
Wow. Venus is very
cool!

4.

"Let's go and see our
earth." "Let's go!"
"Wow". "It looks different.

5.

"Let's go now and see
Mars." "Wait!" I's
that a sock?" "No!
that's Yousef and
Asaa in a spaceship.
"Hi, Yousef, Hi Asaa"

6.

"Let's go, all of us, and
see Mars!" "Wow"!
"Look"! "It has
two moons."

7.

**Figure 12.1**, continued

The skills of grammar and mechanics are handled by Ms. Monas through minilessons, modeling, and on-the-spot conversations as children draft or revise their pieces. Occasionally, Ms. Monas teaches a longer lesson on skills she judges need more time and attention. I admire the way Ms. Monas motivates her children, the way she teaches grammar and mechanics within the context of meaningful writing, and the way she keeps her children growing and glowing. She always has nice words to share with her young writers.

> "The development of power and efficiency with language derives from using language for genuine purposes and not from studying about it. The path to power over language is to use it, use it in genuinely meaningful situations, whether we are reading, listening, writing, or speaking."
> —"Relationship Between Language and Literacy," by Walter Loban, 1979.

**Grammar Enriches Knowledge of the Language**. The humanist argument for the study of grammar operates on the principle that it's good for you. It will help you appreciate the nuance, beauty, and grandeur of language. And language is magnificent. Surely it is humankind's greatest achievement. Everything depends on language. Human knowledge is passed down through the generations through language, and we need it to perform daily interactions with one another. Where would we be without language? Therefore, the argument goes, knowing and appreciating the beauty, structures, categories, and conventions of language is valuable in itself. This humanist argument is not easily refuted, since its premise is aesthetic, not subject to empirical verification. Unfortunately, many children seem not to gain much of an appreciation of language from studying traditional grammar. Children tend to find it boring and confusing.

The intent of the humanist argument is a good one, but it doesn't work well with grammar. Traditional grammar instruction is likely to teach students that language study is uninteresting and perplexing. The better way to develop an appreciation for language is through literature. The humanist argument for appreciating language is more powerfully illustrated in listening to a poem, enjoying a novel, or reading an essay than in sorting out grammatical issues, such as the parts of speech.

**Grammar Helps in Learning Foreign Languages**. It is an article of faith among some advocates of foreign language learning that knowing English grammar makes it easier to learn French or Spanish, for instance. While there is no reliable evidence to sustain this view, the argument has an appealing logic. If you know how nouns and verbs are modified in English, for instance, might not this grammatical awareness help you understand how similar or dissimilar categories work in a foreign language? This seems logical, but the evidence is that few students actually learn how verbs and nouns are modified through a study of traditional English grammar. Moreover, typically children do not acquire enough knowledge from traditional grammar instruction for it to be useful in foreign language learning (Hillocks & Smith, 2003).

## Teaching Grammar in a Reading–Writing Context

Grammar and mechanics have value. Precisely because of this, it is counterproductive to teach them under conditions that inhibit learning them. When grammar and mechanics are disliked, it becomes harder to teach them, even in appropriate contexts. Grammar must be learned, but it is best learned within the context of writing rather than as an isolated subject.

Revision has the most powerful influence on learning to write, and this includes content as well as the mechanics of writing. Cox (1999) makes the point that grammar and conventions must be taught within a writing context: "Grammar and language conventions can be taught as part of the writing process. Doing so is most meaningful during the editing and revising stages of writing" (p. 394). If children have little opportunity to revise and edit their writing, they will not, indeed cannot, discover and correct the grammatical and mechanical errors that are inevitable in early drafts. Finding and correcting miscues in early drafts can take place in different learning settings, such as peer editing. When three or four children work together to read and discuss their work, they are likely to discover flaws they can readily correct. Reading books is another important setting.

> "Keep a collection of children's books that provide good examples of how words can be used. Categorize them based on use of imagery, description, figurative language, and so on.

Children possess more grammatical and mechanical knowledge than they apply in their early drafts. This is not surprising since adult writers have the same problem. Every experienced writer needs editorial support. That is why every major newspaper employs rewrite personnel. Their job is to improve the hastily written drafts of experienced reporters. All writers, including renowned authors such as John Steinbeck and Ernest Hemingway, had editors whose job was to make their writers look better than the submitted manuscripts implied.

Children do not automatically make use of grammatical concepts they have been taught. However, when grammatical concepts are taught in conjunction with reading and writing, they are learned better. Weaver (1998), whose research on teaching and learning grammar is superb, summarizes the case for teaching grammar in a reading–writing context: "teaching *grammar* in the context of writing works better than teaching grammar as a formal system, if our aim is for students to *use* grammar more effectively and conventionally in their writing" (p. 33).

## Point ⇒ Counterpoint

### A Debatable Issue
### Teaching Grammar

**Background**
Traditional school grammar has been taught for centuries in American schools. Research does not appear to support its value for learning to write when taught in isolation. Most children appear not to learn much grammar in school. Why might this be? What ought to be done to change this situation?

**The Debatable Issue**
Grammar should be taught, even though research shows that it has little influence on improving oral and written expression.

**Take a Stand**
Argue the case for or against the debatable issue. Would you teach grammar? If yes, what is your rationale? If no, why not? Marshal your arguments based on research, experience, and your teaching philosophy. After you have discussed these questions among colleagues, consider debating the issue in your class.

## Elements of Grammar

What constitutes the elements of grammar is debatable. For instance the acronym GUMS (grammar, usage, mechanics, spelling) is sometimes used to broadly categorize grammar issues. The mechanics of writing deals chiefly with punctuation and capitalization. These concepts are discussed in a separate section of this chapter. Spelling deals with the orthography of language and is not a grammatical concept; it is discussed in detail in Chapter 13. Three grammatical concepts are discussed in this section: parts of speech, usage, and sentence structures and patterns. This does not exhaust the content of grammatical elements, but it covers three prominent components of traditional grammar instruction.

**Parts of Speech**. Research does not support the belief that knowing the parts of speech helps children learn to read, write, speak, or listen. Therefore, if the parts of speech are to be taught, there must be a reason other than the traditional one. Some say that knowing the parts of speech provides general knowledge about the language and how it works, and appeals to the humanist argument. But since this goal can be better achieved through the study of literature, this reason for teaching the parts of speech seems weak.

Whether useful or not, traditional school grammar usually includes identifying and manipulating the eight typically identified parts of speech: nouns, verbs, pronouns, adverbs, adjectives, prepositions, conjunctions, and interjections. Nouns and verbs are considered the building blocks of sentences. Adjectives, adverbs, and prepositions modify nouns and verbs, and pronouns replace nouns in sentences. For those who are convinced that teaching the parts of speech is essential, it seems best to so in authentic contexts such as writing and oral expression activities. Table 12.1 describes some of the principal functions of nouns and verbs.

### Table 12.1

**Functions of Nouns and Verbs**

| Nouns | Verbs |
|---|---|
| 1. Nouns are often signaled by a determiner: *the* ball, *a* horse, *those* dogs, *my* pig. | 1. Verbs change to agree in number with their subject nouns. |
| 2. Most nouns have a plural and singular form: Nouns are usually pluralized by adding *-s* or *-es*: *toy/toys; patch/patches*. Nouns sometimes change in structure to form plurals: *child/ children*. | 2. Verbs change in tense to indicate time relationships. |
| 3. Possessive nouns are signaled by adding *'s: my friend's book*. Possessive forms can also be signaled by adding *': walruses' tusks*. | 3. Verbs can have suffixes: *-ize, -ify, -en, -ate*. |
| 4. Some nouns take suffixes: *-tion, -ence, -ance, -er, -or, -dom, -age, -hood, -ness*. Less often they take prefixes—*il-, em-, be-, de-* —to form new words or change meaning: *illiteracy, behead*. | 4. Verbs can have prefixes: *be-, re-, dis-*. |
| 5. Nouns can be replaced by pronouns: *Sandy* is smart. *She* writes poetry. | 5. Verbs may end with *-ing*. |
| | 6. Verbs have auxiliaries that change form to show tense or number. |

*Children know the parts of speech implicitly. An argument can be made that knowing the parts of speech adds to one's knowledge of the English language, but it does not add to writing knowledge.*

**Usage**. Usage refers to the customary way in which language is used. But whose customs are elevated as the standard of English expression, and do these customs promote effective communication in all circumstances? The correct way to speak and write, typically called standard English, actually is a "convenient abstraction, like the average man," as G. L. Brooks once said. Sometimes language needs jaws that bite and claws that catch, like Lewis Carroll's Jabberwocky. Though it works well for certain purposes, standard English can be sterile and unevocative when a strong message must be sent. For example, during the Battle of the Bulge of World War II, an American general is said to have replied to a surrender demand, "Nuts." The general could have said, "While our situation is dire, I refuse to acknowledge the possibility of defeat. Therefore, I respectfully decline your invitation to surrender." Such polite words, cast in standard English, do not bite, do not catch the emotion of the word "Nuts." That is why standard English cannot be the only standard by which we determine how language shall be deployed.

Judgement of correct and incorrect usage requires a more complex understanding of language patterns than schools have customarily explored. Usage in one linguistic community might substitute *teached* for *taught; brung* for *brought; hisself* for *himself; she don't* for *she doesn't*. Such usage is sometimes called home or street language. It may represent the speech patterns of a dialect or a bilingual group of speakers of English. When home usage differs from school usage, children need an opportunity to learn alternative usage patterns.

School language can be described as an alternative form of language usage. It is essential that home and street language be recognized as legitimate language. We should not give children the impression that their native language patterns are inferior. There are simply alternative ways of using language: home and street language, school language. Each has its place in communication; each is appropriate for certain purposes.

Children need opportunities to read widely in books that exemplify school language; they need opportunities to hear oral language that exemplifies school language. They need minilessons about and models of how school language sounds orally and appears in writing, and they need to read. Messages that their own language is inadequate are not true, and surely do more harm than good. As such, correcting children's oral language doesn't work well, but modeling school language or standard English is useful and is likely to work better in the long run. Children need to learn standard usage because it is the language of commerce and the academic world. Demonstrate that there are alternative ways to use language and that school or book language is an alternative that has great value.

## Writing Grammatical Sentences

Grammar is mostly concerned with the structures and patterns of sentences. A sentence can be defined as a complete thought, yet a complete thought may also define a word, paragraph, or essay. Another definition says that a sentence is a group of words that includes a subject and predicate, yet successful writers violate this norm every day. Perhaps a sentence is a group of words that starts with a capital letter and ends with a punctuation mark, but this definition also lacks precision. Actually, there is no conclusive definition of a sentence. Even though defining a sentence is difficult, writers have been writing good and bad sentences since the Sumerians invented writing more than 5,000 years ago. There are many ways to write a sentence, and often the choice is determined by purpose and style. Some writers develop a unique style to suit a specific purpose—humor, for instance. Russell Baker, longtime humor columnist for *The New York Times,* often wrote sentences in the following style:

> Grammar funny stuff. Not make sense. Not good to write, "She look good." Why not? Rule say must write, "She looks good." Look good anyway you write it. No? Had grammar teacher in high school. Name, Sarah Fuller. Sarah never look good except at my essay. Look plenty good then. Take bucket red ink pour all over essay. Sarah say, "Fix mistakes Russell!" How? Can't read paper—too much red ink. Grammar sure funny stuff, Sarah.

Sentence sense grows out of legitimate writing experiences during which children are writing stories, poems, essays, and other accounts that are meaningful to them. Children are not starting from scratch; they possess an oral language reservoir of sentence knowledge. The sentence concepts described here already exist in children's oral language. This section discusses three basic sentence concepts: (1) the four sentence types, (2) three sentence patterns, and (3) combining sentences as a way to improve writing.

> "This is the sort of English up with which I will not put."
> —attributed to Winston Churchill, concerning the spurious usage rule forbidding that a sentence end in a preposition

**The Four Sentence Types**. There are four sentence types: statement, question, command or request, and exclamation. Writers need to know how sentences are punctuated, combined, and organized. Children have working concepts of each of the four sentence types, so teaching them the nomenclature is less important than helping them understand how to punctuate and order the sentences into coherent paragraphs and longer pieces of writing.

1. Statement sentences tell, declaim, or state something. They end with a period.

   *Example:* Some children enjoy writing, but others do not.

2. Question sentences ask something. They end with a question mark.

   *Example:* Do you like to write?

3. Command or request sentences give commands or make requests. They end with a period.

   *Example:* Finish your poem. (command)
   
   Please finish your poem. (request)

4. Exclamatory sentences express strong feeling, surprise, or emphasis. They end with an exclamation point. Exclamatory sentences should not be overused. Even though an exclamatory sentence takes the form of a statement, question, or command, it still ends with an exclamation mark.

   *Example:* Come here! (command)
   
   What's the big idea! (question)
   
   I'm mad! (statement)

**Three Sentence Structures.** There are three common sentence structures: simple, compound, and complex. This terminology may confuse children, and they may think they know nothing about such sentences. You can overcome the confusion by demonstrating that children use simple, compound, and complex sentences all the time when they talk. Record sentences children use in classroom conversation, and write them on the board or on a handout as examples of the three sentence structures. For example, point out that independent and subordinate clauses are a natural part of the complex sentences they speak. Keep in mind that it is less important for children to know sentence terminology than to write sentences well. For example, children do not need to identify and label sentence parts because this skill is not essential to good writing. Rather, writing involves transferring oral language knowledge into written language and then transforming and reshaping that language through revision.

Here are descriptions of each sentence type:

1. Simple sentences have a complete subject and predicate.

   *Example:* Ernie mowed the lawn.

   By the way, children do not need to identify predicates and subjects in their sentences. This is gilding the lily. They already have implicit knowledge of subjects and predicates; otherwise they would not be able to utter such sentences in their oral language.

2. Compound sentences join two or more independent clauses. Each clause must have a subject and predicate. Conjunctions such as *and, but, for, or, so,* and *yet* join the simple sentences to make a compound sentence. A comma precedes the conjunction to divide the independent clauses within the compound sentence.

   *Examples:* The girls played basketball, and the boys watched. The game lasted two hours, but everyone stayed to the end.

3. Complex sentences have one independent or main clause and one or more subordinate clauses. The independent clause can stand alone as a sentence, but the dependent clause cannot. Subordinate conjunctions such as *although, after, if, where, when,* and *while* introduce a subordinate clause. A comma separates the subordinate from the independent clause.

   *Examples:* Although it rained, everyone enjoyed the picnic. While sunshine would have been nice, we managed to have fun without it.

**Combining Sentences**. Combining sentences often conveys meaning more economically, and economy aids clarity. Combining sentences often results in better writing and more mature syntactic structures. For instance, Hillocks and Mavrogenes (1986) found that combining sentences improved overall writing quality. Hillocks and Smith (1991) believe this to be the most important finding on sentence combining. While it is clear that sentence combining has a positive influence on writing, researchers do not know how or why it has this effect. Three reasons seem possible:

- It extends conceptual knowledge (Freeman, 1985).
- It leads to increased attention to other aspects of writing (Crowhurst, 1983).
- It has a positive influence on revising and editing (Strong, 1986).

Consider these six procedures for combining sentences.

*Teaching Tip*

1. Two sentences with the same subject but different predicates often make a more economical sentence.

   *Example:* Janet directed the band. She also played the drums.
   Janet directed the band and played the drums.

2. Two sentences with the same predicate but different subjects can also be combined.

   *Example:* Anthony is a fine writer. Jake is a fine writer.
   Anthony and Jake are fine writers.

3. An appositive is a noun or phrase that follows another noun and explains it further. Sentences can be combined by using appositives.

   *Example:* Maria is a fast reader. She just finished reading *War and Peace*.
   Maria, a fast reader, just finished reading *War and Peace*.

4. A preposition and its object make up a prepositional phrase. Sentences can be combined by turning a descriptive sentence into a prepositional phrase.

   *Example:* That girl is a whiz at math. She has a calculator in her hand.
   That girl with the calculator is a whiz at math.

5. When two or more sentences have the same subject and predicate, their modifiers can often be combined.

   *Example:* That music is loud. But that music is fine.
   That music is loud but fine.

6. Combining sentences usually results in more economical writing. Even after combining, cutting unneeded words can improve writing further.

*Example:* Sue prefers friends who are on the intelligent side. She also likes her friends to be funny.

*Combined but not economical:* Sue prefers friends who are funny and on the intelligent side.

*Combined and economical:* Sue prefers funny, intelligent friends.

## Section Summary: Grammar

1. Traditional school grammar (TSG) consists of a complex set of rules and guidelines for spoken and written English.
2. Linguists define grammar as the language patterns that native speakers use automatically. This definition differs from that of traditional school grammar.
3. Research does not support the belief that the study of traditional school grammar improves writing, though this is often cited as a reason for teaching it.
4. Three reasons are typically cited for studying grammar: it makes better writers, enriches knowledge of the language, and helps in learning a foreign language. These reasons are questionable.
5. Grammar is most effectively taught in the context of meaningful writing. Minilessons, revising, modeling, wide reading, and writing conferences are effective ways of teaching grammatical concepts.
6. While teaching the parts of speech is a common practice, little evidence warrants its inclusion in the grammar curriculum.
7. Students need to understand types of sentences and their patterns. Their implicit knowledge of these concepts can be tapped as they master the use of sentences in contexts of writing and reading.
8. Practice in combining sentences within a writing context can improve writing.

## Punctuation and Capitalization

Jamie and Allie were reading drafts of their dinosaur stories to each other in a peer editing conference. Jamie claimed that quotation marks were needed to set off conversations in a story. Allie said, rather heatedly, that she knew that, but she wasn't sure where quotation marks started and ended. "So I left them out," she said. Jamie showed her where he would have put them and then turned to his teacher and asked, "That's right, isn't it Ms. Morgan?" Ms. Morgan confirmed Jamie's assertion, and the two partners went on working. After peer editing ended, Ms. Morgan wrote two examples on the chalkboard of how quotation marks are used in conversation. Her minilesson took no more than three or four minutes and it arose spontaneously as a result of Allie and Jamie's conversation. This episode illustrates the idea of teaching at the point of need and in the context of writing. The combi-

## Grammar Checking

*Connecting Technology to Teaching*

"Help!" I've just finished checking my writing with my computer's grammar check and I'm confused. I thought I did everything right. Is it possible that my grammar program is malfunctioning or speaking another language?" Anyone who has used the grammar feature of word-processing software can relate to this scenario. Since grammar-checking software is notoriously inaccurate, students must learn to use it critically. For example, students can work in small groups and use the grammar check with their own writing, or they can copy and paste writings from the Internet to check. With the teacher or a grammar handbook available, they can determine if the error flagged by the software is really an error. By consulting their teacher or handbook, they can reject or accept the grammar suggestions made by the software.

Although the conventions of writing are best taught in the context of their own writing, some Internet sites that can provide practice based on your classroom objectives. Check these sites to see if they fit your needs.

Daily Grammar (http://www.wordplace.com)
This site provides a free grammar lesson each day of the week.

Be the Editor
(http://www.educationworld.com/a_lesson/02/lp249-04.shtml)
Students search for capitalization, punctuation, spelling, and grammar errors in a work sheet about famous African Americans; designed for grades 3–8.

The Apostrophe
(http://owl.english.purdue.edu/handouts/grammar/g_apost.html)
This site from Purdue University provides instruction, examples, and practice.

*Where the Wild Things Are* by Maurice Sendak
(http://www.successlink.org/great2/g1358.html)
Students learn about adjectives by describing a "wild thing" of their own creation; designed for lower elementary students.

Pop Up Grammar (http://www.brownlee.org/durk/grammar)
Students take online quizzes and receive immediate feedback on their responses; a good resource for students to use independently.

Grammar Review: My Favorite Author from AskERIC
(http://askeric.org/cgibin/printlessons.cgi/Virtual/Lessons/Language_Arts/Writing/WCP0068.html)
Students write about a favorite author and analyze their writing for specific grammar concepts.

Basic Grammar Review using "Jabberwocky" from AskERIC (http://askeric.org/cgi-bin/printlessons.cgi/Virtual/Lessons/Language_Arts/Writing/WCP0004.html)
Designed as a beginning-of-the-year review, this activity helps students identify weaknesses in grammar skills.

Adverbily from AskERIC
(http://askeric.org/cgibin/printlessons.cgi/Virtual/Lessons/Language_Arts/Vocabulary/VOC0020.html)
Students act out verbs and adverbs.

Grammarcise from Kodak®
(http://www.kodak.com/global/en/consumer/education/lessonPlans/lessonPlan067.shtml)
This activity has seventh- and eighth-grade students make slide/tape presentations of the parts of speech.

More Grammar Review Using "Jabberwocky" from AskERIC (http://ericir.syr.edu/cgibin/printlessons.cgi/Virtual/Lessons/Language_Arts/Grammar/GRM0001.html)
An innovative activity has students identify parts of speech.

Contibuted by Lisa Kunkleman

*Faisal and Brad are quite expert with the computer. They are searching the Internet to find information for a research report.*

nation of peer editing and a spontaneous minilesson provided appropriate instruction for a specific writing convention when it was needed.

Punctuation clarifies writing. It helps readers understand the writer's meaning by signaling the logic, rhythm, and structure of writing. When punctuation is used well, it complements and clarifies the writer's meaning. When poorly used, it muddles meaning. It is important, therefore, for children to understand the purpose of punctuation and know how to apply the rules that define its use. Punctuation operates on three levels: flexible conventions, inflexible rules, and personal style or preference:

- Punctuation has some flexible conventions. For example, the last comma in a series is a style choice, not an absolute rule. Some style manuals eliminate it, but others call for it.
- Punctuation has inflexible rules. For example, a period at the end of a statement is not optional.
- Punctuation may sometimes be determined by a writer's personal style, preference, or purpose. For example, in stream of consciousness writing, punctuation may be deliberately ignored to achieve the purpose the writer has in mind. Some poets use little or no punctuation; others use traditional punctuation. But such choices are the prerogative of the sophisticated writer, not the novice.

## Research on Punctuation and Capitalization

How, when, and under what circumstances punctuation skill is acquired has not been researched as fully as other aspects of writing. A few studies give a general picture of how children learn to punctuate their writing. Calkins (1980) compared two third-grade classes to see how children in each class acquired punctuation under different teaching conditions. One teacher taught punctuation in the conventional manner, using isolated drills. The other integrated punctuation instruction with writing. As one might expect, the children taught punctuation in the context of daily writing fared significantly better. Calkins study illustrates how skills learned outside a context of meaningful application are less likely to be learned readily or retained long. Cordeiro, Giacobbe, and Cazden (1983) found that first-grade children appeared to form and test hypotheses about how to use punctuation in their writing. Another finding was that writing provided more opportunities to use punctuation than textbooks or worksheet exercises. Finally, they found that clear, accurate explanations facilitated learning, while abstract explanations caused confusion. Hodges (1991) summed up research on punctuation, capitalization, and segmentation (spaces between words) with this conclusion: "At the present state of understanding, it appears clear that growth of knowledge about functional uses of punctuation, capitalization, and segmentation can be accounted for within the context of the development of general written language ability" (p. 780).

## Teaching Punctuation and Capitalization

Punctuation and capitalization are less abstract and more relevant to writing than are the parts of speech. Careful use of punctuation and capitalization is essential to effective, readable writing. The knowledge and skills required to understand and use these conventions are readily grasped by children, even primary-grade children, when they are taught within the context of meaningful writing.

**The WRITE Context**. When children write early and often, they inevitably discover that their writing differs in certain respects from the writing they see in books or the writing of their teacher. Young writers often invent their own conventions. For instance, they may put stars between words to indicate word boundaries; they may put periods after every word, line, or complete story. They often throw in a punctuation mark in a place where they intuit that it is needed. In other words, they may operate on a best guess basis. Often they are right, but inevitably they make mistakes.

> It is during the revising and editing stages that students apply their . . . knowledge of grammar, punctuation, . . . Children learn to use language by using it. Teachers must keep in mind, however, that the purpose of all these experiences should be to communicate meaning.
> —*Teaching Language Arts,* by Carol Cox, 2000.

Grasping punctuation and capitalization concepts improves slowly. It progresses quite well, for instance, when teachers record dictated stories. Language experience stories are records of children's own words. The taking of a dictated story provides ample opportunity for teachers to comment casually on the mechanical conventions of punctuation and capitalization. A teacher may say, "You see, I put a period at the end of Manuel's statement. A period means STOP. A period shows

*Teaching Tip*

you've come to the end of a sentence or statement." Brief, casual comments about the conventions of written language suffice.

The right attitude about errors will enhance instruction and learning. Errors provide the perfect context for meaningful instruction, but this won't occur if the teacher makes a "big deal" of it. *Errors are expected. Errors are not an occasion for hand wringing.* Rather, they provide an occasion for teaching in the moment of need, when it is most useful.

## Field Notes
### Real-Life Experiences of a Classroom Teacher

We live in the information age, but many teachers continue to teach for the industrial age. We need to prepare children for the age in which they live. I got involved in technology because I saw how motivated my students were to use it. I decided to see how technology could be integrated into the curriculum in a meaningful way. With 28 students and two computers, I wasn't sure if this was feasible. But I found ways to use technology as an instructional tool.

With only two computers, a center approach was my best option. At the center, students could take part in many activities, such as the use of *hotlists*— lists of websites that have been previewed by an adult. The web addresses are categorized to direct students' research. Once a hotlist is created, it can be augmented throughout the year. I looked for sites that covered the third- and fourth-grade curricular units of study—weather, animals, authors online. I previewed websites related to our curriculum so that students only needed to click on the link to be connected to the site.

While at the computer center, students were sometimes instructed to visit specific sections of the hotlists pertaining to our current unit of study. At other times they visited sites of their choice. A form at the Computer Center ensured accountability. The form asked for the title of the site(s) visited and three things students learned from visiting them. They had the option of sharing their new

Ann Llewellyn

knowledge with the class as an extension activity.

Technology can be used for whole group instruction as well. I often use graphics and photos that illustrate topics in the curriculum. For example, I couldn't find sites at a third-grade readability level on the topic of cloud formation, but there were wonderful photos of clouds for them to observe.

I often asked students to do follow-up activities on the computer. For example, when we were studying descriptive language in writing, students wrote descriptive sentences in a program called HyperStudio and then illustrated them on the computer. We printed the pages and made a class book.

There are many great reading activities as well, such as books on CD now and various others can be downloaded. Many give students the option of reading themselves or clicking on unknown words to have the computer "read" for them. This is a great resource for struggling readers. Wiggle Works is a phenomenal program that integrates reading, writing, and spelling. Students are even able to print out the books they read on the computer.

Technology is just a tool to deliver instruction. It should support and reinforce the curriculum. My biggest challenge is to keep up with the skills that are second nature to my students. Technology is a part of their world and will become increasingly vital in the future. Why not use what is already comfortable and motivating for many students?

**Pacing Instruction.** Children explore oral language and make their share of oral errors. Gradually, they sort out the conventions that govern oral language, but first they must go through the exploratory stage where they say things like, "I have two feets." Soon enough, *two feets* disappears and is replaced by *two feet.* The more children explore oral language, the more rapidly they learn. We are accustomed to expecting explorations in oral language and, consequently, we are tolerant of early errors. But why are we so less tolerant of errors that take place in written language? Children sort out the conventions of spoken language because we give them time to do so, all the while expecting errors and often praising early efforts, even if mistaken. Little direct oral language instruction is required. Nevertheless, parents and teachers make appropriate suggestions, mostly by modeling back to the child conventional forms. We can and should do the same thing with early writing conventions.

The speed with which children gain control of written language conventions depends on how frequently children write, our tolerance for errors, and the effectiveness of early instruction in the conventions of writing. When children first begin writing, punctuation may be scarce or missing altogether. A slightly more advanced young writer may sprinkle punctuation here and there, sometimes correctly and sometimes incorrectly. Figure 12.2 shows the writing of a first-grade child in early September. He knows about periods—does he ever. Every word is followed by a period. He capitalizes *I,* but then most of the letters he makes are capital letters. Within a week he drops the period between words—probably only a spacing device—and begins occasionally placing periods at the end of his sentences. The instruction he receives includes frequent writing, minilessons, teacher modeling, writing conferences, and casual comments about the use of punctuation.

> "Learning writing conventions is an individual process, with particular skills being learned and practiced by particular children at particular times . . . Instruction may be more effective if it treats students as individual language learners, with the teacher relying on each student's own written papers for information about what that student knows."
> —*Grammar, Punctuation, and Spelling: Controlling the Conventions of Written English at Ages 9, 13, 17—the Nation's Reportcard,* by A. N. Applebee, J. A. Langer, and I. V. S. Mullis, 1987.

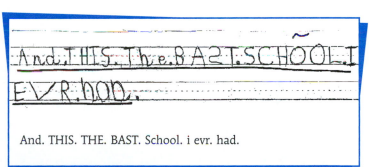

And. THIS. THE. BAST. School. i evr. had.

**Figure 12.2**

**Early Punctuation Effort of a First-Grade Writer**

Young writers make plenty of mistakes in their writing, but the right attitude about mistakes can hasten growth. Where taking a risk brings censure, where mistakes earn red pencil marks, writers will suppress the imagination and take what appears to be the safest path.

Figure 12.3 on page 476 is Alisha's first piece of independent writing, although she had dictated many experience stories. After writing her first story, she said, "I've told lots of stories, but this is the first one I wrote. I like writing stories."

Alisha used quotation marks, a question mark, and an apostrophe. On pages 2, 3, and 4 she used quotation marks. The quotation marks are placed correctly on page 2, incorrectly on page 3, and correctly on page 4. She shows some confusion about whether *said* should be within or outside the quotation marks. *But she has the big idea: quotation marks are used to indicate conversation.* On page 3 Alisha places an apostrophe in the word *not* and gets it wrong, but this indicates that she knows

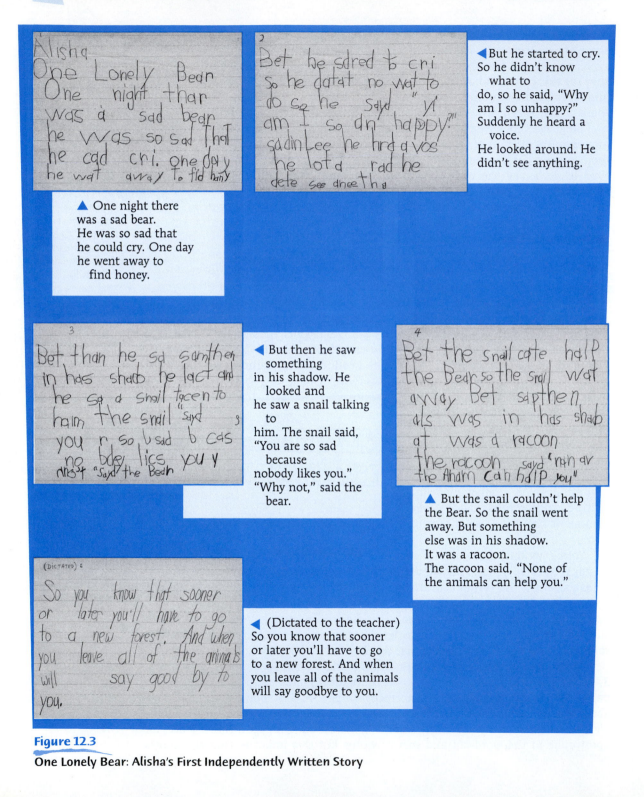

Alisha
One Lonely Bear
One night thar
was a sad bear
he was so sad that
he cad cri. one day
he wat away to fid hany

► One night there
was a sad bear.
He was so sad that
he could cry. One day
he went away to
    find honey.

Bet he sdred to cri
so he datat no wat to
do se he sayd "yi
am I so dn happy?"
sadinLee he hrd a vos
he lotd rad he
dete see dhee tha

◄ But he started to cry.
So he didn't know
    what to
do, so he said, "Why
am I so unhappy?"
Suddenly he heard a
    voice.
He looked around. He
didn't see anything.

Bet than he sa samthen
in has shab he lact and
he sa a snail tacen to
haim the snail "sayd
you r so u sad b cas
no bdey lics you y
nhst "sayd the Bedn

◄ But then he saw
something
in his shadow. He
    looked and
he saw a snail talking
    to
him. The snail said,
"You are so sad
    because
nobody likes you."
"Why not," said the
    bear.

Bet the snail cate half
the Bear so the snail wat
away Bet sapthen
als was in has shab
at was a racoon
the racoon sayd "nan av
the Ahdm cah hdlp you"

▲ But the snail couldn't help
the Bear. So the snail went
away. But something
else was in his shadow.
It was a racoon.
The racoon said, "None of
the animals can help you."

(DICTATED) E
So you know that sooner
or later you'll have to go
to a new forest. And when
you leave all of the animals
will    say good by to
you.

◄ (Dictated to the teacher)
So you know that sooner
or later you'll have to go
to a new forest. And when
you leave all of the animals
will say goodbye to you.

**Figure 12.3**

**One Lonely Bear: Alisha's First Independently Written Story**

something about using an apostrophe. She's thinking of how the apostrophe is used in words such as *do not*. Her errors often show that she is close to understanding some complex punctuation. Remember, this is her first story. You can walk into nearly any high school in the country and find children who have not yet learned how to place quotation marks.

Now here's the question. Alisha has never been formally taught punctuation. She's read a lot; she's dictated many stories. She's observed her teacher using punctuation while recording dictated stories—a form of modeling. She's also heard Ms. Motrick's explanations of why she uses various punctuation marks as she records children's stories. These clues were enough to give Alisha the idea that she could use the conventions, but no one told her to do so. Alisha made rapid progress because she read, wrote, and received direct and indirect instruction from her teacher within the context of writing.

If children write three hours or more per week and if punctuation and capitalization are taught through modeling, revision, and mini-lessons within the context of writing, significant progress can be made, though progress varies widely from child to child. Punctuation clarifies writing, and this is an important concept for children to learn.

### Guidelines for Teaching Punctuation and Capitalization.

What are the best practices for teaching punctuation and capitalization? Research provides some guidance, but it is not definitive. Table 12.2 on page 478 lists the most common punctuation marks, and Table 12.3 on page 479 lists basic capitalization concepts. The following suggestions are derived mostly from the experiences of successful writing teachers and the somewhat limited research.

An informative article on teaching punctuation is "Research Update—When Children Want to Punctuate: Basic Skills Belong in Context" by Lucy Calkins, 1978, *Language Arts, 57*, 567–573.

*Kevin and Danielle are working with magnetic words that represent the various parts of speech. Students are challenged to create sentences using proper capitaization and punctuation.*

- Write frequently, and teach punctuation and capitalization within the context of the writing your children are doing.
- Start with the most common conventions. Gradually move toward the less common ones as progress is made. Periods, question marks, and exclamation marks are among the conventions children use most frequently in their writing. Capitalizing *I* and the first word in the sentence are also common.
- Teach ending punctuation marks before internal ones.

*Teaching Tip*

**Table 12.2**

**Some Common Uses of Punctuation Marks**

**The Period ( . )**

- after a declarative sentence
- after an indirect question
- after most imperative sentences
- after an abbreviation or an initial

**Question Mark ( ? )**

- at the end of a direct or rhetorical question

**Exclamation Mark ( ! )**

- to convey strong emphasis
- after a particularly forceful interjection or imperative sentence
- sparing use

**Comma ( , )**

- before a conjunction (*and, but, for, or, yet*) when it joins the clauses of a compound sentence
- to separate introductory clause or phrase from a main clause
- to separate words in a series and independent clauses
- to separate date from year and city from state
- to set off single-word adverbs, phrases, and clauses (with exceptions)
- after greeting in a friendly letter and closing
- before a quotation

**Colon ( : )**

- to introduce quotations, usually lengthier ones
- to introduce a specification, often a list

**Semicolon ( ; )**

- between certain independent clauses
- in a complex or lengthy series

**Quotation Marks ( " ) and ( " )**

- to set off direct dialogue
- to enclose certain titles and words given in a special sense

**Apostrophe ( ' )**

- to show letters omitted from contractions
- to show ownership

**Dash ( — )**

- to introduce a list
- to show break in thought or speech
- to precede and follow coordinated elements

**Parentheses ( )**

- to enclose less important information within a text

- Evaluate the progress your children are making in their writing to determine when and what conventions should be taught or retaught.
- Teach minilessons, and connect them with problems that have arisen as children write.
- Model the mechanical skills you wish to teach, using your own writing.
- Keep terminology to a minimum. Keep your explanations simple and clear.
- Analyze errors; they are your best guide to future instruction.
- Adjust instruction to suit differing rates of learning. For example, some writers are ready for quotation marks before others have mastered the period.

## Section Summary: Punctuation and Capitalization

1. Punctuation has flexible conventions. Some are optional, some required, and some are determined by a writer's personal preference.

**Table 12.3**

**Capitalization**

| | |
|---|---|
| **First word in a sentence:** | **In the greeting and closing of friendly letter:** |
| —I love reading more than any other activity. | —Greeting: Dear Andy,<br>—Closing: Sincerely yours, |
| **Proper nouns:** | **Abbreviations:** |
| —My teacher, Ms. Patricia Schwartz, says I'm a good reader. | —NY (New York), Ave. (Avenue), Mon. (Monday), Dr. (Doctor) |
| **Proper adjectives:** | **Titles:** |
| —I love Chinese food. | —Mrs. Erin Caldwell, Dr. Toni Walters, General Eisenhower |
| **Names of the days and months** | **First word in a quotation:** |
| —On Saturday, January 26, I went to the dentist. | —Pesildena said, "Reading keeps loneliness at bay." |
| **Initials** | |
| —R. Limon, P. P. Pierson | |
| **Titles of books and periodicals:** | |
| —I read *A Wrinkle in Time* by Madeleine L'Engle.<br>—Jeff subscribes to *The New York Times.* | |

2. Conventions of punctuation and capitalization are best taught within the context of writing, using minilessons, teacher modeling, and conferences.
3. What little research evidence exists supports the value of teaching the conventions within the context of writing.
4. Pace of instruction should suit the level of each child's progress.
5. The most common conventions should be emphasized first, with a gradual move toward the less common.

# Handwriting

A teacher said to me, "My kids can't write a legible sentence." At first, I thought he meant their sentences lacked clarity of thought or were poorly composed. But no. He meant, I soon learned, that their handwriting was illegible. I don't usually make a fuss over terminology (well, sometimes I do), but this is an instance where distinctions matter. Writing and handwriting are entirely different cognitive tasks. Handwriting is transcription, a mechanical task, that once learned can be done without much conscious thought. Writing is the composing of ideas into well-structured sentences and paragraphs. Writing is not a mechanical task at all. Writing requires conscious, thoughtful attention to ideas and language.

Writers must consider what meaning they wish to convey; they must choose words and ideas that express their thoughts; they must consider their audience as

## Standing on the Shoulders of Giants
### Historical Contributions to Literacy
### Ruth Strang

If there were a Hall of Fame for great educators, Teachers College, Columbia University in New York City would be its headquarters. Surely you've heard of John Dewey, Hughes Mearns, and Edmund Burke Huey. But have you heard the name Ruth Strang? Perhaps not.

Ruth Strang taught at Columbia University for nearly four decades and forged another substantial career at the University of Arizona after retirement from Columbia. Her career spanned five decades and left her ranking among the greatest contributors to literacy of the 20th century.

What makes a great university teacher and leader? Two gifts are particularly relevant: scholarly productivity and humane consideration. Professor Ruth Strang excelled in both departments. Scholarly productivity means you have to write. Ruth Strang met that criterion easily. She wrote books, chapters, and articles by the dozens. I count 18 books, but I doubt I have a full list. What surprised me was how many books she wrote in another field—counseling. More important, she led the field in showing the connection between counseling and reading. Her book *Guidance and the Teaching of Reading* is one good example of this connection. Other examples of the extraordinary range of her scholarship include *The Diagnostic Teaching of Reading, The Improvement of Reading, Explorations in Reading*

*Patterns, Helping the Retarded Reader, Helping Your Child Develop His Potentialities, Parent–Teacher Conferences, Making Better Readers, Reading Diagnosis and Remediation,* and *Gateways to Readable Books*. I've named only a few, but they influenced the profession for decades.

But Ruth Strang left an even greater legacy than her scholarship. She guided over 100 students through their doctoral work. I've known about a dozen of her students, and they all tell stories about her kindness, humility, and generosity. Two stories illustrate my point. A poor graduate student and his family discovered a nice house with an absurdly low monthly rent. He couldn't believe his good luck. Years later, he learned that Ruth Strang owned the house. She arranged for him to discover the house and set the rent low so he could pursue his studies without financial worries. Another student was directed to check with the graduate dean about the possibility of a scholarship and stipend. "No problem," the dean announced, "of course we have a scholarship for you." Only later did he learn that the easily obtained scholarship was not funded by the university but by his mentor, Dr. Strang. Ruth Strang's life exemplified both the scholarly and humanistic qualities that left a permanent mark on the profession and the students she cared about so deeply.

they compose. *Writing engages the mind at its core.* Even veteran writers cannot put writing on autopilot. Handwriting is easily put on autopilot, must be put on autopilot, or it will interfere with the writer's message. Putting transcription on autopilot makes fluency possible. The more one must attend to transcription, the less attention can be paid to composing. So, it is in the interest of teachers to help children master the skills of handwriting so that they can get on with the difficult work of creating messages—which is why we learn handwriting in the first place.

## Teaching Handwriting

Handwriting has fallen into disrepair, even disuse, as a means of sending messages. Advances in technology threaten its utility. Voice-recognition software, for instance, is reaching the point where writers compose messages much as children ride bikes: *Look Ma, no hands!* But voice-recognition technology is in its infancy, not fully reliable. Many linguistic subtleties are beyond its capabilities. It restores your faith in the human brain when you realize that a first-grader is way ahead of computer software in parsing the English language.

Computer programmers and teachers have something in common: they both benefit from legible handwriting. Computer makers have developed, but have not perfected, electronic devices that recognize printed and cursive handwriting. But there is a problem. Illegible handwriting gives these devices fits. They can recognize certain barely legible scrawls, but there is a limit. Teachers know what this is like—they too interpret barely legible handwriting but find some beyond their powers of decryption.

It is not just children whose handwriting is illegible; many adults, whose handwriting was once legible, now make unreadable scribbles. Partly this is because there is less need for handwritten messages; most are now created and sent electronically. In our fast-paced lives we do not always take the time to write legibly, though most of us can when pressed. My handwriting deteriorated. After editing students' papers I have been asked more than once, "What does this say?" Technology influences behavior in ways we do not always recognize.

**Legibility**. Legibility is the most important goal of handwriting instruction, which must connect handwriting practice to meaningful writing. Recording children's language, as in dictated accounts, is a place to start. Listening to oral language accounts and recording them in written language enable children to observe the handwriting process. This procedure provides models of handwriting while illustrating the utility of skill. Once children have observed the practical uses of handwriting, more formal instruction can proceed. Formal instruction must be accompanied by practice in composing meaningful messages. For example, have children copy a sentence they have dictated and take it home to their parents. This task motivates students to produce legible copy. The product conveys meaning, and children can see the practical purpose of developing handwriting skill. Teachers have a right to expect legible handwriting. It can be accomplished, but it is not an easy task.

> Teachers are modelers of legible handwriting. They model when they write on the chalkboard, write dictated stories on chart paper, and use wall charts with examples. Another method of modeling is to respond to students in their journals and with written comments (positive and constructive) on students' papers.

Ms. Smart is an excellent first-grade teacher. She expects and gets legible handwriting. As children compose stories, she comments on the ideas and content of writing, yet she does not hesitate to take a moment to show Wendy how to print a lowercase *g* or to suggest to Andrew that his spacing is too crowded. She takes the time to show children how to fix problems. Her on-the-spot instruction is brief, casual, and contextual. Teachers who stress meaningful writing provide the right context for teaching handwriting, since their children have a genuine need for it. Meaningful practice benefits handwriting, just as it does all other skill development.

**Fluency**. Fluency is a familiar concept in reading, and it applies to handwriting as well. An unimpeded flow of handwriting, without conscious attention to the production of the script, enables children to concentrate on ideas and content. Fluency is attained when children have learned to form letters without conscious attention to them. It is developed through an abundance of practice in the context of meaningful writing. Fluent handwriting serves the writer more than the reader, since it enables children to quickly compose their ideas. Legibility primarily serves the reader, since it makes handwriting easy to read. Legibility and fluency are co-equal goals.

Historically, handwriting instruction emphasized the beauty of the script. Calligraphy, the production of beautiful script, is now considered an art form rather than a practical necessity for today's children. Legibility and fluency are the practical goals of handwriting instruction today.

**Manuscript Handwriting**. Children are taught two forms of handwriting: manuscript and cursive. Manuscript is usually taught first, followed by a transition to cursive, usually in the second half of second grade or the first half of third. Manuscript handwriting is what most of us call printing. It is thought to be easier for first-graders to learn manuscript than cursive handwriting because they have not fully developed the fine motor control that cursive handwriting requires. Whether one form is actually easier than another is a question insufficiently examined. Evidence can be cited for one form over another, according to Coon and Palmer (1993). So the tradition of manuscript first seems reasonable. One possible advantage is that books are published in manuscript form, perhaps making it easier for children to move from printed handwriting to printed forms of letters when reading.

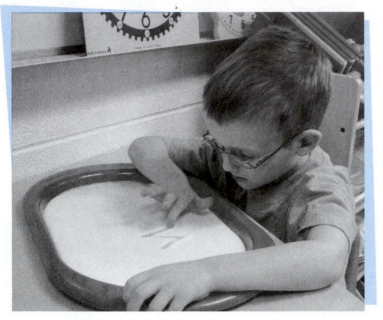

*Brandon is writing letters in a tray of salt, which provides an engaging, tactile experience for practicing letter formation.*

Manuscript handwriting is generally thought of as temporary, since cursive handwriting is intended as a permanent replacement. Actually, many children, as well as adults, use manuscript throughout their lives. Some use it exclusively, and others use both forms, often choosing between the two in a more or less random fashion. Most children are eager to make the transition to cursive handwriting because they think of it as grown-up writing—perhaps reflecting what they have heard adults say about cursive handwriting.

The current emphasis on early composition has influenced handwriting instruction. Many kindergarten children are encouraged to write, using invented spelling; handwriting instruction must therefore begin earlier. Many children come to school these days able to form some letters of the alphabet, if not all of them.

Kindergarten teachers can encourage early manuscript handwriting by having children identify and trace letter shapes. Later, they may practice making letters with a paintbrush or large crayons or chalk. Fine motor control is less of a problem when the instruments of handwriting are large enough for young hands to manipulate.

**Cursive Handwriting**. Cursive handwriting is characterized by flowing script in which letters are joined by connecting strokes. An examination of preliterate handwriting reveals cursive writing in long, flowing, connected lines—minus the letters, of course (see Figure 12.4). You also see attempts to form letters in manuscript (see Figure 12.5). These early efforts reflect children's observation of environmental print, children's television, and home schooling. Young children attempt to reproduce the types of handwriting they see, and they may do so as early as age 2. Early imitative efforts may sometimes occur spontaneously, without benefit of instruction. Once children arrive at school, they begin to form more recognizable handwriting.

**Figure 12.4**

Preliterate Cursive Handwriting

During the transition from manuscript to cursive, children typically produce a mix of manuscript and cursive forms. Some children make the transition readily, abandoning manuscript without regret as they perceive themselves to be producing grown-up handwriting. Other children produce a mixture of forms for a time, and still others mix and match their forms over an extended period of time, in some cases into adulthood.

Though handwriting instruction needs to be associated with the production of meaningful messages, this does not mean that direct instruction in handwriting should not be done. Minilessons can be scattered throughout the instructional day and can also be associated with the use of commercial systems such as those shown in Figures 12.6 on page 484 and 12.7 on page 485. While it is often expedient to have children reproduce specific messages the teacher wishes to convey to parents, it is best to keep such messages to a minimum, substituting instead stories and accounts composed by children independently. Too much practice reproducing other people's messages can become boring, which leads to undesirable attitudes toward schooling in general, and writing in particular.

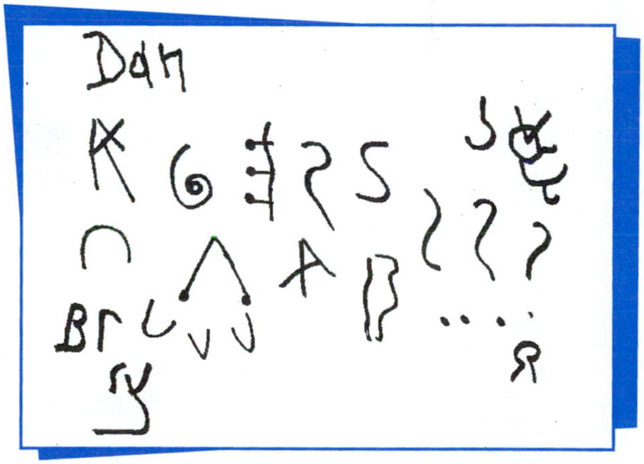

**Figure 12.5**

Preliterate Manuscript Handwriting

Experts suggest six salient characteristics of handwriting: slant, size and proportion, spacing, alignment, line quality, and forming letters. These characteristics enhance legibility and represent goals toward which handwriting instruction should be directed (Hackney, 1993).

- *Slant.* The idea is not that there is only one acceptable way to slant letters, but that the slant should be consistent.
- *Size and proportion.* As students progress up the grades, letter size of uppercase to lowercase letters changes from a ratio of 2:1 to 3:1.
- *Spacing.* Some handwriting systems recommend a specific amount of space between letters and words, although this is less important than providing a consistent amount of space between letters and words.
- *Alignment.* Letters should consistently touch the base of the line on which the letters are resting.
- *Line quality.* Letters should show an unwavering line of even thickness. Using a steady hand while manipulating the writing instrument improves line quality.
- *Forming letters.* Forming letters requires attention to the shape and characteristics that distinguish one letter from another. Forming cursive letters requires particular attention to connecting strokes.

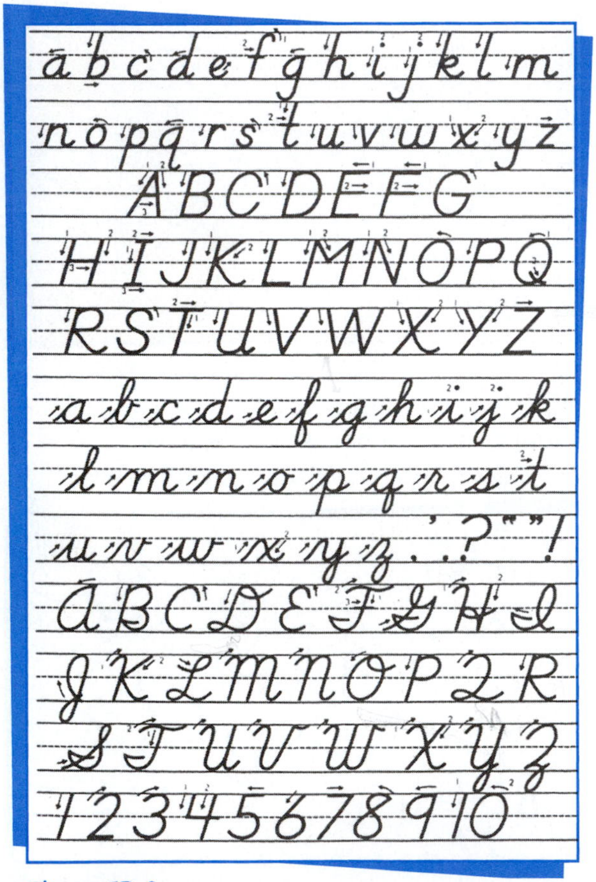

The six characteristics may seem prescriptive, but this need not be the case. It is conceivable that 100 different individuals could produce handwriting that roughly matches the six characteristics described, yet each will produce a distinct handwriting style. It is the distinct style of handwriting that enables handwriting analysts to match handwriting to the individual who produced it. And while handwriting analysis is not an exact science, analysts are able to match handwriting to specific individuals with reasonable accuracy. Distinct handwriting styles are desirable, and it is no doubt inevitable that children will develop their own unique handwriting styles.

**D'Nealian.** D'Nealian handwriting was developed by and named for Donald N. Thurber, a teacher and principal in Michigan. Most D'Nealian manuscript letters are formed in a manner similar to their cursive counterparts, and they maintain the same slant in both forms. The simi-

**Figure 12.6**

**D'Nealian Manuscript and Cursive Handwriting Forms**

*Source:* D'Nealian is a registered trademark of Donald N. Thurber, Copyright © 1987 by Scott, Foresman and Company.

larity of the two forms makes the transition from manuscript to cursive easier. Writers need only add joining strokes to most manuscript letters to produce the cursive form. Five manuscript letters are shaped differently than their cursive forms: *f*, *r*, *s*, *v*, and *z*. D'Nealian handwriting eliminates many of the loops and curves found in other systems of handwriting. Some teachers consider this an advantage; others prefer the fancy flourishes they were taught as children. Many teachers prefer D'Nealian to other systems because of its simplicity, but there is no substantive research evidence that it works better than other methods.

Figure 12.6 illustrates the formation of manuscript and cursive printing as recommended in the D'Nealian system. Figure 12.7 illustrates the formation of manuscript and cursive printing as recommended in the Zaner-Bloser system.

**Left-Handedness**.  By third grade I had a surprise awaiting: *no lefties wanted*. Ms. Bittner made me change hands. I yielded to superior force, and perhaps Ms. Bittner celebrated a victory. But every battle commander knows that strategic retreat can lead to later victories. I am still left-handed.

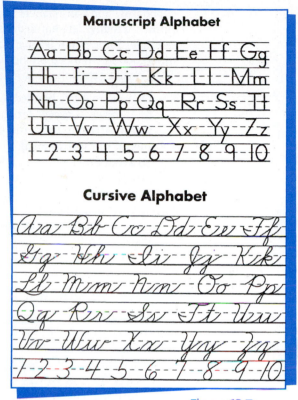

**Figure 12.7**

**Zaner-Bloser Handwriting**

*Source:* Zaner-Bloser, Inc., P.O. Box 16764, Columbus, Ohio. Used by permission of the publisher.

About 10% of children in any classroom are likely to be left-handed. Handedness is usually well established by the time children arrive in kindergarten or first grade. There is no reason to change this normal preference and good reason to honor it. Some children may not have fully established handedness, and a few have mixed dominance—children tend to use their hands interchangeably, depending on the task or activity. Diagnosing handedness is easy. Observe how children use their hands in ordinary activities. Which hand do they use to paint a picture or throw a ball? to reach for a cookie or a book? Give a child a pencil or a crayon and see how he or she uses it to draw or write. Then teach according to the preferred handedness.

Left-handed children should not be considered children with special needs. They tend to write with the wrist hooked in what appears to right handers as an unnatural and uncomfortable position. This hook, while avoidable, is not as unnatural and uncomfortable as it may appear. Left-handers develop it in an attempt to adapt their writing style to right-handed methods. Lefties can avoid the need for hooking the wrist by slanting the paper 30 or so degrees to the right. Right-handed writers slant their paper to the left. If taught early, some left-handed children can avoid developing the hook, but don't count on it. Once free of supervision, left-handed children may revert to adapting their writing to the right-handed world. Left-handers, from infancy, learn to adapt to a *righteous* world. Scissors, doors, cupboards, and can openers are designed for the convenience of the right-handed world. Actually, left-handedness gives an advantage in certain areas—sports, for example. Some major league managers would give their left arm (never their right) for a good left-handed pitcher.

Consider the following ideas for teaching handwriting to left-handers.

*Teaching Tip*

- Do not treat left-handedness as a handicap. Left-handed children are normal in all respects except for their determination to conquer the right-handed world. After all, Leonardo da Vinci, the world's most famous left-hander, turned out well enough.
- To avoid developing the left-handed hook, have lefties slant their paper about 30 degrees to the right, thus avoiding the need for hooking the wrist. Also, allow left-handed children to slant their letters right or left or write them straight up and down.
- Provide suggestions for avoiding hooking the wrist if you wish, but do not insist upon it.

## Section Summary: Handwriting

1. Handwriting is less emphasized than it once was, and this has resulted in a deterioration of handwriting skill generally.
2. Legibility and fluency are the major skills of handwriting. Legibility concerns readability, and fluency concerns producing handwriting automatically, so that writers can focus on their messages, not the mechanics of forming letters.
3. Manuscript handwriting, also known as printing, is taught first to children. While it is intended as temporary until cursive is learned, many writers continue to use it in later childhood and even into adulthood.
4. Cursive handwriting is characterized by flowing script in which letters are joined by connecting strokes.
5. The transition from manuscript to cursive handwriting usually occurs in late second grade and early third grade.
6. Handwriting instruction needs to be associated with the production of meaningful messages.
7. Six characteristics of handwriting include slant, size and proportion, spacing, alignment, line quality, and the formation of letters.
8. D'Nealian is an innovative script intended to ease the burden of transition from manuscript to cursive and to simplify the handwriting process. More traditional forms, including Zaner-Bloser, tend to emphasize loops, circles, and straight lines.
9. Left-handed writers are not handicapped. There are no sound reasons for discouraging left-handed writing. Provisions can made to help lefties avoid the traditional hook.

# Practical Teaching Ideas and Activities

**1.** *Create a handwriting center.* Provide a variety of activities for students to use to practice letter formation and penmanship. Sand or rice trays are very helpful for young children, as are writing in shaving cream and tracing letters on plastic zip-lock bags filled with hair gel. Stencils to develop pencil grip and control are also helpful, as are wipe-off boards and sandpaper letters for tracing and writing practice.

**2.** *Make handwriting cards.* Prepare cards by writing a few lines from poems, songs, and tongue twisters in the appropriate handwriting style. Once or twice a week, during literacy choices, the children copy the poem, song, or tongue twister from one of the cards, paying particular attention to handwriting and letter formation.

**3.** *Make grammar cards.* Write a number of words on index cards, using different colored markers for various parts of speech. For example, write all nouns in red, all verbs in blue, and so on. Provide students with these cards, along with a sentence pocket chart, and challenge them to create complete sentences. As they explore this activity, they will experience firsthand how the various parts of speech are combined to create sentences.

**4.** *Create illustrated adjectives and adverbs.* Demonstrate for students how to write describing words in letters that help depict their meanings. For example, write the word *tiny* in very small letters, and *huge* in balloon letters. Many words lend themselves to this kind of illustrative writing and can help students remember the function and power of descriptive words.

**5.** *Create "thesaurus" posters for adverbs and adjectives.* At the top of a large poster, write in large letters an overused adjective or adverb. Provide students with hot-colored self-adhesive sticky notes, and as they discover a more colorful or interesting word with the same or similar meaning as the "tired" word, have them write it on a note and place it on the poster. Create several of these posters, or perhaps devote a bulletin board for students to fill with interesting words they discover in their reading. Help the students see that these are "hot" words that will spice up their writing!

**6.** *Locate parts of speech within continuous text.* After a minilesson on a particular part of speech, provide students with a paragraph of familiar text, either from a piece of literature or a content area, and have them highlight that part of speech throughout the text. Different parts of speech will lend themselves to further observations, such as where the type of word appears in the sentences, the frequency of certain parts of speech, or the necessity of using various types of words to form sentences.

**7.** *Compare grammatical usage among and across genres.* Various genres use speech differently to convey meaning. A newspaper article may use less descriptive language, be written in a particular verb tense, or utilize simple, direct vocabulary for any objective tone. Poetry certainly uses rich, descriptive language, condenses

*Teaching Tip*

language for stronger impact, and may even sidestep proper grammar for dramatic effect. Share with students various genres, and explore together how language is used differently for different purposes. Help students critically examine their own writing for different tone and level of diction.

**8.** *Have older children write much-needed big books for younger grades.* After the big books are published, the students can introduce the story (as the teacher would) to the class to which they present it. In a meaningful way, they are focusing on handwriting, sentence and story structure, punctuation, and grammar. This activity can motivate older kids to write and produce big books on all sorts of topics for the younger children.

See the Blue Pages at the back of the book and on the Companion Website for additional activities.

## Reflection and Summary

### Reflection

Grammar seems to be popular with teachers, and they feel it should be taught. I agree. But the issue comes down to distinguishing between *should* versus *how*.

> "Grammar is not a set of rules; it is something inherent in the language, and language cannot exist without it. It can be discovered, but not invented."
> —Charlton Laird

Which grammar concepts are useful, and which are not? Those related to writing effective sentences and standard usage are useful and should be taught. Others, such as parts of speech, have less practical benefit, though some justify them on aesthetic grounds. How should grammar be taught? *This is the crucial question*. The traditional approach does not work. What does work is to teach grammar concepts within the context of meaningful oral and written expression.

The mechanics of writing present a different issue. Children do not possess punctuation conventions as part of their oral language. Punctuation conventions cannot be acquired through oral language. But reading and writing help children understand the connection between spoken language and the marks we use to punctuate written language. Punctuation conventions can be acquired only in the context of meaningful reading and writing.

### Summary

This chapter covered three main topics: grammar, punctuation and capitalization, and handwriting.

1. Of the several definitions of grammar, one of the better is that grammar describes the language patterns that native speakers use automatically. Research has shown that teaching traditional grammar does not improve writing, though some believe that such teaching makes for better writers, enriches knowledge and appreciation of language, and aids in learning a foreign language. These reasons have no substantial basis in research.

2. Learning grammar is necessary for effective writing, but it is best learned in the context of writing. Usage has value for written and oral language learning

whereas learning the parts of speech has no such benefit. A practical knowledge of the four types of sentences, three common sentence patterns, and combining sentences can facilitate writing.

3. *Punctuation and capitalization skills facilitate writing. These skills influence the clarity of written language and signal the logic, rhythm, meaning, and structure of writing.* Punctuation should be taught in the context of meaningful writing.

4. Children learn the mechanical skills gradually. Instruction should be paced in harmony with signs of growth in children's writing.

5. *Legibility and fluency are the major skills of handwriting. Legibility concerns readability, and fluency concerns producing handwriting automatically.*

6. Manuscript handwriting, also known as printing, is taught first. The transition from manuscript to cursive handwriting usually occurs in late second grade and early third grade.

7. Handwriting instruction needs to be taught in the context of actual writing. Its six characteristics are slant, size and proportion, spacing, alignment, line quality, and the formation of letters.

8. D'Nealian is innovative script intended to ease the burden of transition. More traditional forms emphasize loops, circles, and straight lines.

9. Left-handed writers are not handicapped. There are no sound reasons for discouraging left-handed writing.

## ◀━ Questions to Challenge Your Thinking ━

1. What are some ways in which grammar is defined?
2. Hillocks and others cite studies showing that traditional school grammar has a negligible influence on writing. Why might this be so?
3. What instructional practices might influence the growth of grammar knowledge in writing?
4. Why teach grammar and punctuation within a writing context?
5. What are some effective ways to teach punctuation?
6. Some say that teaching grammar and punctuation is a waste of time. What arguments can you cite to support, refute, or clarify this claim?
7. What do you now know about grammar and punctuation that you did not know before you read this chapter?
8. What does the author believe about traditional school grammar? Do you agree or disagree? Explain. Does the author believe that grammar and punctuation are useful for learning to write? Explain.
9. Describe two essential goals of handwriting instruction.
10. Should left-handed writers be encouraged to write with the right hand?

## ◀━ A Case Study ━

Patty wrote "Wnsupatm" in kindergarten (see Figure 12.8). She wrote "The cat" in first grade (see Figure 12.9). When she had finished "The cat," she said to her teacher, "This is not a story." Read and analyze each piece. Consider her age and experience at the time she wrote them. Think about the knowledge and skill each piece reveals. Then reflect on the questions below, and discuss them with your classmates or colleagues.

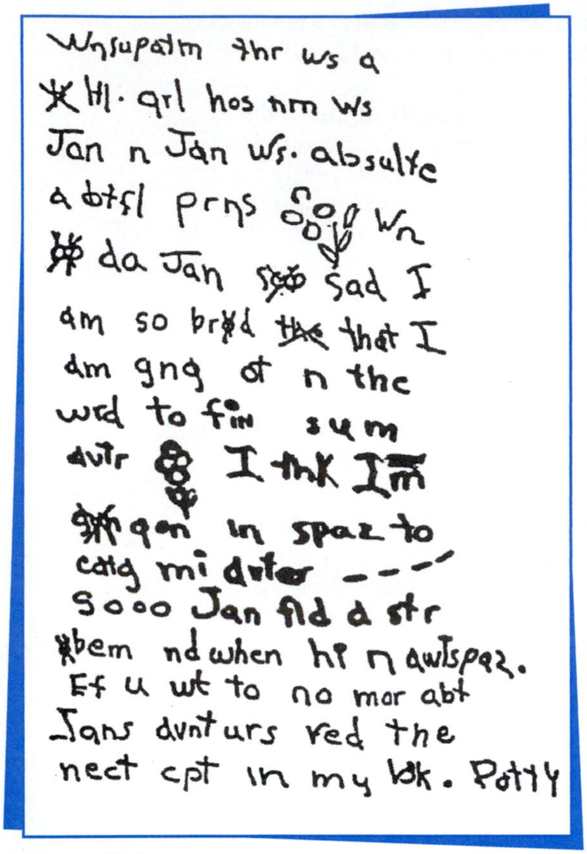

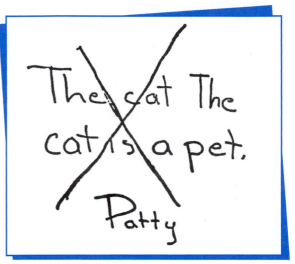

**Figure 12.8**

Wnsupatm (Once Upon a Time): Patty's Kinder-garten Piece

Once upon a time there was a little girl whose name was Jan. And Jan was absolutely a beautiful person. One day Jan said, "I am so bored that I am going out in the world to find some adventure. I think I'm going in space to catch meteor." So Jan found a star beam and went high in outer space. If you want to know more about Jan's adventures, read the next chapter in my book. Patty

**Figure 12.9**

The Cat: Patty's First-Grade Piece

1. What punctuation and capitalization skills does Patty use in each piece?
2. What grammatical knowledge does Patty reveal in each piece?
3. In "Wnsupatm" Patty attempted to spell these words: *absolutely, beautiful, person, adventure, outer space, meteor,* and *chapter,* among many others. Examine the way she spelled each of these words. What do these misspellings reveal about Patty's spelling knowledge?'
4. Compare the two pieces for interest, imagination, and meaning. What does each piece suggest about these characteristics of writing?
5. What can you say about Patty's vocabulary knowledge by examining the words she used in each piece?

6. What do you think Patty meant when she said, "This is not a story"?
7. What may happen to Patty's interest in writing if she continues to write pieces like "The cat"?
8. How would you describe Patty's writing potential?
9. Which piece do you prefer? Give a rationale for your choice.
10. Assume you were Patty's first-grade teacher, and you had seen a copy of her kindergarten piece on the day she began first grade. What would you have done to encourage Patty's writing interest?

## ➤ Revisit the Anticipation Guide

Return to the Anticipation Guide in the chapter opener, and review your original responses to the questions. Complete the guide again, and then consider these questions.

1. Did you change your mind about any items? Why?
2. Think of one major idea with which you disagree. Explain why, and suggest alternative ideas.
3. Think of one major idea with which you agree. Explain why, but suggest alternative ways of thinking about this idea.
4. I have suggested that grammar, punctuation and capitalization, and handwriting should be taught within the context of real-world writing. What do you like or dislike about this philosophy of teaching?

## VideoWorkshop Extra!

If your instructor ordered a package including VideoWorkshop, go to Chapter 12 of the Companion Website (www.ablongman.com/cramer1e) and click on the VideoWorkshop button. Follow the instructions for viewing the appropriate video clip and completing the accompanying exercise. Watch the Companion Website for access to a new interactive teaching portal, My Lab School, currently under construction.

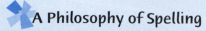

**W**hile we may smile at the T-shirt slogan "Bad spellers of the world untie," we enjoy the humor precisely because it satirizes the folly of inaccurate communication. If children are to enter the door of literacy, effective communication through the written word is crucial. Good spelling is, like good manners, something you notice when it is missing. We do not read to enjoy accurate spelling, yet poor spelling drains the joy from reading. We cannot afford to relegate spelling to an obscure corner of the curriculum. Spelling is not a trivial pursuit. It helps children discover the patterns and structure of English orthography. It is the handmaiden of reading and writing; it serves a useful though subordinate purpose in literacy learning. Good spelling is the result of effectively integrating three components of the literacy curriculum: frequent writing, wide reading, and systematic spelling instruction. When these three components are present in the literacy curriculum, children will be equipped with the "good manners" needed to communicate effectively.

# 13 The Spelling Connection: Integrating Reading, Writing, and Spelling Instruction

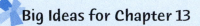**Big Ideas for Chapter 13**

1. Spelling is influenced by reading and writing. Therefore, spelling instruction must be integrated with reading and writing instruction.

2. There are four stages of spelling growth: phonetic, patterns within words, syllable juncture, and meaning derivation.

3. The two most common approaches to spelling are spelling textbooks and individualized spelling. Each approach has many variations.

4. Strategies for learning words include pronunciation, problem parts, visualizing, mnemonic devices, word structure, rhyming, proofreading, and spelling consciousness.

5. Instructional issues in teaching spelling include number of words assigned, how to study troublesome words, spelling tests, review procedures, time on task, and understanding the principles and conventions of spelling.

6. Six criteria for selecting spelling words are developmental appropriateness, frequency, linguistic pattern, frequency of misspelling, content words, and personally chosen words.

7. Invented spelling is necessary since it makes early writing possible. However, it is temporary, and the need for it decreases as spelling skill grows.

8. Spelling assessment is crucial and assessment tests are available. Children must be assigned spelling words appropriate to their instructional spelling level.

### Anticipation Guide

*Consider the following statements, and determine whether you agree or disagree with each. Save your answers and revisit this anticipation guide in the last section of this chapter.*

1. Good spellers are smarter than poor spellers.                                            agree    disagree
2. English spelling is so inconsistent that it should be reformed.                          agree    disagree
3. Reading and writing are closely related.                                                 agree    disagree
4. Good grades on weekly spelling tests are a sure sign of a good speller.                  agree    disagree
5. Meaning is important in learning to spell.                                                agree    disagree
6. Poor spelling is a sign of laziness.                                                      agree    disagree
7. Good readers are more likely to be good spellers than poor readers are.                  agree    disagree
8. Children should choose their own spelling words.                                          agree    disagree
9. Invented spelling leads to poor spelling habits.                                          agree    disagree
10. Poor spelling suggests that a specific learning disability is present.                   agree    disagree

> It's a damned poor mind that can only think of one way to spell a word.
> —*Andrew Jackson*

## A Literacy Story

You're a fly on the wall in a college classroom, circa 1969. You hear a professor calling out names. He's handing back exams. Some students appear anxious, others hopeful. A buzz arises. Angie dances with joy; Esther stifles a tear. One student doesn't get his exam back. Instead, he hears these ominous words: "Richard, please see me in my office."

Seated in the office, Richard hears his professor say, "This is an excellent examination. You are one of nine students who have earned an A in my course this semester. But I've asked you to come here to talk about your spelling. Your examination is the worst example of a college student's spelling I've seen in five years of teaching."

Time passes. The humbled, atrocious speller graduates, goes to graduate school at the University of Virginia, writes a dissertation on spelling, and earns a PhD. He soon publishes a few highly original articles on spelling. Shortly after graduating, he writes a book about spelling. It's a short manuscript, written in the "plain style" that E. B. White so admired. An editor reviews the manuscript, likes it, publishes Richard's book.

In his book, Richard recalls his professor's diagnosis: "Mr. Gentry, anyone as intelligent as you are who can't spell is lazy!" Seventeen years removed from that embarrassing episode, Richard Gentry wrote one of the most widely read books on spelling written in recent times—*Spel Is a Four-Letter Word*. Richard's book tells of his struggle with spelling. Yet in school he worked hard on spelling, and received straight A's, perfect test scores, and third prize in the county spelling bee. Lazy?

Richard Gentry's story raises pedagogical questions: Are poor spellers dumb? Are good spellers smart? Is spelling important? Is spelling overrated? Are poor spellers lazy or are they poorly taught? Do poor spellers have a spelling disability? This chapter touches on each of these questions—and more.

## A MATTER OF STANDARDS

### Spelling Conventions

**Standard 4:** Students adjust their use of spoken, written, and visual language (e.g., conventions, style, vocabulary) to communicate effectively with a variety of audiences and for different purposes.

Standard 4 stresses the importance of conventions, style, and vocabulary, and their use in spoken, written, and visual language. Spelling is one of the more important conventions of written language because of its vital connections to reading and writing. For instance, early writing helps children learn to spell, and it also contributes to growth in word recognition. It also happens that children who write early produce better-quality writing. Early writing plays a vital role in the growth of vocabulary. Children come to school with an enormous oral vocabulary, and early writing provides an opportunity to put that vocabulary to work. But early writing is not possible unless invented spelling is encouraged. This chapter explores the ways in which spelling contributes to reading and writing and the ways in which reading and writing contribute to spelling.

STANDARD

When I was a fifth-grade teacher, I was sometimes asked, "Mr. Cramer, does spelling count?" I'm sorry to say that I didn't have an adequate answer. I should have said, "First, I want you to get your ideas down on paper; ideas are important; what you have to say is important. So, get your ideas on paper; we'll work on spelling when you edit your writing." Instead, I said, "Yes, spelling counts." I gave my children questionable advice. I should have had a better answer, but I hadn't thought through the complexities involved in balancing the importance of good ideas with the value of correct spelling. I wish now that I had said to my children, "No, spelling doesn't count; but it *matters*." Spelling matters as good manners matter. There is a socially correct way of behaving; there is an orthographically correct way of presenting writing. And just as good manners are no substitute for good character, so correct spelling is no substitute for good ideas.

Spelling is, however, highly visible, and it is sometimes assigned a more prominent role in judging literacy and intelligence than it can sustain. When writing is displayed in a public setting, we see the surface features more readily than the deeper meaning that writing conveys. Consequently, poor spelling is sometimes taken as an indicator of low intelligence or illiteracy. Evidence abounds that intelligence and literacy are not necessarily related to spelling. Nevertheless, the media, business, and the general public hang on to this hoary myth. A few decades ago, a vice president of the United States misspelled *potato* (*potatoe*), and the media treated this minor miscue as a metaphor for ignorance. Two decades have passed, and the "potato incident" still plagues this man. Many people of extraordinary achievement were or are mediocre or even atrocious spellers. Edmund Henderson, my mentor and the most eminent spelling researcher in modern times, once told me that his interest in spelling stemmed from curiosity regarding his own spelling inadequacies.

Correct spelling shows that you have taken the trouble to observe the amenities of written language, just as good manners show that you observe the amenities of social intercourse. But spelling matters for more substantive reasons: (1) reading enhances spelling, and spelling enhances reading, particularly word recognition; (2) writing enhances spelling, and spelling enhances writing; (3) spelling conveys knowledge of English etymology, and etymology strengthens vocabulary; (4) spelling enhances children's chances of survival in the economic, academic, and social worlds they will inherit. So it is right to say, "No, spelling doesn't count, but it matters." And we must teach children *how* it matters, *when* it matters, and *why* it matters.

This chapter will discuss the following topics: influences on spelling growth, stages of spelling growth, approaches to teaching spelling, strategies for teaching and learning spelling, instructional issues in spelling, selecting spelling words, invented spelling, and assessing spelling.

## Integrating Reading, Writing, and Spelling Instruction

Poor spelling is not caused by laziness; neither can it be attributed to spelling disability or lack of intelligence. More often than not it results from inadequate instruction. But even good instruction will not turn every child into an excellent speller, nor should it. Differences are normal in all arenas of human achievement.

"Professor Henderson, I was not a lazy speller!"
—Richard Gentry

Accept differences, and you will not be tempted to look for questionable explanations for poor spelling—disability, dyslexia, laziness. You can help every child maximize his or her spelling potential, whatever that may be, by giving excellent reading, writing, and spelling instruction.

Spelling competence is influenced by such instruction. The neglect of any one of these influences can prevent children from reaching their spelling potential. Reading is the cradle of spelling; writing is its playpen. Reading supplies the raw materials—sounds, letters, and words. But exposure to sounds, letters, and words is only background music; children must also manipulate these raw materials. In writing children manipulate and experiment with sounds, letters, and words. Children discover the rules that govern English spelling through writing (Cramer, 2001; Fresch & Wheaton, 1997; Rasinski & Padak, 2000). Given effective reading and meaningful writing, children can begin to invent spellings—temporary approximations that are serviceable until correct spelling is learned. The third influence on spelling is instruction. While some children learn to spell without formal instruction, many do not. Most children need organized spelling instruction focused on words, strategies, conventions, and principles of English spelling. When instruction is given within a context of excellent reading and writing, spelling growth comes along.

### Reading

Reading and spelling share common components, but they are not mirror images of each other. Spelling requires greater control over letter–sound relationships than reading does. The connection between reading and spelling is most pronounced in the primary grades (Blachman, 1984; Juel, Griffith, & Gough, 1986; Mann & Liberman, 1984; Stanovich, 1988; Stanovich, Cunningham, & Cramer, 1984). Knowledge about letters and sounds learned through spelling aids reading; it works the other way, as well. Henderson (1989) found a strong reciprocal relationship between reading and spelling.

Spelling and reading share an overlapping knowledge base. Ball and Blackman (1991) found that phonemic awareness instruction, combined with instruction connecting the phonemic segments to alphabet letters, improved early reading and spelling skills. Word study also contributes to a better understanding of how English orthography works, since it helps children discover patterns and relationships among words (Templeton & Morris, 1999). Since English spelling is far more predictable than is commonly realized, a given pattern discovered in a small set of known words can be applied to dozens of unknown but related words (Fresch & Wheaton, 1997; Gaskins, Ehri, Cress, O'Hara, & Donnelly, 1997).

> "Spelling and word study provide direct teaching of what to attend to in words."
> —Edmund Henderson

## Writing

Only writing provides an authentic forum for *producing* the raw materials of written language (Barr & Johnson, 1997; Wilde, 1987). Readers supply sounds and meaning to decode written language whereas writers encode language by supplying the letters, words, and meaning. Readers are consumers of language already written; writers are creators of written language. Children can write their way to reading knowledge. Chomsky (1971) makes this case quite credibly in her excellent article "Write First, Read Later." By taking the writing path to literacy, children discover how language is encoded and how meaning is communicated through the written word; they also learn how letters and sounds relate and that words exhibit spelling patterns and meaning connections—basic spelling principles. Graves (1983) has found that more children come to school believing they can write than come believing they can read. Children should write on their first day of school and every day thereafter. When this is done, spelling is the beneficiary—and so is reading.

> Carol Chomsky, an early advocate of invented spelling, suggests the provocative idea of starting literacy instruction through writing in her excellent article "Write First, Read Later."

Vanessa Morrison teaches kindergarten in Detroit, Michigan. She knows kindergarten children can write and that writing will strengthen their prospects for reading. In the Field Notes feature on page 498, she discusses writing with her kindergarten children.

## Spelling

Consistent spelling instruction is necessary for most children. Formal instruction should start once children have acquired some fluency in reading and continue through grade 8 for most children. Many would benefit from continued instruction in high school. By grade 8, or sooner, children should be able to fluently spell the vast majority of the words most often used in writing or encountered in reading. Spelling instruction should focus on developing a core spelling vocabulary, princi-

## Field Notes
### Real-Life Experiences of a Classroom Teacher

**W**hen kindergartners write—I listen. The majority of my kindergartners came to school in September confident they knew how to write. They freely expressed this belief on the first day of school in the form of drawings and scribbles. Most of my children could draw and scribble; a few wrote letter strings; three copied environmental print, though they were unable to read it back to me. These three could also write their first and last names. Each of my 24 children operated at a different emerging-writing stage—just what I had anticipated.

Vanessa Morrison

I knew writing would help me get to know my children. I also knew that researchers have provided evidence indicating that writing enhances children's readiness for reading. Visualizing where I wanted the children to be operating by June, I set about devising writing strategies.

From day one, I encouraged my children to draw and write. Usually they generated their own ideas; sometimes I suggested topics, often revolving around books I read to them. I learned about my children's lives outside of the classroom through writing. I discovered their favorite animals, toys, colors, foods, and much more. I learned what made them happy or sad. I'll never forget Andrew's sadness. Looking at his drawing of flowers with stems bent over and petals touching the grass, I asked, "Why does that make you sad, Andrew?" He replied, "'Cause—'cause—it's there no more."

By accepting their drawing and writing, I showed my children I cared about them and what they had to say. Through the action and interaction that comes with writing, a sense of trust and respect developed and continues to grow.

ples and conventions of spelling, and strategies for learning to spell. Whether spelling instruction takes place using spelling textbooks or using an individualized approach is less important than that it take place.

## Section Summary: Integrating Reading, Writing, and Spelling Instruction

1. Spelling competence is influenced by reading, writing, and direct spelling instruction.
2. Reading provides children visual exposure to words and opportunities to manipulate them.
3. Writing is the only authentic forum for producing oral language in its written form—we call it spelling.
4. Most children need direct spelling instruction, which should start once children have acquired some fluency in reading. Spelling instruction should continue until children have acquired a substantial spelling vocabulary.

## The Stages of Spelling Growth

How hard is it to learn to spell? Not as hard as is commonly supposed. English spelling is not chaotic; it has patterns and regularities. English is alphabetic—a writing system whereby one or more letters represent one speech sound or phoneme. Theoretically, the ideal language would have as many graphemes as phonemes. Each letter would stand for only one and consistently the same sound. English does not possess this ideal consistency; nevertheless, it has substantial regularities (Hanna, Hanna, Hodges, & Rudorf, 1966; Venezky, 1999). Some spelling reformers (Benjamin Franklin, George Bernard Shaw, Sir Isaac Pitman) concluded that English spelling is grossly chaotic—so impossibly irregular that it required a complete makeover. But these reformers mistook imperfection for chaos; their reforms failed because of linguistic naiveté and underestimating the cultural resistance that met potential changes in the spelling system.

Learning to spell is developmental; it proceeds through stages of growth (Bear, Templeton, Invernizzi, & Johnston, 2000; Beers & Henderson, 1977; Gentry, 1981). In the earliest stages, children rely primarily on sound. As they move through the five stages of spelling growth, they come to rely on sound, patterns, and meaning relationships. When spelling is taught in ways that enable children to discover the patterns and regularities of the

> "One important issue that has been neglected in studies of spelling stages is the relationship between stages and instruction."
>
> —Linda C. Ehri

Paul Hanna, Jean Hanna, Richard Hodges, and Edwin Rudorf conducted a huge computer study of 17,000 words to map the phoneme–grapheme correspondences in American English. They found that American English spelling is consistent about 85% of the time.

### Spelling and the Reading–Writing Connection

Connecting Technology to Teaching

Spell checkers are often the only way in which technology is connected to spelling instruction. Successful use of spell checkers requires instruction and practice. As students use computers more frequently for reports, assignments, and projects, spelling often seems to be the responsibility of the spell checker. Yet there are ways in which teachers and students can use technology to support spelling growth. Here are a few ideas.

Ideas for Teacher Use

- Create attractive, well-organized word walls.
- Color-code vowels and consonants.
- Print words in alphabetical order.
- Create testing activities using regular or individualized word lists.
- Design computer activities that ask students to edit sentences for spelling.
- Create customized word lists for students.
- Use PowerPoint® or HyperStudio® to flash students' spelling words on the computer monitor.

Ideas for Student Use

- Play hangman and create word searches using simple software programs.
- Design crossword puzzles and anagrams for classmates to solve.
- Play games that encourage spelling practice and word sorting.
- Use a word-processing spell checker to create and use spelling strategies.
- Illustrate your spelling words, using the paint program.

With planning and vision, you can use technology in many ways to support spelling instruction. Try creating your own ideas, too.

Contributed by Lisa Kunkleman

English spelling system, they succeed readily enough. Different names have been used to describe the stages of spelling growth, but the content remains similar. Except for the first stage, the descriptions proposed by Henderson (1989) and his colleagues have been used to describe the stages: prephonetic, phonetic, patterns within words, syllable juncture, and meaning derivation.

## The Prephonetic Stage

There was once an American political party whose major issue was spelling reform. Richard Hodges (1981) tells about the sometimes amusing, sometimes naive, but always interesting attempts to reform the spelling system.

The prephonetic stage occurs before children can associate letters with sounds. Some call this stage *preliterate,* but children at this stage are emerging into literacy and, therefore, the term *prephonetic* seems more appropriate. Children in this stage do not write in the formal alphabetic sense. Rather, they convey messages through drawings, scribbles, wavy lines, alphabet letters, copied words, and an occasional sight word. Their "writing" often includes curves, circles, lines, dots, joining strokes—marks that approximate features of cursive or manuscript writing. Five events mark progress toward formal alphabetic writing: scribbling, drawing, mock writing, printing letters, and concept of word. Concept of word, or word boundary knowledge, is a particularly important indicator of progress toward alphabetic writing (Morris, 1983). During this stage, expect to see writing like that of Figure 13.1 or variations of it.

An important literacy event occurs when a child discovers word boundaries, or concept of word. Darryl Morris (1983) has written the classic article on this event.

Children ages 2 to 5 typically occupy this stage, although some 3- to 5-year-olds may attain a more advanced stage and some older children remain in the prephonetic stage. The following activities can benefit children in the prephonetic stage of development.

*Teaching Tip*

- Teach the alphabet in a variety of ways, such as the alphabet song and alphabet books.
- Teach children to write their names on drawings and other class work.
- Have children "inventory" their knowledge of the alphabet on paper.
- Label objects within the room, and make frequent reference to these labels.
- Have children draw stories about events in their lives and talk about their stories.
- Have childen sort pictures according to initial or final consonant sounds.
- Read nursery rhymes and books that emphasize rhyme.
  - Read stories and poems; then have students draw and write about them.
  - Do choral reading and reader's theater.
  - Collect and display logos children can readily identify.
  - Record a dictated comment on children's drawings; read it back.
  - Model writing with a think-aloud presentation of events of the day, inviting children to read along.

"I want to learn to read and write so that I can take care of myself and those I love."
—A child's response to Ms. Morrison's question "Why do you write?"

## The Phonetic Stage

True alphabetic writing begins with the phonetic stage. Here, for the first time, we see systematic connections between letters and sounds. Initially, children write with consonants and an occasional vowel. For example, Dawn wrote, *i kt fs* for *I caught fish*. Two factors influence spelling during the phonetic stage: the letter name strategy and surrounding speech sounds.

**The Letter Name Strategy**. The sound of a letter's name provides the aural clue that beginning writers need to write it. The pronunciation of most consonants and long vowels approximates the corresponding letter names closely enough for children to make an educated guess. For example, when Carla wrote *i fel hpe* (I feel happy), she spelled the beginning and ending sounds of *feel* correctly. But since the long *e* sound in *feel* is spelled *ee*, her guess was incorrect but close—and easy enough to read.

During the phonetic stage, children correctly represent most single consonants, particularly the ones with the most predictable pronunciations: *b, p, f, v, m, n, t, d, s, k, j, z, l, r*. The consonants with variant pronunciations—*c, g, h, w, y*—are more likely to be spelled incorrectly. Consonant blends and digraphs are more difficult than single consonants. Young writers tend to represent them with one letter. Vowel letters are often missing or incorrect early in the phonetic stage, but toward the middle and end of the phonetic stage, progress is evident.

**Figure 13.1**

**Writing in the Prephonetic Stage of Spelling**
Ajee, a kindergartner, wrote an owl-shaped book with pictures and letters but without letter–sound connections. According to Ajee, her story says, "The little girl and her daddy saw the owl."

**Surrounding Speech Sounds**. The context in which certain letters and sounds appear within words determines whether a child will typically include or omit them. For example, the letters *m* and *n* are often omitted before a final consonant. Thus, *hand* may be spelled *had*, and *lamp* may be spelled *lap*.

Young children's sophisticated understanding of the phonology of English is quite amazing. Charles Read (1971) tells about it in his important article.

Table 13.1 (p. 502) shows some typical phonetic-stage spellings, which are dominated by beginning single and ending consonants and a few vowels. Figure 13.2 (p. 502) is a typical example of early phonetic-stage writing. The following activities are suggested for children who are in this stage of spelling growth.

- Play rhyming games; read rhyming poetry such as Mother Goose rhymes and Dr. Seuss books.
- Make word walls and wall charts of familiar words.
- Match beginning and final single consonants to picture names.
- Start a word bank from language experience stories and other sources.
- Sort known words by features such as beginning, ending, and medial sounds.

*Teaching Tip*

**Table 13.1**

**Phonetic Spelling**

| | | |
|---|---|---|
| md = mad | sd = sound | bg = bug |
| ct *or* kt = caught | pb = people | rmb = remember |
| tat = that | hv = have | y = why |
| wz = was | u = you | rp *or* rop = rope |
| bne *or* bny = bunny | tgr = tiger | cad = could |

- Start word journals or word dictionaries.
- Write phrases and short messages with word bank words.
- Alphabetize words in word banks.
- Sort known words by short and long vowel sounds.
- Contrast words with short vowel sounds with those having long vowel sounds.
- Collect and display logos that children can readily identify.
- Write every day with invented spelling.
- Model writing with a think-aloud presentation of events of the day, inviting children to read along.

## The Patterns Within Words Stage

Many words have predictable spelling patterns within words, hence the name of this stage. During this stage, children learn to spell long vowel patterns, discover silent vowel markers, spell short vowel patterns correctly, and make progress in spelling consonant blends and digraphs. Whereas children's spelling during the phonetic stage centered on one-to-one letter–sound correspondence, it now illustrates a grasp of more complex principles of spelling. The transition from simple to

**Figure 13.2**

**Writing in the Phonetic Stage of Spelling**

Chelsea's written story says, "Leo was a wise, kind king." Her first and last consonant letters are mostly correct; she tries out some vowel spellings, which are not always correct.

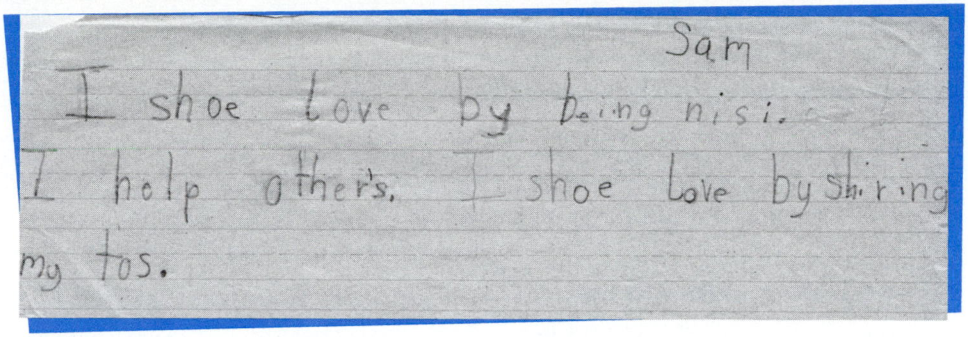

![Sam's handwritten spelling sample: "Sam / I shoe love by being nisi. / I help other's. I shoe Love by shiring / my tos."]

**Figure 13.3**

**The Patterns Within Words Stage of Spelling**

Sam's spelling shows she grasps the "marker" principle, characteristic of this stage: *shoe* for *show, nisi* for *nice,* which are both misspelled but "marked."

complex spelling represents the major spelling discovery of the patterns stage—it represents a stage of transition in reading too. Children move from tentative reading fluency to the fluent reading that will appear in the syllable juncture stage (Bear et al., 2000). Figure 13.3 is a typical example of patterns within words spelling.

Kahlid wrote, "We ate caek and ice crem." In the preceding stage, Kahlid would have written *cak* for *cake*; now he writes *caek.* Kahlid continues to misspell *cake,* but this error represents significant progress. He has discovered the "marker" principle: long vowel sounds are signaled, or "marked," by the presence of a silent vowel. The silent *e* in *cake* and *caek* signals a long sound for the first vowel. This shows that Kahlid has understood an important spelling principle, though he has not yet acquired the correct spelling.

Single short-vowel patterns in one-syllable words spelled correctly also emerge during this stage. Now we are less likely to see *red* spelled *rad,* or *up* spelled *ap.* Another sign of progress is correctly spelled consonant blends and digraphs. Kahlid correctly spelled the *cr* blend when he wrote *crem,* although the word is not yet spelled entirely correctly.

The instructional emphasis during this stage is single-syllable long vowels, short vowels, consonant blends, and consonant digraphs. Activities for children who are in the patterns within words stage may include the following:

- Contrast words with short and long vowel sounds, using picture cards.
- Contrast words with short and long vowel sounds, using known words.
- Contrast single beginning consonant with beginning blends and digraphs. Start with picture sorts, and then move to known words.
- Contrast single ending consonant with ending blends and digraphs. Start with picture sorts, and then move to known words.
- Contrast words with *r* blends to those with *r*-controlled vowels. Start with picture sorts, and then move to known words.

*Teaching Tip*

- Organize word-hunt activities using newspapers and magazines.
- Play board and card games to reinforce word patterns.
- Organize word-sort activities in groups and individually. Model the procedures first.
- Have students record word patterns in a word journal or word dictionary.
- Write every day; allow invented spelling in first-draft writing.
- Teach revision and editing strategies for final-draft writing.

## The Syllable Juncture Stage

A syllable juncture is the place within a word where syllables meet. At the syllable juncture stage, children have a basic spelling vocabulary and command of many long- and short-vowel spelling patterns. Errors occur at syllable junctures because letters may be dropped, doubled, or changed when inflected endings or suffixes are joined to base words: *careing* for *caring*; *steped* for *stepped*; *spys* for *spies* (see Table 13.2). Errors also occur in the internal structure of a word where syllables meet: *midle* for *middle* (see Figure 13.4). Word study during this stage of development focuses on base words, prefixes, suffixes, and syllables. Progress is made in applying rules governing doubling, dropping, and changing letters.

The following activities can be used with children at the syllable juncture stage.

*Teaching Tip*

- Sort known base words that do not change when an ending is added.
- Sort known base words that change when an ending is added.
- Sort words with plural endings -*s* and -*es*.
- Contrast words that are changed when an ending is added to those that remain the same.
- Identify open and closed syllables—the key to doubling or not doubling the final consonant in base words.
- Continue working with word dictionaries.
- Create categories in word journals or dictionaries for doubling, changing, and dropping letters.
- Model word-sort procedures for changes in word endings.
- Write every day; allow invented spelling in first-draft writing.
- Teach revision and editing strategies for final-draft writing.

**Table 13.2**

**Syllable Juncture Errors**

| Dropped | Doubled | Changed |
|---|---|---|
| hated, hatd | bagged, baged | cried, cryd |
| filed, fild | boring, borring | galleries, gallerys |
| tapes, taps | always, allways | juries, jurys |
| named, namd | beginning, begining | bunnies, bunnyes |
| claimed, claimd | planned, planed | earlier, earlyer |

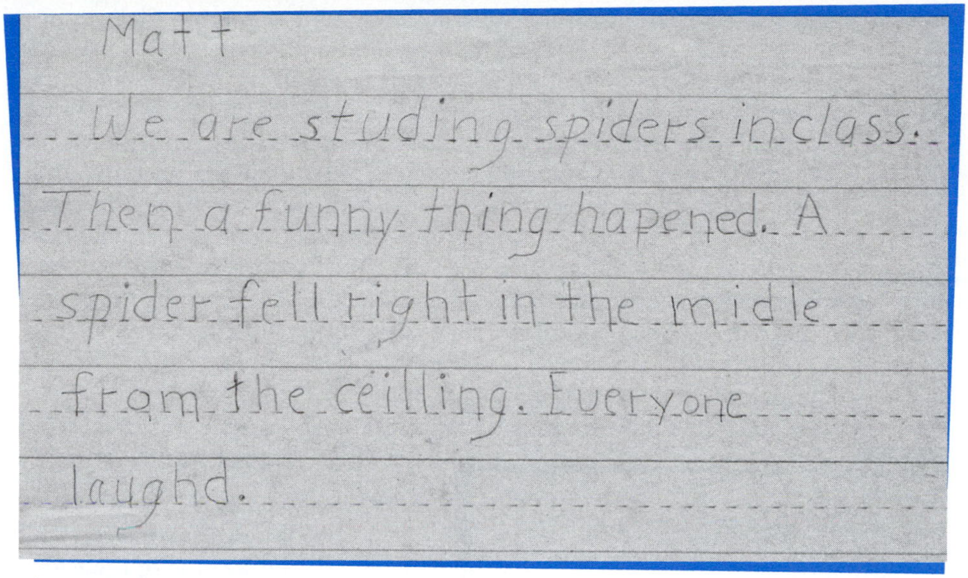

> Matt
> We are studing spiders in class.
> Then a funny thing hapened. A
> spider fell right in the midle
> from the ceilling. Everyone
> laughd.

**Figure 13.4**

**The Syllable Juncture Stage of Spelling**
Matt, a second-grader, has a start on building a core spelling vocabulary, with some typical errors of the syllable juncture stage: *midle* for *middle*, *hapened* for *happened*, *studing* for *studying*, and *ceilling* for *ceiling*.

## The Meaning Derivation Stage

Words related in meaning are often related in spelling, even though the pronunciations of related words may differ. For example, pronounce these three words: *sign, signal, signature*. The sound of *sign* differs in the two related words, but its spelling remains constant. The /g/ is silent in *sign* but sounded in *signal* and *signature*. The /i/ is long in *sign* but short in *signal* and *signature*. But the meaning connection is reflected in the spelling, which remains constant. Children who have progressed through the earlier spelling stages are now ready to examine meaning-related words, many of which are derived from French, Greek, and Latin. Here are some examples.

> Shane Templeton (1992) writes authoritatively on the development of word knowledge among older students. A particularly good example is his article "Theory, Nature, and Pedagogy of Higher-Order Orthographic Development in Older Students."

| | | |
|---|---|---|
| nature, natural | introduce, introduction | admire, admiration |
| observe, observation | act, action | realize, realization |
| compose, composition | affect, affection | exclaim, exclamation |
| combine, combination | generate, generation | relax, relaxation |
| separate, separation | extinct, extinction | magic, magician |
| unit, unite | resign, resignation | memory, memorize |
| obey, obedient | major, majority | labor, laboratory |
| hymn, hymnal | volume, voluminous | magnify, magnificent |

At this stage, children can begin to study homophones—words that are pronounced the same but have a different meaning and a different spelling, such as *tale* and *tail*. Homophones present a major spelling problem, persisting into and through college for some. Cramer and Cipielewski (1995) found that homophones were the most common error category in grades 7 and 8 and the second most common in grades 4–6. Homophone errors are primarily a meaning problem. Many children correctly spell *too, two,* and *to* or *there, their,* and *they're* but use them in the wrong linguistic contexts. Homophone errors would be substantially reduced if just ten of the most common homophones were used correctly (see Table 13.3). Learning the correct usage of homophones takes a long time, much repetition, and effective instruction (Marine, 1995). Figure 13.5 offers a typical example of writing during the meaning derivation stage.

Use the following activities with children who are in the meaning derivation stage of spelling growth.

**Table 13.3**

**Ten Most Commonly Misspelled Homophones**

| | |
|-----|--------|
| to | there |
| too | their |
| two | they're |
| its | your |
| it's | you're |

"Her Room"
By: Susie

She took one last look, coppery eyes flashing with anticipation and the fear of letting go.

Led by a sudden impulse, her eyes darted to the staircase. The young woman set her suitcase down at the foot of the stairs. She slowly ascended the steps.

The Room. No longer her room. Now just a room.

She opened the door and stepped into an unfamiliar world. The Room was so empty. The bed was made. It was immaculately clean.

The one thing that hit her the most was the silence. There were no chaotic family situations, there was no stereo blasting, and there was no phone ringing. This uncomfortable quietness rang in her ears. She longed to hear the echos of her past. The Room seemed like a "ghost town" in a mediocre "western" movie.

- Collect and study sets of meaning-related words in which the spelling of the base word remains constant in the derived form. Use your word collection as examples when modeling meaning-related spelling principles.
- Collect sets of meaning-related words in which the spelling of the base word changes in the derived form. Study these words for clues to spelling the derived form.
- Prefixes, roots, suffixes, and accent of English words are influenced by their origin in other languages. It is helpful, therefore, to look into the etymology of English words for clues to spelling, meaning, and pronunciation.
- Write every day. Teach revision, editing, and proofreading.

**Figure 13.5**

**The Meaning Derivation Stage of Spelling**
Susie, an eighth-grader, is a mature speller at the meaning derivation stage. In this first draft of a story, she spells almost all words correctly.

**Section Summary: The Stages of Spelling Growth**

1. There are five stages of spelling growth: prephonetic, phonetic, patterns within words, syllable juncture, and meaning derivation.
2. The prephonetic stage occurs as children emerge into literacy but before they can associate letters with sounds.
3. The phonetic stage shows children correctly spelling many consonant letters, but vowel sounds tend to be omitted or spelled incorrectly.
4. The patterns within words stage shows children making progress in spelling silent vowels, blends, consonant digraphs, and short-vowel patterns.
5. Spelling errors often occur at the point where letters are dropped, doubled, or changed. This is called the syllable juncture stage of spelling.
6. Many words have a spelling–meaning connection. Spelling patterns within these words remains constant even as sound(s) within the derived form varies.

# Approaches to Teaching Spelling

This section describes two options for directing spelling instruction: spelling textbooks and individualized spelling. Keep in mind that many variations exist within these two approaches to teaching spelling.

## Spelling Textbooks

Teachers often use spelling textbooks for convenience. Preparing spelling lists and activities is time consuming, and many teachers haven't the time or inclination to add another chore to their list of things to do. Others choose spelling textbooks because they have found them as good as or better than other available alternatives. Whatever the reason, most children who are taught spelling at all get their instruction from textbooks.

Spelling textbooks often seem much alike since they have similar salient features. A Lexus and a Yugo also have similar salient features—wheels, transmission, engine. Yet they differ in execution and detail. The same goes for spelling textbooks, even though many provide 36 spelling lessons, a teacher's edition with lesson plans, and ancillary materials keyed to textbook features. Lessons are typically four to six pages long and consist of a word list, a spelling principle, and practice activities revolving around word study, writing, and editing. Some spelling textbooks include provisions for review, diagnostic placement tests, and content-focused lesson plans.

Textbooks are chosen by teacher committees and/or administrators. Sometimes a checklist of criteria guides the selection process. Checklists should reflect a school's or district's curricular goals and standards. Most important, checklists should contain teacher-developed criteria relevant for the children who will use the books. Table 13.4 on page 508 gives a checklist of issues to consider when evaluat-

**Table 13.4**

**Checklist for Evaluating Spelling Textbooks**

| | |
|---|---|
| Spelling lists | Which word-selection criteria used—(1) developmental appropriateness, (2) frequency of occurrence in oral and written language, (3) linguistic pattern, (4) frequency of misspelling, (5) content words, or (6) personally selected words? |
| Major spelling concepts | What provisions are made for teaching spelling strategies, principles, and conventions? |
| Writing | Do the weekly lessons incorporate writing into the mix of activities? |
| Editing and proofreading | Do the lessons incorporate editing and proofreading into the mix of activities? |
| Word study | Are there word study activities revolving around spelling patterns, word structure, and meaning? |
| Personal words | Is there provision for adding personal words to the weekly spelling list? |
| Review | Are key words and spelling concepts reviewed systematically within and across grade levels? |
| Ancillary options | Are ancillary materials compatible with your instructional goals, standards, and perspective? |
| Assessment | Is there a variety of assessment options such as pretests, midweek tests, final tests, review tests, and placement tests? |

ing spelling textbooks, but you should modify it to conform with your own or your school's goals, standards, and perspective.

## Individualized Approaches

There are a variety of individualized approaches to spelling. Some stipulate that children choose their own words; others stipulate that teachers establish the word list. Both approaches have significant deficiencies. I prefer a cooperative individualized approach whereby children and teachers jointly develop spelling lists and activities. Two important tasks are selecting relevant words and organizing meaningful spelling activities. Perhaps the most challenging task in this approach is coordinating instruction across grade levels. If this challenge is met, the approach will work. The following tasks must be accomplished since, by the nature of the approach, there are no ready-made materials available for use.

**Selecting Words.** Students and teachers select spelling words. Words are selected from written work, reading material, and other sources. A major goal is to use words that students choose from their own writing. This is an excellent concept, but a caution is in order. Make sure your children do not feel "punished" for using, but misspelling, their extended vocabularies. For example, Haley, a first-grader, wrote a story she called "Klumsy Bne" (Clumsy Bunny). Haley misspelled 52 words and correctly spelled 23. We do not want 52 words on Haley's personal spelling list. Haley should be asked to pick four or five words from her story that she wants to learn to spell. As time goes on, Haley will learn to monitor her own selections, but the teacher must monitor progress so that children do not become overwhelmed. It is also important for teachers to provide supplemental words. Selection should be guided by teacher-developed criteria coordinated across grade levels.

**Managing Instruction.** The individualized approach works when well managed. Cooperation between students and teachers and among teachers and administrators is crucial. Three prerequisites are essential: effective reading and writing instruction is in place, guidelines for establishing word lists are coordinated across grade levels, and activities for learning words are developed and implemented. These tasks are often neglected at the school or district level, leaving teachers to carry the burden alone. The following tips may be helpful when choosing an approach to spelling instruction.

- Make team decisions about the best approach to spelling for the children in your school or district.
- Align spelling instruction with the reading and writing program in your school or district.
- Make spelling instruction consistent and complementary across grade levels within your school or district.
- Allot sufficient instructional time, and teach spelling regularly.

Spelling instruction must be well managed regardless of the approach chosen. Important questions arise and must be answered: What provisions can be made for individual differences? How is spelling instruction related to reading and writing instruction? How should spelling be assessed? Answers to these questions can be imposed on teachers, but this is a formula for failure. Teachers and administrators must answer these questions as a team and then vigorously pursue implementation.

## Section Summary: Approaches to Teaching Spelling

1. While there are many approaches to spelling instruction, most fall within one of the following two categories: commercial spelling textbooks or individualized spelling programs.
2. Spelling textbooks provide lists and activities in workbooks, as well as ancillary materials keyed to textbook features.
3. Individualized spelling uses spelling words and activities supplied by teachers and children. These lists and activities are often associated with specific reading and writing experiences organized by classroom teachers.

**Background**

Some educators believe that spelling textbooks should not be used to teach spelling; others say an individualized approach is best; still others argue that formal spelling instruction is not necessary.

Most everyone has used a Webster's dictionary. Noah Webster wrote the first American spelling series, compiled dictionaries, and sponsored educational reform. You can read about him in *Noah Webster: The Life and Times of an American Patriot*, by G. H. Unger, 1998.

**The Debatable Issue**

Should teachers use spelling textbooks, organize an individualized spelling program, or depend on spelling growth to come about through frequent writing and wide reading?

**Take a Stand**

Argue the case for spelling textbooks, an individualized approach, or no formal spelling instruction. Marshal your arguments based on your experience, philosophy, and whatever authorities or research seems relevant. Work in teams. After you have discussed the issue with your teammates, debate it in your class or among your colleagues informally.

## Strategies for Teaching and Learning Spelling

A strategy is a plan designed to achieve a particular outcome. The desired outcome of spelling instruction is to get new words into long-term memory and spelling concepts established. Good spellers learn many strategies on their own; poor spellers are less likely to do so, yet they are most in need. Seven strategies students need to know are described below.

### Pronunciation

Some words are misspelled because they are mispronounced or underarticulated (Cramer & Cipielewski, 1995; Templeton & Morris, 1999). For example, failure to fully articulate a word like *probably* may result in this spelling—*probly*. Yet fully articulated pronunciation is helpful for spelling certain words but not others. Words such as *favorite, February, chocolate,* and *different* benefit from clear articulation of the unarticulated or underarticulated troublesome part. It is difficult to know which words fall into this category, but when you suspect a word is misspelled because it is not fully articulated, model how you might say and spell the word.

Ron Cramer and Jim Cipielewski (1995) describe 55 types of spelling errors and their frequency as found in 18,599 children's compositions.

### Problem Parts

Gates (1937) demonstrated that words have "problem parts" that generate a significant proportion of the errors children make in spelling. If a child misspells *laughing* as *lafing,* as they do 57% of the time, then *ugh* is the problem, not the rest of the word. Teach children to locate the place within a word that gives them difficulty; then have them study that part in particular. Locating troublesome parts in a misspelling should be done immediately after pretesting and on other appropriate occasions. Also, children should be taught to locate their own problem parts. Teacher modeling of the process is helpful.

> Arthur Gates was a giant in the field of literacy. His study (1937) of spelling errors remains a classic that has yet to be fully replicated, even though the availability of computers would make replication easier than the hand analysis common in Gates's era.

## Visualizing

Radebaugh (1985) reported that good spellers use visualization far more often than poor spellers do. Poor spellers' overwhelmingly typical strategy was "sounding out," which is useful but limited because it won't take a speller far beyond the phonetic stage of spelling. Visualizing is the creation of a mental picture to help spell a word. It has two dimensions. One may visualize the target word or a related word in its written form. For example, children may be asked to visualize the word *can,* which they know, to help them spell *man,* which may be unknown. Visualizing may also involve creating a mental picture in which images of people, animals, objects, and actions play a role in remembering or imagining the spelling of a word. For example, one might visualize a rat with its tail curled around the letter *e* to recall the *r-a-t* and silent *e* in *separate.* Silly? Of course, but effective nonetheless. Suggestions for coaching in visualization are given in Table 13.5.

## Mnemonic Devices

A mnemonic device is used to aid memory. It can help recall a difficult word or word part. Mnemonic devices are mostly useful for a small number of difficult-to-remember words. They are as effective when they are silly as when they are serious. Children can have fun with mnemonics, so it is good to encourage using them on special situations. Here are some examples.

### Table 13.5
**Visualization Strategies**

| Ask Questions | Make Suggestions | Give Examples |
|---|---|---|
| Which part of the word gives you trouble? | Picture the word in your imagination. | *separate:* picture *a rat* with a tail curled like an *e* as in: |
| Which part is hardest for you to remember? | Your picture may apply to all or part of the word. | *sep A RAT    e* |
| Can you picture the troubling part? | Think of your picture when you write the word. | I know you can spell *cat.* So how might you spell *fat,* which rhymes with *cat?* |
| How does the word look in print? | Your idea has to work for you, not for someone else. | |

| Spelling Problem | Memory Clue |
|---|---|
| *depart* | Hand me *de part.* |
| *attendance* | *At ten* the *dance* starts. |
| *misspell* | *Miss Pell* will never *misspell.* |
| *isolate, notable* | I was *so late,* I was *not able* to meet the President. |

## Word Structure

Words have structural elements: syllables, prefixes, suffixes, roots. Knowing the structure of words, how they relate to one another, and how they influence spelling is crucial information for spelling. Teach children to divide long words into structurally correct parts and conquer the word one element at a time. Words can be divided into affixed parts and root or base word; they can also be broken into syllables. Compounds can be broken at their meaning units. Examples are shown in Table 13.6.

## Rhyming Helper

Rhyming words usually share similar ending features. Words with such features are sometimes called word families because they share a common phonogram, usually a vowel–consonant combination, as in *far, car, star* or *sing, thing, bring.* Rhyming words usually have a similar spelling pattern, but not always, so it is good to make children aware of this. Show them patterns such as *should, could, would, wood*—all the examples sound alike, but one deviates from the spelling pattern. Awareness of inconsistencies is just as important as awareness of consistencies. Three books (Bear et al., 2000; Cunningham, 1995; Pinnell & Fountas, 2001) are especially helpful in dealing with this and other matters related to words and spelling.

## Proofreading

Careful proofreading is a good habit to acquire early. Children who have not yet acquired an extensive spelling vocabulary are limited in their ability to proofread

### Table 13.6

**Word Structure**

| Compound Words (Divide between meaning units) | Affixed Words (Divide between affix and base word) | Syllables (Divide between syllables) |
|---|---|---|
| base/ball | un/need/ed | man/u/script |
| fire/truck | re/fresh/ing | rhet/or/ic |
| street/car | jump/ing | hol/o/caust |
| path/way | manner/ism | sou/ve/nir |
| soy/bean | re/en/act/ment | tech/nol/o/gist |

**Table 13.7**

Developing Spelling Consciousness

| Teach Strategies | Teach Editing and Proofreading | Search Environmental Print |
|---|---|---|
| pronunciation | editor's trick of reading backwards | misspelled signs |
| mnemonic devices | | intentionally misspelled ads |
| spelling consciousness | editing personal writing | newspaper errors |
| visualization | teacher's intentional misspelling | environmental print |
| problem parts | | |
| word structure | class editing | |
| rhyming helpers | editing others' writing | |
| | paired editing with peers | |

effectively. Here are two ideas that may help. First, try a tactic used by professional editors—scan print from right to left, looking only for spelling errors. This takes meaning out of the picture, enabling children to concentrate only on the search for misspelled words. Model the tactic with children before suggesting its use. Second, have children circle words they are sure they have misspelled as well as words they *think* they may have misspelled. Then, in conferences with the teacher or in small peer groups, discuss ways of self-correcting the incorrect and "uncertain" words.

## Spelling Consciousness

Spelling consciousness is a metacognitive strategy, an effort to help children become more aware of what they know, what they may need to know, and how they can come to know it. Good spellers are aware of their spelling knowledge; poor spellers seldom are. The challenge is to help poor spellers develop a self-monitoring stance. Table 13.7 suggests ways to help develop consciousness of techniques for learning to spell and how to monitor the print environment.

"The habits of the good speller are especially needed by the poor speller."

—Edward Dolch

## Section Summary: Strategies for Teaching and Learning Spelling

1. A strategy is a plan designed to achieve a particular outcome. The desired outcome of spelling strategies is to provide children with a variety of ways to practice and learn spelling words and concepts.
2. Pronunciation, problem parts, visualization, mnemonic devices, word structure, rhyming helpers, proofreading, and spelling consciousness are all helpful strategies.

**Instructional Issues**

The Blue Pages at the back of this book suggest many ideas for teaching spelling.

This section deals with day-to-day problems encountered in teaching spelling: number of words assigned, studying troublesome words, taking spelling tests, reviewing words and spelling concepts, time on task, and principles and conventions of spelling.

## Number of Words

There is no reliable research to guide decisions about how many words a child should practice each week, though some traditional notions may serve as a rough guide. Classroom teachers are best able to determine how many words a child can handle in a week, though trial and error may be necessary for a time. Thereafter, monitor progress and adjust the number accordingly. Children who progress well may have more words than those who are having difficulty. Good readers can handle more words than average or slowly progressing readers. The four guidelines offered below help you know when the spelling list needs to be adjusted.

*Teaching Tip*

1. *Monitor achievement.* Children are not ready to handle complex spelling patterns until simpler patterns have been learned. Children who are progressing satisfactorily should routinely score 70% or higher on spelling tests at the end of a study period. When children consistently fall below this level over a 6-week period you have four options:
   - Lower the instructional level.
   - Reduce the number of words assigned.
   - Adjust the level of word complexity.
   - After diagnosing types of errors children make, adjust teaching to correct problems.
2. *Have children read their spelling lists aloud.* They should be able to read their spelling lists fluently.
3. *Spot-check to see if your children know the meanings of their spelling words.* If not, adjust the list.
4. *Satisfactory scores on weekly spelling lists are not sufficient evidence that things are going well.* Check to see if list words are commonly misspelled in daily writing. Performance in daily writing should be consistent with performance on spelling lists and tests. If it is not, reassess the instructional program you are pursuing.

The guidelines in Table 13.8 can help you make an initial estimate of the number of spelling words for each child. But remember, it is an educated guess, not a certain conclusion. Monitoring subsequent performance is the key to getting it right.

## Troublesome Words

Research has shown that certain words continue to be misspelled across grade levels. Cramer and Cipielewski (1995) conducted a study in which they collected

**Table 13.8**

**Number of Spelling Words Assigned Per Week**

| Grade Level | Slowly Progressing Reader–Speller | Average Reader–Speller | Above Average Reader–Speller |
|---|---|---|---|
| 1 | 4–6 | 8–10 | 10–12 |
| 2 | 6–8 | 10–12 | 12–14 |
| 3 | 8–10 | 10–14 | 14–20 |
| 4 | 10–12 | 14–20 | 20–25 |
| 5 | 10–12 | 18–20 | 20–25 |
| 6 | 10–12 | 18–20 | 20–25 |
| 7 | 12–14 | 18–20 | 20–25 |
| 8 | 12–14 | 18–20 | 20–25 |

18,599 compositions written by children in grades 1–8. The sample included children from all states, as well as urban and suburban areas. Analysis of these first-draft compositions yielded lists of words particularly troublesome at each grade level. A method of studying troublesome words is suggested in Table 13.9.

"Words repay the attention they are accorded."
—Joseph Shipley

## Spelling Tests

A properly administered pretest aids learning because it enables children to regulate and direct their learning more efficiently—more metacognitively. It is common practice to administer a pretest, a midweek test, and a final test. A pretest is essential because it tells children what they need to learn. A final test is useful for monitoring progress. A midweek test is optional. Have students work as partners to administer the pretest or midweek test to each other. Self-correction, if monitored effectively,

Peruse the 100 most frequently misspelled words for each grade level, grades 1–8, listed in Figure 13.12 on pages 520–521. These lists are derived from a Scott Foresman–sponsored research project. The results are reported in *Spelling, Research, and Information: An Overview of Current Research and Practices*, 1995.

**Table 13.9**

**Study Procedures for Difficult Words**

| 1. Prepare | Fold a piece of paper into three columns. |
|---|---|
| 2. Study | Study your word until you think you can spell it. Cover it. |
| 3. First writing | Write the word in the first column. Check it. If correct, go to the next step. |
| 4. Second writing | Fold under the first column and write the word in the second column. Check it. If correct, go to step 5. |
| 5. Third writing | Fold under the second column and write the word in the third column. Check it. If correct, stop for now. |
| 6. Error | If you make an error at any point, start again at step 2. |
| 7. Practice | Practice again another time. |

**Table 13.10**

**Procedures for Monitoring a Spelling Pretest**

| | |
|---|---|
| 1. Known words | If you think you've spelled a word correctly, put a check mark beside it. |
| 2. Unknown words | If you think you've probably misspelled a word, put an *X* beside it. |
| 3. Uncertain words | If you don't know whether a word is correct or not, put a question mark beside it. |
| 4. Your pretest | Compare your pretest words with a correct copy, and determine the number you got right. |
| 5. Assessment | How often were you right in your best guesses about words you thought were correct, incorrect, or uncertain? |
| 6. Study | Practice words you missed. |

works well (Hodges, 1981). Teach children to follow the procedures outlined in Table 13.10 *after* they take a pretest but *before* they correct it.

## Review of Words and Spelling Concepts

Research shows that certain words are misspelled across grades 1–8. Therefore, they must be taught and retaught across grade levels. Choose a period of time, say 5–6 weeks, and spend a week reviewing previously taught words. These procedures are helpful: (1) give review tests at regular intervals, (2) monitor writing for frequently misspelled words and review them regularly, and (3) post the correct spelling of problem words for easy reference. Cramer and Cipielewski (1995) identified 100 words that continue to be troublesome regardless of grade level. These words need to be reviewed across and within levels.

There are also spelling principles, conventions, and strategies that all children need to know. Often we assume that they should be learned after one or two exposures. But this does not work for all children. Poor spellers need time to learn strategies and conventions, and even good spellers seldom learn them in a single exposure. It is just as important to review spelling concepts as spelling words. Strategies, principles, and conventions can be applied at different levels and within different contexts, using different words.

## Time on Task

How much time should be devoted to formal spelling instruction? I recommend 60–90 minutes per week, but this can vary depending on how much writing, revising, and reading are done and the approach used. Spelling instruction should be scheduled three to five times a week. Table 13.11 suggests three plans based on 90 minutes per week.

**Table 13.11**

Time Allotted for Spelling Instruction

|            | Day 1 | Day 2 | Day 3 | Day 4 | Day 5 |
|------------|-------|-------|-------|-------|-------|
| 5-day plan | 20    | 15    | 20    | 15    | 20    |
| 4-day plan | 25    | 0     | 25    | 20    | 20    |
| 3-day plan | 35    | 0     | 35    | 0     | 20    |

## Principles and Conventions of Spelling

There are a number of important principles and conventions of spelling, and all are implicated in the spelling errors children make. Children acquire principles and conventions as a by-product of reading and writing and direct instruction. Here are eight common spelling conventions.

1. *Position within word.* The position of one or more letters within a word can influence the sound or placement of one or more other letters. For example, silent *e* influences the long *a* sound in *make*. The *gh* (*ghetto*) never has an /f/ sound at the beginning of a word but can have an /f/ sound in a middle or ending position (*laughing, laugh*).
2. *Meaning-spelling connection.* Many words related in meaning are closely related in spelling in spite of changes in sound in the derived form: *minor, minority.*
3. *Homophone.* This is a word with the same pronunciation as another but with a different meaning, origin, and spelling—*bear, bare.*
4. *Apostrophe.* This mark (') is used to show omission of one or more letters and to show possessive forms: *isn't, is not, Andy's house.*
5. *Compounds.* Two or more words combine in a single meaning unit. There are three types—closed, open, and hyphenated: *bookmark, ice cream, self-portrait.*
6. *Capitalization.* Proper nouns start with a capital letter: *Tom, New York.*
7. *Abbreviation.* A period follows most abbreviated words: *Jan.* for *January.*
8. *One word, not two; two words, not one.* Words such as *alone* and *arise* are one word, not two; terms such as *a lot* and *all right* are two words, not one.

## Section Summary: Instructional Issues

1. Teachers deal with many practical matters related to spelling.
2. These instructional issues include the number of words assigned, study procedures for troublesome words, spelling tests, systematic review of words and spelling concepts, sufficient time each week for studying spelling words and concepts, and adequate coverage of spelling principles and conventions.

## Standing on the Shoulders of Giants
### Historical Contributions to Literacy
## Noah Webster

A baby was born in 1758 in the village of West Hartford, Connecticut. His parents named him after an Old Testament prophet. As a young man, he graduated from Yale and practiced law for a few years. Later he became a teacher. He wrote political pamphlets and edited two Federalist newspapers. He wrote grammars, readers, and spellers and compiled one of the greatest dictionaries of early American English. You see his name on millions of modern dictionaries. Who is he?

Millions of copies of his speller sold well into the 20th century, and his enormous and original linguistic efforts helped standardize spelling and pronunciation in the United States. His great dictionary, *An American Dictionary of the English Language,* appeared in 1828. The dictionary was revised in 1840 and included 12,000 words and

40,000 definitions that had never before appeared in a dictionary. Who is he?

Teacher, philosopher, author, political leader, public official, editor, lexicographer, patriot: he was all of this and more. In 1783, he published a book first known as *A Grammatical Institute of the English Language,* later renamed *The American Spelling Book,* more popularly known as *The Blueback Spellers.* His spelling book changed forever the approach to teaching American children to read, write, speak, and spell. His work touched the lives of the great and the humble, the young and the old, and continues to do so two centuries later. So children, get out your spelling books; teachers, get out your grammars and readers; professors, get out your dictionaries. Noah Webster is the giant on whose shoulders you stand.

## Selecting Spelling Words

There are nearly one million American English words. Fortunately, no one needs to learn even one tenth of them. Here's why a smaller core vocabulary will suffice. If children can spell the 2,000 words most frequently used in writing, they will know enough words to correctly spell about 95% of the words normally used in writing. This is a good start, but insufficient. Add to the 2,000 an additional 10,000–12,000 well-selected words, and a satisfactory spelling vocabulary would be in place. Once a core spelling vocabulary has been acquired and crucial concepts have been learned, additional thousands of derived and analogous words can be spelled that have never been taught. The spelling of rare or seldom-used words can be left to dictionary searches and spell checkers.

Researchers cannot agree on the seemingly simple question "What is a word?" For instance, are big, bigger, biggest three different words or one word with two derived forms? As a result, not only is it difficult to count the actual number of words in language, but it is even more difficult to decide what to count.

Six criteria should be used when building spelling lists from which basic spelling concepts can be illustrated and practiced: developmentally appropriate words, high-frequency words, linguistically patterned words, frequently misspelled words, content related words, and personally selected words. A brief description of each criterion follows.

## Developmentally Appropriate Words

Children should learn spelling words that match their stage of growth in reading, writing, and oral language. Researchers, principally under the leadership of Edmund Henderson, have identified five stages of spelling development. Each stage implicitly suggests the need for the introduction of certain orthographic concepts and the avoidance of others. Word lists should be constrained by the boundaries of knowledge children have acquired as they proceed through the stages of spelling growth.

## Frequency in Oral and Written Language

A core spelling vocabulary of 2,000 or so of the most common words used in writing and reading is crucial to selecting and sequencing spelling lists. Frequency lists abound, but each list was developed for different reasons and drawn from different sources. No single list will suffice. The best advice is to consult the frequency list references shown in Figure 13.6. If it were only a matter of selecting high-frequency words, the task would be easy. A major problem in constructing spelling lists is integrating words of the highest frequency with other word selection criteria. It is a herculean task to compile a list of 10,000–12,000 words and honor all relevant criteria.

## Linguistic Pattern

Linguistic pattern is the organizing principle around which other word selection criteria revolve. Linguistic features, such as meaning, sound, structure, and etymology, provide insight into how words are spelled. For example, there is an

---

Carroll, J., et al. *The American heritage word frequency book.* Boston: Houghton Mifflin, 1971. Contains 86,741 different words sampled from textbooks, novels, encyclopedias, magazines, and other grades 3–9 sources.

Dolch, E. A basic sight vocabulary. *Elementary School Journal,* 1936. Contains 220 high-frequency words.

Dolch, E. The 2,000 commonest words for spelling. *Better Spelling.* Champaign, IL: The Garrard Press, 1942. Lists the 2,000 most common spelling words.

Harris, A., & Jacobson, M. *Basic reading vocabularies.* New York: Macmillan, 1982. Contains 10,000 high-frequency words from running text in eight basal reading series.

Thorndike, E., & Lorge, I. *The teachers' word book of 30,000 words.* New York: Columbia University, 1944. Contains 30,000 words arranged alphabetically. Frequency of occurrence for a word in general is given, as well as its frequency in four different sets of reading matter.

Edward Thorndike and Irving Lorge were giants in the field of word-frequency counts. Their book on the frequencies of 30,000 words set the standard for many years. Pity the poor graduate assistants who had to do the counting!

**Figure 13.6**

**Word-Frequency References**

**Figure 13.7**

**Frequently Misspelled Words**: **Relevant Studies**

Cramer, R., Beers, J., Hammond, D., Cipielewski, J., & Marine, K. *The Scott-Foresman research in action project: A study of spelling errors in 18,599 written compositions of children in grades 1–8*. Glenview, IL: Scott, Foresman Addison Wesley, 1995. Screened 1,584,758 words to determine most frequently misspelled words across and within grade levels 1–8 and categorizes 55 different types of spelling-error patterns across eight grade levels.

Farr, R., et al. *An analysis of the spelling patterns of children in grades 2–8*. Center for Reading and Language Studies: Indiana State University, 1989. Identifies words children often misspell and reports patterns of spelling errors.

Gates, A. *A list of spelling difficulties in 3,876 words, showing the "hard-spots," common misspellings, average spelling-grade placement, and comprehension grade ratings for each word*. New York: Bureau of Publications, Teachers College, Columbia University, 1937. Early study of spelling difficulties that locates the features within words, which are most likely to generate spelling errors.

important link between meaning and spelling, vowel patterns and spelling, word structure and spelling, etymology and spelling. Good spelling lists consider all of these linguistic features. While this makes list construction challenging, it is the best way to organize learning. Organizing lists by linguistic features does not preclude considering other criteria for word selection, though it adds to the complexity of list construction.

## Frequently Misspelled Words

Error analysis research can aid word selection. Certain words are difficult to learn and are thus troublesome across many grade levels. Frequently misspelled words are invariably high-frequency words, so working them into spelling lists is not especially difficult. Knowing which words are most frequently misspelled tells you which words must be recycled within and across grade levels. The three word studies shown in Figure 13.7 can help you determine which words have proven difficult for children to learn.

Table 13.12 contains a list of the 100 most frequently misspelled words across grades 1–8. Words are listed in order of their frequency of misspelling.

### Table 13.12

**100 Most Frequently Misspelled Words, Grades 1–8**

| | | | |
|---|---|---|---|
| 1. too | 8. it's | 15. they're | 22. finally |
| 2. a lot | 9. when | 16. said | 23. where |
| 3. because | 10. favorite | 17. know | 24. again |
| 4. there | 11. went | 18. you're | 25. then |
| 5. their | 12. Christmas | 19. friend | 26. didn't |
| 6. that's | 13. were | 20. friends | 27. people |
| 7. they | 14. our | 21. really | 28. until |

## Table 13.12, continued

| | | | |
|---|---|---|---|
| 29. with | 47. Halloween | 65. Easter | 83. started |
| 30. different | 48. house | 66. what | 84. was |
| 31. outside | 49. once | 67. there's | 85. which |
| 32. we're | 50. to | 68. little | 86. stopped |
| 33. through | 51. like | 69. doesn't | 87. two |
| 34. upon | 52. whole | 70. usually | 88. Dad |
| 35. probably | 53. another | 71. clothes | 89. took |
| 36. don't | 54. believe | 72. scared | 90. friend's |
| 37. sometimes | 55. I'm | 73. everyone | 91. presents |
| 38. off | 56. thought | 74. have | 92. are |
| 39. everybody | 57. let's | 75. swimming | 93. morning |
| 40. heard | 58. before | 76. about | 94. could |
| 41. always | 59. beautiful | 77. first | 95. around |
| 42. I | 60. everything | 78. happened | 96. buy |
| 43. something | 61. very | 79. Mom | 97. maybe |
| 44. would | 62. into | 80. especially | 98. family |
| 45. want | 63. caught | 81. school | 99. pretty |
| 46. and | 64. one | 82. getting | 100. tried |

## Content Words

Math, science, social studies, English, reading, and other subjects have key vocabularies, which change as children move from grade to grade. It is important for children to learn these vocabularies. Consequently, content words should be included on spelling lists. There are two options for dealing with content words. They can be worked into weekly lists, or they can be taught separately. If incorporated into

*Content words like* Mississippi *can be learned through mnemonic devices. Many children find these seemingly difficult words easier to spell than homophones such as to, too, and two.*

PEANUTS reprinted by permission of United Feature Syndicate, Inc.

**Table 13.13**

**Sample Lists of Content Words**

| Science | Math | Reading | Social Studies |
|---|---|---|---|
| carnivore | division | meaning | neighborhood |
| dinosaur | multiply | pronounce | community |
| magnet | remainder | sounds | oceans |
| Fahrenheit | geometry | letters | continent |
| volcano | vertex | thinking | Earth |
| retina | intersecting | strategy | globe |
| humidity | parallel | brainstorm | Pilgrims |
| compass | mathematics | library | Indians |
| predator | quotient | research | plains |
| prey | divisible | context | geography |

weekly lists, they must fit a linguistic pattern. While this is not difficult to do, it does scatter content words across many lessons. If incorporated into separate spelling lessons, they can be taught at the time teachers want them taught. Since there is a dearth of useful studies to guide selection of content words, one has to rely on subject matter textbooks, content lists in spelling textbooks, and other such sources. Table 13.13 contains sample lists of content words.

## Personal Words

Personal words are selected from writing or reading *by children with teacher assistance.* Each list is specific to the child who selects it. Personal words should constitute a proportion of the words children study each week. Which words to choose, and how many, can become a problem. Two criteria apply: (1) personal words should be ones a child misspells in written work or encounters in reading, and (2) personal words should be within a child's meaning and word recognition vocabulary. If these two criteria are met, problems are unlikely.

Children sometimes enjoy choosing exotic words such as *antidisestablishmentarianism.* There is no harm in such choices and much fun. Still, most personal choices should be functional rather than exotic. Choosing the right number of personal words is important, since you do not want students to be overchallenged or underchallenged. If you are using spelling textbooks, most programs suggest three to five personal words per week. If you are following an individualized spelling approach, establish a balance between the number of personal words selected and the number of teacher-assigned words.

## Section Summary: Selecting Spelling Words

1. Words must be developmentally appropriate so as to match children's stage of growth in reading, writing, and oral language.
2. Select words according to their frequency in oral and written language.
3. Organize spelling lists based on linguistic patterns.
4. Include words that tend to be frequently misspelled.
5. Include key content words in spelling lists.
6. Encourage children to add personally selected words to their lists, drawn from their reading and writing.

# Invented Spelling

Invented spelling can be thought of as a temporary crutch, useful for a period of time, abandoned when no longer needed. When an incorrect attempt to spell an unknown word is made, the resulting spelling is said to have been invented. Invented spelling supports reading, writing, and spelling because it strengthens children's command of these crucial elements of literacy: phonemic awareness, phonetics, letter–sound relationships, word analysis and synthesis, control, confidence, hypotheses construction, and curiosity.

See "A Retrospective on Invented Spelling and a Look Forward," by R. Gentry, 2000, *The Reading Teacher, 54*(3).

Spelling impedes writing for children who do not have a core spelling vocabulary. First-graders may have oral vocabularies ranging from 5,000–15,000 words, but they can spell perhaps 5–500 words. Used wisely, children's oral language hastens literacy. Children who write early make progress in reading, writing, and spelling, not in spite of invented spelling but because of it. Picture in your mind an imaginary first-grader; let's call her Anna. Anna has a 10,000-word oral vocabulary but can spell only 5 words. She wants to write a story. What kind of a story can Anna write with 5 spelling words at her command? An impoverished one or none at all. But if Anna is encouraged to use invented spelling, her story can be as rich as her imagination and oral vocabulary will allow.

Think of invented spelling as an anvil on which children shape their knowledge of English orthography. Children must go through a long process of forging their knowledge of the spelling system. Some will become "master blacksmiths" of spelling, others journeymen. Regardless of eventual status, each child must lay hands on the tools of spelling. Mistakes will be made, must be made, but they are merely the slippery rungs on a ladder that leads upward. Letter by letter, word by word, concept by concept, children forge their knowledge of English orthography. And invented spelling plays a crucial role in making the links.

Consider this long chain of invented spelling forged by a first-grade child: EFUKANOPNKAZIWILGEVUAKANOPENR (if you can open cans, I will give you a can opener) (Chomsky, 1979). Only 2 correct spellings in 12 words attempted—*I* and *a* are spelled correctly. Yet this piece can be read easily by an experienced teacher. And it is a first effort. It doesn't matter how many words are spelled correctly. Children who begin at this stage will soon produce words closer and closer to standard spelling, and more and more of their words will be correctly spelled.

## Research on Invented Spelling

Cramer (1970) conducted a study of first-grade children's spelling as part of a larger study comparing the language experience approach to a basal reader approach. He found that first-grade children who used invented spelling quickly became superior spellers, far better than their basal reader counterparts who did not use it. The language experience children also performed better in reading and writing than did their basal reader counterparts, and they maintained their superior literacy achievement across six years (Stauffer, Hammond, Oehlkers, & Houseman,

1972). Clarke (1989) studied the effects of invented spelling versus traditional spelling among first-grade children. She measured reading, writing, and spelling achievement. While achievement in reading was similar, children using invented spelling showed superior spelling and phonetic analysis skill. Low-achieving children benefited most from invented spelling. Healy (1991) compared the effects of invented spelling and traditional spelling on growth in reading and writing among first-graders. The invented spelling group produced better and more writing than children in the traditional spelling group. Garcia (1997) investigated the effects of invented spelling on first-graders' reading, writing, and spelling growth. Results showed that invented spelling had a beneficial influence on word attack skills, vocabulary knowledge, and writing.

Read (1975) provided the linguistic explanation for invented spelling. He studied invented spelling among preschoolers and discovered that different children invented the same system of spelling and that their inventions were systematic and uniform from child to child. He showed that children classify sounds into categories based on perceived similarities; they used their knowledge of letter–sound relationships to produce approximations of words. He found that their spelling inventions were consistent with the underlying phonemic system of English. Finally, he found that invented spelling flourished where parents enjoyed and appreciated their children's writing. Research on invented spelling supports the following generalizations, which have implications for teaching children to read, write, and spell:

- Children in an invented spelling program spell better than their counterparts in traditional spelling programs (Cramer, 1970; Healy, 1991).
- Children in an invented spelling program read better than their counterparts in traditional language arts programs (Garcia, 1997; Stauffer et al., 1972).
- Children in an invented spelling program produce more and better writing than their counterparts in traditional language arts programs (Cramer, 1970; Healy, 1991).
- No reliable research has shown that invented spelling has a negative influence on reading, writing, and spelling.

## How Invented Spelling Works: Its Linguistic Features

The features of early invented spelling described and summarized here are extrapolated from research conducted across three decades.

- Long vowels are spelled by the name of the letter that matches the sound. This is called the letter-name strategy: *rak* for *rake*; *got* for *goat*; *tru* for *true*.
- Short vowels are spelled by the letter name that has the sound closest in point of articulation to the one being replaced: *fes* for *fish*, *git* for *got*.
- Two nasal sounds, *m* and *n*, are omitted when they occur just before another consonant: *bopy* for *bumpy*, *plat* for *plant*.
- Syllable sonorants (*l*, *m*, *n*) carry the vowel sound in a syllable: *batl* for *battle*; *btm* for *bottom*; *opn* for *open*.
- R-controlled vowels are omitted: *grl* for *girl*; *hrd* for *heard*.

- Past tense marker *-ed* is spelled with a *t* or *d*: *lokt* for *looked*; *stpt* for *stopped*; *klid* for *climbed*; *brd* for *bored*.
- Sounds made by doubled letters *t* and *d* are spelled with one letter: *ltl* for *little*; *mdl* for *middle*; *padl* for *paddle*.
- Affricative sounds such as *tr, dr,* and *ch* are spelled *jr, gr, ch,* and *chr*: *jran* for *train*; *griv* for *drive*; *chran* for *train*; *wht* for *watched*.
- One or more letters may stand for an entire word. This is called letter-name spelling: *u* for *you*; *r* for *are*; *yl* for *while*; *nhr* for *nature*.

These generalizations apply in most instances, but not all. Thus, while one child may spell *train* as *jran*, another may spell it *trn* or *tran*. How children spell a given word depends on their spelling stage, progress made within a stage (early, middle, late), and variation attributable to individual differences. As children move through the stages of spelling growth, they become less dependent on sounds and more dependent on broader spelling concepts: patterns within words, rules of syllable juncture, and principles of meaning derivation. Teachers need not know all of the technical details in order to use invented spelling, although it is useful to understand the basic concepts. For instance, if you see *bumpy* spelled *bopy* and *troubles* spelled *chribls*, you might think the child is way off in understanding how to connect letters with sounds. But if you are aware of these early features of invented spelling, you will know that there is a linguistic reason for the seemingly strange spelling you have observed.

## Explaining Invented Spelling to Parents

Spelling is a visible symbol of literacy, so when parents are told that invented spelling is just another example of dumbing down the curriculum, they may be ready to believe it. Looking at the issue from the standpoint of parents, it is not surprising that some are alarmed. Critics tell them that invented spelling will handicap their children with poor spelling habits from which they may never recover. Yet most parents want to believe that their children's teachers are upholding educational standards. Therefore, teachers must explain why invented spelling makes sense. Parents can be persuaded, but they want evidence. The most persuasive evidence is the success their children are experiencing in learning to read, write, and spell. But we can't just tell them; we must show them. Examples of their children's writing can be persuasive. It also helps to explain what invented spelling is all about, how it works, and how it benefits reading and writing.

Inform parents that invented spelling is temporary and will gradually be replaced with correct spelling. As children progress through the stages of spelling, their temporary spellings move gradually toward standard spelling. For example, when their child writes *name* as *nm*, this spelling is temporary and will soon be spelled correctly. On the other hand, if a first-grader spells *absolutely* as *ablule*, the parent should know that this is an excellent guess and suggests that the child is progressing well beyond first-grade standards.

Help parents understand why early reading and writing are important. Once parents understand that spelling is a barrier to progress in reading and writing, they are more likely to understand the value of invented spelling. If writing is delayed until spelling is acquired, children have no way of practicing the spelling words they are learning in their weekly spelling lesson. Inform parents that invented spelling builds reading knowledge. The reader decodes and the writer encodes. The given for the reader is the visible word, and readers must supply the sounds to decode the words they see. It works the other way around for spelling. The writer has the sounds but must supply the letters. Thus, practice in writing reinforces knowledge needed for reading and spelling; practice in reading and spelling reinforces knowledge needed for writing.

Finally, assure parents that you are teaching standard spelling. Many schools have abandoned systematic spelling instruction, but this should never be the case. Poor spelling is bound to attract critics. Invented spelling is an inviting target to take the blame. But invented spelling does not account for poor spelling achievement. Abandonment of effective spelling instruction is the culprit. Assure parents that along with invented spelling, you are teaching standard spelling.

## Section Summary: Invented Spelling

1. Invented spellings are temporary best guesses at spelling words. Research shows that invented spelling increases reading, writing, and standard spelling achievement. The features of invented spelling, categorized by Read (1975), show that they are systematic and uniform across different children.
2. Teachers need to explain the value of invented spelling and assure parents that they are teaching standard spelling.

# Assessment of Spelling

Spelling assessment is sometimes neglected because teachers may feel uncertain about how to chart progress. Yet it is crucial to understand how to assess progress and determine appropriate placement for spelling. This section provides case studies in how to assess progress and determine placement levels.

## Early Spelling Growth and Assessment

A good way to assess early spelling growth is to administer the Morris Spelling Test. This test is especially useful for children in K–3 or those whose reading acquisition is substantially delayed. A teacher can confidently make one of three decisions about performance on the Morris Test:

1. Progress is delayed.
2. Progress is moderate.
3. Progress is rapid.

After deciding which category is appropriate, we must ask, *What does the information suggest for future instruction?* Testing is a waste of time unless this question is answered. It need not be answered perfectly. Diagnosis is always tentative and subject to follow-up observation.

Look at Asa, Jacob, and Linda's spelling performance on the Morris Test in February of their first-grade year, as shown in Table 13.14. Each child exhibits a different pattern: Asa exhibits slow progress, Jacob's progress is moderate, and Linda's progress is rapid. Review the analysis of each case below. Tentative conclusions about their performances have been made, and suggestions provided for how the information can be used to plan future instruction.

**Case 1: Asa, Delayed Progress.** Asa is at the earliest level of the phonetic stage of spelling.

### Tentative Conclusions

- At the beginning of the phonetic stage of spelling
- Beginning to make letter–sound connections
- Makes letter sound connections with beginning consonants only
- Does not have a fully established concept of word

### Recommendations for Instruction

- Instruction on letter–sound relationships, phonemic awareness
- Word sort activities focused on beginning and ending consonant sounds
- Writing with invented spelling every day
- Basic reading instruction, probably at a beginning level
- Dictate, read, and reread stories—group and individual
- Read shared books aloud in groups
- Read aloud to Asa every day

### Follow-up

- Observe performance in reading and writing; make adjustments as needed.
- Administer Morris Test again in April or May.

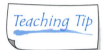
*Teaching Tip*

**Table 13.14**

**Performance on the Morris Test**

| Word | Asa | Jacob | Linda |
|------|-----|-------|-------|
| back | b | bay | back |
| sink | c | ski | suck |
| mail | m | meal | mail |
| dress | j | jay | dries |
| table | t | tall | table |
| side | c | sod | side |
| feet | f | fret | feet |
| stamp | c | shape | stamp |
| letter | l | lath | letter |
| stick | c | sic | stir |
| bike | b | bit | bike |
| seed | s | sued | suede |
| monster | m | mistreat | monster |
| elevator | TV | liver | elevator |

**Case 2: Jacob, Moderate Progress.** Jacob is at the phonetic stage of spelling, though he is further into this stage than Asa.

### Tentative Conclusions

- Middle to late phonetic stage
- Solid grasp of letter–sound connections
- Beginning and ending single consonant always present, usually correct
- Consonant blends not fully established, but may be close—*st* in *monster*
- Always honors vowel sounds; on the cusp of grasping marking principle
- Concept of word established
- Most likely making satisfactory progress in reading

### Recommendations for Instruction

- Word sorts focused on consonant blends, digraphs, short vowel patterns
- Writing with invented spelling every day
- Dictate, read, and reread personal stories
- Individualized reading from trade books
- Group comprehension instruction
- Read aloud to Jacob every day

### Follow-up

- Observe performance in reading and writing; make adjustments as needed.
- Administer Morris Test again in April or May.

**Case 3: Linda, Rapid Progress.** Linda is progressing from the late phonetic stage to the early patterns within words stage of spelling.

### Tentative Conclusions

- Excellent grasp of letter–sound connections
- Good start on a spelling vocabulary
- Consonant blends and digraphs solidly established
- Aware of silent vowel marker principle
- Concept of word fully established
- Most likely making satisfactory progress in reading and writing

### Recommendations for Instruction

- Word sorts focused on long vowels, contrasting vowels
- Writing with invented spelling every day
- Individualized reading from trade books
- Group comprehension instruction
- Read aloud to Linda every day

### Follow-up

- Observe performance in reading and writing; make adjustments as needed.
- Administer Morris Test again in April or May.

Asa, Jacob, and Linda are typical of what one might expect of first-graders. Each child exhibits a different pattern of growth. Administer the Morris Test three times a year, preferably in November, February, and May. I know of a school that administered a similar test starting in kindergarten and continued through third grade. Teachers gained valuable information about spelling and word recognition growth among their children over a four-year period.

## Placement for Instruction

Placing children at their correct spelling level accelerates growth; placing them at their independent level slows growth; placing them at their frustration level stops growth. You can determine placement levels by giving the Spelling Placement

Inventory. Although placement inventories yield reasonably good estimates, misplacement happens. It is necessary, therefore, to monitor spelling performance for 5–6 weeks following initial placement. Adjust placement up or down when children consistently perform above or below their placement level.

**Administering the Placement Inventory**. A spelling inventory is easy to administer. Start at an independent level and test until a frustration level is reached. Since you cannot know the independent level (if there is one) in advance, start the inventory two grade levels below current grade placement. Typically, a third-grader would start with the first-grade list, a fifth-grader with a third-grade list, an eighth-grader with a sixth-grade list. Slowly progressing readers may need to start at the easiest level or, in some cases, postpone spelling instruction until further reading

*Teacher Gizelle Rey helps Nicholas search for patterns among words from his word bank. Words can be sorted by sound, structure, or meaning.*

progress is evident. Administer the inventory in small groups, using two or more sittings if necessary. Continue testing until each student is missing about half of the words on a list—the frustration level.

**Interpreting Scores**. Each correctly spelled word on the inventory is worth 5 points. Multiply the number of correct words on each list by 5. Use this score to determine the independent, instructional, and frustration levels, as shown in Table 13.15.

An independent level is reached when a child achieves a score of 85–100%. Not all children have an independent level; others will have independent scores across two or more grade levels. Do not place children at their independent level as it is not sufficiently challenging.

**Table 13.15**

**Criteria for Determining Spelling Levels, Using a Spelling Placement Inventory**

| Level | Criteria Scores | What It Means |
|---|---|---|
| Independent | 85–100 | Do not place at this level. Not challenging enough; does not need teacher support. |
| Instructional | 65–80 | Place at this level. Just right; growth can occur; needs teacher support. |
| Frustration | 60 or Lower | Do not place at this level; too hard; growth will be slowed or stopped; even teacher support will not suffice. |

The instructional level is the point of instruction at which children are challenged but can manage the task with teacher support or *scaffolding,* as it is sometimes called. The instructional level is akin to what Vygotsky (1962) calls the zone of proximal development.

Lev Vygotsky (1962) was a Russian psychologist who died quite young. His most important work, *Thought and Language,* has influenced the way educators think about teaching and learning with children.

The instructional spelling level is reached when a child achieves a score of 65–80%. Some children achieve instructional level scores spanning two or more grades. Placement is normally at the highest instructional level achieved. An instructional level should be challenging but not so difficult that frustration is encountered.

The frustration level is reached when a child scores 60% or less. Do not place children at this level as it is too difficult, and learning will almost certainly be impeded. And keep in mind Richard Gentry's (1987) experience. Some children are quite good at rote memory of spelling words, holding words in memory just long enough to pass the weekly spelling test.

Table 13.15 identifies criteria for interpreting scores received on the Spelling Placement Inventory. Placement is a tentative decision. It must be adjusted upward or downward if subsequent monitoring of performance indicates that the initial placement was too low or too high.

## Section Summary: Assessment of Spelling

1. The Morris Test provides an easily administered list of words that is helpful in determining whether spelling progress is delayed, moderate, or rapid. Assessment that provides no blueprint for instruction is useless. Testing must be followed by analysis of performance to determine an appropriate spelling program for every child.

2. Determining a student's instructional level involves use of a placement inventory and observation during instruction. Placement at the independent level is not sufficiently challenging; placement at a frustration level ensures lack of growth. Children learn best at their instructional level since this level is challenging without being too easy or too hard.

## Practical Teaching Ideas and Activities

*Teaching Tip*

**1.** *Pretest with a buddy.* Before they study a week's list of words, have students take a pretest; tell children to test themselves so they'll know which words they know how to spell and which they do not know. First, they give the test to a buddy; then their buddy tests them. Students correct their test themselves first; then their buddy checks their work.

**2.** *Make "fruitflake" words.* Compound words are two words joined to make a word with a distinct meaning: *football, tennis court; vice-president.* But these are ordinary, sensible compounds. Children can do better than that! What's a fruitflake word? Maybe they can think of what it might mean. Have them work with a buddy or a small team to make fruitflake compounds and then define them.

**3.** *Meaning schmeaning!* When students have trouble spelling big words tell them that knowing how to spell a smaller related word can help. For example, if someone knows how to spell *sign*, he or she can spell *signal* even though the sounds in *sign* change when they say *signal*. Challenge students to tell what meaning-related word goes in the second column.

| Meaning of Missing Word | Missing Word |
| --- | --- |
| 1. One's name | has *sign* in it |
| 2. Book of songs | has *hymn* in it |
| 3. When you quit your job | has *resign* in it |
| 4. Where animals live | has *habit* in it |
| 5. More than 50% | has *major* in it |

Then have students write five more puzzlers using these words: *minor, labor, combine, compete, memory.*

**4.** *Make lists of words for writing.* Let's suppose the child decides to write a story about a holiday, such as Halloween. It helps to have a list of words that might be needed. For Halloween, he or she might want to spell words such as *ghost, scarecrow, haunted house, trick, treat, mask, costume,* and so on. As they write their stories, encourage the use of invented spellings for words they don't know how to spell. When they are ready to proofread for spelling, they ask the teacher to put a list of Halloween words on the board. Or they can work with their friends to see if they can find the correct spellings, using dictionaries and other sources.

**5.** *Play art smart.* Make a collage of words that have something in common. For example, search for words that start with the same letter, end with the same two letters, rhyme, have three syllables, and so on. They can put whatever type of words they want in their collage.

**6.** *Write homophone sentences.* Working with a partner, children make a list of ten homophones that they have recently studied. Let them write each homophone in a sentence, making sure they have used the homophone correctly. Then have them dictate their sentences to their partner; next, they write their partner's sentences, and finally check each other's work.

See the Blue Pages at the back of the book and on the Companion Website for additional activities.

## Reflection and Summary

### Reflection

My spelling is tolerable, but I can't spell nearly as well as my daughter Jenny can. This, despite decades of studying and writing about spelling. Sometimes I feel like Pooh Bear when he said, "My spelling is wobbly. It's good spelling but it wobbles and the letters get in the wrong places." Pooh Bear's problem isn't a disability; it's merely a difference. Learning differences are normal, and it is time for educators to understand that differences are not disabilities. The band of normal behavior and achievement is broad, not narrow. Obviously, we want children to learn to spell, but it's abnormal to expect everyone to be an excellent speller, just as it would be abnormal to expect everyone to run fast, jump high, or think brilliantly. Let us instead strive to help most children spell adequately or better and some children to spell excellently. Most differences of achievement in spelling, reading, and writing should be thought of as differences, not disabilities.

## Summary

This chapter has presented the following main ideas:

1. There are three major influences on spelling growth: reading, writing, and explicit instruction.
2. Spelling knowledge develops through stages: (a) prephonetic: children experiment with drawings, letters, and letterlike forms; (b) phonetic: children invent spellings, using mostly consonants and some vowels; (c) patterns within words: children discover orderly structures within words; (d) syllable juncture: children discover principles of spelling associated with affixing words—dropping, doubling, and changing; (e) meaning derivation: children learn that the spelling of derived forms and homographs is associated with meaning and structural principles.
3. Approaches to teaching spelling include the textbook approach, which uses commercially prepared materials, and an individualized approach, in which teachers and children jointly select words and devise activities for spelling.
4. Strategies aid learning to spell. They include pronunciation, problem parts, rhyming helpers, visualization, mnemonic devices, word structure, proofreading, and spelling consciousness.
5. Instructional issues in spelling involve number of words assigned, troublesome words, spelling tests, review of words and spelling concepts, time on task, and principles and conventions of spelling.
6. Spelling words should be chosen according to six criteria. Words should be developmentally appropriate, high in frequency, linguistically patterned, frequently misspelled, content oriented, and, in part, personally selected.
7. Invented spelling is a temporary best guess at spelling until standard spelling is learned. Research has shown that it benefits reading, writing, and spelling growth.
8. Assessment of spelling achievement helps teachers understand how children are progressing and how to place them for instructional purposes.

# ◀━ Questions to Challenge Your Thinking ━━

1. Spelling achievement is influenced by reading, writing, and instruction. What contribution does each of these influences make to spelling growth?
2. Spelling growth proceeds through five stages of growth. What important changes transpire between the first and last stages?
3. What advantages and disadvantages do you see in choosing an individualized spelling approach over a textbook approach?
4. What is the purpose of teaching spelling strategies? Give examples of how specific strategies might aid spelling.
5. Why is it necessary to review spelling principles, strategies, and conventions across grade levels?
6. Which three word-selection criteria do you

think are most important? Defend your choices.

7. First- and second-graders may have 5,000–12,000 words in their oral vocabularies. How does invented spelling take advantage of this wealth of oral language?

8. Why is it crucial to teach children spelling at their instructional level?

## A Case Study

Study Shokelle's writing shown in Figure 13.8. Consider the ideas and information presented in this chapter and then answer the questions below.

Shokelle is a 5-year-old kindergarten child. She writes every day and enjoys writing. She used invented spelling to write her story. Her teacher, Ms. Vanessa Morrison, read a book, *Leo the Lion*, and Shokelle's story is in response to the book. Shokelle's story translates like this: *Leo the Lion was, he too busy doing, he was doing his job.*

1. Identify Shokelle's spelling stage. What evidence do you have for your decision?
2. What strengths do you recognize in Shokelle's work?
3. What does Shokelle's work tell you about her reading and writing knowledge?
4. What instructional support and encouragement would you provide for Shokelle over the next few months? Why?

**Figure 13.8**   **Shokelle: A Case Study**

5. How might invented spelling help Shokelle become a better reader, writer, and speller?
6. What prediction would you make about Shokelle's readiness for first grade? Explain.

## Revisit the Anticipation Guide

Return to the Anticipation Guide in the chapter opener, and review your original responses to the questions. Complete the guide again, and then consider these questions.

1. Did you change your mind about any items that you had agreed or disagreed with earlier? If so, why?

2. How close are your current ideas about the major chapter topics to those you held before reading this chapter? Explain.
3. Has reading this chapter changed or confirmed what you knew before you read this chapter? Explain what has changed or been confirmed.

## VideoWorkshop Extra!

If your instructor ordered a package including VideoWorkshop, go to Chapter 13 of the Companion Website (www.ablongman.com/cramer1e) and click on the VideoWorkshop button. Follow the instructions for viewing the appropriate video clip and completing the accompanying exercise. Watch the Companion Website for access to a new interactive teaching portal, My Lab School, currently under construction.

# The Blue Pages

## Teaching Activities, Children's Literature, and Professional Resources

## 1 Foundations and Approaches to Teaching the Language Arts

### Teaching Activities

**1.** *Focus on language arts in staff development and staff meetings.* As a staff, choose one or two specific areas of language arts on which to focus the entire year of teacher in-servicing and focus studies. Ask your principal or building administrator to regularly set aside 10 to 15 minutes of each staff meeting for substantive conversation about language arts instruction. Teachers could share specific classroom experiences, model lessons, or discuss a prechosen topic.

**2.** *Establish a professional library.* Ask the teachers in your building to share their professional literature. Create a teachers' resource library, with a checkout system, in an easily accessible area such as the teachers' lounge, workroom, or designated section of the media center.

**3.** *Start a book study group.* Get together with other teachers in your building for ongoing dialogue about professional readings. Choose a professional book or series of articles that seem pertinent to your school's needs, and set aside time weekly or biweekly to discuss, question, and analyze assigned sections. Make this an after-school social gathering for relaxed, in-depth discussion.

**4.** *Create a support network.* Coordinate a language arts group of teachers within your building, district, or across your county; plan to meet monthly or bimonthly. Use this opportunity to exchange ideas, share experiences and teaching practices, inquire, gain multiple insights, and plan in a collaborative manner. Inspiration, empowerment, and effective growth and change often result from opportunities in which teachers collaborate and learn from one another.

**5.** *Review research with a critical lens.* Use these questions as you evaluate a piece of research:
- What exactly was accomplished by the study?
- What population was used?
- At what time of the school year was it done?
- How long was the study?
- Can the results be replicated?
- How are posttest results measured?

**6.** *Outline a literacy framework.* Based on what is workable in your own classroom and district, develop a week-long outline that includes a routine framework of reading and writing activities. These meaningful literacy activities should include reading aloud, literature discussion and response, modeled writing, shared reading, guided reading, shared writing, guided writing, writing workshop, independent reading, independent writing, and word study. In doing this, you can be assured that you are including a balance of approaches and techniques to support children's literacy learning. This framework will also serve as a guide in integrating these instructional processes with the content areas.

**7.** *Infuse language arts into all content areas.* Sketch a year's overview of content area themes, and align language arts themes and topics with these as much as possible. Social studies and science can be easily integrated with read-alouds, shared reading, oral language activities, and writing. Integrate reading and writing materials into multiple areas of the classroom. Put written book talks, literature extensions, and books written by children in the reading corner. In the science center, rotate books for further investigation, and include writing materials for note taking and recording observations. In the art center, books provide wonderful examples of various art media along with other pertinent information; access to writing materials encourages children to include labels or annotations with their art projects. When writing materials are included in construction centers with Legos and blocks, children have the opportunity to record directions for building favorite structures.

**8.** *Keep a record of explicit and implicit phonics instruction.* In a balanced literacy program, the word work children engage in should stem from a meaningful context. To effectively communicate your direct phonics instruction to parents, administrators, community members, or politicians, keep a record of the phonics skills you have taught through these meaningful, authentic literacy experiences.

**9.** *Stand up as an influential professional.* Become an advocate for your children and school on local issues. Keep informed on current happenings that reflect on educational policy at the state and national level. Take an active role in curricular and political decision making across school, district, state, and national levels.

**10.** *Cultivate a strong home–school connection.* Establish a partnership with the parents in your classroom. Avoiding educational terms and jargon, thoroughly explain to parents the how and why behind all of the teaching that you do. Communicate and demonstrate to parents how they can effectively support their child at home. Here are some examples of ways to convey this information:

- Designate a section of your weekly newsletter to thoroughly explain a specific area in children's literacy development or a teaching practice.
- Extend open invitations for parents to visit your classroom to observe and, when possible, get involved in the literacy experiences.
- Continually steer parents toward, or make available to them, relevant parent resources to support their understanding of literacy development.
- Host parent workshops to demonstrate strategies and techniques that can be used in the home to support their child's growth, such as reading with a child, bookmaking workshops, writing with a child, or word study through meaningful experiences at home.

# Children's Literature Selections

Ackerman, K. (1988). *Song and dance man.* New York: Knopf. A grandfather shows three children how to enjoy life by dancing and singing for them. Grades K–3.

Asch, F. (1985). *Bear shadow.* Englewood Cliffs, NJ: Prentice Hall. Bear's shadow is interfering with his fishing, so Bear cleverly tries to outsmart it by hiding, nailing it to the ground, and other tricks; however, his tricks are unsuccessful. Grades Pre-K–1.

Burton, V. (1942). *The little house.* Boston: Houghton Mifflin. A little house experiences changes from country life to city life as times evolve and people's lives become busier. The house dreams of the simple country life and is finally granted this wish at the end of this classic story. Grades 1–3.

Dahl, R. (1970). *Fantastic Mr. Fox.* New York: Knopf. A delightful story of three nasty farmers who try to outsmart a fox because they think he is trying to steal their stock. Grades 4–6.

Keats, E. J. (1962). *The snowy day.* New York: Viking. This Caldecott Medal winner tells the story of a boy's experiences in the first snowfall of the year. He makes angels, a snowman, and even attempts to save a snowball in his pocket when he's called inside. Although he is disappointed when it melts, a brand new snowfall brings excitement and adventure for another day. Grades Pre-K–1.

Lionni, L. (1997). *Frederick.* New York: Random House. In this beautiful picture book, winter is approaching and it seems a field mouse isn't paying attention to the upcoming change of weather. Grades Pre-K–2.

Mathis, S. B. (1975). *The hundred penny box.* New York: Viking. A boy's great-great-aunt tells the story of each penny she has collected, one for every year of her life. Children will get a better understanding of elderly people through this very moving book. Grades 2–4.

McKissack, P. (1986). *Flossie and the fox.* New York: Dial Books for Young Readers. A clever young girl pretends not to notice a sly fox who is trying to steal eggs from her. Children will love Flossie and her continued attempts to outsmart the fox. Grades 1–3.

Morsel, A. (1968). *Tikki tikki tembo.* New York: Holt. This tale explains why the Chinese no longer use long names, all because of two sons who are intrigued by a deep well. The repetition of the names captures young listeners in this classic picture book. Grades K–2.

Orwell, G. (1951). *Animal farm.* New York: Penguin. In one of the most famous political allegories ever written, animals take over a farm and enjoy life to the fullest. One day the pigs decide on a different agenda and chaos begins. Grades 8–12.

Paterson, K. (1980). *Jacob have I loved.* New York: Crowell. This young adult book is a Newbery Medal winner about a young girl, Louise, who finally overcomes sadness and obstacles in her personal and school life. Grades 6–8.

Potter, B. (1989). *The complete tales of Peter Rabbit.* New York: Frederick Warne. This collection of the classic tales of Peter Rabbit and his adventures includes "The Tale of Peter Rabbit," "The Tale of Benjamin Bunny," "The Tale of the Flopsy Bunnies," and "The Tale of Mr. Toad." Grades K–3.

Rylant, C. (1985). *The relatives came.* New York: Bradbury. This rich picture book details the events when relatives visit from another state, going full circle from when they start out, to their arrival, the fun shared together with the family, and then the trip back home. Grades K–3.

Sendak, M. (1963). *Where the wild things are.* New York: Harper & Row. This highly popular Caldecott Medal winner presents Max, a mischievous boy who has been sent to his room, and all the imaginative goings on that then occur. Monsters play a major role, helping draw children to the humor and illustrations of this classic book. Grades K–3.

Shaw, C. G. (1947). *It looked like spilt milk.* New York: Harper & Row. A new silhouette is presented on each page for readers to identify. The repetitive pattern and predictable format are enjoyable. Grades Pre-K–1.

Slobodkina, E. (1968). *Caps for sale.* New York: Harper & Row. This folktale details the frustration of a peddler whose wares are stolen by a band of monkeys. The peddler's reaction is engaging to young children as he attempts to get his caps back from the thieves. Grades K–2.

Steinbeck, J. (1993). *Of mice and men.* New York: Penguin. George Milton and Lennie Small, two migrant laborers in central California, dream of owning their own farm someday, yet tragedy snatches that dream away. Grades 10–12. (Originally published in 1937.)

Stevenson, R. L. (1981). *Treasure Island.* New York: Scribner's. After Jim Hawkins finds the map leading to Captain Flint's treasure, he encounters pirates and other obstacles in this classic novel set in the 18th century. Grades 5–12.

Voigt, C. (1984). *Building blocks.* New York: Macmillan. In this moving novel a boy meets another child in a fortress that his father built for him, but the child is really his father when he was growing up. Grades 5–8.

Yolen, J. (1987). *Owl moon.* New York: Scholastic. Through its beautiful language and illustrations, this Caldecott Medal winner draws the reader into a young child's nighttime search with his father for an owl; readers can imagine the cold of the winter air, the quiet patience, and the anticipation of discovering an owl. Grades Pre-K–6.

# Professional Resources

Adams, D., & Hamm, M. (2001). *Literacy in a multimedia age.* Norwood, MA: Christopher-Gordon. The authors of this book provide a guide for K–12 teachers to aid them in using technology to enhance their teaching. Practical suggestions for using technology as a supportive tool are provided, with a focus on literacy issues and educational trends.

Au, K. H. (1997). Literacy steps for all students: Ten steps toward making a difference. *The Reading Teacher, 51,* 186–194. The author urges new teachers to examine their personal philosophies on literacy and teaching, describing measures teachers can take to ensure a constructive search for literacy understanding and effective instruction.

Booth, D. (Ed.). (1996). *Literacy techniques for building successful readers and writers.* Portland, ME: Stenhouse. This collection of proven and effective literacy techniques helps create successful readers and writers. Some of the many topics addressed include revision, punctuation, collaborative learning, grammar, portfolios, and literature circles,

Calkins, L. M. (1997). *Raising lifelong learners: A parent's guide.* Reading, MA: Perseus Books. Emphasizing that literacy begins before school, this book was written for parents but is also a good resource for teachers, explaining how the significant adults in a child's life play a crucial role in providing an exciting foundation for literacy learning. It offers advice for turning homes into literature-rich environments and discusses the importance of oral language through conversation and shared stories.

Campbell, R. (2001). *Read-alouds with young children.* Newark, DE: International Reading Association. Interactive read-alouds require the listener to be actively engaged and a contributing member of the learning process, extending the child's personal experience with books. The author explores reading aloud to young children in home and school settings and suggests activities that can grow naturally out of the reading experience.

Carreiro, P. (1998). *Tales of thinking: Multiple intelligences in the classroom.* Portland, ME: Stenhouse. The author describes how to incorporate Howard Gardner's work on multiple intelligences into a kindergarten classroom. Specific strategies demonstrate that children are perceptive and capable when prompted appropriately by a discerning teacher.

Cousin, P. T., Dembrow, M. P., & Molldrem-Shamel, J. (1997). Inquiry about learners and learning. *The Reading Teacher, 51,* 162–164. The process of inquiry focuses our thinking and encourages problem solving. This article presents clear steps for teachers to follow as they examine their own beliefs about teaching in a format that calls for planning, collecting information, and reflection.

Daniels, H. (2001) *Literature circles: Voice and choice in book clubs and reading groups* (2nd ed.). Portland,

ME: Stenhouse. K–12 teachers learn how to organize student-led discussions while sidestepping potential obstacles. Detailed examples are provided to assist in scheduling, management, and assessment.

Foster, G., Sawicki, E., Schaeffer, H., & Zelinski, V. (2002). *I think, therefore I learn!* Portland, ME: Stenhouse. Children need to be cognizant of their own thinking in order to know when and what they are learning. This comprehensive book emphasizes practical ways teachers can reflect on and monitor their instruction and help students analyze their thoughts.

Goodman, K. E. (Ed.). (1998). *In defense of good teaching: What teachers need to know about the "reading wars."* Portland, ME: Stenhouse. Much has been written and said about the "reading wars" in the past few years. The author suggests the debate between systematic phonics instruction and whole language could be politically based and reflective of outside economic interests.

Hahn, M. L. (2002). *Reconsidering read-aloud.* Portland, ME: Stenhouse. This book shows how to make read-alouds come alive through student conversation around the book. Teaching strategies can be effectively used to make the most of this proven and powerful strategy.

Hammond, W. D., & Raphael, T. E. (Eds.). (1999). *Early literacy for the new millennium.* Ann Arbor, MI: Center for the Improvement of Early Reading Achievement (CIERA). This book is the result of the collaboration of six Michigan educators who demystify and explain the complex and politically charged topic of teaching literacy. Major topics include a balanced approach to literacy, diverse learners, and strong home–school relationships.

Hoffman, J. V. (1998). When bad things happen to good ideas in literacy education: Professional dilemmas, personal decisions, and political traps. *The Reading Teacher, 52,* 102–112. The author describes the history of literacy reforms over the last few decades as he makes his case for classroom teachers to embrace the ongoing search to improve instruction and not be threatened by change.

Morrison, I. (1991). *Getting it together: Linking reading theory to practice.* Bothell, WA: The Wright Group. This little book explains in simple language the elements of a balanced reading program and ongoing assessment. Through planning and strategic instruction, classroom teachers can influence student learning, reflecting the teacher's understanding of the reading process and personal literacy philosophy.

Pappas, C. C., Kiefer, B. Z., & Levstik, L. S. (1999). *Integrated language perspective in the elementary school: An action approach* (3rd ed.). Boston: Allyn & Bacon. The authors present practical, research-based guidance on implementing an integrated classroom, enabling students to experience the reciprocity between language and their own learning. The needs of children in the daily life of classrooms are addressed through curriculum theory, assessment, and instruction.

Pennac, D. (1999). *Better than life.* Portland, ME: Stenhouse. This book is a must for teachers who understand the enchantment of young children discovering books and who want to understand how it can turn into disillusionment in the adolescent reader. The author draws on personal experience as reader, parent, writer, and teacher to work to restore the magic in reading.

Raphael, T. E., & Hiebert, E. H. (1996). *Creating an integrated approach to literacy instruction.* New York: Harcourt Brace. The authors present the social-constructivist perspective on instruction through an integrated approach that stresses the reading–writing connection and the importance of talk in the classroom. Theory is presented along with real classroom settings and examples.

Smith, J. & Elley, W. (1998). *How children learn to write.* London: Paul Chapman. This book describes how children best learn to write, based on teacher understanding of the layers of development in the writing process. It encourages classroom teachers to examine their existing personal philosophy about teaching writing and meeting student needs and to extend their knowledge base by considering the beliefs of educational theorists such as Vygotsky, Graves, and Cambourne.

Strickland, D. S., Ganske, K., & Monroe, J. K. (2001). *Supporting struggling readers and writers: Strategies for classroom intervention, 3–6.* Portland, ME: Stenhouse. This book contains effective teaching strategies for reaching even struggling literacy students through integrated interventions in the regular classroom. The authors explore how to help these students through systematic, ongoing approaches that motivate and intrigue.

Szymusiak, K., & Sibberson, F. (2001). *Beyond leveled books: Supporting transitional readers in grades 2–5.* Portland, ME: Stenhouse. Ways for strengthening the home–school connection to create stronger student readers are discussed, including strategies to build and strengthen a parent–teacher partnership to foster comprehension.

Whitmore, K. F., & Goodman, Y. M. (Eds.). (1996). *Whole language voices in teacher education.* Portland, ME: Stenhouse. This book offers a theoretical framework as well as practical advice for teachers and in-service directors on whole language principles. Chapters are in narrative form and discuss the realities of success and failure and the challenge of whole language.

Worthy, J., Broaddus, K., & Ivey, G. (2001). *Pathways to independence: Reading, writing, and learning in grades 3–8.* New York: Guilford. This book focuses on the "middle" learners. Reading teachers will find it informative and specific to the needs of the older student.

# 2 Organizing Learning Environments: Language, Learning, and Diversity

## Teaching Activities

**1.** *Create a student task board.* Create a task board to outline the activities available or expected to be completed during the literacy block. This will guide students as they work independently, with a partner, or in a small group, while the teacher works with guided reading or writing groups. Divide students into flexible, heterogeneous groups and assign them a symbol to identify with and follow on the task board. Create a number of cards that designate activities and centers in the classroom, and post them on the task board. An easy way to maintain the board for a week at a time is to vertically assign four to five tasks in each of five columns; each day, move the student groups across the top of the task board. That will ensure that every student has the opportunity to work in each area of the classroom.

**2.** *Construct a job chart.* As a community, brainstorm necessary jobs for day-to-day routine and maintenance in your classroom. Display this collaborative list of required roles. Job assignments can be managed in a variety of ways: leave all jobs open for "helping hand" volunteers to place their name by the task they are willing to complete for a day or week; randomly draw students' names and, as they are called out, allow them to choose an open job; or assign the children yourself to the specific jobs, rotating them weekly. Keeping the children involved with classroom jobs will not only keep the classroom in good order but will instill good citizenship in the classroom community.

**3.** *Make a family celebration scrapbook.* Celebrate the diversity of families in your classroom by having each family send in several pictures that represent a family tradition or celebration. Designate a page in the scrapbook for each celebration, and record captions as each child shares his or her pictures. Place this book in the classroom library for children to read and revisit throughout the year.

**4.** *Create a world map reflecting the diversity within your classroom.* On a large bulletin board, display a world map. Ask students and families to work together to create a family tree that indicates where family members were born, tracing back to their grandparents' generation. Assign each generation a colored pushpin; for example, the student's pin might be red, the parents' blue, and the grandparents' green. Pin onto the map according to the place of birth. Display the family trees, indicating the students' names and family origin, around the map. Use this map throughout the year to connect to literature, social studies, and other content areas. Consider having students research their family's country or state of origin and write a report to share with the class; post the report with the map.

**5.** *Assess the classroom library for cultural diversity.* Does your classroom collection of books and magazines reflect not only the diversity within your classroom but also the various cultures of our society? If not, do some research to identify titles to supplement your library. Then fill in the gaps with requests to parents, book club orders, library book sales, or solicited grant money that may be available specifically to provide multicultural materials for classrooms.

**6.** *Create photo journals.* Throughout the year, take numerous candid pictures of children engaged in regular learning activities, special events, field trips, and events that involve parents. Create photo journals with captions written through shared or interactive writing experiences. Leave the journals out for children to revisit all year. Oral language skills will be encouraged as children discuss these journals and recall the experiences. You may also want to rotate the journals for children to take home and share with their families. Parents will appreciate this opportunity to connect with their child's classroom experience.

**7.** *Create a climate respectful of differences.* Read the book *We Are All Alike, We Are All Different*, written and illustrated by the kindergartners at Cheltenham Elementary School, to prompt discussion of ways that the children in your class are both alike and different. Provide access to multicultural paint, crayons, and paper, and have the children create self-portraits. Celebrate the diversity in your classroom, and emphasize community effort by creating a classroom quilt that displays these self-portraits, along with recordings of the similarities and differences brought up in the literature discussion. To emphasize the principle that every community has stories to tell and each child is an important character in these stories that develop over the year, begin a Character Wall, with the children's painted portraits and names representing "classroom characters." As you share in the enjoyment of favorite stories or connect with book characters, continue to update the wall with portraits of literary characters and their names.

**8.** *Organize parent volunteers.* Collaborate as a building to organize and host a volunteer orientation workshop early in the school year. At various stations have teachers demonstrate the use of equipment such as the laminator, book binder, and copy machine. Show them where supplies are kept. Teachers can model various volunteer support strategies such as reading with children or helping publish writing. This time can also be used to share policies and procedures pertaining to your building that parents should be aware of as school volunteers.

**9.** *Construct "the giving tree"—a classroom wish list.* Hang a poster or cutout of a bare tree near the entrance of your classroom; attach leaf shapes to the branches with an easily removable adhesive such as sticky-tack or tape. Use the leaf cutouts to write items needed for the classroom, such as Kleenex, paper products, or craft supplies. Parents who would like to contribute can take a leaf from the tree and send in the requested supplies. By posting this display near the doorway, parents can easily see what is needed at open house, when they are picking up their child, or when passing by in the hallway. Acknowledge parents' contributions by thanking them in a designated section of your class newsletter.

**10.** *Organize the classroom library for optimal student use.* In order for students to freely, actively, frequently, and wisely use this important center, it is essential that it be highly organized, with as much student input as possible. Involve the students in sorting the books according to readability as well as by genre, theme, and author collections. Use color-coded stickers as well as coordinating tape, tubs, or baskets to keep books organized. Designate a tub or box for returned books, and assign a student librarian to reshelve books.

## Children's Literature Selections

Aesop. (1984). *The hare and the tortoise.* New York: Holiday House. This is a beautiful retelling of the classic tale of a race between an overconfident hare and a hopeful tortoise. Grades K–3.

Babbitt, N. (1975). *Tuck everlasting.* New York: FSG. A Newbery Medal–winning young adult novel examines the issue of immortality when a young girl befriends a family and shares their extraordinary secret. Grades 4–6.

Brown, M. (1979). *Arthur's nose.* Boston: Little, Brown. Arthur the aardvark is very unhappy with his nose; even his schoolmates and friends laugh at it. Arthur decides to get a new nose, and when he steps out of the doctor's office, his friends are very surprised. Grades K–2.

Brown, M. W. (1972). *The runaway bunny.* New York: Harper & Row. A young bunny tries to defy his mother, yet she lets him know that she will always be there for him, no matter what. The bunny comes to know that he is loved unconditionally. Grades Pre-K–1.

Burnett, F. H. (1962). *The secret garden.* New York: Harper & Row. When an orphaned girl is forced to live with her cold uncle in the English moors, she encounters an invalid child hidden in the uncle's mansion and an intriguingly locked and abandoned garden. Grades 3–6.

Carle, E. (1984). *The mixed-up chameleon.* New York: Harper & Row. A chameleon searches for his true identity. Grades Pre-K–2.

Cheltenham Elementary School Kindergartners. (2002). *We are all alike, we are all different.* New York: Scholastic. Teachers and children alike love the authentic text and illustrations that are the product of a rich exploration of diversity. Grades Pre-K–3.

Dahl, R. (1961). *James and the giant peach.* New York: Knopf. A boy living with his cruel and selfish aunts is given a magical potion. When James accidentally drops the portion, some insects and a peach grow to enormous size. James develops a strong friendship with the insects, and they have incredible adventures living in the peach. Grades 4–6.

Dahl, R. (1964). *Charlie and the chocolate factory*. New York: Knopf. Charlie and four other children win invitations to visit the magical candy factory that belongs to the mysterious Willie Wonka. There are unusual lessons to be learned by many of the selfish and greedy visitors, yet Charlie's innocence and loving nature allow him to receive the grandest prize of all. Grades 4–6.

Gannett, R. (1948). *My father's dragon*. New York: Random House. A boy named Elmer Elevator has many adventures away from home with a dragon in need of help. Grades 4–6.

Keats, E. J. (1964). *Whistle for Willie*. New York: Viking. Peter, a young boy living in the city, is trying to learn to whistle so he can teach his dog to come whenever he hears that sound. Grades Pre-K–1.

Kraus, R. (1971). *Leo the late bloomer*. Old Tappan, NJ: Windmill Books. Leo's parents are convinced that Leo can't do many things because he is a late bloomer. But just when hope is fading, Leo's time arrives and he shines. Grades 1–4.

Lowry, L. (1993). *The giver*. Boston: Houghton Mifflin. This Newbery Medal winner describes a civilization wherein strict rules and rites of passage are dictated to all. A boy who once accepted this way of life discovers that a different world lies beyond, filled with choices, pain, and happiness; and he must decide whether to stay or to travel to this unknown world. Grades 5–8.

McCloskey, R. (1941). *Make way for ducklings*. New York: Viking. In this Caldecott Medal winner, Mr. and Mrs. Mallard try to find a safe area for their ducklings in Boston. With the help of their policeman friend, Michael, they find their way. Grades Pre-K–3.

Naylor, P. (1997). *Saving Shiloh*. New York: Atheneum. In the last of the Shiloh trilogy, young Marty Preston struggles to decide whether people can change from bad to good. With the love of his dog, Shiloh, Marty embarks on an exciting and meaningful journey to answer this difficult question. Grades 5–8.

Nelson, D. (1999). *Buzzy the bee*. Chelsea, MI: Sleeping Bear Press. Unfortunately, when Buzzy reads in a book that bees are not meant to fly, he believes the words even though he's flown many times before. Readers learn what doubt can do to minds and spirits and how to overcome fears. Grades K–2.

O'Dell, S. (1960). *Island of the blue dolphins*. Boston: Houghton Mifflin. A young girl living on an island in the 1800s becomes stranded after the people in her village flee from dangerous strangers. Her years alone are filled with beauty, danger, and self-realization. This story is a Newbery Medal winner. Grades 5–8.

Paterson, K. (1977). *Bridge to Terabithia*. New York: Harper Collins. This novel, a Newbery Medal winner, explores what happens when a boy named Jess loses his best friend, Leslie, in an accident. This story captures childhood through everyday experiences with sports, school, friends, peers, and all of life's uncertainties. Grades 6–8.

Stevens, J. (1987). *The three billy goats gruff*. San Diego: Harcourt Brace. In the tale of the three billy goats who attempt to cross over a bridge guarded by a mean and ugly troll, the clever billy goats outsmart the troll and reach the green grass on the other side. Grades Pre-K–2.

Stolz, M. (1963). *The bully of Barkham Street*. New York: Harper & Row. To 11-year-old Martin, life seems totally unfair. He feels frustrated by his parents, teachers, and peers and yet finds that slowly changing his perspective can lead to a happier existence. Grades 4–8.

Wilder, L. I. (1953). *Little house in the big woods*. New York: Harper & Row. In the story of a pioneer family making their home in Wisconsin in the 1800s, the narrator, Laura, describes their struggles and triumphs as they settle into their new surroundings. Grades 4–7.

## Professional Resources

Allen, J., & Gonzalez, K. (1998). *There's room for me here: Literacy workshop in the middle school*. Portland, ME: Stenhouse. This book offers theory-based, practical strategies for helping struggling students. Detailed suggestions are given for setting up a literacy workshop, effective record keeping, and helping students establish goals and self-evaluate.

Booth, D. (2001). *Reading and writing in the middle years.* Portland, ME: Stenhouse. This book contains comprehensive information on the latest methods for teaching students reading and writing in grades 4–8. Practical suggestions are given to help relate the adolescent's world to written text.

Buehl, D. (2001). *Classroom strategies for interactive learning* (2nd ed.). Newark, DE: International Reading Association. Educators are discovering the importance of helping adolescent strategic readers and writers effectively process material in content areas. This book includes many strategies and examples to help classroom teachers become better prepared to meet the literacy needs of the older student.

Calkins, L. M. (2001). *The art of teaching reading.* New York: Longman. The author discusses the whys and hows of a comprehensive balanced reading program that relies on teacher know-how, creativity, preparation, and resilience. Reflecting years of classroom research, this book demonstrates the social nature of literacy learning and the evolution of classroom change to meet the needs of children.

Cambourne, B. (2000/2001). Conditions for literacy learning—turning learning theory into classroom instruction: A minicase study. *The Reading Teacher, 54,* 414–417. Teachers know that theory is only as good as its relevance to real classrooms. This article shows how to have meaningful dialogue within a school literacy team to produce practical, workable strategies.

Cantrell, S. C. (1998/1999). Effective teaching and literacy learning: A look inside primary classrooms. *The Reading Teacher, 52,* 370–378. This article describes the classrooms of four Kentucky teachers who successfully moved from traditional literacy instruction to implement comprehensive reformed practices. Their literature-based programs engaged students in a variety of open-ended writing activities and meaningful reading experiences.

Chapman, C. (1993). *If the shoe fits: How to develop multiple intelligences in the classroom.* Arlington Heights, IL: Skylight Professional Development. The author presents a practical approach to implementing Gardner's theory of multiple intelligences. The first chapter describes the theory and the elements necessary to create a brain-compatible classroom, while successive chapters define the intelligences and offer ready-to-use activities adaptable across all grade levels.

Cunningham, D. H., & Sigmon, C. M. (1999). *The teacher's guide to the Four Blocks.* Greensboro, NC: Carson-Delosa. This resource provides teachers with a summary of the Four Blocks model and step-by-step directions for setting up an organized, purposeful literacy environment for grades 1–3. Instruction is multileveled and systematic as children learn through reading and writing activities.

Cunningham, P. M., & Allington, R. L. (2003). *Classrooms that work: They can all read and write* (3rd ed.). New York: Longman. The premise of this book is that employing many strategies, instead of relying on a single approach, will have a greater chance of reaching the diverse learners in our classrooms. It provides a framework for high-quality literacy instruction and stresses a balanced approach that engages children in meaningful activities.

Dahl, K. L., Scharer, P. L., Lawson, L. L., & Grogan, P. R. (2001). *Rethinking phonics: Making the best teaching decisions.* Portsmouth, NH: Heinemann. The premise of this book is that once children understand that print carries meaning, phonics instruction can meet the needs of individual students through appropriate lessons in whole group, small group and individual settings. Activities from eight successful first-grade classrooms are provided.

Fountas, I. C., & Pinnell, G. S. (1996). *Guided reading: Good first teaching for all children.* Portsmouth, NH: Heinemann. This book is an excellent resource for teachers who want to organize and manage balanced literacy classrooms. The authors carefully present the philosophy and purpose of guided reading, providing many practical, interactive ideas for teaching and assessing emergent and early readers.

Graves, M., & Graves, B. (2002). *Scaffolding reading experiences: Designs for student success* (2nd ed.). New York: Christopher-Gordon. This book offers activities for all stages of the reading experience. Teachers (K–8) are given practical ideas for incorporating effective scaffolds in their classrooms to enhance and support real learning.

Hill, B. C., Schlick Noe, K. L., & Johnson, N. J. (2001). *Literature Circles resource guide: Teaching suggestions, forms, sample book lists, and database.* Norwood, MA: Christopher-Gordon. This is a valuable resource for setting up literature circles and helping students think deeply about their reading. The authors provide ready-made planning forms, teacher-developed guidelines, plus ideas for organization and written response.

Hindley, J. (1996). *In the company of children*. Portland, ME: Stenhouse. This book contains many ideas and strategies on how to conduct effective literacy workshops and make the most of time during the school day. Clear directions are given for productive reading and writing workshops, minilessons, writer's notebook, and how to assess student progress.

Krueger, E., & Braun, B. (1998/1999). Books and buddies: Peers tutor peers. *The Reading Teacher, 52,* 410–414. Second language learners can be empowered through literacy, raising confidence and self-esteem. This article describes a second- and third-grade project, "Books and Buddies," a program that focuses on peer interaction, providing opportunities to talk, listen, read, and write English through peer interaction.

Martens, P. (1998). Using retrospective miscue analysis to inquire: Learning from Michael. *The Reading Teacher, 52,* 176–180. Readers follow a teacher's journey with Michael, a third-grade student with learning disabilities, and look at his processing through conversation and miscue analysis. As he learns that reading is meaning-based, he develops flexible strategies that support his efforts.

Morrow, L. M. (2002). *The literacy center: Contexts for reading and writing* (2nd ed.). Portland, ME: Sten-

house. The author outlines how to make reading and writing meaningful and relevant through the use of literacy centers. This is a practical handbook for elementary school teachers who want to learn how to establish and maintain literacy centers.

Parker, D. (1997). *Jamie: A literacy story*. Portland, ME: Stenhouse. Reflective, caring teaching affects all students, especially those with special needs. The author takes the reader into her classroom where she worked for three years (K–2) to empower Jamie, a student with spinal muscular atrophy, with literacy knowledge and understanding.

Patterson, L. & Mallow, F. E. (2001). *Teaching every child: A guide for literacy teams*. Norwood, MA: Christopher-Gordon. Here is a book that shows school literacy teams how to collaborate and solve problems to help children (K–3) become proficient readers. Emphasis is on supporting the struggling student.

Weaver, C. (Ed.). (1998). *Practicing what we know*. Urbana, IL: National Council of Teachers of English. This book offers detailed instruction for classroom teachers who want to provide sound, research-based reading instruction. Its collection of 33 essays representing the best teaching practices covers a cross-section of reading instruction today. Topics include miscue analysis, phonics, word skills, literature, students with special needs, and more.

# 3 — Assessing Writing and Reading

## Teaching Activities

**1.** *Organize a systematic assessment schedule.* A systematic assessment schedule provides a highly organized framework for assessing children regularly, through multidimensional measures. Meaningful evaluation is integral to the teaching and learning process. In order for assessment to be useful to both student and teacher, it must be authentic—integrated with daily learning experiences and relevant to the task at hand. Authentic assessment then becomes a natural extension of teaching and learning. Through daily experiences, teachers observe what the child is doing consistently (behavioral evidence of skills and strategies the child has under control), *and* what the child is attempting to do, in order to determine what is needed to help the child move forward. Organizing for this meaningful, ongoing assessment is critical; it must be efficiently integrated with daily instruction rather than isolated. Checklists can be developed and used as prompts to effectively record information gained through observations during whole or small group time. Blocks of independent work time can be utilized for observation, one-on-one student conferences, and other evaluation procedures. In addition, many opportunities arise out of regular classroom routines (such as pulling a child aside to conduct an interview or do a running record during regular morning routine). Through this seamless integration, purposeful assessment and guided instruction go hand in hand. Outline an organizing framework for collecting assessment data, based on your district's benchmarks, and integrate it into your regularly scheduled literacy experiences. Include a time frame for the assessment measures, along with specific methods of collecting and documenting the information.

**2.** *Explore convenient ways to keep student evaluation materials organized.* In addition to the use of ring binders, consider using all or some of the following to gather information about each student:

- Use a clipboard with observation checklists and formatted grids for self-adhesive notes or mailing labels. When the sheets are full, the information can be separated and filed appropriately for each student.
- Keep a file card for each student on a ring to record assessment data; file the card when it is full.
- Checklists, and other record grids with the whole class on the same page, allow you to get a glimpse of the range of literacy development for the class as a whole, noting patterns and trends that can guide your group or small group instruction.

**3.** *Be an excellent observer.* The most powerful assessment tool for understanding children's literacy abilities is observation. Learning to step back and be an excellent observer (or "kid-watcher," as Yetta Goodman calls it) may be the most valuable thing teachers can do as expert evaluators and informed decision makers. Excellent observation is integral to guiding instruction based on students' strengths and needs. We need to know what to look for, based on a solid understanding of the literacy developmental process and sequential benchmarks. Because we are so busy, we can easily neglect student observation. The key here is to *consciously plan* to observe students. Write it into your lesson plan! Keep careful records to ensure that certain children are not overlooked.

**4.** *Set goals with students.* Assessment can be a powerful learning experience for students when the teacher supports and guides them through the process of reflecting on their strengths and then setting goals for further growth and learning. Our ultimate goal in assessing children is to deepen our understanding of where they are as individual learners in order to continually raise the bar and effectively guide them toward where they need to go. Establish regular goal-setting conferences with each individual child to involve him or her in this process. These conferences provide opportunities to reflect on strengths and literacy development, to set new learning goals, and to evaluate the process of moving toward new goals and expectations.

**5.** *Enlist collegial support in utilizing rubrics to analyze children's writing.* Collaborate with a network of teachers in your building to analyze children's writing samples using a rubric, either a commercially published one or one developed through building or districtwide collaboration. For each writing piece, work together to discuss areas of strengths and behaviors the child seems to have under control; also discuss skills the writer is just beginning to use, which point the way to the next area to be developed. Discuss the rationale for scoring each area of writing on the rubric. This ongoing dialogue can foster some consistency in scoring and expectations within a building or across a district.

**6.** *Enlist collegial support in analyzing several running records of children's oral reading.* As suggested by Fountas and Pinnell (1996), collaborate with a network of teachers in your building to analyze several running records collected within your group of classrooms. Examine them for the use of strategic processing strategies. Consider the following analysis questions:

- Was the text at an appropriate level of difficulty for this child?
- What sources of information (meaning, structural, visual cuing systems) did the child use or neglect?
- Did the child notice an error and actively work to make a "sources of information" (MSV) match? What does he/she do at point of error?
- Is there evidence of phrasing and fluency?
- Is there evidence that the child is reading with understanding?

You may want to keep a copy of these prompts on an index card, located on a guided reading clipboard in your classroom; refer to them when analyzing your children's reading behaviors until you internalize these points of consideration.

**7.** *Construct "What a Good Reader Does" and "What a Good Writer Does" strategy lists.* As a shared writing activity, collaborate as a group about what good readers do to process text while maintaining meaning. Create a list of these strategies, using the children's natural language so it will be a meaningful resource for them; display the list in the classroom, and encourage students to continuously refer to it when reading. Create a writing strategies reference list in the same manner. The charts developed through this process will provide visual reminders for the children to refer to in order to independently solve problems, increasing their reading and writing powers. In addition, this collaborative process will foster metacognitive awareness of strategic literacy processes. This will serve as the foundation for self-assessment.

**8.** *Develop child-friendly rubrics and checklists.* Develop rubrics and checklists for students to apply to their reading and writing experiences. Design these to fit the grade and developmental level of your students. Even kindergarten children are able to evaluate their own writing and drawing when given clear criteria in a checklist picture format. These rubrics should be clear and concise so that students can target specific areas and skills before completing an assignment. In this way, the students are encouraged to take charge of some of their own learning and are better able to see growth over time.

**9.** *Hold weekly writing conferences.* Writing develops quickly when the teacher gives the students frequent, specific feedback directed at their individual strengths and needs. One-on-one writing conferences can serve a variety of purposes, including assisting the child in stimulating ideas, solving problems, working with editing and revision, discussing publication, and evaluation and goal setting. However, it can be difficult for busy teachers to regularly meet with each student. Consider creating five heterogeneous groups for the daily writing block, and each day meet with a different group for conferencing. A writing work board (similar to what many teachers use to manage literacy centers) is an effective way to manage the rotation of writing groups. With a class divided into five groups, a weekly rotation might look like this: one group works at a table with the teacher for conferencing and guided support; one group is publishing (after conferencing with the teacher the day before); and the other three groups are engaged in various steps of the writing process. This method ensures every child has a quality, one-on-one conference for support and guidance in his or her writing development. These conferences also allow the teacher to evaluate the child's written work, noting behavioral evidence of emerging writing development and how best to support the next steps of growth.

**10.** *Encourage peer conferencing.* Revision conferences between children can be very effective. The writer reads the text to another child, who acts as the audience. Thus the writers' purpose is to help the listeners make sense of their writing; in addition, they are encouraged to critically self-evaluate what they have written and will often make spontaneous revisions while reading to their partner. The listener has an evaluator role as well and is encouraged to give specific feedback on the writing. Establishing routines and expectations and teaching the children how to provide effective feedback in a noncritical manner are paramount! The teacher needs to model this process frequently. It is very helpful to provide a chart to prompt effective comment starters such as these:

- *I like the way . . .*
- *The best part for me was . . .*
- *That made me think about . . .*
- *I am still wondering . . .*

## Children's Literature Selections

Ahlberg, J., & Ahlberg, A. (1986). *The Jolly Postman; or, Other people's letters.* Boston: Little, Brown. Children can join the Jolly Postman as he makes his rounds, delivering mail to Goldilocks, Cinderella, Jack's Giant, and other fairy tale characters. Tiny letters can be pulled from the pages so children can actually hold the mail. Grades K–2.

Barton, B. (1993). *The little red hen.* New York: Harper-Collins. A group of animals refuses to assist their friend the hen to plant seeds, gather and grind wheat, and bake bread. When the bread is finished, the hen's friends think they can share in her hard work, but they are sadly mistaken. Grades Pre-K–1.

Bayer, J. (1984). *My name is Alice.* New York: Dial. This book is based on the familiar jump rope game, creating sentences using the same letter in each phrase. The rhyme and repetition make this book fun for children. Grades K–2.

Blos, J. (1979). *A gathering of days: A New England girl's journal, 1830–32.* New York: Scribner. A 13-year-old girl growing up in a New Hampshire town writes in her diary about her daily life, her father's remarriage, and the death of her best friend. This is a Newbery Medal winner for Grades 5–8.

Byars, B. (1970). *Summer of the swans.* New York: Viking. Fourteen-year-old Sara faces the disappearance of her younger, mentally impaired brother. This novel won the Newbery Award for its realistic characters and moving theme. Grades 6–12.

Cleary, B. (1983). *Dear Mr. Henshaw.* New York: Morrow. A discouraged boy seeks the wisdom of a writer he admires by writing him letters in this Newbery Medal–winning book. Grades 4–7.

de Paola, T. (1979). *Oliver Button is a sissy.* San Diego, CA: Harcourt Brace Jovanovich. This is a persuasive story about a boy who loves to read, write, draw, and dance. Even though he is teased by classmates, he is a star in the end because he never swerves from doing the things he loves. Grades 1–3.

Fitzhugh, L. (1964). *Harriet the spy.* New York: Harper & Row. Harriet's only dream in life is to become a spy. She follows family, friends, and classmates around, making personal observations in her spy notebook. All goes well with her new career until others read that notebook. Grades 4–6.

Hoban, T. (1983). *I read signs.* New York: Greenwillow. The author's photographs illustrate traffic and street signs encountered in our daily life. This is an excellent book to use with emergent readers. Grades K–2.

L'Engle, M. (1962). *A wrinkle in time.* New York: Farrar, Straus, & Giroux. One dark and stormy night a stranger appears at the home of Meg and Charles. She claims that she knows about something called a "tesseract," which is a wrinkle in time. Soon the children's father is lost in his time machine and it is up to them to find him. Grades 5–8.

Lewis, C. S. (1950). *The lion, the witch, and the wardrobe.* New York: MacMillan. Four children discover another world called Narnia hidden in an old wardrobe closet. In this mystical kingdom they encounter heroes, witches, princes, and much more. This is the first of the seven extraordinary books in the Narnia series. Grades 4–6.

Lowry, L. (1979). *Anastasia Krupnick.* Boston: Houghton Mifflin. A very intelligent 10-year-old finds life confusing, especially when her parents announce they are going to have a baby. Written with much humor, this novel is very appealing to children. Grades 4–6.

MacLachlan, P. (1985). *Sarah, plain and tall.* New York: Harper & Row. When their father orders a bride through the mail, Sara and her brother, Caleb, discover how wonderful she is and hope she will stay with them. Grades 2–5.

Mayer, M. (1974). *Frog goes to dinner.* New York: Dial. In one of a hilarious series of wordless picture books, Frog creates quite a disturbance when he appears in a restaurant after stowing away in a boy's pocket. Grades K–2.

Mayer, M. (1981). *Liverwurst is missing*. New York: Four Winds Press. In a humorous story that is quite out of the ordinary, a rhinoceros named Liverwurst travels from a farm to circus life but is abducted. Grades 1–3.

Schwartz, A. (1984). *In a dark, dark room*. New York: Harper & Row. Children will be captivated by the eeriness of these chilling stories. Grades 4–6.

Van Allsburg, C. (1981). *Jumanji*. Boston: Houghton Mifflin. A jungle world comes alive during a board game two children are playing. Suddenly their home is overrun by snakes, monkeys, lions, insects, and flood waters. Grades 2–5.

Viorst, J. (1972). *Alexander and the terrible, horrible, no good, very bad day*. New York: Atheneum. A young boy wakes up in the morning to realize disappointment from the start. Throughout his day he encounters more and more misfortune and feels frustrated and angry. Grades K–2.

Wood, A. (1982). *I'm as quick as a cricket*. San Diego: Child's Play. A young boy describes himself in this beautiful picture book, detailing his many talents and traits by comparing himself to different animals. Grades Pre-K–2.

Zolotow, C. (1972). *William's doll*. New York: Harper & Row. More than any other toy in the world, young William wants a doll. He is teased by his brother, his friends, and even his father. None of this changes William's mind and in the end his grandmother finds the perfect solution. Grades Pre-K–2.

## Professional Resources

Ainsworth, L., & Christinson, J. (1998). *Student generated rubrics: An assessment model to help all students succeed*. Palo Alto, CA: Dale Seymour. This is an excellent resource for involving primary and intermediate students more fully in their own learning. The authors' organization is easy to understand and follow in linking instruction with assessment through task-specific rubrics that students and teachers create.

Anthony, R. J., Johnson, T. D., Mickelson, N. L., & Preece, A. (1991). *Evaluating literacy: A perspective for change*. Portsmouth, NH: Heinemann. This book looks at many of the myths of assessment that have shaped how we evaluate children's learning. The authors show that instruction and assessment are interdependent and must reflect the clear educational goals of the teacher.

Barr, R., Blachowicz, C. L. Z., Katz, C., & Kaufman, B. (2002). *Reading diagnosis for teachers: An instructional approach* (4th ed.). Boston: Allyn & Bacon. In this well-organized book the authors help teachers understand the nature of literacy development and how to become good observers of their students in order to learn their strengths and the nature of any learning problems.

Bratcher, S. (1994). *Evaluating children' writing: A handbook of communication choices for classroom teachers*. New York: St. Martin's Press. This book for elementary teachers is a good reference tool to have on hand. It explores options for evaluating students' writing, stressing intentional, instructive evaluation methods that encourage, rather than discourage.

Bridges, L. (1996). *Assessment: Continuous learning*. Portland, ME: Stenhouse. This book is filled with suggestions and checklists for making the most of student-led conferences through portfolios, rubrics, and self-evaluation profiles. Also included are teacher field notes that offer helpful tips.

Drummond, M. J. (1994). *Learning to see: Assessment through observation*. Portland, ME: Stenhouse. Teachers must understand how children learn and what to look for in order to understand assessment. This theory-based book tells how to closely observe children as an integral part of a meaningful assessment process.

Farr, B. P., & Trumbull, E. (1996). *Assessment alternatives for diverse classrooms*. Norwood, MA: Christopher-Gordon. Chapters include topics on the challenges of assessment equity in a diverse society, the role of language in assessment, and sociopolitical issues. Teachers can examine fair assessment practices that support meaningful learning in their classrooms as they look through the eyes of experts.

Glazer, S. M., & Brown, C. S. (1993). *Portfolios and beyond: Collaborative assessment in reading and writing*. Norwood, MA: Christopher-Gordon. The authors show how to link instruction to assessment in all grades. Teachers are shown how to organize their instruction and manage the materials generated by authentic instruction in the classroom.

Goodman, Y., Watson, D. J., & Burke, C. L. (1987). *Reading miscue inventory: Alternative procedures.* New York: Owen. Based on Ken Goodman's theory that reading is cued and errors reflect the reader's language and personal experience, this book explains in detail how to do a miscue analysis. Teachers will learn how to collect and assess technical data so they can make insightful teaching decisions that meet the specific needs of students.

Hansen, J. (1998). *When learners evaluate.* Portsmouth, NH: Heinemann. This book explains the importance of teachers who value students' voices and encourage them to be responsible for their own learning. The teacher serves as guide as students evaluate, plan, and document their work, creating powerful learning in the writing process.

Harp, B. (2000). *The handbook of literacy assessment and evaluation* (2nd ed.). Norwood, MA: Christopher-Gordon. This updated handbook provides popular informal and published literacy evaluation tools. Information is easy to find. Many blackline masters are included.

Hill, B. C. (2001). *Development continuums: A framework for literacy instruction and assessment, K–8.* Norwood, MA: Christopher-Gordon. The author links literacy assessments with developmental benchmarks. National, state, and district standards are addressed, along with current understanding of literacy acquisition. A CD-ROM is included.

Hinchman, K. A., & Michel, P. (1999). Reconciling polarity: Toward a responsive model of evaluating literacy performance. *The Reading Teacher, 52,* 578–587. Student understanding is crucial and must inform instructional decision making. The authors show how to gather a variety of data, interpret it critically, and develop teaching strategies to effect student learning.

Lipson, M. Y., & Wixson, K. K. (2003). *Assessment and instruction of reading and writing difficulties: An interactive approach* (3rd ed.). Boston: Allyn & Bacon. Here is a comprehensive look at the theoretical foundation and rationale for tying assessment and instruction together, from a constructivist perspective. Case studies and graphic overviews provide understanding and step-by-step assessment instruction.

Rickards, D., & Cheek, E., Jr. (1999). *Designing rubrics for K-6 classroom assessment.* Norwood, MA: Christopher-Gordon. The use of rubrics can be a highly effective tool for both children and teachers. This book addresses how to foster reading and writing proficiency by using rubrics as an agent for growth. Student examples are provided.

Serafini, F. (2000/2001). Three paradigms of assessment: Measurement, procedure, and inquiry. *The Reading Teacher, 54,* 384–393. Teachers can make informed decisions about their instruction when assessment becomes a process of inquiry. The author focuses on the need for educators to investigate various assessment frameworks and to view student assessments as an interpretive process.

Tierney, R. J. (1998). Literacy assessment reform: Shifting beliefs, principled possibilities, and emerging practices. *The Reading Teacher, 51,* 374–390. Assessment must be thoughtful and have instructional purpose. The author clearly states his views on literacy assessment and on 13 key principles for making it child-centered and developmental.

# 4 — Listening and Talking

## Teaching Activities

**1.** *Use sharing circles.* Opportunities for sharing foster a sense of the value of community as students learn to respect diverse individuals. A sharing circle is a valuable way to end all workshop blocks of time in the learning day: reading, writing, math, science, and social studies. Setting aside this consistent, predictable time fosters reflection on learning and creates an opportunity to listen to the ideas and opinions of other individuals within the learning community.

**2.** *Listen for images in poetry.* Explain to students that poetry can create pictures in the mind. Select a poem with strong visual images, and ask students to close their eyes and create an image in their heads as you read aloud. After reading the poem a couple of times, ask the students to share their visual interpretations and to write about or illustrate it. Publish the poem on a bulletin board or in book form, including students' illustrations.

**3.** *Share wordless books.* In wordless books, the story is carried entirely by the pictures. The child has the opportunity to formulate the story through his or her individual interpretation of the pictures. These provide exceptional opportunities for the development of oral language, including story structure and language. Children really enjoy the opportunity to tape-record their story. You can put these tapes in a listening center with the book. Using the overhead projector to project enlarged pictures is another variation of this experience that works well for small or whole group retellings.

**4.** *Practice storytelling.* Oral language development and rich dialogue are fostered through small, cooperative groups' use of language to dramatize a favorite story. Collaborating on the creation of original dialogue to tell a simple story is a valuable experience as well. Groups can construct their own puppets and determine characters, puppet voices, and personalities. A variation of creating dialogue and narration would be to present information based on a theme the class has been studying. Provide the opportunity for the cooperative group to present the play in front of the class or any other audience. Items such as felt boards, puppets, and prop-stories (in which a box contains stuffed animals and other artifacts representing characters and events in the story) all enhance the story-telling process.

**5.** *Appoint a "current events reporter."* Each day allow a different student to share something about a current event topic. This activity will usually bring about meaningful group discussion of issues related to the topic.

**6.** *Go for a listening walk.* Provide the students with a clipboard and paper, or a notebook. Go for a walk inside the school or, if possible, outdoors. Have students record the things they hear. You can extend this activity and fine-tune the students' listening skills by giving them categories of sound to listen for, such as man-made and natural sounds. Older students could choose one sound they heard and do a writing extension, such as a poem or a descriptive paragraph.

**7.** *Utilize buddy reading.* Buddy reading provides the opportunity for children to read together, sharing thoughts, reactions, and connections in response to what they read. The focus is on making meaning from the text, together, through social interaction. Other values inherent in buddy reading experiences include

- Active engagement in reading for sustained periods of time
- Increased independence as partners collaborate on integrating strategic problem-solving strategies
- Stimulating purpose for enjoyable, successful interactions with books
- Sharpening of listening and speaking skills

**8.** *Discuss "encouragers and discouragers."* Engage students in reflecting on how small group discussions are going and creating commonly understood expectations for group members. Divide a chart into two columns labeled *Behaviors That Encourage Discussion* and *Behaviors That Discourage Discussion*. Using students' language, record their thoughts and ideas. Keep this chart prominently displayed so it can be revisited, revised, or added to when needed. It will also provide a guide for students in the self-evaluation and group evaluation process at the end of each discussion cycle.

**9.** *Select a "friend of the week."* Many teachers highlight a different student weekly, encouraging the chosen child to bring in a poster or photographs that illustrate his or her experiences and interests. This activity can be deeply enriched by incorporating oral language. Have the designated student share the poster or photos with the whole class, giving some basic information, and then talking about the pictures to introduce important people and interests. Have classmates ask questions to find out more. This encourages students to be good listeners as well as users of oral

language. Next, have students identify new information that they learned about this friend. They could write a retelling about the "friend of the week."

**10.** *Distinguish between asking questions and telling statements.* Internalizing the distinction between asking questions and telling statements is an important process for young children; it helps them understand their role of being an "audience" that asks appropriate questions. Through frequent discussions, develop a list of question words to post near the sharing area. Common question words include *are, can, did, do, does, how, if, is, should, was, what, when, where, who, why,* and *will.*

## Children's Literature Selections

Achebe, C. (1984). *Things fall apart.* New York: Doubleday. This novel details Nigeria's colonial period and its impact on the story's main character, Okonkwo. Upon being banished from his village for killing a clansman, Okonkwo returns after seven years to find his tribe changed. Grades 8–12.

Bang, M. (1980). *The grey lady and the strawberry snatcher.* New York: Four Winds Press. This story is a wordless allegory that depicts an elderly lady buying strawberries. An unsettling figure pursues her to try to steal her berries. Grades 1–12.

Barrett, J. (1978). *Cloudy with a chance of meatballs.* New York: Macmillan. Food and drink fall from the sky instead of raindrops in the land of Chewandswallow. At breakfast, lunch, and dinner, food appropriate to the meal showers down upon the people of the village, leaving them quite overwhelmed in this imaginative story. Grades K–3.

Bunting, E. (1979). *The big red barn.* San Diego, CA: Harcourt Brace Jovanovich. Upon his mother's death, a young boy finds comfort in their barn. He again hides there after his father remarries. When a terrible fire destroys the barn, the boy realizes life often means change. Grades 1–4.

Burton, V. L. (1939). *Mike Mulligan and his steam shovel.* Boston: Houghton Mifflin. This is a story of devotion and determination when a dedicated steam shovel is replaced by a modern machine. Because of the bond between Mike and his steam shovel, they overcome their misfortune and prove that they are still worthwhile. Grades K–3.

Curtis, C. P. (1995). *The Watsons go to Birmingham, 1963.* New York: Delacorte. A moving novel filled with laughter describes a family's trip from Michigan to Alabama. Their unique relationships and outrageous interactions engage the reader humorously while presenting a very meaningful lesson. Grades 4–8.

de Paola, T. (Ed.). (1988). *Tomie de Paola's book of poems.* New York: Putnam. Children who love Tomie de Paola won't be able to resist this collection of poems for all occasions. Grades K–6.

Dorros, A. (1995). *Abuela.* New York: Dutton. A fantasy of a Hispanic American child who imagines she is rising in the air and soaring with her Abuela (grandmother). They fly over Manhattan, taking in all the sights. The text is printed in both Spanish and English. Grades K–3.

Gardner, B. (1985). *Guess what?* New York: Lothrup, Lee & Shepard. A small portion of an animal picture is displayed in color, inviting the reader to guess its identity. The full view of the animal is on the next page. Grades Pre-K–2.

Goble, P. (1978). *The girl who loved wild horses.* New York: Macmillan. The Caldecott Medal–winning story of a Native American girl and her love of wild horses is rich with illustration and beautiful language. When the girl is caught in a storm, she is rescued by a beautiful stallion. Grades K–2.

Knight, E. (1940). *Lassie, come home.* New York: Holt. This heart-warming story describes the struggle of a collie dog to return from Scotland to her young master in England. Devotion, frustration, and courage characterize the dog, who longs to be home again. Grades 4–7.

MacDonald, B. (1947). *Mrs. Piggle Wiggle.* New York: Lippincott. A simple woman offers many unusual cures to help children with naughty habits when they are sent to her magical farm. Grades 2–5.

Mayer, M. (1987). *There's an alligator under my bed.* New York: Dial Books for Young Readers. A boy's predicament with an alligator leads to creative measures to rid his room and house of this creature. Grades K–2.

Numeroff, J. (1991). *If you give a moose a muffin.* New York: HarperCollins. A big moose receives a muffin and makes himself at home by asking for jam to go with it. The story continues as the moose makes more and more requests, ending full circle. Grades K–2.

Park, B. (1996). *Mick Harte was here.* New York: Knopf. Phoebe loses her brother, Mick, in a bicycle accident, and her struggles to accept his death are examined in this beautifully written novel. Grades 6–12.

Rowling, J. K. (1997). *Harry Potter and the sorcerer's stone.* New York: Scholastic. This is the first of a series of tales about a young wizard in training.

Harry Potter, an unpopular kid in school, discovers friends, magical powers, and his destiny. Grades 4–8.

Sachan, L. (1991). *Dogs don't tell jokes.* New York: Knopf. Twelve-year-old Gary Boone dreams of being a comedian, but not all his classmates agree that he'd succeed. Gary decides to try out for the talent show to prove them wrong, and it's almost a disaster. Grades 3–6.

Seuss, Dr. (1950). *If I ran the zoo.* New York: Random House. A boy finds it boring at the local zoo after comparing the animals to those in the zoo in his imagination, with unusual animals such as a Gusset, a Gherkin, a Gasket, and a Gootch. Grades Pre-K–4.

Shulevitz, U. (1978). *The treasure.* New York: Farrar, Straus & Giroux. This is a retelling of an enchanting folktale. When Isaac dreams three times of going to look for a treasure, he decides he must see if the dream will come true. Grades 6–8.

Spier, P. (1978). *Oh, were they ever happy.* New York: Doubleday. Parents go out, telling their children that the sitter will arrive in a few minutes. When she never shows up, the children decide to paint the house. Grades K–3.

# Professional Resources

Chambers, A. (1996). *Tell me: Children, reading, and talk.* Portland, ME: Stenhouse. Oral language has the power to help children process and organize their thoughts about reading. This book shows how to teach children to listen and talk effectively, clarifying their thoughts in order to communicate them. A framework of oral prompts to encourage book talking is provided, as are guidelines for avoiding mistakes. It is a companion to *The Reading Environment.*

Flood, J., & Lapp, D. (1997/1998). Broadening conceptualization of literacy: The visual and communicative arts. *The Reading Teacher, 51,* 342–344. Children are exposed to multiple sources of information as they develop language skills. The authors present their view of how visual arts form an integral part of the literacy curriculum; teachers who understand their importance broaden and deepen literacy learning.

Flood, J., & Lapp, D. (Eds.); Wood, K. (Coauthor). (1998). Viewing: The neglected communication process, or "When what you see isn't what you get." *The Reading Teacher, 52,* 300–304. When teachers deliberately structure lessons through visual information, students become actively engaged. This article describes a collaborative listening–viewing guide (CLVG), similar to the directed reading activity for printed material, which promotes student attention and interest in visual literacy.

Goldberg, M. (2001). *Arts and learning: An integrated approach to teaching and learning in multicultural and multilingual settings* (2nd ed.). Boston: Allyn & Bacon. This book explores ways in which learning occurs through the visual, literary, and performing arts. It stresses integrating these arts across the curriculum and shows teachers how to engage children's natural inclination toward creativity and critical thinking.

Hansen, J. (2001). *When writers read* (2nd ed.). Portsmouth, NH: Heinemann. When writers read, they read as authors themselves. This book describes five central concepts writers actively use to be effective readers: look for author's voice, make constant mental decisions about the text, read abundantly, respond critically and thoughtfully, and use self-discipline.

Kruise, C. S. (1987). *Those bloomin' books: A handbook for extending thinking skills*. Littleton, CO: Libraries Unlimited. Using Bloom's taxonomy of higher thinking skills, the author develops questions and activities for elementary school teachers, using children's literature as a springboard to encourage and support thinking skills. Teachers will learn how to develop and monitor their own questioning techniques to foster in-depth comprehension and critical thinking.

Miyata, C. (2001). *Speaking rules! Classroom games, exercises, and activities for creating masterful speakers and presenters*. Portland, ME: Stenhouse. Speaking before an audience can be nonthreatening, even liberating. Part one of this book focuses on oral communication, with strategies for improving listening, exploring voice, and interpretation. Part two shows how to develop content, coach student performers, and evaluate. Many games and exercises are provided.

Moline, S. (1995). *I see what you mean: Children at work with visual information*. Portland, ME: Stenhouse. This book describes how students acquire strategies that require communicating graphically. It is filled with activities for struggling writers and contains over a hundred student examples that illustrate how conventional written text can be enhanced with purpose and utility. This would be a particularly helpful resource for creating an integrated curriculum and thematic instruction.

Morrow, L. M. (1997). *Literacy development in the early years: Helping children read and write* (3rd ed.). Boston: Allyn & Bacon. This prolific author offers a wide variety of theory-based activities for integrating the language arts in the early school years.

Parsons, L. (2001). *Response journals revisited: Maximizing learning through reading, writing, viewing, discussing, and thinking*. Portland, ME: Stenhouse. This book offers step-by-step explanations about response journals and why they are effective literacy tools. Students will learn how to explore ideas they are reading, viewing, or discussing. A catalog of teacher questions is provided to prompt personal responses. Organization tips, checklists, and evaluation forms for both students and teachers are included.

Routman, R. (1999). *Conversations: Strategies for teaching, learning, and evaluating*. Portsmouth, NH: Heinemann. Routman continues the discussion she began in the best-selling *Invitations*, further exploring an effective language arts and literacy program across the curriculum.

# 5 — Emerging Literacy

## Teaching Activities

**1.** *Develop phonemic awareness through nursery rhymes.* Nursery rhymes are an enjoyable and beneficial context for demonstrating rhyming, repetition, and manipulation of phonemes. Make a big book of nursery rhymes, and provide the children with individual copies of the book as well. Play with the sounds and sound patterns through rhyme and manipulation of sounds. Create additional verses to the rhymes, and experiment with word substitutions through shared and interactive writing experiences. Clap out the words in the rhyme, or match the words and syllables to physical movement such as marching or walking to the words in the rhyme. This rhythmic movement activity develops children's awareness of speech segments. Have the children identify the rhymes or talk about what makes them rhyme. You can also use self-adhesive notes to cover the second word in rhyming pairs so the children can guess the missing rhyming words in the passage. Substitute beginning sounds and adapt the rhymes to focus on sounds and letters by writing them on a dry-erase board where the letter and word beginnings can be changed.

**2.** *Use oral cloze.* Skilled readers anticipate the text ahead. You can help beginning readers internalize this strategy in shared reading experiences by stopping at strategic points to have the children fill in the next word. Meaningful predictions are based on the children's knowledge of the meaning of the text, along with their oral language and understanding of the structure of language. This activity encourages children to utilize the nonvisual cuing systems—syntactic (language structure) and semantic (meaning).

**3.** *Learn the alphabet through purposeful and enjoyable experiences.* Teaching letters in isolation or a prescribed sequence is an ineffective and inefficient use of literacy teaching and learning time. The difficult task in early reading and writing is not isolated letter identification, but rather applying letter and sound knowledge when reading and writing continuous text. When these emergent literates are learning about letters, it is important to point out the same information in mul-

tiple contexts to guide them in the transfer and application of their letter knowledge. Some alphabet activity ideas include the following:

- Display a collaborative "alphabet wall," adding to it continuously; teach children how to use it.
- Provide a variety of alphabet books and dictionaries, and show children how to use them.
- Make a class alphabet big book.
- Provide each child with a personal alphabet reference card. As an alternative, have the children make their own alphabet books, using their own drawings or magazine cutouts to illustrate the written words. This year-long project can be continually updated.
- Sing songs and provide shared reading experiences that use alphabet rhymes and games.
- Play alphabet games, such as "I Spy," that link letter names and words with words from shared reading texts to locate particular letters.
- Provide tactile, hands-on experiences manipulating and forming letters, using magnetic letters, letter tiles, clay, and sandpaper.
- Each child in the class is given his or her Letter Day. On that child's day, display his or her initials, and have the children stay on alert to find those letters in their environment.

**4.** *Environmental print.* Children's surrounding oral language environment influences oral language growth. In a similar way, children's surrounding environmental print influences reading and writing. If you have beginning readers and writers or struggling readers and writers, it is important to enrich the environmental print in your classroom. For instance, label key items in your room with a printed card and an accompanying picture. Place banners and posters in prominent places in your room. *One caution is in order.* We quickly become so accustomed to items within our environment that for all practical purposes, we are blind to their existence. Environmental print does little good unless a specific and vigorous effort is made to connect print with reading and writing experiences.

Therefore, it is necessary to call children's attention to the print you want them to notice.

**5.** *Highlight print information in the context of shared reading and writing experiences.* For young children, early attempts at reading require increased attention to the print details, since they have to process most of the information on the page. Teachers can most effectively draw attention to print details and characteristics of written text and demonstrate new learning in the context of meaningful, purposeful reading and writing of continuous text. These concepts can be effectively highlighted through the use of a pointer or masking device to direct children's attention to print features and skills such as these:

- Book conventions
- Layout of text
- Directional movement
- One-to-one match
- Distinctive features of letters
- Isolating individual letters or clusters of letters
- Isolating individual words (high-frequency and high-interest words)
- Knowledge and understanding of spelling patterns
- Punctuation

**6.** *Use names as a high-meaning entrant into print concepts.* Children's own names are of the highest interest to them, and usually they are the first words a child learns to recognize in print. Capitalize on this by writing their names on appropriate items around the room, playing phonological games with their names, and writing their names into simple LEA stories.

**7.** *Transform sing-alongs into shared reading experiences.* Print the words to favorite songs on large chart paper or in blank big books. As you sing along together, point to the words on the chart so the children can match the visual representation of the word with the spoken word.

**8.** *Revisit familiar text.* Frequent opportunities to read familiar material are integral to the process of "learning to be a reader." Through these experiences beginning readers start integrating complex reading behaviors effectively. Texts used for shared reading experiences, text constructed through shared writing experiences, or rereadings of pieces children have written themselves support beginning readers as they move toward increased independence, developing seamless

integration of multiple reading behaviors. Familiar language structure and meaning allow children to focus on the visual details of print, matching the spoken word with the written word.

**9.** *Encourage and support emergent "reading" of books.* First, it is important to set up an inviting reading area. Consider providing child-sized furniture, pillows, and rugs to create a cozy, inviting space. Placing this area next to the windows helps both with light and aesthetics. Books for children at this level should be displayed so they can see the attractive front covers. Provide a variety of picture books including stories; concept books that deal with number, color, the alphabet, and shapes; and information books. All books should be read aloud before placing them in the reading area, so that students are familiar with them. Support "reading reenactment" to encourage children to engage in reading behaviors: they tend to mimic the experiences and reading behaviors of the adults in the classroom and tend to be more interested in books with which they are familiar. Emergent readers retell the story in a trade book as though they are actually reading it on their own. This "pretend reading" is a valuable approximation, a prelude to actual beginning reading that should be encouraged in early literacy classrooms. Children are imitating reading behavior that has been frequently modeled for them.

**10.** *Retell familiar stories with manipulatives.* Provide concrete story props, such as flannel board pieces and objects representative of story elements, to allow children to build on the structure and patterns of familiar books. Such supported retellings help children develop a sense of story by internalizing elements such as character, setting, plot, theme, problem and solution, and sequence of events. Place props for a given folk or fairy tale in the block center. Provide figures to represent characters, as well as a few essential props. For example, for *The Three Bears,* provide three bear figures of different sizes, a Goldilocks figure, and three small bowls. Encourage the children to build the appropriate setting with the blocks. This will help them think through the essential elements of the setting. Providing a sequence chart created with the students and posted in the block center will assist oral retelling for students who need this support. You can also leave a copy of the story in the area for student reference.

## Children's Literature Selections

Ahlberg, J., & Ahlberg, A. (1978). *Each peach pear plum.* New York: Viking Kestrel. This sequence book displays wonderful scenes, each hiding a nursery rhyme character. It can be used to support activities that expand language skills. Grades Pre-K–K.

Asch, F. (1979). *Sand cake.* New York: Parents Magazine Press. A little bear becomes frustrated at the beach, and Father asks him if he will eat a cake Father makes. The little bear agrees and, after his father makes it, he cleverly comes up with a way to get back at his father. Grades K–2.

Brown, M. W. (1947). *Goodnight moon.* New York: Harper & Row. This classic is a calming book about a little rabbit's bedtime ritual of bidding objects around him goodnight. Colored pages alternate with black and white to create a peaceful bedtime story. Grade Pre-K–K.

Carle, E. (1969). *The very hungry caterpillar.* New York: Philomel Books. This concept book uses days of the week and counting food items in the patterned text. It also describes the stages of the caterpillar's life with a delightful ending. Grades Pre-K–2.

Fleming, D. (1988). *Mama cat.* New York: Scholastic. Predictable text depicts a kitten's lack of routine with his mother and siblings. Children can easily read along with this comical picture book. Grades Pre-K–1.

Freeman, D. (1968). *Corduroy.* New York: Viking. A teddy bear searches a department store, wishing for a friend, and a little girl buys him with her own money in this classic story. Grades Pre-K–2.

Hawkins, C., & Hawkins, J. (1987). *I know an old lady who swallowed a fly.* New York: Putnam. An old woman begins by swallowing a fly and, in succession, swallows something unusual and a little bigger than the previous edible. Sequencing and fluency skills grow stronger with this old favorite. Grades K–3.

Hennessy, B. G. (1991). *The missing tarts.* New York: Viking. This clever story uses nursery rhyme characters to discover who stole the Queen of Hearts' fresh-baked tarts. Grades Pre-K–2.

Hines, A. G. (1986). *Daddy makes the best spaghetti.* New York: Clarion. The story follows young Corey from when his daddy picks him up from day care to bedtime. Grades Pre-K–K.

Hutchins. P. (1997). *Changes, changes.* New York: Simon & Schuster. Wooden dolls arrange and rearrange wood blocks to create interesting objects in this intriguing wordless picture book. Grades Pre-K–1.

Keats, E. J. (1971). *Over in the meadow.* New York: Four Winds Press. Many different animals are illustrated in their natural environment in this beautiful book. Counting, rhyme, and repetition are all used to engage children in interaction with the story line. Grades Pre-K–2.

Krauss, R. (1945). *The carrot seed.* New York: Harper & Row. Simple illustrations express the true faith and hope of a young boy. When he plants a carrot seed, no one believes it will grow, not even his parents. The child continues to care for his seed, and one day his beliefs overcome everything. Grades Pre-K–K.

Langstaff, J. (1955). *Frog went a courting.* New York: Harcourt Brace Jovanovich. This old Scottish song can be read, sung, and used for choral reading experiences. Grades K–2.

Martin, B. (1983). *Brown bear, brown bear, what do you see?* Orlando, FL: Holt, Rinehart & Winston. This sing-song text in a question-and-answer format lets young children name brightly colored animals on each page. At the end of the book all the animals are illustrated for the children to label in succession. Grades Pre-K–1.

McGovern, A. (1967). *Too much noise.* Boston: Houghton Mifflin. An old man, annoyed with all the animal sounds, seeks the aid of a wise man to help him solve his problem. Grades K–2.

Numeroff, J. (1988). *If you give a mouse a cookie.* New York: Harper & Row. A demanding mouse makes a series of requests after receiving a cookie from a boy. This excellent read-aloud book teaches sequencing, storytelling, and prediction. Grades Pre-K–2.

Peppe, R. (1970). *This is the house that Jack built.* New York: Delacorte Press. This familiar nursery rhyme engages children as it describes the house and its inhabitants. The text builds on fluency and auditory memory. Grades Pre-K–2.

Piper, W. (1979). *The little engine that could.* New York: Scholastic. One of the most famous children's stories, a little engine conquers a most difficult obstacle with positive thinking. Grades Pre-K–2.

Walker, B. K. (1969). *I packed my trunk.* Chicago IL: Follett. A boy packs a trunk to take along with him on a visit. In his trunk are things that begin with the letters of the alphabet. He begins with an apple, then a book, and so it goes until he gets to *z*. This is an excellent book to encourage memory and fluency as children try to recall the items in the trunk. Grades 1–5.

Wood, A. (1984). *The napping house.* San Diego, CA: Harcourt Brace Jovanovich. This predictable book

of a boy napping with his granny, dog, cat, and mouse is an excellent story for young listeners. The strongly patterned text also demonstrates the use of adjectives and sequencing in its rhyming text. Grades K–3.

# Professional Resources

Askew, B. J., & Fountas, I. C. (1998). Building an early reading process: Active from the start! *The Reading Teacher, 52,* 126–134. The authors show why it is important to understand what emergent readers do as they actively engage in reading and writing tasks, and how to become better observers. Three early actions for children are discussed: fostering early independence, establishing expectations, and encouraging active learning.

Campbell, R. (Ed.). (1998). *Facilitating preschool literacy.* Newark, DE: International Reading Association. Literacy begins before formal schooling. This book explores how very young children construct literacy meaning in their lives in the context of home and family. The roles of parents and caregivers are discussed, supporting literacy development and guiding new discoveries for meaningful learning.

Campbell, R. (2001). *Read-alouds with young children.* Newark, DE: International Reading Association. This book explores read-alouds in home and school settings and extending children's literacy development through interactive involvement with books; it presents multiple opportunities for related activities. Its premise is founded in research, describing the enjoyment children receive through read-alouds, which encourage lifelong readers.

Clay, M. M. (1975). *What did I write? Beginning writing behavior.* Portsmouth, NH: Heinemann. This book explicates the thinking processes that very young children go through as they first learn to record their thoughts on paper. Specific examples show the various stages of understanding the writing process. The reader is encouraged to hypothesize what strengths and abilities the child possesses in order to scaffold the next developmentally appropriate step in learning.

Clay, M. M. (1991). *Becoming literate: The construction of inner control.* Portsmouth, NH: Heinemann. Clay argues that successful readers gradually gain an inner control over methods of working with print through interaction with parents and teachers, slowly building to personal independence.

Donaghue, M. R., (2001). *Using literature activities to teach content areas to emergent readers.* Boston: Allyn & Bacon. Integration of emergent literacy across the curriculum is a natural extension of how young children learn. This book is a useful supplement for teachers who want to connect children's literature with math, social studies, and science content strands. It presents over a hundred fiction and nonfiction books and related activities, emphasizing developmental levels, interests, and abilities of young children as they learn communication skills.

Hicks, C. P., & Villaume, S. K. (2000/2001). Finding our own way: Critical reflections on the literacy development of two Reading Recovery children. *The Reading Teacher, 54,* 398–412. This article is a thoughtful account of the journey two first-graders take with their Reading Recovery teacher as they explore print and its meaning. Readers will come to understand the Reading Recovery framework and many particular confusions children must overcome to learn to orchestrate their cue sources and construct meaning from the text.

Jalongo, M. R, (2003). *Early childhood language arts* (3rd ed.). Boston: Allyn & Bacon. This text takes a comprehensive look at early childhood literacy and the integrated language arts in our diverse population. Information on brain research, bilingual education, technology, and media influences on young children are discussed along with current research on emerging literacy. Teacher concerns and self-assessment are outlined as they relate to each chapter.

Morrow, L. M. (2001 ). *Literacy development in the early years: Helping children read and write* (4th ed.). Boston: Allyn & Bacon. This comprehensive look at language and literacy development in today's world covers a range of literacy topics, including the role children's literature plays, the importance of family members who value literacy, and ways to provide young children with models for language learning. Each chapter ends with suggested activities for classroom teachers.

Neuman, S. B., & Dickinson, D. K. (Eds.) (2001). *Handbook of early literacy research.* New York: Guilford. Teachers, researchers, and administrators interested in the findings of leading developmentalists and literacy experts will find this an informative book. Diverse perspectives are presented with interesting analyses and theories.

Pressley, M., Allington, R. L., Wharton-McDonald, R., Block, C. C., & Morrow, L. M. (2001). *Learning to read: Lessons from exemplary first-grade classrooms.* New York: Guilford. Enjoyable to read, this book offers teachers practical solutions in a comprehensive, student-centered literacy program. Readers are taken into first-grade classrooms and learn from the best as they observe student learning.

Schwartz, R. M. (1997). Self-monitoring in beginning reading. *The Reading Teacher, 51,* 40–48. This article provides clear examples and explanation of the new reader's use of a monitoring system that controls early reading behaviors. Emergent and early readers must become aware of their thinking.

Strommen, L. T., & Mates, B. F. (1997). What readers do: Young children's ideas about the nature of reading. *The Reading Teacher, 51,* 98–107. This article describes a three-year study on emergent literacy and how young children's perception of reading expands and evolves. Results of the study show a strong interdependence between children's reading growth and their understanding of constructing meaning as they use multiple strategies. Teachers should ask themselves what the child is attending to and why.

Taberski, S. (2000). *On solid ground: Strategies for teaching reading, K–3.* Portsmouth, NH: Heinemann. This book encourages teachers to establish goals with purpose as they develop a comprehensive literacy program that is balanced and flexible in meeting students' needs. Enjoyable to read, it contains practical know-how from real classrooms. Many examples, figures, and student samples are provided.

Vukelich, C., Christie, J., & Enz, B. (2002). *Helping young children learn language and literacy.* Boston: Allyn & Bacon. This book about teaching the language arts to the young child (2–5 years) stresses the connections among reading, writing, speaking, and listening. Based on social constructivist learning theory, it shows the relationship between theory and real life through case studies.

# 6 Literature and Literacy

## Teaching Activities

**1.** *Hold author studies.* A collection of books written by the same author can be a powerful teaching tool. The goal of an author study is to support students in making a connection between a book and an author's life, while identifying unique aspects of a particular author's style and craft. This shows students that authors are real people, develops motivation to seek out other works by the same author, and hopefully inspires students to write and use what they learn in their own writing. Each month a designated bulletin board ("Spotlight On . . .") could display artifacts, books, book reviews, and various collaborative discoveries and insights, such as similarities in an author's craft across several books.

**2.** *Compare picture books to other modes of storytelling.* When we read, we create pictures in our own minds of what characters and scenery look like. We also pay attention to different parts of the story according to our background and interests. Watching a movie is very different, since we experience the viewpoint of the person who made the movie. Help students see this difference and experience for themselves the richness and variety of their own point of view in relation to the story. Choose a novel or piece of literature that has also been made into a movie. Read the literature together, discussing its elements and themes as you would at any other time. Then view the movie together. Afterward, compare the two experiences, discussing point of view. Encourage discussion about what the students liked and disliked in each version. Help the students identify the elements of each and how point of view impacts the story.

**3.** *Teach story elements to young children even before they themselves are independent readers.* Begin with stories that have very clear story elements, such as folk or fairy tales. One way to help young children see how all of the elements add up to create one whole story is to use a visual aid, such as a story glove with the heading of each element (setting, characters, plot, problem, resolution) on each finger of the glove. The theme can be represented as a heart in the palm of the glove, representing the unifying thread of the story.

**4.** *Introduce poetry in thematic units.* Choose either a unifying theme or a poet study. Point out the different "voices" of poets as they explore the same theme or topic. Help students identify how poets' voices are expressed through word choice, structure, and topic.

**5.** *Teach children to give book talks.* When children are immersed in literature-rich classrooms, informal book talks should occur regularly as a way for students to recommend good books to one another. Recommendations should include a description of why they liked the book and why they think others will enjoy it. Some suggested points to mention include the following:

- Retelling some events (without including the ending)
- The child's favorite part or character and the reason for this choice
- How the book is similar to or different from others by the same author

If the child wishes, he or she can make a poster to advertise the book and display it in the reading area.

**6.** *Send books home and back.* Hold students accountable for nightly reading homework, with the time varying according to grade level. Every day, provide students with access to a wide variety of literature through a home checkout system, by which they can borrow a book from the classroom to read and respond to in a literature log. Help students take responsibility for checking books in and out. Literature logs should be designated for students to process their nightly reading homework and prepare to share with others by recording thoughts, ideas, and connections made during the reading. Each morning, allow approximately 15 minutes for students to gather in pairs to share the book they read and their response. Have students keep an ongoing record of the books checked out and rate each selection with a star system and comments, if desired. Through discussion in individual reading conferences, encourage them to look for trends in their reading by identifying favorite styles, genres, and authors.

**7.** *Foster literature response.* These activities are designed to extend and complement literature and help students explore it on a deeper level. Through shared experiences, students are collaboratively extending the literature in meaningful ways. Keep in mind, however, that children shouldn't spend too much time responding because it will take away from actual reading. Introduce and model a variety of ways in which readers make connections to what they are reading. Post these ideas in the front of the room, and allow the students to choose a form of response. The following are a few suggestions:

- Paint a picture to illustrate scenes or characters from the story.
- Make puppets and turn the story into a play.
- Retell the story.
- Collaborate innovatively on the story.
- Make a comparison chart on multiple versions of a tale.
- Present a dramatic interpretation of the story.
- Rewrite the story as a reader's theater script.

**8.** *Share the very best of literature.* Introduce children to award-winning literature they might not discover on their own. Adult critics award the Newbery Medal annually to the author who made "the most distinguished contribution to American literature for children," while the Caldecott Medal is presented annually to "the artist of the most distinguished American picture book for children." The Coretta Scott King Award is given annually to an African American author and an African American illustrator for "outstanding inspirational and educational contributions to literature for children." Children and young adults across the country vote for their favorite books of the preceding year, with the winners being listed as Children's Choices and Young Adult Choices in the October issue of *The Reading Teacher* and the November issue of *The Journal of Adolescent and Young Adult Literacy,* respectively. When children read several books from the same year, they can hold mock award competitions to decide if they agree with the critics' choices. Children delight in holding mock award competitions with books published in the current year, before the awards are announced in January of the following year. (Of course, exercises such as these also strengthen literary response skills, since the students have to defend their choices orally or in writing.) The winners of the Newbery and Caldecott Medals and the Coretta Scott King Awards for the past 30 years are listed below.

### Newbery Medal Winners

| | |
|---|---|
| 1970 | *Sounder* by William H. Armstrong |
| 1971 | *Summer of the Swans* by Betsy Byars |
| 1972 | *Mrs. Frisby and the Rats of NIMH* by Robert C. O'Brien |
| 1973 | *Julie of the Wolves* by Jean Craighead George |
| 1974 | *The Slave Dancer* by Paula Fox |
| 1975 | *M. C. Higgins the Great* by Virginia Hamilton |
| 1976 | *The Grey King* by Susan Cooper |
| 1977 | *Roll of Thunder, Hear My Cry* by Mildred D. Taylor |
| 1978 | *Bridge to Terabithia* by Katherine Paterson |
| 1979 | *The Westing Game* by Ellen Raskin |
| 1980 | *A Gathering of Days: A New England Girl's Journal, 1830–32* by Joan W. Blos |
| 1981 | *Jacob Have I Loved* by Katherine Paterson |
| 1982 | *A Visit to William Blake's Inn: Poems for Innocent and Experienced Travelers* by Nancy Willard |
| 1983 | *Dicey's Song* by Cynthia Voigt |
| 1984 | *Dear Mr. Henshaw* by Beverly Cleary |
| 1985 | *The Hero and the Crown* by Robin McKinley |
| 1986 | *Sarah, Plain and Tall* by Patricia MacLachlan |
| 1987 | *The Whipping Boy* by Sid Fleischman |
| 1988 | *Lincoln: A Photobiography* by Russell Freedman |
| 1989 | *Joyful Noises: Poems for Two Voices* by Paul Fleischman |
| 1990 | *Number the Stars* by Lois Lowry |
| 1991 | *Maniac Magee* by Jerry Spinelli |
| 1992 | *Shiloh* by Phyllis Reynolds Naylor |
| 1993 | *Missing May* by Cynthia Rylant |
| 1994 | *The Giver* by Lois Lowry |
| 1995 | *Walk Two Moons* by Sharon Creech |
| 1996 | *The Midwife's Apprentice* by Karen Cushman |
| 1997 | *The View from Saturday* by E. L. Konigsburg |
| 1998 | *Out of the Dust* by Karen Hesse |
| 1999 | *Holes* by Louis Sachar |
| 2000 | *Bud, Not Buddy* by Christopher Paul Curtis |
| 2001 | *A Year Down Yonder* by Richard Peck |
| 2002 | *A Single Shard* by Linda Sue Park |
| 2003 | *Crispin: The Cross of Lead* by Avi |

### Caldecott Medal Winners

| | |
|---|---|
| 1970 | *Sylvester and the Magic Pebble* by William Steig |

1971 *A Story, a Story* by Gail E. Haley

1972 *One Fine Day* by Nonny Hogrogian

1973 *The Funny Little Woman* by Arlene Mosel, illustrated by Blair Lent

1974 *Duffy and the Devil* by Harve Zemach, illustrated by Margot Zemach

1975 *Arrow to the Sun,* adapted and illustrated by Gerald McDermott

1976 *Why Mosquitos Buzz in People's Ears* by Verna Aardema, illustrated by Leo and Diane Dillon

1977 *Ashanti to Zulu: African Traditions* by Margaret Musgrove, illustrated by Leo and Diane Dillon

1978 *Noah's Ark* by Peter Spier

1979 *The Girl Who Loved Wild Horses* by Paul Goble

1980 *Ox-Cart Man* by Donald Hall, illustrated by Barbara Cooney

1981 *Fables* by Arnold Lobel

1982 *Jumanji* by Chris Van Allsburg

1983 *Shadow* by Blaise Cendrars, illustrated by Marcia Brown

1984 *The Glorious Flight: Across the Channel with Louis Bleriot, July 25, 1909* by Alice and Martin Provensen

1985 *Saint George and the Dragon,* adapted by Margaret Hodges, illustrated by Trina Schart Hyman

1986 *Polar Express* by Chris Van Allsburg

1987 *Hey Al* by Arthur Yorinks, illustrated by Richard Edielski

1988 *Owl Moon* by Jane Yolen, illustrated by John Schoenherr

1989 *Song and Dance Man* by Karen Ackerman, illustrated by Stephen Gammell

1990 *Lon Po Po: A Red Riding Hood Story,* adapted and illustrated by Ed Young

1991 *Black and White* by David Macaulay

1992 *Tuesday* by David Wiesner

1993 *Mirette on the High Wire* by Emily Arnold McCully

1994 *Grandfather's Journey* by Allen Say

1995 *Smoky Night* by Eve Bunting, illustrated by David Diaz

1996 *Officer Buckle and Gloria* by Peggy Rathman

1997 *Golem* by David Wisniewski

1998 *Rapunzel* by Paul O. Zelinsky

1999 *Snowflake Bentley* by Jacqueline Briggs Martin

2000 *Joseph Had a Little Overcoat* by Sims Taback

2001 *So You Want to Be President* by Judith St. George, illustrated by David Diaz

2002 *The Three Pigs* by David Wiesner

2003 *My Friend Rabbit* by Eric Rohmann

### Coretta Scott King Award Winners (Authors)

1970 *Martin Luther King, Man of Peace* by Lillie Patterson

1971 *Black Troubador: Langston Hughes* by Charlemae Rollins

1972 *Seventeen Black Artists* by Elton C. Fax

1973 *I Never Had It Made* by Jackie Robinson, as told to Alfred Duckett

1974 *Ray Charles* by Sharon Bell Mathis

1975 *The Legend of Africania* by Dorothy Robinson

1976 *Duey's Tale* by Pearl Bailey

1977 *The Story of Stevie Wonder* by James Haskins

1978 *Africa Dream* by Eloise Greenfield

1979 *Escape to Freedom* by Ossie Davis

1980 *The Young Landlords* by Walter Dean Myers

1981 *This Life* by Sidney Poitier

1982 *Let the Circle Be Unbroken* by Mildred Taylor

1983 *Sweet Whispers, Brother Rush* by Virginia Hamilton

1984 *Everett Anderson's Goodbye* by Lucille Clifton

1985 *Motown and Didi* by Water Dean Meyers

1986 *The People Could Fly: American Black Folktales* by Virginia Hamilton

1987 *Justin and the Best Biscuits in the World* by Mildred Pitts Walter

1988 *The Friendship* by Mildred Taylor

1989 *Fallen Angels* by Walter Dean Myers

1990 *A Long Hard Journey: The Story of the Pullman Porter* By Patricia C. & Frederick L. McKissack

1991 *The Road to Memphis* by Mildred Taylor

1992 *Now Is Your Time! The African American Struggle for Freedom* by Walter Dean Myers

1993 *The Dark Thirty: Southern Tales of the Supernatural* by Patricia C. McKissack

1994 *Toning the Sweep* by Angela Johnson

1995 *Christmas in the Big House, Christmas in the Quarters* by Patricia C. and Frederick L. McKissack

1996 *Her Stories: African American Folktales, Fairy Tales, and True Tales* by Virginia Hamilton

1997 *Slam* by Walter Dean Myers

1998 *Forged by Fire* by Sharon M. Draper

1999 *Heaven* by Angela Johnson

2000 *Bud, Not Buddy* by Christopher Paul Curtis

2001    *Miracle's Boys* by Jacqueline Woodson
2002    *The Land* by Mildred D. Taylor
2003    *Bronx Masquerade* by Nikki Grimes

### Coretta Scott King Award Winners (Illustrator)

1970–1973    none
1974    *Ray Charles* by Sharon Bell Mathis, illustrated by George Ford
1975–1977    none
1978    *Africa Dream* by Eloise Greenfield, illustrated by Carole Bayard
1979    *Something on My Mind* by Nikki Grimes, illustrated by Tom Feelings
1980    *Cornrows* by Camille Yarbrough, illustrated by Carole Bayard
1981    *Beat the Story Drum, Pum-Pum* by Ashley Bryan
1982    *Mother Crocodile* by John Steptoe
1983    *Black Child* by Peter Magubane
1984    *My Mama Needs Me* by Mildred P. Walter, illustrated by Pat Cummings
1985    none
1986    *The Patchwork Quilt* by Valerie Flourney, illustrated by Jerry Pinkney
1987    *Half a Moon and One Whole Star* by Crescent Dragonwagon, illustrated by Jerry Pinkney
1988    *Mufaro's Beuatiful Daughters: An African Tale* by John Steptoe
1989    *Mirandy and Brother Wind* by Patricia McKissack, illustrated by Jerry Pinkney

1990    *Nathaniel Talking* by Eloise Greenfield, illustrated by Jan Gilchrist
1991    *Aida* told by Leontyne Price, illustrated by Leo and Diane Dillon
1992    *Tar Beach* by Faith Ringgold
1993    *The Origin of Life on Earth: An African Creation Myth* retold by David Anderson, illustrated by Kathleen Atkins Wilson
1994    *Soul Looks Back in Wonder* by Tom Feelings
1995    *The Creation* by James Weldon Johnson, illustrated by James E. Ransome
1996    *The Middle Passage: White Ships Black Cargo* by Tom Feelings
1997    *Minty: A Story of Harriet Tubman* by Alan Schroeder, illustrated by Jerry Pinkney
1998    *In Daddy's Arms I Am Tall* by Alan Schroeder, illustrated by Javaka Steptoe
1999    *I See the Rhythm* by Toyomi Igus, illustrated by Michele Wood
2000    *In the Time of the Drums* by Kim L. Siegelson, illustrated by Brian Pinkney
2001    *Uptown* by Bryan Collier
2002    *Goin' Someplace Special* by Patricia C. McKissack, illustrated by Jerry Pinkney
2003    *Talkin' About Bessie: The Story of Aviator Elizabeth Coleman* by Nikki Grimes, illustrated by E. B. Lewis

## Children's Literature Selections

Allard, H. (1977). *Miss Nelson is missing!* Boston: Houghton Mifflin. The children in Miss Nelson's class are horribly behaved in spite of her sweet nature. But when she is absent, their substitute teacher, Miss Viola Swamp, is more wicked than they could have ever imagined, and they wonder if Miss Nelson will ever return. Grades K–2.

Armstrong, W. H. (1969). *Sounder.* New York: Harper & Row. A boy must accept injury to his beloved dog as he tries to stop the arrest of his father. Through the years the boy and his family hope for the father's return; while they wait, the boy discovers himself and the value of learning. Grades 6–8.

Brett, J. (1994). *Town mouse, country mouse.* New York: Penguin. Two pairs of mice decide to trade lifestyles in this Aesop fable retold with a little twist. The mice living in the country realize that town isn't as wonderful as they imagined, and the town mice feel the same about country life. Grades K–2.

Brown, M. (1982). *Stone soup.* New York: MacMillan. This French tale about a group of very hungry soldiers is a classic. Through their cleverness they are able to create a delicious soup by using stones. Grades 1–4.

Cleary, B. (1950). *Henry Huggins.* New York: Morrow. This is a charming story about a young boy and a dog who find one another outside a drugstore. Henry names him Ribsy, and the two develop a strong bond that children will love. Grades 3–5.

Crossle-Holland, K. (2001). *The seeing stone.* New York: Scholastic. This story takes place in medieval times as a 13-year-old girl travels back to the days of King Arthur. Grades 7–12.

Cushman, K. (1995). *The midwife's apprentice.* New York: Clarion. A young homeless woman in the Middle Ages discovers her inner strength and finally finds peace after convincing a midwife to take her into her home and profession. Grades 7–12.

Farley, W. (1944). *The black stallion.* New York: Random House. This is an amazing novel uniting a young boy and a wild horse. Their bond enables them to overcome many obstacles. Grades 2–6.

Matas, C. (1993). *Daniel's story.* New York: Scholastic. Fourteen-year-old Daniel is stunned and terrified when the horrors of the Holocaust sweep him and his family away. Grades 6–12.

Minarik, E. H. (1957). *Little bear.* New York: Harper & Row. Four charming stories about a little bear and his mother; her love and wisdom help him learn along the way. Grades Pre-K–1.

O'Brien, R. C. (1971). *Mrs. Frisby and the rats of NIMH.* New York: Atheneum. In an exciting fantasy tale, rats become highly intelligent through a secret experiment. Grades 4–6.

Seuss, Dr. (1978). *I can read with my eyes shut!* New York: Random House. The joys of reading are described in unusual fashion by the beloved Cat in the Hat, as he tries to convince a young cat about the joys of reading. Grades Pre-K–3.

Silverstein, S. (1964). *The giving tree.* New York: Harper & Row. The relationship of a young boy and a tree is observed as time passes and the boy grows into manhood. The gift of giving and the depth of love are the true messages in this beautiful story. Grades K–4.

Taylor, M. D. (2001). *The land.* New York: Penguin. This historical novel deals with issues of racism and also the beauty of friendship and family, as Paul, the son of a white man and a black woman, tries to determine his identity after the Civil War. Grades 7–12.

White, E. B. (1945). *Stuart Little.* New York: Harper & Row. A charming mouse, Stuart Little, lives with a human family. When his friend is missing, Stuart tries to find her, leading to many adventures. Grades 2–4.

White, E. B. (1952). *Charlotte's web.* New York: Harper & Row. This deeply beloved classic tells the story of a deep friendship between a pig and a spider. Grades 3–5.

# Professional Resources

Barton, R. (2000). *Telling stories your way: Storytelling and reading aloud in the classroom.* Ontario: Pembroke. The author shares his expertise in using storytelling in the classroom. Teachers will learn how to find and select stories, develop their own technique, and evaluate results.

Booth, D., & Barton, R. (2000). *Story works: How teachers can use shared stories in the new curriculum.* Ontario: Pembroke. Using literature can be a powerful tool in both language learning and achievement. The authors argue that in our fast-paced, media-drenched world, children need the structure and elements of story more than ever. They describe how to present them with follow-up activities.

Daniels, H. (2002). *Literature circles: Voice and choice in book clubs and reading groups* (2nd ed.). Portland, ME: Stenhouse. This book contains new resources and procedures based upon ten years of research using literature circles. After covering the basics for starting to use literature circles, it discusses how to handle the mature reader who needs advanced work with literature.

Fox, M. *Reading magic.* (2001). New York: Harcourt. Children need to bond to a book, and the adult reading it needs to feel comfortable and excited about reading. This book is for parents and teachers who want to understand why reading aloud to children can work magic and set children on the road to emerging literacy. It is fast and enjoyable reading.

Frank, C. R., Dixon, C. N., & Brandts, L. R. (2001). Bears, trolls, and pagemasters: Learning about learners in book clubs. *The Reading Teacher, 54,* 448–462. Children become interested, motivated participants when engaged in literary conversations. This article describes a student-centered second-grade classroom and a two-year ethnographic study. Readers will discover the power of literature discussion groups and how one teacher structured and organized her learning environment.

Harris, V. J. (Ed.). (1997). *Using multiethnic literature in grades K–8*. Norwood, MA: Christopher-Gordon. This book explores the creation, publication, and dissemination of multiethnic literature for children. Issues related to sharing the literature in K–8 classrooms are discussed.

Oster, L. (2001). Using the think-aloud for reading instruction. *The Reading Teacher, 55,* 64–69. The premise of this article is that through the process of student think-alouds, teachers can assess how students are making sense of literature, and monitor their instruction. A seventh-grade classroom experience with Steinbeck's *The Pearl* is used to illustrate how metacognitive awareness is a crucial component of reading.

Routman, R. (2000). *Conversations: Strategies for teaching, learning, and evaluating*. Portsmouth, NH: Heinemann. This book describes and demonstrates theory and practice in a comprehensive literacy program. Its intent is to help teachers become more effective and knowledgeable professionals.

Serafini, F. (2001). *The reading workshop: Creating space for readers*. Portsmouth, NH: Heinemann. With so many different approaches to teaching reading, how can you make sense of the best paths available? When Serafini describes his day-to-day schedule and gives an overview of how the workshop operates over time, he provides a flexible framework teachers can adapt and implement to suit their needs. His love of literature shines through his writing.

Short, K. G. (1997). *Literature as a way of knowing*. Portland, ME: Stenhouse. This book gives a rationale and direction for using real literature in a dynamic reading program. Student understanding will be enhanced and extended through practical suggestions and varied approaches with peers or independent reading.

Spiegel, D. L. (1998). Silver bullets, babies, and bath water: Literature response groups in a balanced literacy program. *The Reading Teacher, 52,* 114–124. A balanced approach to literacy recognizes the contributions of many successful literacy approaches. The author's message is that we cannot afford the destructive tendency to throw out everything "old" when we embrace the new.

Trelease, J. (2001). *The read aloud handbook* (5th ed.). New York: Penguin. This is a wonderful resource for both parents and teachers, providing a rationale for why reading to children is crucial. Topics include stages of read-alouds, the impact of television, sustained silent reading, and libraries. A large treasury of high-quality books is provided, each with a summary, suggested age level, and related books.

# 7 Content Literacy: Reading and Writing in the Content Areas

## Teaching Activities

**1.** *Promote active participation in content area learning through informal "quick writes."* Quick writes are simple, brief writing activities used for a variety of purposes: predicting and anticipating, building background knowledge, processing new learning, questioning, and reflective evaluation. Informal quick writes can be utilized in the content areas in numerous ways:

- At the end of a piece of text, have students take a few minutes to record a few things they remember or a few thoughts or feelings.
- When introducing a thematic topic, have students take 3 minutes or so to write down all of the words they think of when they hear this theme mentioned.
- Take 5 minutes to write everything you know about a particular topic before beginning an investigation.
- Spend 3 minutes recording predictions for a science experiment.
- Select a concept that you explored that day, and give students 2 minutes to write a definition in their own words.
- At the end of an investigation, have students quickly list at least one thing they still don't understand or something they are left wondering about.
- At the conclusion of a thematic unit, have students quickly write down three to four things they learned through the study.

**2.** *Utilize shared reading.* Shared reading is an approach developed by Don Holdaway, in which the teacher and a group of students read a piece of text together. This is a common approach in the early grades; however, it is often neglected in upper grades. For older students, shared reading helps make difficult texts accessible for all students, regardless of their reading ability. The emphasis shifts from focusing on the print and word level with young readers to supporting older students in interpreting, analyzing, and gaining new knowledge from more challenging texts.

Shared reading provides effective means to learn in all curricular areas, particularly expository text. Examples include study and analysis of poetry, or shared reading of a science text so all students can take part. It is important that all students are able to see the text clearly; use big books, write text out on large chart paper, or copy text onto overhead transparencies.

**3.** *Introduce a thematic unit.* At the beginning of a thematic unit such as insects, collaborate as a class on questions pertaining to the topic of focus or areas of inquiry and record them on a KWL chart. Investigate answers to these questions, and explore new information in a variety of nonfiction texts that have been added to a thematic book tub in your classroom library. Refer to the KWL chart and update it regularly with new information learned, questions answered, and new questions that have arisen through the thematic study. Have the children write about and illustrate what they have learned.

**4.** *Use written retellings to strengthen informational text reading.* Following the reading of an article or section of content area literature, ask students to do a written retelling. This can be used as an instructional piece, with the teacher modeling and engaging students in shared writing experiences. Later, as students become competent at this task, it can be used as an authentic assessment task to determine students' understanding of the main idea and supporting details of the content that was read.

**5.** *Create alphabet books.* Alphabet books can provide a comprehensive extension or application opportunity during a thematic focused inquiry or content-area unit. They are often used as a culminating activity at the end of a unit of study, such as oceans or plants. These books can be created by the whole group, small groups, or individuals as an extension project or long-term focus. Prior to students creating their own, provide numerous models of alphabet trade books, and discuss the way the text and illustrations are laid out. When students are ready to create their own, follow this suggested sequence:

- Brainstorm a list. Write the letters down the left side of a chart.
- Divide letters among the number of students working on the project.
- Agree on a common structure or format.
- Use the writing process: draft, conference, revise, and edit.

**6.** *Utilize poetry.* Numerous poems and songs written for children can be effectively used to teach content area topics. These serve as an engaging context through which students can learn new information. Students can also be encouraged to write their own poems and songs related to the topic of study.

**7.** *Write through a mask—simulated journals.* A simulated journal can be used to assume another's role and write from that person or object's viewpoint. Students can assume the role of a historical figure or famous person, picking key dates in that person's life and writing entries from this simulated perspective. Another possibility is to take on the perspective of a science concept such as a raindrop passing through the water cycle.

**8.** *Use read–share–write.* This activity not only fosters focused comprehension but enables students to develop the ability to articulate their ideas by putting their learning in their own words. This leads to internalization of information and an increased transfer and application. As students are reading expository text for thematic or content area learning, they use the following process:

- Read a selected passage and close the book.
- Share and discuss what you just read with a partner.
- Record what you learned in a learning log.
- Buddy-read the passage again to ensure important information wasn't left out or misinterpreted.

**9.** *Write informational text.* The most authentic expository writing experience for students takes place within the context of learning about science and social studies themes or topics of study. Young children can start out writing "All About . . ." books, in which they write about information on a familiar topic. A whole class collaboration on a big book or thematic mural is most effective for K–2 students. This activity should be started a few weeks into an in-depth thematic focus, allowing students to acquire new information about the focus topic. Collaborate on the formulation of factual statements about what has been learned. Spread multiple statements out in order to effectively group them to form cohesive and fluid book sections. Name the book sections, sequence them, and create a table of contents before publishing the book. For older children, small, cooperative groups can work together to create their own expository text as an informational picture book, resulting in multiple books within one class. Each group writes and publishes a book (in the same manner mentioned above) to inform others about the focus topic. Each group member generates several facts pertaining to the topic of study, based on memory or a review of a learning log. The group collaborates to sort each statement into related groups. Each section of the book can be labeled and sequenced on a long strip of paper; a draft is created as each section is labeled with the sequenced statements attached down the strip. Each group should go through the proofreading and editing process, followed by publishing and storing the text for rereading.

**10.** *Make a weekly alphabet research book.* Each week students complete five research areas related to a single letter of the alphabet and one personal response. The information is recorded on two facing pages in a notebook. Research materials include an atlas, encyclopedias, the weekly newspaper, and an English or math text. Some suggested research topics may include language, math, current events, states, poets and poetry, an author, a famous person, or a country. The following example illustrates some topics researched for the letter *M*:

- *Language.* Metaphor: The comparison of one thing to another without the use of the word like or as. For example, in *Tuck Everlasting,* "A dragonfly, a brilliant blue jewel, darted up and paused over the lily pads."
- *Math.* Mirror symmetry: From points on one side, draw perpendicular lines to the mirror line and extend them an equal distance beyond.
- *Current Events.* Mail Call! November 14, 2000: The U.S. Postal Service is raising the cost of a first-class stamp by 1¢. This increase will create $1 billion for the U.S.P.S. next year. The increase will go into effect on January 7, 2001.

# Children's Literature Selections

Benchley, N. (1977). *George the drummer boy*. New York: Harper & Row. George, a British drummer boy, is involved in the first battle of the American Revolution. The story takes his viewpoint and shares his confusion and fear over what he is witnessing. Grades 1–4.

Berger, M. (1986). *Germs make me sick*. New York: Harper & Row. In this clever picture book, bacteria and viruses are examined, describing how they can make people sick. Grades Pre-K–3.

Bishop, C. H. (1952). *Twenty and ten*. New York: Viking. In France, 20 courageous fifth-graders hide 10 Jewish refugee children during World War II. This exceptional story examines what life was like during this fearful time in history. Grades 4–7.

Branley, F. M. (1987). *It's raining cats and dogs: All kinds of weather and why we have it*. Boston: Houghton Mifflin. In addition to giving scientific accounts of our weather, this book examines strange happenings that may occur in nature, such as pink and green snowstorms. Grades 3–6.

Cleary, B. (1990). *Henry and Beezus*. New York: HarperCollins. Henry wants to buy a new bicycle, so he tries to earn money by delivering papers and selling bubble gum—but he only ends up with more problems. Beezus, his old friend, has a plan that may lead to more trouble or great success. This humorous story can also enhance children's conceptual understanding of money. Grades 2–6.

Defoe, D. (2002). *Robinson Crusoe*. New York: Viking Press. Based on a real-life incident, this story portrays a man who tries to escape his mundane life by setting sail for adventure. Stranded on an island after a terrible storm, his survival is at risk since he has few possessions. This story of solitude and problem solving provides a classic look at humanity's basic instincts of survival and hope. Grades 8–12.

Ebsensen, B. J. (1996). *Echoes for the eye: Poems to celebrate patterns in nature*. New York: HarperCollins. In this collection of 25 original poems, geometry is presented by describing patterns in nature. This is an excellent resource for math, science, and reading activities. Grades 3–6.

Ehlert, L. (1987). *Growing vegetable soup*. San Diego, CA: Harcourt Brace Jovanovich. In a garden a child and his father plant, water, and watch seeds grow. They pick their vegetables and make a special soup together. Grades K–2.

Fritz, J. (1980). *Where do you think you're going, Christopher Columbus?* New York: Putnam. Christopher Columbus's personality traits are examined in this enriching informational picture book. He thought he had reached India even though he really landed in the New World. Grades 3–6.

Geehan, W. (1999). *Sir Cumference and the dragon of pi*. Watertown, MA: Charlesbridge. Sir Cumference drinks a potion that turns him into a dragon, and his son must search for the magic number "pi" to restore his father to his original shape. This is an amusing story to teach math skills. Grades 3–6.

Heller, R. (1981). *Chickens aren't the only ones*. New York: Putnam. The many living things that lay eggs are explored in this simple information book. Grades K–3.

Hinton, S. E. (1978). *The outsiders*. New York: Viking. A teenage boy named Ponyboy narrates this chilling story of rival gangs, the Socs and the Greasers. Ponyboy desperately tries to be tough on the outside to fit in with the others, but inside he is scared and confused. This story has impacted readers for decades and its message still resonates with today's young adults. Grades 9–12.

Hutchins, P. (1989). *The doorbell rang*. New York: Greenwillow. When their doorbell rings repeatedly, Victoria and Sam must divide the dozen cookies their Ma just baked with their unexpected visitors. This is an excellent story to use when introducing division, as well as a delightful book about sharing. Grades K–3.

Hutchins, P. (1994). *Clocks and more clocks*. New York: Simon & Schuster. Mr. Higgins tries desperately to figure out which of his clocks has the correct time. Finally, a clockmaster teaches Mr. Higgins a few things about how to read his clocks. This is an excellent book to introduce telling time. Grades K–2.

Levinson, N. S. (1990). *Clara and the bookwagon*. New York: HarperCollins. Young Clara dreams of reading, but her father believes it is unimportant for farm life. When Miss Mary travels to their farm in her bookwagon, Clara's father is persuaded that reading is important. Grades K–3.

Lewis, P. J. (2002). *A world of wonders: Geographic travels in verse and rhyme.* New York: Penguin. This is a fact-filled collection of poems that makes geography interesting, humorous, and intriguing. Grades 3–7.

Lionni, L. (1960). *Inch by inch.* New York: Scholastic. A worm takes pride in measuring everything around him. When a hungry bird comes along, ready to eat him, the worm cleverly uses measuring to outsmart the bird. Grades Pre-K-2.

London, J. (1970). *The call of the wild.* New York: Scholastic. Buck, a dog who has led a sheltered life, is shipped off to the Klondike to be a sled dog. His survival instincts are tested with challenges unknown to him before. This classic story of overcoming obstacles is a must to share with readers. Grades 7–12.

Matthews, L. (1993). *Bunches and bunches of bunnies.* New York: Scholastic. Busy bunnies and a simple text introduce the multiplication tables from 1 to 12—a fun-filled picture book to introduce multiplication concepts. Grades K–2.

Scieszka, J. (1995). *Math curse.* New York: Viking. Math seems to fill a young girl's life after her teacher tells the class that math problems are all around them. At home, she sorts clothes, calculates time, and even thinks of measurement while eating pancakes. This humorous book relays to children that we need math every day. Grades 3–6.

## Professional Resources

Fountas, I. C., & Pinnell, G. S. (2001). *Guiding readers and writers, grades 3–6: Teaching comprehension, genre, and content literacy.* Portsmouth, NH: Heinemann. The authors of *Guided Reading* continue their discussion of guided literacy for readers and writers in upper elementary grades.

Freeman, E. B., & Person, D. G. (1998). *Connecting informational children's books with content area learning.* Boston: Allyn & Bacon. Methods of encouraging problem solving are modeled in an atmosphere of inquiry, within the context of national standards and usable teaching methods. This book stresses making the most of informational reading in integrated, thematic units. Sample units and lesson plans are provided.

Graves, D. H. (1989). *Investigate nonfiction.* Portsmouth, NH: Heinemann. One title in the *Reading/Writing Teachers* series, this book suggests actions teachers can take and reflect upon as they experiment with how to inspire children to write meaningful nonfiction. It examines a range of nonfiction genres and how to engage children with purpose and voice.

Harvey, S. (1998). *Nonfiction matters: Reading, writing, and research in grades 3–8.* Portland, ME: Stenhouse. This book discusses ways to help students read and write expository text. It suggests inquiry-based projects that require thoughtful research and organization, as well as providing ideas for teacher modeling and assessment. Also included are helpful bibliographies of nonfiction books by subject and genre.

Headley, K. N., & Dunston, P. J. (2000). Teachers' Choices books and comprehension strategies as transaction tools. *The Reading Teacher, 54,* 260–268. This article describes three interactive comprehension strategies to be used with books for enhancing literacy learning: KWL plus, the directed listening thinking activity, and discussion webs. Teachers are shown how to help students construct meaning before, during, and after reading Teachers' Choice trade books (a project of the International Reading Association).

Hoyt, L. (2002). *Make it real: Strategies for success with informational texts.* Portsmouth, NH: Heinemann. Informational literacy is critical to students. The author discusses a range of instructional strategies, making content text more understandable to students. Modeled, shared, and guided reading and writing are discussed as teachers are shown how to scaffold content-specific words and ideas.

Irvin, J. L., Buehl, D. R., & Klemp, R. M. (2003). *Reading and the high school student: Strategies to enhance literacy.* Boston: Allyn & Bacon. This book is specifically geared to improving reading strategies in the content areas for the struggling older student. Ways to develop a literacy program are discussed. This book is a good complement to *Reading and the Middle School* by Judith Irvin.

Lake, J. (2000). *Literature and science breakthroughs—connecting language and science skills in the elementary classroom*. Ontario: Pembroke. Here is a practical and useful book for incorporating children's literature with real life science learning. Teachers will learn to go beyond simply reading about science concepts to providing students with activities that engage and internalize learning. The book is organized according to five major science strands.

Moore, D. W., Moore, S. A., Cunningham, P. M., & Cunningham, J. W. (2003). *Developing readers and writers in the content areas, K–12* (4th ed.). Boston: Allyn & Bacon. This practical, engaging book introduces teachers to content reading instruction. Chapters address topics such as comprehension, vocabulary, writing, and studying informational texts, with focus on building literacy through content learning.

Moyer, P. S. (2000). Communicating mathematically: Children's literature as a natural connection. *The Reading Teacher, 4*, 246–255. Classroom teachers will learn how to effectively integrate language and literature with developing mathematical concepts to mirror the natural way children learn. Classroom activities and conversations are used to illustrate the process of connecting real-life math with children's life experiences through stories.

Murray, D. M. (2000). *Write to learn* (7th ed.). Boston: Heinle & Heinle. This is a classic text, a must-have for teachers who want to use writing in the content areas.

Sadler, C. R. (2001). *Comprehension strategies for middle grade learners: A handbook for content area teachers*. Newark, DE: International Reading Association. This book contains a collection of classroom-tested strategies geared for students who lack strong literacy skills. They are presented in a single-page layout with a brief description, easy-to-follow procedures, and suggestions for assessment. Teachers will appreciate how students will connect new learning to personal background knowledge and interests.

Stephens, E. C., & Brown, J. E. (1999). *A handbook of content literacy strategies: 75 practical reading and writing ideas*. Norwood, MA: Christopher-Gordon. Teachers (grades 4–12) will find practical tools for integrating reading and writing into the content areas in this book. The authors provide strategies to form a partnership between literacy learning and content learning, while dealing with the realities of implementation.

Walpole, S. (1998/1999). Changing texts, changing thinking: Comprehension demands of new science textbooks. *The Reading Teacher, 52*, 358–369. This article helps teachers consider the structure of ideas and students' background knowledge when bridging the gap between children and texts. As science textbooks change, there is a growing need to support student learning with instruction based on teacher inquiry into student processing.

# 8 Teaching Children to Comprehend Written Text

## Teaching Activities

**1.** *Utilize interactive read-alouds.* Throughout a read-aloud, encourage students to share predictions, comments, insights, and connections. The students and teacher are actively processing the text together, through engaging discussion; students aren't listening silently and passively.

**2.** *Open-ended questions initiate rich dialogue.* Be thoughtful regarding the questions you ask children after reading. Often, we ask inauthentic, superficial questions that stifle thoughtful discussion of a piece of literature. To avoid a "teacher asks, students respond" interaction, initiate a discussion with open-ended prompts:

- What did this remind you of?
- How did that make you feel?
- Tell us what you thought of this.
- What did you notice?
- What do you wonder?
- What is your opinion?

**3.** *Involve students in frequent small group discussions about text being read.* Often, discussions about literature take place in the whole group, with the teacher directing and one student at a time speaking. To facilitate more active engagement with much more student involvement, arrange students in small "buzz groups." Giving a focus for the discussion will be important at first; however, with more experience, students will begin to focus these student-led discussions on their own.

**4.** *Create a common dialogue about effective reading.* A common set of prompts should be used consistently within a classroom, across grade levels in a school, and at home as well. These prompts guide students towards strategic problem solving when meaning breaks down. When the same language is used across the contexts in which students are reading, they begin to internalize it, making the same language part of their repertoire of problem-solving strategies. Collaborate as a building, or better yet as a district, to generate common terminology with consistent, clear explanations for each strategy. When used across grade levels, this language

empowers students to increase the flexibility of their independent use of these strategies as they approach more challenging levels of text and various genres. This cumulative effect is significant!

**5.** *Make connections.* Each reader has a unique way of experiencing a book, making personal, individual connections. There are three categories of connections that readers make to enhance understanding:

- *Text-to-self connection.* A personal connection between the book and the reader's own life experiences
- *Text-to-text connection.* Connecting an author's craft, themes, characters, and events from one book to another
- *Text-to-world connection.* Connecting what is read to the issues or concepts in the larger world

Comprehension strategy instruction should begin with making connections, the foundation for constructing meaning. Model each connection separately, several times, by thinking aloud while you are reading to the students. Consider posting three large charts with a connection heading on each: text-to-self, text-to-text, and text-to-world. As students begin to voice these connections in your literature discussions, record them on the appropriate poster.

**6.** *Collaborate on genre charts.* As you study particular genres, collaborate to create a large display chart listing specific features of various types of text. Refer to the chart regularly, making revisions and additions as needed. As the children explore multiple genres throughout the year, this large chart will serve as a genre comparison reference that can be utilized to support understanding of text features during reading or writing.

**7.** *Explore the elements of literature.* Bring the various elements of literature to students' conscious attention: parts of a book, author's purpose, setting, characters, illustrations, point of view, plot, symbols, mood, and theme. Keep in mind that these elements are not ends in themselves but rather tools for deepening one's understanding of a story. When these terms become a significant part of a group's language, a common vocabulary is created that supports discussion. Students move beyond a superficial level of comprehension to better understand the author's craft and how to use the elements to explore and discuss a piece of literature. Introduce each element of literature separately. For each one, develop a chart to record collaborative definitions and descriptions that arise through discussions as a community of readers. (Adapted from Serafini, 2001.)

**8.** *Teach students how and when to apply visual comprehension aids.* Students experience many ways to organize information. However, all too often teachers assign the use of a particular graphic organizer rather than gradually releasing responsibility to the students to use these tools independently. After many interactive experiences using KWL, Venn diagrams, story maps, webs, and other comprehension organizers, begin to teach students how and when to apply the most effective organizer to new text. With practice, students should become adept at applying these tools for themselves, which is really the goal of comprehension instruction.

**9.** *Help students reflect on learning from expository text.* Teach students to be reflective readers and actively search for new understanding or learning. Help students internalize the following prereading questions:

- What is my purpose for reading on this particular topic?
- What do I already know?
- What do I need to know?

As students read expository text and gain new understanding, guide them to internalize the following questions:

- What new information did I learn about the topic?
- Can I put it into my own words?
- Were my questions answered?
- How has my thinking changed?
- Do I want to pursue this topic further?

(Adapted from Wilson, 2002.)

**10.** *Express new vocabulary with art.* Tricky vocabulary may impede understanding. One way to help students to make a connection to unfamiliar words is to have them illustrate the words. After deriving the meaning of a word through context clues, predicting, and looking it up in the dictionary, ask students to draw a picture to make a connection to the word. This often helps them clarify their understanding of the meaning as well as recall the word for later use.

## Children's Literature Selections

Bang, M. (1985). *The paper crane.* New York: Greenwillow. Owners of a poor restaurant serve a customer as if he were royalty; however, he is also poor and is unable to pay his bill. To make up for what he owes, he transforms a folded napkin into a beautiful bird and magically it comes alive. People are drawn to the restaurant from that day on to see the crane. Grades 2–5.

Brown, A. (1986). *Piggybook.* New York: Knopf. Mrs. Piggett takes care of her husband and sons by cleaning and cooking for them. One day she becomes weary of this routine and leaves them to do their own chores. This is an excellent story to probe inferences and have students give reasons why the pigs behaved in a certain manner. Grades 3–5.

Burningham, J. (1977). *Come away from the water, Shirley.* New York: Crowell. This is a story of an ongoing dialogue between a young girl and her parents at the beach. Her proximity to the water makes them nervous, but Shirley only can see a grand adventure as she uses her imagination. Grades 1–4.

Cendras, B. (1982). *Shadows.* New York: Scribner's. Based on an African folktale, this story is about shadows and their wonders, and is translated by Marcia Brown. Analyzing the text and sharing ideas about the impression the story had on the reader are ways to extend the reading of this book. This is a Caldecott Medal winner. Grades 6–8.

Gage, W. (1976). *Squash pie.* New York: Greenwillow. A farmer's squash crop continues to be spoiled by a thief. This puzzle never really is answered in the story, allowing readers to come up with their own theories. Grades 1–5.

Green, N. (1974). *A hole in the dike.* New York: Crowell. This is a tale retold by Norma Green about a young Dutch boy who discovers a hole in the dike on his way home. The brave child places his finger into the hole to stop the water and saves the people of his village. Children can examine this story and discuss why they think he risked his life. Grades 1–3.

Gwynne, F. (1976). *A chocolate moose for dinner.* Englewood Cliffs, NJ: Prentice Hall. A collection of clever homonyms amuses children with the multiple meanings of our language. One example is "toasting daddy." Grades 2–5.

Hall-Ets, M. (1955). *Play with me.* New York: Viking. A little girl in a meadow seeks to find a playmate, but the little creatures she encounters fly, swim, or run away from her. She decides to sit on a rock for a while and discovers something magical. Grades K–2.

Isadora, R. (1979). *Ben's trumpet.* New York: Greenwillow. A young boy who wants to be a musician is mentored by a trumpeter from the neighborhood Zig Zag Night Club. This story engages readers while aiding them in making inferences and asking "why" questions about the events. Grades 6–8.

Lawrence, J. (1968). *Harriet and the promised land.* New York: Simon & Schuster. Short verses accompanied by beautiful pictures tell the story of Harriet Tubman who finally discovered a life of freedom from slavery. Grades 6–12.

Leaf, M. (1936). *The story of Ferdinand.* New York: Viking. This is the classic tale of a bull who would rather sit among the flowers than enter a bull ring in Spain. It is a charming story to engage discussions. Grades Pre-K–2.

Macaulay, D. (1985). *Baaa.* Boston: Houghton Mifflin. A flock of sheep remains in a deserted town after the human race has died out. The sheep learn to read and write from watching television and eventually become like humans and build a flourishing civilization. In the end, they make the same mistakes that humans did and disappear as well. Grades 7–12.

Marshall, E. (1985). *Four on the shore.* New York: Dial Books for Young Readers. Lolly, Sam, and Spider try to scare Spider's little brother, Willie, so he'll stop bothering them. They decide to tell Willie scary stories so he'll go away, but Willie ends up telling the best story of all. This is an excellent book to use when teaching about stories within stories. Grades 2–5.

Patterson, F. (1985). *Koko's kitten.* New York: Scholastic. This nonfiction book tells of a gorilla that is taught to communicate by using sign language. Discussions of the characters involved, how the research was developed, and how this research affected others will be rich. Grades 1–5.

Turner, A. (1985). *Dakota dugout.* New York: Macmillan. In short poetic verses, a grandmother shares with her granddaughter what life was like on the Dakota prairie a century ago. Grades 4–6.

Viorst, J. (1978). *Alexander, who used to be rich last Sunday.* New York: Atheneum. This story examines why Alexander only has bus tokens when his brothers have real money. This is a wonderful story to use with inferencing. Grades 2–5.

Wells, R. (1973). *Noisy Nora.* New York: Dial Books for Young Readers. Nora uses naughty ways to get her mother's attention. Grades Pre-K–K.

Yorinks, A. (1986). *Hey, Al.* New York: Farrar, Straus, & Giroux. Al and his dog are unhappy living in a one-room apartment. Then a huge, colorful bird comes to their window and takes them to a beautiful island, but Al realizes that it's not as wonderful as he imagined. Grades 4–5.

Zukman, S., & Edelman, H. (1987). *It's a good thing.* Los Angeles: Price, Stern, & Sloan. In this humorous book, children need to figure out answers to unusual questions such as why it is a good thing giraffes don't need haircuts. Picture clues will help students solve these puzzles. Grades 1–3.

## Professional Resources

Blachowicz, C., & Ogle, D. (2001). *Reading comprehension: Strategies for independent learners.* New York: Guilford. This explanation of how to scaffold student learning through an expansive number of comprehension strategies is clear and comprehensive. Classroom teachers will learn to use the strategies effectively in a comprehensive literacy program.

Bryan, J. (1998). K-W-W-L: Questioning the known. *The Reading Teacher, 51,* 618–619. This short, to-the-point article suggests how to extend the familiar KWL comprehension strategy to help students develop appropriate questions about text. A classroom example illustrates the teacher's thinking process as students are led to respond and consider new relevant and meaningful ideas.

Fountas, I. C., & Pinnell, G. S. (2000). *Guiding readers and writers (grades 3–6): Teaching comprehension, genre, and content literacy.* Portsmouth, NH: Heinemann. This is a companion volume to *Guided Reading* for teachers in the intermediate grades who want to provide effective help for all students. Presenting the basic structure of literacy learning through independent reading, guided reading, and literature study, the authors explain how to enhance reading comprehension and word study by tapping the interrelationship of reading and writing.

Harvey, S., & Goudvis, A. (2000). *Strategies that work: Teaching comprehension to enhance understanding.* Portland, ME: Stenhouse. The authors of this practical and easy-to-read book show K–8 teachers how to model specific comprehension strategies to engage students in active processing. Forty strategy lessons are provided along with suggestions for enhancing comprehension in content areas. Extensive appendices and examples of student work are provided.

Keene, E. O., & Zimmerman, S. (1997). *Mosaic of thought: Teaching comprehension in a reader's workshop.* Portsmouth, NH: Heinemann. The authors take the K–12 classroom teacher on an enjoyable journey into the reader's mind and the individual thought processes that occur as the text unfolds. The tone is informal and relies heavily on real classroom experiences. Its focus is deepening comprehension of literature, activating background knowledge, and valuing personal response.

Marshall, J. C. (2002). *Are they really reading?* Expanding SSR in the middle grades. Portland, ME: Stenhouse. Classroom teachers are guided into making sustained silent reading time instructionally sound and effective. The author gives clear directions on how to plan and implement a meaningful program, build a classroom library, and motivate and scaffold readers, using examples from her own classroom experience.

Miller, D. (2002). *Reading with meaning: Teaching comprehension in the primary grades.* Portland, ME: Stenhouse. This book shows teachers how to motivate and engage readers in classrooms designed to foster both independence and collaboration. Examples from a real classroom demonstrate how to plan and execute explicit instruction, model comprehension strategies, set up book clubs, and encourage children's response to literature.

Sadler, C. R. (2001). *Comprehension strategies for middle-grade learners: A handbook for content area teachers.* Newark, DE: International Reading Association. Teachers of content areas face the educational dilemma of how to help struggling readers comprehend. This book provides practical tools to help students understand their assigned readings and use strategies that promote independent learning.

Serafini, F. (2001). *The reading workshop: Creating space for readers.* Portsmouth, NH: Heinemann. Using a reader's workshop format, Serafini shows teachers how to help children learn to read because they want to read.

Tovani, C. (2000). *I read it, but I don't get it: Comprehension strategies for adolescent readers.* Portland, ME: Stenhouse. This book is as enjoyable to read as it is insightful. Readers are drawn into the minds of adolescent readers who don't comprehend their reading but have learned to "fake it." Teachers will learn how to help students develop comprehension skills that are constructive and reliable, and in the process convey the sole purpose of reading—personal understanding.

Wilhelm, J. D. (2001). *Improving comprehension with think-aloud strategies.* New York: Scholastic. This book is for upper elementary and middle school teachers who want to learn how to model strategic decision making and interpretive processes through think-alouds. The seven chapters provide methods to help students navigate text features and monitor their own comprehension.

Wilson, L. (2002). *Reading to live: How to teach reading for today's world.* Portsmouth, NH: Heinemann. Wilson makes a strong case for preserving integrated, holistic reading programs, debunking one-size-fits-all instruction. She offers easy-to-use strategies that build on the life experiences and language that children bring with them to school.

Worthy, J., & Broaddus, K. (2001/2002). Fluency beyond the primary grades: From group performance to silent, independent reading. *The Reading Teacher, 55,* 334–342. A reader's fluency has tremendous impact on comprehension. This article explores how to teach reading fluency through modeling, explicit instruction, and independent practice on a variety of texts. Performance activities for fostering student interest and engagement, such as reader's theater, poetry read-alouds, and buddy reading, are discussed.

# 9

# Word Study: Word Recognition, Dictionary Skills, and Vocabulary Skills

## Teaching Activities

**1.** *Develop awareness of syllables through clapping.* As students move beyond the early emergent stage of reading, they need to work through longer and more complicated words. Begin only with aural experiences for young children. Involve them in clapping their names, or clapping out the beats of familiar rhymes. Add interest by pounding a drum to mark each syllable. Use the children's name cards; as each name is clapped, sort them into groups according to the number of syllables heard. As readers mature, begin connecting the aural experiences with familiar print. Clap out syllables in words and beats in rhymes, and then show children how the printed words can be divided into syllable parts. This will help students take apart words in reading and writing contexts.

**2.** *Make a name chart.* Word study should begin with children's names. Create a name chart with all of the children's names in the room. This is a highly valuable reference point when talking about letters and sounds and eventually more complex phonics concepts.

**3.** *Use guided and interactive writing.* The teacher is guiding the writing process as the group interacts collaboratively to construct the text. Children participate in representing sounds with letters. For example, the teacher might prompt them as follows: "Say *fun* out loud, slowly. What do you hear first? What letter is this? What do you hear next?"

**4.** *Develop phonemic awareness through "I Spy."* Collect miniature objects. With a small group of children, play "I Spy" by saying, "I spy with my little eye something that begins like *ball.*" Invite the students to guess the correct object from the collection. Continue in the same manner with the rest of the objects. The teacher can vary this game by voicing the object's beginning sound (such as /b/). Other variations include listening for ending sounds, rhyming sounds, or number of syllables.

**5.** *Create personal word banks.* As students build a reading vocabulary, have them write new words on small cards (cut from tagboard or index cards). These words can be drawn from a variety of contexts: special or meaningful words, groups of words from word study lessons, and theme or content area studies. Store these in word banks made by the child from index file boxes or margarine tubs. Use the words for various word sorts or for the child to independently read or share with a buddy during center time. Encourage students to study the patterns in these words: beginning and ending sounds, rhymes, blends and digraphs, vowel sounds, spelling patterns, prefixes and suffixes, and so on.

**6.** *Use magnetic letters.* These letters provide a very effective, hands-on experience in which the students physically manipulate letters to form words. Cookie sheets make small portable surfaces that students can use anywhere in the room. Store the letters in a fishing tackle box, labeled at the back of each opening, so learning time is not spent searching for the appropriate letter.

**7.** *Making words.* In this active, hands-on activity, students manipulate alphabet letters as they are guided through the spelling of a group of words. As they manipulate the letter cards, they review and practice phonics and spelling concepts, discovering sound–letter correspondences and learn to identify spelling patterns in words. This multilevel task can be done with all learners in a classroom. The teacher leads the group through a series of progressively longer words until all of the letter cards are arranged to make the chosen word (teacher-selected from a content area unit or to exemplify a particular spelling pattern). Students can review this throughout the week as they repeat the lesson in a center.

**8.** *Begin with morning message.* Skill and strategy instruction can be temporarily isolated and then taken back into meaningful written contexts.

- Prior to students' arrival, the teacher composes a message for a "what can you show us" activity. The students attempt to read the message upon arrival, taking the message apart by focusing on what they know. Students individually volunteer to show something they know about the displayed piece of text including letters, clusters, words, sound–letter correspondences, spelling patterns, punctuation, and text features.

- The teacher composes the message and incorporates problems such as errors in punctuation, capitalization, spelling, grammar, or sentence structure. The students work together or individually to edit the message.
- The teacher asks children to share experiences in a morning meeting and then chooses one message to write. The students participate in determining letter–sound associations. The teacher thinks aloud while writing, thus modeling the process proficient writers use to compose text.

**9.** *Create alternative word lists.* Expand students' vocabulary through the exploration of multiple words with similar meanings. Display a sentence on a chart that includes a common, overused word, such as "He said that he didn't want to go." Start a collaborative list of related words that could be used as alternatives, and have students continuously add to it (*stated, replied, suggested . . .*).

**10.** *Make a vocabulary wall.* Identify a few interesting words from read-alouds, and post them on a chart. Encourage students to be on the alert for the selected words in reading, writing, and talking contexts. Each time one comes up, they bring it to one another's attention and put a tally mark by the word. The students start looking for and listening for these words everywhere and attempt to use them! (Adapted from Taberski, 2000.)

## Children's Literature Selections

Allen, P. (1982). *Who sank the boat?* New York: Coward McCann. Readers must make predictions about how a boat sank as a cow, donkey, sheep, pig, and mouse get into a rowboat. Grades 1–5.

Babbitt, N. (1974). *The search for delicious.* New York: Farrar, Strauss, & Giroux. An intense argument develops between a king, queen, and their court over the meaning of *delicious.* The adopted son of the Prime Minister is instructed to poll the kingdom to determine the true meaning. Grades 3–7.

Brown, M. (1996). *Arthur's reading race.* Boston: Little, Brown. Arthur believes he can get out of buying his younger sister an ice cream cone by challenging her to read ten words. To his surprise, she quickly reads signs and wins her cone. Grades K–2.

Brown, M. (1980). *Pickle things.* New York: Parents Magazine Press. This rhyming book describes things that can be pickled. A sample of the text is "A pickle ear, a pickle nose, pickle hair, and pickle toes." Children can create their own pickle rhymes and other variations of expressive words. Grades 1–5.

Burchers, S. (1998). *Vocabulary cartoons: Word power made easy.* Punta Gorda, FL: New Monic Books. With cartoon memory aids, words are presented in a humorous and clever manner to increase children's vocabulary. This is an excellent extension to help children build their vocabularies in their daily lives. Grades K–4.

DeGross, M. (1987). *Donavan's word jar.* New York: HarperCollins. When a boy collects printed words that he can read in a glass jar, he discovers that his jar is full and he is faced with a dilemma. When Donavan's grandmother visits, they find a solution. Grades 2–5.

Duncans, P., & Edwards, D. (1999). *The wacky wedding.* New York: Hyperion. This inventive alphabet book begins with two ants about to marry. Each page has words beginning with the same letter, which makes the text lively and fun. Grades 4–7.

Elting, M., & Folsom, M. (1980). *Q is for Duck.* Boston: Houghton Mifflin. This book is filled with amusing riddles for readers to answer regarding the alphabet. Readers must use their prior knowledge to discover the correct response. Grades Pre-K–2.

Frasier, D. (2000). *Miss Alaineus: A vocabulary disaster.* San Diego: Harcourt Brace Jovanovich. Sage mishears or misunderstands one of her vocabulary words and the mistake leads to a potential disaster at school. Teachers will find this is an excellent story that aids vocabulary development. Grades K–6.

Hunt, B. K. (1976). *The whatchamacallit book.* New York: Putnam. Readers are presented with silly riddles such as "Whachamalcallits you might see on a trip," ". . . the feelers of insects," and ". . . the roller in a typewriter" to answer in this humorous book of definitions. Grades 2–5.

Hutchins, P. (1974). *The wind blew.* New York: Puffin Books. The wind blows away the townspeople's belongings, creating chaos. Readers learn to recognize past tense verbs such as blew, grabbed, lifted, tossed, and whirled. Grades pre-K–2.

Pomerantz, C. (1974). *The piggy in the puddle.* New York: Macmillan. The predictable text in this story is a nonsense tongue twister about a "piggy in the middle of a puddle" and how his family tries to get him out. Young readers enjoy playing with language in this wonderful picture book. Grades Pre-K–1.

Scarry, R. (1976). *Richard Scarry's best picture dictionary ever.* New York: Golden Books. This dictionary has more than 2,500 words that children will have fun learning, with characters such as Squigley Worm and Hilda Hippo. Grades K–3.

Sendak, M. (1962). *Alligators all around.* New York: Harper & Row. Alligators do silly things in this unusual alphabet book, which helps children learn to read verbs in predictable sentences. Grades 1–2.

Seuss, Dr. (1998). *I am not going to read any words today!* Learn about rhyming letters. New York: Random House. Word recognition skills are reinforced as children read and rhyme their way through this wonderful book on words. Grades Pre-K–2.

Shaw, N. (1997). *Sheep in a shop.* Boston: Houghton Mifflin. Sheep search for a birthday gift but cause chaos instead. Rhyming and alliteration enhance awareness for young readers. Grades Pre-K–2.

Stock, C. (1988). *Alexander's midnight snack: A little elephant's ABC.* Boston: Houghton Mifflin. When an elephant awakes, he encounters a variety of foods. The alphabet is highlighted in varying parts of speech. Grades K–3.

Terban, M. (1981). *Mad as a wet hen.* Boston: Houghton Mifflin. Children will love these playful idioms while learning how language can describe feelings and situations. Grades 5–8.

Terban, M. (1991). *Superdupers: Really funny words.* Boston: Houghton Mifflin. One hundred nonsense words that exist in the English language are listed in this humorous and colorful book for older readers. Unusual words such as hobnob, tutti frutti, and rah rah are grouped by similarities and given definitions. Grades 6–12.

Wildsmith, B. (1978). *What the moon saw.* New York: Oxford University Press. The concept of opposites, including *many/few, heavy/light,* and *patterned/ plain,* is presented in this one-sentence text. Grades 1–2.

## Professional Resources

Allen, J. (1999). *Words, words, words: Teaching vocabulary in grades 4–12.* Portland, ME: Stenhouse. This book offers teachers practical, research-based information on how to make word study an important part of their literacy program. Detailed strategy lessons include building concept knowledge, using word and structural analysis, and studying words to enhance reading comprehension. Its tone is down to earth and easy to relate to.

Blevins, W. (2001). *Teaching phonics and word study in the intermediate grades: A complete source book.* New York: Scholastic. In this helpful reference for teachers in grades 3–8, strategies that involve structural analysis, critical reading, and complex spelling patterns are addressed to encourage students to gain insight into automatic word recognition and reading fluency.

Cramer, R. L. (1998). *The spelling connection: Integrating reading, writing, and spelling instruction.* New York: Guilford. This book shows teachers how to strategically incorporate reading, writing, and spelling instruction within the larger context of language arts. It uses case studies to illustrate the stages of spelling, leading to effective teaching strategies. In addition, it shows readers how to assess authentic spelling achievement.

Cunningham, P. M., & Hall, D. P. (1994). *Making big words.* Torrance, CA: Good Apple. In this companion book to *Making Words* for older children (grades 3–6), the step-by-step lessons encourage student discovery of letter patterns and strengthen spelling skills.

Cunningham, P. M., & Hall, D. P. (1994). *Making words.* Torrance, CA: Good Apple. This activity book for primary teachers offers hands-on, sequential spelling and phonics lessons for young children as they work with letters and their various combinations. During the 15-minute lessons, students manipulate letters to make words and learn about letter–sound relationships and spelling patterns. Warm-up lessons are included, along with oral directions and scaffolds.

Fountas, I. C., & Pinnell, G. S. (Eds.). (1999). *Voices on word matters: Learning about phonics and spelling in the literacy classroom.* Portsmouth, NH: Heinemann. This sequel to *Word Matters: Teaching phonics and Spelling in the Reading/Writing Classroom* presents a rich collection of word study instruction. The authors of the essays help children explore letter and word learning in a variety of contexts. Articles also address detailed observations of young readers, analyze classroom processes, and provide samples of student work.

Gunning, T. G. (2001). *Building words: A resource manual for teaching word analysis and spelling strategies.* Boston: Allyn & Bacon. This manual gives an overview of word analysis and effective strategies to apply. Its hands-on, practical approach offers a variety of tools and techniques for teachers to build independence and confidence in analyzing words.

Johnson, D. D. (2001). *Vocabulary in the elementary and middle school.* Boston: Allyn & Bacon. With its clear description of vocabulary instruction and the classroom teacher's role, this is a good resource to have on hand for examples, classroom applications, and aspects of the study of words.

Pinnell, G. S., & Fountas, I. C. (1998). *Word matters: Teaching phonics and spelling in the reading/writing classroom.* Portsmouth, NH: Heinemann. In a companion volume to *Guided Reading,* the authors present teachers with a variety of activities for a systematic literacy program to help young children learn about letter-sound relationships and words. Emphasis is on meaningful utilization and enjoyment.

Rasinski, T. V., Padak, N. D, Church, B. W., Fawcett, G., Hendershot, J., Henry, J. M., Moss, B. G., Peck, J. K., Pryor, E., & Roskos, K. A. (Eds.). (2000). *Teaching word recognition, spelling, and vocabulary: Strategies from* The Reading Teacher. Newark, DE: The International Reading Association. Teachers will appreciate this collection of 17 articles from *The Reading Teacher* that share ideas for helping students learn about words. Topics include phonemic awareness, psycholinguistics, spelling development, scaffolding, and more.

Rosencrans, G. (1998). *The spelling book: Teaching children how to spell, not what to spell.* Newark, DE: The International Reading Association. This book is geared toward intermediate grade teachers, outlining a methodology that combines whole language principles with phonetic strategies. Lessons and activities are easy to adapt to existing programs. Student independence is stressed.

Rupley, W. H., Logan, J. W., & Nichols, W. D. (1998/1999). Vocabulary instruction in a balanced reading program. *The Reading Teacher, 52,* 336–346. Teacher-directed vocabulary instruction that is built on student background knowledge is an important part of a successful reading program. The authors explore its role in reading development and offer suggestions for student motivation through classroom-tested approaches.

Taberski, S. (2000). *On solid ground: Strategies for teaching reading, K–3.* Portsmouth, NH: Heinemann. This well-written book covers areas critical to teaching beginning literacy, such as how to conduct guided reading sessions, how to develop vocabulary skills, and how to assess progress.

Towell, J. (1997/1998). Fun with vocabulary. *The Reading Teacher, 51,* 356–358. This article describes ten classroom tested strategies and activities that motivate and engage students in active vocabulary instruction. Teachers will appreciate the clear descriptions, directions, and practical suggestions.

# 10   The Writing Process in a Workshop Environment

## Teaching Activities

**1.** *Emphasize writing leads.* A lead is the opening sentence of a piece of writing. Leads are especially important in newspaper writing and stories. A lead is intended to "hook" the interest of the reader and keep the reader reading. Ask students to choose three stories or books and read the opening sentence. Which opening sentence did they like best? Why? Then have individuals write three or four leads to a story they want to write or rewrite the lead sentence in a story already written.

**2.** *Explain that stories do not have to be told in words.* Cave dwellers wrote with pictures. Cave writings are stories about hunting, seeking food, and daily living. Have students draw a series of pictures that tell a story—one made up by the student or a retelling of a story from a book or movie, such as *Frankenstein's Monster, The Bride of Frankenstein, Star Wars, E. T., Home Alone, Cinderella,* or *The Three Little Pigs.* After drawing, have children tell their picture stories to their classmates.

**3.** *Tell tall tales.* Mountain men loved to tell exaggerated accounts of their deeds—tall tales, as they sometimes called them. Many of these men would have made good members of a "liar's club." Have students pretend to be members of a "liar's club," getting ready for the annual meeting. Have them write an elaborate, entertaining whopper. Prepare children for this activity by reading tall tales to them.

**4.** *Choose precise words.* Precise words improve writing. Have students look for imprecise words, such as *stuff* and *things,* in a recent piece of writing. Challenge them to replace such words with more precise ones. For example, "*All kinds of stuff* sat on the garage shelves" is greatly improved by using specific words and details: "Paint and cans, bolts and nails, jars and rope sat on the garage shelves."

**5.** *Feedback for student writing.* Writing is personal, so when giving feedback to students about their writing, be careful what you say and how you say it. For instance, if a child's story is confusing, you might

be tempted to say, "I don't get it." More neutral comments work better. For instance, try using generic questions and comments, such as "I wonder . . . ," "I notice . . . ," "Can you tell me more about . . . ". Such questions and comments signal the writer that something needs further consideration and that you are interested in what that something might be. Further, such questions and comments are likely to get an oral response from the writer, which can provide an opportunity for you to make a positive suggestion.

**6.** *Build a writers' library.* Look around the room. Undoubtedly, there are books lying here and there. Are any written by someone you know? Perhaps not. You can change that quickly. Start a class project that will make the writing done in your classroom available to everyone. Make bound books, and start a class library featuring writing produced in your classroom.

**7.** *Teach students how to conduct peer conferences for editing and revision.* An important part of the writing process is editing. After students have completed some self-editing, have them do peer editing before conferencing with the teacher. Minilessons on revising and editing will be necessary, as well as lessons on how to constructively share conferences with one another.

**8.** *Invite authors to share their writing process with your students.* Meeting a published author or illustrator is a powerful experience. Consider inviting one to your school to share how he or she writes and publishes his or her work. Often authors have slide or video presentations showing the steps they go through in their own writing process. This is an unforgettable experience for students and teachers alike!

**9.** *Pay close attention to the prewriting stage.* Very often students struggle with the composition aspect of writing. They just can't seem to formulate their thoughts or even choose a topic for their writing! Engaging students in whole group, small group, or partner discussions prior to the writing task will help them explore ideas before dealing with the mechanics of writing. If students seem reluctant to begin writing, take a good long look at the prewriting experiences you are offering the students. Make sure this time is filled with kid talk, rather than teacher talk!

**10.** *Have quarterly publishing parties.* Celebrate children's work as writers. Provide each child the opportunity to read aloud his or her published piece to an audience. Celebrate writing by inviting parents to an authors' tea. An invitation to a book celebration such as this communicates a powerful message to family members: we not only value writing, we celebrate it! This enables them to see and listen to their child as an author.

## Children's Literature Selections

Anno, M. (1977). *Anno's journey.* New York: Philomel Books. A journey through northern Europe is detailed through illustrations in this wordless book. Children can attempt to guess the countries on each page as well as write stories to accompany each scene. Grades 4–6.

Banyai, I. (1995). *Zoom.* New York: Viking. This is an intriguing wordless book that begins with a close-up of a rooster's comb and pulls back, like a camera, farther and farther until viewers are in outer space, looking at the dot of light that is Earth. The book provides a concrete example to use when discussing the importance of point of view and detail in writing. Grades K–12.

Brown, M. W. (1949). *The important book.* New York: Harper & Row. This book helps children use their senses to describe words. Its pattern format allows children to think of various ways to describe things and then bring the main point back into focus. Grades Pre-K–1.

Brown, R. (1981). *A dark dark tale.* New York: Dial Books for Young Readers. Using sequencing, prepositions, and adjectives, this spooky story takes the reader through a house with great anticipation. Grades 1–3.

Bunting, E. (1994). *The night tree.* San Diego: Harcourt Brace Jovanovich. A family decorates a tree in the forest in this excellent example of rich, descriptive language. Grades K–3.

DeJong, M. (1953). *Hurry home, Candy.* New York: Harper. This moving story is about the life of a dog from birth to adulthood. It describes the people it encounters, as well as the love and fear it experiences as it searches for a home. Grades 2–6.

Eckert, A. W. (1971). *Incident at Hawk's Hill.* New York: Little, Brown. A young boy is adopted by a badger, very much reflecting Mowgli's experience in *The Jungle Book.* Eventually this wild child is captured. Grades 6–12.

Johnson, C. (1955). *Harold and the purple crayon.* New York: HarperCollins. Harold and his magical purple crayon go for a walk, which leads him from nature, to a hot-air balloon ride, and into a big city. All Harold wants to do is find his home again, and finally he realizes he has the answer in his hands. Grades K–3.

Kraus, R. (1952). *A hole is to dig.* New York: Harper & Row. This book has a strong influence on children as the author allows them to think of their own meanings for words. This is an excellent book to generate original definitions for classroom words. Grades Pre-K–1.

Lobel, A. (1980). *Fables.* New York: Harper & Row. This excellent book consists of short fables such as "The Camel Dances" and "The Ostrich in Love." Hidden morals can be used to teach the art of excellent storytelling. Grades 2–5.

Mayer, M. (1974). *The great cat chase.* New York: Four Winds Press. In this wordless story three children try to capture their cat. This never-ending chase allows children to predict what will happen and to create sentences of their own. Grades Pre-K–1.

McDermott, G. (1980). *Sunflight.* New York: Four Winds Press. This is a retelling of the Greek myth about Daedalus and his son, Icarus. The two escape King Minos and create wings from wax. Icarus doesn't listen to his father's warning and flies too close to the sun. Grades 3–5.

Moss, M. (1995). *Amelia's notebook.* Middleton, WI: Pleasant Company. Nine-year-old Amelia writes and draws all over the pages of her journal as she captures feelings, thoughts, and questions in the haphazard fashion of a true writing journal. Grades 3–5.

Moss, M. (1999). *Amelia writes again.* Middleton, WI: Pleasant Company. Amelia begins a second journal after her first one is filled. Like its predecessor, this book strongly demonstrates the real purpose of a writer's notebook—to capture impressions of the world as they occur to the writer. This is not always easy to demonstrate to young writers, and Amelia does it beautifully. Grades 3–5.

Murphy, R. (1964). *The pond*. New York: Dutton. This moving novel is about the history of suburban and urban life in America in 1917. A young boy realizes the good and evil in life. Grades 6–12.

O'Dell, S. (1980). *Sarah Bishop*. Boston: Houghton Mifflin. This novel is based on an actual incident during the outbreak of the Revolutionary War. A young girl flees Long Island after her brother and father are killed. She begins her new life in a cave in the wilderness. Grades 5–12.

O'Neill, M. (1989). *Hailstones and halibut bones: Adventures in color*. New York: Philomel. A well-loved collection of color poems that begs for children to write their own takeoffs. They can then return to the book to appreciate the craft that lies behind each poem. Grades K–12.

Pinkwater, D. M. (1977). *The big orange splot*. New York: Scholastic. A neighborhood is disrupted by Mr. Plumbean's decision to paint his house to represent the colors of his dreams. This is a wonderful story to teach story elements. Grades 2–4.

Sams, C. R., & Stoick, J. (2000). *Stranger in the woods*. Milford, MI: Friesens of Altona. The beautiful photographs convey the fright and curiosity of animals in a forest when they spy a strange new occupant. The imagination used in this story provides a wonderful example of how images can create a story. Grades K–3.

Stearns, P. (1976). *Into the painted bear lair*. Boston: Houghton Mifflin. This is a very imaginative story of a boy who enters another world and cannot find his way back to the toy store where this transformation occurred. A female knight and a ferocious bear help the boy discover how choices can lead to happiness. Grades 3–6.

Van Allsburg, C. (1984). *The mysteries of Harris Burdick*. Boston: Houghton Mifflin. This book presents drawings with their own titles and captions. Some of the pictures are eerie and others may bring a smile. An excellent book to prompt creative writing to accompany the pictures. Grades 4–9.

# Professional Resources

Bullock, R. (Ed.). (1998). *Why workshop? Changing course in 7–12 English*. Portland, ME: Stenhouse. Classroom teachers wrote the nine essays in this book, which examine how to make the philosophies and elements of literacy workshops work. Its methods and strategies give a clear overview of successful elements and what to avoid.

Calkins, L. M. (1994). *The art of teaching writing* (new ed.). Portsmouth, NH: Heinemann. Teaching writing is a complex task with many nuances. This comprehensive book looks at the writing workshop as the foundation of language arts education. The author draws upon the latest research and her own reflections to address the writing process.

Dorn, L. J., & Soffos, C. (2001). *Scaffolding young writers: A writer's workshop approach*. Portland, ME: Stenhouse. Students need the guidance and perception of someone more knowledgeable to lead them into new learning, building on existing background knowledge or understanding. This book shows teachers how to provide clear and purposeful scaffolds, which foster independent learners.

Edwards, S. A., Maloy, R. W., & Verock-O'Loughlin, R. E. (2003). *Ways of writing with young kids: Teaching creativity and conventions unconventionally*. Boston: Allyn & Bacon. This book shows how to help young children (K–3) explore the power of writing and express their thoughts in many genres and styles. The authors use "The Five C's of Children's Writing" system to motivate, instruct, and support: coaching, creativity, conventions, choice, and confidence. Ideas are adaptable and encourage teachers to be inventive.

Glazer, S. M. (2001). *Teaching all children to write: A little comprehensive guide*. Norwood, MA: Christopher-Gordon. Teachers of young children (K–3) will appreciate the opportunities to learn about themselves as teachers and learners when they read this guide to providing children with quality writing experiences. Some chapters include information on dialogue and literature journals, recording content information, and writing as a developmental process.

Gillet, J. W., & Beverly, L. (2001). *Directing the writing workshop: An elementary teacher's handbook*. New York: Guilford. This practical and comprehensive book shows teachers how to guide students through the many stages of writing development. Mini-lessons and guidelines are provided, along with helpful appendices.

Goldstein, J. M., & Johnson, B. (2002). *Voices and values: A reader for writers*. West Berlin, NJ: Townsend Press. This book for high school teachers consists of a collection of 40 essays that celebrate human values. It contains a wide range of writing assignments that encourage personal response on an emotional level. Attention is given to vocabulary and using the writing process.

Johnson, P. (1990). *A book of one's own: Developing literacy through making books*. Portsmouth, NH: Heinemann. This book gives detailed directions for student-made books. Teachers will learn how children explore story meaning and how to open the doors of their imaginations by creating books that reflect their ideas. Many illustrations are provided.

Lensmire, T. J. (1994). *When children write: Critical revisions of the writing workshop*. New York: Teachers College Press. The author details the changes he feels must be made in many writing workshops in order to meet the demands and needs of the child writer.

Madigan, D., & Koivu-Rybicki, V. T. (1997). *The writing lives of children*. Portland, ME: Stenhouse. How children approach writing is as varied as the individuals themselves, and teachers can guide them to express their unique voices. This book, the result of a study of third- and fourth-grade writers in an inner-city school, is composed of essays about ten individual children who learn to speak for themselves in writing as they learn about their worlds.

McCarrier, A., Pinnell, G. S., & Fountas, I. C. (2000). *Interactive writing: How language and literacy come together, K–2*. Portsmouth, NH: Heinemann. The authors discuss in detail the components of interactive writing with the young child as they learn how to communicate their thoughts, explore letter–sound relationships, and grasp the role of spacing and other conventions. It discusses how young writers engage in the writing process and explore its many features to convey meaning.

New Zealand Staff Ministry of Education. (1992). *Dancing with the pen: The learner as a writer*. Wellington, New Zealand: Learning Media (distributed in the U.S. by Pacific Learning). This book describes teachers' beliefs about literacy and the writing process. It outlines how to immerse young children in written language, encourage approximations, and engage children on a level that is personal and relevant to them.

Parsons, L. (2001). *Revising and editing: Using models and checklists to promote successful writing experiences*. Portland, ME: Stenhouse. This book addresses the two distinct practices of revising and editing. By exploring their principles and goals, the author clarifies how to help students rethink the writing process to achieve their desired outcome. Other topics include evaluation, writing in the computer age, student and peer-led conferences, and parent involvement. Student samples are provided.

Smith, F. (1994). *Writing and the writer* (2nd ed.). Hillsdale, NJ: Erlbaum. This book explores the relationship between the writer and what happens psychologically during the writing process. Filled with thought-provoking theory, it provides in-depth understanding of language, the writing process, and how the human brain perceives new learning.

Spandel, V. (2001). *Creating writers through 6-trait writing assessment and instruction* (3rd ed.). New York: Longman. The author argues that timely assessment of writing by teacher and student will lead to increased revision and higher quality writing. Discussion uses the 6-trait writing model for narrative and expository writing: ideas, organization, voice, word choice, sentence fluency, and conventions.

Willis, M. S. (1993). *Deep revision: A guide for teachers, students, and other writers*. New York: Teachers and Writers Collaborative. This book treats revision as a natural, enjoyable process that can be viewed from many perspectives. A large number of specific, inventive revision exercises will broaden the writer's views on improving a written work and the learning experience as a whole.

# 11 Poetry for Children

## Teaching Activities

**1.** *Use simple poems and finger rhymes as part of the shared reading experience.* Early elementary classrooms often use big books for shared reading experiences. Consider charting simple poems, songs, and finger-plays for shared reading experiences as well. Collect these over the course of the year, and encourage students to revisit them during literacy center time.

**2.** *Create a poetry center.* If you use literacy centers in your classroom, be sure to set aside space to develop a poetry center. For emergent readers, post a sentence-strip pocket chart to house the shared reading poem for the week. Every day revisit the poem as a shared reading experience, exploring the various concepts about print children need to learn. Use the poem for word study, highlighting features such as rhyme, patterns, and high-frequency words. During center time, students can match words or sentence strips into the pockets, or take the poem apart and resequence it. Students can also have a typed copy of the poem to glue into their own poetry notebook and then illustrate the poem at the poetry center.

**3.** *Model poetry writing for and with students.* Writing poetry can be intimidating for many students. To help them get a feel for it, as well as the process a poet experiences, do modeled or shared writing every time you ask students to write poetry. This is not a teaching practice reserved for lower elementary grades. It is very effective all the way through high school, not only helping students to be successful writers but also helping teachers better understand and appreciate the difficulties and joys of what we ask students to do when writing.

**4.** *Collect inspiring poetry topics.* Ideas for poems are all around us! Encourage students to keep a list of poetry topics in their writing notebook as ideas come to mind when they are looking and listening. Other suggestions to gather topic ideas include the following:

- Ideas from memories
- Ideas from an observation stroll

- A poetry suitcase filled with stuff (crazy stuff, cute stuff like a stuffed animal, everyday stuff like a pair of sunglasses or glove) to peruse, which might trigger a memory or inspire a thought.

(Adapted from Janeczko, 1999.)

**5.** *Publish a poetry anthology.* Student poems can be published by typing them and having the students illustrate them; then photocopy and bind them into a booklet for each individual child or as a classroom anthology. The student's best work can be self-selected for a general anthology. Theme-based or topic-focused anthologies also work well. These student anthologies will be influential in encouraging young poets.

**6.** *Hold an annual poetry reading.* Introduce a wide variety of poetry for children to read. Provide opportunities for children to write in varied poetic forms. Choose pieces to publish. Create a class poetry anthology. Invite parents for a poetry reading, letting the students choose a piece they want to read.

**7.** *Do a study of song lyrics as poetry.* Many songs consist of both wonderful music and inspired, humorous, or thought-provoking lyrics. Lyrics often take the form of poetry and offer students a way to connect to the poetic form. Ask students to bring in examples of song lyrics to share with the class. Be sure to include examples that cross musical genres.

**8.** *Read students picture books with illustrated poems to connect imagery to words.* There are many examples of beautiful picture books in which an illustrator has taken a single poem and illustrated each line to create a collection of images evoked by the poem. These books are a wonderful way for students to develop their own ability to visualize while reading and to create images in their own writing.

**9.** *Have students create their own illustrated poem in book form.* After exploring picture books that illustrate individual poems, have students choose a poem with strong visual images and create their own illustrated picture book. If they have a lot of experience writing poetry, perhaps they can choose from their own collection. Consider displaying these books in the school library or sharing them with lower elementary students.

**10.** *Introduce literature discussion groups with poetry.* Select poetry that can be read in a single sitting; however, be sure it is rich enough to sustain a meaningful discussion. Students read the same poem and then convene to share their own interpretations, thoughts, and reactions. Read the poem together. Discuss various images created in the students' minds during reading. You can use an overhead transparency to locate particularly powerful parts for evoking these images and discuss vocabulary that may impede understanding.

# Children's Literature Selections

Carle, E. (1989). *Animals, animals.* New York: Philomel. Here is an exuberant collection of poems about animals. Grades K–2.

Cole, W. (1978). *Oh such foolishness.* New York: Lippincott. Cole has collected 57 poems of all kinds. Readers will find a range of humorous to spooky passages in this book. Grades 1–6.

Fisher, A. (1980). *Out in the dark and daylight.* New York: Harper. Poems of nature and animals are related to the childhood experience in these 140 poems. Arranged by seasons and holidays so the reader captures the sense of time and change. Grades Pre-K–5.

Fleischman, P. (1985). *I am phoenix: Poems for two voices.* New York: Harper & Row. These beautiful poems are to be read simultaneously by two people or groups, creating a harmonic sound. Grades 5–12.

Fleischman, P. (1988). *Joyful noise: Poems for two voices.* New York: Harper & Row. Like *I am phoenix,* these insect poems should be read by two people or groups simultaneously. Grades 5–12.

Greenfield, E. (1978). *Honey, I love.* New York: Crowell. Children will love these 16 short poems about friends, family, music, treasures, and even their mothers' clothes. Grades Pre-K–3.

Hoberman, M. A. (1978). *A house is a house for me.* New York: Viking. This imaginative rhyming book uses metaphors as it describes various houses in the world, such as "a rose is a house for a smell" or "cartons are houses for crackers." An excellent resource for teaching descriptive poetry. Grades Pre-K–6.

Holman, F. (1976). *At the top of my voice.* New York: Scribner. Childhood is examined in these 18 poems as wonders, fears, triumphs, and disasters are rhymed in a witty and meaningful fashion. Grades K–6.

Jacobs, L. B. (1967). *Is somewhere always far away?* New York: Holt. A collection of 41 short poems touching on living in the city or country. Grades Pre-K–4.

Lindgreen, B. (1981). *The wild baby.* New York: Greenwillow. This is a rhyming story of a naughty and mischievous child; yet his mother's love for him never lessens. It is adapted from the Swedish by American poet Jack Prelutsky. Grades K–2.

Lobel, A. (1985). *Whiskers and rhymes.* New York: Greenwillow Books. This wonderful series of poems allows children to play with language and rhyme with everyday words. Grades 1–4.

McMillan, B. (1990). *One sun.* New York: Scholastic. Beginning poetic patterns are presented in this photographic book for young readers. The word rhymes focus on objects on a beach, such as "tan man" and "snail pail." Grades Pre-K–2.

O'Neill, M. (1966). *Hailstones and halibut bones.* New York: Doubleday. Children can think of their own identities when reading this classic book of poems about colors. Common objects are seen in their true colors. Grades 3–5.

Prelutsky, J. (1976). *Nightmares: Poems to trouble your sleep.* New York: Greenwillow. Children will be drawn to these creepy poems about bogeymen, trolls, and vampires and amused by their silliness as well. Grades 4–8.

Prelutsky, J. (1986). *Read aloud rhymes for the very young.* New York: Knopf. More than 200 poems are written to appeal to young children. The book is structured by a child's daily activities such as waking up, getting dressed, playing outside, going to the zoo, and then bedtime rituals. Grades Pre-K–2.

Silverstein, S. (1981). *A light in the attic.* New York: Harper Row. A classic treasury of humorous poems by a beloved children's poet. Grades K–8.

Stepanek, M. (2001). *Journey through heartsongs.* New York: Hyperion. Mattie Stepanek has muscular dystrophy; he has been writing poetry since he was 3 years old. In this book of poetry he writes of fears, life and death, and the loss of loved ones. He also inspires with poetry of hope and joy. Grades 5–12.

Untermeyer, L. (1959). *The golden treasury of poetry.* New York: Golden Books. This is an extraordinary collection of 379 poems written by the world's most highly regarded poets. Many styles are presented to share and to help teach the elements of poetry. Grades Pre-K–12.

Van Laan, N. (1996). *Mouse is in my house.* New York: Hyperion. A house seems to be taken over by an assortment of animals. In the end of the story, it is revealed that the event was all in the boy's imagi-

nation. This rhyming chant will appeal to young children. Grades Pre-K–2.

Viorst, J. (1981). *If I were in charge of the world and other worries.* New York: Atheneum. Humor and an introspective voice allow readers young and old to identify with themselves and others a little better. Grades 3–adult.

## Professional Resources

Calkins, L. M. (2000). *The art of teaching reading.* New York: Longman. Among many other topics, this text examines how reading aloud to children helps them become proficient, interested readers who want to know more.

Cullinan, B. E., Scala, M. C., & Schroeder, V. C. (1995). *Three voices: An invitation to poetry across the curriculum.* Portland, ME: Stenhouse. This informative and insightful book shares how to motivate children to read and write poetry across the day's curriculum. Proven teaching strategies are provided, along with hundreds of specific teaching ideas. Teachers will appreciate the descriptions of poetry forms, checklist for choosing poems, and learning extensions for their classrooms.

Flynn, N., & McPhillips, S. (2000). *A note slipped under the door: Teaching from poems we love.* Portland, ME: Stenhouse. This book shows how to make poetry an integral part of elementary and middle school classrooms. Students are led by inquiry through the stages of writing poetry, with glimpses into writer's workshops for specific elements to inform instruction. Teachers will learn from the inspirations of some popular poets and student writing samples.

Hadaway, N. L., Vardell, S. M., & Young, T. A. (2001). Scaffolding oral language development through poetry for students learning English. *The Reading Teacher, 54,* 796–806. This article discusses the importance of providing opportunities for listening and talking, particularly for ESL students. By sharing and responding to poetry's unique qualities, students can actively engage their oral language skills while enjoying the emotional connections.

Heard, G. (1998). *Awakening the heart: Exploring poetry in elementary and middle school.* Portsmouth, NH: Heinemann. This creative handbook discusses the joy and power of sharing poetry with children.

It provides teachers with useful tools and examples for creating writing environments children feel safe in, enabling them to express their inner selves. Emphasis is on transitioning from reading to producing poetry.

Janeczko, P. B. (1999). *Favorite poetry lessons (Grades 4–8).* New York: Scholastic. This book shows how to immerse your middle grade students in a learning environment that honors poetry and its reflections of the world. It describes how to begin creating a poetry-friendly classroom, in which the teacher explores reading and writing poetry along with the students.

Koch, K. (1994). *Rose, where did you get that red?* Teaching great poetry to children. Vancouver, WA: Vintage. This book is both an anthology and instructor's guide, providing a framework for inspiring children to record their thoughts on paper with both thoughtfulness and abandon. (Originally published in 1973.)

Perfect, K. A. (1999). Rhyme and reason: Poetry for the heart and head. *The Reading Teacher, 52,* 728–737. This article is for teachers who love poetry and realize it is a powerful tool in a literacy program. By immersing children in poems in an environment that is accepting and safe, children will want to explore writing and become part of a shared community of poets.

Routman, R. (2000). *Kids' poems: Teaching first graders to love writing poetry.* New York: Scholastic. Written to inspire classroom teachers, part one of this delightful book describes the joy and simplicity of teaching poetry to children. Part two is a collection of poems, shown in the original and final forms, by real first-graders who learned to trust their inner voices and write with confidence. There are similar books for subsequent grades.

# 12

# The Mechanics of Writing: Grammar, Punctuation, Capitalization, and Handwriting

## Teaching Activities

**1.** *Use body percussion to signal punctuation in shared reading experiences.* Often, big book stories and other shared reading texts are read several times over the course of a week, and various aspects of the text are highlighted. One way to help emergent readers "see" punctuation is to assign a sound to each mark. For example, periods are represented with a clap, question marks with a slap on the legs, and commas with finger snaps. As you chorally read a piece, have the students produce this body percussion as punctuation appears in the text.

**2.** *Teach older children the fine art of calligraphy for publishing special pieces.* Many brands of felt-tipped calligraphy pens are available for purchase. These pens usually contain basic directions on how to write in different calligraphy styles. This kind of writing for the purpose of publishing can be an incentive to improve handwriting as well as exposing students to another art form.

**3.** *Read Ruth Heller's wonderful collection of picture grammar books.* This author–illustrator has published several picture books demonstrating a particular part of speech. These are written to capture the interest of students from kindergarten through high school. Each of these beautifully illustrated books can serve as a springboard for the study of a particular part of speech, as well as an example of how really wonderful the English language can be!

**4.** *Teach students to edit and revise for one aspect of their writing at a time.* Teach students that revision is about clarifying meaning in their writing. This is where word choice, embellishment, reduction, and sequencing come into play. Connect lessons about grammar to the very real task of revising a student's own writing. After revision comes editing. Teach students that this process cleans up a piece of writing so that others can read it without impediment. Editing is the polishing of punctuation, spelling, and, sometimes, handwriting. Because the process of revision and editing can seem overwhelming, teach students to revise and edit for one thing at a time.

**5.** *Demonstrate functional grammar.* Using shared reading of familiar text, cover some of the words (for example, *sand,* a noun; *crayon,* a noun; *her,* a pronoun; *furiously,* an adverb; *jump,* a verb). For each covered word, the children suggest substitutes that would still make sense. Reread the whole sentence with the substitute word, and verify if it still makes sense. This provides an opportunity for students to demonstrate understanding and discuss functional grammar, even though they may not know the terminology.

**6.** *Create big book innovations.* Based on a familiar big book, use a similar structure that mirrors the original big book text. For instance, *Brown Bear, Brown Bear, What Do You See?* by Bill Martin Jr. has a repeated pattern with only minor changes in the wording as you move from page to page. Innovations on Martin's repetitive pattern would be: (1) *Second-Graders, Second-Graders, What Do You Hear?* (2) *Alligator, Alligator, What Do You Eat?* (3) *Mama, Mama, Where Are You Going?* It is best to write your big book first as a class writing project since this will allow the teacher to comment on the way your book differs from the original. For example, "Our big book uses different naming words" (nouns).

**7.** *Create a morning message.* Write a "grammar-gram" to your children each morning. Write a message that deliberately incorporates a specific number of grammatical, punctuation, and spelling errors. The children's task is to find as many of the mistakes as possible by the end of the day. Establish incentives to maintain the motivation to participate. For instance, recognize different levels of achievement: *all correct, all correct for five days in a row.* Also, create awards and incentives for children who are less likely to find all of the mistakes.

**8.** *Help students combine sentences.* Research shows that one of the more effective grammatical experiences is to practice combining sentences. Here is an example of a sentence combining activity that can improve writing while illustrating a grammatical concept and more efficient sentence structure. Write a brief passage and have your children rewrite it by combining sentences. Here are two examples:

- The wolves surrounded the buffalo. The buffalo was big.
  The wolves surrounded the big buffalo. (*combined by moving an adjective*)
- The calf trembled. The calf stood beside its mother.
  The calf trembled and stood beside its mother. (*combined by creating a compound predicate*)

**9.** *Work on sentence fragments.* Children often have trouble writing complete sentences, producing instead a sentence fragment—a piece of a sentence. Sentence fragments rank among the more common sentence-writing problems that children experience at all grade levels. The best way to overcome it is to have children write frequently and take their writing through the revision process. Another way to work on the fragment problem is to take examples of fragments from everyday writing without identifying the name of the writers. Write these sentence fragments on the board, and model how they can be corrected. Then provide practice. For example, suppose you found this fragment in one of your children's pieces of writing: *I ride my bike to school. Because I don't like to walk.* After modeling how to correct the sentence fragment (*I ride my bike to school because I don't like to walk*), give a few additional examples. Finally, have children examine a recent piece of their own writing, looking for sentence fragments.

**10.** *Conquer run-on sentences.* Writers sometimes run two or more sentences together when they should have been punctuated as separate sentences or should have been made into a compound sentence. The procedure for helping children overcome this problem is similar to the one described for sentence fragments. First, model how run-on sentences are corrected, using examples drawn from children's writing. Then provide practice. For example, suppose you found this run-on sentence in a child's writing: *Ronnie looked out the window he couldn't see his dog anywhere.* This run-on sentence can be corrected in two ways: (1) two separately punctuated sentences: *Ronnie looked out the window. He couldn't see his dog anywhere;* or (2) a compound sentence: *Ronnie looked out the window, but he couldn't see his dog anywhere.*

## Children's Literature Selections

Burningham, J. (1984). *Skip, trip.* New York: Viking. Verbs are the focus of this picture book for young listeners. Choices are presented to corresponding pictures such as hop, kick, throw, slip, and trip. This is an excellent extension to model and shape sentences. Grades Pre-K–2.

Carroll, L. (1989). *Jabberwocky: From the looking glass.* New York: Abrams. Here is an excellent poem to identify the various mechanics of our language for older children. Grades 8–12.

Charlip, R. (1964). *Fortunately.* New York: Parents Magazine Press. Ned encounters a series of fortunes and misfortunes which lead him to a big surprise. This is an excellent book to introduce adverbs that contain the prefix *un-.* Grades 1–4.

Cleary, B. (2000). *Hairy, scary, ordinary: What is an adjective?* Minneapolis, MN: Lerner. In this rhyming text, descriptive words are presented humorously. Grades 2–4.

Eastman, P. D. (1976). *Are you my mother?* New York: Random House. A mother bird leaves her nest to find some food, and while she is away, her egg hatches. The baby bird decides to search for her, and along the way he asks a variety of things, "Are you my mother?" This book provides an excellent introduction to the use of quotation marks. Grades K–2.

Emberly, E. (1992). *Go away, big green monster!* Boston: Little, Brown. Adjectives are used to describe a monster's scary face in this fun-filled picture book. Repetition of colors, sizes, and parts of the face reinforces reading sight words. Grades Pre-K–2.

Heller, R. (1997). *Mine, all mine: A book about pronouns.* New York: Putnam. In this rhyming story, pronouns are explained and examples are given of the many ways they are used in language. Grades 1–6.

Heller, R. (2000). *Fantastic! wow! and unreal!: A book about interjections and conjunctions.* New York: Puffin. This clever book allows readers to learn about interjections and conjunctions through colorful dragons, rainbow-striped zebras, and mysterious sea creatures. Grades 1–6.

Hutchins, P. (1985). *The very worst monster.* New York:

Greenwillow. Hazel experiences sibling rivalry and attempts to prove she is the worst monster. Present progressive tense as well as adjectives such as *bad, worse,* and *worst* can be used as lessons. Grades K–2.

Lalicki, B. (1994). *If there were dreams to sell.* New York: Simon & Schuster. This is a reissue of a collection of classic prose from 1984. Letters are associated with the way they are used in key words that people view in phrases and lines from excellent literature. Grades 6–12.

Lesieg, T., & McKie, R. (1993). *I can write!—a book by me, myself.* New York: Random House. The book begins with pages for the child to trace. Throughout the rhyming story the child has the opportunity to practice printing words. Grades K–1.

Maestro, B. C. (1992). *All aboard overnight: A book of compound words.* Boston: Houghton Mifflin. A young girl and her mother set off to the railroad station to visit her grandparents. Throughout this picture book, compound words are used during the girl's trip. Grades K–2.

Many, P. (2002). *The great pancake escape.* New York: Walker. A magician accidentally makes pancakes, using the wrong book. The pancakes take flight, and children try to capture their breakfast. This

wonderful rhyming story teaches nouns by naming items used for making pancakes, as well as people, places, and things. Grades K–3.

Martin, B., Jr. (1983) *Brown bear, brown bear, what do you see?* New York: Holt. A classic example of engaging patterned text, this book is a must for every emergent classroom as it supports repeated readings. Grades Pre-K–1.

Terban, M. (1991). *Your foot's on my feet!* Boston: Houghton Mifflin. This book presents irregular nouns and their plural forms in a clear yet humorous manner. Such words as *elf/elves, foot/feet,* and *moose/moose* are presented. Grades 1–4.

Wells, R. (2001). *Ready to read.* New York: Putnam. Timothy, Yoko, and friends learn about letter-sound relationships, rhyming, and upper and lower case letters. Included in this book are activities for writing, learning initial consonants, and using context clues. Grades Pre-K–1.

Yabuuchi, M. (1985). *Whose footprints?* New York: Philomel Books. Illustrations show different footprints, and readers must guess which kind of animal created them, reinforcing the concept of possessive nouns such as "a duck's." Grades 1–2.

# Professional Resources

Barnitz, J. G. (1998). Revising grammar instruction for authentic composing and comprehending. *The Reading Teacher, 51,* 608–611. The author reviews some current practices used to improve language structure that make literacy instruction authentic and viable. He suggests that teachers reflect on their past experiences in school, consider what was meaningful, and use that awareness to enliven and improve syntactic instruction.

Kane, S. (1997). Favorite sentences: Grammar in action (teaching skills with meaningful contexts). *The Reading Teacher, 51,* 70–72. Our own teaching patterns often mirror ineffective past learning experiences. This article is entertaining and thought-provoking in its simplicity. The author discusses her past experiences in learning grammar and her enjoyment of reading literature, noting that they do not always coincide.

Smith, F. (1994). *Learning the technicalities.* In *Writing and the writer* (2nd ed.). Hillsdale, NJ: Erlbaum. In this chapter the author addresses features of written composition, conventions of written text, and the role of spelling, punctuation, and grammar in service to the writing process. Learned over time with practice, descriptions and explanations of the writing technicalities are clear and specific.

Umstatter, J. (2001). *Grammar grabbers: Ready-to-use games and activities for improving basic writing skills.* New York: Prentice Hall. Children learn naturally when they perceive relevance to themselves. Learning grammar can be fun and exciting as children play games that sharpen awareness of grammar in the writing process. Over 200 games and activities are provided.

# 13 The Spelling Connection: Integrating Reading, Writing, and Spelling Instruction

## Teaching Activities

**1.** *Create word sorts.* Use index cards to make word-sort games. Put one word on each card. For instance, write words on the cards with beginning or ending consonants, blends, or other phonic elements. Then have children sort the cards and arrange them to match the phonic elements you have written on the board. Children can work in pairs, teams, or individually. After arranging words by sounds, encourage children to sort their cards by other word features they can find within their words—meaning, number of syllables, prefixes, suffixes, and so on.

**2.** *Foster visual discrimination.* Early spelling is most closely associated with auditory cues, but it is useful to direct children's attention to visual clues as well. For example, prepare word cards that have only a one-letter visual distinction as in *bat/bet, hat/hit, sit/sat.* Other visual discrimination tasks can be devised, such as those based on shape and length.

**3.** *Have a "talking toys day."* Have children bring their favorite toy or stuffed animal to class. Line up the toys and stuffed animals along the board, and draw a speech balloon above the toy or stuffed animal. Have children write dialogue for their animal in the speech balloon. Encourage them to use as many of the week's spelling words as possible.

**4.** *Consistently work with frequently misspelled words.* Table 13.12 lists the 100 most frequently misspelled words. The Blue Pages for this chapter has an even longer list. Make class charts listing these words, and post them conspicuously within your room. Each week choose a few words from the charts that are particularly troublesome for your children. Then create challenges and incentives for learning the selected words. For example, (1) challenge children to use the week's chosen words in their daily writing, (2) challenge them to find the words during their daily reading activities, and (3) challenge them to show whether they can spell the chosen words by the end of the week.

**5.** *Help children learn difficult words.* Make a wall chart of the procedures (Word Study Procedures for Troublesome Words), and put it in a conspicuous place in your classroom. The chart suggests steps for learning especially difficult words. Encourage children to use these procedures for any word they have had trouble spelling. Keep in mind that the procedures are most effective when children use them as they are described. Consequently, it is worth taking time to help children learn to follow the procedures carefully.

**6.** *Work with content words.* Content words are words frequently used within a given field of study—science, health, social studies, math, reading, literature, writing. There are an enormous number of possible content words that children need to know how to spell. So it is best to be selective, and choose only those most crucial to your curricular goals. Children having difficulty with key content words can learn to spell content words using the procedures described in item 5 above for frequently misspelled words.

**7.** *Connect word recognition and spelling.* Spelling skill is closely associated with word recognition skill. Most children cannot learn and *retain* spelling words in advance of their word recognition skills. For example, if Andy's word recognition level is second grade, his spelling level is likely to be half a year behind his word recognition knowledge. Consequently, do not expect children, such as Andy, to learn spelling words at levels beyond their word recognition capabilities. While children can often temporarily test well on words through rote memory, they are often unable to retain this spelling knowledge over time. This is one of the major reasons why children do well on their weekly spelling tests but do not correctly spell the same words in their daily writing activities.

**8.** *Testing spelling knowledge.* The Blue Pages for this chapter contain a spelling placement test. Directions are provided for administering and scoring it. Administer this spelling placement test at the beginning of the school year and more often if necessary. Make sure your children are placed at their appropriate instructional spelling level. When children are misplaced, spelling will be too easy for them (independent level) or too difficult (frustration level).

**9.** *Play Off the Wall.* Place spelling charts on your classroom walls. For example, you might have a chart of frequently misspelled words, content words, and homophones. Once or twice a week, play "Off the Wall." The game goes like this. Start with a clue that identifies the chart on which the word can be found:

- Clue 1: This word can be found in the first column of the homophone chart.
- Clue 2: This word has only one syllable.
- Clue 3: This word ends with the silent *e.*
- Clue 4: The homophone of this word means "simple, ordinary, a broad, flat place such as a prairie."
- Clue 5: This word describes a carpenter's tool or a machine to fly in (plane).

**10.** *Introduce an unusual word of the week.* Words can be fascinating to children, particularly when teachers work to make children word-conscious. Often children are fascinated by "big" words, which usually means multisyllabic words. Encourage children to notice big words in and out of school contexts. Have them bring their candidate for Big Word of the Week to school. Find different ways to make the big word interesting: check its meaning in the dictionary, break it into syllables, study its history, and create occasions to use the big word at unexpected times during the day. It is not necessarily a good idea to require children to learn to spell the big word since this may be too challenging for some children. Big Word of the Week is a good way to develop word awareness. Incidentally, the best way to interest children in words is show them how fascinated you are with words.

## Children's Literature Selections

Ambrus, V. (1978). *Mishka.* New York: Frederick Warne. A story of Mishka's rise from studying violin living on his grandfather's farm to playing for a grand circus. Twenty simple sentences allow beginning readers to read with confidence. Grades 6–12.

Base, G. (1986). *Animalia.* New York: Abrams. This truly amazing alphabet book creatively presents animals for each letter. Words that begin with each animal's letter are illustrated in ways that capture children's imagination. Grades 1–5.

Burningham, J. (1984). *Jangle, twang.* New York: Viking. Words such as *boom, clash, strum,* and *scrape* are accompanied by a picture of the action. This book is a fun way to identify sight and action words. Grades Pre-K–2.

Chitwood, S. (2002). *Wake up, big barn.* New York: Scholastic. Life on a farm is described in a fun-filled rhyming book. Grades Pre-K–1.

de Paola, T. (1985). *Hey diddle diddle and other Mother Goose rhymes.* New York: Putnam. This selection of ever-popular nursery rhymes strengthens a child's memory for similar sounds as well as understanding word patterns. Grades Pre-K–K.

de Paola, T. (1973). *Andy: That's my name.* Englewood Cliffs, NJ: Prentice Hall. Andy uses his wagon to carry intriguing items that represent the letters of his name. Grades Pre-K–1.

Emberley, E. (1967). *Drummer Hoff.* Englewood Cliffs, NJ: Prentice Hall. This rhyming folk verse about building a cannon using soldiers to bring the parts to assemble it won the Caldecott Medal. Repetition and sequencing are reinforced. Grades Pre-K–1.

Fleishman, P. (1988). *Joyful noise: Poems for two voices.* New York: Harper & Row. Poems about insects are written for two voices in this Newbery Medal winner. The beauty of the words is astonishing. Grades 5–12.

Hanson, J. (1973). *Homographic homophones.* Minneapolis, MN: Lerner. Illustrations show the multiple meanings of homophones, such as having characters row a boat and then stand in a row. Grades 1–4.

Hayward, L. (1973). *Letters, sounds, and words: A phonic dictionary.* New York: Platt & Munk. The alphabet and its sounds are presented in this amazing dictionary. Letters with one or more sounds, blends, or special sounds are presented to aid mastery of spelling patterns. Grades K–2.

Hoben, T. (1981). *More than one.* New York: Greenwillow. This book of photographs can be used with all ages. The reader recognizes or guesses how two words can have the same meaning. Grades 1–12.

Hoguet, S. R. (1983). *I unpacked my grandmother's trunk.* New York: Dutton. This story challenges the reader to recite the items from grandmother's trunk, beginning with *A* and ending with *Z.* Grades 1–5.

Lobel, A. (1962). *A zoo for Mister Muster.* New York: Harper & Brothers. Mister Muster loves to walk in the zoo and visit all the animals. One night, animals steal the keys from the zookeeper so they can visit Mister Muster. This is an excellent book to target specific phonetic sounds. Grades 1–3.

Parrish, P. (1970). *Amelia Bedelia*. New York: Scholastic. Amelia seems to take life literally, which makes things quite strange. She "puts the lights out" on the clothesline and when she "dresses the turkey," it ends up in shorts. This book leads to enjoyable discussions of homonyms and idioms. Grades 2–4.

Roffey, M. (1984). *Look, there's my hat.* New York: Putnam. This is an upbeat book about ownership. Articles include a hat, shoes, an umbrella, a belt, and a coat—a wonderful categorizing book to extend classroom activities. Grades K–2.

Russell, Y. (1979). *Words in my world: The I-can-look-it-up book.* Skokee, IL: Rand McNally. More than 300 words that children commonly use are written and illustrated in this book. The words are catego-rized, such as playthings, house items, and types of clothing. Grades Pre-K–K.

Sendak, M. (1962). *Alligators all around.* New York: Harper & Row. In this wonderful alphabet chant, absurd things occur to a gang of alligators. Grades Pre-K–2.

Sendak, M. (1962). *Chicken soup with rice.* New York: Harper & Row. Each picture of this book has a different action and scene, and its words rhyme and are repetitive in nature. Each page models sentence structure and offers various sound production lessons. Grades 1–3.

Seuss, Dr. (1976). *Hop on Pop.* New York: Random House. Dr. Seuss uses rhyme and patterning to describe simple text; cleverly placed words allow children to view the similarities in spelling. Grades Pre-K–2.

## Professional Resources

Aiken, A. G., & Bayer, L. They love words. *The Reading Teacher, 56,* 68–74. This article looks at using a spelling–decoding instructional strategy (Making Words) with first graders within their language arts curriculum. Emphasis is on emerging processes based on meaningful, authentic literacy experiences.

Bear, D. R., & Templeton, S. (1998). Explorations in developmental spelling: Foundations for learning and teaching phonics, spelling, and vocabulary. *The Reading Teacher, 52,* 222–242. The authors discuss current understandings of spelling instruction and learning, how it fits within the broader spectrum of literacy development, and the implications for teaching word study. When approached from the perspective of student discovery through exploration, children can navigate through perceived spelling "traps" in the English language, which frustrate and discourage.

Bear, D. R., Templeton, S., Invernizzi, M., & Johnston, F. (2000). *Words their way: Word study for phonics, vocabulary, and spelling instruction* (2nd ed.). Columbus, OH: Merrill. An outstanding book describing many word study activities keyed to spelling stages.

Beers, J. W., & Henderson, E. H. (1977). A study of developing orthographic concepts among first grade children. *Research in the Teaching of English, 2,* 190–197. This is the earliest explication of stage theory in spelling development.

Cramer, R. L. (1998). *The spelling connection: Integrating reading, writing, and spelling instruction.* New York: Guilford. The book focuses on the interrelatedness of spelling, reading, and writing.

Cramer, R., & Cipielewski, J. (1995). A study of spelling errors in 18,599 written compositions of children in grades 1–8. In *Spelling research and information: An overview of current research and practices* (pp. 11–52). Glenview, IL: Scott Foresman. Based on an extremely large study, the 54 categories of spelling errors are identified, including frequencies of error types and frequency of misspelled words.

Cunningham, P. M. (1995). *Phonics they use: Words for reading and writing* (2nd ed.). New York: HarperCollins. This is an excellent and sensible look at the role of phonics in reading and spelling. Practical classroom ideas and activities are suggested.

Fresch, M. J., & Wheaton, A. (1997). Sort, search, and discover: Spelling in the child-centered classroom. *The Reading Teacher, 51,* 20–31. Children who participated in the child-centered program Sort, Search and Discover (SSD) became more aware of their thinking about spelling and its rules. The program is based on the belief that instruction needs to be built on what children know and then extended on that knowledge so they can make informed decisions in their writing.

Gentry, J. R. (1989). *Spel . . . is a four-letter word.* Portsmouth, NH: Heinemann. A brief, personal account of spelling and how it might be better taught and learned, this readable book gives suggestions to teachers and parents for supporting children's progress in spelling. Teachers are urged to reconsider the traditional spelling model and adopt a more balanced, research-based theory.

Heald-Taylor, G. B. (1998). Three paradigms of spelling instruction in grades 3 to 6. *The Reading Teacher, 51,* 404–413. Three paradigms of spelling instruction in the intermediate grades are discussed in this article: traditional, transitional, and student-oriented. Theory and research behind each practice are explained, along with implications for teaching. The different theoretical perspectives provide a framework for teachers to examine their own instruction methods.

Henderson, E. H. (1989). *Teaching spelling* (2nd ed.). Boston: Houghton Mifflin. A seminal work on spelling development, this book provides a historical look at English spelling and explains the theory supporting stages of spelling growth.

Read, C. (1971). Preschool children's knowledge of English phonology. *Harvard Educational Review, 41,* 1–34. This article supplies the linguistic rationale that explains and supports the invented spelling phenomenon.

Templeton, S., & Bear, D. R. (Eds.). (1992). *Development of orthographic knowledge and the foundations of literacy: A memorial Festschrift for Edmund H. Henderson.* Hillsdale, NJ: Erlbaum. Edmond H. Henderson's students and colleagues describe their research and explain how it fits into a coherent theory of word knowledge.

Templeton, S., & Morris, D. (1999). Questions teachers ask about spelling. *Reading Research Quarterly, 34,* 102–112. The authors give thoughtful answers to typical questions teachers ask about spelling instruction and spelling development among children.

## Blue Pages Figure 1

### Spelling Placement Test

| Grade 1 | Grade 2 | Grade 3 | Grade 4 |
|---|---|---|---|
| 1. at | 1. ten | 1. must | 1. picture |
| 2. run | 2. has | 2. winter | 2. doctor |
| 3. up | 3. hold | 3. fine | 3. rockets |
| 4. go | 4. like | 4. don't | 4. followed |
| 5. flag | 5. keep | 5. threw | 5. easier |
| 6. men | 6. room | 6. point | 6. playful |
| 7. pet | 7. grow | 7. first | 7. reason |
| 8. name | 8. far | 8. taking | 8. mistake |
| 9. gave | 9. hiding | 9. inside | 9. turned |
| 10. use | 10. player | 10. Friday | 10. ground |
| 11. stop | 11. bell | 11. uncle | 11. village |
| 12. big | 12. last | 12. ever | 12. computer |
| 13. keep | 13. even | 13. skate | 13. marbles |
| 14. slow | 14. lake | 14. aren't | 14. singing |
| 15. ship | 15. mean | 15. flew | 15. meaner |
| 16. top | 16. bloom | 16. boil | 16. graceful |
| 17. time | 17. load | 17. early | 17. season |
| 18. tree | 18. bark | 18. tasting | 18. lemonade |
| 19. bikes | 19. dancing | 19. airport | 19. pressed |
| 20. when | 20. farmer | 20. Thursday | 20. country |

| Grade 5 | Grade 6 | Grade 7 | Grade 8 |
|---|---|---|---|
| 1. danger | 1. equal | 1. mumble | 1. cashier |
| 2. prize | 2. settle | 2. hurried | 2. skis |
| 3. practice | 3. already | 3. engage | 3. laying |
| 4. huge | 4. defense | 4. received | 4. grouchy |
| 5. strawberry | 5. compare | 5. edition | 5. approximate |
| 6. destroy | 6. horrible | 6. college | 6. difficult |
| 7. careless | 7. entrance | 7. admiration | 7. universe |
| 8. nearly | 8. thieves | 8. imperfect | 8. selective |
| 9. unfair | 9. logic | 9. attractive | 9. weapon |
| 10. argue | 10. student | 10. disease | 10. contractor |
| 11. hurricane | 11. angel | 11. whimper | 11. dividend |
| 12. squeezed | 12. pistol | 12. where's | 12. octopuses |
| 13. camera | 13. leisure | 13. enable | 13. betrays |
| 14. balloons | 14. decent | 14. pliers | 14. accountant |
| 15. karate | 15. committee | 15. compression | 15. revolutionary |
| 16. appointed | 16. lovable | 16. agility | 16. aggravate |
| 17. colorful | 17. enclose | 17. complication | 17. monotonous |
| 18. surely | 18. liberties | 18. illiterate | 18. appreciative |
| 19. inaccurate | 19. public | 19. achievement | 19. metropolitan |
| 20. repair | 20. ancient | 20. beneath | 20. technician |

Number Correct

_____     _____     _____     _____

Equals Score of

_____     _____     _____     _____

*Formula:* Number Correct × 5 = Percentage Score
*Example:* 17 × 5 = 85%

## Blue Pages Table 1

### 265 Words Often Misspelled at Every Grade Level 1-8:
### Scott Foresman Spelling Research Project (List Derived from 18,599 Unedited Written Compositions)

| | | | | | |
|---|---|---|---|---|---|
| a lot | chocolate | Florida | know | really | to |
| about | Christmas | for | let's | relatives | together |
| after | clothes | found | license | remember | told |
| again | college | Friday | like | restaurant | tomorrow |
| against | come | friend | little | right | too |
| allowed | coming | friends | lose | said | took |
| almost | could | friend's | love | Saturday | tried |
| already | couldn't | funny | made | saw | trying |
| always | cousin | get | maybe | scared | turned |
| and | cousin's | getting | met | school | TV |
| animals | Dad | girl | might | second | two |
| another | Dad's | going | minutes | separated | until |
| anything | decided | going to | Mom | should | upon |
| anyway | definitely | good | Mom's | since | upstairs |
| are | didn't | got | morning | sister | usually |
| aren't | different | grabbed | much | some | vacation |
| around | dinosaurs | Grandma's | my | someone | very |
| aunt | doesn't | great | myself | something | want |
| awhile | dollars | guess | next | sometimes | wanted |
| babies | don't | Halloween | nice | special | was |
| back | down | happened | night | started | wasn't |
| backyard | downstairs | happily | no | stopped | watch |
| baseball | Easter | haunted | no one | stuff | wear |
| basketball | elementary | have | now | supposed | weird |
| beautiful | end | having | nowhere | surprised | went |
| because | enough | Hawaii | of | swimming | were |
| before | environment | he's | off | teacher | we're |
| beginning | especially | hear | once | than | what |
| believe | every | heard | one | thank | what's |
| bird | every day | her | opened | that | when |
| birthday | everybody | him | other | that's | where |
| bored | everyone | himself | our | the | whether |
| bought | everything | his | out | their | which |
| break | everywhere | home | outside | them | who |
| brother | except | hospital | part | themselves | whole |
| brought | excited | house | party | then | will |
| business | exciting | hurt | people | there | witch |
| but | experience | I | piece | there's | with |
| buy | families | I'm | planet | they | without |
| came | family | I've | play | they're | world |
| can't | favorite | into | played | think | would |
| cannot | field | is | presents | thought | wouldn't |
| caught | finally | it's | pretty | threw | your |
| cheese | first | knew | probably | through | you're |
| children | | | | | |

# Glossary

**accountability:** The idea that schools and teachers are responsible for student achievement, which is often measured by students' scores on standardized tests. See also *high-stakes testing*.

**advance organizer:** A teaching strategy used prior to reading to help students organize their thinking about a text before reading it. An advance organizer could consist of key vocabulary words used to predict text content.

**aesthetic reading:** Louise Rosenblatt's (1978) term to describe reading for pleasure. In aesthetic reading, a reader's response is driven by personal feelings evoked by interaction and transaction with text.

**affix:** A word part added at the beginning (prefix) or end (suffix) of a word; affixes change the meaning of a word (*un-* in *unhappy; -est* in *smallest*).

**alliteration:** Repetition of the initial sound(s) or letter(s) in a group of words such as a line of prose or poetry: *Craig loved his fuzzy, furry ferret.*

**alphabetic principle:** The view that each speech sound (phoneme) should be represented by its own corresponding grapheme (letter). Such a language system would, in theory, result in one-to-one correspondence between letters and sounds.

**alphabetic writing:** A writing system in which one or more letters represent a phoneme (single speech sound) but not a syllable or morpheme.

**analytic phonics:** An approach to phonics instruction in which teaching proceeds from whole to part. For example, students first learn a few sight words and then learn phonetic elements and generalizations based on the known whole, or sight, words.

**analytic scoring:** Detailed assessment of narrative and expository writing, including content, organization, word choice, mechanics, and so on. Analytic scoring contrasts with holistic scoring, which focuses on an overall assessment.

**anticipation guide:** Prediction questions used to activate prior knowledge and encourage readers to anticipate concepts they will encounter in text. These guides often include true–false or agree–disagree questions, though other types may be used.

**antonym:** A word that means the opposite of another word; for example, *hot* is an antonym for *cold*.

**assessment:** Gathering data through direct observation or formal and informal testing in order to determine students' strengths and needs in the language arts.

**authentic:** In teaching, a term used to designate materials and activities thought to represent the real world in which learning occurs. For example, reading unaltered literature is considered more authentic than reading a "Dick and Jane" story.

**automaticity:** The rapid and fluent recognition of words requiring only a minimum of effort and attention. Automatic processing of information applies to comprehension and other tasks as well.

**balanced literacy approach:** An approach to literacy that brings together diverse philosophies and practices. These include writing process, word study, comprehension, a literature-based curriculum, and the recognition of the diverse needs of children.

**basal reading program:** Reading and writing materials consisting of student textbooks and workbooks, teachers' manuals, and ancillary materials. Basal programs are usually prepared for kindergarten through middle school.

**base word:** A word to which affixes and inflected endings may be added to form related words such as *think, thinking,* and *rethink*.

**bidialectalism:** The ability to communicate effectively in more than one dialect of a language.

**big books:** An enlarged version of a picture book used in reading instruction, especially in small group settings.

**bilingualism:** The ability to speak one's native language and another language with some degree of proficiency.

**blend:** In phonics instruction, the act of combining, or blending, the sounds represented by two or more consonants: *sp* in *spell, spr* in *sprint*. See also *digraph*.

**book club:** An instructional model in which independent groups of students discuss high-quality literature.

**bookmaking:** The practice of publishing children's compositions in the form of a book.

**book talk:** A teacher-led discussion intended to introduce books to students and to induce them to select their own to read.

**brainstorming:** A learning strategy designed to solve a problem or elicit ideas and information on a topic in an open-discussion format that accepts all contributions.

**case study:** A method of investigation often associated with qualitative research whereby an investigator collects and analyzes data about a single event, group, or situation.

**censorship:** An attempt to limit people's access to or presentation of ideas and information in speech, books, and other forms of communication.

**character:** The individuals, human or not, who come to life in a narrative. Writers reveal the nature of their characters through speech, thought, and action.

**children's literature:** Literature intended specifically for children, as well as literature that children have chosen to make their own.

**chunking:** Breaking words into pronounceable units, such as prefixes, suffixes, base words, and syllables, as an aid to pronunciation. See also *structural analysis*.

**closed syllable:** A syllable ending with one or more consonants, such as *bad, grasp*.

**cloze procedure:** An instructional strategy whereby students fill in missing words in written or oral utterances.

**cognition:** A term used as a synonym for *knowing, thinking,* or *reasoning.*

**collaborative learning:** Learning that results from working together with members of a group, often resulting in a jointly created process or product.

**compound word:** Two or more words combined to create a new word with its own meaning yet related to the words that form it. There are three types of compounds: closed (*footprint*), open (*dry ice*), and hyphenated (*ready-to-wear*).

**comprehension:** Constructing meaning by using information from a text, prior knowledge, and reasoning.

**concepts about print:** Conventions about how print is oriented and presented in a language. Emergent readers of English must learn print awareness conventions such as directionality, word boundaries, print versus manuscript, and so on.

**concrete poetry:** Poetry in which the arrangement, shape, or juxtaposition of words suggests the poet's theme or meaning.

**consonant:** a letter representing sounds made in complex ways within the vocal system. Consonants are most commonly thought of as all letters of the alphabet other than the vowel letters *a, e, i, o, u; y* may function as a consonant (*yam*) or a vowel (*thyme*).

**consonant digraph:** Two consonant letters that together represent a single speech sound, such as *th* in *them, ch* in *chat, sh* in *wish, ph* in *phone, gh* in *rough*. See also *blend*.

**construction of meaning:** As it relates to comprehension, a theory maintaining that readers build, or construct, meaning by using prior knowledge, information from a text, and reasoning.

**constructivism:** A theory maintaining that one's prior knowledge, belief structures, and mental schemata are instrumental in constructing, building, or interpreting all types of texts and experiences.

**content reading:** Reading instruction that focuses on strategies, skills, and procedures especially useful for reading expository texts in subject areas such as math, history, health, English, and other content subjects.

**context:** The linguistic environment in which a word or phrase is embedded in oral or written language.

**contextual analysis:** Using the surrounding linguistic environment to determine the meaning and/or pronunciation of an unknown word; one of four components in word recognition instruction: sight words and contextual, structural, and phonetic analysis.

**contextualized:** The quality of the environment in which an activity, experience, or process takes place. Students learn the conventions of writing more readily in a contextual setting in which meaningful personal writing choices are provided rather than workbook exercises, for example.

**conventions:** In talking and writing, the rules, traditions, and standards that may enhance clarity of expression; in writing, the term *conventions* usually refers to grammar, usage, mechanics, and spelling (GUMS).

**creative thinking:** Thinking characterized by solving problems in new or unexpected ways. Creative thinking is more intuitive and subjective than critical thinking. Creative thinkers see the world in nontraditional ways; for example, the impressionist artists departed from the techniques of the well-established realistic artists.

**critical thinking:** Thinking characterized by logic and inclined toward the use of empirical evidence and scientific inquiry. Critical thinkers seek to confirm or falsify ideas and theories and define the boundaries of logical thought processes.

**culture:** The customs, traditions, knowledge, skills, arts, and beliefs of a nation, group, region, civilization, or people.

**curriculum:** A formal program of study adopted within a school unit; all the educational experiences planned for students within a given educational institution.

**cursive writing:** Handwriting in which the letters are joined within a word in a flowing, continuous fashion.

**decoding:** To analyze spoken or graphic symbols (letters) to determine their pronunciation and/or meaning; among teachers and other reading professionals, an alternative description of word identification.

**decontextualized:** A term that describes reading materials and exercises that have insufficient meaningful context.

**denotation:** The explicit meaning of a word as opposed to its associative, or connotative, meaning. For example, the denotative meaning of *mother* is a "female parent" whereas the connotative meaning may imply kindness and love.

**developmentally appropriate:** The idea that materials and instruction should match the educational characteristics of individual learners so that children can progress according to their capabilities.

**diagnosis:** The process of determining the nature of a difficulty or disorder in the language arts. Its broader meaning includes planning and implementing an instructional program to correct a difficulty or disorder.

**dialect:** A form of spoken language peculiar to a region, community, or social group. Dialects vary in phonology, syntax, and word choice. For example, English-speaking New Englanders and Texans may utter different sounds, sentence structures, and words in specific situations, and these are considered dialect differences.

**dictated language experience story:** An account dictated by a student to a teacher who records it, usually in manuscript printing. The account is subsequently read and reread and used to develop a bank of words for word recognition instruction.

**digraph:** Two letters that represent one sound. There are consonant digraphs as well as vowel digraphs: *sh* in *push* and *oa* in *boat*.

**diphthong:** A vowel sound produced as the tongue glides from one vowel sound to another, such as in *oy* in *joy, ou* in *mouse,* and *ow* in *cow.*

**directed reading activity (DRA):** A set of procedures developed by Emmet Betts (1946) for directing reading instruction including how and when to teach oral and silent reading, word recognition, comprehension and other pertinent instructional matters.

**directed reading thinking activity (DRTA):** A systematic procedure for presenting a fiction or nonfiction reading lesson originated by Russell Stauffer (1969). A DRTA differs from a DRA in its emphasis on purpose setting through prediction and verification of prediction validity.

**direct instruction:** Systematic explicit instruction of a strategy, concept, or skill. For example, one might directly teach the conventions of writing; they might also be taught indirectly by providing meaningful personal writing experiences.

**diversity:** The term literally means "different" or "dissimilar" but has taken on a broader cultural meaning. Diversity in this context refers to the value of teaching and promoting appreciation and understanding of cultural, racial, ethnic, linguistic, gender, and other differences that exist in society.

**drafting:** The second stage of the writing process, which emphasizes getting ideas on paper as rapidly and fluently as possible without worrying about the conventions, which can be attended to during the revision process.

**dyslexia:** A reading disability thought to be inborn. Symptoms include difficulty with decoding and spelling among readers of normal or above-average intelligence. Some authorities question the validity of the concept, suggesting that it is normal for some readers to learn more slowly and with greater difficulty than others.

**eclectic:** Incorporating concepts and strategies from various sources and approaches into a coherent instructional program. In this sense, the balanced literacy approach can be described as eclectic.

**editing:** A component part of revision occurring during the third stage of the writing process. Editing focuses on refining the language of a piece and answers to the writer's question, "How can I best say what I have in mind to say?"

**efferent reading:** Louise Rosenblatt's (1978) term for reading that focuses on abstracting, analyzing, and structuring information and ideas gained from reading.

**emerging literacy:** Reading and writing behaviors observable in young children prior to conventional literacy. Emergent literacy behaviors include scribbling, mock writing, invented spelling, pretend reading, and so on. Elizabeth Sulzby and William Teale (1986) researched and popularized this concept.

**environmental print:** Print and other graphic symbols displayed throughout a child's home, school, and community environment. It includes signs, logos, labels, books, and other written language. It is the written counterpart to a child's oral language environment.

**essay:** A literacy composition giving a personal perspective on the writer's chosen topic. An essay may be brief or lengthy, depending on the forum, and is usually presented in prose.

**etymology:** The study of word histories, including their meaning, structure, and derivation across time.

**explicit comprehension:** Instruction that focuses on the literal aspects of comprehending text, as opposed to inferential aspects. Explicit comprehension provides some of the crucial information needed for higher-order comprehension.

**family literacy:** Activities that help parents foster literacy among their children. In some definitions, it also includes fostering literacy for parents, which enables parents to help their children acquire literacy.

**fiction:** A literary work portraying imagined events and characters; typical genres include novels and short stories.

**figure of speech:** A nonliteral expression such as a simile (fast as a cheetah), metaphor (the lake is a blue jewel), or image (fire in the eye).

**flexible reading:** Reading that takes account of the reader's purpose and the nature of the materials. Flexible readers skim, scan, study, or survey materials according to their purpose and the difficulty of the text.

**fluency:** In reading, smooth, easy reading unimpeded by problems with word recognition; in writing, the free flow of words and ideas when drafting; in oral expression, the seemingly effortless reading of a passage aloud.

**folktale:** A story handed down orally from generation to generation among the "common folk." A folktale usually has legendary or mythical elements, and its original authorship is often unknown.

**formative evaluation:** In teaching, assessment aimed at improving instruction by monitoring the learning progress of students.

**freewrite:** A strategy to aid fluency whereby children write for a stipulated period of time without stopping or even lifting pencil from paper. Freewriting is a cousin to brainstorming.

**frustration reading level:** A reading level that a student would find too difficult because of deficiencies related to word recognition, vocabulary, concepts, or prior knowledge. At this level word recognition is 89% or lower, comprehension below 70%. Placing children at frustration level is likely to result in little or no reading growth.

**genre:** A classification system for literary works based on form, technique, or content. There are genre classifications for children's literature (picture book, folktale) literary works (play, poem), and social uses of language (sermon, lecture).

**grammar:** A description of the language patterns that native speakers use automatically; the system of word structures and word arrangements in a language.

**grapheme:** A letter or group of letters that represents a phoneme or sound. For instance, *t* represents /t/ in *toy,* and *oy* represents /oi/ in *toy.*

**guided reading:** Reading instruction directed by a teacher with a specific purpose and structure and focused on small groups of children reading at the same level and having similar needs.

**handedness:** Consistent or dominant preference for using either the left or right hand.

**Head Start:** A federally funded educational program primarily for children from low-income families and intended to help advance children's intellectual, physical, and emotional growth.

**high-frequency word:** A word that appears in written or oral language more often than most other words. Edward Dolch (1942) and others compiled lists of high-frequency words in written and oral language.

**high-stakes testing:** The use of standardized tests to determine whether schools have met local, state, or federal standards. Failure to score at mandated levels might result in sanctions for teachers, schools, or school districts.

**holistic scoring:** A writing assessment technique that judges the adequacy of a composition on its overall merit. Holistic scoring is guided by criteria and the use of anchor compositions that represent different levels of performance. See also *analytic scoring*.

**homograph:** A word with the same spelling as another word but having a different meaning and origin. Homographs may have different pronunciations but the same spelling: he wore a *bow* tie; take a *bow*. They may, however, also have the same pronunciation and the same spelling: hand me the *pen*; put the pigs in their *pen*.

**homonym:** A word with the same pronunciation and often the same spelling as another word but with a different origin and meaning: *deer* and *dear* (same oral form but different spellings); *bear* and *bear* (same oral form and same spelling). According to this definition, homonyms include homophones and homographs.

**homophone:** A word having a different origin and meaning but the same pronunciation as another word, whether or not spelled alike: *ring* and *wring*; *scale* and *scale*.

**HyperStudio:** A commercially developed and distributed authoring program that allows nonprogrammers to create multimedia and hypermedia materials; published by Roger Wagner Publishing (http://www.hyperstudio.com/).

**hypermedia:** Linked online resources that may include audio, video, animations, or graphic media in addition to text. Some authorities use the term to refer to any linked collection of materials, thus relating it closely to the definition of *hypertext*.

**hypertext:** Nonsequential text that branches and allows choice to the reader; hypertext is best read on an interactive screen. The links and pages of the World Wide Web are the most widely known and used form of hypertext today.

**illiteracy:** The inability to read or write a language; according to some definitions, the inability to use reading and writing with a certain level of facility, also called *functional illiteracy*.

**imagery:** The forming of mental pictures or images while reading or listening; in writing the use of expressive language to create an image involving one or more of the five senses.

**implicit comprehension:** Comprehension of ideas and information implied but not directly or literally expressed in a text; implicit comprehension results from a combination of text, prior knowledge, and reasoning.

**independent reading level:** The highest level at which a child can read materials without teacher assis-

tance; word recognition is 96% or higher, comprehension 90% or higher. Since a child may have more than one independent level, the highest level is the one at which independent reading is recommended.

**individualized reading:** An approach emphasizing self-selection of reading materials, primarily of trade books. Under the guidance of a teacher, children pace their reading, engage in literature discussions, and write. Lyman Hunt (1971), Jeanette Veatch (1976), and Walter Barbe (1961) were early advocates of individualized reading.

**inflected ending:** A word ending that expresses plurality or possession when added to a noun (*friends, friend's*), comparison when added to an adjective and some adverbs (*finer, finest*), and tense when added to a verb (*jumped, jumping*).

**informal reading inventory (IRI):** A graded series of passages of increasing difficulty used to determine independent, instructional, frustration, and listening capacity levels by assessing word recognition in context and comprehension. Emmett Betts (1946) developed this assessment procedure.

**instructional level:** The highest level at which a child can read with instructional assistance from a teacher. Word recognition is 90–95%; comprehension ranges from 70% to 89%. Since a child may have more than one instructional level, the highest instructional level is the one at which instruction is recommended.

**integrated language arts:** An approach to teaching reading, writing, talking, listening, viewing, and visual representation so that the components mutually reinforce one another. In this conception of language arts instruction, the components are seen as a unified core rather than separate skills or subjects.

**International Reading Association (IRA):** An association of teachers and other reading professionals. IRA sponsors conferences and publishes professional journals and books. (IRA, 800 Barksdale Road, P.O. Box 8139, Newark, DE 19714-8139; www.reading.org)

**invented spelling:** Spelling miscues resulting from attempts to spell words not yet known. Spellers base their attempts on incomplete knowledge of the spelling system, using phonological, structural, and meaning cues. Also called *temporary spelling*.

**journaling:** The practice of writing in journals. The many kinds of journal writing include personal, learning, double-entry, content, and dialogue.

**KWL:** A reading strategy to help children establish purposes for reading. Three questions are asked: What do you Know? What do you Want to know? What did you Learn? Donna Ogle (1989) developed this strategy.

**language arts:** Traditional language arts instruction included the development of four school subjects or skills: reading, writing, talking, and listening. Recently visually representing and viewing have been described as components of the language arts.

**language experience approach (LEA):** An approach to language arts instruction emphasizing the integration of the language arts into all instructional activities. Oral composition, or dictation, is an important early activity in the LEA, but dictation is only one of many principles and practices of LEA.

**learning log:** A journal-like record of learning kept by students to encourage evaluation of current learning, planning future learning, and other ideas related to learning experiences.

**letter–sound correspondence:** The representation of a sound by a letter or combination of letters.

**listening:** The act of receiving and understanding spoken language; in teaching, a crucial component of integrated language arts instruction.

**listening capacity:** The highest grade level at which a child can comprehend text read aloud. A score of 70% or higher identifies this level. The capacity level is used to estimate the difference between reading achievement (instructional level) and potential achievement (capacity).

**literacy:** The ability to read and write; also used to describe other skills such as computer literacy and workplace literacy. The terms *functional literacy* and *advanced literacy* denote different levels of literacy accomplishment, but precise definitions of each are not agreed upon.

**literature:** Descriptions of literature abound, but few are as poetic and satisfying as this definition: "The imaginative shaping of life and thought into the forms and structures of language" (Huck, Hepler, & Hickman, 1993, p. 6).

**literature-based curriculum:** A language arts curriculum wherein the dominant materials and concepts of instruction are works of literature.

**literature circle:** An approach to reading instruction in which small groups of students read and respond to literature, usually under teacher guidance.

**long vowel:** In teaching tradition, vowel sounds that are also names of the five letters *a, e, i, o, u*: /a/ as in *bake*, /e/ as in *heat*, /i/ as in *nice*, /o/ as in *boat*, and /u/as in *unit*.

**lowercase letters:** Manuscript or cursive handwriting smaller than and usually formed differently from uppercase letters.

**manuscript writing:** A handwriting style wherein letters are not connected; traditionally called *print*.

**mapping:** An instructional strategy graphically depicting relationships or connections between and among words, phrases, ideas, or topics. Other related strategies include clustering, semantic mapping, word mapping, and webbing.

**mechanics:** A term loosely and inconsistently used to refer to the conventions of writing such as grammar, usage, punctuation, capitalization, and spelling.

**metacognition:** Awareness and knowledge of one's own mental processes; the process of monitoring, controlling, and regulating one's own learning.

**metaphor:** A figure of speech containing an implied comparison in which a noun or noun phrase is applied to an unrelated noun, as in *life is a river*.

**minilesson:** Instruction on any topic, skill, or concept that supportive teaching may require. Minilessons are brief, explicit, and focused and may be presented to an individual, small group, or whole class.

**miscue:** A deviation from text during oral reading; used as a synonym, among some reading professionals, for an oral reading error.

**miscue analysis:** A method of coding, analyzing, and interpreting reading miscues to determine strengths and needs of readers; the concept was developed by Ken Goodman (1969) and Yetta Goodman and Carolyn Burke (1972).

**mnemonic:** A strategy, device, or memory trick to aid recall of information.

**model:** A standard or example to be imitated. For example, a teacher may model the writing of a poem; a book may model style and content for readers.

**modeling:** The act of serving as an example for others to follow or imitate.

**morpheme:** A meaningful linguistic unit that cannot be divided into smaller meaningful units. For example, the word *tank* is a meaningful linguistic unit; the *s* in *tanks* is also a meaningful linguistic unit since it forms the plural of the word *tank*.

**motivation:** The internal force within individuals that arouses and directs behavior.

**multiple intelligences:** Howard Gardner (1983) proposed the idea of seven intelligences: verbal–linguistic, logical–mathematical, visual–spatial, kinesthetic, musical, interpersonal, and intrapersonal. Gardner argues that society overvalues verbal–mathematical intelligence and neglects others.

**multisyllabic:** A word containing more than one syllable, also called *polysyllabic*. The word *carefully* is multisyllabic since it has three syllables: *care, ful, ly.*

**narrative:** A story, real or imagined, expressed orally or in writing. Folktales, for example, are narratives passed down orally from generation to generation and eventually recorded in written form; a novel is a written narrative.

**National Council of Teachers of English (NCTE):** An association of teachers and other language arts professionals with local and state affiliates. NCTE sponsors conferences featuring the language arts and publishes professional journals and books (see www.ncte.org).

**National Reading Conference (NRC):** An association of reading professionals. NRC sponsors a national conference, publishes a yearbook, and promotes research in reading and the language arts. (NRC, 7044 South 13th Street, Oak Creek, WI 53154-1429; www.nrconline.org)

**nonfiction:** Prose that argues, explains, or describes and is intended to be based on fact or logic; prose that is specifically not fiction. However, nonfiction materials may, in some instances, have fictional elements. Nonfiction is not necessarily "true."

**objective:** Without bias or prejudice; detached or impersonal. The construction and scoring of a multiple-choice test is said to be objective whereas an essay test is said to be subjective. Some educational authorities question the claim that standardized tests reflect a high level of objectivity.

**onomatopoeia:** Use of words that imitate the sound associated with their meaning; for example, *buzz, hum,* and *splat.*

**onset:** The consonants preceding the vowel in a syllable, such as *st* in *sting.*

**open syllable:** A syllable ending in a vowel sound rather than a consonant, such as *ra* in *radar.*

**oral reading:** Reading aloud to communicate to an audience; a dramatic reading that interprets a text.

**oral vocabulary:** One's spoken vocabulary; distinct from other vocabularies such as listening, writing,

and reading vocabularies. Each type differs in size, quality, and other factors.

**orthography:** Spelling in accord with conventional usage; spelling as a subject of study.

**peer conference:** In teaching, small groups of children meet to listen to and critique each other's compositions or other work; peer conferences may take place before, during, or after a composition has been completed.

**personalized reading:** The term used by Walter Barbe (1961) and others as an alternative for *individualized reading.*

**phenomenon:** Any fact, experience, or circumstance apparent to the senses; an extraordinary thing or event.

**philosophy:** One's general principles, practices, and beliefs in a field of knowledge such as education; principles that govern conduct in life.

**phoneme:** A minimal sound unit in speech. Linguists identify 44 English phonemes.

**phoneme–grapheme correspondence:** In phonics, the relationship between sounds and letters; in technical language, the relationship between a phoneme and its graphemic representation.

**phonemic awareness:** In teaching practice, the ability to orally segment and manipulate speech sounds within words. It is a good predictor of reading success in first grade, and some authorities believe it is prerequisite to learning to read.

**phonetic analysis:** In teaching practice, associating speech sounds with letters and blending them to pronounce words; some authorities say it is technically incorrect to use the term *phonetic analysis,* preferring the term *phonic analysis.*

**phonics:** In teaching practice, associating speech sounds with letters and blending them to pronounce words; in popular usage, a misnomer for *word recognition* or *word identification.*

**phonogram:** A sequence of letters comprised of a vowel spelling and an ending consonant: *ed* in *bed* and *ake* in *take.*

**phonology:** The study of the unified system of the speech sounds of a language and how they work.

**plot:** What happens in a narrative; the plan of events, action, and consequences.

**poetry:** Some dictionaries define *poetry* as a collection of poems—not very satisfying, but not many definitions are. The Welsh poet Dylan Thomas defined it as "Statements made on the way to the grave." Let's settle provisionally for that thought-provoking definition (see Chapter 11).

**poetic license:** Freedom for poets and writers to disregard conventional rules, forms, and style of poetry and other types of writing; a metaphor for freedom to disregard traditions and conventions in other avenues of life.

**point of view:** The perspective of the narrator who tells a story, usually discussed in regard to fiction. Two common perspectives are the *limited* point of view, wherein the narrator knows only what he or she sees, hears, knows, or is told, and the *omniscient* point of view, wherein the author–narrator knows, sees, feels, and hears all.

**portfolio:** A selection of work in a variety of subjects; portfolios usually include items that represent the student's best work across a period of time.

**portfolio assessment:** Using the contents of a student's portfolio to determine educational progress, often as an alternative to assessing performance through standardized tests or other measures.

**pragmatics:** The study of the language choices people make in social settings and the influence such choices have on others; in semiotics, the study of the relationship between signs and their objects.

**prediction strategy:** Encouraging readers to predict what may happen in a story and in nonfiction by making an educated guess based on prior knowledge and text clues, as in a DRTA or KWL. Prediction establishes purposes for reading and provides opportunity for verification during and after reading.

**prewriting:** Planning for writing before drafting; prewriting activities include reading, brainstorming, taking notes, mapping, searching the Internet, and organizing information and ideas.

**primary trait scoring:** Assessing writing by focusing on a single characteristic or trait. One might, for example, assess a composition for organization, ignoring other features. It can be used for a specific instructional purpose such as determining whether students need help in organizing their writing.

**prior knowledge:** The store of knowledge, concepts, and information one possesses; also called world knowledge. Readers call on their prior knowledge to comprehend and interpret text; teachers use strategies to help readers activate their prior knowledge before and during reading.

**proofreading:** A component of revision whereby writers make final changes prior to publishing. Proofreading involves searching for mechanical defects in writing, but since writers often find more serious defects while proofreading, they may need to make more significant changes than proofreading normally entails.

**publishing:** The final stage of the writing process, wherein students prepare their writing to share with an audience or for public display.

**punctuation marks:** Graphic symbols used in writing to clarify meaning and signal the writer's intent. Punctuation gives speech characteristics to written language.

**qualitative research:** Research conducted in naturalistic settings in order to interpret behavior, phenomena, or cultural practices, as in case studies, interviews, teacher research, and other observations where quantitative data is unavailable or undesirable.

**quantitative research:** Research that tests hypotheses, describes findings in numerical terms, and tests hypotheses, using statistics to determine the significance of findings.

**readability formula:** A formula for estimating the difficulty of text, usually in terms of grade-level difficulty. Readability formulas tend to use linguistic features to determine difficulty: word length, word frequency, sentence length, sentence complexity, and so on.

**reader response:** Louise Rosenblatt's (1978) theory that reader and literacy text transact and interact through efferent and aesthetic responses to text. The transaction between reader and text is an act of creation.

**Reader's Theater:** Oral interpretation of literature such as stories, plays, or poetry; other oral expressive read-aloud experiences.

**reading:** A complex activity of the mind, involving the construction of meaning using information from a text, prior knowledge, and reasoning. Harris and Hodges (1995) list 20 historical definitions of reading, giving the impression that an entirely satisfactory and stable definition remains elusive.

**reading–writing connection:** The idea that reading and writing should be taught, learned, and used together because they mutually reinforce the acquisition of literacy.

**reasoning:** The drawing of inferences and conclusions from acquired information and experience; often used as a synonym for thinking.

**recursiveness:** In writing, the idea that writing does not move in a linear fashion from prewriting to publication. Instead, writers move back and forth from one stage of the writing process to another in any order that suits their purpose and needs as they construct their compositions.

**reflective thinking:** The process of thinking about how to respond to an issue or solve a problem in order to reach a reasonable, balanced, and just solution.

**reinforcement:** In teaching, the process of strengthening a desired learning outcome by giving students information about how they have performed on a learning task so that they may improve their performance on subsequent occasions.

**research:** Systematic study and investigation undertaken to discover, establish, or propose theories and principles that may advance practice within a particular field of knowledge.

**retelling:** A comprehension and assessment procedure in which readers are asked to tell, in summary fashion, what happened in a recently read passage.

**reversal:** Immature readers may reverse words or letters, such as saying *saw* for *was*. Single letters, particularly *b, p, q, d, n,* and *j,* may also be reversed. Thought by some to be symptomatic of dyslexia, most reversals are a temporary problem that disappears as reading skill grows.

**revising:** Changes made in written text during the third stage of the writing process. Four changes are possible: adding, deleting, substituting, and rearranging. This text argues that editing and proofreading are part of the revision process, not separate stages of the writing process.

**rhyme:** An identical or similar recurring final sound in words, usually at the end of two or more lines of a poem and sometimes within lines of a poem.

**rime:** A vowel and any following consonant(s) of a syllable, as *ong* in *song* or *et* in *set.*

**sanctions:** With respect to the standards movement, a penalty for failing to meet a specified level of performance regarded as a standard.

**scaffolding:** A metaphor for supportive teaching usually ascribed to the psychologist Jerome Bruner (1970). In modeling a writing skill, teachers scaffold children through supportive teaching and then gradually withdraw support as they show evidence of independence in the skill.

**schema (plural: schemata):** An abstract cognitive structure stored in memory. Schemata represent an individual's existing knowledge of events and concepts acquired through the whole of one's experience, including reading.

**schema theory:** A theory describing the process by which meaning is constructed by connecting existing knowledge with new knowledge encountered in text.

**schwa:** An unstressed or unaccented vowel sound represented by the symbol ə, as in *pencil* (*pehn səl*).

**second language learners:** Individuals in the process of learning a language different from their native language.

**semantics:** The meaning system of a language; the study of the meaning of language, including the meaning of words, phrases, sentences, and whole text.

**setting:** The time, place, and circumstances in which a narrative take place.

**shared reading:** An instructional strategy whereby a teacher reads aloud to students and students follow along in the text. Often a big book is used so students can easily follow the text.

**short vowels:** In instructional practice, the sounds /a/, /e/, /i/, /o/, and /u/ as heard in the following key words: *hat, set, hit, hot, pup.*

**show and tell:** A classroom activity, most often in primary grades, in which children talk about things that interest them, such as a trip taken with their parents. Show and tell may also include talking about an object such as a new book or toy.

**sight word:** A word immediately recognized upon seeing it, whether in context or isolation. Since sight words are embedded in long-term memory, they do not require word analysis unless a miscue has occurred on a known sight word.

**silent *e* (also called final *e*):** An English spelling pattern in which *e* is the last letter in a word but does not represent the final sound; silent or final *e* often signals a long vowel in the preceding vowel letter, as in *snake* and *bite.*

**silent reading:** Subvocalized reading in which the words are inaudible to an audience.

**simile:** A comparison expressed using *like* or *as,* such as *slow as molasses.*

**social constructivism:** A theory that views learning as a product of social interaction and collaboration. Lev Vygotsky (1962), a Russian psychologist, is one of the chief proponents of this theory.

**speaking:** The act of communicating through speech; in teaching, one of the crucial components of intergrated language arts instruction; in this text, the terms speaking and talking are often used interchangeably when describing the components of language arts instruction.

**spelling:** The study of the conventional spelling of words, involving correct letter selection and sequencing.

**standard:** In teaching, a written statement describing an educational goal. Attainment of standards is usually measured with a standardized test. Failure to meet standards may result in sanctions for states, schools, or teachers.

**standardized test:** A test with specific tasks, standards, and procedures that enable comparisons of groups of students across time and geographical regions. Such tests purport to be objective, though subjective elements inevitably are part of the make up of all standardized tests.

**standard language:** The language of the dominant culture and the well educated; the language recognized by grammars, dictionaries, and the educated class as correct. Some linguists consider standard English as one dialect among others, no more correct or useful for communicating among its users than other dialects.

**standards movement:** A movement energized by legislators and educators in response to the perceived failure of schools to provide an adequate education to children. The movement has resulted in federal, state, and local standards, mandating certain levels of achievement that, if not met, may result in sanctions.

**strategy:** In teaching, a specific plan, activity, process, or procedure intended to improve performance in a particular skill or subject. For example, predicting and self-monitoring are strategies intended to improve reading comprehension.

**structural analysis:** A component of word recognition wherein readers examine words to identify the pronunciation and meaning of structural parts such as syllables, prefixes, suffixes, and base words.

**style:** A writer's distinctive voice, individuality, and imagination; the unique way writers express ideas in prose or poetry.

**subjective:** Existing in the mind; concerning one's thoughts and feelings; the opposite of *objective,* often considered a more scientific and factual viewpoint. Thus, multiple-choice tests are said to be objective and essay tests subjective. This view oversimplifies the issues involved in subjective and objective assessment.

**summative evaluation:** Assessment intended to determine the degree to which the goals and objectives of an enterprise have been met, often with the goal of reporting progress to an outside audience, such as reporting to parents how a school district has fared in a statewide assessment of reading.

**syllable:** A word or part of a word pronounced as a unit and having only one vowel sound. A syllable consists of a vowel alone or a vowel with one or more consonants. For example, *event* has two syllables: the *e* alone is the first syllable, and *vent* is the second syllable.

**symbol:** Something that stands for and represents something else; letters stand for sounds, a lion symbolizes courage, and a lamb is a symbol of meekness.

**synonym:** A word that means the same or nearly the same as another word. For example, *little, small,* and *tiny* are synonyms for one another.

**syntax:** The study of how sentences are formed and the rules that govern word order within sentences.

**synthetic phonics:** An approach to phonics that proceeds from part to whole. Children are first taught letter–sound combinations and blending and then use this phonics knowledge to pronounce whole words. Synthetic phonics is the counterpart to analytic phonics, which proceeds from whole to part.

**tactile:** Referring to the sense of touch as a learning method. For example, tracing letters in sand or on sandpaper produces a tactile sensation. Grace Fernald (1943) developed the VAKT strategy, combining the **v**isual, **a**uditory, **k**inesthetic, and **t**actile senses in one learning technique.

**talking:** The act of producing oral speech. In language arts texts, *talking* is a synonym for the language arts component also known as *speaking.*

**technology:** Mechanical devices used for learning and work. Computers and multimedia are commonly thought of as technology, yet tools such as plows and hammers are also technological devices and were once cutting-edge technology.

**test item:** A single question, statement, or problem in a test. Some tests consist mostly of items said to be objective; essay questions are said to be subjective because they require the analytical judgment of a human reader. This distinction is questionable if not incorrect.

**theme:** The central idea running through a story, such as a moral or lesson; a major idea that informs the full scope of a literary work.

**think aloud:** In teaching, a modeling strategy in which teachers verbalize aloud how they think as they demonstrate a literacy skill, such as comprehending text and other language arts skills.

**thinking:** The use of the mind to consider information and ideas; to reflect, reason, or imagine.

**traditional school grammar (TSG):** The system of grammatical rules taught in American schools for two or more centuries, derived in part from Latin and Greek grammars.

**uppercase letters:** Letters, used in both manuscript and cursive writing, that are larger than lowercase letters. They differ not only in size but also in shape: *A, a; B, b.*

**USSR:** Uninterrupted sustained silent reading, a strategy for encouraging silent reading for a sustained period of time. Teachers often start USSR with a 5-minute period. Over time, they increase the period to 30 minutes or more. No interruptions are tolerated.

**viewing:** The teaching of strategies for interpreting and analyzing visual data and images, integrating the skills of text comprehension; critical analysis of viewing experiences.

**visually representing:** Depicting or portraying an image or likeness through arts, crafts, and other forms of image making. Visual representation arouses, stimulates, and enlarges interest and knowledge, enlists mind and body in the portrayal of imaginative ideas, augments the growth of language, and advances the development of multiple intelligences.

**vocabulary:** Primarily a term that refers to words one knows the meaning of, not words one can pronounce without knowing their meanings; vocabularies referred to in the language arts include listening, speaking, reading, and writing vocabularies, which differ in quality and quantity.

**whole language approach:** A philosophy applied to teaching and learning the language arts. While there are whole language instructional practices, the beliefs and intentions of whole language teachers distinguish it from other approaches, according to Altwerger, Edelsky, and Flores (1989).

**word family:** Words that share a common phonic element, such as *ake* in *take, ot* in *hot.* A word family and a phonogram generally refer to the same phonic element.

**word identification:** An alternative term to describe the elements associated with learning to pronounce words. Some authorities distinguish between word identification and word recognition, but this technical argument has little relevance to teaching the skills.

**word recognition:** The process of determining the pronunciation and meaning of words not known by sight. Its three major components are phonic analysis, structural analysis, and contextual analysis. Sight-word knowledge is also associated with word recognition instruction.

**word sort:** A word study activity wherein words written on cards are classified or sorted according to phonic, structural, meaning, and spelling patterns.

**word wall:** Words posted on classroom walls for a variety of instructional purposes. Word walls may include word families, high-frequency words, words often misspelled, and so on.

**writing:** Recording ideas and information in written form, often with particular emphasis on the process of doing writing and the product that results from writing. Writing is one of four major aspects of language arts instruction: listening, talking, writing, and reading.

**writing conference:** A conversation between a writer and another individual to help the writer evaluate a composition and obtain suggestions and reactions of a friendly reader, often the teacher or a peer.

**writing process:** A particular method of doing writing, which includes theories, procedures, and activities that emphasize the operations by which writing is accomplished rather than the product. Typically, four stages are identified: prewriting, drafting, revising, and publishing or sharing.

**writing workshop:** An approach to writing instruction and learning that honors writing and writers, based on the procedures and stages of the writing process. It emphasizes self-selection of topics and purposes, author's chair, bookmaking, conferences, modeling, revision, and student ownership of writing.

**zone of proximal development (ZPD):** The distance between children's current level of development and their next potential level of development. This potential level is achieved through supportive adult instruction and collaboration with capable peers, according to Lev Vygotsky (1962).

# References

Adams, M. J. (1990). *Beginning to read: Thinking and learning about print.* Cambridge, MA: MIT Press.

Allington, R. L. (2001). *What matters for struggling readers: Designing research-based programs.* New York: Addison Wesley Longman.

Allington, R. L. (2002). *Big brother and the national reading curriculum: How ideology trumped evidence.* Portsmouth, NH: Heinemann.

Allington, R. L., & Johnson, P. (2000). *Exemplary fourth-grade reading instruction.* Paper presented at the American Educational Research Association, New Orleans.

Altwerger, B., Edelsky, C., & Flores, B. M. (1989). Whole language: What's new? In G. Manning and M. Manning (Eds.), *Whole language: Beliefs and practices, K-8,* Washington, DC: National Education Association.

Ames, W. (1966). The development of a classification scheme for contextual aids. *Reading Research Quarterly, 2,* 57–82.

Anderson, D. R. (2002). Creative teachers' risk, responsibility, love. *Journal of Education, 47* (1), 33–48.

Anderson, N. A. (2002). *Elementary children's literature: The basics for teachers and parents.* Boston: Allyn & Bacon.

Anderson, R. C. & Nagy, W. E. (1992). The vocabulary conundrum. *American Educator,* Vol. 16 14–18, 44–47.

Anderson, R., Hiebert, E., Scott, J., & Wilkinson, I. (1985). *Becoming a nation of readers.* Bloomington, IN: The Center for the Study of Reading.

Applebee A. (1978). *The child's concept of story.* Chicago: University of Chicago Press.

Ashton-Warner, S. (1963). *Teacher.* New York: Simon and Schuster.

Atwell, N. (1998). *In the middle: New understandings about writing, reading, and learning* (2nd ed.). Portsmouth, NH: Boynton/Cook.

Au, K. H. (1997). Literacy steps for all students: Ten steps toward making a difference. *The Reading Teacher, 51* (3), 186–194.

Ayres, L. (1993). *The efficacy of three training conditions on phonological awareness of kindergarten children and the longitudinal effect of each on later reading acquisition.* Unpublished doctoral dissertation, Oakland University, Rochester, MI.

Bader, L. A. (2002). *Bader reading and language inventory* (4th ed.). Columbus, OH: Merrill Prentice Hall.

Ball, E. W., & Blachman, B. A. (1991). Does phoneme awareness training in kindergarten make a difference in early word recognition and spelling development? *Reading Research Quarterly,* (26) 1:49–64.

Barbe, W. (1961). *Educator's guide to personalized reading instruction.* Englewood Cliffs, NJ: Prentice Hall.

Barr, R., & Johnson, B. (1997). *Teaching reading and writing in elementary classrooms.* New York: Longman.

Bear, D., Templeton, S., Invernizzi, M., & Johnston, F. (2000). *Words their way: Word study for phonics, vocabulary, and spelling instruction* (2nd ed.). Columbus, OH: Merrill.

Beers, J. W., & Henderson, E. H. (1977). A study of developing orthographic concepts among first grade children. *Research in the Teaching of English, 2* (2), 190–197.

Betts, E. (1947). *Foundations of reading instruction.* Englewood Cliffs, NJ: Prentice Hall.

Betts, E. A. (1946). *Foundations of reading instruction.* New York: American Book Co.

Bissett, D. (1969). *The amount and effect of recreational reading in selected fifth-grade classes.* Doctoral dissertation, Syracuse University.

Blachman, B. A. (1984). Language analysis skills and early reading acquisition. In G. Wallach & K. Butler (Eds.), *Language learning disabilities in school age children* (pp. 271–287). Baltimore, MD: Williams and Wilkins.

Blachowicz, C., Fisher, P., Wohlreich, J., & Guastafeste, P. (1990). *Children using dictionaries: A think-aloud study.* Paper presented at the American Educational Research Association Annual Convention, Boston.

Blachowicz, C., & Fisher, P. (2002). *Teaching vocabulary in all classrooms* (2nd ed.). Columbus, OH: Merrill Prentice Hall.

Bradbury, R. (1996). *Zen in the art of writing*. Santa Barbara: Joshua Odell Editions.

Braddock, R., Lloyd-Jones, R., & Schoer, L. (1963). *Research in written composition*. Champaign, IL: National Council of Teachers of English.

Bradley, L., & Bryant, P. E. (1983). Categorizing sounds and learning to read—a causal connection. *Nature, 301,* 419–421.

Brown, H., & Camborne, B. (1989). *Read and retell: A strategy for the whole language/natural learning classroom*. Portsmouth, NH: Heinemann.

Brown, J. (1985). Some tests of the decay theory of immediate memory. *Quarterly Journal of Experimental Psychology, 10,* 12–21.

Brown, R., Postal, P., Bellugi, V., Chomsky, C. (1972). *Language and learning: Investigations and interpretations*. Cambridge, MA: Harvard Educational Publishing Group.

Bruner, J. (1962). *On knowing*. Cambridge, MA: Harvard University Press.

Bruner, J. (1966). *The process of education*. Cambridge, MA: Harvard University Press.

Bruner, J. (1966). *Toward a theory of instruction*. Cambridge, MA: Harvard University Press.

Bruner, J. (1970). *Acts of meaning*. Cambridge, MA: Harvard University Press.

Burt, D. (2001). *The literary 100*. New York: Checkmark Books.

Busink, R. (1997). Gender and grade level differences in the development of concepts about print. *Reading Psychology, 12,* 309–328.

Calkins, L. M. (1980). Research update—when children want to punctuate: Basic skills belong in context. *Language Arts, 57* (5), 67–73.

Calkins, L. M. (1994). *The art of teaching writing*. (2nd ed.) Portsmouth, N. H.: Heinemann.

Camborne, B. (1995). Toward an educationally relevant theory of literacy learning: Twenty years of inquiry. *The Reading Teacher, 43* (3), 182–190.

Carreiro, P. (1998). *Tales of thinking: Multiple intelligences in the classroom*. York, ME: Stenhouse.

Center for English Language Arts (1998). *Newsletter*. Albany, NY: State University of New York.

Chall, J. (1967). *Learning to read: The great debate*. New York: McGraw-Hill.

Chapman, C. (1993). *If the shoe fits: How to develop multiple intelligences in the classroom*. Arlington Heights, IL: Skylight Professional Development.

Chomsky, C. (1971a). Reading, writing, and phonology. *Harvard Educational Review, 40,* 287–309.

Chomsky, C. (1971b). Write first, read later. *Childhood Education, 47,* 269–299.

Chomsky, C. (1972). Stages in language development and reading achievement. *Harvard Educational Review, 42,* 1–33.

Chomsky, C. (1979). Approaching reading through invented spelling. In L. B. Resnick & P. A. Weaver (Eds.), *Theory and practice of early reading* (Vol. 2, pp. 43–65). Hillsdale, NJ: Erlbaum.

Chomsky, N. (1959). Review of B. F. Skinner. *Verbal Behavior. Language, 35,* pp. 26–57.

Chomsky, N. (1968). *Language and mind*. NY: Harcourt and World.

Clarke, L. K. (1988). Encouraging invented spelling in first graders' writing: Effects on learning to spell and read. *Research in the Teaching of English, 22* (3), 281–309.

Clarke, L. K. (1989). Encouraging invented spelling in first graders' writing: Effects on learning to spell and read. *Research in the Teaching of English, 22* (3), 281–309.

Clay, M. M. (1975). *What did I write?* Auckland, New Zealand: Heinemann.

Clay, M. M. (2000). *Running records for classroom teachers*. Portsmouth, NH: Heinemann.

Clay, M. M. (2001). *Change over time: In children's literacy development*. Portsmouth, NH: Heinemann.

Clymer, T. (1963/1996). The utility of phonic generalizations in the primary grades. *The Reading Teacher, 16,* 252–258; *50,* 182–187.

Coon, G. E., & Palmer, G. M. (1993). *Handwriting research and information: An administrator's handbook*. Glenview, IL: Scott Foresman.

Cordeiro, P., Giacobbe, M. E., & Cazden, C. (1983). Apostrophes, quotation marks, and periods: Learning punctuation in the first grade. *Language Arts, 60,* 323–332.

Cottrell, M. (1953). Wild dog. In Helen Miller & Nell Murphy (Eds.), *Let's read: Book 1—Reading for fun*. New York: Holt, Rinehart and Winston.

Cox, C. (1999). *Teaching language arts*. Boston: Allyn & Bacon.

Cramer, B. B. (1985). *The effects of writing with invented spelling on general linguistic awareness and phonemic segmentation ability in kindergartners*. Unpublished doctoral dissertation, Oakland University, Rochester, MI.

Cramer, R. L. (1970). An investigation of first grade

spelling achievement. *Elementary English, 47* (2), 230–237.

Cramer, R. L. (1971). "Dialectology: A case for language experience." *The Reading Teacher, 25* (1), 33–39.

Cramer, R. L. (1979). *Children's writing and language growth.* Columbus, OH: Merrill.

Cramer, R. L. (1998). *The spelling connection: Integrating reading, writing, and spelling instruction.* New York: Guilford.

Cramer, R. L. (2001). *Creative power: The nature and nurture of children's writing.* New York: Addison Wesley Longman.

Cramer, R. L., & Hammond, W. D. (1970). *Directed listening thinking activity: An extension of Stauffer's directed reading thinking activity.* Mimeographed. Oakland University, Rochester, MI.

Cramer, R., & Cipielewski, J. (1995) A study of spelling errors in 18,599 written compositions of children in grades 1–8. In *Spelling research and information: An overview of current research and practices.* Glenview, IL: Scott Foresman.

Crowhurst, M. (1983). Sentence combining: Maintaining realistic expectations. *College Composition and Communication, 34,* 62–72.

Cunningham, A. E., & Stanovich, K. E. (1990). Tracking the unique effects of print exposure in children: Associations with vocabulary, general knowledge, and spelling. *Journal of Educational Psychology, 83,* 264–274.

Cunningham, A. E., & Stanovich, K. E. (1997). Early reading acquisition and its relation to reading experience and ability 10 years later. *Developmental Psychology, 33* (6), 934–945.

Cunningham, A. E., & Stanovich, K. E. (2003). Reading matters: How reading engagement influences cognition. In F. Flood, D. Lapp, J. R. Squire, & J. M. Jensen (Eds.), *Handbook of research on teaching the English language arts* (2nd ed., pp. 660–667). Mahwah, NJ: Erlbaum.

Cunningham, P. (1995). *Phonics they use.* New York: HarperCollins.

Cunningham, P. M. (2000). *Phonics they use* (3rd ed.). New York: Longman.

Cunningham, P. M., & Hall, D. P. (1994). *Making big words: Multilevel, hands-on spelling and phonics activities.* Torrance, CA: Good Apple.

Daiute, C. (1985). *Writing and computers.* Reading, MA: Addison Wesley.

Davis, F. B. (1944). Fundamental factors of comprehension in reading. *Psychometrika,* 185–197.

Delpit, L. (1995). *Other people's children.* Paper presented at the National Reading Conference, New Orleans, LA.

Dickens, C. (1992). *Great expectations.* Hertfordshire, UK: Wordsworth Editions Limited.

Dickinson, E. (1955). *The complete poems of Emily Dickinson.* Thomas H. Johnson, (Ed.), Boston: Little, Brown.

Dolch, E. W. (1942). *Better spelling.* Champaign, IL: Garrard Press.

Doyle, A. C. (1905). *The complete Sherlock Holmes.* New York: Doubleday.

Drury, J. (1991). *Creating poetry.* Cincinnati, OH: Writer's Digest Books.

Durkin, D. (1979). What classroom observations reveal about reading comprehension instruction. *Reading Research Quarterly, 14* (4), 481–533.

Dyson, A. H. (1988). Appreciate the drawing and dictating of young children. *Young Children, 43,* 25–32.

Dyson, A. H. (1997). *Writing superheroes: Contemporary childhood, popular culture, and classroom literacy.* New York: Teachers College Press.

Dyson, A. H., & Freedman, S. W. (1991). Writing. In J. Flood, J. M. Jensen, D. Lapp, & J. R. Squire (Eds.), *Handbook of research on teaching the English language arts* (pp. 754–774). New York: Macmillan.

Elley, W. B. (1992). *How in the world do students read?* Newark, DE: International Reading Association.

Elley, W. B., Barham, I. H., Lamb, H., & Wyllie, M. (1976). The role of grammar in a secondary school English curriculum. *Research in the Teaching of English, 10,* 5–21.

Elson, P. D. (1990). *An investigation of the revision processes of fifth grade children.* Unpublished doctoral dissertation, Oakland University, Rochester, MI.

Emans, R. (1967). The usefulness of phonic generalizations above the primary grades. *The Reading Teacher, 20,* 419–425.

Emig, J. (1971). *The composing processes of twelfth graders.* Urbana, IL: National Council of Teachers of English.

Evans, K. S. (2001). *Literature discussion groups in the intermediate grades: Dilemmas and possibilities.* Newark, DE: International Reading Association.

Faigley, L., & Witte, S. P. (1984). Measuring the effects of revision on text structure. In R. Beach & L. Birdwell (Eds.), *New directions in composition research* (pp. 53–71). New York: Guilford.

Fernald, G. M. (1943). *Remedial techniques in basic school subjects.* New York: McGraw-Hill, 1943.

Feuer, M. J., Holland, P. W., Green, B. F., Bertenthal, M. W., & Hemphill, F. C. (1999). *Uncommon measures: Equivalence and linkage among educational tests.* Washington, DC: National Academy Press.

Flood, J. (1986). The text, the student, and the teacher: Learning exposition in the middle school. *The Reading Teacher, 39,* 784–791.

Flynt, E. S., & Cooter, R. B. (2001). *Reading inventory for the classroom* (4th ed.). Upper Saddle River, NJ: Merrill Prentice Hall.

Foster, G., Sawicki, E., Schaeffer, H., & Zelinski, V. (2002). *I think, therefore I learn.* Portland, ME: Stenhouse Publishers.

Freeman, A. K. (1985). Sentence combining: Some questions. In A. K. Freedman (Ed.), *Carleton papers in applied language studies* (Vol. 2, pp. 17–32). ERIC Document Reproduction Service No. ED 267 602.

Fresch, M. J. (2001). Journal entries as a window on spelling knowledge. *The Reading Teacher 54* (5), 500–513.

Fresch, M. J., & Wheaton, A. (1997). Sort, search, and discover: Spelling in the child centered classroom. *The Reading Teacher, 51,* 20–31.

Frost, R. (1964). Stopping by woods on a snowy evening. In *The poetry of Robert Frost,* Edward Connery Lathem (Ed.), New York: Holt Rinehart and Winston.

Frost, Robert, 1874–1963. *The poetry of Robert Frost.* Edited by Edward Connery Lathem. New York: Holt, Rinehart, & Winston, (1969).

Fry, S. (2002, July 20). Forget ideas, Mr. Author, what kind of pen do you use? *The New York Times,* pp. B1–B2.

Gaffney, J. S., & Askew, B. J. (1999). *Stirring the waters: The influence of Marie Clay.* Portsmouth, NH: Heinemann.

Garcia, C. A. (1997). *The effect of two types of spelling instruction on first grade reading, writing, and spelling achievement.* Unpublished doctoral dissertation, Oakland University, Rochester, MI.

Gardner, H. (1991a). *To open minds.* New York: Basic Books.

Gardner, H. (1991b). *The unschooled mind: How children think and how schools should teach.* New York: Basic Books.

Gardner, H. (1993). *Multiple intelligences: The theory in practice.* New York: Basic Books.

Garrison, W. (1992). Why you say it. New York: MJF Books.

Gaskins, I. W., Ehri, L. C., Cress, C., O'Hara, C., & Donnelly, K. (1997). Procedures for word learning:

Making discoveries about words. *The Reading Teacher, 50,* 312–327.

Gates, A. I. (1937). *Generalization and transfer in spelling.* New York: Bureau of Publications, Teachers College, Columbia University. A thorough pre-computer study of spelling errors within words, it provides a basis for identifying the location within words where errors most often occur.

Gavelek, J., Raphael, T., Biondo, S., & Wang, D. (2000). Integrated literacy instruction. In M. L. Kamil, P. B. Mosenthal, P. D. Pearson, & R. Barr (Eds.), *Handbook of reading research: Volume III* (pp. 587–607). Mahwah, NJ: Erlbaum.

Gentry, J. R. (1981). Learning to spell developmentally. *The Reading Teacher, 34,* 378–381.

Gentry, J. R. (1987). *Spel is a four-letter word.* Portsmouth, NH: Heinemann.

Gilbar, S. (1989). *The open door.* Boston: Godine.

Gillespie, J. T., & Naden, C. J. (1990). *Best books for children: Preschool through grade 6* (4th ed.). New York: R. R. Bowker.

Ginott, H. (1965). *Between parent and child.* New York: Macmillan.

Giovanni, N. (1987). *Spin a soft black song.* New York: Farrar, Straus & Giroux.

Goodman, K. (1965). "Dialect barriers to reading comprehension." *Elementary English, 42,* 853–860.

Goodman, K. (1969). An analysis of reading miscues: Applied psycholinguistics. *Reading Research Quarterly, 5,* 9–30.

Goodman, K. (1986). *What's whole about whole language?* Portsmouth, NH: Heinemann.

Goodman, K. (1996). *On Reading: A common sense look at the nature of language and the science of reading.* Portsmouth, NH: Heinemann.

Goodman, Y. M., Watson, D. J., & Burke, C. L. (1987). *Reading miscue inventory.* New York: Owen.

Goodman, Y., & Burke, C. (1972). *Reading miscue inventory.* New York: Owen.

Gould, S. (1996). *The mismeasurement of man: Revised and expanded.* New York: Norton.

Graves, D. H. (1983). *Writing: Teachers and children at work.* Exeter, NH: Heinemann Educational Books.

Graves, D. H. (1994). *A fresh look at writing.* Portsmouth, NH: Heinemann.

Graves, D. S. (2002). *Testing is not teaching: What should count in education.* Portsmouth, NH: Heinemann.

Guthrie, J. T. (2002). Preparing students for high-stakes test taking in reading. In A. E. Farstrup & S. J. Samuels (Eds.), *What research has to say about reading instruction* (3rd ed., pp. 370–391). Newark, DE: International Reading Association.

Guthrie, J. T., & McCann, A. D. (1997). Characteristics of classrooms that promote motivations and strategies for learning. In J. T. Guthrie & A. Wigfield (Eds.), *Reading engagement: Motivating readers through integrated instruction* (pp. 128–148). Newark, DE: International Reading Association.

Hackney, C. (1993). *Zaner-Bloser handwriting.* Columbus, OH: Zaner-Bloser, Inc.

Hall, M. A. (1970). *Teaching reading as a language experience.* Columbus, OH: Merrill.

Halliday, M. (1973). *Explorations in the functions of language.* New York: Elsevier.

Halliday, M. (1975). *Explorations in the functions of language.* New York: Elsevier.

Halliday, M. A. K. (1975). *Learning how to mean.* London: Edward Arnold.

Hanna, P. R., Hanna, J. S., Hodges, R. E., & Rudorf, E. H., Jr. (1966). *Phoneme–grapheme correspondences as cues to spelling improvement.* Washington, DC: U.S. Department of Health, Education, and Welfare, Office of Education.

Harris, R. (1962). *An experimental inquiry into the functions and value of formal grammar in the teaching of English.* Unpublished doctoral dissertation, University of London.

Harris, T. L., & Hodges, R. E. (1995). *The literacy dictionary: The vocabulary of reading and writing.* Newark, DE: International Reading Association.

Hartwell, P. (1985). Grammar, grammars, and the teaching of grammar. *College English, 47,* 105–127.

Hayden, R. (1997). Those winter Sundays. In D. Ray & J. Ray (Eds.), *Father's: A collection of poems.* New York: St. Martin's Press.

Head, B. B. (2000). *Revision instruction and quality of writing by eighth grade students using paper and pencil or word processing.* Unpublished doctoral dissertation, Oakland University, Rochester, MI.

Healy, N. A. (1991). *First-graders writing with invented or traditional spelling: Effects on the development of decoding ability and writing skill.* Unpublished doctoral dissertation, University of Minnesota, Duluth, Morris, and Twin Cities, MN.

Henderson, E. H. (1989). *Teaching spelling* (2nd ed.). Boston: Houghton Mifflin.

Hennings, D. (1999). *Reading with meaning: Strategies for college reading.* Upper Saddle River, NJ: Prentice Hall.

Hesser, A. (2002, July 31). In the clover, a bee nirvana. *The New York Times,* dining out section.

Heubert, J. P., & Hauser, R. M. (Eds.), (1999). *High stakes: Testing for tracking, promotion, and graduation.* Washington, DC: National Academy Press.

Hillocks, G. Jr., & Smith, M. W. (2003). Grammar and literacy learning. In J. Flood, J. M. Jensen, D. Lapp, & J. R. Squire (Eds.), *Handbook on teaching the English language arts* (2nd ed., pp. 721–737). New York: Macmillan.

Hillocks, G., Jr. (1986). *Research on written composition: New directions for teaching.* Urbana, IL: ERIC and NCTE.

Hillocks, G., Jr., & Mavrogenes, N. (1986). Sentence combining. In *Research in written composition: New directions for teaching* (pp. 142–146). Urbana, IL: National Council of Teachers of English.

Hirsch, E. D., Jr., Kett, J. F., & Trefil, J. (1988). *The dictionary of cultural literacy.* Boston: Houghton Mifflin.

Hodges, R. (1991). The conventions of writing. In F. Flood, J. M. Jensen, D. Lapp, & J. R. Squire (Eds.), *Handbook of research on teaching the English language arts.* New York: Macmillan.

Hodges, R. E. (1981). *Learning to spell.* The ERIC Clearinghouse on Reading and Communication Skills and the NCTE, Urbana, IL.

Holdaway, D. (1979). *The foundations of literacy.* Portsmouth, NH: Heinemann.

Huck, C. S., Helper, S., & Hickman, J. (1993). *Children's literature in the elementary school* (5th ed.). New York: Brown & Benchmark.

Hunt, L. (1966). The individualized reading program: A guide for classroom teaching. In *Proceedings of the International Reading Association* (Vol. 2, Part 3). Newark, DE: International Reading Association.

Hunt, L. C. (1957). Can we measure specific factors associated with reading comprehension? *Journal of Educational Research, 51,* 161–171.

Hunt, L. C. (1971). Six steps to the individualized reading program (IRP). *Elementary English, 48,* 27–32.

Hurst, B., Wilson, C., Camp, D., & Cramer, G. (2002). *Creating independent readers: Developing word recognition skills in K-12 classrooms.* Scottsdale, AZ: Holcomb Hathaway.

Jalongo, M. R. (1995). Promoting active listening in the classroom. *Childhood Education, 72* (1), 13–18.

Janeczko, P. B. (1997). *Favorite poetry lessons (grades 4-8).* New York: Scholastic.

Janeczko, P. B. (2001). *A poke in the I.* Illustrated by Chris Raschka. Cambridge, MA: Candlewick.

Johns, J. L. (2001). *Basic reading inventory* (7th ed.). Dubuque, IA: Kendall/Hunt.

Johnston, P. (1997). *Knowing literacy: Constructive literacy assessment.* York, ME: Stenhouse.

Juel, C., Griffith, P., & Gough, P. B. (1986). Acquisition of literacy: A longitudinal study of children in first and second grade. *Journal of Educational Psychology, 87,* 243–255.

Jursted, R., Koutras, M., & Kurstedt, R. (2000). *Teaching writing with picture books as models.* New York: Scholastic.

Kane, T. S. (1988). *The new Oxford guide to writing.* New York: Oxford University Press.

Katiper, K., & Wilson, P. (1993). Updating poetry preferences: A look at the poetry children really like. *The Reading Teacher, 47* (1), 28–35.

Kennedy, X. J. (1986). *An introduction to poetry* (6th ed.). Glenview, IL: Scott Foresman.

Kirkpatrick, H., & Cuban, L. (1998). Computers make kids smarter—right? *Technos Quarterly for Education and Technology.* Retrieved May 1, 2003, from http://www.technos.net/journal/volume7/2cuban.htm.

Koestler, A. (1941). *Darkness at noon.* New York: Macmillan.

Krashen, S. (1999). *Three arguments against whole language and why they are wrong.* Portsmouth, NH: Heinemann.

Lagna, J. R. (1972). *The development, implementation, and evaluation of a model for teaching composition which utilizes individualized learning and peer grouping.* Unpublished doctoral dissertation, University of Pittsburgh.

Lane, B. (1993). *After the end: Teaching and learning creative revision.* Portsmouth, NH: Heinemann.

Langer, J. A. (1985). What eight-year-olds know about expository writing. *Educational Perspectives, 23,* (3), 27–33.

Langer, J. A. (1986). Learning through writing: Study skills in the content areas. *Journal of Reading, 19,* 400–406.

Langer, J. A. (1995). *Envisioning literature: Literary understanding and literature instruction.* New York: Teachers College Press.

Langer, J. A., & Applebee, A. N. (1987). *How writing shapes thinking: A study of teaching and learning.* Urbana, IL: National Council of Teachers of English.

Laudner, T. K. (1998). Learning and representing verbal meaning: The latent semantic analysis theory. *Current Directions in Psychological Science, 7,* 161–164.

Lederer, R. (1989). *Crazy English.* New York: Pocketbooks.

Lederer, R. (1991). *The miracle of language.* New York: Pocketbooks.

Lee, H. (1960). *To kill a mockingbird.* Philadelphia: Lippincott.

Lennenberg, E. H. (1967). *Biological foundations of language.* New York: Wiley.

Lesesne, T. S. (1997). Reading aloud: All the possible ways. In *Into Focus* by Kylene Beers and Bobbi Samuels. Boston, MA: Christopher Gordon Publishers.

Leslie, L., & Jett-Simpson, M. (1997). *Authentic literacy assessment: An ecological approach.* New York: Longman.

Lewis, R. (Ed.), (1966). *Miracles: Poems by children of the English-speaking world.* New York: Simon & Schuster.

Light, S. (1991). *Parents reading aloud to their third-grade children and its influence on vocabulary, comprehension, and attitudes.* Unpublished doctoral dissertation, Oakland University, Rochester, Michigan.

Lipson, E. R. (2002). *Zena Sutherland: Expert on literature for children.* New York: New York Times, p. A27.

Loban, W. (1963). *The language of elementary school children.* Urbana, IL: National Council of Teachers of English.

Lobel, A. (1980). *Fables.* New York: HarperCollins.

Mailer, Norman (1991). *Harlot's ghost.* New York: Random House.

Mandler, J., & Johnson, N. (1987). Remembrance of things parsed: Story structure and recall. *Cognitive Psychology, 9,* 111–151.

Mann, V. A., & Liberman, I. Y. (1984). Phonological awareness and verbal short-term memory: Can they presage early reading problems? *Journal of Learning Disabilities, 17,* 592–599.

Marine, K. (1995). Using the research: Developing a spelling curriculum. In *Spelling research and information: An overview of current research and practices* (pp. 41–52). Glenview, IL: Scott Foresman.

Mason, J. M., Stahl, S. A., Au, K. H., & Herman, P. A. (2003). Reading: Childrens developing knowledge of words. In F. Flood, D. Lapp, J. R. Squire, & J. M. Jensen (Eds.), *Handbook of research on teaching the English language arts* (2nd ed., pp. 914–930). Mahwah, NJ: Erlbaum.

May, F. B., & Rizzardi, L. (2002). *Reading as communication.* Upper Saddle River, NJ: Merrill Prentice Hall.

Mearns, H. (1929, 1958). *Creative power: The education of youth in the creative arts*. New York: Dover.

Miller, G. A., & Gildea, P. M. (1987). How children learn words. *Scientific American, 257* (3), 94–99.

Millman, J., & Bishop, C. H. (1965). An analysis of test-wiseness. *Educational and Psychological Measurements, 25*, 707–717.

Moffett, J., & Wagner, B. J. (1983). *Student-centered language arts and reading, K-13* (3rd ed.). Boston: Houghton Mifflin.

Morris, D. (1980). Beginning readers concept of word. In E. Henderson & J. Beers (Eds.), *Developmental and cognitive aspects of learning to spell* (pp. 97–111). Newark, DE: International Reading Association.

Morris, D. (1983). Concept of word and phoneme awareness in the beginning reader. *Research in the teaching of English, 17* (4), 359–373.

Morrow, L. (1986). Effects of structural guidance in story retelling on children's dictation of original stories. *Journal of Reading Behavior, 18*, 131–151.

Morrow, L. M. (1997). *Literacy development in the early years: Helping children read and write*. Boston: Allyn & Bacon.

Murray, D. M. (1985). *A writer teaches writing* (2nd ed.). Boston: Houghton Mifflin.

Nagy, W. E., & Anderson, R. C. (1984). How many words are there in printed school English? *Reading Research Quarterly, 19*, 304–350.

Nagy, W. E., Herman, P. A., & Anderson, R. C. (1987). Learning words from context. *Reading Research Quarterly, 20* (2), 233–253.

Newell, G. (1984). Learning from writing in two content areas: A case study/protocol analysis. *Research in the Teaching of English, 18*, 205–287.

O'Conner, P. T. (1996). *Woe is I: The grammarphobe's guide to better English in plain English*. New York: Grosset/Putnam.

O'Dell, S. (1960). *Island of the blue dolphins*. New York: Dell Yearling.

O'Dell, S. (1970). *Sing down the moon*. Boston: Houghton Mifflin.

Ogle, D. (1986). KWL: A teaching model that develops active reading of expository text. *The Reading Teacher, 39*, 564–570.

Ogle, D. M. (1989). The know, want to know, learn strategy. In K. D. Muth (Ed.)., *Children's comprehension of text* (pp. 205–223). Newark, DE: International Reading Association.

Owston, R. D., Murphy, S., & Wideman, H. H. (1992). The effects of word processing on students' writing quality and revision strategies. *Research in the Teaching of English, 26* (3), 249–276.

Padgett, R. (1987). *The teachers and writers handbook of poetic forms*. New York: Teachers and Writers Collaborative.

Padgett, R. (2000). *The teachers and writers handbook of poetic forms* (2nd ed.). New York: Teachers and Writers Collaborative.

Pappas, C. C., Kiefer, B. Z., & Levstik, L. S. (1999). *Integrated language perspective in the elementary school: An action approach* (3rd ed.). Boston: Allyn & Bacon.

Paris, S. G., Lawton, T., Turner, J., & Roth, J. (1991). A developmental perspective in standardized achievement testing. *Educational Researcher, 20*, 12–20.

Pavonetti, L. (2002). *Readers theater for the 21st century: Engaged reading for middle and high school students*. Mimeographed. Oakland University, Rochester, MI.

Pearson, P. D., & Johnson, D. D. (1978). *Teaching reading comprehension*. New York: Holt, Rinehart and Winston, 1978.

Pearson, P. D., & Raphael, T. (1999). Toward a more complex view of balance in the literacy curriculum. In D. Hammond & T. Raphael (Eds.), *Early literacy instruction for the new millennium*. Grand Rapids, MI: Michigan Reading Association and Center for the Improvement of Early Reading Achievement.

Peterson, R., & Eeds, M. (1990). *Grand conversations: Literature groups in action*. New York: Scholastic.

Piaget, J. (1955). *The language and thought of the child*. New York: Meridian Books.

Piaget, J. (1981). *Intelligence and affectivity: Their relationship during child development*. (T. A. Brown & E. E. Kaegi, Trans.). Palo Alto, CA: Annual Reviews Inc.

Pinker, S. (2002). *The blank slate*. New York: Viking.

Pinnell, G. S., & Fountas, I. C. (1998). *Word matters*. Portsmouth, NH: Heinemann.

Pinnell, G. S., & Jaggar, A. M. (1991). Oral language: Speaking and listening in the classroom. In F. Flood, J. M. Jensen, D. Lapp, & J. Squire (Eds.), *Handbook of research on the teaching of the English language arts* (pp. 691–742). New York: Macmillan.

Prelutsky, J. (1984). *The new kid on the block*. New York: Greenwillow.

Pressley, M. (1998). *Reading instruction that works*. New York: Guilford.

Pressley, M. (2000). What should comprehension instruction be the instruction of? In M. L. Kamil, P. B. Mosenthal, P. D. Pearson, & R. Barr (Eds.), *Handbook of reading research* (Vol. 2, pp. 545–56). Mahwah, NJ: Erlbaum.

Pressley, M. (2002). *Reading instruction that works: The*

*case for balanced teaching* (2nd ed.). New York: Guilford.

Quindlen, A. (1998). *How reading changed my life.* New York: Ballantine.

Radebaugh, M. R. (1985). Good spellers use more visual imagery than poor spellers. *The Reading Teacher, 38* (6), 532–536.

Rankin, E., & Overholzer, B. (1969). Reaction of intermediate grade children to contextual clues. *Journal of Reading Behavior, 1,* 50–73.

Raphael, T. (1986). Question/answer strategies for children. *The Reading Teacher, 35,* 186–190.

Raphael, T. E., & McMahon, S. I. (1994). Book club: An alternative framework for reading instruction. *The Reading Teacher, 48,* 102–116.

Rapp-Ruddell, M. (1993). *Teaching content reading and writing.* Boston: Allyn & Bacon.

Rasinski, T., & Padak (2000). *Reading strategies: Teaching children who find reading difficult* (2nd ed.). Columbus, OH: Merrill.

Read, C. (1971). Pre-school children's knowledge of English phonology. *Harvard Educational Review, 41* (1), 1–34.

Read, C. (1975). *Children's categorization of speech sounds in English.* NCTE Research Reports No. 17, Urbana, IL: National Council of Teachers of English.

Robinson, S. E. (1973). *Predicting early reading progress.* Master's thesis, University of Auckland Library.

Rosenblatt, L. (1938, 1983). *Literature as exploration.* New York: Modern Language Association.

Rosenblatt, L. (1978). *The reader, the text, the poem: The transactional theory of the literary work.* Carbondale, IL: Southern Illinois University Press.

Routman, R. (1991). *Invitations.* Portsmouth, NH: Heinemann.

Routman, R. (2000). *Conversations.* Portsmouth, NH: Heinemann.

Ruddell, R. B. (1999). *Teaching children to read and write: Becoming an influential teacher* (2nd ed.). Boston: Allyn & Bacon.

Samuels, S. J. (1988). Decoding and automaticity: Helping poor readers become automatic at word recognition. *The Reading Teacher, 411,* 756–760.

Schatz, E. I., & Baldwin, R. S. (1986). Context clues are unreliable predictors of word meaning. *Reading Research Quarterly, 21,* 439–453.

Schwartz, L. S. (1996). *Ruined by reading: A life in books.* Boston: Beacon Press.

Schwartz, R. M. (1988). Learning to learn vocabulary in content area textbooks. *Journal of Reading, 20* (20), 108–118.

Schwartz, R. M., & Cramer, R. L. (1988). Planning process lessons: A guide to independent learning. *Research Studies in Education.* Rochester, MI: Oakland University.

Serafini, F., Funke, J., & Wiley, R. (2001). Talk is sharing: Creating space for sharing in the writing circle. In P. Smith (Ed.), *Talking classrooms: Shaping children's learning through oral language instruction.* Newark, DE: International Reading Association.

Shanahan, T. (1980). *A canonical correlational analysis of learning to read and learning to write: An exploratory analysis.* Unpublished doctoral dissertation, University of Delaware, Newark.

Shanahan, T. (1984). The nature of reading-writing relations: An exploratory multivariate analysis. *Journal of Educational Psychology, 76,* 357–363.

Shanahan, T. (1988). The reading–writing relationship: Seven instructional principles. *The Reading Teacher, 41,* 636–647.

Shaughnessy, M. P. (1977). *Errors and expectations: A guide for the teacher of basic writing.* New York: Oxford University Press.

Silvaroli, N. J., & Wheelock, W. H. (2000). *Classroom reading inventory* (9th ed.). New York: McGraw-Hill.

Silverstein, S. (1974). *Where the sidewalk ends.* New York: Harper & Row.

Silverstein, S. (1981). *A light in the attic.* New York: Harper & Row.

Skinner, B. F. (1957). *Verbal behavior.* NY: Appleton Century-Crofts.

Slobin, D. I. (1968). "Imitation and grammatical development." In N. S. Endure, L. R. Boulder, & H. Oscar (Eds.), *Contemporary issues in developmental psychology.* New York: Holt, Rinehart, and Winston.

Smith, J. W. A., & Elley, W. B. (1997). *How children learn to write.* Katonah, NY: Owen.

Stahl, S. A., & Fairbanks, M. M. (1986). The effects of vocabulary instruction: A model-based meta-analysis. *Review of Educational Research, 56* (1), 72–110.

Stanley, A. G. (1988). *Revision in third grade.* Unpublished master's thesis. Oakland University, Rochester, MI.

Stanovich, K. E. (1986). Matthew effects in reading: Some consequences of individual differences in the acquisition of literacy. *Reading Research Quarterly, 21,* 360–407.

Stanovich, K. E. (1988). *Children's reading and the development of phonological awareness.* Detroit, MI: Wayne State University Press.

Stanovich, K. E. (2000). *Progress in understanding reading: Scientific foundations of new frontiers.* New York: Guilford.

Stanovich, K. E., & West, R. F. (1989). Word recognition: Changing perspectives. In R. Barr, M. L. Kamil, P. B. Mosenthal, & P. D. Pearson (Eds.), *Handbook of reading research* (Vol. 2, pp. 418–452). White Plains, NY: Longman.

Stanovich, K. E., Cunningham, A. E., & Cramer, B. B. (1984). Assessing phonological awareness in kindergarten children: Issues of task comparability. *Journal of Experimental Child Psychology, 38,* 175–190.

Stauffer, R. G. (1969). *Directing reading maturity as a cognitive process.* New York: Harper & Row.

Stauffer, R. G. (1970). *The language-experience approach to the teaching of reading* (2nd ed.). New York: Harper & Row.

Stauffer, R., Hammond, D., Oehlkers, W., & Houseman, A. (1972). *Effectiveness of a language-arts and basic-reader approach to first grade reading instruction extended into sixth grade.* Newark, DE: Cooperative Research Project 3276, University of Delaware.

Stein, N. L. (1979). How children understand stories: A developmental analysis. In L. Katz (Ed.), *Current topics in early childhood education* (p. 974). Norwood, NJ: Ablex.

Steiner, G. (1995). *Paris Review, 137.* New York: Drew Heinz.

Steptoe, J. (1997). *In Daddy's arms I am tall: African Americans celebrate fathers.* New York: Lee & Low Books.

Sternberg, R. J. (1985). *Beyond IQ: A triarchic theory of human intelligence.* Cambridge, UK: Cambridge University Press.

Sticht, T. G., & James, J. H. (1984). Listening and reading. In P. D. Pearson, R. Barr, L. Kamil, & P. Mosenthal (Eds.), *Handbook of reading research* (pp. 293–317). New York: Longman.

Stotsky, S. (1983). Research of reading/writing relationships: A synthesis and suggested directions. *Language Arts, 60,* 568–580.

Strong, W. (1986). *Creative approaches to sentence combining.* Urbana, IL: National Council of Teachers of English.

Sutherland, Z., & Arbuthnot, M. H. *Children & Books* (7th ed.). Glenview, IL: Scott, Foresman & Company.

Teale, W., & Sulzby, E. (1986). Emergent literacy as a perspective for examining how young children become writers and readers. In W. Teale & E. Sulzby (Eds.), *Emergent literacy: Writing and reading* (pp. 727–757). Norwood, NJ: Ablex.

Temple, C., Martinez, M., Yokota, J., & Naylor, A. (2001). *Children's books in children's hands: An introduction to their literature* (2nd ed.). Boston: Allyn & Bacon.

Temple, C., Nathan R., Temple, F., & Burris, N. A. (1993). *The beginnings of writing* (3rd ed.). Boston: Allyn & Bacon.

Templeton, S., & Bear, D. (1992). Theory, nature, and pedagogy of higher-order orthographic development in older students. In S. Templeton & D. Bear (Eds.), *Development of orthographic knowledge and the foundations of literacy: A memorial Festschrift for Edmund H. Henderson* (pp. 130–186). Hillsdale, NJ: Erlbaum.

Templeton, S., & Morris, D. (1999). Questions teachers ask about spelling. *Reading Research Quarterly 34* (1), 102–112.

Tierney, R. J. (1990). Learning to connect reading and writing: Critical thinking through transactions with one's own subjectivity. In Timothy Shanahan (Ed.), *Reading and writing together: New perspectives for the classroom* (pp. 131–143). Norwood, MA: Christopher-Gordon.

Tierney, R., & Leys, M. (1984). *What is the value of connecting reading and writing?* (Reading Education Report No. 55). Urbana-Champaign, IL: Center for the Study of Reading, University of Illinois.

Tierney, R., & Shanahan, T. (2002). Research on the reading writing relationship: Interactions, transactions, and outcomes. In R. Barr, M. L. Kamil, P. B. Mosenthal, & P. D. Pearson (Eds.), *Handbook of reading research* (Vol. 2, pp. 246–280). Hillsdale, NJ: Erlbaum.

Tough, J. (1973). *Focus on meaning.* London: Allen & Unwin.

Trelease, J. (1995). *The read-aloud handbook* (4th ed.). New York: Viking Penguin.

Unger, G. H. (1998). *Noah Webster: The life and times of an American patriot.* New York: Wiley.

Van Allen, R. V. (1976). *Language experiences in communication.* Boston: Houghton Mifflin.

Veatch, J. (1959). *Individualizing your reading program.* New York: Putnam.

Veatch, J. (1976). *Individualizing your reading program.* New York: Putnam.

Veatch, J., Sawicki, F., Elliott, G., Barnette, E., & Blakey, J. (1973). *Key words to reading: The language experience approach begins.* Columbus, OH: Merrill.

Venezky, R. (1999). *The American way of spelling: The structure and origins of American English orthography*. New York: Guilford.

Voigt, C. (1983). *Dicey's song*. New York: Atheneum.

Volavkova, H. (Ed.), (1993). *I never saw another butterfly: Children's drawings and writings from Terezin Concentration Camp, 1942-1944* (2nd ed.). New York: Schocken.

Vygotsky, L. S. (1962). *Thought and language*. Cambridge, MA: MIT Press.

Vygotsky, L. S. (1978). *Mind in society: The development of higher psychological processes* (M. Cole, V. John-Steiner, S. Scribner, & E. Souberman, Eds. and Trans.). Cambridge, MA: Harvard University Press.

Walter, N. W. (1962). *Let them write poetry*. New York: Holt, Rinehart and Winston.

Walters, T. S. (1990). Note taking while reading a textbook. *Michigan Reading Journal, 23*, 34–37.

Walters, T., Webster, P., & Cramer, A. (1998). *A never ending, never done bibliography of multicultural literature for younger and older children*. ERIC document ED 407-388, Rochester, MI: Oakland University.

Weaver, C. (1998). Teaching grammar in the context of writing. In C. Weaver (Ed.), *Lessons to share: On teaching grammar in context* (pp. 18–38). Portsmouth, NH: Heinemann.

Wiencek, B. J. (2001). *Guided reading*. Mimeo. Rochester, MI: Oakland University.

Wilde, S. (1987). *Program in language and literacy*. Tucson, AZ: Occasional Paper, University of Arizona, Division of Language, Reading, and Culture.

Wilson, L. (2001). *Reading to live: how to teach reading in today's world*. Portsmouth, NH: Heinemann.

Yen, W., & Ferrara, S. (1997). The Maryland school performance assessment program. *Journal of Educational and Psychological Measurement, 57*, 60–84.

Yopp, H. K. (1988). The validity and reliability of phonemic awareness tests. *Reading Research Quarterly, 23*, 159–177.

Yopp, H. K. (1992). Developing phonemic awareness in young children. *The Reading Teacher, 45*, 696–703.

# Index